HOW FAR ACROSS THE RIVER?

Stanford Studies in International Economics and Development

Stephen H. Haber and John H. Pencavel, *editors*

The process of international economic integration has both ardent advocates and energetic detractors. Over the last half-century, the dramatic expansion of international trade and capital flows has been linked with unprecedented economic advances. At the same time, many view these closer economic ties as a major complicating factor in macroeconomic management, as well as a leading cause of financial crises. Moreover, nations share unevenly in global prosperity. Despite some conspicuous successes, many countries remain mired in underdevelopment and want. While supporters of integration attribute these failures mainly to deficiencies in developing countries' own policies, its opponents often attribute the failures to the self-same factors that help make some countries rich.

These live and vital issues are the focus of the Stanford Studies in International Economics and Development. This series, which will include single- and co-authored books as well as edited collections of scholarly papers, deals with a broad spectrum of policy issues that influence the economic performance of low-income countries, including those engaged in the transition from command to market economies. The series concerns itself with the policy reforms that are urgently needed to raise the living standards of the world's poor, to enhance global cooperation and security, and to foster broader participation in the benefits engendered by growth in the global economy.

HOW FAR ACROSS
THE RIVER?

Chinese Policy Reform
at the Millennium

Edited by

*Nicholas C. Hope, Dennis Tao Yang,
and Mu Yang Li*

Stanford University Press
Stanford, California 2003

Stanford University Press
Stanford, California

Printed in the United States of America
on acid-free, archival-quality paper

Library of Congress Cataloging-in-Publication Data

How far across the river? : Chinese policy reform at the millennium /
edited by Nicholas C. Hope, Dennis Tao Yang, and Mu Yang Li.
p. cm.
Includes bibliographical references and index.
ISBN 0-8047-4766-0 (alk. paper)
1. China—Economic policy—1976–2000.   2. China—Economic
policy—2000–.   3. China—Economic conditions—1976–2000.
4. China—Economic conditions—2000–   5. China—Social
conditions—1976–2000.   6. China—Social conditions—2000–.
I. Hope, Nicholas C.   II. Yang, Dennis Tao.   III. Yang Li, Mu.

HC427.92   .H675 2003
330.951—dc21   2003009659

Typeset by G & S Typesetters in 10/12 Bembo

Original Printing 2003
Last figure below indicates year of this printing:
12   11   10   09   08   07   06   05   04   03

Special discounts for bulk quantities of Stanford University Press
books are available to corporations, professional associations, and
other organizations. For details and discount information, contact
the special sales department of Stanford University Press.
Tel: (650) 736-1783, Fax: (650) 736-1784

Stanford Center for International Development
(*formerly the Center for Research on Economic Development and Policy Reform*)

To the memory of Ken MacLeod, who had the vision

CONTENTS

Figures   ix
Tables   xi
Acknowledgments   xv
About the Contributors   xvii

1   Economic Policy Reform in China   1
Nicholas C. Hope, Dennis Tao Yang, and Mu Yang Li

PART I: POLICY REFORM IN CHINA:
WHAT IS NEEDED NEXT?   29

2   China's Transition to a Market Economy:
How Far Across the River?   31
Yingyi Qian and Jinglian Wu

PART II: BUILDING MARKET-SUPPORTING
INSTITUTIONS   65

3   When Will China's Financial System Meet China's Needs?   67
Nicholas R. Lardy

4   Thriving on a Tilted Playing Field: China's Nonstate
Enterprises in the Reform Era   97
Chong-En Bai, David D. Li, and Yijiang Wang

5   The More Law, the More . . . ? Measuring Legal Reform
in the People's Republic of China   122
William P. Alford

PART III: TOWARD GREATER ECONOMIC
INTEGRATION   151

6   Trade Policy, Structural Change, and China's Trade Growth   153
*William Martin, Betina Dimaranan, Thomas W. Hertel,
and Elena Ianchovichina*

7   Sizing Up Foreign Direct Investment in China and India   178
Shang-jin Wei

8   How Much Can Regional Integration Do to Unify
China's Markets?   204
Barry Naughton

PART IV: SHARING RISING INCOMES   233

9   China's War on Poverty   235
Scott Rozelle, Linxiu Zhang, and Jikun Huang

10   Social Welfare in China in the Context of Three Transitions   273
Athar Hussain

11   Housing Reform in Urban China   313
Jeffrey S. Zax

PART V: SUSTAINING POLICY REFORM   351

12   Can China Grow and Safeguard Its Environment?
The Case of Industrial Pollution   353
David Wheeler, Hua Wang, and Susmita Dasgupta

13   The Political Economy of China's Rural–Urban Divide   389
Dennis Tao Yang and Cai Fang

14   What Will Make Chinese Agriculture More Productive?   417
Jikun Huang, Justin Y. Lin, and Scott Rozelle

15   Bending Without Breaking: The Adaptability of Chinese
Political Institutions   450
Jean C. Oi

PART VI: FURTHER RESEARCH   469

16   Agenda for Future Research   471
Nicholas C. Hope, Dennis Tao Yang, and Mu Yang Li

Index   483

FIGURES

1.1   Transformation of the Sectoral Structure of the Chinese
Economy   7
1.2   China in the World Economy   8
6.1   China's Share of World Exports   155
6.2   The Share of Exports of Goods and Nonfactor Services in GDP   155
6.3   Changes in the Composition of Exports from China   156
8.1   Outflows and Exports, Twenty-Five Provinces   210
8.2   Inflows and Imports, Twenty-Five Provinces   211
8.3   Total Provincial Outflows, 1987 and 1992   212
8.4   Total Provincial Inflows, 1987 and 1992   213
8.5   Energy and Transport Intensity of GDP   219
8.6   Infrastructure Investment: Major Trends   220
9.1   Investment-to-Wage Spending Ratio in Shaanxi, 1982–92   243
9.2   Poverty Alleviation Investment Per Capita and Proportion of
Investment by Source in Forty-Three Sample Counties in
Shaanxi, 1986–91   244
9.3   Poverty Alleviation Investment Per Capita and Proportion of
Investment by Users in Forty-Three Sample Counties in Shaanxi,
1986–90   246
9.4   Total Provincial Poverty Investment in Sichuan, 1991–95   247
9.5   Provincial Investment of Total Poverty Funds, by Target Sector, in
Sichuan, 1991–93   248
9.6   Total Provincial Poverty Investments in Industry, by Program in
Sichuan, 1991–93   249
9.7   Total Provincial Investments in Agricultural Infrastructure, by
Program in Sichuan, 1991–93   249

9.8   Total Provincial Poverty Investments in Transportation Infrastructure, by Program in Sichuan, 1991–93   250

9.9   Total Provincial Poverty Investments in Other Sectors, by Program in Sichuan, 1991–93   250

9.10   Gross Per Capita Income in Sichuan's Poor and Nonpoor Counties, 1985–95   255

9.11   Net Per Capita Income in Sichuan's Poor and Nonpoor Counties, 1985–95   257

12.1 SO_2 Emissions and Atmospheric Concentration in Chinese Cities, 1991–93   354

12.2   Projected Deaths from Air Pollution, 1997–2020   355

12.3   Provincial Pollution Intensities   356

12.4   Provincial Pollution Levies   357

12.5   Provincial Differences in Citizen Environmental Complaints   359

12.6   COD Intensity Factors: Effect and Significance   360

12.7 SO_2 Intensity Factors: Effect and Significance   360

12.8   Output Share of Large Plants   361

12.9 SO_2-Intensive Sectors: Manufacturing Share   362

12.10   Trend in the Output Share of the Five Dirtiest Industrial Sectors, 1977–92   363

12.11   Trend in Net Imports from Pollution-Intensive Industries, 1987–94   363

12.12   Consumption-Production Ratio of Polluting Products, 1987–92   364

12.13   Particulate Marginal Abatement Costs: Large Plants   366

12.14   Particulate Marginal Abatement Costs: Small Plants   366

12.15   COD Loads in Three Scenarios   374

12.16   Industrial SO_2 Loads in China   376

12.17   Lives Saved by SO_2 Regulation, 1997–2020   377

12.18   Total Deaths from Industrial Air Pollution, 1997–2020   378

12.19   Additional SO_2 Abatement in Zengzhou: Marginal Benefits and Costs   382

13.1   Ratio of Urban to Rural Consumption and Income   396

13.2   Changes in Relative Agricultural Price and Relative SOE Wage Growth   402

13.3   Shares of Government Expenditures and Loans to Agriculture   407

TABLES

2.1   Ownership Composition in Industrial Output   53

2.2   Ownership Composition in Retail Sales of Consumer Goods   53

2.3   State-Owned Industrial Enterprises by Size, 1993   55

3.1   Interest Outlays on Domestic Treasury Debt, 1993–98   76

3.2   Financial Sustainability in China, 1998–2008, Base Scenario   79

3.3   Fiscal Sustainability in China, 1998–2008, Revenue
Enhancement   81

3.4   Fiscal Sustainability in China, 1998–2008, Commercial Bank
Behavior   82

3.5   Fiscal Sustainability in China, 1998–2008, Revenue Enhancement
and Commercial Bank Behavior   84

3.6   Working Capital Lending, 1991–99   87

3.7   Price Changes, 1994–98   88

4.1   Growth Rates of Industrial Output: State Sector versus Nonstate
Sector   100

4.2   Development of TVEs, 1980–95   101

4.3   Growth Rate of TVEs Output and Employment, 1981–95   102

4.4   Share of Nonagricultural Employment: State Sector versus Nonstate
Sector   103

4.5   Share of Industrial Output: State Sector versus Nonstate Sector   103

4.6   Share Contributed to Industrial Growth: State Sector versus Nonstate
Sector   104

4.7   Types of Entry Barriers by Firm Size   105

4.8   Share of Total Fixed Investment: State Sector versus Nonstate
Sector   106

4.9   The Nonstate Sector's Share in Total Short-Term Loans from State
Banks   107

4.10   Sources of Private Firms' Initial Investment   107
4.11   How Private Firms Deal with Business Disputes   108
4.12   Most Important Social Problems Troubling the Operation of Private
          Firms   109
4.13   State versus Nonstate Sector: Government Budgetary Revenue   113
6.1   Share of Goods Sold at State-Fixed Prices, 1978–93   159
6.2   Contribution of Different Firms to China's Trade, 1994   160
6.3   Products Covered by State Trading and Designated Trading   162
6.4   Share of Imports Protected by NTBs in 1996, Using 1992 Trade
          Weights   163
6.5   Changes in Average Tariff Rates in China, 1992–98   164
6.6   Final Tariff Bindings on Selected Agricultural Products   168
6.7   Cumulative Percentage Growth Rates, 1995–2005   170
6.8   Weighted Average Tariffs in China with and Without WTO
          Accession   172
6.9   Output, Exports, and Imports as a Share of the World Economy   173
7.1   Business Environment in Selected Countries, 1990s   179
7.2   Realized Foreign Direct Investment in China and India   181
7.3   Evolution of Laws and Regulations in FDI in China and India   183
7.4   Sources of Foreign Direct Investment in China   188
7.5   Foreign Direct Investment Flow into China: Chinese versus Source
          Country Statistics   190
7.6   China as a Host for FDI Compared to Its Potential   194
7.7   Adding Public Policies and Public Institutions   195
7.8   Inflow of FDI   197
7.9   Hong Kong Connection for FDI Stock   198
7.10   Hong Kong Connection for FDI Flow   199
7.11   Increment in FDI as a Result of Reducing Corruption and Red
          Tape   201
8.1   Domestic and Foreign Trade Ratios, 1992   209
8.2   Interprovincial Trade, 1987 and 1992   211
8.3   Characteristics of Goods in Interprovincial Trade   217
8.4   Provincial Priority Industries Selected for the Ninth Five-Year
          Plan   223
9.1   National Government's Investment in China's Poor Areas by
          Program, 1986–97   239
9.2   Estimates of the Number of Poor in Rural China, 1984–98   251
9.3   Annual Growth Rates of Key Sectors in China's Rural Economy,
          1970–95   252
9.4   Gross Per Capita Income (deflated) in Sichuan Counties, Grouped by
          Income Levels and Poverty Designation, 1985–95   254

9.5 Net Per Capita Income (deflated) in Sichuan Counties, Grouped by Income Levels and Poverty Designation, 1985–95 256

9.6 Income Levels and Program Designation of Sichuan Province's Poorest Counties 257

9.7 Results from Growth Regressions on County-Level Per Capita Incomes 258

9.8 Ordinary Least Squares Regression Explaining Income Levels and Growth in Sichuan Province, 1990–95 261

10.1 Population Profile, 1998 and 2020 275

10.2 Age Structure of Working-Age Adults, 1982 and 1998 278

10.3 Sectoral Distribution of Labor Force 281

10.4 Causes of Death in Urban and Rural China 297

10.5 Sources of Health Financing 302

11.1 Dwelling Unit Size in 1988 and 1995 318

11.2 Other Housing Characteristics in 1988 and 1995 319

11.3 Tenure Type in 1988 and 1995 319

11.4 Monthly Rents and Housing Subsidies in 1988 and 1995 320

11.5 Actual and Estimated Market Monthly Rents in 1995 321

11.6 Correlations Between Estimated Market Rents and Actual Rents in 1995 321

11.7 Housing Finance for Owner-Occupied Housing in 1995 322

11.8 Correlations Between Estimated Market Values and Estimated Market Rents in 1995 323

11.9 Estimates of Housing Construction Costs 325

11.10 Estimates of Subsidized and Market Housing Sale Prices 326

11.11 Comparisons Between Housing Costs or Prices and Average Incomes 327

12.1 Projected Annual Deaths from Industrial SO_2 Pollution 377

12.2 Industrial SO_2 Abatement in Five Cities 380

13.1 Per Capita Consumption of Rural and Urban Residents 1952–97 393

13.2 Total Per Capita Disposable Income and Its Components for Urban Residents 395

13.3 Real Per Capita Total Income for Rural and Urban Residents 396

13.4 The Ratio of Nonagricultural Income to Agricultural Income: An International Comparison 397

13.5 Regional Development Policies and Their Geographical Coverage 403

14.1 Annual Growth Rates of China's Economy, 1970–98 419

14.2 Changes in the Structure of China's Economy, 1970–97 420

14.3 Annual Growth Rate of Agricultural Economy by Sector and Selected Agricultural Commodity, 1970–97 421

14.4   Capital Flow (billion yuan in 1985 price) from Agricultural/Rural to
        Industry/Urban Through Fiscal, Financial (banking), and Grain
        Procurement Systems   423
14.5   Nominal and Effective Real Protection Rates of Grain, 1985–98   425
14.6   Rural Enterprise (RE) Development in China, 1980–97   428
14.7   Agricultural Labor Productivity in China, 1978–97   429
14.8   Agricultural Research and Extension Expenditures in China,
        1985–96   432
14.9   Trends of Output, Input, and Total Productivity for Rice, Wheat,
        Soybean, and Maize in China, 1979–95   433
14.10   Experiment Station Yields, Actual Yields, and the Yield Gap in
        Sample Provinces in China, 1980–95   436
14.11   Elasticities of TFP with Respect to Technology, Extension, and
        Other Factors for Rice, Wheat, Soybean, and Maize for China,
        1982–95   438
14.12   Projections of Grain Production, Demand, and Net Imports Under
        Various Scenarios, 2005–2020   441
14.13   Grain Self-Sufficiency Rates Under Various Scenarios,
        1994–2020   443
15.1   Toward Political Change in China   452

ACKNOWLEDGMENTS

This volume emerged from the conference on Chinese policy reform that the Center for Research on Economic Development and Policy Reform (CREDPR) of Stanford University hosted at Stanford in November 1999. Beyond the authors of the chapters included in this volume, the chief intellectual debt we owe is to the other participants in the conference who, as formal discussants of papers, chairs of sessions, or general commentators, enlivened the proceedings and contributed through the vigor of the debate to the revisions of the original papers. We thank, in particular, Professor Gregory Chow of Princeton University, the late Professor D. Gale Johnson of the University of Chicago, and Professor Lawrence Lau of Stanford University for contributions before, during, and after the conference that assisted us greatly in our task. We are grateful as well to Vice Minister Li Jiange of China's State Council Office for the Reform of the Economic System for attending the conference and delivering a keynote speech on the path of Chinese reform and the implications for China's economy.

We owe a particular debt to Professor Anne Krueger, the founding director of CREDPR, who contributed both her vision of what the Center should be and her perceptions on how best to achieve that vision. At every step, she guided and gave impetus to our endeavor; she also helped shape the final form of the volume without being responsible in any way for the deficiencies that remain. The staffs of the Stanford Institute for Economic Policy Research (SIEPR) and CREDPR arranged the conference and supported the ensuing work.

The Center would like to express its gratitude for the generous financial support that made the conference and ultimately this volume possible. We appreciate greatly contributions from the Bechtel Initiative on Global Growth and Change (of the Institute for International Studies of Stanford University); E. M. Warburg Pincus and Co. Asia, Ltd. (now Warburg Pincus LLC); Exxon (now

Exxon-Mobil) Corporation; the Ford Foundation (Beijing); Goldman Sachs (Asia) LLC; the Hong Kong Stock Exchange; the Hong Kong University of Science and Technology; and the Koret Foundation (through SIEPR). We are grateful, too, for the funding provided by Stanford University to the Center.

Finally, we acknowledge the contributions to this volume, and to the series in which it is published, of the late Ken MacLeod. We greatly regret his untimely passing.

ABOUT THE CONTRIBUTORS

The Editors

Nicholas C. Hope is deputy director of the Center for Research on Economic Development and Policy Reform, Stanford University. Prior to joining Stanford in 2000, he had had a lengthy career at the World Bank, holding among others, the positions of chief of the External Debt Division, director of resident staff in Indonesia, and country director, China and Mongolia. A Rhodes Scholar from Tasmania in 1965, he received his Ph.D. in economics from Princeton University in 1975. His research interests include banking and enterprise reform in China.

Dennis Tao Yang is associate professor of economics at the Virginia Polytechnic Institute and State University. Prior to that, he was assistant professor at Duke University, where he became Senior Research Fellow at the Center for Demographic Studies at Duke in 1999. He received his Ph.D. in economics from Chicago in 1994, and his research emphasizes China's labor markets and microeconomic development. His recent publications are on China's rural–urban disparity and population policies.

Mu Yang Li has provided research assistance at the Stanford University's Center for Research on Economic Development and Policy Reform since 1998. Her interests are comparative institutional analysis, international economics, and the Chinese economy. She earned her doctorate in economics in 2003 and is a postdoctoral research associate at the Center for Entrepreneurial Studies, Stanford Graduate School of Business.

The Contributors

William P. Alford is the Henry L. Stimson Professor of Law, director of East Asian legal studies, and associate dean for the graduate program and international legal studies at Harvard Law School. After obtaining graduate training in Chinese studies and Chinese history at Yale University, he completed his J.D. at Harvard University in 1977. He specializes in Chinese law and legal history, comparative law, and international trade law. His many professional distinctions include his most recent ABE fellowship at the Social Science Research Council. Legal development and environmental law in China have been the focus of his most recent publications.

Chong-En Bai, initially trained as a mathematician, received his Ph.D. in mathematics from the University of California, San Diego, in 1988. Five years later, he graduated from Harvard with a Ph.D. in economics. He taught at Boston College from 1992 until he joined the School of Economics and Finance, University of Hong Kong, in 1999. He is a research fellow of the William Davidson Institute at the University of Michigan Business School and the National Center for Economic Research at Tsinghua University. His research interests lie primarily in the economics of organization and the economics of development and transition.

Cai Fang is professor and director of the Institute of Population Studies, Chinese Academy of Social Sciences (CASS), and dean of the Department of Population Studies, at the CASS graduate school. His areas of expertise are economic development, agricultural policies, and economic reform in China. He is one of the most internationally distinguished Chinese scholars in these fields.

Susmita Dasgupta is senior economist on the Infrastructure/Environment Team of the Development Research Group at the World Bank, with a specialization in empirical research. Her current research focus is on environmental management and the prospects of Internet diffusion for developing countries. Originally trained as an econometrician, with a Ph.D. in economics from the State University of New York at Albany, she taught at American University and SUNY-Albany before joining the World Bank in 1992.

Betina Dimaranan is research associate with the Center for Global Trade Analysis Project (GTAP) at Purdue University. She received her Ph.D. in agricultural economics from Purdue. Her research interests are in the areas of international trade, trade reform, economic development, general equilibrium analysis, and agricultural protectionism. She has coauthored several papers that used the GTAP framework to conduct comparative static analyses of trade issues involving the

Uruguay Round of GATT negotiations, agriculture and food, the Asia–Pacific region, and China.

Thomas W. Hertel is professor of agricultural economics and founding director of the Global Trade Analysis Project (GTAP) at Purdue University. He received his Ph.D. in resource economics from Cornell University in 1983. His research in the economywide analysis of trade policies has led to numerous journal articles. He is currently on the editorial board of the *Australian Journal of Agricultural and Resource Economics* and has served as a consultant to the World Bank, the OECD, the European Commission, the Ford Foundation, and the Australian Productivity Commission.

Jikun Huang is professor and director of the Center for Chinese Agricultural Policy, Institute of Geographical Sciences and Natural Resources Research, Chinese Academy of Sciences. In addition to his academic career, he has been a policy adviser to the Ministry of Agriculture and various provincial governments as well as a consultant for a number of leading international development organizations. He received his Ph.D. in agricultural economics at University of the Philippines at Los Baños College in 1990. Because of his outstanding and prolific research in agricultural economics and rural development, he was recognized as one of seventeen National Outstanding Young (Chinese) Scientists in 1998.

Athar Hussain is senior research fellow at the London School of Economics, as well as the deputy director of the Asia Research Center there. He is also a member of the Economic and Social Committee for Overseas Research in the Department for International Development of the United Kingdom. Previously, his professional engagements included positions at the Asian Development Bank, the European Commission, and the World Bank. He has coauthored and edited numerous books on economic development in China and has written many journal articles in the area of economic development.

Elena Ianchovichina is an economist at the World Bank. She received her Ph.D. in production and international economics from Purdue University in 1998, after which she joined the faculty of Kansas State University as an assistant professor in international trade. Her research has focused on technological progress in agriculture and land use in a global context and the recovery of the East Asian economies from the Asian economic crisis of the late 1990s.

Nicholas R. Lardy is senior fellow for foreign policy studies at the Brookings Institution and Frederick Frank Adjunct Professor of International Trade and Finance at Yale University's School of Management. He received his Ph.D. in economics from University of Michigan in 1975. He has published extensively on his area of expertise, the Chinese economy, including two recent books, *Integrating China into the Global Economy* (Brookings Institution, 2002) and *China's Unfinished Economic Revolution* (Brookings Institution, 1998).

David D. Li is associate professor of economics at the Hong Kong University of Science and Technology. After completing his Ph.D. at Harvard University in 1992, he taught at the University of Michigan, during which time he was a Hoover National Fellow. His research interests include corporate governance and enterprise reform in China.

Justin Y. Lin is professor and founding director of the China Center for Economic Research at Peking University, professor at the Hong Kong University of Science and Technology, and adjunct professor at the Australian National University. Trained at the University of Chicago, where he earned his Ph.D. in 1986, he has written six books, including *The China Miracle: Development Strategy and Economic Reform* (Chinese University, 1996), with Li Zhou, and numerous journal articles on history, development, and transition in China. He serves as a member of the editorial boards of nine international academic journals and is also a member of the National Committee of the Chinese People's Political Consultation Conference.

William Martin is principal economist for the Development Research Group at the World Bank. He obtained his Ph.D. from Iowa State University in 1982. Before joining the World Bank in 1991 as an economist in the International Trade Division, he was a senior research fellow at the National Center for Development Studies, Australian National University. He has held a seat on the Global Trade Analysis Project Consortium Board since 1993. His prolific publications focus on trade and development and on multilateral trade agreements.

Barry Naughton is So Kwanlok Professor of Chinese and International Affairs in the Graduate School of International Relations and Pacific Studies at the University of California, San Diego. He received his Ph.D. in economics from Yale University in 1986. His expertise in the Chinese economy has led him to publish *Grow Out of the Plan: Chinese Economic Reform, 1978–1993* (Cambridge University Press, 1995), as well as numerous journal articles in this field. His current research interests lie in China's technology policy formulation and economic and political integration.

Jean C. Oi is associate professor of political science and director of the Center for East Asian Studies at Stanford University. She received her Ph.D. in political science from the University of Michigan in 1980. Her research interests are corporate governance in China's reform of state-owned enterprises; Chinese politics, institutions, and transitional systems; and the state and development. She was a 1990–91 National Fellow at the Hoover Institution.

Yingyi Qian is professor of economics at the University of California, Berkeley. He received his Ph.D. in economics from Harvard University in 1990. He taught previously at Stanford University, where he was a Hoover National Fellow and a McNamara Faculty Fellow, and at the University of Maryland. He specializes in comparative institutional analysis and economies in transition. Recent publications include articles on Chinese-style federalism and dynamics of institutional reform.

Scott Rozelle is associate professor of agricultural and resource economics at the University of California, Davis. After receiving his Ph.D. in agricultural economics from Cornell University in 1990), he held positions at the Food Research Institute and subsequently the Economics Department at Stanford University. He was a National Fellow of the Hoover Institution and a recipient of a Ford Foundation grant for research on poverty alleviation in China. His research is primarily on China's agriculture and rural development, a field in which he has published extensively.

Hua Wang is environmental and resource economist with the Development Research Group at the World Bank. Trained at the School of Public Health at the University of North Carolina at Chapel Hill, where he earned his Ph.D. in 1997, he has worked extensively on industrial pollution control in China and has written numerous journal articles.

Yijiang Wang is associate professor at the Industrial Relations Center, Carlson School of Management, University of Minnesota, and received his Ph.D. in economics from Harvard University in 1991. His research focuses on industrial relations, labor economics, and economies in transition. His professional affiliations include a research fellowship with the William Davidson Institute.

Shang-jin Wei is economic adviser at the International Monetary Fund and faculty research fellow at the National Bureau of Economic Research. He is senior fellow and the New Century Chair at the Brookings Institution and senior fellow at the Center for Economic Policy Research (Europe). His research focuses on international finance and macroeconomics and on reforms in former centrally planned economies. His current research interests include corruption and international economic and political integration. He was also a consultant at the World Bank and the Board of Governors of the Federal Reserve System. He received his Ph.D. from the University of California, Berkeley, in 1992.

David Wheeler is lead economist in the Infrastructure/Environment Team of the World Bank's Development Research Group, where he directs a team that works on policy and research issues in collaboration with national and state pollution control agencies. He received his Ph.D. in economics from the Massachusetts Institute of Technology in 1974. Before joining the World Bank, he was a professor of economics at Boston University. He was the director of the Development Studies Project in Jakarta, Indonesia, and is a cofounder of the Boston Institute for Developing Economies. He has published numerous books and journal articles on issues related to development and environment.

Jinglian Wu is senior research fellow at the Development Research Center of the State Council of the People's Republic of China and professor of economics at the graduate school of the Chinese Academy of Social Sciences. He was formerly executive director of the Economic Research Center (now the Development Research Center) of the State Council. His other prominent governmental positions have included membership of the Standing Committee of the Chinese People's Political Consultative Conference. As a major architect of China's economic reform, he has published many policy-oriented articles both domestically and internationally. His current research and policy interests center on state sector restructuring and private sector development.

Jeffrey S. Zax is associate professor of economics at the University of Colorado in Boulder. He received his Ph.D. from Harvard University in 1984 and has taught at the City University of New York and has served as a research economist with the National Bureau of Economic Research. Specializing in labor economics, he has published numerous articles on urban labor in China.

Linxiu Zhang is associate professor and deputy director of the Center for Chinese Agricultural Policy at the Institute of Geographical Sciences and Natural Resources Research, Chinese Academy of Sciences (CAS). Her current responsibilities are primarily the supervision of the International Food Policy Research Institute's Beijing office and coordination of its research activities with Chinese partners. After receiving her Ph.D. in agricultural economics from the University of Reading, England, in 1995, she took up her position at CAS, spearheading various projects on agriculture and rural households. She has conducted extensive research on household food security, gender, and poverty.

1

Economic Policy Reform in China

Nicholas C. Hope, Dennis Tao Yang, and Mu Yang Li

Two decades into an era of sustained reform, China is a country transformed. Twenty years of growth at an average of about 9 percent a year has quadrupled gross domestic product and made China a U.S.$1 trillion economy. Admittedly, that impressive output level looks less so alongside China's huge population of more than 1.3 billion. But it is a remarkable accomplishment nevertheless, especially considering the condition of the Chinese economy in 1979, when market-oriented reforms began in earnest. China's ongoing and largely successful efforts to transition from a command economy to a "socialist market economy" have contrasted starkly with the erratic progress under the command system that is being dismantled.

Attempts to build an efficient command economy began at the founding of the People's Republic of China in 1949. To the extent that the economic statistics of the period convey meaningful measures of the economy, the attempts achieved some success, with annual growth rates averaging about 15 percent during the initial period of 1952–58.[1] The Communist government replaced the market with the plan, communized the farms, established state ownership of industrial enterprises, and instituted price controls in order to transform agricultural surplus into industrial investment. As a result, the industrial sector, especially heavy industries, quickly emerged from near nonexistence in the nation's underdeveloped agrarian economy. From 1953 to 1959, crude steel output grew by 40 percent, coal by 30 percent, cement by 20 percent, and metal-cutting machine tools and electric power by almost 30 percent.[2]

Despite the bias toward heavy industry, agriculture grew fast too. Total grain output increased from 113 million metric tons in 1949 to 214 million in 1966, representing a 38 percent increase in per capita output.[3] Socialist distribution also channeled resources into improving the material welfare of the people in a number of ways. According to such indicators of social well-being as life expectancy and infant mortality, China outperformed most other countries at comparable levels of per capita income.[4]

However, these initial accomplishments were soon followed by nearly twenty years of economic and political turmoil. The Great Leap Forward (1958–61), an unprecedented attempt to achieve fast industrialization, had disastrous outcomes. Grain output in China fell precipitously in 1959 and 1960, and the value of industrial output also fell sharply in 1961–62. The resulting famine in China claimed as many as twenty to thirty million lives. After an all-too-brief recovery, China entered another period of political upheaval, the Cultural Revolution (1966–76).[5] Throughout nearly two decades of disastrous performance, China continued to pursue a development strategy centered on heavy industry, despite the gross economic inefficiency that imposed on its centrally planned economy.

In the aftermath of the Cultural Revolution, the senior leadership recognized that inefficiency resulting from distorted incentives and wasteful investment was a powerful inhibitor of economic development. Not only were the prospects for sustaining fast growth becoming increasingly bleak, but also the growth pattern itself had sacrificed wage goods and led to only modest improvements in living standards. After three decades of seemingly respectable growth, China was still undeniably poor. And China's poverty was all the more evident when contrasted with the growing prosperity of the "Four Dragons of Asia"—Hong Kong, Korea, Singapore, and Taiwan—as well as the other rapidly industrializing countries of Southeast Asia.

Reform as an Imperative

During the Third Plenum of the Eleventh Party Congress (December 18–22, 1978), the Chinese leadership made the landmark decision to attempt an unprecedented transition from a centrally planned economy to a more market-oriented economy, or a "planned socialist commodity economy." Although the transition began without a clear long-term agenda other than the desire to increase productivity and raise standards of living, the reform proceeded under then paramount leader Deng Xiaoping's call to "cross the river by touching the stones."

Deng's famous phrase captures how reforms in China were introduced gradually and sequentially, often following small-scale experimentation. Bolder experiments were permitted, and a process of trial and error ultimately led to a succession of approved small steps toward the far riverbank. China's ability to introduce change gradually and as a conscious choice seems almost a luxury when its experience is compared to that of other command economies engaged in tumultuous transitions to the market. Where it is possible, gradualism seems greatly to be desired if it enables governments to build and sustain political support for reform.

In China's case, that support has been won by establishing at the outset that far more people would gain than lose from reform policies and by maintaining a sense of the familiar throughout a dramatic and deceptively speedy transformation. China's progress in establishing the institutional underpinnings of a market economy has been halting, but it has avoided the alienation of support that might have occurred if unfamiliar institutions had been imposed on a resisting populace. The "best practice" institutions that will ultimately be needed to complete China's transition to a market economy might have proved too exotic to flourish in the comparatively hostile environment to be found in China when the first tentative steps into the river were taken.

The most significant early reform was the introduction of the so-called Household Responsibility System in agriculture. It replaced the old collectivized communes and allowed rural households to market surplus output in excess of the plan. This improved incentives at the margin and unleashed vigorous growth in agricultural production and productivity. Rising rural incomes from the partial liberalization of agricultural markets stimulated demand for wage goods. Together with the restoration in the early 1980s of private user rights for land, that spurred massive rural industrialization, in which the township and village enterprises (TVEs) began to supply consumer goods. At the same time, the TVEs absorbed 100 million rural workers and became the driving force behind the growth of Chinese industrial production.[6]

As the success of the Household Responsibility System became apparent, essentially similar reforms were introduced in the cities. Municipal officials and local plant managers were granted more discretion to organize the productive activities of a wide variety of small-scale enterprises in services and light manufacturing. Numerous price controls were gradually removed or relaxed. As the share of production directed by the plan continued to shrink, fewer and fewer products were distributed through state-controlled channels. What began as small-scale experiments in partial market liberalization extended gradually to give farmers and nonagricultural enterprises much greater freedom to determine the composition and pricing of their products and to retain and decide on the disposition of their profits. Better incentives encouraged competition and improved performance even in the state-owned sector. At the same time, the economy became more and more open to foreign trade and foreign investment.

As China entered the 1990s, a limited program of economic liberalization in rural areas gradually became a much broader process of social change involving virtually all areas of human endeavor, including the arts, education, sports, religion, defense, and systems of governance. China's entire institutional framework was gradually being overhauled. Administrative and fiscal decentralization transferred greater discretion and gave better incentives to local governments to plan and manage economic activities. The institutional changes accompanying decentralization, as summarized by Yingyi Qian, consisted mainly of "regional decentralization of government, entry and expansion of nonstate enterprises, financial stability through financial dualism, and a dual-track approach to market liberalization."[7] One of the most important outcomes of reform was China's almost complete transition from planning and control. Goods markets proliferated, and people's livelihoods greatly improved.

Deepening Reforms

Despite the prevalence and success of market-oriented reforms, by the early 1990s China had become a much more complex economy that still depended on a clumsy system of administrative controls to maintain macroeconomic balance. Many reforms had been incomplete, experimental, and local and had failed to tackle systemic macroeconomic concerns. Macroeconomic management was essentially limited to direct credit and investment controls. Economic instability through booms and then (comparative) busts became increasingly frequent, and led to public unrest. In 1989, the Tiananmen Square incident dampened the internal momentum of reform and soured many foreign observers on the Chinese experiment.

The surge in inflation (to 20 percent or more a year) that followed Deng Xiaoping's historic visit to South China in early 1992 clearly exposed the systemic weaknesses stemming from ad hoc reforms. His post-Tiananmen "southern tour" reaffirmed the commitment of the Chinese Communist Party (CCP) to economic reforms and induced a flood of nonstate and state investment in manufacturing, real estate, and service industries. Much of the investment was financed, sometimes indirectly, by domestic state banks and was often refinanced by the central bank (the People's Bank of China—PBC). Efforts to control the runaway investment boom and associated inflation were frustrated by the high degree of fiscal and monetary decentralization that had resulted from the delegation of administrative power in the 1980s.

Almost certainly not coincidentally, the reform path took a pivotal turn in 1993. After much internal debate, a consensus emerged within the CCP on the need to employ drastic macrostabilization measures and to develop rule-based macroeconomic management and regulatory mechanisms. In November 1993, the Third Plenum of the Fourteenth Party Congress enacted the "Decision on Issues Concerning the Establishment of a Socialist Market Economic Structure," which articulated the goal of establishing a "socialist market economy," an initially ill-defined replacement for the vague earlier concept of a "market economy with Chinese characteristics."[8] The "Decision" called for coordinated reforms in different areas to create a rule-based market system and a level playing field. In fact, it grouped fifty separate decisions under ten headings—enterprise reform, market system, macroeconomic management, national incomes policy and social security system, rural economic reform, international economic relations, science and technology policy, legal reform, and Party leadership—to form the blueprint for policymaking and institution building for ensuing decades.

In the area of fiscal management, the goal was to replace the existing revenue contracting arrangements by central and local taxation systems with clearly defined sources of revenue. A series of measures soon after the "Decision" were enacted to realize this goal. In 1994, a national tax bureau and local tax bureaus were established, with separate jurisdiction over clearly specified national and local sources of revenue. These tax reforms put an end to the persistent erosion of central government revenue that had resulted from prior fiscal decentralization. In 1995, the Budget Law prohibited the central government from borrowing from the central bank and allowed it to finance its deficits only by the issuance of public debt. Similar fiscal discipline was imposed on local governments.

Monetary centralization and some important financial reforms constituted another major initiative following the "Decision." Independent monetary authority was given to the PBC, and the four large state banks were to be more substantially exposed to commercial principles. In 1993, the PBC severed the personnel link between the management of its branches and the local governments. The Central Bank Law of 1995 gave the People's Bank the sole mandate for monetary policy, to the exclusion of local governments. Further institutional change occurred when the thirty provincial branches of the PBC were succeeded by nine regional branches, a configuration clearly influenced by the Federal Reserve System of the United States.

Some progress was made to introduce commercial principles to the four large state banks. Three policy banks were created in 1994 in an attempt to eliminate policy lending from the state commercial banks' portfolios. In 1995, preparations began to develop a nationally integrated interbank market, and a phased interest rate liberalization program started in January 1996. To tackle the worsening problem of nonperforming loans (NPLs), in 1999 four asset management companies (AMCs) were established—each with 10 billion reminbi (RMB) yuan initial capital provided by the Ministry of Finance—to take on much of the burden of the NPLs in the banking sector.[9] Upon acquiring these assets, the AMCs assumed the right to dispose of them on a commercial basis, including the possibility of swapping the debts for equity in the indebted state-owned enterprises (SOEs). Since their inception, they have completed the purchase of about 1.39 trillion yuan of NPLs from the state banks. By the end of 2001, they had disposed of NPLs worth 178.1 billion yuan (U.S.$21.51 billion) and recovered 36.88 billion yuan (U.S.$4.45 billion) in cash.[10] In return for shedding bad loans and boosting their capital, the banks were required to begin to implement stricter accounting standards and observe market discipline under a series of new banking regulations.

The unification of the foreign exchange rate in 1994 and the subsequent early introduction of convertibility on the current account of the balance of payments was one of the major accomplishments of recent Chinese reform. Before 1994, a dual-track foreign exchange system had been in operation: some transactions occurred at "swap" market exchange rates instead of at the official rate. But the share of foreign exchange allocated under the plan was allowed to fall gradually — to less than 20 percent by 1993 — and the official and swap rates were unified remarkably smoothly into a single market rate on January 1, 1994. The foreign exchange rate, represented by the U.S. dollar–RMB yuan rate, appreciated from 8.7 to 8.3 and has since remained stable. Current account convertibility followed in December 1996.

Another breakthrough of the "Decision" was the official recognition of the positive role played by nonstate ownership. Although it stresses the significance of continued public ownership of the key means of production and main service organizations, at the same time, the "Decision" paved the way for further enterprise reform both by mandating the change of system, *zhuanzhi*, for the numerous medium and small SOEs and by permitting the private sector to flourish. Since then, there has been greater acceptance of, and even reliance on, the development of private enterprises and the privatization of public assets.

The Fifteenth Party Congress convened in September 1997 went beyond the 1993 "Decision" in elevating the status of private ownership to "an important component of the economy," from the previous status of "a supplementary component." The revision was written into an amendment to the constitution in March 1999. Private ownership, which was nonexistent before the reform, has thrived in an increasingly market-oriented economy. Private enterprises, *siying qiye*, and self-employed households, *getihu*, contributed approximately 18 percent of total gross industrial output in 1999, while the broadly defined nonstate sector, including private enterprises, shareholding corporations, foreign-funded firms, and collectives, accounted for 72 percent. With employment by the SOEs and collectives decreasing steadily since 1996, the share of urban employment by private firms (both *siying qiye* and *getihu*), foreign-funded firms, and shareholding corporations had risen from 4 percent in 1990 to 24 percent in 1999.[11] Even more important, private enterprises comprise the most vibrant sector of the economy, outperforming both the state-owned enterprises and nonstate collectives in both output and productivity growth.

The more than quadrupling of real GDP since 1979 understates the sweeping changes that have taken place within the economy. By 1999, only 15 percent of GDP came from agricultural production, while about 50 percent was contributed by the industrial sector and 35 percent by the service sector. This structural shift in the economy is also reflected in the sectoral composition of a labor force of seven hundred million people, about half of whom are now employed in agriculture, a quarter in industry, and the remaining quarter in services (see Figure 1.1).

FIGURE 1.1
Transformation of the Sectoral Structure of the Chinese Economy

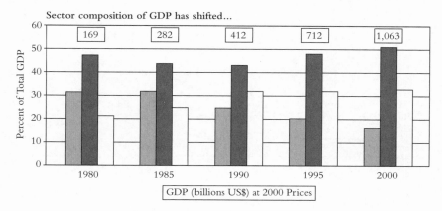

Sector composition of GDP has shifted...

GDP (billions US$) at 2000 Prices

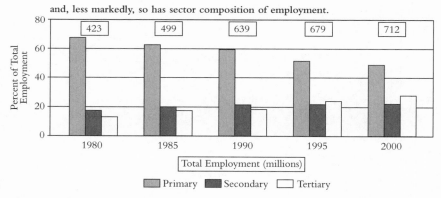

and, less markedly, so has sector composition of employment.

Total Employment (millions)

▨ Primary   ■ Secondary   ☐ Tertiary

SOURCE: State Statistical Bureau, *China Statistical Yearbook, 2001* (Beijing: State Statistical Publishing House, 2001).

From a state of virtual isolation from the world economy in 1979, the Chinese economy has also become substantially involved in the international flow of commodities, services, and capital. In 2002, total trade, measured as the sum of imports and exports, amounted to about 50 percent of GDP. Contingent on a number of factors, China's share of world export (and import) markets could rise from around 3.5 percent in 1995 to over 6 percent by 2005 (see Chapter Six). China has also become a major host of foreign direct investment (FDI), consistently attracting over one-third of FDI to the developing countries. Net FDI has risen from less than $5 billion a year in the early 1990s to exceed $50 billion

FIGURE 1.2
China in the World Economy

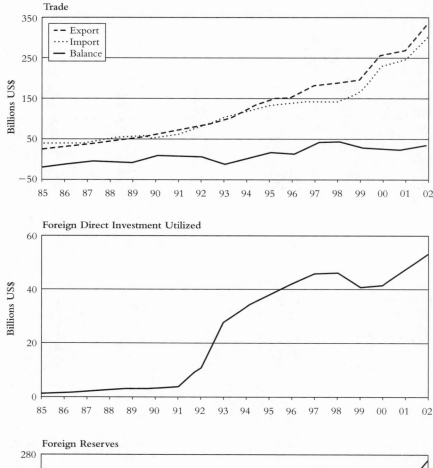

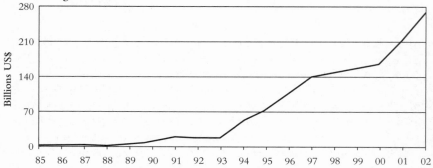

SOURCES: 1985–99 data from State Statistical Bureau, *Chinese Statistical Yearbook, 1996, 1998, 2000* (Beijing: State Statistical Publishing House, 1996, 1998, 2000); 2000 data from a report published by the National Bureau of Statistics on March 26, 2001.

in 2002. Balanced import and export growth, coupled with continued inflow of FDI, has led to sustained growth of Chinese foreign exchange reserves, which passed $285 billion at the end of 2002 (see Figure 1.2).

Notwithstanding these developments and China's vigorous efforts to implement the ambitious blueprint outlined in the "Decision," many observers would argue that uncertainty clouds the prospects for continued progress in reform. Despite some impressive achievements, reforms still seem to be falling short of what was promised. China remains poor—more than half its people live on less than $2 a day. Difficult institutional reforms, such as financial restructuring and the perennial problem of enterprise reform, seem to encounter mounting resistance. A widening rural–urban divide and diverging incomes across socio-economic groups are straining the fabric of a society that is yet to experience the pressures of the deeper reforms that are needed before the river is forded.

To outside observers, China's reform process appears fragile because of its partial, incomplete nature. Most observers, insiders and outsiders alike, would probably conclude, however, that a China that completes its reforms successfully and becomes increasingly prosperous would have much to offer the world. The chapters in this book represent a stocktaking of how much of the river has been traversed and how to complete the rest of the journey.

What Pressing Issues Remain?

No single volume could hope to cover exhaustively the breadth of China's experience with the multiplicity of reforms that have been initiated in the past twenty years. But selectively, for some important broad areas, the contributions presented in this volume assess China's progress and propose directions for further reforms, fifty years after the founding of the People's Republic and two decades into China's remarkable experiment in how best to emerge from a deprivation that its leaders finally recognized was largely self-imposed. The authors of the chapters are a multidisciplinary group drawn from both China and abroad, representing academia, government, private business, and multilateral organizations.

In Chapter Two, the authors evaluate the overall status of Chinese policy reform and present their views on the most urgent areas for new reforms. The volume then groups its analysis of specific issues into four broad areas. Within them, individual authors have chosen how narrowly or broadly to define the scope of their research. The first group of issues is concerned with how reforms have shaped market-supporting institutions. Three important areas for institutional reform are analyzed—the financial system, the enterprise system, and the legal system—with the objective of helping China build market-friendly institutions.

The second topic area examines how to extend Chinese participation in markets, domestically and internationally, and considers the implications of greater integration. China's accession to the World Trade Organization (WTO) adds urgency to the need for better understanding of the issues involved for China, as well as its trading and investment partners. China is in the front ranks of global trading powers and an ever-stronger magnet for direct investment. In turn, greater integration in the global economy can be a powerful force for greater integration of domestic markets and the gains in efficiency that will bring.

The third broad topic area investigates who benefits from China's growth. The first contribution examines the effectiveness of China's poverty reduction programs in extending the benefits of rapid growth to China's poor. The other two topics—reforming social welfare and housing—directly influence the quality of life of most people and also facilitate reforms in other areas, which are constrained by the absence of both an affordable social safety net to assist those affected adversely by change and a functioning labor market.

The final set of issues concerns how to sustain the benefits of growth. The long-term stability of China's reforms depends in large measure on meeting the pressing challenges posed by the rapidly deteriorating physical environment, declining agricultural productivity growth, widening rural-urban disparities, and the limited adaptability of political institutions. The authors of the four chapters in this section evaluate how each of these challenges might threaten future reforms and how best to remove the threats.

The book ends with a summary, drawn from the earlier chapters, of research priorities that promise to do the most to inform further policy reforms.

Policy Reform in China: What Is Needed Next?

In Chapter Two, Yingyi Qian and Jinglian Wu present their assessment of Chinese reform over the past twenty years. They conclude that early reforms, starting in 1979, substantially achieved the objectives of raising productivity and improving living standards. Successful reforms also contributed importantly to a self-sustaining momentum for further reform by adapting existing institutions to support market-friendly policies. The second main wave of reform, beginning in 1992–93, signaled a shift in policy from experimentation with incremental reforms to a more focused endeavor to build a comprehensive modern market system.

Qian and Wu evaluate progress on the five main economic reforms targeted by the 1993 "Decision." Progress in unifying the foreign exchange market has been excellent. Tax and fiscal reforms are proceeding well, although far-reaching institutional reform is yet to be rewarded—as it promises to be—by dramatic improvements in raising revenue. Experience in the financial sector has been mixed, in that significant improvements in the framework for monetary management have yet to be matched by equivalent improvement in the performance of the banking system. The enterprise system has seen uneven progress, with a fairly dramatic transformation of small firms but no real breakthroughs in the governance and management of large ones. To date, reform of the social safety net has been slow and focused on urban areas.

Without saying explicitly how much of the river remains to be forded, Qian and Wu imply that a considerable body of water still lies ahead, and the far shore might be partially shrouded in mist. A long list of necessary reforms remains, even in areas that have already seen considerable progress: taxation, the financial system, the social safety net, social equality, regulation, foreign trade and investment in the context of membership in the WTO, and so on. Further reform is needed by most of China's market-supporting institutions, as well as to revamp the systems of both national and enterprise governance. From their long list, Qian and Wu identify two priorities for China in the early years of the new century: the reform of the state sector and the establishment of a competitive enterprise system. The key ingredient for the second of these is to establish an arm's-length relationship between governments at all levels and business.

Qian and Wu find considerable cause for optimism in recent government actions. They single out the central government's formal approval of private ownership; endorsement of the rule of law; continuing experiments with reform of the social safety net, which should partly relieve enterprises from the burden of providing for the welfare of current and former employees; and creation of asset management companies to help clean up the portfolios of the state-owned banks.

Building Market-Supporting Institutions

The importance of institutional reform in China is underlined by the judgment of Qian and Wu that establishment of the rule of law and continuing reform of the financial and enterprise systems are the most important challenges confronting the government.

The next section of this volume considers aspects of institutional reform in each of three areas where reform has lagged and where the government seems irresolute in its efforts to implement change, even where new policy directions have been charted.

Reforming the Financial System

One costly legacy of China's old command system is that its four large state-owned commercial banks are unequal to the task of performing the functions of modern banking institutions in a market economy. Their portfolios are burdened with unsustainably high shares of nonperforming loans, a consequence both of their role in implementing the centrally mandated credit plan and of their lack of skills in the techniques of commercial banking. Nicholas Lardy, in analyzing aspects of the deficiencies remaining in China's financial system, identifies severe misallocation of investment as an important indicator of the continuing inefficiency of financial intermediation. Despite the important financial reforms that have been introduced in recent years, the lack of related institutional reform and inadequate competition in the financial and capital markets have contributed to slow improvement in performance.

Lardy analyzes the banking system and the implications for the public finances of the extremely weak portfolios of the (state-owned) commercial banks. He identifies several actions that represent significant headway in improving the framework for the banking system. The functions and structure of the People's Bank of China have been reorganized, and the state-owned commercial banks have been freed (at least to some extent) from policy lending through the formation of specialized policy banks and the dismantling of the credit plan. The banks have been partially recapitalized, and some of their nonperforming loans have been assigned to the recently created asset management companies. Nonetheless, these changes have failed so far to lead to the emergence of a truly commercial credit culture in China's banking system.

Until such a culture emerges, China's banks remain vulnerable to the risk that the tradition of bad lending will continue. Cleaning up the stock of bad assets is of less immediate importance to the long-run health of the banking system than is ensuring that new lending accords with the principles of sound banking. But even assuming that new lending is soundly based, the legacy of the past has important fiscal consequences for the Chinese government, which at some point will need to put its banks on a sound financial footing if they are to compete with a developing private banking sector foreshadowed by China's WTO membership. By analyzing financial outcomes under three scenarios, Lardy concludes that both revenue buoyancy and an effective credit culture are necessary components of a solution to that part of the government's public finance dilemma due to the poor performance of its banks.

How Fair Is Competition Among Enterprises?

The second chapter on institutional change considers the need for further adjustment to China's competition policy, notwithstanding the fact that much of the impetus for industrial growth in the past two decades has stemmed from the extraordinary activity of the nonstate sector (which includes the TVEs). Chong-En Bai, David Li, and Yijiang Wang analyze factors that inhibit continued growth of collectively owned enterprises as they endeavor to acquire sufficient size to compete effectively with state-owned firms and increasingly with foreign and domestic privately owned firms.

Aspects of the tilted playing field, especially "ambiguous ownership," that worked in favor of small, dynamic firms during the early stages of transition to a market economy are much less to their advantage now. The reasons are that

firms find themselves with compromised property rights and, partly as a consequence, with severe constraints on their access to formal credit and on the protections they receive under the commercial law. These impediments are especially detrimental to the emergence of larger firms, as empirical findings in other
studies of private sector development have indicated. For instance, data from a
panel of economies in transition show that early in the transition, entrepreneurs
were able to overcome the constraints to the rapid emergence of new firms
through their self-help. However, as transition proceeded, they came to need assistance from the state in providing contract enforcement and access to finance.[12]

The chapter authors analyze the difficulties that the managers of firms now
confront in clarifying ownership rights, especially the problems of "buying off"
the bureaucrats who have acquired rights as "stakeholders."

The Rule of Law

By common consensus, China's legal system is inadequately developed to foster
the emergence of a modern market economy. Many analysts have called for the
establishment of the "rule of law" in China; as William Alford makes clear in
Chapter Five, that remains a daunting task. To establish the rule of law and so relieve the ills of uncertainty and lack of contractual clarity (stressed in the earlier
chapters) requires much work over many years. China needs to introduce new
laws, win acceptance of them at the grassroots level, train lawyers and jurists, and
develop a body of case law that allows investors in general and foreign investors
in particular to be confident about how they will fare if they put Chinese law to
the test.

Alford analyzes the role that more formal legal institutions, rules, and trained
personnel will play in inculcating the greater respect for the rule of law that many
see as an essential underpinning of sustained economic growth. Choosing the
"best" commercial laws that work well in the wealthy countries is no guarantee
that they can be implemented effectively in a "top-down" manner in China. In
China, as elsewhere, laws are likely to do the job intended only when they are
"societally generated."[13] We tend to speak of the rule of law when we mean rule
by law, and China needs a cultural change in which people first embrace amendments to accepted rules and then accept that "rules matter more than the people
who make them."

An important thesis of Alford's chapter is the infeasibility of establishing rule
by law in a society where the Chinese Communist Party exempts itself from formal and informal legal restraints. Although many observers might question legitimately whether the CCP is communist in anything but name, it remains the
sole functioning political organization in China, and it has made the law an instrument of state power, in the important sense that the government now does
by law what it did previously by administrative fiat. Although progress has been

made, and the government has introduced sensible rules that increasingly recognize commercial and other rights, politics and the CCP win out when the
rules conflict with Party interests.

Alford contends that discretion in interpreting the law needs to be reduced;
at the same time, the system has to retain its ability to adapt laws and regulations
to a rapidly changing society. New research might investigate why law matters to
the Chinese economy, beyond simple devotion to the rule of law, with the priority being to examine the interplay between formal rules and informal norms
and how they interact within Chinese society.

Toward Greater Economic Integration

In 1997, the World Bank considered what the Chinese economy might look like
in 2020.[14] Sustained rapid growth could see China's share in world trade triple to
10 percent, which would make China the second-largest trading nation by the
end of the second decade of the new century. This outcome promises significant
welfare gains, for China and its trading partners and for foreign investors in the
Chinese economy, but those gains depend on sustained reforms and continued
liberalization of the regime for movement of goods, services, and capital internationally. In this section of the volume, authors analyze the implications of
continuing growth in China for its links with the international economy, as well
as for the integration of its internal markets.

China's Growing Role in World Trade

As we have seen, policy reform has carried China from virtual autarky to its position as a major international trading power. In Chapter Six, William Martin,
Betina Dimaranan, Thomas Hertel, and Elena Ianchovichina recognize the very
considerable adjustments that have accompanied China's rapid integration into
the world economy during its twenty-plus years of reform. They describe the
important developments that have eroded the dominance of a few large state
trading companies as literally thousands of new firms have begun to trade internationally and led to a pronounced reduction in the use of nontariff barriers
to trade to protect favored domestic industries. The authors analyze the implications of membership of the WTO, and the core of the chapter is the projections they obtain from a global general equilibrium model of the likely changes
as the world adjusts to China in the WTO.

With China in the WTO, its resources will shift more in accordance with
global comparative advantage. The WTO agreements require China to make
rapid progress in liberalizing agricultural imports and in opening the domestic
markets to foreign competition, especially in the telecommunications and financial service industries. The authors warn against taking their modeling results too

literally but assert that the results provide valuable insights into how powerful economic forces for structural change will reshape China's production and trade patterns in coming years. China will become an even more competitive force in the market for apparel and an emerging presence in trade in such relatively high-technology sectors as automobiles and electronics. Its trading partners can expect to capture rising shares of the Chinese markets for agricultural products, telecommunications, and services. Clearly, the extent to which liberalization proceeds will affect the growth of China's export market share; one of this chapter's contributions is to highlight the many factors that will determine how effectively China's growing role in world trade delivers promised benefits to all participants.

The Outlook for Foreign Investment in China

In analyzing China's involvement with the international capital markets, Shang-jin Wei takes an innovative approach in Chapter Seven. By the mid-1990s, China, although still a relatively modest borrower from the banks and bond markets,[15] had become the dominant host among developing nations for FDI. China was second only to the United States as a magnet for FDI; direct investment inflows have now surpassed U.S.$55 billion a year.[16] Instead of analyzing how China had become such a star performer, Wei emphasizes that China received much less investment than it might have received had it offered a more attractive climate to investors, especially to those from countries other than Hong Kong and Taiwan. He advances the proposition that good governance can be a more important factor in attracting FDI than the cheap labor or tax holidays that are often thought to be primary determinants of FDI flows. The implication drawn from his analysis is that China will attract more FDI in coming years if it concentrates on improving the institutional environment in which foreign investors operate rather than granting short-term economic incentives.

Wei identifies data discrepancies that lend uncertainty to China's own data on investment inflows. To support his contention that China is an underachieving host for direct investment from traditional major source countries, he uses cross-country data to estimate the potential inward FDI for a host country with China's economic and policy characteristics. His analysis establishes a huge gap between China's potential direct investment inflows and what has been achieved. Wei contends that if China could create a more transparent regime for foreign investors and eliminate corruption, substantially more FDI would flow to China than has been the case to date.

Integrating the Internal Market

One of the unfortunate legacies of the command economy is the wasteful excess capacity that exists throughout China. Some analysts depict China as a group of insufficiently specialized regional economies, marked by considerable local protection of markets. In their view, national economic integration has been hampered by the unwillingness of local officials to accept the consequences of more integration of markets on their locally owned SOEs. But using a new data set, Barry Naughton shows in Chapter Eight that interprovincial trade was large as far back as 1992 and large in comparison with trade within the European Union and between the members of ASEAN. Among the provinces, only Guangdong and Fujian trade more with other countries than they do with other Chinese provinces. In internal exchange of final commodities, China behaves much more like a single country than a close-knit trading bloc, notwithstanding a distribution infrastructure that remains underdeveloped. He contends that the relatively high share of intraindustry trade is a result of economic development, not of poor infrastructure for transporting bulk goods and raw materials.

Naughton's conclusions thus challenge the commonly held notion that regional protection was and is pervasive, although he asserts, despite data deficiencies that prevent firm conclusions, that significant barriers still impede the movement of factors of production and trade in services and intermediate goods. In value terms, differentiated manufactured goods for final consumption dominate trade between the provinces. Clearly, China has experienced a considerable buildup of internal competition, with evidence of significant restructuring at the local level.

Even if trade between provinces is larger than the literature to date might suggest, there still remains the question of whether the trade that takes place is predominantly regional rather than countrywide. Other studies have suggested recently that China's internal market is becoming less integrated and that greater mobility of labor, if not capital, should reduce the need for trade in goods.[17] Nevertheless, Naughton makes a convincing case, and casual observation reveals how commonly goods from all over China now can be found in local markets. Despite deficiencies in the data, the enterprise model seems to have changed from the single location–multiproduct model typical of the early 1980s to the mutilocation–single product model much more in evidence today. The chapter offers strong support to the view that China is progressing from an enterprise system based on inappropriate specialization to one founded on appropriate specialization.

Sharing Rising Incomes

China's leaders have accepted that income will be less equally distributed as an inevitable consequence of the move to a market economy in the pursuit of faster growth. At the same time, throughout the 1990s, the government has made poverty reduction a central objective of policy. In 1993, under the so-called 8–7 Program for poverty alleviation, it adopted the specific goal of lifting the eighty million people subsisting on unacceptably low levels of income and consumption from poverty by 2000.[18] In three chapters in this section, researchers tackle aspects of three issues that affect the distribution of the benefits of growth: how much success China has had in eliminating poverty, how effective China is in providing a social safety net for the economically disadvantaged, and how China is progressing in supplying its people with satisfactory housing.

Providing for the Poor

The chapter by Scott Rozelle, Linxiu Zhang, and Jikun Huang acknowledges at the outset China's impressive achievements in poverty reduction during the reform era. However, poverty alleviation continues to be a major policy challenge. The government's figures show that China had at least forty million rural poor at the turn of the century; World Bank estimates of rural poverty based on international comparisons exceed one hundred million. And on a consumption basis, more than two hundred million Chinese could still be considered poor in 2000.

The authors note that 698 poor counties had received targeted assistance under poverty programs by 1998. Even while agreeing that the government has done well in identifying poor areas, they call attention to the limitations of programs that neglect the poor who reside in nonpoor counties, including the growing incidence of poverty in urban areas. A distinction could be made here between transient and chronic poverty. The former might occur in a single year because of a weather-induced failure of the harvest. The latter is far more serious and is the hallmark of the resource-deficient areas where every year is a bad one. Data problems complicate the analysis of poverty issues, but a plausible hypothesis is that overall economic growth and regional poverty alleviation programs have both done about as much as can be done to tackle hard-core poverty in severely resource-deprived rural areas.

The authors' analysis supports this hypothesis. They analyze data from case studies of two provinces—Sichuan and Shaanxi—to determine how well China's poverty programs target the poor and how effectively those poverty programs have stimulated growth and employment. Their analysis leads them to conclude that poverty reduction can largely be attributed to China's fast growth. Imperfect targeting, inadequacies in design, and insufficient funding have limited the effectiveness of targeted programs in alleviating poverty. They contend that success has been greater in programs that finance household-based projects and that reach local agencies directly.

The chapter's authors also note that China's poverty programs are largely designed to deal with poverty *in situ*. They argue persuasively and powerfully that continuing progress in reducing hard-core poverty requires greater attention to formation of human capital over the longer term. That means more and better education for the children of poor rural families, which will equip them for better-paying jobs off the land.

To the extent that programs to create local infrastructure are sustained, they will fare better if local officials make the expenditure decisions that benefit the poor in their localities. Decisions made by bureaucrats from afar all too often have little relevance to the actual circumstances of the intended beneficiaries. No doubt, investment programs will continue to be needed in poor areas—to spur agricultural development, for example, and to supply services that make life less dreadful while investment in human capital enhancement is under way. Ultimately, more investment in human capital along with migration to jobs in urban areas is likely to have more success in reducing rural poverty than low-return investments in local physical infrastructure.

Erecting a Social Safety Net

Athar Hussain's chapter provides a comprehensive review of China's capacity to extend the basic elements of a social security system, especially to its urban population.[19] He emphasizes the three transitions with which successful policy reform must contend: from a command to a market economy, from a predominantly rural to a predominantly urban population, and from a youthful to an elderly demographic profile. The first of these requires the abolition of the enterprise-centered welfare system; the second, an income-generating asset that substitutes for access to land in supporting the aged population in towns and cities; and the third, a system of caring for the aged that replaces the traditional role played by children, especially sons.

He also emphasizes two major constraints in introducing a social security system: lack of fiscal resources, which is a problem throughout China, but more acutely so in poorer areas, and administrative capacity, which promises to be an even more important constraint than money in the next several years. He notes that China's one-child policy is unlikely to raise the dependency ratio[20] in the near future; in fact, it is projected to be lower in 2020 than in 1998 because the declining share of children in the population offsets the rising share of the elderly.

Hussain observes that rural areas are largely unaffected by the collapse of the enterprise-centered welfare system, and he identifies the priorities in rural areas as "establishing income maintenance schemes and health care insurance almost from scratch." In urban areas, the priorities are to replace the inherited social security system and to tackle the problem of emerging urban poverty, which has been neglected to date. The financing of urban social security is now based on universally accepted contributory principles, but the designs are flawed, in particular, by providing unaffordably generous benefits and neglecting to make special provision for current or soon-to-be retirees. Reliance on pay-as-you-go principles taxes the current labor force (and enterprises) heavily to provide for both its own benefits and those of earlier generations of workers and encourages evasion and inappropriate substitution away from labor in the factor mix.

Pooling across different benefits and regions could improve financial viability, and the overall system could be affordable once the problem of how to fund the benefits of current retirees is solved. The Ministry of Labor had ruled out an earlier attempt to replace a pay-as-you-go system with a fully funded system, preferring to try to collect high levies from existing workers. That has resulted in some serious problems, most notably evasion, which have caused the government to look more favorably on the option of using sales of state property to compensate retirees. But there are problems even if sales of state assets could establish pension funds that would provide some of the benefits promised to retirees. The limited assets currently available for investment would pose problems for fund managers, whose performance would in turn have to respond to appropriate incentives through yet-to-be-developed governance structures.

The transitions Hussain emphasizes mean that by 2020, China's populace will be grayer, more urban, more mobile, more oriented toward supplying services, and more vulnerable to unemployment. This implies that China needs to tackle the problems of how to extend the system (to all urban, and ultimately all rural, workers) and how to scale it down (from the benefit levels provided in the past by governments and state-owned enterprises). As it tackles these problems, he advises China to be wise enough not to extend the system and benefits prematurely and concludes that a universal social security system for the whole country, "although desirable, is infeasible in the immediate future for financial and administrative reasons."

Improving China's Housing

One of the most important nonwage benefits that China's work units have traditionally supplied to their employees is housing. For most of the Communist era, internal labor migration in China has been administratively restricted or even prohibited. The transition to a market economy has seen greater internal movement of workers, but the absence of a functioning housing market has heightened the immobility of the labor force. Few workers could afford to leave their residences to seek new jobs without an assurance that they would find affordable places to live. Creating a housing market will be an important building block both in establishing an effective labor market and in raising the quality of Chinese housing services.

In Chapter Eleven, Jeffrey Zax attributes the massive increase over the past twenty years in China's housing stock mainly to the equally massive investment in housing by work units. Although housing rents are rising, and rising even as a share of income, rental prices charged by work units are still far below the economic value of the lodgings provided. Low rents are essentially fully offset by depressed wages, but both of these factors work against home ownership: workers who qualify for low-rent dwellings have no incentive to leave them and incur the costs of buying homes, the more so because their wages are too low to enable them to afford houses at market prices. Home ownership is growing mainly because work units have turned over their real estate assets to worker-occupiers at very low or zero cost.

Zax emphasizes that the unquestioned improvements in both the quantity and quality of housing in the reform era owed little to the intrusion of market forces. Actual housing rents and house prices are far below plausible estimates of market prices, and "most ownership transactions are independent of market considerations." Using data from 1988 and 1995, Zax observes significant improvements in indicators of housing quality but finds little evidence to suggest that market forces were playing any meaningful role in allocating housing services or drawing investment to the sector. He stresses the immediate need for the "commoditization" of housing and the elimination of subsidies, with equity issues being tackled subsequently through tax policy. And he concludes provocatively that the dramatic improvement in the quality of the urban housing stock has been associated with a deteriorating policy regime: "almost no new construction [of housing] . . . is economically sensible."

There is clear evidence in the suburbs around major cities, however, that private developers are actively supplying new housing, and casual observation suggests that in such major cities as Beijing, Shanghai, Shenzhen, and Guangzhou, the private housing market seems to be thriving. Far from an oversupply of private housing, most new units in these cities seem to be finding buyers without apparent difficulty.[21] Even some government agencies have held successful sales of their housing assets, though prices were undoubtedly discounted relative to true market value. Increasingly, banks are willing to make loans for housing purchases, so mortgage financing is emerging rapidly. Unfortunately, currently available data are unable to quantify the extent to which these new developments are influencing the overall housing market.

Sustaining Policy Reform

In this section, authors consider how twenty years of reform have led to emerging stresses in China and investigate the potential for some of them to disrupt reform. Four topic areas are studied: the impact of growth on China's physical environment, the persistent gulf between the income and consumption levels of rural citizens compared with those enjoyed by their urban counterparts, the capacity of Chinese agriculture to support rising wages for agricultural workers, and the compatibility of China's seemingly static political system with its rapidly evolving economic system.

Growth and the Environment

Rapid growth has exacted a toll on China's environment. Travelers in China's north and west can attest to the drastic depletion of natural resources, especially water and forest, due to poor husbandry, bad policies, and population pressure. In the cities, pollution from emissions into air and water has become a serious threat to health. The chapter by David Wheeler, Hua Wang, and Susmita Dasgupta focuses mainly on the air pollution (principally from particulates and sulfur) that has accompanied rapid industrial growth in urban areas. Heavy use of coal for power, heating, and cooking has contributed to a high incidence of respiratory diseases and resulted in many premature deaths. Most waterways in urban areas are also highly polluted with human and industrial wastes that make them unusable for recreation, and extensive, costly treatment of water is required to render it safe for household or commercial use.

The authors document the severely adverse environmental effects that have resulted from rapid industrialization, but they note as well that experience in the 1990s shows that the damage can be reduced substantially at modest cost. They contend that reforms resulting in changes in the sectoral composition, ownership, and scale of production, along with stricter regulation, have contributed to keeping pollution below levels it had the potential to reach. Rising incomes will lead to calls for less pollution and create a capacity to pay for it, and education also has an important role to play in alerting the public to the dangers to health that accompany the fouling of air and water.

The chapter's authors reach the encouraging conclusion that rapid development will promote stricter pollution control. And growth resulting from further reform is likely to moderate the pace of environmental degradation. Even if this is the case, however, their modeling of policy options shows that even more stringent regulation of emissions would be cost-effective in reducing the pollution load further. A result would be cleaner waterways and sharply lower death rates caused by airborne emissions. Finally, the authors observe that their analysis could be extended usefully to shed light on the similar issues involved in natural resource degradation, agricultural pollution, and solid waste generation. Research in these areas can make use of "China's impressive investment in environmental, social, and economic data."

Richer Towns, Poorer Countryside

Historically, Chinese farmers and agricultural workers have earned and consumed less than their urban counterparts. This was probably the case before the founding of the People's Republic, it remained the case during the era of central planning, and it continues to be the case twenty years into the transition to a market economy.[22] In virtually all countries, rural workers earn less than their urban counterparts, but in Chapter Thirteen, Dennis Tao Yang and Cai Fang show that China lies in the group of countries that exhibit high inequality of income favoring urban over rural dwellers. They assert that this high degree of inequality has its roots in political economy. During the central planning period, inequality resulted from an industrial development policy that emphasized city-based production of capital goods. To support the policy, low official prices for agricultural outputs effectively transferred resources away from agriculture, and taxation and other policies reinforced that tendency. The resulting rapid industrial growth, both in absolute terms and relative to the rest of the economy, was achieved at the cost of allocative and technical inefficiencies, as well as lower agricultural incomes.

With the inception of reform, farm incomes began to rise relative to those in urban areas as a result of the early liberalization of agricultural prices. But the comparative gains were short-lived. According to Yang and Fang, the maintenance of the large gap was due to the emergence of political pressure groups in the cities with the power to persuade government at all levels to manipulate policies in their favor. Policies that protected incomes of urban dwellers included direct price subsidies for food and other consumption goods, large subsidies and direct financial transfers to state-owned enterprises, and continuing restrictions on migration from rural areas to the cities. The authors contend that an important consequence of the government's urban bias, apart from the potential for social instability if rural people become dissatisfied with the situation, is ongoing misallocation of labor and other factors of production across sectors. Failure to remove the policy distortions threatens to slow China's growth in the longer run.

Yang and Fang conclude, "The most compelling reason for eliminating the rural–urban income gap is to improve economic efficiency." They state that this "is not a hypothesis but a proven fact of past growth" and cite studies that attribute from one-sixth to one-fifth of Chinese economic growth to the movement of labor from low-productivity to higher-productivity occupations. Essentially that means moving surplus agricultural workers into industrial and service jobs.

They conclude as well, however, that greater mobility of rural workers will be difficult to achieve.[23] There are political obstacles to eliminating restrictions on labor mobility and lifting the controls that have depressed agriculture's access to credit. Similar obstacles will impede the elimination of income subsidies to urban residents; a useful first step would be to replace market distortions with direct transfer payments to protect urban incomes. Raising the efficiency of factor markets itself would spur growth and help create the resources to make such transfer payments affordable.

Boosting Agricultural Productivity

Simply reducing the numbers of people employed in agriculture is likely to raise agricultural productivity and rural incomes as the average farmworker cultivates more land. But the interlinked objectives of food security, raising farm incomes, and boosting agricultural productivity pose more complex problems than changes in the factor mix. Jikun Huang, Justin Lin, and Scott Rozelle investigate those issues in Chapter Fourteen and identify what has worked well and what not so well in reforming Chinese agriculture.

China prides itself on its ability to feed one-fifth of the global population from one-fourteenth of the world's arable land. The authors observe that limitations on natural resources notwithstanding, in the past four decades, China has raised per capita food consumption, improved nutrition, and added greatly to household food security for a population that doubled over the same period. Higher domestic production has been the overwhelmingly predominant factor in expanding food availability.

As incomes rise further, China's grain consumption will continue to increase, and much of the increase might be provided most efficiently by increasing imports.[24] Although most of the easy gains from reforming agricultural prices and freeing agricultural markets and farmers from the burdens of the command system have already been reaped, the authors look to further benefits from improving water control investments, pricing policies, and institutional arrangements (especially the compulsory grain procurement system).

The two areas that offer the most hope for higher productivity in agriculture are specialization in production to conform to China's comparative advantage and a much greater emphasis on research. As a member of the WTO, China will be required to liberalize agricultural imports (see Chapter Six); China could profit from the regime change by permitting the market to play a greater role in determining output and trade patterns. The consequence would be increased agricultural trade, between provinces domestically as well as internationally, with China importing more land-intensive agricultural products and exporting products that are intensive in labor input. Farmers would need to be freed from the requirements to grow grain, especially on land only marginally suited to the purpose, but even in areas that are highly suitable for grain production, farmers should be free to produce the highest-value-added products as determined by the markets.

Huang, Lin, and Rozelle argue that China's agricultural research system was the main driver of its rapid agricultural growth since World War II and "has produced a steady flow of new crop varieties and other technologies since the 1950s." The combination of research funds and improved incentives largely explains why China's food production has more than kept pace with its population growth. But the government's fiscal problems have undermined budget support for the research system. Agricultural research now needs to be invigorated by a substantial resource infusion to achieve its potential. Greater attention also needs to be paid to the delivery of extension services, the system for which has become increasingly fragile, and to other institutional reforms that will support the research system.

Can China's Political System Accommodate Further Economic Reform?

Objective observers of China's political scene probably would concede that the Chinese Communist Party is misnamed. The changes that successive governments have introduced to promote economic development and facilitate the transition to a market economy have stripped away many of the fundamental tenets customarily associated with communism. What remains is a single party with a monopoly on power. It has demonstrated little willingness to share power and has responded ruthlessly on occasions when its power has been challenged.

Despite this, Jean Oi's chapter describes a political scene that is undergoing change. China has avoided both economic and political "big bangs" but has cautiously introduced modest political changes that lag, even while they complement, the more dramatic changes occurring in the economy. Her chapter investigates the flexibility that the regime has displayed in trying to mute the sources of political disruption actually or potentially resulting from economic reform in order to illuminate the big question: "Is the political system up to the task of dealing with the mounting economic and political demands?"

On this question, Oi reports that the jury is still out. Her chapter presents clearly the mix of problems and solutions confronting the political leadership, and she invites her readers to choose if the glass is "half-empty or half-full." The system has evolved considerably. There has been a relaxation of control over citizens, due to decentralization and the restoration of markets. There have been changes in the center-local balance of power, partly as a result of fiscal reform. Individuals increasingly enjoy positions of status and power deriving from their wealth and economic success, as opposed to position in the Party hierarchy. And in a striking development, the government displays a growing tolerance of articulate, overt dissent.[25]

In assessing the likelihood of serious political trouble, Oi observes that political reform is not a priority of the peasants. And the highly publicized unemployment accompanying restructuring of the governments and the SOEs is less of a political liability than casual observation might suggest. Many laid-off workers secure higher-paying jobs, and some of the SOEs have improved performance considerably, thereby restoring some sense of security in employment. Her analysis draws attention again to the gradual adaptability of institutions, many of which, although being transformed only slowly, are already far advanced from what they used to be.

Another source of stability lies in the central Party elite's successful transfer of blame for failures from themselves to local leaders, meaning that expressions of discontent still tend to be localized rather than nationally directed. One of the best examples of this phenomenon is the introduction of a true village electoral system. The choice is still between party members, but village voters have real power to dismiss rascals. This lends stability to the system, as it protects the Party from the damage its reputation suffers when its appointees behave badly.

All of this amounts to a "bending without breaking" strategy whereby the Party endeavors to relieve political tension and preserve legitimacy. Oi concludes that scope remains for political maneuvering through gradual political reform. Whether the system bends or breaks depends on how willing the Party is to accept the changes to political institutions required by new realities.

What Lies Ahead?

Although the analysis of Chinese policy reforms presented in this volume is less than comprehensive, the chapters collected here amount to an impressive body of work that conveys accurately a sense of the complexity of the process under way in China. Even allowing for the narrow focus of some chapters dealing with issues that could have been interpreted much more broadly, the richness of the agenda that still confronts Chinese policymakers is immediately apparent.

The gradual nature of the Chinese reform process means that many areas of reform are incomplete. The unifying theme of all the chapters is the distance that still needs to be traveled before the river is forded. In building institutions, adapting policies, amending laws, introducing market-oriented regulations, and enhancing the performance of public bodies, the sense is of a journey well begun but far from over. Though Deng Xiaoping might view what he helped bring about with justifiable pride and gratification, he would recognize the potential slipperiness of the stones that must still be trod to complete the crossing.

One of the purposes of preparing this volume was to help illuminate the choices of Chinese policymakers. Another was to point researchers in the direction of fruitful areas of inquiry. The final chapter, in the final section of the book, presents a summary agenda for research drawn from the contributions of the scholars whose work is presented here.

Notes

1. Growth rates are based on national income figures. State Statistical Bureau, *China Statistical Yearbook, 1988* (Beijing: State Statistical Publishing House, 1988), p. 39.

2. George N. Ecklund, *Financing the Chinese Government Budget, Mainland China, 1950–1959* (Chicago: Aldine, 1966).

3. Ibid.

4. State Statistical Bureau, *China Statistical Yearbook, 2000* (Beijing: State Statistical Publishing House, 2000), p. 870.

5. On the impact of those events, see, for example, Gregory Chow, "Estimating Eco-

nomic Effects of Political Movements in China," *Journal of Comparative Economics* 23 (1996): 192–208.

6. See Pieter Bottelier, "The First Lian Huang Memorial Lecture: China's Economic Transition and the Significance of WTO Membership," Center for Research on Economic Development and Policy Reform, Stanford University, 1999.

7. Yingyi Qian, "The Institutional Foundations of China's Market Transition," in Boris Pleskovic and Joseph Stiglitz (eds.), *Annual World Bank Conference of Development Economics,* 1999 (Washington, D.C.: World Bank, 2000).

8. The ideological breakthrough came in September 1992, where the CCP endorsed, for the first time, the "socialist market economy" as the goal of China's reform.

9. Four asset-management companies—Cinda, Great Wall, Dongfang, and Huarong —correspond, respectively, to the China Construction Bank, the Agricultural Bank of China, the Bank of China, and the Industrial and Commercial Bank of China. On this and other aspects of financial reform, see, for example, People's Bank of China, *China Financial Outlook 2000,* pp. 62–68.

10. *China Daily,* April 2, 2002.

11. Data on industrial output and employment have been obtained from State Statistical Bureau, *China Statistical Yearbook* (Beijing: State Statistical Publishing House, published annually), various issues.

12. John McMillan and Christopher Woodruff, "Entrepreneurs in Economic Reform," Working Paper No. 102, Center for Research on Economic Development and Policy Reform, Stanford University, 2001.

13. In common with other contributors, Alford emphasizes that gradualism in Chinese reform extends to institutional change as well as policy change. For example, Yingyi Qian (see note 7) argues that China was able to support reforms through progressive modification of institutions and thereby avoid the problems with public acceptance that might have emerged if "best practice" institutions had been introduced prematurely. He recognizes that to complete the reform agenda, however, the institutional framework will have to evolve eventually to something that constitutes best practice in the Chinese context.

14. World Bank, *China 2020,* Volume 1: *Development Challenges in the New Century* (Washington, D.C.: World Bank, 1997). See the studies in the other six volumes, especially Volume 7: *China Engaged: Integration with the Global Economy* (Washington, D.C.: World Bank, 1997).

15. China was a major borrower of official finance, however, and it became the World Bank's largest borrower, with lending commitments of around U.S.$3 billion a year in 1993–97.

16. After a slowdown in FDI approvals, associated by many observers with the uncertainties of the East Asian currency and financial turmoil that arose in 1997, Minister Zeng Peiyan of the State Development Planning Commission reported to the Ninth National People's Congress (March 6, 2001) that utilization of FDI again exceeded U.S.$40 billion in 2000.

17. The opposite point also might be made: greater movement of goods has enabled officials to sustain barriers to factor mobility.

18. Using standardized international measurements of poverty, China had many more than eighty million poor people in 1993. The 8-7 Program was extremely ambitious, especially considering the limited budget that it received. Detailed information is unavailable, but one might guess that it was successful in reducing the official figure for (rural) poverty to no more than forty million in 2000.

19. Reforms of the social security system continue to be a hotly debated issue in

China. A pilot program for urban areas was introduced during 2001 in Liaoning province. Liaoning, in the northeastern "rust belt," was chosen because it has the highest proportion of urban residents of any province and because the severity of its problems means that a pilot that succeeds there is likely to provide a robust model for a nationwide system.

20. Hussain defines the dependency ratio conventionally as the ratio of the population under age fifteen and over age sixty-five to the total population. This ratio might have limited analytical value when applied to China, where current retirement ages are sixty for men, fifty-five for women in managerial positions, and fifty for women in other positions. Retirement is possible at even younger ages for workers in hazardous occupations.

21. Support for this position can be found in the report by Minister Zeng Peiyan (see note 16), who noted that sales of commercial housing to individuals increased by more than 50 percent in 2000, accounting for 85 percent of total sales of commercial housing. Elsewhere the government reported that the biggest increase (approaching half) in credit from financial institutions in 2000 was for consumer lending "for the purchase of houses, for durable goods, and for education purposes."

22. D. Gale Johnson, in "The Second Huang Lian Memorial Lecture: The Urban-Rural Disparities in China: Implications for the Future of Rural China," Center for Research on Economic Development and Policy Reform, Stanford University, 1999, observes that in 1952, per capita consumption in urban areas was 2.4 times its level in rural areas, and that was probably an inheritance from prerevolutionary China. He notes that despite Chairman Mao's commitment to equality, the ratio continued to rise, reaching 2.9 in 1978. In his report to the NPC on March 6, 2001, Prime Minister Zhu Rongji noted that urban incomes continued to grow faster than rural incomes in 2000.

23. Despite these difficulties, there is clear evidence that the government is in the process of easing the household registration policy (*hukou*) that had impeded more flexible labor migration. The Xinhua News Agency reported on August 17, 2001, that the *hukou* system will be phased out in the next five years in the coastal provinces.

24. The authors suggest that grain imports might rise by up to 60 million metric tons in 2005 under varying assumptions about trade liberalization, food security policies, and investment in agricultural research. A more plausible figure is about 20 million tons a year in 2005–20.

25. It is less tolerant of demonstrations in the cities than it is of farmers' protests in rural areas; organizations like Falun Gong, however, continue to invoke highly repressive responses.

Part I

POLICY REFORM IN CHINA: WHAT IS NEEDED NEXT?

2

China's Transition to a Market Economy

How Far Across the River?

Yingyi Qian and Jinglian Wu

It was the best of times, it was the worst of times, it was the age of wisdom, it was the age of foolishness, it was the epoch of belief, it was the epoch of incredulity, it was the season of Light, it was the season of Darkness, it was the spring of hope, it was the winter of despair, we had everything before us, we had nothing before us, we were all going direct to Heaven, we were all going direct the other way.
—Charles Dickens, *A Tale of Two Cities*

By the end of 1998, China's economic reform had gone through two full decades. China's transition from a planned to a market economy has often been portrayed as a gradual and experimental process, or in Deng Xiaoping's widely quoted phrase, "crossing the river by groping for stones." But how far has China progressed across the river? How tough is the remaining journey? And how will China navigate to the other side of the river? This chapter will give some assessment of these important questions.

We view China's transition to the market economy as an evolutionary process in two stages, where the first stage spanned about fifteen years between 1978 and 1993 and the second stage began in 1994. Although the two stages have much continuity between them, the division is quite clear, the watershed being the historic "Decision on Issues Concerning the Establishment of a Socialist Market Economic Structure," adopted by the Third Plenum of the Fourteenth Congress of the Chinese Communist Party in November 1993.

To better understand the significance of this decision, we need to review the nature of the first stage reform, which we do in the opening part of this chapter. In that stage, while the basic institutional framework of central planning remained intact, the reform was carried out incrementally to improve incentives and to expand the scope of the market for resource allocation. The incremental reform achieved most success outside rather than inside the state sector. It was a great success: it generated rapid growth, dramatically improved people's living standards, and eliminated shortages, the common symptom of all planned economies. Its significance can be understood only when compared with the seemingly similar reforms in Eastern Europe prior to 1990. The most remarkable example is Hungary, which pioneered a serious economic reform by abolishing mandatory planning targets for enterprises as early as in 1968 and became a role model for the Chinese reformers in the early 1980s. However, the Hungarian reform failed to eliminate shortages, and the Hungarian economy stagnated in the 1980s (Kornai, 1986). Similar stories might be told for Poland and the Soviet Union. The failures of economic reform in Eastern Europe provided an impetus for a more radical approach to reform, which only became possible and was put into practice after the fall of the Communist parties from the power around 1990. Against this background, the extent of China's success in its incremental reforms between 1978 and 1993 was surprising, and it has pioneered an alternative way to transit from plan to market.

The November 1993 decision is a historic document because it represents a strategic shift in the course of China's reforms. For the first time and in essence, China decided to abolish the planning system altogether and set the goal of reform to be the establishment of a modern market system and eventually to incorporate international institutions recognized as "best practices." This made the second stage of China's reform beginning in 1994 comparable to that in Eastern Europe after 1990 and in the former Soviet Union countries after 1992, although the political and economic background leading to such reforms was quite different. As is well known, in all countries of Eastern Europe and the former Soviet Union, transition to markets began after political democratization. By contrast, China entered the transition stage without such a political reform. We will examine the process of change in the mind-set of the leadership and its political, economic, and intellectual basis.

In the five years after 1994, China attempted several radical reforms according to the November 1993 decision. The major ones include unification of exchange rates and convertibility under the current account; overhaul of the tax and fiscal systems, with the separation of national and local tax administrations; and reorganization of the central bank, including establishing cross-province (regional) central bank branches. China also started to privatize small-scale state-owned enterprises (SOEs), to lay off excess state employees, and to establish a social safety net. Subsequently, we will provide a critical evaluation of the progress in these areas between 1994 and 1998.

Despite the impressive achievements, China still has a long way to go on its progression toward the other side of the river—a modern market economy. To investigate the remaining challenges, one is often tempted to prepare a long and comprehensive menu covering many issues, all of which seem to be important.

But what is the core issue? We shall argue that the core issue is the change of the government-business relationship to an arm's-length type with the establishment of a free and competitive enterprise system. This is the foundation of any modern market system. No one would deny the importance of tax reform, financial reform, or external sector reform, for example, but without this foundation, no tax or financial system can function well. To fundamentally change the government-business relationship, we consider three tasks necessary: (1) transforming state-owned enterprises, (2) promoting private enterprises, and (3) establishing the rule of law to govern the government-business relationship. In each case, we describe the current status, analyze the opportunities and the difficulties, and examine possible development trends.

There is no precedent for a country under the rule of a communist party to make a successful transition to a full-fledged market economy. Nor is there a precedent under which a centrally planned economy reformed successfully in an incremental way, as China did in its first fifteen years of reform. No existing theory would predict either success or failure in China's second stage of reform. China faces many difficult challenges, but it also has many opportunities. One new favorable factor is China's accession to the World Trade Organization (WTO), which we argue provides an important and timely impetus for its future reform. We are cautiously optimistic about China's capacity to make a quantum leap during the next decade in its transition to a modern market economy.

The Nature of the Reform in the First Stage

Compared to the dismal economic performance of the Eastern European reforms in the 1970s and 1980s, China's incremental reform between 1978 and 1993 was a remarkable success. During this period, China's GDP grew at an average annual rate of about 9 percent, or 7.5 percent on a per capita basis. The living standards of ordinary Chinese people improved significantly. For example, the average Chinese consumer increased consumption of edible vegetable oil, pork, and eggs about threefold. Per-person living space has doubled in urban areas and more than doubled in rural areas, and total household bank deposits, measured against GDP, increased from less than 6 percent in 1978 to more than 40 percent in 1993. The number of people living in absolute poverty was substantially reduced from over 250 million to less than 100 million in this period. By the end of 1993, reform was supported by people in all walks of life simply because almost everybody benefited from it. This contrasted sharply with the frustration of Eastern European reformers in the late 1980s, who saw only a dead end to the reform efforts of decades (Kornai, 1986, 1992).

Why was China able to avoid the failures of Eastern European reform? The answer is that China made deeper institutional changes than those in Eastern Europe (Qian, 2000; Wu, 1999). These changes take the form of "incremental reform" (*zengliang gaige*), that is, introducing dramatic changes outside rather than inside the existing core of central planning. The most significant is the rapid rise of a sector outside the state sector, known as the "nonstate sector" (Qian and Xu, 1993; Wu, 1999). Since the early 1980s, nearly all agricultural activity has been organized by households. In nonagriculture activities, the nonstate sector includes enterprises of a variety of ownership forms, including collectives, cooperatives, private businesses, joint ventures with foreign firms, and foreign-owned firms. Unlike SOEs, nonstate enterprises operated outside the purview of central planning, and they were subject to harder budget constraints and faced more competition than SOEs. The nonstate enterprises soon became the engine of growth and industrialization. In 1978, the state sector in industrial output accounted for 78 percent of the national total; by 1993, it was down to only 43 percent. The share of the state sector in commerce was 55 percent in 1978, and it was down to 40 percent by 1993. Because of the absence of privatization of SOEs during this period, the increase in the relative weight of the nonstate sector was entirely due to its fast growth. In contrast, despite decades of reform in the Eastern European countries, by the late 1980s, their state sectors continued to dominate the economy and their "second economy" (that is, the nonstate sector) remained insignificant, especially in industry (Kornai, 1986). However, it is worth noting that during this period, foreign direct investment in China was insignificant, accounting for less than 5 percent of total investment in the early 1990s. Furthermore, domestic private firms were also insignificant; most of the nonstate firms were actually local government-controlled collective enterprises, such as rural township and village enterprises (TVEs).

Accompanying the rise of the nonstate sector was the development of markets. Price reform was started in what is known as the "dual track" mechanism: prices were freed up at the margin while planned prices were maintained for planned quantities, which were frozen for some time (Wu and Zhao, 1987; Lau, Qian, and Roland, 2000). Again, this is a form of incremental reform. As a result, true domestic market prices for all goods were established quickly and as early as in the mid-1980s. The planned track was largely phased out in the early 1990s, and by 1993, more than 90 percent of prices (in terms of industrial output values) were determined by market forces, rather than by the government. By contrast, in Hungary, despite the fact that mandatory planning targets were abolished as early as in 1968, most prices continued to be "administered" by bureaucrats in the late 1980s (Kornai, 1986). China's market development was also pushed by its fast expansion of foreign trade. Due to the "opening" policy, both exports and imports increased much faster than GDP. For example, the export-to-GDP ratio increased from less than 5 percent in 1978 to more than 20 percent by the early 1990s. The expansion of foreign markets interacted with domestic market development, which helped achieve the convergence of the two tracks.

In essence, the achievements up to 1993 were made through innovative incremental reforms, which differed significantly from the Eastern European reforms up to 1989. On the other hand, these reforms were often ad hoc responses to particular constraints of the planning system or took advantage of the loopholes in it. For example, "contracting" between different levels of government and between government and enterprises or households prevailed. Although such contracting was effective in eroding central planning, these contracts were ad hoc and were subject to frequent renegotiations and change. However, in the final analysis, by the early 1990s, the core of central planning remained.

Lenin, in his famous book *State and Revolution*, characterizes a centrally planned economy as a state "syndicate" and as "Party-State Inc." Lenin's original description refers to the situation in which the entire society becomes one factory and all the people become employees of the Party-State. In its narrow sense, this description does not apply even to prereform China (or the former Soviet Union), because the complex internal organizational structure involved both the state and collective sectors. But the essential point of Lenin's Party-State remained valid for both prereform and postreform China. The Party-State is reflected in three areas. First, SOEs are still controlled by the state and the Party in an old-fashioned way—if not in their daily operations, then certainly in their strategic decisions. No single state enterprise was privatized, and almost none went bankrupt. No state employees were ever laid off for economic reasons. The Party appointed top managers in state enterprises. Although the state sector shrank significantly in relative terms, it expanded in absolute terms in employment, output, and assets. Second, truly private enterprises did not develop at a healthy pace. Truly private enterprises accounted for less than 15 percent of industrial output by the end of 1993, and almost all of the domestic private enterprises had fewer than eight employees. Most nonstate enterprises, such as TVEs, were collective or joint ventures, which were essentially controlled by local governments and hence not truly private. Third, new market-supporting institutions were not built to replace the old planning institutions. China did not have a market-supporting fiscal system, financial system, system of corporate governance, social security system, or a modern legal system, for example. Fundamentally, there was no rule of law, and the state and the Party, not laws, were governing the economy.

Essence of the November 1993 Decision and Reasons for the Change

The November 1993 decision marks a watershed change, indicating the beginning of a new direction of economic reform. To understand the significance of this turning point, we start by discussing the main contents of this decision and several follow-up decisions. We then analyze the political and economic reasons that led the leadership to make such a strategic shift as well as the intellectual inputs contributing to the change.

The Decision and Subsequent Ideological Changes

At the outset of reform, China desired change in order to increase productivity and improve living standards, but at no time did the leadership think of introducing a full-fledged market system (Perkins, 1994). During the first fifteen years of reform, the official ideology was one of "combining plan and market together."

In the early 1990s, the mind-set of the leadership started to change. In the spring of 1992, Deng Xiaoping made his famous southern tour to mobilize local support for further and more radical reform. The big ideological breakthrough occurred afterward at the Fourteenth Party Congress held in September 1992 when the Party, for the first time, endorsed the "socialist market economy" as the goal of reform. It is important to distinguish the Chinese socialist market economy from "market socialism" as advocated by some Eastern European reformers in the 1970s and 1980s. In market socialism, the market is a simulated one, which is to serve the purpose of socialism based on public ownership (Kornai, 1992). In contrast, in a socialist market economy, the word *socialist* is the adjective, and the goal is a *market economy*. Therefore, a socialist market economy differs from market socialism in a fundamental way.

The components of the transition to a socialist market economy became clearer one year later. In 1993, the Communist Party's Economics and Finance Leading Group, headed by Party Secretary General Jiang Zemin, worked together with economists to prepare a grand strategy of transition to a market system. Several research teams were formed to study various aspects of the transition, ranging from taxation, the fiscal system, the financial system, and enterprises to foreign trade. The final output was the "Decision on Issues Concerning the Establishment of a Socialist Market Economic Structure" adopted by the Third Plenum of the Fourteenth Party Congress in November 1993 (*China Daily,* November 17, 1993).

The essence of the November 1993 decision was to replace China's centrally planned system with a modern market system and eventually to incorporate international institutions recognized as "best practices." This landmark document marked a turning point on China's road to a market economy, for it made two major breakthroughs. First, the decision called for building of market-supporting institutions, such as formal fiscal federalism, a centralized monetary system, and a social safety net. For example, separation of central and local taxes and their administration was a crucial step in moving toward formal fiscal federalism. Revenue transfers between the central and provincial governments were to be based on a fixed formula rather than bargaining. It represented the beginning of a rule-based system.

Second, the decision addressed the enterprise reform issue in a more fundamental way by emphasizing property rights and ownership. It decided to transform SOEs into "modern enterprises" with "clarified property rights, clearly defined responsibility and authority, separation of enterprises from the government, and scientific internal management." Also, for the first time, it left the door open regarding the privatization of SOEs: "As for the small state-owned enterprises, the management of some can be contracted out or leased; others can be shifted to the partnership system in the form of stock sharing, or sold to collectives and individuals." But a further breakthrough on ownership issues had to wait a while.

In the November 1993 decision, state ownership was still regarded as a "principal component of the economy" while private ownership was a "supplementary component of the economy." The Fifteenth Party Congress held in September 1997 made a major change regarding ownership issues: state ownership was downgraded to a "pillar of the economy" and private ownership was elevated to an "important component of the economy." In Chinese politics, these subtle changes of rhetoric reflect a big change in ideology. The document recognized that "varieties of ownership should develop together," but because private ownership was discriminated against for decades, the only new information here was that private ownership had gained legitimacy. Furthermore, although the rhetoric of public ownership was maintained, its meaning was redefined, because public ownership may have many "different realization forms," such as joint stock corporations with investment by several owners rather than a single owner.

The second major breakthrough of the Fifteenth Party Congress, somewhat overshadowed by the ownership issue but nevertheless more important, was its explicit emphasis on the rule of law. As always in China, the meaning of the rule of law will evolve over time. The rule of law does not necessarily entail democracy. For example, the two most free market economies, Hong Kong and Singapore, have the rule of law but are not democracies by Western standards. Chinese leadership seemed to decide to give priority to the rule of law rather than democracy. It is not hard to understand: the rule of law is clearly a cornerstone of a modern market economy but does not directly and instantaneously threaten the governing power of the Party.

Both private ownership and the rule of law were formally incorporated into the Chinese constitution in March 1999.[1] An amendment of Article 11 of the constitution placed private businesses on an equal footing with the public sector by changing the original clause "the private economy is a supplement to public ownership" to "the nonpublic sector, including individual and private businesses, is an important component of the socialist market economy." Moreover, Article 5 of the constitution was amended to include the principle of "governing the country according to law and establishing a socialist, rule-of-law country." These amendments are a major step for China's transition toward a full market system based on the rule of law.

The failure of the pre-1990 Eastern European reform has led to persuasive arguments for the need for democratic reform to precede economic transition (Kornai, 1992). The Communist Parties there were unwilling to change their ideology. The collapse of the Communist Parties in Eastern Europe was the logical consequence. China provides an example that proved impossible in Eastern Europe and elsewhere: the Chinese Communist Party voluntarily made the ideological shift. As a result, China has become the first country where the ruling Communist Party has voluntarily changed its official ideology to embrace a market economy and private ownership. This raises a fundamental question: What brought about the change in the mind-set of the Chinese leadership? We shall attempt to answer this question from the political, economic, and intellectual perspectives.

The Political Will

The primary political objective of the Party is to maintain its power. The political will of the leadership for economic reform is shaped by both domestic political events and geopolitics. It is based on the following central proposition: economic reform is good for economic development, which is in turn good for maintaining the Party's power.

In this regard, we highlight the important legacy of the 1966–76 Cultural Revolution. The Cultural Revolution taught the Chinese leadership the important lesson that economic development is the key to maintaining its power. During the Cultural Revolution, the central focus of the Party was "political movement," which resulted in disastrous consequences for the national economy and the living standards of the people. Lack of economic development fueled mass resentment toward the Party, although officially such resentment was targeted toward the Gang of Four. The experience of the Cultural Revolution has had an enormous effect on the mind-set of some top leaders. They were convinced that without economic development, the Party could not survive; in other words, economic development was a necessary condition for maintaining the Party's power and retaining popular support. To a large extent, the displacement of the dogmatic ideology in favor of pragmatism was due to the backlash of the Cultural Revolution. The proposition of economic development became even more compelling after the 1989 Tiananmen Square incident, because it was the only source from which the government would gain its legitimacy. In Deng Xiaoping's own words, "[Economic] development is the hard rule."

After the Cultural Revolution, reverting to the Soviet type of central planning was out of the question because such a system was abandoned by China after 1958. The debate was only about the scope of the market relative to central planning and the extent of opening. The information arriving from its neighbors provided strong evidence in favor of increasing the role of markets and opening. Most Chinese were stunned by the fast economic development of Japan and the "Four Little Tigers" of Hong Kong, Taiwan, Singapore, and South Korea during the period of the Cultural Revolution. Referring to the success of Hong Kong, Deng reportedly said that although he did not have a good knowledge of economics, he could tell a good economy when he saw it.

The commitment to economic development for the purpose of maintaining power had an enormous impact on the course of economic reform. When the Party felt that deepening reforms was necessary to sustain economic growth, it pushed for more reforms. The start of economic reform in 1979 followed the so-called emancipation of mind in 1977 and 1978. The same mentality of the Party was behind the change that led to the November 1993 decision.

At the same time, the political will of the Party is also shaped by geopolitics. By the early 1990s, the pressure from East Asian countries was growing, with the perceived "East Asian miracle" and increased foreign investment from that region. More important, the collapse of the Soviet Union at the end of 1991 changed geopolitics forever. Both Eastern European countries and the republics of the former Soviet Union started a radical transition to markets. The Party felt that its power would be undermined if those newly democratized countries quickly caught up with China in terms of economic development.

The Economic Motivation

The political will of the leadership also faced the economic reality. From the late 1970s to the early 1990s, the economic landscape of China had changed dramatically. In the late 1970s, the state sector was a dominating sector. This was no longer true fifteen years later. The nonstate sector became the engine of growth. At first, there was a great success in agriculture when the commune system was dismantled and replaced by household farming. Then came the boom in the industrial and service sectors. By the early 1990s, the shares of the state in both industrial output and retail commerce accounted for less than 50 percent of the national total. Such a change in the economic landscape created new pressures for more radical reforms. What were the pressing economic problems in the early 1990s?

First, the problem of the state sector became increasingly serious. State-owned enterprises underwent successive reforms for more than ten years along the line of "expanding enterprise autonomy and increasing profit incentives." But their performance remained disappointing despite disproportional resource allocation in their favor. For example, the ratio of total profits and taxes to capital in state-owned enterprises declined from 24.2 percent in 1978 to below 10 percent in 1993. Losses from SOEs increased dramatically, and nonperforming loans accumulated in the state banks, reportedly accounting for more than 20 percent of total outstanding loans. Moreover, the rise of the nonstate sector increased the competitive pressure, which made holding on to SOEs more costly than before. The incremental reform of expanding enterprise autonomy and increasing profit incentives was not enough; more radical reforms were needed to address the key issues of property rights, ownership, and corporate governance.

Second, even the TVEs needed to be reformed, including privatization. Although the TVEs played an important role in generating growth in the early phase of reform, as they grew and the market matured, many problems arose because of the lack of clearly defined property rights and good corporate governance. The weakness of TVEs became more and more obvious in the early 1990s, especially, for example, in southern Jiangsu. One problem concerned their internal organizations. As TVEs grew large, they became increasingly bureaucratic in their management and started resembling the SOEs. Another problem came from the increased pressure of market competition. In the managerial labor market, TVEs started to lose good managers to foreign and joint venture firms as the latter paid their managers higher salaries and even gave them shares in the corporation. In the product market, the rapid entry of domestic private enterprises and foreign firms changed the existing seller's market to a buyer's market, eroding the profit margins that the TVEs had enjoyed in the 1980s as early starters.

Third, the old-style administrative control under central planning could no longer ensure macroeconomic stability in an increasingly decentralized economy. Inflation began again to rise sharply in late 1992 and early 1993, which also put pressure on the exchange rate. Both the state and nonstate sectors were responsible for this overheating, and the government had little control over it, in part because of the excessive monetary decentralization of the 1980s. A more comprehensive and indirect (or market-oriented) approach to macroeconomic management was imperative (Lou, 1997), requiring reforms of the tax and fiscal system, monetary system, financial system, and exchange rate to manage an increasingly decentralized and market-oriented economy. This was one of the immediate reasons for the November 1993 decision, but the broad scope of the decision shows that it was by no means the only reason.

Fourth, the mixture of a market economy and a planned economy led to rampant corruption and rent-seeking activities. Government officials at all levels used their power to divert income to themselves and strip assets from enterprises for personal gain. They also used their power to collect bribes through granting licenses and land use rights, approving IPOs, exempting taxes, and many other means. The problem was due to the lack of market-supporting institutions based on the rule of law to constrain the government. As a result, corruption and rent-seeking created a major bottleneck for China's sustained economic growth.

The Intellectual Inputs

The economic factors combined with the political will of the leadership explain the demand for a strategic shift in the mind-set of the leadership. Ideas from economists, on the other hand, provided important intellectual inputs to the November 1993 decision.

Unlike most countries of Eastern European and the former Soviet Union, Chinese reform has never relied on foreign economic advice. China's reform agenda has been shaped by the Chinese themselves. However, the influence of Chinese domestic economists (and some foreign economists) is considerable. Throughout the 1980s, academic exchange with the West and Eastern European countries and new economics education had an enormous impact on all generations of Chinese economists. So-called Western economics has gradually replaced Soviet-style economics in education and research and taken root in the economics profession. After more than a decade of economic reform and academic exchanges, the body of knowledge in China on the market economy and reform had increased impressively.

These ideas had an important intellectual impact on the 1993 November decision. In fact, this decision incorporated many ideas coming out of research done in the early 1990s. Some of the key research results were later collected and published in a collective volume (Wu, Zhou, Rong, et al., 1996). Starting in 1990, at the low point of economic reform after the Tiananmen incident, a group of researchers worked on the medium-term integrated design of reforms. The research focused on several key areas for reform, including detailed studies on new fiscal and monetary systems, monetary policy in transition, currency convertibility, reforms of state commercial banks, financial restructuring of enterprises and banks, social safety net, corporatization, and the changing role of government in the economy. These studies drew on the body of economics knowledge developed in the West, including both neoclassical economics and new institutional economics. In addition, they also incorporated the lessons learned from the reform experience in China and Eastern Europe in the 1980s. The fusion of economic theory with the reform experience made these studies applicable to the Chinese reality and suitable for policy purposes.

Many important ideas can be traced to the period of intellectual debates on reform strategies in the 1980s. One of the key ingredients of the decision, building market-supporting institutions (such as the tax system and the financial system), has its intellectual roots in the "integrated reform" school (Wu, Zhou, Lou, et al., 1988). This group of economists recognized early on the shortcomings of piecemeal reforms and emphasized the importance of coordinated reform in such key areas as liberalization of prices, building a market-oriented tax and fiscal system, and monetary and financial reforms. They were in favor of a systematic approach and considered a "mini-bang" reform the key to the establishment of a market system. Their proposals were initially accepted but later rejected by the leadership in the 1980s. However, their intellectual contribution influenced the later economic thinking and had a specific impact on the formulation of the November 1993 decision.

Another key ingredient of the decision involved reform of ownership and property rights, which also had its intellectual roots in the 1980s. Dong Furen (1979) was the first to recognize the importance of ownership reform. The idea of property rights, ownership, and shareholding companies was introduced to the Chinese economists' circle in the 1980s and that of corporate governance in the early 1990s. Increased knowledge of how corporations work in the West influenced the thinking on enterprise reform. The limits of the practice of profit contracting in the 1980s together with the knowledge of the functioning of Western corporations and the stock market contributed to the subsequent decisions on corporatization, diversification of ownership structure, and development of securities markets.

Progress During the Second Stage

Starting in January 1994, a series of reforms was launched in keeping with the November 1993 decision, primarily in five areas: (1) foreign exchange and external sector reform, (2) tax and fiscal reform, (3) financial reform, (4) SOE reform, and (5) establishment of a social safety net. We shall evaluate the progress made in the first five years in these areas.

Foreign Exchange and External Sector Reform

Before 1994, liberalization of foreign exchange markets, like many other markets, followed a dual-track approach, and there existed both an "official" rate and a "swap" rate (the market rate). Because of the dramatic growth of the market track, by 1993 the share of plan-allocated foreign exchange had fallen to less than 20 percent of the total. On January 1, 1994, plan allocation of foreign exchange was completely abolished, and the two tracks were merged into a single market track. However, for organizations that were used to receiving cheap foreign exchange, annual lump-sum subsidies in the domestic currency, sufficient to enable the purchase of the previous allocation of foreign exchange, were offered for a period of three years to compensate for their losses. In December 1996, China went one step further and announced current account convertibility of its currency. However, it did not move to capital account convertibility and retained capital controls. This is one important reason why China weathered the Asian financial crisis well, given its weak financial system.

We rate the foreign exchange reform as excellent. Between 1994 and 1998, the exchange rate remained stable and even appreciated slightly from 8.7 yuan per U.S. dollar to 8.3 yuan per dollar. Following the reform, both exports and foreign direct investment (FDI) increased dramatically, and the country's foreign reserves increased from U.S.$21 billion to U.S.$145 billion in 1998. Despite the Asian financial crisis, China continued to attract FDI of about U.S.$45 billion annually in 1997 and 1998.

The Tax and Fiscal Reform

Before 1994, the fiscal contracting system had played a positive role by providing badly needed incentives for local governments. But fiscal contracting was ad hoc. Under central planning, China had never had a national tax bureau, and there was no such need because all taxes were collected by local governments and turned over to the central government. After the 1979 reform, local governments often used their authority to reduce or exempt taxes that were supposed to be paid to the central government.

On January 1, 1994, China introduced major tax and fiscal reforms more aligned with international practices. These reforms introduced a clear distinction between national and local taxes and established a national tax bureau and local tax bureaus, each responsible for its own tax collection. This tax reform has made it very difficult for local governments to erode national taxes as they did in the past (Dong, 1997). The reform also established fixed tax rules between the national and local governments. For example, under the new system, the value-added tax became the major indirect tax shared by the national and local governments at a fixed ratio of 75:25. But local governments were compensated for their revenue losses for three years.

In 1995, the new Budget Law took effect. It prohibited the central government from borrowing from the central bank and from deficit-financing its current account. The central government could use deficit financing only in its capital account, although it had to finance the deficit with government bonds. It also imposed more stringent restrictions on local governments: local governments at all levels were required to have their budgets balanced (as before), and the law strictly controlled their bond issuance and restricted their borrowing in the financial market (a change from the past). To ensure enforcement of the Budget Law, an independent auditing system was introduced. For example, in 1996, the State Auditing Agency audited the Ministry of Finance's implementation of the state budget for the first time since the founding of the People's Republic in 1949 (Dong, 1997). Tax reform, together with the implementation of the Budget Law, made local governments' budget constraints much harder.

The 1994 fiscal reforms were perhaps the most profound and comprehensive institutional transformation made in that period. The government budgetary revenue as share of GDP stopped declining and started to recover. This share declined from 11.2 percent in 1994 to 10.7 percent in 1995 but then increased to 10.9 percent in 1996, 11.6 percent in 1997, and 12.4 percent in 1998 (State Statistical Bureau, 1999). The share surpassed 13 percent in 1999 and has continued to rise subsequently. On the other hand, there remain many unresolved thorny issues, the most important of which are revenue transfer issues between the central and local governments, the troubling subprovincial tax and fiscal system, and the problems related to extrabudgetary and off-budget fees and funds.

We can only say that the progress in fiscal reforms had a reasonably good start, but the reform remains far from complete.

The Monetary and Financial Reform

China's monetary system before 1994 was in a bad shape. Before 1994, some 70 percent of the central bank's loans to state commercial banks were made by the central bank's local branches, which were heavily influenced by the local governments. In 1993, after Vice Premier Zhu Rongji became its governor, the central bank centralized its operations. Since then, its local branches have been supervised only by the headquarters of the central bank, without any interference from the local governments. In 1995, China passed the Central Bank Law, which gave the central bank the mandate to determine monetary policy independent of the local government. These reforms substantially reduced the local governments' influence on monetary policy and credit allocation decisions (Xie, 1996). This is one of the main reasons that the overall budget constraints of the local governments became much harder in the 1990s compared to the 1980s: through fiscal channels, because of the tax reform, and through financial channels because of the monetary reform. In 1998, the central bank further replaced its thirty provincial branches with nine cross-province regional branches, as in the U.S. Federal Reserve System. The nine regional branches are located in Shenyang, Tianjin, Jinan, Nanjing, Shanghai, Guangzhou, Wuhan, Chengdu, and Xi'an. This reform further minimized the local governments' influence on monetary policy. We commend the monetary reform.

In contrast, we consider the banking and financial sector reforms very limited and unsatisfactory. Since 1994, limited progress has been made to commercialize four major state banks—the Industrial and Commercial Bank of China, the Agricultural Bank of China, the Bank of China, and the Construction Bank of China—which account for more than 80 percent of total outstanding loans. After the passing of the Commercial Banking Law in 1995, these banks began to adopt international accounting standards for bank assets and risk management and became more conscious of profitability and the quality of loans. They also started to compete with each other when their business dealings overlapped. Their operations came one step closer to those of conventional commercial banks after the central bank in 1998 abandoned the credit allocation ceilings and replaced them with standard reserve requirements, asset-liability management, and interest rate regulations. They faced no real competition from foreign banks, even though foreign banks were allowed to open branches in China, because the latter could not conduct local-currency business and were mostly restricted to special economic zones and some major cities.

On prudential regulation, China has basically followed the old U.S. model along the lines of its Glass-Steagall Act; not only is commercial banking separated from investment banking, but commercial banks cannot own equities in companies. Three different government agencies now separately regulate commercial banks, security firms, and insurance companies. In 1998, for the first time, several high-profile banks and investment companies, such as Hainan Development Bank and Guangdong International Trust Investment Company (GITIC), went bankrupt and were closed down.

Despite the large amount of capital infusion into the four state banks in 1999, the banking and financial system was perhaps even more fragile than it was in 1994. This is mainly because of tardy reform of SOEs and the governance of state banks. The lack of SOE reform has meant that the nonperforming loan problem continues to worsen. The governance of the four state banks has not improved significantly: they remain 100 percent state-owned and administratively subordinated to the central bank.

The SOE Reform

China did not privatize any state-owned enterprises prior to 1992. China's industrial SOEs were dominated by small and medium-sized enterprises. Most of these enterprises were under the supervision of county and city governments. Privatization of small SOEs began to emerge on a large scale in 1995 (Cao, Qian, and Weingast, 1999).[2] It began as an experiment initiated by local governments in a few provinces, including Shandong, Guangdong, and Sichuan, as early as 1992. Later in 1995, the central government endorsed it with the slogan "grasping the large and releasing the small" (*zhuada fangxiao*). Although the process slowed down in 1998 partly because of the Asian economic crisis, the speed of privatization picked up again in 1999. Overall, privatization of small SOEs proceeded at a very uneven pace across provinces, with some provinces (Zhejiang, Guangdong, and Shandong) moving very fast and others (especially in the Northeast) lagging behind.

Many SOEs are either not viable or are overwhelmed with excess workers, and for them, reallocation of labor is the main concern. About ten million workers from SOEs and urban collectives were laid off each year between 1996 and 1998. Ironically, such massive layoffs and the associated unemployment were often painted as serious problems of the Chinese reform by the mass media. In fact, they should be viewed as significant achievements of the second stage reform: never before were state employees laid off and state enterprises closed down, and layoffs are the essential first step in any serious SOE reform. In contrast, the lack of labor shedding in Russian enterprises even after privatization is a clear sign of failure rather than achievement. Total state employment in China has started to shrink after reaching a peak in 1995 and has declined to below one hundred million (including government agencies and state enterprises), the level of the late 1980s (State Statistical Bureau, 1999).

However, on ownership and governance issues, reforms in large state-owned enterprises had no breakthroughs. But the failure of several attempts in past years was quite revealing. First, in 1997, there was an experimental reform of one hundred large state-owned enterprises. The original purpose was to corporatize these SOEs by introducing several investors in each of them, but it ended up with more than eighty of them remaining solely state-owned. Second, many corporatized SOEs, including those already listed on China's two stock exchanges, suffered from the conflict between the so-called three old committees (the Party Committee, the employee representative committee, and the workers' union) and three new committees (meetings of the shareholders, meetings of the board of directors, and meetings of the supervisory committee). In some cases, the conflict between the Party secretary and the top manager was so severe that it interfered with the enterprise's normal operation. Third, in response, some enterprises opted to place the same person in the positions of Party secretary and chairman of the board. But this led to another problem: insider's control. Fourth, to address this problem, starting in 1998, hundreds of external "special inspectors" (*jicha tepaiyuan*) were sent by the central government to large SOEs to supervise their operations. However, these inspectors were mostly retired high-level bureaucrats who had no knowledge of business operations or financial accounting. Not surprisingly, they could play no constructive role in addressing the corporate governance problem. Fifth, after abolishing the special inspectors, the government came up with another solution—setting up the Large Enterprise Working Committee (*daqiye gongwei*) inside the Party's Central Committee responsible for directly appointing top managers in large SOEs (in collaboration with the Ministry of Personnel). It was sad to see that after so many years of reform of large SOEs, China went full circle and almost returned to where it had started.

Establishment of the Social Safety Net

The establishment of a social safety net is regarded as essential for both more radical reform of SOEs and the healthy development of private enterprises. In China, the existing social safety net mainly concerns urban residents and consists of four programs: pensions, health care, unemployment insurance, and minimum living standard support. So far, China does not have a unified national social security program. Rather, provincial and municipal governments are responsible for implementing their own local programs to establish a social safety net.

Financially, the most costly programs are the ones for pensions and health care, especially the former. The general goal of the pension reform, according to the November 1993 decision, is to move from the enterprise-based pension system under central planning to one combining "social responsibility" and "individual accounts"; the former follows the "pay as you go" principle, and the latter is a "fully funded" program. After several years of effort, such a pension scheme already covers, at least nominally, the employees in almost all SOEs and urban collective enterprises and in more than half of the private enterprises. However, two serious problems remain. The first concerns the division between the social responsibility and individual accounts. Some authorities advocate a small social account and a big individual account, while others advocate the opposite. The related second problem is the compensation issue for old and retired employees, who cannot contribute a sufficient amount to their individual accounts. Many old industrial cities with high proportions of old and retired employees face serious challenges in pension reform (also see Chapter Ten), and they are inclined to go for smaller individual accounts in order to pay for the immediate obligations toward current retirees.

In 1997, the State Council introduced the following framework: a mandatory amount of 11 percent of payroll should go to individual accounts, of which 8 percent is contributed by employees and 3 percent by the enterprises, and the local governments decide on the amount of social responsibility, often around 17 percent of payroll. Under this framework, individuals contribute 8 percent and enterprises contribute a total of 20 percent of payroll. This poses two problems. The total tax rate for pension purposes is too high, at around 28 percent of the payroll, dramatically increasing the labor costs of enterprises. Second, the compensation problem for old and retired employees is unsolved. The original proposal of using a part of state assets or government bonds for compensation has not been implemented. As a result, most individual accounts of old employees are still empty, and they continue to rely on the pay-as-you-go mechanism. This practice also erodes the individual accounts of new employees, because some of their contributions are used to pay the current retirees. This will certainly create problems in the future, defeating the original purpose in creating fully funded individual accounts.

Challenges Ahead

In the new century, China faces pressing needs for further reform for two basic reasons. First, China's economic growth slowed in the late 1990s, partly due to the Asian financial crisis but also because of the sluggishness of reform in key areas. To revitalize China's economy, the government must speed up the unfinished reforms. The second reason is China's accession to the WTO. The nature of the agreements between China and other countries on the terms of accession urgently require that China push its domestic reform more rapidly; otherwise, foreign competition could deal several sectors a devastating blow. Optimistically, the pressure from joining the WTO provides political momentum for further economic reform. Therefore, now is a good time to push for the next wave of reform along the path laid out in the November 1993 decision and subsequent decisions.

What Is the Core Issue?

Our assessment of the first five years of reform since 1994 is mixed. Although the reform was on the right track and made several impressive strides, it was disappointing in many areas. To complete its transition to a modern market economy and realize its full potential, China faces numerous challenges. One might prescribe a long list of what should be done. For example, each of the five areas we have analyzed has an unfinished agenda, and to that list one may add reforms in regulation and competition policy, improvement in social equality, the need to crack down on corruption, and so on. But instead of studying a comprehensive list of issues, we prefer to pose the following question: What is the core issue?

In our view, the core issue, which is linked to many of the other issues we have discussed, is to establish a system of free and competitive enterprises wherein the nature of the government-business relationship is changed into one at arm's length. Specifically, addressing the core issue requires undertaking the following three tasks: (1) transforming existing state-owned enterprises, (2) promoting new private enterprises, and (3) establishing the rule of law. If the first two concern the governance of firms, the last one concerns the governance of the economy as a whole. The three tasks are closely related. Without transformation, SOEs will continue to divert resources away from private enterprises and impede their growth. Moreover, the development of private enterprises also requires the rule of law, because the government needs to be constrained by law and the market needs a level playing field. In the end, solving the core issue means the dismantling of Lenin's Party-State Inc. and the establishment of an economy insulated from politics.

Scholars studying the institutional foundations of economic development emphasize the nature of the government-business relationship. Economic historians, such as North (1981) and Rosenberg and Birdzell (1986), have attributed the rise of the West in the eighteenth and nineteenth centuries to the fundamental change in the government-business relationship. They cite a sequence of events, such as the Glorious Revolution in England in 1688 and the development of commercial codes and company laws later, as responsible for insulating business and commerce from arbitrary interventions by the government. Through this institutional evolution, the governments in the West were eventually able to keep an arm's-length distance from economic activities. This provided room for entrepreneurial activities that were largely free from government intrusions. Scholars of contemporary economic systems drew similar lessons, although from a different context. For example, in his study of socialist economies, Kornai (1992) considered the Party-State control over the economy and the resulting bureaucratic coordination of economic activities as the main cause of the recurrent problems in those economies.

Addressing the core issue provides a key link to many other reform issues. Take government fiscal revenue, for example. Some economists tend to regard the insufficiency of government revenue as the source of many problems such as inflation, regional inequality, or lack of a social safety net. But a deeper problem behind the fiscal revenue issue is the problem of state-owned enterprises: SOEs are the governments' main source of revenue and also their main fiscal burden. The problems of the financial sector have deep roots in state-owned enterprises as well because the SOEs have accumulated massive bad loans; moreover, the state banks that extended these loans are themselves state enterprises. Consider the issue of establishing a social safety net. The main obstacle concerns the compensation for old and retired employees, the removal of which requires part of state assets to be endowed in individual accounts. This again requires enterprise reform. As for external reform and further opening up, if domestic reforms lag behind and the government continues to stand in the way of business, domestic enterprises would lose to foreign firms in competition. This would lead to a backlash against opening up. Finally, addressing the core issue also benefits some social objectives; for example, the establishment of the rule of law is an instrument to fight corruption.

Transforming State-Owned Enterprises

The first task of severing the close relationship between the government and business enterprises concerns transforming SOEs. State-owned enterprises still account for about one-quarter of industrial output and much more in such services as wholesale commerce, transportation, communications, and banking. The state has a virtual ownership monopoly in sectors such as airlines, telecommunications, and banking. Large SOEs still constitute the backbone of the economy. The state sector continues to place a disproportionally large claim on economic resources. For instance, SOEs' share of bank lending remained near 60 percent by the end of 1998. Although SOEs are still a major revenue source for the government, they also represent a big financial burden. Despite two decades of reforms, the financial performance of SOEs continues to decline and is ultimately responsible for the financial sector's difficulties.

The document on SOE reform adopted by the Fourth Plenum of the Fifteenth Party Central Committee in September 1999 (*China Daily*, September 27, 1999) set the stage for a major breakthrough. Three new policies were most significant. The first, and perhaps most important, new policy was "readjustment of the layout of the state economy" in the sense of narrowing its scope dramatically. Specifically, the state has decided to concentrate its control over enterprises of four main types while gradually withdrawing from other areas. The specified four areas for control are (1) industries related to national security, (2) natural monopolies, (3) industries providing important public goods and services, and (4) pillar industries and backbone enterprises in high-tech and new-tech industries. Currently, SOEs are operating in almost all sectors of the economy, ranging from fighter plane production to hotel operation, from bookselling to toymaking. Committing the government to withdrawing from most industrial and service sectors is a significant and encouraging step forward in transforming the state sector in the economy.

However, we note that this new policy could have been improved. The most controversial aspect concerns the fourth area, the pillar and technology industries. The inclusion of this provision appears to be a political compromise. The vague definition could admit many industries, such as banking, telecommunications, or the Internet. We should not be surprised if politicians use this vagueness as a loophole to retard privatization.

The second new policy concerns the diversification of ownership structure for enterprises over which the state still wants to maintain control. Except for a few in which the state intends to retain sole ownership, all other enterprises will become joint stock companies with multiple owners. These new owners can be either domestic private investors or foreign investors. The government's regulatory body, the China Securities Regulatory Commission, has already been authorized to promulgate the regulations on selling state shares. This policy change is also quite significant. Just a couple of years ago, when the government selected one hundred large SOEs for reform experiments, as many as eighty of them ended up with the state as their sole owner.

Diversification of ownership structure of large SOEs had already started in 1999. We give three examples. The state telecommunications monopoly was broken up early that year. Four companies were formed, and each of them actively seeks listings abroad. With the abolition of oil and chemical ministries, the reorganization produced two national petrochemical companies: the China National Petroleum Corporation (CNPC) and the China Petrochemical Corporation (SINOPEC). The IPO of PetroChina, a subsidiary of CNPC, was completed in early 2000. The third example concerns Legend Group, the largest maker of personal computers in China. Established in 1984, the company was fully state-owned. Early in 2000, the company distributed 35 percent of its shares to its managers, engineers, and other employees. Legend Group has set a precedent for other state high-tech companies to distribute shares to their employees.

The third new policy concerns the establishment of corporate governance, a topic mentioned in a Party document for the first time. Once a firm has several investors, the demand for corporate governance emerges. Corporate governance is a set of institutional arrangements governing the relationships among investors (shareholders and creditors), managers, and workers. The structure of corporate governance concerns (1) how control rights are allocated and exercised, (2) how boards of directors and top managers are selected and monitored, and (3) how incentives are designed and enforced. In market economies, major issues of corporate governance concern legal rules limiting agency problems, protecting shareholders and creditors, and providing room for managerial initiatives.

Of the three new policies affecting SOEs, we expect corporate governance reform to be the most difficult to implement. The difficulty arises because of the political position of the Chinese Communist Party. Although previous SOE reforms changed numerous policies, the fundamental principle of the Party's controlling personnel remained unchallenged. The Party not only appoints cadres to administrative posts but also appoints managers of state-owned enterprises. The combination of expanding enterprise autonomy and the power of the Party over personnel has led to a dilemma (Qian, 1996): delegating more effective control rights to managers provides them with incentives to increase current production but also enables them to plunder state assets, which results in high agency costs. On the other hand, maintaining Party control over the selection and dismissal of managers serves to check managerial asset stripping somewhat but is also the ultimate source of political interference.

As for the Party's role in corporate governance, the recent decision on SOE reform sent out a mixed signal. On the one hand, the government intends to follow common international practices in hiring, empowering, and rewarding top managers of its enterprises, including giving them stock. On the other hand, the decision reiterated the fundamental principle of the Party's control of personnel, although it also said that the control methods would be improved. Party control gives the enterprise Party Committee extraordinary power in making strategic decisions, and thus it presents a fundamental problem in corporate governance.

In the coming years, we will see conflicting forces contend over reforming corporate governance. Withdrawing the Party from managerial appointments is the first test of the political limits of economic reform. Unless the state, institutional investors, and individual investors are put on an equal footing, political intervention by the government will continue to plague the performance of these firms. The issue of the Party's role must be addressed before the goal of "separation of government and enterprise" can be achieved. For this reason, corporate governance for large state-controlled enterprises remains one of the thorniest issues.

The Special Case of Reforming the State Banks

Many studies of the financial system's problems focus on nonperforming loans. But the ultimate problems of the financial system are SOEs and state-owned banks. State banks are simply state-owned enterprises in the banking business. Currently, the state owns 100 percent of all four state commercial banks, which account for more than 80 percent of total outstanding loans, through the legal form known as "sole state ownership" (*guoyou duzi*). A useful reform would be diversification of the banks' ownership structure to make them truly commercial banks and further to improve their corporate governance. In this regard, we expect one of two possibilities, each of which can find a precedent in China's own experience.

The first possibility is a partial diversification of state ownership through the issuance of bank shares to the public in the domestic or overseas stock markets.

In 1999, Pudong Development Bank of Shanghai issued 400 million yuan (U.S.$48 million) worth of shares to the public and listed the bank on the Shanghai Stock Exchange. Traditionally, households in developing countries favor bank stocks and regard them as "blue chips." Issuance of bank shares may also invigorate the Chinese stock market. Therefore, the experience of Pudong Development Bank provides one possible model for the four major state commercial banks. Diversification of ownership to include the public is one way to force a bank to set up better corporate governance.

The second possibility is to follow the example of the Communication Bank of China. Established in 1987, this bank is the fifth-largest bank in China. It is arguably the best-run bank as well, being the most profitable and having the lowest proportion of nonperforming loans in its assets. This bank is a joint stock bank (but is not listed on the stock market), and its shareholders are other state-owned enterprises and organizations. These investors have a strong financial interest in the healthy operation of the bank, although ultimately all the shares of the bank are owned by the state. The corporate governance of this bank is quite different from that of the four major state banks; this bank does not have a direct administrative link to a particular government agency, whereas the others do. Diversification of ownership to include multiple institutional investors is another way leading to better corporate governance because one state administrative organ would no longer possess monopoly control.

We expect the state to continue to hold majority shares in the four major banks in the near future, through one method or the other. Nevertheless, the performance of these banks still could be improved with better corporate governance and more competition, especially competition from foreign banks after China's accession to the WTO. In many other countries, privatization of banks often came after privatization of industrial firms. In Taiwan, for example, most banks are state-owned. Also in Germany, more than half of the banks (in terms of assets) are still publicly owned, mostly by local governments. These banks do not appear to perform too badly when compared to private banks. This is perhaps because banks have to be regulated by the government anyway and thus the entrepreneurial scope for operating a bank is smaller than that of operating an unregulated firm, provided that the regulations are well enforced.

The Chinese government launched two reform programs to clean up the accumulated nonperforming loans in state banks. The first is the creation of four asset management companies (AMCs)—Cinda, Dongfang, Changchong, and Huarong—to take over nonperforming loans of the Construction Bank of China, the Bank of China, the Agricultural Bank of China, and the Industrial and Commercial Bank of China, respectively. The second and related program is the "debt-equity" swap, which is intended to reduce the debt burden of selected SOEs. Because the Chinese banking law does not allow commercial banks to hold equity, the newly established AMCs are made responsible for implementing the debt-equity swaps.

While both AMCs and debt-equity swaps can be useful, they are not substitutes for the banking reform we have described; moreover, we have serious concerns about their implementation. Transferring bad debts from state banks to AMCs and debt-equity swaps by themselves are merely accounting exercises, because the state still owns the bad assets of SOEs through its ownership of AMCs. These exercises by themselves do not address the crucial problem of banking reform, the governance of state banks. Worse, large-scale transfers of bad debts and debt-equity swaps might introduce a greater moral hazard problem to state banks and state enterprises. When done unconditionally, the state is actually handing out cash, like an emergency blood transfusion, to save troubled banks and enterprises.

Promoting Private Enterprises

The second task of establishing an arm's-length relationship between government and business is the promotion of private enterprises, especially small and medium-size enterprises (SMEs). By 1998, private enterprises accounted for 37 percent of total industrial output (see Table 2.1). Although private enterprises accounted for more than 50 percent of retail sales of consumer goods (see Table 2.2), they accounted for much less in other services. For example, in ser-

TABLE 2.1

Ownership Composition in Industrial Output

(percent)

Enterprise	1978	1980	1985	1990	1995	1998
State-owned or controlled	77.6	76.0	64.9	54.6	32.6	27.0
Collectives	22.4	23.5	32.1	35.6	35.6	36.3
Private	0.0	0.5	3.1	9.7	31.8	36.8

NOTE: State-owned means complete state ownership, and state-controlled means the state has 51 percent or more of the shares in joint ventures or joint stock companies. Collectives refers to urban collective enterprises and rural township-village enterprises. Private refers to the rest, including foreign firms.
SOURCE: *China Statistical Yearbook,* various years.

TABLE 2.2

Ownership Composition in Retail Sales of Consumer Goods

(percent)

Enterprise	1978	1980	1985	1990	1995	1998
State-owned or controlled	54.6	51.4	40.4	39.6	39.8	20.7
Collectives	43.3	44.6	37.2	31.7	19.3	16.6
Private	2.1	4.0	22.4	28.7	40.9	62.7

NOTE: State-owned means complete state ownership, and state-controlled means the state has 51 percent or more of the shares in joint ventures or joint stock companies. Collectives refers to urban collective enterprises and rural township-village enterprises. Private refers to the rest, including foreign firms.
SOURCE: *China Statistical Yearbook,* various years.

vice sectors such as telecommunications and banking, private enterprises virtually do not exist.

Ten years ago, at the beginning of the transition in Eastern Europe, economists paid great attention to mass privatization of large state-owned enterprises, and they believed that such a privatization would soon lead to superior performance. Voicing a minority opinion, Kornai (1990) argued that rather than focusing on mass privatization of existing state-owned enterprises, transition economies would be better off promoting new ventures of private entrepreneurs. Because entrepreneurial firms always start small and entrepreneurs have a substantial personal stake in their firms, they would be better positioned to avoid many of the pitfalls in governance that beset large firms at the initial stage of transition.

Evidence from Eastern European transitions over the past decade demonstrates that growth indeed came from new private enterprises, which were mostly SMEs. The striking example is Poland, which had not implemented any mass privatization of large state-owned enterprises because of workers' opposition—not a surprise in a country where unions exert strong political power. Despite (or because of) this, Poland is one of the most successful transition economies, due mostly to the newly created private enterprises. Like their counterparts in Eastern Europe, Chinese economists in the past two decades spent much time and energy debating ways to reform large state-owned enterprises, including privatization. China's experience demonstrates that the growth impetus comes mainly from small and medium-sized enterprises, the phenomenal growth of TVEs being a good example.

Even in market economies in developed or developing countries, newly created small and medium-sized firms play an important role in economic growth. The boom of the U.S. economy in the 1990s benefited greatly from the deregulation and structural changes in the 1980s, when more and more small enterprises entered previously monopolized industries and new high-tech companies mushroomed. In California's Silicon Valley, new start-up firms emerged at a record rate, becoming the pillars of the Internet revolution. In Taiwan, the phenomenal growth of the high-tech industries was driven largely by entrepreneurial small and medium-sized firms. In recent years, Taiwan's electronics industry overtook that of South Korea, which relied more heavily on a few big conglomerates (*chaebol*), to become the third-largest producer in the world, after the United States and Japan.

Development of private enterprises in China may take three forms. The first is new ventures started by entrepreneurs. The Chinese do not lack entrepreneurship; the stumbling block has been inadequate legal protection for entrepreneurial activities. Recently, China's National People's Congress passed the Law on Individually Owned Enterprises, which provides, for the first time, legal protection for entrepreneurial firms.

TABLE 2.3

State-Owned Industrial Enterprises by Size, 1993

(percent)

Size	Number	Output	Employment
Large	4.7	56.7	43.2
Medium	12.9	23.6	25.6
Small	82.3	19.7	31.1

NOTE: The precise definition of the size of an enterprise varies by industry. Large enterprises are subdivided into "large I" (very large) and "large II," and medium enterprises are subdivided into "medium I" and "medium II." For details, see Appendix III of *China Industrial Economic Statistical Yearbook, 1988.*
SOURCE: Table 1 in Cao, Qian, and Weingast (1999).

A second avenue comes from privatized small and medium-sized state-owned enterprises. The 1995 government policy of "releasing the small" was further relaxed to "releasing the small and the medium" in the decision of September 1999 on SOE reforms (*China Daily*, September 27, 1999). Its impact on the development of private enterprises can be quite significant. This is because in China, unlike Eastern Europe, the distribution of SOEs by size is skewed toward small enterprises. In 1993, small and medium-sized state firms employed about 67 percent of state workers and produced about 43 percent of state industrial output (see Table 2.3). Even without privatization of large state-owned enterprises, the release of the small and medium-sized SOEs would reduce the share of state industry by almost half.

The third option is privatized collective enterprises. By 1998, collective enterprises accounted for about 36 percent of total industrial output, and most of them were TVEs. The TVEs were the growth engine of the 1980s and early 1990s, but their competitive advantage gradually declined. Since 1995, more and more TVEs have been transformed into "stock cooperatives" or have been privatized outright.

Private enterprises will develop faster if the government can provide a better institutional environment. We highlight two policy issues. The foremost concerns further liberalization to eliminate ideological and political discrimination against private enterprises. Notwithstanding the constitutional amendment that established private ownership as an important component of the economy, various types of discrimination against private ownership remain. For example, the initial capital requirement for registration of a limited liability company in China is about $60,000, one of the highest in the world. In addition, China also has one of the most complicated bureaucratic procedures to open a private business. The second issue concerns the creation of more favorable financing channels for small enterprises. Smaller banks and credit cooperatives may have advantages in financing local small firms. In restructuring financial institutions, the government should not focus exclusively on the large banks but should give adequate attention to the financing needs of small enterprises.

The Case of Zhejiang Province

The development of private small and medium-sized enterprises will likely become the new growth engine and the brightest spot of the Chinese economy in coming years. Our optimism is supported by recent evidence from Zhejiang province, which has the fastest development of private enterprises and in which we see the likely pattern of future development for the rest of the country.

Zhejiang province, immediately south of Shanghai, marks the midpoint of China's coastline. It has a population of forty-four million, the same as South Korea. For some time before 1978, Zhejiang was a median performer among twenty-nine provinces in terms of economic development. Two decades later, however, Zhejiang jumped to fourth position in terms of total GDP. It accounted for 10 percent of the national industrial output, ranking third behind Guangdong and Jiangsu provinces. In 1998 and 1999, while the national economy slowed down, Zhejiang kept its momentum and became the star province of China. In 1998, for example, its GDP grew at 10.1 percent, compared to the national average of 7.8 percent.

Zhejiang's outstanding economic performance can be attributed to the exceptionally fast development of its private enterprises. In the 1990s, private enterprises grew at an amazing speed. By 1998, the shares of industrial output in the state, collective, domestic private, and other types of enterprises (including foreign enterprises and joint ventures) were 11 percent, 32 percent, 45 percent, and 12 percent, respectively. In 1998, for the first time in its history, the private sector on its own contributed more than half of Zhejiang's industrial output. Zhejiang has become the first of thirty-one provinces in which private industry accounts for more than half of industrial output.[3] Not surprisingly, Zhejiang province has the lowest share of state industry in the country as well (*Zhejiang Online*, September 1, 1999). The share of private industry exceeds half in more than two-thirds of the twenty fastest-growing counties in Zhejiang.

Even more interesting, private enterprises in Zhejiang have started to take over ailing state enterprises. For example, in 1999, Renmin Electronic Equipment Group, a private enterprise from Wenzhou, bought 230 *mu* (about 38 acres) of land in the Pudong area of Shanghai for its electronic equipment manufacturing facility. At the same time, it acquired 34 SOEs in Shanghai. Most of these SOEs are loss-making but are endowed with premium locations and some advantages in terms of technological and human capital. The private enterprise had six subsidiaries and more than three hundred sales companies all over China, with total sales of 300 million yuan ($36 million) in 1998 (*People's Daily*, September 17, 1999).

Several other features of private enterprise development in Zhejiang are worth mentioning. First, private enterprises in rural areas are the main driving force in

Zhejiang's industrialization. Between 1992 and 1997, three-quarters of the increase of industrial value added came from rural enterprises. A further breakdown in 1997 shows that private enterprises accounted for two-thirds of rural enterprise output (*Zhejiang Online*, September 1, 1999). Second, for a coastal province, Zhejiang does not have a particularly impressive record in attracting foreign direct investment, which contributes less than 10 percent of industrial output. Domestic private enterprises have been the primary force in its impressive development. Third, Zhejiang also relies mainly on domestic markets, not exports, for its development. Zhejiang's development seems to fit into neither the strategy of import substitution nor that of export orientation.

Zhejiang represents China's future. In historical perspective, Zhejiang had led the country in ownership changes. In 1984, the share of nonstate industrial output (collective and private) in Zhejiang was already more than 50 percent, at a time when the national average was 35 percent. Eight years later, in 1992, the national average of nonstate industrial output rose to over 50 percent. In 1998, the share of private industry surpassed 50 percent in Zhejiang while the national average stood at 37 percent. Recently, many provinces have sent out study groups to visit Zhejiang to find out why it grew faster than other provinces. To us, the lesson is clear: faster development of private enterprises. With other provinces learning from Zhejiang's experience, we would not be surprised to see the share of private industrial output at the national level surpass 50 percent within the next decade.

Establishing the Rule of Law

Both transforming state-owned enterprises and developing private firms require fundamental changes in the rules of the game. Ultimately, changing the government-business relationship to an arm's-length type requires the establishment of the rule of law. Interestingly, the Chinese government has separated legal reform from other "political reforms," which allowed it to make considerable progress in the 1990s. In 1996, China's parliament passed the Lawyers' Law, which many observers consider a milestone in legal reform. Public hearings, open trials, and even live TV coverage of trials followed, although these are still limited but growing in scope. The constitutional amendment of March 1999 that incorporates the principle of the rule of law is another major development.

The economic advantages of the rule of law over ad hoc arrangements are transparency, predictability, and uniformity, which reduce idiosyncratic risks, rent-seeking, and corruption. These features will in turn reduce transaction costs and increase economic efficiency. Therefore, the rule of law is more than putting the government's words into public codes; it fundamentally concerns the rules in a modern economy that govern the relationship between the state and markets in the way most conducive to economic development.

The rule of law has two economic roles. The first requires that law should apply to government—governments need to be constrained by law vis-à-vis other economic agents in the market. Through the rule of law, the government binds itself and thus makes a credible commitment to the provision of private incentives, which are the ultimate force driving economic development. This role of the rule of law provides a foundation for a limited government and secures private property rights against government intrusion. By reducing government discretion, the rule of law is also a powerful instrument to limit corruption and rent-seeking.[4] Under the rule of law, individuals have the right to sue governments. Recently, private businessmen and farmers have begun to use legal means to protect themselves against excess fees. For example, the *Wall Street Journal* (March 25, 1999) reported the case of Peijiawan village in Shaanxi province, where twelve thousand farmers in 1996 filed a class-action lawsuit against the local government for levying excess fees of $75,000. In the fall of 1998, the local court made an initial ruling in favor of the farmers.

The second economic role of the rule of law is to enable governments to protect private property rights, to enforce contracts, to create a level playing field for competition, and to regulate the market, if necessary. To achieve these goals, governments need to become a neutral third party, making a fundamental shift from the role of manager or administrator of economic activities under central planning. In early 1998, a major reform to streamline the government bureaucracy took place. The number of ministries in the central government was trimmed from forty-five to twenty-nine, and the number of civil servants was cut by half, from eight million to four million. Most of the former industrial branch ministries were downgraded to bureau status and placed under the jurisdiction of the State Economic and Trade Commission. Their previous enterprise management functions were removed, and their direct administrative links with state enterprises were severed. One example is the Ministry of Information Industry. This ministry used to directly administer China Telecom, the telephone monopoly in China. After the breakup of China Telecom, the ministry became the regulatory agency for the telecommunications industry, playing the part of the U.S. Federal Communications Commission. Another example concerns the government's regulation of financial institutions and markets. With China's accession to the WTO and its commitment to grant market access to foreign banks and insurance companies, the need for prudential regulation has become urgent.

The rule of law is not just a collection of legal codes, which can in principle be copied from other countries or even downloaded from the Internet. In China, as in many other transitional and developing countries, the most troubling aspect of implementing the rule of law is not enacting laws but enforcing them. The impartial enforcement of laws and contracts requires an independent and uncorrupted judicial system. This raises a profound question: Is it possible to establish an independent judiciary within the basic framework of a one-party political system?

The two most serious problems in contract and law enforcement are in fact judiciary corruption and local protectionism. We will focus our discussion here on the latter. China is a very large country. As a result of two decades of reform and decentralization, most economic decisions are made by enterprises or other organizations connected to local rather than central government. Xiao Yang, chairman of China's Supreme People's Court, felt that local protectionism was the main reason for difficulties in law enforcement, leading to what he called "judiciary localism" (*People's Daily*, September 3, 1999). Local judiciary protectionism biases judgments in dispute resolution in favor of the party within the jurisdiction of the court conducting the deliberations. In a typical contract dispute between firm A in province 1 and firm B in province 2, the court in province 1 likely rules in favor of firm A and the court in province 2 likely rules in favor of firm B. Under local judiciary protectionism, legal enforcement is not impartial.

The Case for a Two-Tier Judiciary System

The nature of the problem suggests a solution. Because the central government now usually has an arm's-length relationship with local business transactions, we consider it possible to create a two-tier judicial system to overcome the problem of local judiciary protectionism. In such a way, the judicial system can be made substantially (but not entirely) independent from government influence. Because most business transactions are local, the rule of law can be implemented substantially, even within a one-party political framework.

In the two-tier judiciary system, the local tier consists of the current local courts: each province (or city and county) maintains its own courts responsible to the corresponding People's Congress under the Chinese constitution. On top of that, another tier—the central or federal tier, consisting of the Supreme Court and cross-province circuit courts under it—may be established. Currently, China's Supreme People's Court, as part of the central government, does not have the facilities to rule on disputes involving different provinces. Cross-province circuit courts have no interest in the local economy and consequently would be less influenced by local governments. Thus compared to the current system, a two-tier judiciary system could better ensure impartiality in the enforcement of laws and contracts. It appears to be politically feasible as well.

The proposed two-tier judicial system reform shares some features with the fiscal and central bank reforms of the 1990s. In the fiscal reform, a two-tier tax administration system was established whereby national and local tax bureaus replaced the single tax administration. In the central bank reform, the central bank established nine cross-province regional branches to replace previous provincial branches. In these cases, the reforms substantially reduced local political influence on tax collection and monetary policies. A parallel judicial reform could have similar beneficial effects on contract and law enforcement.

Can the Current Political Institutions Accommodate the Change?

We have discussed the three major areas of importance to the core issue. But can these desirable reforms be implemented within China's prevailing political system? There is no easy answer to this important question, for several reasons. First, political institutions will respond to economic development and structural change—the classical endogeneity problem. Indeed, as in the past, we may see in the future more far-reaching political changes in responding to demands emerging from economic growth. Second, the meaning of political reform also changes over time. For example, legal reform used to be considered a part of political reform but no longer is. Third, even if one takes political institutions and political reform as a fixed concept, there is no uniform answer to the question because different reforms face different political constraints.

We group the reforms into three categories according to current political feasibility. In the first category, reforms are implementable now, meaning that the current political institution imposes no significant constraint. Such reforms include developing small and medium-sized private enterprises, introducing multiple investors in large state-controlled enterprises, and public listing and ownership diversification of major state commercial banks.

The second category concerns reforms that are openly debated now but on which consensus has yet to form. For example, in connection with SOE reform, the issue of reducing the Party's decision-making role in large state-controlled enterprises is much debated. Many people favor adopting the practice according to the Company Law, in which no special role is given to the Party. In fact, as far back as 1980, Deng Xiaoping himself pushed the idea that the Party Committee (*dangwei*) in SOEs should not be involved in the day-to-day decisions of the enterprises (Deng, 1993). But others still insist otherwise.

The third category includes reforms that are not being openly discussed right now but present promising indirect resolutions that could realistically be adopted. An example is judiciary independence; the very concept has been avoided in newspapers. Interestingly, "legal reform" in China has been separated from "political reform." Just like the concept of "market economy," the rule of law is also written into the Chinese constitution. Political reform, which is currently not on the agenda, mainly refers to free elections and freedom of political association. How far legal reform can go without political reform is unclear. But the possibility exists that substantial judiciary independence can be adopted through innovative legal reforms.

Concluding Remarks

In 1998, China marked the twentieth year of reform of its economy in the transition from plan to markets. One of the most significant events in the twenty-year history of reform was the adoption, in November 1993, of a program to guide China to a "socialist market economy." Since then, China's reform has entered the second stage of building market-supporting institutions systematically and resolving the problem of state-owned enterprises.

In our analysis of the economic reforms implemented since 1994, we observe a clear trend developing in some areas (such as private enterprise development); in other areas, we expect to see multiple possibilities unfolding (such as corporate governance of large state-controlled enterprises); and in yet other areas, we see only the beginning of change (such as the rule of law).

China has good prospects to continue to grow rapidly in coming years. However, whether the growth potential can be realized depends on whether reform is able to keep pace with economic development. We see great difficulties ahead. But we are cautiously optimistic about China's future reforms. After more than two decades of successful reforms, the nonstate sector has already become the bulk of the economy, and popular support for further reforms has remained strong. These are the fundamental domestic factors that are favorable to further reforms.

Our optimistic view on Chinese reform is bolstered by a particular new factor—China's accession to the WTO. The rules of the WTO are the rule of law for global market competition. By joining the WTO, China will become more integrated into the global economy. To survive in the global marketplace, China has no choice but to accelerate its transition to a full-fledged market system by adopting international best practices. Thus China's accession to the WTO will likely tilt the domestic political balance in favor of further and faster reform. Already, the demand inside China for quickening its transformation of SOEs, developing private enterprises, and establishing the rule of law has become stronger than it ever was in the past. Therefore, the WTO factor will provide an important and timely impetus for China's transition to a market economy.

History is never short on surprises. Twenty years ago, few observers predicted the enormous success of China's economic reform in the subsequent two decades. Past performance is no guarantee of future results, and there are always contingencies that are beyond anyone's predictions. But barring catastrophic events, we remain cautiously optimistic about China's remaining journey toward the other side of the river—a modern market economy.

Notes

1. "Top lawmakers yesterday overwhelmingly endorsed China's landmark constitutional amendments, which enshrine the 'rule of law' and bolster the status of private businesses" (*China Daily*, March 16, 1999).

2. The Chinese do not use the term *privatization*, relying on several other expressions, such as "transformation of ownership" (*zhuanzhi*) or "readjustment of ownership structure" (*suoyouzhi jiegou tiaozheng*). Similarly, the Chinese often use "nonpublic ownership" as a substitute for "private ownership."

3. The two new "provincial-level" entities since 1998 are Chongqing and Hainan.

4. Democracy is another way to limit corruption. China has held elections only at the village level.

References

Cao, Yuanzheng, Yingyi Qian, and Barry R. Weingast. "From Federalism, Chinese Style, to Privatization, Chinese Style." *Economics of Transition*, March 1999, 7(1): 103–31.

Deng Xiaoping. *Selected Works of Deng Xiaoping*, vol. 2 [in Chinese]. Beijing: People's Press, 1993.

Dong Furen. "*Yusuanfa he Yinghua Zhengfu de Yusuan*" ["The Budget Law and Hardening Government Budget Constraints"], in Tianqing Xu and Jinyan Li (eds.), *Zhongguo de Shuizhi Gaige* [*China's Tax Reform*]. Beijing: China Economics Publishing House, 1997.

———. "*Guanyu woguo shehuizhuyi suiyouzhi xingshi wenti*" ["On China's Socialist Ownership Form Problem"]. *Economic Research*, 1979, 1.

Kornai, Janos. "The Hungarian Reform Process: Visions, Hopes, and Reality." *Journal of Economic Literature*, December 1986, 24(4): 1687–1737.

———. *The Road to a Free Economy*. New York: Norton, 1990.

———. *The Socialist System: The Political Economy of Communism*. Princeton, N.J.: Princeton University Press, 1992.

Lau, Laurence, Yingyi Qian, and Gérard Roland. "Reform Without Losers: An Interpretation of China's Dual-Track Approach to Transition." *Journal of Political Economy*, February 2000, 108(1): 120–43.

Lou, Jiwei (ed.). *Macroeconomic Reform in China: Laying the Foundation for a Socialist Market Economy*. World Bank Discussion Paper No. 374. Washington, D.C.: World Bank, 1997. Translated from Chinese: *Hongguan Jingji Gaigem, 1992–1994: Beijing, Shexiang, Fangan, Sanzuo*. Beijing: Enterprise Management Publishing House, 1995.

North, Douglass C. *Structure and Change in Economic History*. New York: Norton, 1981.

Perkins, Dwight. "Completing China's Move to the Market." *Journal of Economic Perspectives*, Spring 1994, 8(2): 23–46.

Qian, Yingyi. "Enterprise Reform in China: Agency Problems and Political Control." *Economics of Transition*, October 1996, 4(2): 427–47.

———. "The Institutional Foundations of China's Market Transition," in Boris Pleskovic and Joseph Stiglitz (eds.), *Proceedings of the World Bank's Annual Conference on Development Economics, 1999*. Washington, D.C.: World Bank, 2000.

Qian, Yingyi, and Chenggang Xu. "Why China's Economic Reforms Differ: The M-Form Hierarchy and Entry/Expansion of the Nonstate Sector." *Economics of Transition*, June 1993, 1(2): 135–70.

Rosenberg, Nathan, and L. E. Birdzell. *How the West Grew Rich: The Economic Transformation of the Industrial World*. New York: Basic Books, 1986.

Shirk, Susan. *The Political Logic of Economic Reform in China*. Berkeley: University of California Press, 1993.

State Statistical Bureau. *China Statistical Yearbook, 1999* (Beijing: State Statistical Publishing House, 1999)

State Statistical Bureau. *A Statistical Survey of China* [in Chinese]. Beijing: State Statistical Publishing House, various years.

Wu, Jinglian. *Dangdai Zhongguo Jingji Gaige: Zhanlue Yu Shishi* [*The Contemporary Chinese Economic Reform: Strategy and Implementation*]. Shanghai: Shanghai Far East Publishing House, 1999.

Wu, Jinglian, and Renwei Zhao. "The Dual Pricing System in China's Industry." *Journal of Comparative Economics*, September 1987, *11*(3): 309–18.

Wu, Jinglian, Xiaochuan Zhou, Jiwei Lou, et al. *Zhongguo Jingji Gaige de Zhengti Sheji* [*The Integrated Design of China's Economic Reform*]. Beijing: China Outlook Publishing House, 1988.

Wu, Jinglian, Xiaochuan Zhou, Jingben Rong, et al. *Jianshe Shichang Jingji de Zongti Gouxiang Yu Fangan Sheji* [*The Road to a Market Economy: Comprehensive Framework and Working Proposals*]. Beijing: Central Compilation and Translation Press, 1996.

Xie Ping. *Zhongguo Jinrong Tizhi de Xuanze* [*The Choice of China's Financial System*]. Shanghai: Far East Publishing House, 1996.

Part II

BUILDING MARKET-SUPPORTING INSTITUTIONS

3

When Will China's Financial System Meet China's Needs?

Nicholas R. Lardy

The development of a modern, commercially oriented financial system in China is an important precondition for sustaining fast economic growth and moving more decisively toward a market economy. In this chapter, I review evidence showing that financial intermediation in the first two decades of reform, particularly in the 1990s, was relatively inefficient. Excessive real resources were poured into property development, creating by the mid-1990s a major property bubble; into excess production capacity in manufacturing, leading to unusually low levels of capacity utilization; and into a massive buildup of inventories.

As a result of these sources of inefficiency, the rate of return on real assets in the state-owned manufacturing sector fell continuously. By the end of two decades of reform, the return on assets was only 5 percent, quite low for a rapidly growing emerging market.[1] Moreover, excess investment led to systematic deflation in the producer goods sector. Deflation began in the first half of 1997, well before the onset of the Asian financial crisis, and three years later showed little sign of abating. Inefficient intermediation is also reflected in a continuous decline, well into negative territory, in the rate of return on assets of China's largest state-owned banks, which dominate the financial system.[2] I also analyze China's financial reform program, including the partial recapitalization of the four largest state-owned banks in the second half of 1998, the reorganization of the central bank and related institutional reforms, and the establishment of asset management companies to deal with the accumulation of nonperforming assets in the banking system.

Finally, I critique several aspects of the emerging financial reform program. First, related institutional reforms, such as the development of a modern bankruptcy law, are lagging. Second is the crucial need to develop larger and more efficient capital markets to provide additional competition in financial markets and a more stable source of funding for long-term investment projects and to raise the likely rate of recovery on nonperforming loans that are being taken over by the asset management companies. Third is the emerging fiscal challenge of bank restructuring. It is commonplace to argue that the ratio of domestic treasury debt to gross domestic product in China is low, leaving considerable room for additional government bond issuance to finance the write-off of non-performing loans in the state-owned banking system. I argue that the conventional wisdom fails to consider adequately both the limited fiscal capacity of the central government and the rapid growth in recent years of government debt, both treasury debt and other debt obligations of the central government. This analysis suggests that a successful program of financial sector restructuring will depend critically on both further fiscal reform and the rapid development of a commercial credit culture in the financial system.

Efficiency of Intermediation

A growing body of evidence suggests that China's financial system has become an increasingly inefficient intermediator of funds. Because the savings rate has risen and there are few alternative financial assets, the flow of funds into the banking system has been prodigious, masking the insolvency of several of the largest state-owned banks. By the end of 1999, household savings alone reached 6 trillion RMB yuan, more than 280 times the 21.06 billion yuan at the end of 1978.[3] These deposits are the principal source of funds for bank lending. By the end of 1999, loans outstanding from all financial institutions reached 9.4 trillion yuan, over 110 percent of gross domestic product and well over twice the 50 percent lending-to-GDP ratio prevailing in 1978.[4]

A significant portion of the resources financed by this lending has been misallocated. This judgment is based in part on evidence of waste of real resources in real estate and manufacturing and in part on the worsening financial performance of the lending institutions themselves.

Property

Massive investment in real estate and property created an enormous property bubble. By the end of the decade, there were tens of millions of square feet of completed but unoccupied first-class office space in cities such as Beijing, Shanghai, and Shenzhen. Based on current rates of market absorption of new space, it will be years before most of this space is occupied and the developers begin to earn the cash flow that will allow them to service their debt. Prices have been falling since 1995. In Beijing, for example, the rental price of grade A office space peaked at U.S.$5 to $6 per square foot in 1995. By January 1998, the price had fallen to below $4 and by October 1999 to under $2. Given a vacancy rate of 32 percent and substantial additional space nearing completion, prolonged lower prices were inevitable.[5]

Overbuilding was even more severe in Pudong, Shanghai, where building began at a feverish pace in 1992. Not only were many finished buildings unoccupied, but construction on more than a dozen partially finished office towers came to a halt in 1997–98. Since some of the buildings are joint ventures with Asian partners, in part this reflected the Asian financial crisis. But many of the buildings were financed by Chinese companies that simply ran out of money.

Nevertheless, the air has not yet come out of the property bubble. Lenders have not foreclosed on property loans, either because of the legal difficulties of seizing and liquidating the collateral underlying the loans or the lenders' judgment that they are better off holding the nonperforming loans than selling the collateral and recovering only a very small portion of the original loan amount.

In addition to real estate development geared toward foreign business, the Ministry of Construction acknowledged that nationally at the end of 1998 there were almost a billion square feet of completed but unsold residential property. Most of this was built for domestic residents, at a cost of about 600 billion yuan. The housing glut was acknowledged to "have tied up large quantities of bank loans and affected the banks' normal operation."[6] Another 850 million square feet of retail space also sat vacant.[7]

Excess Capacity

In addition to financing a property bubble, the banks have financed excess capacity across a broad range of industries. China's 1995 industrial census showed that rates of capacity utilization for dozens of major consumer and producer goods were well under 50 percent.[8] Although China has sustained reasonably strong economic growth since the census, capacity utilization rates appeared to have fallen further by the late 1990s.[9]

Inventories

Compared to market economies, where average inventory growth is typically minuscule, a relatively large share of output in China goes unsold. In the period 1990–98, additions to inventories averaged 5.7 percent of GDP.[10] On average, annual additions to inventories were the equivalent of 42 percent of incremental output. In the United States, the comparable figures were 0.4 percent and 7 percent, respectively.[11] Because most state-owned firms have no working capital other than that borrowed from banks, much of this inventory growth has been financed by increased borrowing.[12] The increase in inventories since 1978, if financed entirely by borrowing, would have absorbed one-third of the increase in credit provided by all types of financial institutions in the reform period. This is clearly a significant contributor to the rapid growth of lending relative to GDP that has occurred over the past twenty years.

Financial Sector

Given the developments in the real economy, it is not surprising that the performance of the financial sector also has deteriorated. The rate of return on assets of China's four largest state-owned banks fell from 1.4 percent in 1985 to only 0.2 percent in 1997.[13] The situation worsened in 1998. Profits of the Bank of China, the best managed and by far the most profitable of the four large banks, fell 40 percent in 1998 compared with 1997.[14] Financial conditions in the largest state-owned banks appear to have worsened further during 1999. In the late summer, the Communist Party newspaper carried an article reporting that the portion of borrowers not paying interest on their bank loans had risen and that the share of bank assets that was nonperforming continued to increase.[15]

Moreover, these official numbers overstate the profitability of Chinese banks. Interest income is exaggerated because of accrual of interest on nonperforming loans, inadequate provisioning for nonperforming loans, and possibly the shifting of unprofitable activities to subsidiaries, such as securities firms and trust and investment companies, whose results are not always consolidated with those of the parent bank. On a realistic accounting basis, several of the largest state-owned banks have been unprofitable in recent years.

In light of sinking profitability, it is not surprising that the ratio of capital relative to assets of the largest banks has shrunk. Unweighted capital adequacy of the four largest state-owned banks fell from 13.2 percent of assets in 1985 to only 2.8 percent of assets at the end of 1997. Again, the official numbers are somewhat misleading since the Ministry of Finance restricts the amount of bad assets that the banks are allowed to write off in order to be able to collect more tax revenues. Realistic loan write-offs would lower bank operating earnings and thus their tax payments. The Ministry of Finance requires banks, for example, to continue to list as assets on their balance sheets some loans to firms that have gone through bankruptcy and liquidation on which the banks recovered nothing. In 1997, in the four largest state-owned banks, these so-called dead loans were approximately equal to the net worth of the banks. Because the banks held other nonperforming loans on which the ultimate recovery rate will certainly be less than 100 percent, the banks as a group were insolvent. An injection of 270 billion yuan in the second half of 1998 probably raised the capital of the banks into positive territory. But using the internationally agreed risk-weighting methodology, the capital of the four largest state-owned banks is almost certainly less than the 8 percent Basel standard the central bank adopted in 1994, a standard that was subsequently incorporated into the Commercial Bank Law.[16]

The financial condition both of banks other than the big four and of nonbank financial institutions is also deteriorating. For example, conditions worsened in 1998 at several of the smaller new banks that are generally thought to be less encumbered with policy loans. Nonperforming loans at both the Everbright Bank and the Shenzhen Development Bank, for example, jumped sharply in 1998 compared to 1997.[17] In 1999, the bankruptcies of several nonbank financial institutions, including the Guangdong International Trust and Investment Company (GITIC), the Guangzhou International Trust and Investment Company (GZITIC), and Guangdong Enterprises, attracted substantial international press coverage.

Less well understood is that nonbank financial institutions as a group, which include not only trust and investment companies but also credit cooperatives, finance companies, and leasing companies, had nonperforming assets equal to 50 percent of their total assets as early as 1996. In the same year, the nonperforming loans of rural credit cooperatives comprised 38 percent of their loan portfolios and were equal to 4.4 times their capital.[18] The financial condition of rural credit cooperatives has dramatically worsened since. The capital of rural credit cooperatives plunged from 63.72 billion yuan at the end of the second quarter of 1996 to a negative 11.76 billion yuan at the end of the third quarter of 1999.[19] This is the first time the People's Bank of China has acknowledged that a major component of China's financial system is insolvent. The risks this insolvency poses are substantial since rural households have more than one trillion yuan deposited in savings accounts in these institutions. Finally, the Chinese government has also launched a program to close failing rural credit funds. These funds, also called foundations, were initially established in the 1980s to manage the assets of the disbanded collective agricultural system. But in the 1990s, they expanded the scope of their business by taking deposits and offering loans. The financial cost of closing these institutions is difficult to estimate.[20]

The Financial Reform Program

To address the problems summarized so far, the authorities have embarked on a far-reaching financial reform program. Its key elements are enhanced central bank regulation and supervision, the adoption of incentives to encourage commercial behavior by large state-owned banks, and the rehabilitation of bank balance sheets.

The key to strengthened central bank regulation and supervision was the reorganization of the regional branch structure of the People's Bank of China along supraprovincial lines in 1998. Historically, provincial offices of the People's Bank were unduly influenced by government and party leaders at the provincial level, most of whom were more interested in ensuring a generous flow of bank credit to support their favorite projects than in the soundness of the banks that operated in their jurisdictions. Presidents of the regional branches of the People's

Bank now outrank provincial governors and first party secretaries and should be more able to rebuff requests for political loans that are directed to banks that they supervise. The People's Bank in 1998 also began to introduce a risk-based system of classifying bank loans. Since it is more forward-looking than the payment-based classification system it replaces, when fully implemented it will constitute an important tool of the central bank in supervising banks.

The government has also sought to stimulate commercial behavior on the part of large state-owned banks. In 1994, three policy banks were established in order to allow the four large state-owned banks to concentrate on commercial lending. The Commercial Bank Law, which was passed by the Standing Committee of the National People's Congress on May 10, 1995, and took effect on July 1 of that year, reinforced this by requiring state-owned banks to "assume exclusive responsibility for profits and losses."

Finally, the financial reform program seeks to rehabilitate the balance sheets of the four largest state-owned banks. The first step, as noted, was the injection of 270 million yuan in capital in August 1998. The state in 1999 also created four asset management companies—Cinda, Huarong, Changchong, and Dongfang—to deal with the nonperforming loans that clog the balance sheets of the four large state-owned banks. These companies, which are being financed by issuing government-backed bonds, are purchasing nonperforming loans at face value from the banks in exchange for equity positions in the borrowing firms. The asset management companies will seek to recover as much as possible through a combination of liquidation, auction, securitization, sale of equity, mergers and acquisitions, and private placements of the assets they acquire. Although the asset management companies are said to be loosely modeled on the Resolution Trust Corporation in the United States, initial indications are that the companies will try to recover more though sale of equity via initial public offerings rather than relying, as Resolution Trust did, primarily on auction and liquidation.

Institutional Constraints

While the planned rehabilitation of its four largest state banks draws on the experience of other countries that have endured banking crises, there are several features of China's institutional landscape that may lead to outcomes that are less favorable than, for example, the Resolution Trust Corporation in the United States. First, China's bankruptcy procedures are deeply flawed. Several laws give Chinese banks and other creditors the highest priority for the distribution of proceeds from the liquidation of bankruptcy assets. But these laws have been undermined by a State Council regulation assigning priority to meeting pension and social welfare obligations of workers in firms that are liquidated.[21] When firms go through bankruptcy and liquidation, the extent of financial recovery by creditors is low, around 10 to 15 percent.[22] As a result, banks rarely initiate bankruptcy proceedings. This pattern suggests that the asset management companies may recover relatively little if they liquidate the collateral securing the nonperforming loans they take over from the banks or if they sell the assets at auction.

Institutional constraints may also lead to relatively low rates of recovery on the assets purchased by Cinda and the other asset management companies. Cinda has acquired large equity stakes in exchange for canceling the bank debt of the borrowing firms.[23] Cinda's expectation is that after restructuring and streamlining these companies in three to five years, it will sell its equity stake to investors by listing the firms on the Shanghai or Shenzhen stock market. However, at least in the first year of its operation, Cinda appeared not to have exercised its ownership rights in these firms by installing new managers who are strongly incentivized to improve profitability and by appointing new independent directors to oversee the companies. Indeed, the manager of the first firm to conclude a debt equity agreement stated that despite its 70 percent ownership stake, Cinda would be unable to change the firm's management.[24] In the absence of significant restructuring, the market value of these companies may be depressed when they are listed on Chinese stock markets.

A second institutional constraint that could lead to a low rate of recovery is that China lacks the large pension funds, mutual funds, and insurance companies that could provide the diversification and professional management that could facilitate a substantial increase in equity ownership by households, the likely ultimate owners of the stock in the companies that the asset management companies will be selling.[25]

Finally, the underdeveloped domestic government bond market may impede the government's strategy of recapitalization of the financial system. Initially, Cinda and the other asset management companies are issuing bonds to the banks in exchange for loans, which they then swap for equity. But since the proceeds from the eventual sale of this equity will inevitably fall far short of the face value of the bonds, ultimately the Ministry of Finance will have to sell bonds to make up the difference. In addition, the ministry will have to provide funds to rehabilitate the balance sheets of nonbank financial institutions and perhaps banks other than the big four. The bonds that must be sold to finance the rehabilitation of China's financial sector will likely amount to 30 percent or more of GDP.

Although the stock of government debt has grown rapidly in recent years, it is not clear that markets will easily absorb what will amount to more than a doubling of the stock of treasury debt. Since the mid-1990s, the Ministry of Finance has moved away from auction markets for the initial distribution of bonds, preferring to issue bonds at a fixed spread above the interest rate on bank deposits of similar maturity rather than at market-determined interest rates; the maturity spectrum of bonds has become more compressed, and a large share of treasury bonds sold are nontradable. In short, China lacks a deep and highly liquid government bond market that would facilitate the dramatic increase in the issuance of bonds that will be necessary to finance the recapitalization of the financial system.[26]

Fiscal Sustainability

Even if the institutional obstacles could be overcome and asset management companies work smoothly, bank recapitalization and related reforms will pose a considerable fiscal challenge for China's central government. This judgment differs from that offered by some analysts. For example, the chief economist and director of global economics at Morgan Stanley Dean Witter believed that "China's non-performing loan problem should properly be viewed as a government solvency issue—hardly problematic with total government debt unlikely to exceed 50 percent of GDP at any point in the next five years."[27] This view fails to take into account four factors: the low level of government revenues relative to gross domestic product, the very substantial growth of treasury debt in recent years, the existence and continued growth of a large stock of nontreasury government debt, and the possibility that even if the large initial recapitalization of banks and other financial institutions can be financed, the emergence of new nonperforming loans will create a burden that ultimately exceeds the state's fiscal capacity.

Revenues

From the beginning of reform in 1978 until the mid-1990s, there was a long-term decline in government revenues relative to gross domestic product, from 28.4 percent in 1978 to a low of 10.7 percent in 1995.[28] There has been some recovery in response to a major reform of the fiscal system initiated in 1994, but consolidated fiscal revenues at all levels of government in 1998 were only 12.4 percent of GDP, and the budgeted revenue share in 1999 was only 12.9 percent. In most emerging markets, the government's revenue share is about twice as large. Even in Russia, which defaulted on its domestic debt in the fall of 1998, the government's consolidated fiscal revenues relative to GDP were twice those in China.[29]

The central government encountered some difficulty in raising additional revenues in 1998 and 1999. There are two cases—the fuel tax and the tax on interest income. The Ministry of Finance proposed amending the Highway Law by replacing ad hoc automobile and road fees collected by provincial and local governments with a uniform national tax of 1 yuan per liter of diesel fuel and 1.2 yuan per liter of gasoline.[30] Based on the levels of consumption of these fuels at the time, the tax revenue generated by this reform would have been about 100 billion yuan, an increase of a little over 10 percent in government budgetary revenues.[31] The amendment was first considered by the Standing Committee of the National People's Congress in late October 1998. Because of insufficient support, a vote on the amendment was postponed until the next session. But at the next legislative session, in December 1998, the vote was postponed again. In the spring of 1999, when a vote finally occurred, 29 of 154 members did not attend the meeting, 42 of those attending abstained, and 6 voted against. Although 77 members voted in favor of the government's proposal, since passage requires a majority of all members rather than just of those present, 77 affirmative votes was one vote shy of the number required to pass the amendment. It was only the second time in the history of the National People's Congress, traditionally regarded as a rubber-stamp legislative body, that a government proposal was voted down.[32] Not until October 31, 1999, did the National People's Congress Standing Committee pass the amendment to the Highway Law. Passage was due in part to a new provision exempting farmers from the gasoline tax. Further difficulties delayed implementation of the tax beyond the anticipated starting date of early 2000.

The tax on interest income, approved by the Standing Committee of the National People's Congress in the late summer of 1999, was easier. Unlike the amendment to the Highway Law, there was no loss of revenues to provincial and local governments, and the bill passed on its first reading. But the revenues that can be anticipated from the tax on interest income are relatively modest.[33]

Government Debt

Given the slow growth of revenues relative to expenditures, the government budget was continually in deficit for most of the first two decades of economic reform. Initially, a large part of the deficit was financed by borrowing from the central bank. But beginning in 1994, the government was precluded from such borrowing to finance its budget deficit. Initially, this was an administrative decision, but it was codified in the Central Bank Law, which took effect in 1995. As a result, the average annual quantity of treasury bonds sold jumped from under 40 billion yuan in 1991–93 to 150 billion yuan in 1994–96 and over 300 billion yuan in 1997–98.[34] Thus the stock of outstanding treasury debt attributable to the budget deficit climbed steadily, from 106 billion yuan, or 4.9 percent of GDP, in 1991 to 726 billion yuan, or 9.1 percent of GDP, at the end of 1998.[35] In addition, in 1998, the government issued 270 billion yuan in thirty-year "special treasury bonds" to the four major state-owned banks as part of a recapitalization program. Although these bonds are not included in official compilations of treasury debt, they clearly should be regarded as part of government debt, bringing the total to 996 billion yuan, or 12.5 percent of GDP, at the end of 1998.

The dependence of the central government on debt to finance its expenditures grew significantly between 1993 and 1998. Net issuance of treasury debt as a percentage of central government expenditures, the latter inclusive of interest expenditures, increased from 19 percent in 1993 to 46 percent in 1998.[36]

TABLE 3.1

Interest Outlays on Domestic Treasury Debt, 1993–98

Year	Interest Outlays (billions of RMB yuan)	Central Expenditures (billions of RMB yuan)	Interest Burden (percent)
1993	5.2	136	3.8
1994	12.5	188	6.6
1995	28.2	228	12.4
1996	38.7	254	15.2
1997	49.1	302	16.2
1998	57.3	370	15.5

NOTES: Interest outlays for 1998 are estimated based on an assumed average interest rate of 9 percent on outstanding treasury debt. Nine percent is a rough guess based on the magnitude of maturing older bonds with higher interest rates that were redeemed and the volume of issuance of new bonds, which because of declining inflation rates pay lower nominal rates of interests. Central government expenditures are actual central government outlays as reported by the Ministry of Finance plus interest outlays on the outstanding domestic debt. The latter have not been included in the Ministry's published data on central expenditures since the mid-1990s. The latter adjustment is consistent with IMF GFS standards.
SOURCES: *US$1,000,000,000 People's Republic of China 7.3% Bonds Due 2008* (Crédit Suisse First Boston and Goldman, Sachs & Co.); Prospectus dated December 9, 1998, p. 59. Finance Yearbook of China Editorial Commission, *Finance Yearbook of China, 1998* (Beijing, 1998), p. 462. Finance Minister Xiang Huaicheng, "Report on the Execution of the Central and Local Budgets for 1998 and on the Draft Central and Local Budgets for 1999," delivered to the second session of the Ninth National People's Congress, March 6, 1999. Xinhua News Agency, March 18, 1999, in FBIS-CHI-1999-0320.

The interest burden of treasury debt, reflected in Table 3.1, has also grown substantially. Interest payments on treasury debt in 1998 are estimated to have been 57.3 billion yuan, compared to 5.2 billion yuan in 1992, a tenfold increase in five years. The third column shows that the interest burden of the treasury debt, expressed as a percentage of central government outlays, quadrupled from 3.8 percent in 1993 to 15.5 percent in 1998.[37]

Nontreasury Government Debt

In addition to treasury bonds and the special treasury bonds issued by the Ministry of Finance to provide additional capital to the four largest state-owned banks, the debt of the state-owned policy banks established in the mid-1990s is appropriately considered as a direct government obligation for several reasons. First, the China Development Bank, which is by far the largest of the three policy banks, undertakes only investment projects identified by the State Development and Planning Commission and other central government entities.[38] Second, the China Development Bank operates with virtually no capital.[39] Thus its ability to absorb losses on its portfolio of loans is extremely limited. Third, the bonds of the policy banks, which are the principal source of funding for their lending programs, are not sold on the market to willing buyers. Rather the bonds are "placed" with the large state-owned banks and, to a lesser extent, other newer, smaller banks. Placement appears to be necessary because the interest rate on the bonds does not include a risk premium commensurate with the purposes for which the funds are re-lent, particularly in the case of the China Development Bank. An auction market would presumably result in a significant risk premium over treasury debt, given the policy nature of the China Development Bank's lending. There can be little doubt that in the event that any of the policy banks defaulted on their debt, the bondholders would expect the state to compensate them for their losses. Alternatively, one could argue that no risk premium is needed to get financial institutions to hold the bonds since they are implicitly guaranteed by the central government. In either case, the conclusion is the same—the debt of the China Development Bank and the other policy banks is appropriately regarded as direct central government debt, similar to treasury bonds.

The balance outstanding of the bonds issued by the policy banks at the end of 1998 was 511.7 billion yuan, or 6.4 percent of GDP.[40] Thus, inclusive of treasury bonds, the special treasury bonds issued in 1998 to provide funds for bank recapitalization and the financial bonds of the China Development Bank and other policy banks, by the end of 1998, government debt was 1.507 trillion yuan. That was 18.9 percent of GDP, more than three times the comparable ratio in 1993.[41]

This estimate of government debt excludes corporate bonds issued by state-owned manufacturing firms, as well as other contingent and implicit government liabilities. These include nonperforming loans extended by state-owned banks, pension arrears of the government and government-owned firms, and unfunded pension liabilities of current employees of the government and government-owned firms. It also excludes implicit liabilities of local governments, such as guarantees for construction projects and local borrowings from trust companies, rural credit cooperatives, rural credit funds, and city trust cooperatives. Xiang Huaicheng, minister of finance in the fall of 1999, warned of the problem of local government debt, stating that "in some regions a debt risk has already started to appear clearly and is becoming a burden on local government."[42]

The magnitude of these excluded items ranges from quite small to substantial. The issuance of new corporate bonds has shrunk substantially in recent years, in part because some state-owned firms have defaulted on maturing bonds.[43] Nonetheless, there were still 56.4 billion yuan of government enterprise bonds outstanding at the end of 1998, an amount equivalent to 0.7 percent of GDP.[44]

The implicit state pension debt is much larger, about 50 percent of GDP in 1994 according to an estimate of the World Bank.[45] As the financial performance of state-owned enterprises has weakened since then, a growing number of firms have discontinued or delayed making contributions to local pension pools. As a result, China's pension system recorded a deficit in 1997 for the first time since 1984.[46] At the end of March 1999, total social premium arrears of enterprises, including contributions both for pensions and unemployment insurance funds, were 33 billion yuan.[47] In an effort to deal with this and to mitigate the resulting pressure on the state budget, the State Council in early 1999 promulgated two new regulations providing substantial new penalties for firms that fail to make required contributions to pension and other social funds.[48]

According to an estimate of the World Bank, in the mid-1990s, the market value of housing owned by state-owned enterprises was roughly equal to the magnitude of their unfunded pension liabilities. That suggested that over a period of time, enterprises could sell their housing to meet the pension obligations then outstanding. That would free up the flow of ongoing contributions, which had historically been used to finance the pay-as-you-go pension scheme. These flows could be allocated to a funded pension program for current workers, in effect paying down the state's massive unfunded pension liabilities.

It now appears, however, that the bulk of the housing stock owned by state-owned enterprises in most cities has been sold at such highly subsidized prices that it has generated only modest revenues and that even these proceeds have not been allocated to meet pension obligations. As early as 1995, some 29 percent of all urban families were living in housing units they had purchased from their work units since housing reform began. But more than nine-tenths of these families purchased their units at subsidized prices that averaged less than a fourth of the market price.[49] Anecdotal evidence suggests that in many cities, most public housing was sold at highly subsidized prices by the end of 1999. Thus it would appear that the value of housing assets of state-owned firms now falls significantly short of the value of these firms' unfunded pension liabilities.

Thus the magnitude of the pension problem has grown substantially since the time of the World Bank's comprehensive study. Because regular government tax revenues are now being used to meet a portion of the pension obligations of state-owned companies,[50] there is a strong case for including China's implicit pension debt as a direct obligation of the central government. This is not done, however, in the scenarios presented next, which look at the question of the fiscal sustainability of China's bank balance sheet rehabilitation in more detail.

Scenarios

Contrary to the assertion that government debt is unlikely to exceed 50 percent of gross domestic product any time in the next five years, the analysis presented here suggests that any serious attempt to recapitalize China's financial system will push the level of government debt to well over 50 percent of output. This is made clear in Table 3.2, which provides the first of several scenarios to judge the fiscal sustainability of financial sector restructuring over the next decade. In the baseline scenario, the key assumptions are as follows:

- The government revenue share is assumed to stay at 12.4 percent of GDP, as in 1998, and the shares of central and local government revenue remain unchanged.[51]

TABLE 3.2

Financial Sustainability in China, 1998–2008: Base Scenario

(billions of RMB yuan)

	1998	1999	2000	2001	2002	2003	2004	2005	2006	2007	2008
Government revenue	12.40	12.40	12.40	12.40	12.40	12.40	12.40	12.40	12.40	12.40	12.40
Government expenditure	13.50	13.45	15.21	15.41	15.63	15.87	16.13	16.41	16.71	17.04	17.39
of which:											
Noninterest	12.70	12.70	12.70	12.70	12.70	12.70	12.70	12.70	12.70	12.70	12.70
Interest	0.80	0.75	2.51	2.71	2.93	3.17	3.43	3.71	4.01	4.34	4.69
Incremental	0.00	0.00	0.00	0.00	0.00	0.00	0.00	0.00	0.00	0.00	0.00
Budget balance	**-1.10**	**-1.05**	**-2.81**	**-3.01**	**-3.23**	**-3.47**	**-3.73**	**-4.01**	**-4.31**	**-4.64**	**-4.99**
Total debt/GDP	**0.19**	**0.52**	**0.57**	**0.63**	**0.68**	**0.74**	**0.81**	**0.87**	**0.94**	**1.01**	**1.09**
Interest/Central government revenue		0.12	0.41	0.44	0.48	0.52	0.56	0.60	0.65	0.71	0.76
Memo items:											
Increments to government debt of which:											
Budget deficit	87.51	88.28	250.83	285.40	324.82	369.80	421.15	479.77	546.73	623.25	710.70
New policy bank debt	297.02	177.08	187.70	198.97	210.90	223.56	236.97	251.19	266.26	282.24	299.17
Special treasury bonds/Loan write-off	270.00										
Total Government debt	1507.36	4368.32	5105.34	5932.97	6863.45	7910.79	9090.97	10422.31	11925.74	13625.22	15548.19
of which:											
Treasury debt	725.69	2595.60	3958.89	4587.55	5307.13	6130.91	7074.12	8154.27	9391.44	10808.69	12432.49
Policy bank debt	511.67	688.75	876.45	1075.42	1286.32	1509.88	1746.85	1998.04	2264.30	2546.54	2845.71
Special treasury debt	270.00	270.00	270.00	270.00	270.00	270.00	270.00	270.00	270.00	270.00	270.00
Interest on treasury debt	57.30	43.54	204.57	237.53	275.25	318.43	367.85	424.45	489.26	563.49	648.52
Interest on special treasury debt	19.44	19.44	19.44	19.44	19.44	19.44	19.44	19.44	19.44	19.44	19.44
Gross domestic product	7955.00	8432.30	8938.24	9474.53	10043.00	10645.58	11284.32	11961.38	12679.06	13439.81	14246.19
Government revenue	985.30	1045.61	1108.34	1174.84	1245.33	1320.05	1399.26	1483.21	1572.20	1666.54	1766.53
of which:											
Central	488.50	518.62	549.74	582.72	617.68	654.75	694.03	735.67	779.81	826.60	876.20
Local	496.80	526.99	558.60	592.12	627.65	665.31	705.22	747.54	792.39	839.93	890.33
Government expenditure	1077.10	1133.88	1359.17	1460.24	1570.15	1689.86	1820.40	1962.98	2118.94	2289.78	2477.23
Loans outstanding	8652.00	9949.80	11442.27	13158.61	15132.40	17402.26	20012.60	23014.49	26466.66	30436.67	35002.17

- Noninterest government budgetary expenditures for existing programs remain at 12.7 percent of GDP, as in 1998.
- The interest financed through the government budget each year is equal to the sum of 6 percent of the prior year's treasury debt outstanding and the interest due on 270 billion yuan of special treasury bonds issued in 1998.[52]
- The budget deficit each year is financed entirely by an increase in treasury debt.
- The net issuance of bonds by the policy banks relative to GDP continues at a rate equal to the average in 1996–98, and the interest cost of this debt continues to be borne by the issuer, not directly by the government budget.[53]
- The cost of recapitalizing the financial system is equal to 25 percent of all loans outstanding from all financial institutions at the end of 1998 plus 20 percent of the value of new loans issued beginning in the year 2000.
- The rate of GDP growth is 6 percent per year.
- Loans continue to grow such that the ratio of loans outstanding to GDP expands at the same pace as in 1995–98.[54]

This set of assumptions is designed to capture key elements of the financial situation prevailing as of late 1998.

As can be seen from the time-series values for the budget balance, the ratio of total debt to gross domestic product, and interest as a share of central government revenues, simply recapitalizing the financial system without any other changes in the financial and fiscal systems is doomed to fail. In the baseline scenario, the budget deficit as a share of GDP almost quintuples and the debt ratio explodes from an initial level of 19 percent to 109 percent of GDP, and still rising sharply, in 2008. Interest on the treasury debt plus the special treasury debt as a share of central government revenues increases sharply, from 12 percent in the base year to 76 percent and still rising in 2008. This scenario is clearly not fiscally sustainable.

Table 3.3 presents the first of two alternative scenarios. In this alternative, the government succeeds in continuing to increase government revenues relative to GDP at the same rate achieved from 1995 through 1998.[55] Under this scenario, government revenues relative to GDP increase by almost half by 2008. However, increased revenues are not assumed to lead to a one-for-one reduction in the government budget deficit. Half of the incremental revenue growth is allocated to meet what the World Bank argues are urgently needed additional budgetary outlays for health, education, poverty alleviation, pensions, social insurance, infrastructure, and the environment.[56] Compared to the baseline scenario, the rise in the ratio of debt to GDP is more moderate, and interest expenditures on the treasury and special treasury debt outstanding rise much more slowly, to 45 percent by the end of the ten-year period. But the overall path is probably not fiscally sustainable. Although the budget deficit declines after 2000, the debt ratio exceeds 90 percent of GDP and is still rising in 2008. The interest burden also continues to rise through 2008. Eventually, this path will be unsustainable,

TABLE 3.3

Fiscal Sustainability in China, 1998–2008: Revenue Enhancement

(billions of RMB yuan)

	1998	1999	2000	2001	2002	2003	2004	2005	2006	2007	2008
Government revenue	12.40	12.96	13.52	14.08	14.64	15.20	15.76	16.32	16.88	17.44	18.00
Government expenditure	13.50	13.73	15.75	16.20	16.66	17.12	17.57	18.04	18.51	18.99	19.48
of which:											
Noninterest	12.70	12.70	12.70	12.70	12.70	12.70	12.70	12.70	12.70	12.70	12.70
Interest	0.80	0.75	2.49	2.66	2.84	3.02	3.19	3.38	3.57	3.77	3.98
Incremental	0.00	0.28	0.56	0.84	1.12	1.40	1.68	1.96	2.24	2.52	2.80
Budget balance	**−1.10**	**−0.77**	**−2.23**	**−2.12**	**−2.02**	**−1.92**	**−1.81**	**−1.72**	**−1.63**	**−1.55**	**−1.48**
Total debt/GDP	**0.19**	**0.52**	**0.56**	**0.61**	**0.66**	**0.70**	**0.75**	**0.79**	**0.84**	**0.89**	**0.94**
Interest/Central government revenue		**0.12**	**0.37**	**0.38**	**0.39**	**0.40**	**0.41**	**0.42**	**0.43**	**0.44**	**0.45**
Memo items:											
Increments to government debt											
of which:											
Budget deficit	87.51	64.67	199.36	201.31	202.79	203.89	204.74	205.52	206.46	207.88	210.20
New policy bank debt	297.02	177.08	187.70	198.97	210.90	223.56	236.97	251.19	266.26	282.24	299.17
Special treasury bonds/Loan write-off	270.00	2595.60	298.49	343.27	394.76	453.97	522.07	600.38	690.43	794.00	913.10
Total government debt	1507.36	4344.70	5030.26	5773.80	6582.25	7463.67	8427.46	9484.54	10647.69	11931.81	13354.28
of which:											
Treasury debt	725.69	3385.95	3883.81	4428.38	5025.93	5683.79	6410.61	7216.50	8113.39	9115.27	10238.57
Policy bank debt	511.67	688.75	876.45	1075.42	1286.32	1509.88	1746.85	1998.04	2264.30	2546.54	2845.71
Special treasury debt	270.00	270.00	270.00	270.00	270.00	270.00	270.00	270.00	270.00	270.00	270.00
Interest on treasury debt	57.30	43.54	203.16	233.03	265.70	301.56	341.03	384.64	432.99	486.80	546.92
Interest on special treasury debt	19.44	19.44	19.44	19.44	19.44	19.44	19.44	19.44	19.44	19.44	19.44
Gross domestic product	7955.00	8432.30	8938.24	9474.53	10043.00	10645.58	11284.32	11961.38	12679.06	13439.81	14246.19
Government revenue	985.30	1092.83	1208.45	1334.01	1470.30	1618.13	1778.41	1952.10	2140.23	2343.90	2564.31
of which:											
Central	488.50	542.04	599.39	661.67	729.27	802.59	882.09	968.24	1061.55	1162.58	1271.90
Local	496.80	550.78	609.06	672.34	741.03	815.54	896.32	983.86	1078.67	1181.33	1292.41
Government expenditure	1077.10	1157.49	1407.81	1535.32	1673.09	1822.02	1983.15	2157.61	2346.68	2551.78	2774.52
Loans outstanding	8652.00	9949.80	11442.27	13158.61	15132.40	17402.26	20012.60	23014.49	26466.67	30436.67	35002.17

TABLE 3.4

Fiscal Sustainability in China, 1998–2008: Commercial Bank Behavior

(billions of RMB yuan)

	1998	1999	2000	2001	2002	2003	2004	2005	2006	2007	2008
Government revenue	12.40	12.40	12.40	12.40	12.40	12.40	12.40	12.40	12.40	12.40	12.40
Government expenditure	13.50	13.45	15.21	15.37	15.51	15.64	15.75	15.84	15.91	15.95	15.97
of which:											
Noninterest	12.70	12.70	12.70	12.70	12.70	12.70	12.70	12.70	12.70	12.70	12.70
Interest	0.80	0.75	2.51	2.67	2.81	2.94	3.05	3.14	3.21	3.25	3.27
Incremental	0.00	0.00	0.00	0.00	0.00	0.00	0.00	0.00	0.00	0.00	0.00
Budget balance	**−1.10**	**−1.05**	**−2.81**	**−2.97**	**−3.11**	**−3.24**	**−3.35**	**−3.44**	**−3.51**	**−3.55**	**−3.57**
Total debt/GDP	**0.19**	**0.52**	**0.56**	**0.60**	**0.64**	**0.67**	**0.70**	**0.73**	**0.75**	**0.76**	**0.78**
Interest/Central government revenue		**0.12**	**0.41**	**0.43**	**0.46**	**0.48**	**0.50**	**0.51**	**0.52**	**0.53**	**0.53**
Memo items:											
Increments to government debt											
of which:											
Budget deficit	87.51	88.28	250.83	281.64	312.37	344.48	377.62	411.31	444.89	477.52	508.59
New policy bank debt	297.02	177.08	187.70	198.97	210.90	223.56	236.97	251.19	266.26	282.24	299.17
Special treasury bonds/Loan write-off	270.00	2595.60	235.81	202.20	192.70	175.92	149.94	112.48	60.87	0.00	0.00
Total government debt	1507.36	4368.32	5042.66	5725.46	6441.43	7185.38	7949.92	8724.90	9496.92	10256.67	11064.43
of which:											
Treasury debt	725.69	3409.56	3896.20	4380.04	4885.10	5405.50	5933.07	6456.86	6962.62	7440.13	7948.72
Policy bank debt	511.67	688.75	876.45	1075.42	1286.32	1509.88	1746.85	1998.04	2264.30	2546.54	2845.71
Special treasury debt	270.00	270.00	270.00	270.00	270.00	270.00	270.00	270.00	270.00	270.00	270.00
Interest on treasury debt	57.30	43.54	204.57	233.77	262.80	293.11	324.33	355.98	387.41	417.76	446.41
Interest on special treasury debt	19.44	19.44	19.44	19.44	19.44	19.44	19.44	19.44	19.44	19.44	19.44
Gross domestic product	7955.00	8432.30	8938.24	9474.53	10043.00	10645.58	11284.32	11961.38	12679.06	13439.81	14246.19
Government revenue	985.30	1045.61	1108.34	1174.84	1245.33	1320.05	1399.26	1483.21	1572.20	1666.54	1766.53
of which:											
Central	488.50	518.62	549.74	582.72	617.68	654.75	694.03	735.67	779.81	826.60	876.20
Local	496.80	526.99	558.60	592.12	627.65	665.31	705.22	747.54	792.39	839.93	890.33
Government expenditure	1077.10	1133.88	1359.17	1456.48	1557.70	1664.54	1776.88	1894.52	2017.09	2144.05	2275.11
Loans outstanding	8652.00	9949.80	11423.61	13108.60	15035.56	17234.512	19733.52	22545.54	25589.19	28659.89	32099.08

either because the growth of revenues relative to output cannot be sustained indefinitely or because the government might have to assume some direct responsibility for the debt of the policy banks, which by 2008 is projected to be equal to one-fifth of GDP.

The second alternative scenario, presented in Table 3.4, differs from the baseline scenario by assuming that following the initial recapitalization of financial institutions at the end of 1999, banks operate on increasingly commercial terms going forward. Thus the volume of loans that needs to be written off, either as a result of deterioration of the stock of loans banks are left with after the asset management companies purchase their bad loans or new loans that go bad, falls rapidly, and by 2007, all loan losses can be absorbed from loan loss reserves without impairing bank capital adequacy.[57]

In this second alternative scenario, the debt-to-GDP ratio approaches 80 percent, and debt service absorbs over half of central government revenue in 2008. More important, both the budget imbalance and the debt ratio are still rising slowly in 2008, suggesting that this scenario too is not fiscally sustainable.

A final scenario, presented in Table 3.5, combines the first two—the government's revenue share grows by half over the ten-year period, government expenditures rise by half this amount, and banks operate on an increasingly commercial basis beginning in 2000. Under this happy combination of circumstances, the budget is basically balanced by 2008, the debt-to-GDP ratio peaks at about two-thirds in 2005–06 and then declines, and the interest burden of treasury debt peaks at under 40 percent of central government revenues in 2001 and then declines slowly. This path is clearly fiscally sustainable.[58]

These scenarios suggest that a successful recapitalization of China's financial system will require both significant revenue buoyancy and a significant change in the behavior of banks going forward after the asset management companies absorb the nonperforming loans of the banking system and arrangements are made to write-off nonperforming assets in other financial institutions. Revenue buoyancy alone is not enough. Neither is commercial bank behavior.

Of course, these results are only suggestive. They show the effects of changing only two variables, the government revenues relative to gross domestic product and the efficiency of intermediation by the banking system. All other parameters and assumptions remain fixed. Different results can be generated by alternative assumptions about the amount of bad loans that must be written off, the ability of the policy banks to continue to finance the interest on their rapidly growing stock of debt, the need of the government to finance pension obligations of state-owned companies, and so forth. Among the most important of these are the assumed rates of economic growth and the interest rate the government must pay to sell its bonds. In the scenarios, these are assumed to be equal at 6 percent in order to focus the analysis on the effects of alternative paths of revenue growth and efficiency of intermediation of funds. If the government were able to sustain

TABLE 3.5

Fiscal Sustainability in China, 1998–2008: Revenue Enhancement and Commercial Bank Behavior

(billions of RMB yuan)

	1998	1999	2000	2001	2002	2003	2004	2005	2006	2007	2008
Government revenue	12.40	12.96	13.52	14.08	14.64	15.2	15.76	16.32	16.88	17.44	18.00
Government expenditure	13.50	13.73	15.75	16.17	16.54	16.88	17.19	17.47	17.71	17.90	18.06
of which:											
Noninterest	12.70	12.70	12.70	12.70	12.70	12.70	12.70	12.70	12.70	12.70	12.70
Interest	0.80	0.75	2.49	2.63	2.72	2.78	2.81	2.81	2.77	2.68	2.56
Incremental	0.00	0.28	0.56	0.84	1.12	1.40	1.68	1.96	2.24	2.52	2.80
Budget balance	**-1.10**	**-0.77**	**-2.23**	**-2.09**	**-1.90**	**-1.68**	**-1.43**	**-1.15**	**-0.83**	**-0.46**	**-0.06**
Total debt/GDP	**0.19**	**0.52**	**0.56**	**0.59**	**0.61**	**0.63**	**0.65**	**0.65**	**0.65**	**0.64**	**0.62**
Interest/Central government revenue		**0.12**	**0.37**	**0.38**	**0.37**	**0.37**	**0.36**	**0.35**	**0.33**	**0.31**	**0.29**
Memo items:											
Increments to government debt											
of which:											
Budget deficit	87.51	64.67	199.36	197.54	190.34	178.57	161.22	137.05	104.61	62.15	8.09
New policy bank debt	297.02	177.08	187.70	198.97	210.90	223.56	236.97	251.19	266.26	282.24	299.17
Special treasury bonds/Loan write-off	270.00	2595.60	235.81	202.20	192.70	175.92	149.94	112.48	60.87	0.00	0.00
Total government debt	1507.36	4344.70	4967.58	5566.28	6160.22	6738.27	7286.40	7787.12	8218.87	8563.25	8870.51
of which:											
Treasury debt	725.69	3385.95	3821.12	4220.86	4603.90	4958.39	5269.55	5519.08	5684.57	5746.72	5754.81
Policy bank debt	511.67	688.75	876.45	1075.42	1286.32	1509.88	1746.85	1998.04	2264.30	2546.54	2845.71
Special treasury debt	270.00	270.00	270.00	270.00	270.00	270.00	270.00	270.00	270.00	270.00	270.00
Interest on treasury debt	57.30	43.54	203.16	229.27	253.25	276.23	297.50	316.17	331.15	341.07	344.80
Interest on special treasury debt	19.44	19.44	19.44	19.44	19.44	19.44	19.44	19.44	19.44	19.44	19.44
Gross domestic product	7955.00	8432.30	8938.24	9474.53	10043.00	10645.58	11284.32	11961.38	12679.06	13439.81	14246.19
Government revenue	985.30	1092.83	1208.45	1334.01	1470.30	1618.13	1778.41	1952.10	2140.23	2343.90	2564.31
of which:											
Central	488.50	542.04	599.39	661.67	729.27	802.59	882.09	968.24	1061.55	1162.58	1271.90
Local	496.80	550.78	609.06	672.34	741.03	815.54	896.32	983.86	1078.67	1181.33	1292.41
Government expenditure	1077.10	1157.49	1407.81	1531.56	1660.64	1796.70	1939.63	2089.15	2244.84	2406.05	2572.40
Loans outstanding	8652.00	9949.80	11423.61	13108.60	15035.56	17234.512	19733.51	22545.54	25589.19	28659.89	32099.08

a growth rate above the real rate of interest, all of the outcomes are more favorable to fiscal sustainability.

However, a sensitivity analysis of the baseline scenario shows that the gains to the government from an ability to finance its treasury debt at a lower real rate of interest are modest. For example, changing the base scenario so that the real interest rate is only 3 percent, in the year 2008, the budget deficit at 2.4 percent, the debt ratio at 95 percent, and the interest burden at 34 percent are all lower.[59] But they are all still rising, suggesting that even in this favorable scenario, the fiscal situation is unsustainable over the long run.[60]

The scenarios do not examine alternative policies to support the recapitalization of state-owned banks. For example, if fiscal reforms are incapable of generating rising revenues relative to GDP, perhaps the sale of state assets could generate funds to pay for the expected cost of bank recapitalization. The state raised funds averaging the equivalent of 1.5 percent of GDP in 1997 and 1998 through the sale of shares in state-owned companies on stock markets in China and Hong Kong, amounts more than twice the assumed annual rise in fiscal revenues in the revenue enhancement scenario.[61]

Creating a Credit Culture

Reform pressures have presumably forced banks to become more selective in their lending, stimulating the development of commercially oriented lending practices. The World Bank reflects this view, opining that "by 1997 . . . bank managers became more reluctant to lend to loss-making enterprises."[62] Media reports of toughened credit approval procedures are commonplace.[63]

It is difficult to evaluate the extent to which a commercial culture is already emerging in the financial system. Evidence already summarized of a continuing erosion in both the quality of bank assets and the rate of return on bank capital is not definitive, since it may simply reflect a deterioration in the stock of previously existing loans rather than poor recent lending decisions.

Other evidence, both institutional and empirical, suggests that the development of a commercial credit culture is at an early stage. On the institutional side, it is notable that although the state has for several years promoted the goal of banks' assuming responsibility for their profit and losses, the banks themselves do not yet appear to have adopted this as their primary objective. The annual reports of the largest state-owned banks, with the exception of the Bank of China, rarely even mention selectivity in their lending or any indicator of improvements in their financial performance that might follow from increasing selectivity. Rather these reports continue to emphasize the growth of lending and deposit taking rather than the rate of return on equity, the rate of return on capital, the share of nonperforming loans in loan portfolios, or any other measure of the efficiency of their operations.

Similarly, the annual reports of most large state-owned banks fail to provide any information on their efforts to come into compliance with the basic prudential ratios set forth in the Commercial Bank Law in 1995.[64] Interested readers of the annual reports of these banks, of course, can calculate each bank's compliance with some of the prudential ratios using data that appear in each bank's profit-and-loss statement and balance sheet. But the absence of any information on capital adequacy or on loan concentration, which cannot be calculated from disclosed information, is disturbing.

Even some of the newer banks, which are generally thought to be more commercially oriented, exhibit some of the same problems. For example, in the 1998 annual report of the Bank of Shanghai, the president's message mentions profitability in passing, choosing to focus on the magnitude and growth of the bank's deposit taking and lending businesses and the bank's share of these activities among the seven biggest banks in the city.

On the quantitative side, there are also several indicators worth examining that bear on the depth of commitment to commercially oriented lending. First, the continued rapid growth of lending relative to gross domestic output suggests that a commercial credit culture has yet to emerge. In 1999, the quantity of loans outstanding rose by just over 1 trillion yuan. The rate of growth of lending—12.5 percent—was well above the officially reported 7.1 percent expansion of the economy. As argued elsewhere, much of this rapid growth in lending appears to have been used to finance the losses of enterprises that cannot cover their costs from the sale of their product. Loans are used to pay for inputs, workers' wages, pensions of retirees, and additions to inventories.[65]

A second quantitative indicator that points to slow progress of the large state-owned banks in developing a commercial credit culture is the continued allocation of a disproportionately large share of loans to state- and collectively owned companies. The failure of China's largest bank, the Industrial and Commercial Bank of China, to provide significant credit to private and individual firms is indicative of the problem. This is particularly striking given the large role these firms have played in generating output and especially employment since the early 1990s. At the end of June 1998, working capital loans to private and individual firms by the bank totaled only 7.6 billion yuan, an astoundingly small 0.49 percent of the bank's working capital loans outstanding to industrial and commercial firms.[66]

The same pattern is true at the other banks and at nonbank financial institutions. As shown in Table 3.6, working-capital lending to the private sector has grown dramatically in absolute terms over the previous decade but at the end of 1999 remained under 1 percent of working-capital loans outstanding from the financial system.[67] In short, access to credit by individual and privately run companies remains quite limited, particularly in light of the rapid development of

TABLE 3.6

Working Capital Lending, 1991–99

Year	Loans Outstanding from All Financial Institutions (billions of RMB yuan)	Loans to Private Sector (billions of RMB yuan/percent)
1991	1,829.3	4.9 (0.27)
1992	2,239.8	6.8 (0.30)
1993	2,774.6	10.9 (0.39)
1994	3,276.9	15.6 (0.47)
1995	4,039.7	19.6 (0.49)
1996	4,899.9	28.0 (0.57)
1997	5,541.8	38.7 (0.70)
1998	6,061.3	47.2 (0.78)
1999	6,388.8	57.9 (0.91)

NOTE: The private sector includes what the Chinese authorities classify as *geti*, translated as "individual" or "self-employed" workers, and *siying qiye*, translated as "privately managed firms."
SOURCES: *Almanac of China's Finance and Banking 1998*, p. 508. *China Financial Outlook '98*, p. 92. "China's Financial Industry Is Developing Steadily Under Reform," *Jinrong Shibao* (Financial News), January 25, 1999, p. 1. "Sources and Uses of Credit Funds of Financial Institutions, Fourth Quarter 1999," *Jinrong Shibao* (Financial News) January 13, 2000, p. 2.

the sector. The share of industrial output produced by these firms in 1997 was 18 percent, three times their share in 1991.[68] Equally important, these firms have also become the principal sources of employment growth. Indeed, since 1994, these firms have created more jobs than state, collective, and foreign-invested firms combined.[69] The further development of a commercial credit culture would presumably lead to significantly more lending to the private sector, thus easing the financial constraint that appears currently to inhibit its growth. This will require training in credit skills and risk management in the banks. And it will also require a fundamental change in the state policy of implicitly guaranteeing most lending to state-owned companies while requiring the banks to absorb from their own profits any losses from bad loans to private borrowers.

Perhaps the most interesting evidence suggesting that financial reforms to date have not succeeded in creating a credit culture is the policy response to the deflation that emerged in China in the mid-1990s. The relevant data are summarized in Table 3.7. At the retail level, prices began declining in the fall of 1997. The fall in producer goods prices started earlier, in January 1997.[70] In 1998, the broadest measure of price trends, the implicit GDP deflator, also turned downward for the first time since the early 1960s.[71]

In response, the state cut interest rates on both deposits and loans to encourage consumption and investment, organized cartels to reduce production, and introduced price floors for many products in excess supply. None of these measures appears to have had its intended effect. Consumption and investment ap-

TABLE 3.7

Price Changes, 1994–98

(percent)

Year	Retail Prices	Industrial Products	Of Which Producer Goods	Of Which Steel Products
1994	21.7	19.5	16.7	−0.4
1995	14.8	14.9	13.6	−9.3
1996	6.1	2.9	3.5	−1.8
1997	0.8	−0.3	−0.3	−1.7
1998	−2.6	−4.1	−4.6	−5.0

SOURCES: State Statistical Bureau, *China Statistical Yearbook, 1998* (Beijing: Statistical Publishing House, 1998), pp. 302 and 317; *Statistical Survey of China, 1996* (Beijing: Statistical Publishing House, 1996), p. 50; *Statistical Survey of China, 1998* (Beijing: Statistical Publishing House, 1998), p. 74; *Statistical Survey of China, 1999* (Beijing: Statistical Publishing House, 1999), pp. 73 and 76.

pear to have responded only sluggishly to interest-rate cuts, and the government was unable to enforce price floors for most commodities.

The State Economic and Trade Commission initiated another administrative approach to the problem of deflation in the summer of 1999. It issued a new regulation prohibiting any new fixed-asset investment that would increase productive capacity for 201 goods for which existing capacity was already seriously underutilized.[72] The scope of the list was broad, covering sixteen sectors including steel, petrochemicals, pharmaceuticals, construction materials, machinery, electronics, light industry, textiles, and shipbuilding. In each sector, there is a list of specific products for which no new fixed-asset investment is authorized.

One good example of overinvestment and excess capacity is the steel industry. China became the world's number one producer in 1996 when output hit 101 million metric tons. Production in 1998 grew to 116 million metric tons. But the annual production capacity of the industry was a staggering 190 million metric tons, 60 percent more than output.[73] China's unutilized capacity exceeds the output of almost all of the world's other large producers. The State Economic and Trade Commission's order prohibits new investment in productive capacity of sixteen different types of steel products.

Significant new capacity was added in the second half of the 1990s, even though capacity utilization in the industry was already low in 1995.[74] While the industry added aggressively to basic steelmaking capacity, demand continued to exceed supply for a number of specialized steel products, leading to large imports of specialized steel products throughout the second half of the decade.

If Chinese banks and other financial institutions were operating on a commercial basis, the State Economic and Trade Commission's order prohibiting these institutions from making loans for such projects would be redundant. Lending officers making loan decisions on a commercial basis would be very unlikely to extend credit to firms seeking to build additional productive capacity in product lines in which capacity utilization rates of existing firms were frequently below 50 percent and sometimes below 25 percent and in which prices had already been falling for three or more years. The order implies that state banks either have yet to develop commercial credit skills or, perhaps more likely, that they are still pressured by government and party officials to make loans that do not meet commercial standards.

Other policies may also tend to inhibit the development of a commercial credit culture. For example, the state has notified state-owned banks they must assume responsibility for their own profits and losses and that the acquisition of nonperforming loans by the asset management companies is a onetime event, never to be repeated. The state at the same time, however, still requires banks to make additional loans to heavily indebted, money-losing companies. One example of this type of lending is "closed-end loans" (*fengbi daikuan*). In principle, these loans are to be limited to financing specific profitable activities of heavily indebted money-losing firms.[75] For example, unprofitable firms with signed contracts to produce goods for the export market are eligible for closed-end loans if the exports are expected to be profitable.

The potential shortcomings of this program are obvious. First, it presumes a degree of accounting skill at the enterprise level and a degree of bank control of enterprise expenditure that may not exist. The former is essential to determine the profitability of a subset of any firm's activities. The latter is also needed since funds lent under this program are not supposed to be diverted to other purposes, such as paying back taxes or wage arrears. Second, because firms tend to regard labor as a fixed cost, lending for activities in which firms can more than cover what they define to be their variable costs could still be value-subtracting, thus reducing the net worth of the firm and hence the bank's likely ultimate rate of recovery on previously outstanding loans to the firm. Third, the program may be abused. For example, some commentators have suggested that closed-end loans be used to finance the noncore activities that are stripped out of a firm's profitable core manufacturing, frequently in preparation for a public listing.[76] Since current regulations require firms to be profitable prior to listing, noncore activities, which are rarely profitable, are excluded to boost the profitability of the to-be-listed company. This proposed use of closed-end loans would further reduce the quality of bank loan portfolios.

A second example of a central government policy that could tend to undermine the development of a commercial credit culture in the banks is the credit guarantee system that the State Economic and Trade Commission launched in early 1999 to encourage banks to lend to small and medium-sized firms. The loan guarantee program is one of several steps the government has taken to encourage the development of these firms. But guaranteeing bank lending to small and medium-sized firms may well undermine any incentive the banks have to lend on the basis of creditworthiness. Why invest scarce resources in credit analysis if the loan is guaranteed? Finally, the guarantees are being provided by provincial and municipal governments, suggesting that the program is an open invitation to abuse of banks, undermining efforts of recent years to insulate banks from interference in lending decisions by local political and government authorities.

Conclusion

China's financial system is unlikely to allocate resources more efficiently and contribute to sustained economic growth unless the balance sheets of the existing financial institutions are rehabilitated and a commercial credit culture takes hold. I have sought to shed light on the magnitude of the fiscal challenge of the former and to identify government policies that appear to have the potential for undermining the achievement of the latter. Further research and in some cases better data are needed before more definitive conclusions can be drawn. At the most basic level, the information available to judge the magnitude of nonperforming loans in banks and in nonbank financial institutions and the likely rate of recovery on these loans is inadequate. The People's Bank began to introduce a more realistic loan classification system based more closely on international standards in 1998, but no systematic information on nonperforming loans as measured by this new system has been made available. Similarly, systematic and timely information on government interest outlays on its domestic debt is unavailable.[77] Substantial additional research is needed to evaluate the magnitude of China's property bubble; the authority of the asset management companies to restructure firms in which they acquire a majority or dominant ownership share; the prospects for an accelerated sale of state assets through stock listings, particularly sales that involve a divestiture of state ownership and real improvements in corporate governance, rather than simply the sale of minority shares to private owners; the sources of growth of the private sector in recent years and the likelihood that this growth can be sustained over time;[78] the likely magnitude of the additional fiscal resources the state will need to meet unfunded pension obligations of state-owned enterprises, particularly those that will be forced to shrink dramatically or to go out of business as banks are allowed and are able to develop commercial lending practices; and the prospects for achieving revenue buoyancy through improvements in tax administration, expansion of the coverage of the value-added tax, or other means. Each of these will have a substantial bearing on either the ultimate cost of restructuring the banking system and state-owned enterprises or the ability of the government to raise the funds to finance these costs.

Notes

1. The rate of return on assets is calculated as the ratio of pretax profits to the sum of the depreciated value of fixed assets plus working capital for state-owned industrial enterprises with independent financial accounting. State Statistical Bureau, *China Statistical Yearbook, 1999* (Beijing: State Statistical Publishing House, 1999), pp. 432–35. A decade earlier, the return on assets was 17 percent; by 1996, it had fallen to 6.5 percent. Nicholas R. Lardy, *China's Unfinished Economic Revolution* (Washington, D.C.: Brookings Institution, 1998), p. 48.

2. The banks are the Industrial and Commercial Bank of China, the Bank of China, China Construction Bank, and the Agricultural Bank of China.

3. Yang Shuang, "The Striking Results of Monetary Policy," *Jinrong Shibao* [Financial News], January 13, 2000, p. 1; Lardy, *China's Unfinished Economic Revolution*, p. 132.

4. The increase from 50 to more than 110 percent understates the growth of lending because in 1999, asset management companies purchased loans from the largest state-owned banks as part of the state's program to rehabilitate the banks. In addition, the China Development Bank on its own also swapped loans for equity in some of its borrowers. Both types of transactions reduced the value of loans on the books of the banks. The implied value of such transactions in 1999 was 320 billion yuan. Shuang, "Striking Results," p. 1; Yang Shuang, "The Stable Development of China's Financial Industry Under Reform," *Jinrong Shibao* [Financial News], January 25, 1999, p. 1. If these loans had remained on the balance sheets of the banks, the loan-to-GDP ratio at the end of 1999 would have been 117 percent.

5. Economist Intelligence Unit, "The One Good Thing About Beijing," *Business China*, October 25, 1999, pp. 1–2.

6. "Vacant Housing Glut Can't Find Buyers," *China Daily*, October 18, 1999.

7. "No More Blind Investment," *China Daily*, February 19, 2000, p. 4.

8. For a summary of the industrial census, see State Statistical Bureau, *China Statistical Yearbook, 1997* (Beijing: State Statistical Publishing House, 1997), pp. 454–55.

9. Thomas G. Rawski, "China's Move to Market: How Far? What Next?" Paper presented at the conference "The PRC at Fifty," Cato Institute, September 9, 1999.

10. State Statistical Bureau, *China Statistical Yearbook, 1999*, pp. 67–68.

11. U.S. Bureau of the Census, *Statistical Abstract of the United States, 1998* (Washington, D.C.: Government Printing Office, 1998), p. 451.

12. In 1995, for example, 97 percent of the working capital of state-owned enterprises was borrowed. Lardy, *China's Unfinished Economic Revolution*, p. 42.

13. Ibid., p. 100.

14. Bank of China, *Annual Report, 1998*, p. 35.

15. Shi Mingshen, "Expansive Monetary Supply Is the Way," *People's Daily*, August 16, 1999. However, in early 2000, these banks reported substantially higher profits for 1999 than for 1998. Some of the increase may be due to interest paid on the banks' holdings of special treasury bonds. These bonds were issued in the fall of 1998, making 1999 the first year in which the banks would receive interest payments on the bonds for a full year. At the announced interest rate of 7.5 percent, the payments in 1999 would have been 20.25 billion yuan.

16. China's risk-weighting system diverges substantially from international standards, resulting in a substantial overstatement of capital adequacy in Chinese banks. For example, loans extended to central government public utility enterprises such as post and telegram, telecommunications, roads, transportation, water, and power and gas carry a risk weighting of 20 percent rather than the 100 percent required by the Basel Agreement.

17. At Everbright Bank, the increase was from 11 percent of outstanding loans in 1997 to 16 percent in 1998. At Shenzhen Development Bank, the numbers were 18 percent and 22 percent, respectively. Moody's Investors Service, *Banking System Outlook China: The Start of a Long March* (New York: Moody's Investors Service, 1999), p. 18.

18. Nicholas R. Lardy, "The Challenge of Bank Restructuring in China," in *Strengthening the Banking System in China: Issues and Experience*, Policy Paper No. 7 (Basel: Bank for International Settlements, 1999), p. 31.

19. People's Bank of China, *Quarterly Statistical Bulletin* 4 (1999), p. 25.

20. Because rural credit funds are not part of the formal financial system, they are not supervised by the central bank. Thus there is no reporting on these funds in the annual *Almanac of China's Finance and Banking* and other publications originating with the People's Bank of China. For reporting on the inability of farmers in Baimashi village in Liaoning province to withdraw their funds from a local failed rural credit fund see Feng Yuxing, "Foundation Fails Farmers' Investment," *China Daily*, November 27, 1999, p. 2.

21. Donald Clarke, "State Council Nullifies Statutory Rights of Creditors," *East Asian Executive Reports*, April 15, 1997, pp. 9–15.

22. Lardy, *China's Unfinished Economic Revolution*, pp. 142–43, 274.

23. These include the acquisition of large equity stakes in the Beijing Cement Company, the Shanghai Jiaohua Company (a natural gas supplier), the Meishan Iron and Steel Company (a subsidiary of Baoshan Iron and Steel Company), and the Jiangxi Guixi Fertilizer Plant.

24. Mure Dickie, "Asset Transfers Offer Lifeline to China's Ailing State Ventures," *Financial Times*, October 28, 1999, p. 6.

25. In 1999, China had only ten asset management companies. They managed closed-end funds with a market capitalization in late 1999 of only 2 billion yuan, about 0.1 percent of domestic stock market capitalization. Chooi Tow Kwan, "China Opens New Funding Channels for Brokerages," *Dow Jones Newswire*, September 22, 1999. Assets of insurance companies are also modest. Lardy, *China's Unfinished Economic Revolution*, pp. 224–25. Moreover, until 1999, insurance companies were precluded from holding any of their assets in stocks of listed companies. They were allowed to hold only government bonds or savings deposits in state-owned banks in their portfolios. Beginning in April 1999, they were allowed to place a portion of their funds in selected corporate bonds issued by state-owned companies, and in October 1999, the China Securities Regulatory Commission and the China Insurance Regulatory Commission announced that they would be able to own shares. However, they are not allowed to purchase shares directly but only to purchase shares in listed mutual funds. "China Insurers to Enter Stock Market via Mutual Funds," *Dow Jones Newswire*, October 26, 1999.

26. Daily transaction volume in the spot market for government bonds in September 1999 was only 100 million yuan.

27. Stephen Roach, "Land of the Rising Dragon," *Financial Times*, March 4, 1998, p. 12.

28. *Finance Yearbook of China, 1998* (Beijing: Finance Yearbook of China Editorial Commission, 1998), p. 444.

29. The revenue share in Russia was 27.8 percent of GDP in 1997 and 24.5 percent in 1998. *Interfax Statistical Report*, March 13, 1999, 3(12), tab. 2. I am indebted to Cliff Gaddy for providing this information.

30. James Harding, "Beijing to Introduce Fuel Tax," *Financial Times*, April 7, 1999, p. 8.

31. The estimated tax revenue if the fuel tax had existed in 1997, the most recent year for which data on consumption of gasoline and diesel are available, is 106 billion yuan.

State Statistical Bureau, *China Statistical Yearbook, 1999*, pp. 252–53. The conversion factor for both diesel and gasoline is 1,149 liters per metric ton. Total energy consumption in 1998 was 98.43 percent of the level in 1997. State Statistical Bureau, *A Statistical Survey of China, 1999* (Beijing: State Statistical Publishing House, 1999), pp. 112. If the share of total energy consumption derived from consumption of diesel and gasoline did not change compared to 1997, the fuel tax would have generated 104 billion yuan in 1998.

32. Yang Xu, "Road Bill Negation Written in History," *China Daily*, April 30, 1999, p. 1.

33. The tax is 20 percent of interest earnings, although interest income on certain types of savings is exempt. Based on midyear savings account balances of 4.99 trillion yuan, of which roughly 20 percent was in demand deposits earning 0.99 percent per annum and 80 percent was in time deposits earning 2.25 percent per annum, if the tax had been in place for all of 1999, it would have raised about 25 billion yuan. This estimate does not take into account exemptions.

34. Treasury bonds include treasury bills, financial bonds, state construction bonds, key construction bonds, special bonds, special purchase bonds, and price index bonds. These bonds share three characteristics: all are issued by the Ministry of Finance, funds raised through these bonds are disbursed through the government budget, and interest payments and repayment of principal also are financed through the government budget. China Securities Regulatory Commission, *China Securities and Futures Statistical Yearbook, 1999* (Beijing: China Financial and Economic Publishing Housing, 1999), pp. 8–9.

35. Ibid.; State Statistical Bureau, *Statistical Survey*, p. 11.

36. Net issuance of treasury debt was 25.8 billion yuan in 1993 and 174.8 billion yuan in 1998. Ibid. The percentage figures in the text are calculated based on the central expenditure data in Table 3.1.

37. Since the stock of nominal treasury debt in 1998 grew at a multiple of the nominal rate of expansion of GDP, the reduction in the interest rate burden in 1998 compared to 1997 is entirely a function of an average lower interest rate on the stock of outstanding government debt. Note that the estimated interest outlays in 1998 do not include the interest on the 270 billion yuan "special treasury bond" issued in August 1998 to finance a partial bank recapitalization. The interest rate on these bonds is 7.2 percent. It is not clear if the Ministry of Finance is actually making interest payments on these bonds, which are held by the four largest state-owned banks, and if so, what the source of the funds is.

38. The China Development Bank was originally called the State Development Bank.

39. For further discussion, see Lardy, *China's Unfinished Economic Revolution*, pp. 178–79.

40. China Securities Regulatory Commission, *China Securities and Futures Statistical Yearbook, 1998*, pp. 8–11.

41. Treasury debt outstanding in 1993 was 154.1 billion yuan, or 4.45 percent of GDP. In the comparison in the text, the value of other government bonds, in addition to those discussed in the text, are included in the measure of government debt outstanding in 1993. These are state investment bonds, issued in 1991 and 1992 by the Construction Bank of China and guaranteed by the Ministry of Finance; state investment company bonds issued in 1987–92 by six investment companies that were under the State Planning Commission (these companies were incorporated into the China Development Bank when it was established in 1995); and general financial bonds issued by state-owned commercial banks in 1986–92. The yearbook of the China Securities Regulatory Commission no longer reports on the amounts of these bonds redeemed and outstanding. The sum of the bonds of these types outstanding in the last year for which in-

formation was published (either 1996 or 1997) was 40.75 billion yuan. It is possible that some of these bonds were still outstanding at the end of 1998.

42. *Xinxi Ribao,* July 16, 1999.

43. Dong Furen, "Meticulously Develop the Stock Market," *People's Daily,* July 3, 1999, p. 8, in FBIS-CHI-1999-0727.

44. Chinese Securities Regulatory Commission, *Chinese Securities and Futures Statistical Yearbook, 1998,* pp. 8–11.

45. World Bank, *China: Pension System Reform* (Washington, D.C.: World Bank, 1996), p. 26.

46. Huang Ying, "Firms to Pay for Insurance Funds," *China Daily,* February 27, 1999. Since there are still regions that have a surplus of pension funds, this presumably means that the total losses in regions with deficits exceeded the total surpluses in other regions.

47. Huang Ying, "Premium Collection to Be Better Regulated," *China Daily,* May 25, 1999, p. 3.

48. Huang Ying, "Firms to Pay."

49. Jeffrey S. Zax, "The Evolution of Housing Stock and Housing Markets in Urban China, 1988-1995," paper presented at the conference on Policy Reform in China, Stanford University, November 18–20, 1999. See Chapter Eleven.

50. In 1998, the government allocated 16.8 billion yuan from the budget to ensure that living expenses of laid-off workers and pensions for retirees were paid. Xiang Huaicheng, "Report on the Execution of the Central and Local Budgets for 1998 and on the Draft Central and Local Budgets for 1999," presented at the second session of the Ninth National People's Congress, March 6, 1999, per Xinhua News Agency, March 18, 1999, in FBIS-CHI-1999-0320.

51. Ibid. Note that the government's fiscal revenues already reflect seignorage gains. For further discussion, see Lardy, *China's Unfinished Economic Revolution,* pp. 11–15, 237. By 2002, the government revenue share exceeded 16 percent of GDP, and you will note other significant divergences between these assumptions and the outcomes through 2002.

52. Six percent is approximately the real rate of interest on the longest-term government bonds, ten years, issued in the fall of 1999. On December 21, the yield on the bonds was 3.6 percent and deflation was running at 2.0 to 2.5 percent annually. Ramoncito de la Cruz, "China Government Bonds End Higher; Stock Money Shifts to Bonds," *Wall Street Journal,* December 22, 1999.

53. Net debt issuance by the policy banks was 79 billion yuan (1.2 percent of GDP) in 1996, 109 billion yuan (1.5 percent of GDP) in 1997, and 297 billion yuan (3.7 percent of GDP) in 1998. Chinese Securities Regulatory Commission, *Chinese Securities and Futures Statistical Yearbook, 1998,* pp. 8–9.

54. The ratio of loans to GDP expanded from 86 percent at the end of 1995 to 109 percent at the end of 1998, or 8.2 percent per year. Lardy, *China's Unfinished Economic Revolution,* p. 78; Yang Shuang, "Stable Development," p. 1. If GDP expands at 6 percent per annum, loans must grow at 15 percent per annum to continue the same upward trend in the loan-to-GDP ratio observed in 1995–98.

55. The revenue share rose from 10.7 percent in 1995 to 12.4 percent in 1998, an average increase of 0.57 percent per annum.

56. World Bank, *China 2020: Development Challenges in the New Century* (Washington, D.C.: World Bank, 1997), pp. 25–26.

57. Compared to the baseline scenario, additional lending is reduced over time as banks become increasingly commercialized and the quantity of loans assumed to require write-off declines.

58. China's growth rate has exceeded the real rate of interest on Chinese government bonds during 1999–2002.

59. The reason the debt-to-GDP ratio shows the least improvement is that it is driven in part by the assumption that the policy banks' net bond issuance continues at a rate of 2.1 percent of GDP per year, the average rate of bond issuance in 1996–98.

60. Specifically, interest payments as a share of central government revenues trace the following path starting in 2000: 0.22, 0.23, 0.24, 0.25, 0.27, 0.28, 0.30, 0.32, and 0.34.

61. Chinese Securities Regulatory Commission, *Chinese Securities and Futures Statistical Yearbook, 1999*, p. 17. It is worth noting, however, that the proceeds from the sale of these shares were invested in the underlying businesses. If the proceeds from share sales become government revenue, the price investors would be willing to pay for shares would presumably be lower.

62. World Bank, *China: Weathering the Storm and Learning the Lessons* (Washington, D.C.: World Bank, 1999), p. 29.

63. See Kathy Wilhelm and Trish Saywell, "Mission Critical," *Far Eastern Economic Review*, September 9, 1999, pp. 75–77.

64. The law set forth four specific prudential ratios: minimum capital adequacy is 8 percent, the ratio of loans to deposits is not to exceed 75 percent, the ratio of current assets to current liabilities is not to be less than 25 percent, and the total loans to a single borrower cannot exceed 10 percent of a bank's total capital. Few, if any, banks met these standards when the law was promulgated. The time period within which these banks would have to comply with the provisions was not specified in the law.

65. Lardy, *China's Unfinished Economic Revolution*, p. 43.

66. Chen Zhiqiang, "An Investigation of the Situation of the State-Owned Commercial Banks Service of the Development of China's Small and Medium Enterprises," *Gaige* [Reform], 1999, 1: 53. I am grateful for Thomas G. Rawski for drawing this article to my attention.

67. At the end of 1999, working-capital lending accounted for 68 percent of all loans from the financial system. There is no systematic information available on the allocation of the balance, fixed-asset loans, by ownership.

68. State Statistical Bureau, *China Statistical Yearbook, 1998*, pp. 433, 435.

69. Thomas G. Rawski, "China's Move to Market: How Far? What Next?" Paper presented at the conference "The PRC at Fifty," Cato Institute, September 9, 1999.

70. Sun Shangwu, "Price Falls Bring Challenges," *China Daily*, July 5, 1999, p. 1.

71. In 1998, nominal GDP grew from 7.477 trillion yuan to 7. 955 trillion yuan, or 6.4 percent. Growth in constant prices was 7.8 percent, implying an implicit GDP of 0.978; that is, prices fell 2.2 percent. State Statistical Bureau, *A Statistical Survey of China, 1999* (Beijing: State Statistical Publishing House, 1999), pp. 11, 16.

72. State Economic and Trade Commission, "A Catalogue of Domestic Industrial and Commercial Investment to Stop Duplicate Construction (First Installment)," Order No. 14, August 9, 1999. The list of products was also published in *Jinrong Shibao* [Financial News], August 17, 1999, p. 2.

73. "Steel Output Cut to Boost Development," *China Daily*, June 23, 1999, p. 4.

74. Rawski, "China's Move to Market."

75. People's Bank of China, State Economic and Trade Commission, State Planning Commission, Ministry of Finance, and State General Bureau of Taxation, "Interim Procedures on Closed-End Loan Management," July 26, 1999.

76. Wang Zhuo, "Unburden State-Owned Enterprises of 'Historical Loads,'" *Dagongbao*, August 30, 1999, p. D8, in FBIS-CHI-1999-0916.

77. The data on interest outlays in Table 3.1 for the years 1993–97 comes from a pro-

spectus for a Chinese sovereign bond issue, the only available openly published source of this information. But sovereign bond issues occur at irregular intervals. As of early 2000, there had been no sovereign bond issue since the fall of 1998, so the last year for which information was available on interest outlays on treasury debt was 1997. The Ministry of Finance publishes a yearbook that runs to almost nine hundred pages, but it contains no information on interest expenditure on domestic debt.

78. Much of the dramatic growth of private enterprise in the 1990s results from the sale of collective enterprises, particularly township and village enterprises, to their workers and managers. Consequently, judging the underlying rate of growth of output and employment in this sector, as opposed to growth resulting from reclassification of output and workers that statisticians previously included in the collective sector, is difficult.

4

Thriving on a Tilted Playing Field
China's Nonstate Enterprises in the Reform Era

Chong-En Bai, David D. Li, and Yijiang Wang

In the past two decades, China's nonstate sector, which generally encompasses all production units not directly owned or controlled by the state, achieved a growth record unparalleled by other transitional economies. With its growth far outpacing that of the state sector, the share of China's total industrial output produced by the nonstate sector rose from about 35 percent in 1985 to more than 72 percent in 1999. During this period, the share of the nonstate sector's contribution to total industrial growth increased from about 55 percent to 72 percent. The outstanding performance of the nonstate sector is indeed a feature that distinguishes China's reform experience from that of other transitional economies. Given the share of the nonstate sector in China's economy, there is little question that this sector has become a major factor in determining the overall performance of the economy.

This chapter reviews the experience of China's nonstate enterprises in the past two decades by analyzing three closely related questions. First, does the outstanding performance of China's nonstate sector imply a better economic environment for nonstate enterprises (NSEs) than enjoyed by state–owned enterprises (SOEs) during the reform? We will argue that the answer to this question is no, on the grounds that financial, legal, and other discrimination against the NSEs is persistent and pervasive. We will argue that such discrimination is detrimental to the NSEs' development because it means high entry barriers for potential entrants, poorly protected property rights for the existing NSEs, and distorted internal governance. All these lead inevitably to losses of efficiency.

Our second question is a puzzle resulting from the answer to the first question. If the playing field is tilted so disadvantageously for the NSEs, how did they manage to grow so rapidly in the past two decades? We believe that the answer to this question lies in an understanding of China's transitional institutions. One such transitional institution is fiscal and intragovernmental decentralization. The relative fiscal and administrative independence of local governments from the center allows the former (collectively, and officials individually) to benefit from the rapid growth of the NSEs in multiple ways, including better employment opportunities and increased (retainable) tax revenues. Another transitional institution has been the vague and ambiguous property right arrangements in many NSEs. In the early stages of their development, many NSEs voluntarily chose a government agency as a partner. By yielding some benefit and control rights to the government agency and its bureaucrats, these NSEs obtained better protection from the local bureaucrats and avoided many of the financial (e.g., tax and credit), administrative (e.g., red tape), and legal difficulties that less well protected enterprises find hard to overcome.

The third question has great policy significance: Are the existing transitional institutions adequate to support continued rapid growth of China's nonstate sector? We believe the answer is, again, no. There are several reasons for this. First, the playing field remains tilted against the NSEs, and the impact is becoming more severe as the NSEs strive to expand. The transitional institutions are no longer equipped to support those firms' continued growth. Second, due to important institutional changes concerning the NSEs during the 1990s, the main benefits of transitional institutions are fading away. Third, some accumulated distortionary effects of the transitional institutions are difficult to correct and therefore likely to persist. A case in point is the difficulty in privatizing NSEs that were initially established as collective or ambiguously owned firms. Until they are privatized, these NSEs will find it difficult even to compete in the market place, let alone to expand. Finally, severe difficulties exist for many indigenous private enterprises to grow into large, modern enterprises. The difficulties multiply due to the absence of the rule of law.

In this chapter, we will clarify the concept of the nonstate sector in China and summarize its performance over the past two decades. We then explain why we believe that during the reform era, the playing field has tilted against the NSEs in China. Next we look at the institutional arrangements responsible for the rapid growth of the nonstate sector during most of the reform era and then examine why those institutional arrangements are now inadequate and unlikely to propel further success of China's nonstate sector in coming years. In the last section, we explore policy implications of our study and identify needed further research.

The Nonstate Sector as the Engine of China's Growth

Defining the Nonstate Sector

We follow the official definition of the nonstate sector in publications such as the *Almanac of China's Economy* (published annually by the State Development Research Center), which is that the nonstate sector includes all the production units that are not controlled and owned by the state or a government agency. In other words, the concept of the nonstate sector is simply all production units not in the state sector. Under this definition, formal SOEs undergoing major owner-ship changes—for example, by issuing equity shares in the stock market—are still considered SOEs, as long as the state maintains controlling ownership.

Within this rather broad definition, the nonstate sector can be divided into collective enterprises, private enterprises, and enterprises of other ownership forms. Nominally, a collective enterprise is owned either by workers employed in the firm or by a group of community members, such as all the residents in an administrative jurisdiction. In reality, collective enterprises are under close con-trol of a government. Major investment and employment decisions could not be made without government direction or approval.

Unlike collective enterprises, private enterprises are owned by private indi-viduals. Private enterprises can be further classified into "individually owned" (*getihu*) and "privately owned" (*siying qiye*) enterprises. The difference between these two types of enterprises is that the former type either involves no hired la-bor or hires immediate family members only, whereas the latter hires nonfamily members. From the mid-1950s, when private enterprises had been nationalized, until the start of the reform, the government adopted a very hostile attitude to-ward private businesses, including individually owned businesses. In a series of political campaigns, private enterprises were confiscated and their owners per-secuted. Individually owned businesses did not really reemerge in China until after the market-oriented reforms were introduced in 1979.

Enterprises of other ownership types include foreign-invested companies and shareholding enterprises without government as the major shareholder (other-wise, they are called state-owned shareholding enterprises, a new category of state enterprises). Typically, joint ventures between state-owned enterprises and foreign investors are also categorized as nonstate enterprises.

China's nonstate sector can also be classified by geographical location as rural or urban. In rural areas, thanks to the rapid decollectivization reform in the early 1980s, all agricultural production, except that of the few state-owned farms, be-longs to the nonstate sector. As for industrial activities in rural areas, the most prominent are those of the township and village enterprises (TVEs). The TVEs originated as industrial accessories to collective farming units established un-der the People's Commune system (collectivized agriculture). They were ini-tially termed "commune and brigade enterprises." Given their accessory posi-tion, most commune and brigade enterprises did not even have independent accounting. Strictly speaking, these early commune and brigade enterprises were community-owned collective enterprises. The TVEs acquired their current name in 1983 when the People's Commune system was abolished and Chinese agriculture was essentially decollectivized. However, in most cases, the township (corresponding to the commune) and village (corresponding to the brigade) governments continued to control the TVEs as closely as the commune and brigade administrations did. In many TVEs, it is not clear who are the owners, who are the investors and how much they have invested, and who has what control rights. These aspects merit discussion, and we will return to them later.

In urban areas, the nonstate sector consists of collectives, private enterprises, and firms involving foreign investors. The firms with foreign investment can be either solely owned by foreign investors or jointly owned by foreign investors and their Chinese partners. The Chinese partner of a joint venture could be a state-owned enterprise or a nonstate enterprise. Because of their many unique features, these firms are typically excluded from official statistics of the nonstate sector and treated separately. For the same reason, we omit them in our discussion.

Rapid Growth of China's Nonstate Sector

China's nonstate sector has developed very rapidly, and this has been the most important factor driving the country's economic growth for the past two decades. One may argue about the accuracy of the statistics, but anecdotal evidence and casual observations do suggest that the orders of magnitude portrayed in the official statistics are close to reality. Table 4.1 lists the annual growth rates

TABLE 4.1

Growth Rates of Industrial Output: State Sector versus Nonstate Sector

(percent)

Year	State-Owned Enterprises	Non-State Enterprises	
		Collective	Other
1986	6.2	18.0	67.6
1987	11.3	23.2	56.6
1988	12.6	28.2	47.3
1989	3.9	10.5	23.8
1990	3.0	9.0	21.1
1991	8.6	18.4	25.3
1992	12.4	33.3	47.0
1993	5.7	35.0	66.2
1994	6.5	24.9	56.2
1995	8.2	15.2	51.5
1996	5.1	20.9	20.0
1997	1.0	10.2	15.4
1998	0.1	9.1	14.7
1999	8.8	6.0	14.4
Average	6.7	18.7	37.7

NOTES:
1. The growth rates are in real terms.
2. Foreign investment firms and Sino-foreign joint ventures are omitted.
SOURCE: Table 13-4 of *China Statistical Yearbook, 2000.*

TABLE 4.2

Development of TVEs, 1980–95

Year	Number of TVEs (million)	Gross Output of TVEs (billion RMB yuan)	Employees in TVEs (million)	Total Rural Labor Force (million)	TVE Employees/ Rural Labor Forces (percent) = 100 × (4)/(5)
(1)	(2)	(3)	(4)	(5)	(6)
1980	1.4	65.7	30.0	318.4	9.4
1981	1.3	74.5	29.7	326.7	9.1
1982	1.4	85.3	31.1	338.7	9.2
1983	1.4	101.7	32.4	346.9	9.3
1984	6.1	171.0	52.1	359.7	14.5
1985	12.2	272.8	69.8	370.7	18.8
1986	15.2	354.1	79.4	379.9	20.9
1987	17.5	476.4	88.1	390.0	22.6
1988	18.9	649.6	95.5	400.7	23.8
1989	18.7	742.8	93.7	409.4	22.9
1990	18.5	846.2	92.7	420.1	22.1
1991	19.1	1,047.8	96.1	430.9	22.3
1992	20.8	1,594.2	105.8	438.0	24.2
1993	24.5	2,785.5	123.5	442.6	27.9
1994	25.0	3,761.2	120.2	446.5	26.9
1995	22.0	5,609.2	128.6	450.4	28.6

NOTES:
1. The gross output is in constant prices of 1980.
2. Before 1983, the data included just the collective enterprises. For 1984–1995, the data included all TVEs.
3. The 1980 price = the 1990 price/1.1323, where 1.1323 comes from 958.11/846.16, 958.11 is the 1990's gross output of TVEs in 1990 price, and 846.16 is 1980 price. (See Source 4 below.)
SOURCES:
1. 1980–92 data of column 2 are from *China Statistical Yearbook, 1993*, p. 395, and 1985–95 data is from *China Statistical Yearbook, 1996*, p. 387.
2. 1980–92 data of column 4 are from *China Statistical Yearbook, 1993*, p. 395, and 1985–95 data is from *China Statistical Yearbook, 1996*, p. 388.
3. 1985–95 data of column 5 are from *China Statistical Yearbook, 1996*, p. 353, and 1980–1984 data is from *China Statistical Yearbook, 1983, China Statistical Yearbook, 1984*, and *China Statistical Yearbook, 1985*.
4. 1980–90 data (1980 price) of column 3 are from *China TVE Statistical Yearbook, 1991*, p. 136. Data of years 1990, 1991, 1992, 1993, 1994, and 1995 in 1990 price are from *China TVE Statistical Yearbook, 1991*, p.140, *China TVE Statistical Yearbook, 1992*, p. 140, *China TVE Statistical Yearbook, 1993*, p. 152, *China TVE Statistical Yearbook, 1994*, p. 178, *China TVE Statistical Yearbook, 1995*, p. 89, and *China TVE Statistical Yearbook, 1996*, p. 114, respectively.

of the state sector and nonstate sector in total output and employment. As can be seen, from 1986 to 1999, the average annual growth rate of industrial output of collective enterprises and private enterprises was about 19 percent and 38 percent, respectively. During the same period, output of the state enterprises grew only 7 percent a year.

The fast growth of the nonstate sector can also be illustrated by the development of TVEs in rural areas. From Tables 4.2 and 4.3, one can see that from

TABLE 4.3

Growth Rate of TVEs Output and Employment, 1981–95

(percent)

Year	Gross Output	Employment
1981	13.5	−1.0
1982	14.5	4.8
1983	19.2	3.9
1984	68.2	61.0
1985	59.6	34.0
1986	29.8	13.7
1987	34.6	10.9
1988	36.3	8.4
1989	14.4	−1.9
1990	13.9	−1.1
1991	23.8	3.7
1992	52.1	10.1
1993	74.7	16.7
1994	35.0	−2.6
1995	49.1	7.0
Average annual growth rate, 1980–95	34.5	10.2

SOURCES: See Table 4.2.

1980 through 1995, the output of the TVE sector grew at an average annual rate of 34.5 percent in real terms: the output of the TVEs in 1989 was more than eleven times that of 1980 in real terms. In 1995, the output of TVEs was more than six times that of 1990. From 1980 to 1995, total employment in TVEs more than quadrupled, increasing from 30 million to nearly 130 million. The average annual growth rate of employment exceeds 10 percent.

As a consequence of the very rapid growth of the nonstate sector and at the same time the much slower growth of the state sector, the landscape of the Chinese economy has completely changed in the twenty years since the inception of economic reform. Table 4.4 gives the share of nonagricultural employment of the nonstate sector. It shows that in 1985, when economic reform was first introduced in the urban areas, the state-owned enterprises employed about 70 percent of nonagricultural workers. By 1999, the share was reduced to about 41 percent. Measured by output, the picture is even more striking. According to Table 4.5, the share of SOEs in the country's industrial output shrank from 65 percent in 1985 to just over 28 percent in 1999.

With its very rapid growth, the nonstate sector has become the most important engine of growth of the Chinese economy. There are different ways to project this picture. Table 4.6 decomposes each year's increase in industrial output into that from the state sector and nonstate sector, respectively. As can be

TABLE 4.4

Share of Nonagricultural Employment: State Sector versus Nonstate Sector

(percent)

| Year | State-Owned Enterprises | Nonstate Enterprises | | |
		Collective	Other	Total
1985	70.0	26.1	3.9	30.0
1990	62.3	21.5	16.2	37.7
1995	59.1	16.4	24.6	41.0
1997	54.8	14.1	31.0	45.1
1998	43.8	9.5	46.7	56.2
1999	40.8	8.2	51.1	59.3

NOTE: Each year's total nonagricultural employment is scaled to 100.
SOURCE: Calculated from Table 2-3 of *China Statistical Yearbook, 1998* (before 1998) and Table 5-1 of *China Statistical Yearbook, 2000* (after 1998).

TABLE 4.5

Share of Industrial Output: State Sector versus Nonstate Sector

(percent)

| Year | State-Owned Enterprises | Nonstate Enterprises | | |
		Collective	Other	Other Enterprises
1985	64.9	32.1	1.8	1.2
1986	62.3	33.5	2.8	1.4
1987	59.7	34.6	3.6	2.1
1988	56.8	36.1	4.3	2.8
1989	56.1	35.7	4.8	3.4
1990	54.6	35.6	5.4	4.4
1991	56.2	33.0	4.8	6.0
1992	51.5	35.1	5.8	7.6
1993	47.0	34.0	8.0	11.0
1994	37.3	37.7	10.1	14.9
1995	34.0	36.6	12.9	16.5
1996	36.3	39.4	15.5	8.8
1997	31.6	38.1	17.9	12.4
1998	28.2	38.4	17.1	16.3
1999	28.2	35.4	18.2	18.2

NOTES:
1. Each year's total employment is 100.
2. "Other Enterprises" include foreign-invested firms and Sino-foreign joint ventures.
SOURCE: Table 13-6 of *China Statistical Yearbook, 1998* (for data before 1990) and Table 13-3 of *China Statistical Yearbook, 2000* (for data from 1990 onward).

TABLE 4.6

*Share Contributed to Industrial Growth: State Sector
versus Nonstate Sector*

(percent)

Year	State-Owned Enterprises	Nonstate Enterprises	
		Collective	Other
1986	45.3	42.9	11.8
1987	48.8	39.3	11.8
1988	47.6	40.9	11.4
1989	52.5	33.5	14.0
1990	37.8	34.8	27.4
1991	43.7	36.1	20.1
1992	32.5	45.5	21.9
1993	31.4	39.1	29.5
1994	14.4	46.3	39.3
1995	33.5	14.6	51.9
1996	8.8	57.7	33.5
1997	4.7	29.1	66.2
1998	−44.1	44.8	99.3
1999	27.6	−15.9	88.3

NOTES:
1. Each year's total increase in industrial output is scaled to 100.
2. The negative share of contribution is partly due to changes of ownership forms of many enterprises in 1998, from state-owned enterprises to collective enterprises and from collective enterprises to private enterprises, respectively.
SOURCE: Calculated from Table 13-3 of *China Statistical Yearbook, 2000.*

seen from the table, before 1990, the state sector's contribution to the increase in industrial output fluctuated around 50 percent. Since 1996, the share of the state sector's contribution has been significantly lower.[1]

How Level Is the Playing Field?

Does the very rapid growth of the nonstate sector in the past two decades imply that China has created a level (or even more favorable) playing field for the sector? We argue that, to the contrary, the playing field has been tilted to the disadvantage of the nonstate enterprises, especially the indigenous and small private enterprises. The tilted playing field has prevented the nonstate sector from growing at its full potential. More recently, it has caused a dramatic slowdown of the growth of the nonstate sector.

Legal and Bureaucratic Restrictions to Entry

One major disadvantage of the nonstate sector is a government ban on the NSEs in many sectors of the economy: the NSEs are not allowed to enter certain in-

TABLE 4.7

Types of Entry Barriers by Firm Size

(percent of responses)

Size of Employment	Licenses	Policy Restriction	Local Protection	Industry Monopoly	Market Size
Less than 51	22.6	29.0	6.6	29.0	12.9
51–100	50.0	12.5	12.5	25.0	0.0
100–500	37.5	37.5	18.8	0.0	6.3
More than 500	80.0	0.0	20.0	0.0	0.0

NOTE: Based on interviews with CEOs of 338 private enterprises in Beijing, Shunde (Guangdong province), Chengdu (Sichuan province), and Wenzhou (Zhejiang province) in the summer of 1999.

SOURCE: Table 4.1 on page 59 of *International Finance Corporation* (2000).

dustries. A partial list of these sectors includes telecommunications, commercial and investment banking, insurance, import and export trade, and wholesale trade. In many cases, the NSEs' inability to enter these sectors of high profit margins and high growth potential is due to complicated bureaucratic approval procedures or entry requirements that are too hard for nonstate enterprises to meet. For example, until recently, it was very difficult for NSEs to complete the bureaucratic procedures needed to obtain import permits (Jiang, 1999). Without direct channels of imports, many potentially profitable operations are not viable for the NSEs. As another example, many high-tech NSEs are now looking to become contractors for the national defense industry, which enjoys high profit margins. But it is very difficult for a NSE to clear the security scrutiny of the government and therefore to be approved to enter the industry. Table 4.7 shows the result of a survey of 338 private enterprises in 1999 by the International Finance Corporation. More than half of all types of enterprises indicated that the most important entry barriers are license requirements and government policy restrictions. Moreover, for larger private enterprises (over five hundred employees), by far the most important barrier for them to enter an industry of their choice is obtaining a license. This shows that the larger the private enterprise, the more prominent the constraint of government restriction on entry.

Recently, China's commitments for membership of the WTO have created an interesting new twist to government restrictions on the entry of the NSEs into certain industries. Under the accession agreements, China is required to phase out restrictions on foreign companies' entry into Chinese markets. The liberalization, however, does not apply to domestic private enterprises. In addition to the unequal treatment that disadvantaged the NSEs compared with the SOEs, the indigenous NSEs will be disadvantaged with respect to foreign corporations as well. This awkward situation prompted many Chinese economists to argue and petition on behalf of the indigenous NSEs for the equal treatment of domestic private firms and foreign companies (under the interesting slogan "National Treatment for National Industries"). Some argued that markets should be opened first to domestic private firms to allow them time to prepare for anticipated foreign competition and not yield too much market share to foreign entrants after the WTO accession. Reasonable as these proposals were, Chinese policymakers are yet to adopt them universally; nevertheless, the climate for private enterprise has improved markedly since WTO accession.

Credit Restriction

Another often-mentioned form of discrimination against nonstate enterprises is state banks' credit allocation. As many Chinese economists have observed (e.g., Jiang, 1999; Fan, 1999), a disproportionately low amount of bank credit has been allocated to nonstate enterprises. Table 4.8 shows that during the reform era, the state sector has been obtaining more funds for fixed investment than the nonstate sector. This pattern of state banks' credit allocation favoring SOEs continued even as their share of output diminished dramatically. Table 4.9 is even

TABLE 4.8

Share of Total Fixed Investment: State Sector versus Nonstate Sector

(percent)

Year	State-Owned Enterprises	Nonstate Enterprises	
		Collective	Other
1980	81.9	5.0	13.1
1981	69.5	12.0	18.6
1982	68.7	14.2	17.1
1983	66.6	10.9	22.5
1984	64.7	13.0	22.3
1985	66.1	12.9	21.0
1986	66.6	12.6	20.8
1987	64.6	14.4	21.0
1988	63.5	15.0	21.5
1989	63.7	13.0	23.4
1990	66.1	11.7	22.2
1991	66.4	12.5	21.1
1992	68.1	16.8	15.1
1993	60.6	17.7	21.6
1994	56.4	16.2	27.4
1995	54.4	16.4	29.1
1996	52.4	15.9	31.7
1997	52.5	15.4	32.1
1998	53.4	14.8	31.8
1999	54.1	14.5	31.4

SOURCE: Table 6-3 of *China Statistical Yearbook, 2000.*

TABLE 4.9

The Nonstate Sector's Share in Total Short-Term
Loans from State Banks

(percent)

Year	Collectives	Private Enterprises	Sino–Foreign Joint Ventures
1994	7.4	0.6	2.9
1995	7.5	0.6	3.0
1996	7.0	0.7	3.3
1997	9.1	0.7	3.4
1998	9.2	0.8	4.1
1999	9.6	0.9	4.7

NOTE: Each year's total short-term loan is scaled to 100.
SOURCE: Calculated from Table 18-3 of *China Statistical Yearbook,*
1998, and Table 19-3 of *China Statistical Yearbook, 2000.*

TABLE 4.10

Sources of Private Firms' Initial Investment

(percentage of total amount)

Year of Operation by Mid-1999	Self-Financing	Bank Loans	Institution	Other
Less than 3	92.4	2.7	2.2	2.7
3–5	92.1	3.5	0.0	3.8
5–10	89.0	6.3	1.5	3.0
More than 10	83.1	5.7	9.9	1.3

NOTE: Based on interviews with CEOs of 338 private enterprises in Beijing, Shunde
(Guangdong province), Chengdu (Sichuan province), and Wenzhou (Zhejiang province) in the summer of 1999.
SOURCE: Compiled from Table 5.1 on page 67 of *International Finance Corporation*
(2000).

more telling on this point. It shows that from 1994 through 1999, the nonstate
sector each year obtained no more than 15 percent of total short-term loans and
almost no long-term loans from the state banks while contributing over 65 percent of the country's growth of industrial output during the same period!

To illustrate the problem of credit constraint, let us look at the source of enterprises' initial investment funds. Not surprisingly, China's NSEs relied primarily on self-financing for their initial investments. Naturally, this restricts the
size of their operations, at least at the beginning. Table 4.10 also reports results
from the survey of 338 private enterprises in the summer of 1999 by the International Finance Corporation and shows, on average, that well over 80 percent
of the cost of initial investments was self-financed. Less than 6 percent came
from bank loans. Interestingly, the newer enterprises in the survey seem to have

relied more heavily on self-financing than the older ones, indicating that in recent years, credit constraints have not eased for China's NSEs.

Poor Legal Protection

Poor legal protection of their property rights is another major problem faced by nonstate enterprises, especially the indigenous enterprises. As is well known, China has yet to develop an independent judiciary system, so legal protection of rights is generally ad hoc. This is not nearly as much of a problem for the SOEs as it is for the NSEs because the former group is itself part of the government apparatus and has close relations with administrative branches. Therefore, it is easy to understand why a nonstate enterprise rarely gets a fair ruling when engaged in a dispute with a state-owned enterprise. Because of this concern, nonstate enterprises typically avoid legal cases against state enterprises, even when that entails an unfavorable settlement outside the legal system. For example, in a survey of 1,171 private enterprises in 1993 and 1995, two Chinese researchers from the Chinese Academy of Social Sciences (CASS), Zhang and Ming (1999), found that when facing business disputes, the overwhelming majority of the managers (71 percent) tried to deal with the disputes on their own. Only 6.5 percent of those surveyed said that they would resort to legal means (see Table 4.11). There are no similar statistics for the SOEs, but anecdotal evidence suggests that the proportion resorting to legal means for dispute settlement is considerably higher.

Meanwhile, China's regulatory agencies typically have the (biased) perspective that nonstate enterprises thrive by violating government regulations and evading taxes. The agencies are therefore much more stringent on nonstate enterprise. Frequent inspections generate opportunities for extortion that in turn induce more frequent inspections. Thus the regulatory burden on nonstate enterprises is disproportionately higher than that on state enterprises.

TABLE 4.11

How Private Firms Deal with Business Disputes

(percent)

Approach	Response
Ignore them	0.6
Deal with them by the firm itself	71.4
Seek help from government	6.1
Resort to legal means	6.5
No response	15.2

NOTE: Based on a survey of 1,171 private enterprises in 1993 and 1995.
SOURCE: Table 15 on page 150 of Zhang and Ming (1999).

TABLE 4.12

Most Important Social Problems Troubling the Operation of Private Firms

(percent)

Social Problems	Responses in 1995	Responses in 1997
Unfair income distribution	5.1	9.9
Trade between bureaucratic power and money (corruption)	37.3	37.6
Public crimes	20.6	41.1
Arbitrary taxes and fees	31.4	6.3
Others	10.7	5.2

NOTE: Based on a survey of 1,171 private enterprises in 1993 and 1995.
SOURCE: Table 13 on page 148 of Zhang and Ming (1999).

Poor protection of the NSEs' property leaves them vulnerable to several forms of predatory behavior. One problem is excessive taxation and fees. Another is the demand by bureaucrats for bribes before they provide services and protection. In the same survey of 1,171 private enterprises mentioned earlier, Zhang and Ming (1999) found that over 37 percent of private enterprise managers interviewed listed "trade between bureaucratic power and money" (corruption) as a major factor slowing down their business. Interestingly, in 1995, arbitrary taxation was a major concern, but in 1997, it was less so. But corruption remained consistently important between the two survey periods (see Table 4.12).

Tilted Playing Field: A Further Comment

During the reform period, it was often said that the SOEs are disadvantaged in many ways in their competition with NSEs. They are subject in some areas to stricter regulations. Government interference in SOEs' operational decisions is also more direct and probably more frequent. As a consequence, the SOEs cannot shed surplus labor as easily, for example. They need to pay their workers (even those with no work to do) well enough to maintain a basic standard of living and thereby help maintain social stability. But they are not allowed to pay wages high enough to compete with private and foreign employers for special talents, such as managerial and technical professionals. Prompt and timely decisions are also more difficult to make because of strict bureaucratic review and approval procedures. Based on these observations, some people argue that when all the distortions are considered and averaged out, the playing field *is* level for NSEs or possibly even tilted to their advantage.

Granted, the SOEs have their own problems, but it is a gross misperception to think that their problems essentially offset those of the NSEs and conclude that the playing field is level after all. It would be even worse to assume that no further effort is needed to create an environment more conducive to the survival and growth of the NSEs. The institutional constraints under which the SOEs operate and the associated problems caused thereby are not a consequence of the NSEs. These constraints are long-standing; they existed well before the NSEs became a major force in the Chinese economy. Policy reform is needed to eliminate constraints detrimental to both the SOEs and the NSEs. In both cases, constraints cause inefficiencies. Both cases need to be resolved in the process of further reforms, with the government-business relationship and the country's legal systems at the core.

NSEs Thriving on the Tilted Field: The Role of Transitional Institutions

With all the discrimination against the NSEs, it is puzzling that China's nonstate sector could have achieved such rapid growth over the past two decades. We argue here that several transitional institutional arrangements played an essential role in promoting the development of the nonstate sector.

Intragovernment Decentralization

Decentralization within government itself was a main thrust of China's political reform in the past two decades. That reform provided incentives for local governments to help their local NSEs and proved to be indispensable in promoting the growth of the nonstate sector. From the mid-1980s to mid-1990s, fiscal decentralization was implemented in China. In the fiscal reform, governments at different levels (the center and the provinces, provinces and municipalities, etc.) first negotiated a set of revenue-sharing rules among themselves. Also, in the mid-1980s, local government agencies were granted the right to create their own business entities. The fiscal and administrative decentralization provided local governments both incentives and latitude to develop local businesses.

But for at least two reasons, local governments' incentives for local economic development did not directly lead to a friendly environment for the development of private enterprises. First, many policies that discriminate against private enterprises extend directly from the center, and it is beyond local governments' power to remove them. Examples are sector entry restrictions and discriminatory access to credit. Second, rent-seeking motivations, in the form of either more tax revenues or more private benefits, mean that local governments' real interests lie less in creating an environment in which private enterprises can prosper than in extracting benefits from them.

One result has been that local government officials and entrepreneurs created many NSEs with ambiguous property rights, in terms of both control rights and distribution of benefits (Weitzman and Xu, 1994; Chang and Wang, 1994; Li, 1996; Che and Qian, 1998). Under ambiguous property rights arrangements, a local government will offer an NSE its protection and facilitation. Local governments have helped steer the NSEs away from many existing and burdensome regulations, taxes, fees, and harassment. They have also used their own power to grant land use rights to the NSEs, lobby on their behalf for bank loans, and secure low-priced raw materials and transportation services for the NSEs within their jurisdictions. Meanwhile, the arrangements allow the entrepreneurs to operate their enterprises. In exchange, the NSE will yield to the local government some of its control and economic benefit.

Given the discriminatory environment faced by the NSEs, the protection and facilitation that local governments had to offer were valuable contributions, making the exchange worthwhile. In the 1980s and early 1990s, it was very common for a private founder of an NSE to choose to register the firm as a collective rather than a private firm, even though the latter option was officially also available. The popularity of the unusual ambiguous property rights arrangements is reflected in aggregate data. In fact, for most of the reform era, the rapid growth of the nonstate sector was attributable mainly to that of "collective" enterprises. In contrast, before 1993, private enterprises had constituted a relatively small proportion of the nonstate sector. As data in Table 4.5 show, before 1993, the private enterprises' share of industrial output was no more than 6 percent.

How did local governments benefit from the rapid growth of the nonstate sector? They did so in two ways—political and economic—thanks to the institutional arrangements that we have just described. By directly controlling the NSEs in its jurisdiction, a local government found it easy to collect taxes and fees from the enterprises. More tax revenues meant more tax contributions to higher-level governments. It also meant more investments in local public goods. Also, the development of the NSEs led to more employment. This is especially important in areas with few SOEs (so that the emergence of nonstate enterprises does not crowd out existing state enterprises and the net employment gain is large). Rising employment mitigated problems of social instability. Tax contributions, public goods, low unemployment, and social stability are all measurable and valued indicators of the political achievements of local government officials and as bases for promotion. Rapid growth of nonstate enterprises can indeed lay a solid foundation for the successful political career of a local government official.

The second benefit to local officials of rapid growth of the nonstate sector is economic. More tax revenue can easily be transformed into more on-the-job consumption, such as better offices and cars, as well as more resources under the control of the government official in general. In many cases, local government officials were able to find ways, legally or illegally, to convert a considerable portion of the newly created community wealth into their own personal wealth.

Information Decentralization

As we noted earlier, the lack of legal protection leads to discriminatory taxes and fees on NSEs. To a certain extent, the problem is mitigated by the ambiguous property rights arrangement, since NSEs can rely on their sponsoring government agencies to fend off arbitrary taxes and fees from other agencies. However, the sponsoring government agencies themselves often demand excessive taxes, fees, and profit remittances. In fact, many NSEs surveyed complained that the demand (not actual payment) for taxes and fees exceeded their total operating revenue.[2] Table 4.12 shows that one of the top two concerns of private managers surveyed in 1995 was arbitrary taxation.[3] This raises the question, How could any business survive, let alone prosper, under such heavy burdens of government taxation?

An important transitional institution that has helped China's NSEs in fending off arbitrary taxes and fees is information decentralization. Information decentralization greatly reduced the amount of information available to government agencies on NSEs' transactions and profitability and therefore limited the ability of the agencies to collect arbitrary taxes and fees from them. The major institutional arrangement of information decentralization is what we call anonymous banking (Bai, Li, Qian, and Wang, 2000). That means that in the reform era, the Chinese government gradually but steadily loosened monitoring of enterprise transactions by the banking sector, which had been an essential part of the socialist central planning system. Not only was cash permitted for most business transactions, but anonymous bank accounts were also allowed for NSEs. Before the reform, enterprises had to conduct virtually all of their transactions in real-name bank accounts, with the use of cash and anonymous bank accounts restricted mainly to households.

Reform enabled the NSEs to hide their transactions and profits from governments, which in turn served the purpose of evading taxes and fees. Thus although the government and its various branches and agencies at different levels have the coercive power to collect arbitrary taxes, in practice, taxes, especially on smaller NSEs, were difficult to collect. Effective tax rates are therefore much lower than what they are officially. This is clear from Table 4.13, which shows that although toward the end of the 1990s, the nonstate sector annually produced about twice as much industrial output as the state sector, its contribution to government fiscal revenues remained less than half that of the SOEs. Despite accounting for less than a third of total industrial output and being generally in poor financial shape, SOEs still contributed 70 percent of Chinese government tax revenues annually during this period. The low effective tax rates provide some de facto protection of NSEs' property and incentives for private businesses to grow.

TABLE 4.13

State Sector versus Nonstate Sector: Government Budgetary Revenue

	Budgetary Revenue (billion yuan)	Budgetary Revenue from State Ownership (billion yuan)	Share of Budgetary Revenue from State Ownership (%)	Share of State Industrial Output (%)
1978	113.2	98.5	87.01	77.6
1979	114.6	100.2	87.43	78.5
1980	116.0	100.7	86.81	76.0
1981	117.6	101.7	86.48	74.8
1982	121.2	103.3	85.23	74.4
1983	136.7	114.7	83.91	73.4
1984	164.3	136.0	82.78	69.1
1985	200.5	155.6	77.61	64.9
1986	212.2	166.2	78.32	62.3
1987	219.9	162.1	73.72	59.7
1988	235.7	168.8	71.62	56.8
1989	266.5	187.7	70.43	56.1
1990	293.7	209.5	71.33	54.6
1991	314.9	224.6	71.32	56.2
1992	348.3	248.3	71.29	51.5
1993	434.9	311.6	71.65	47.0
1994	521.8	372.7	71.43	37.3
1995	624.2	444.1	71.15	32.6
1996	740.8			28.5

NOTE: Column one: Government budgetary revenue is net of planned subsidies for the losses of state–owned enterprises.

SOURCE: *China Statistical Yearbook, 1997*, pp. 235, 237, 238, 413. *China Industrial Statistical Yearbook, 1994*, p. 27.

Transitional Institutions as Obstacles to the Nonstate Sector's Further Growth

Since the mid– to late 1990s, China's nonstate sector has begun to show signs of slowing down. The pattern can be discerned from aggregate statistics. From Table 4.1, one can see that between 1986 and 1996, the average growth rate of industrial output of the collective enterprises was 23 percent; it was 8.3 percent between 1997 and 1999 and decreased year by year. For private industrial enterprises, the average growth rate from 1986 to 1996 was 43 percent; it was 14.8 percent from 1997 to 1999 and also decreased year by year. A contributing factor is of course the macroeconomic shock due to the Asian financial crisis. But more worrisome are major institutional reasons underlying the aggregate statistics.

One of the major and positive measures in China's overall reform effort in the mid-1990s is the 1994 tax reform. However, the tax reform also had the unintended effect of reducing local governments' incentives to promote the development of the nonstate sector. Freer products and labor markets had similar effects. Meanwhile, continued local government interference has turned many collective enterprises into mini–SOEs laden with many of such long-lasting problems typical of the SOEs as poor incentives, inflexibility in adjusting employment levels, soft budget constraints, and persistent financial losses. Difficulties in securing bank credits are limiting the NSEs' growth more than ever before as the bigger NSEs find greater difficulty in relying on the informal financial sector to satisfy their financial needs.

The slowdown since the mid-1990s raises the question as to whether the transitional institutions we have discussed here can support continued growth of the nonstate sector. We shall argue that this is unlikely to be the case since the transitional institutions themselves have become increasingly ineffective in dealing with the difficulties faced by the nonstate enterprises. Moreover, while facilitating rapid growth of nonstate enterprises in the past, the transitional institutions have generated distortions of their own—notably, ambiguous property rights in many nonstate enterprises. For the nonstate sector to develop further, distortions must be eliminated, and there are substantial obstacles to overcome.

Increased Adverse Impact of the Tilted Playing Field

As we have argued, the playing field has never been level for China's nonstate enterprises. However, in the early years of the reform, most of the start-up nonstate enterprises were able to overcome many government-created difficulties quite successfully by relying on the transitional institutions, as evidenced by the rapid entry of nonstate enterprises that we have observed.

The situation is very different now, as many nonstate enterprises have gone beyond the start-up stage and are aspiring to grow larger. The negative impact of the tilted playing field now becomes much more prominent. The transitional institutions are much less helpful for the growing nonstate enterprises than they were in the past.

To understand the deepening impact of the tilted playing field, let us first look at the issue of entry barriers. Twenty years ago, the prohibition of entry to the high-profit-margin sectors, such as financial services, telecommunications, wholesale trade, and import and export trade, had more nominal than real impact on the development of the nonstate sector, as most small start-up NSEs did not target those sectors for entry. Indeed, their top choices for entry were restaurants, small hotels, light manufacturing plants, small retail outlets, and the like, and the barriers in these sectors were much lower. Today, however, competition in these sectors has become fierce, and many successful nonstate firms aspire to enter such high-profit-margin sectors as financial services and telecommunications but are unable to do so. Thus legal prohibition of NSEs' entry into these sectors is now much more restrictive on nonstate firms than in the early years of reform.

Similarly, today's nonstate sector suffers more from restricted access to bank credit and financial markets. Twenty years ago, when start-up nonstate enterprises needed to raise capital, they bypassed the state-controlled financial institutions by relying on personal savings and borrowing from close relatives and friends. Since the initial capital requirement for a start-up was rather small and often below the minimal lending amount of a bank or other financial institution, the lack of access to formal financial services was not a fatal restriction for many of the new NSEs. But for a currently successful nonstate enterprise to grow bigger, the amount of capital needed far exceeds what can normally be raised from the informal financial sector. Thus the lack of access to bank credit and formal financial markets has become more damaging.

The same can be said about the earlier lack of impact of discriminatory regulations and the inadequate legal framework on the NSEs. We noted earlier that many NSEs were able to protect themselves from government discrimination and intrusion by hiding their transactions and wealth, and this was possible because information in the economy was decentralized. It is more difficult for the NSEs to do the same thing nowadays, for two reasons. First, many of them are much bigger than before, and the government scrutinizes them more carefully. Second, institutions such as anonymous banking have been abolished as part of China's effort to modernize its economic institutions and adapt itself to WTO membership.

As the effects of a tilted playing field become increasingly prominent, local governments, which used to be very supportive of nonstate sector development and actively assisted NSEs to overcome the restrictions, are less effective in this regard. The reason is that the restrictions that today's nonstate enterprises face are mostly sectorwide and nationwide and are very difficult for individual local government agencies to change. For example, the sector entry prohibitions are set by national government agencies and are virtually impossible to evade by local agencies. Likewise, the policies and institutional arrangements of the central bank and nationwide state commercial banks have hindered the efforts of nonstate enterprises to obtain needed bank credit and to gain access to formal financial markets. Such restrictions are much more difficult to evade than those on land use, tax rates, and business registration, even with the help of a local government.

The Diminishing Role of the Transitional Institutions

The transitional institutions responsible for the rapid growth of the nonstate sector are themselves evolving. This reflects a number of important changes; in particular, the 1994 tax reform and the emergence of cross-regional labor migration led to major changes in the economic incentives of governments. The 1994 tax reform aimed to consolidate taxation and return to the central government a much larger share of tax revenue. The centerpiece of the reform was the establishment of a value-added tax (VAT) of 17 percent collected by the central government tax agencies residing in local areas. As much as 70 percent of the VAT goes to the central government. Moreover, the VAT, unlike taxes collected previously in the Chinese economy, is easy for the tax authorities to collect thanks to the possibility of cross-checking among enterprises. Although the merits of the 1994 tax reform need to be judged by its long-run effects and warrant separate study, a prominent near-term impact is the diminished interest of local governments in promoting nonstate enterprises. Much of the tax contribution of these enterprises goes to the central government, while the cost of efforts to promote their growth remains with local government officials. As a consequence, local government officials are less motivated to promote the growth of the NSEs and rationally divert their efforts to other areas.

Recent years have seen increased cross-regional labor migration in China. Again, while this is good for China's long-run efforts to establish a market economy, it has a negative effect on local governments' incentives to promote nonstate enterprises. Historically, nonstate enterprises, especially TVEs, served to mitigate local unemployment pressure. Reducing unemployment among local residents by increasing employment in the nonstate sector is a major policy objective of many local governments. In recent years, relaxed domicile control, improved transportation, and better information flow are three of many factors that have contributed to increased interregional labor migration. As a result, a typical labor-intensive nonstate enterprise hires mostly cheap labor from outside the region in which it resides. Meanwhile, local residents have the option to seek employment in other regions. Thus nonstate enterprises are less effective in providing jobs for local residents, further reducing the interests of local government officials in promoting the growth of NSEs.

A number of political events also contributed to the diminished interests of local government officials in nonstate enterprises. The most obvious is the intensified anticorruption campaign of recent years. The motivation for quelling corruption is strictly political: to secure political support and shore up the legitimacy of the Communist Party. Although the anticorruption campaign should bring some long-term economic benefit, there is a short-term economic cost. For local government officials, personally benefiting from the development of the NSEs is now more risky. This is more so since antireform factions often employ the anticorruption campaign to oust reformers with little respect for rules or appropriate legal procedures. Government officials who are most supportive of nonstate enterprises and most heavily involved in their development often find themselves the targets of ill-intentioned anticorruption campaigners. As a result, nonstate enterprises suffer.

Another prominent political development in recent years is the so-called three-emphasis (*san jiang*) campaign. It requires all government officials to make an explicit commitment to putting the proper emphasis on politics, professional knowledge acquisition, and maintaining high moral standards. In connection with this campaign, the promotion of government officials is no longer based solely on local economic development criteria, thus changing officials' performance incentives. Much abated is their interest in promoting nonstate enterprises and in spurring local economic development in order to secure faster career advancement.

Difficulties in the Privatization Effort

As convenient as they were during the early years of reform, the ambiguous property rights arrangements of the nonstate enterprises are becoming liabilities to the enterprises. The reason is that as the reforms have progressed, production inputs are now more readily available from markets. Assistance and protection from local governments are much less valuable than before. Demanding profit shares and wielding bureaucratic influence, governments now represent more trouble than help to nonstate enterprises. As a result, under the aegis of "clarifying property rights," many nonstate enterprises want to part company from local governments. Effectively, they are trying to take back control rights from government bureaucrats or to privatize their enterprises.

However, there are substantial difficulties in "clarifying property rights" in nonstate enterprises. For example, in Bolou County, in Guangdong province, a rather economically liberal and prosperous region, by April 1998, years after the call for privatization, 74 percent of the registered collective firms that should have been established as private enterprises were yet to be privatized (Zhang and Ming, 1999, p. 241).

The reason for the slow pace and difficulty of privatization is that officials cannot be forced to relinquish their hold on an enterprise, since they still enjoy the power to block the proper operation of the enterprise. Instead, entrepreneurs have to negotiate with bureaucrats to induce the latter to give up their control rights. As several studies have shown (e.g., Li and Zhang, 2000; Qing, 1998), the biggest difficulty is that it is often impossible to buy out incumbent bureaucrats from their enterprises. The central problem is how to compensate the bureaucrats for their lost control rights in the enterprises. In some cases, acceptable arrangements were negotiated to convert collective enterprises into private ones. In more cases, privatization stalled.

To understand the difficulty in compensating bureaucrats, consider the following. When a bureaucrat controls an enterprise, he enjoys a benefit from control that is inalienable. To induce him to give up his control rights, a high enough monetary payoff has to be provided. By definition, the increase in profit of the enterprise after the departure of the bureaucrats should be higher than the bureaucrat's private benefit of control. Therefore, the entrepreneur should be willing to make a monetary payment adequate to compensate for the bureaucrat's loss of the control right. However, the bureaucrat is unlikely to be able to enjoy all of the monetary payment. Nominally, the bureaucrat is not an owner of the collective firm; he is supposed to represent the government agency that is nominally a part owner of the firm. Therefore, he is not nominally entitled to any payment from the entrepreneur to buy out the control right. Instead, any payment to the bureaucrat himself would be considered illegal and a bribe—particularly in light of the ongoing anticorruption campaign. Even if the payment is declared legal, it may be taken in whole or in part by other government officials with greater power because the payment is monetary and hence alienable. If a payment is made to the government agency as a nominal owner of the firm, the bureaucrat, as only one member of the agency among many, therefore can enjoy only a relatively small share of the monetary transfer offered by the entrepreneur. The result could be that the bureaucrat prefers the status quo, in which he reaps a private benefit from the control right, rather than agreeing to privatization of the enterprise.

Although there are several immediate reasons for the lack of progress in privatizing nonstate enterprises, we feel that this explanation is of considerable direct relevance to many failed privatization attempts in China. A common explanation for the failure of the nonstate enterprises to buy out the incumbent bureaucrats is a liquidity constraint. This may be the case for small and newly established firms, but for larger and more mature collective enterprises, it is less likely to be a relevant reason.

Establishing Modern Enterprises Without the Rule of Law?

Today's nonstate enterprises in China, except those invested by foreign investors, face great challenges in growing into larger, modern enterprises. In the 1980s and early 1990s, they began as small operations and were able to grow rapidly thanks to the market opportunities created by the inefficiency of the SOEs. After twenty years of reforms, market competition has substantially increased, and the small, primitive, family-run nonstate enterprises find it difficult to survive.

Establishing a modern enterprise without the benefit of the rule of law poses particular challenges to today's nonstate enterprises in China. The most prominent issue concerns corporate governance. Corporate governance, specifically defined, refers to institutions that assure outside investors that the corporations they invest in will exert all best efforts to provide a return on their investment. Based on the experience of modern market economies, the most effective means of corporate governance is legal protection of investor interests. This includes a large array of company laws and security and exchange regulations. China's legal system is transparently inadequate in this regard. Thus today's nonstate enterprises are trapped in a difficult situation. They need outside investments, but without a working legal system, they cannot credibly convince outside investors that they will not misuse the investment funds. Thus they cannot obtain the needed capital and therefore cannot grow into large, modern corporations. Many of them remain small family-run enterprises.

The difficulties due to the lack of legal protections are much more acute for nonstate enterprises than for state enterprises and are in fact more damaging now than before. For state enterprises, investment brings with it the help of government intervention (including implicit government guarantee in the case of bank loans). Also, state enterprises are subject to rather tight government monitoring. In a way, for state enterprises, political governance replaces corporate governance (Li, 1998). Managerial abuse of outside investment funds is monitored and controlled without formal legal institutions. For nonstate enterprises, government control is much looser, and there is a pressing need for legal institutions to bind enterprise insiders in order for them to be credible in raising capital from unaffiliated investors. Moreover, in comparison with early years, today's nonstate enterprises are much thirstier for outside capital. Hence the absence of the rule of law is more damaging for today's nonstate enterprises than for both yesterday's nonstate enterprises and today's state enterprises.

Policy Implications and Further Research

China's nonstate sector has achieved rapid growth in the past twenty years. However, this was achieved on a tilted playing field. During the early days of reform, a set of transitional institutions helped start-up nonstate enterprises overcome difficulties stemming from this disadvantaged position. However, such transitional institutions do not provide long-term solutions for the problems facing China's nonstate enterprises. While helping many nonstate firms to get started on a small scale, the transitional institutions offer little help to the NSEs as they struggle to grow and modernize. The transitional institutions also create their own distortions. Consequently, we have seen signs of slowdown in China's nonstate sector.

The policy implications of our analysis are very clear. Leveling the playing field for all enterprises should be the top priority of the government in order to spur further growth of the nonstate sector. This involves reforms on many fronts. Entry restrictions must be lifted. Credit evaluation and supply must be based on market principles. Privatization of ambiguously owned collectives must be fully encouraged and pushed ahead in many regions. Finally and very important, China must establish the rule of law, especially laws protecting outside investors. The absence of the rule of law is most damaging for nonstate enterprises in their efforts to become large, modern enterprises.

Further research is needed to advance our understanding of a few crucial aspects of China's nonstate enterprises. We need good politicoeconomic research on government incentives in maintaining a tilted playing field. This can elucidate the conditions that make it possible for the government to level the playing field. We need empirical research on effective mechanisms to privatize ambiguously owned nonstate enterprises. Finally, an interesting area for study is the incentives of central and local government officials in supporting or obstructing the implementation of laws protecting corporate investors.

Notes

1. One reason for the diminishing share of SOEs' contribution to industrial output is privatization, which transformed some SOEs into collective or private enterprises. We do not think this is all the reason. In fact, privatization was not adopted as a major policy until mid-1997 but the share of SOEs' contribution to output growth has been consistently lower than that before 1990. Poor performance of existing SOEs is a major reason for this.

2. According to Zhang and Ming (1999), the amount of fees paid by NSEs was as high as 30 percent of formal taxes. Some Chinese authors claim that the ratio is 170 percent. Also, the number of different fees collected by local governments was more than 18,200. A newspaper article revealed that one local government collected fees based on the measure of "air density" (Zhang and Ming, 1999, p. 140).

3. In the 1997 survey, complaints on arbitrary taxation were much less than the 1995 survey. We suspect that this was due to the tax reform of 1994, which began to take effect after the three-year phase-in period. (We discuss this later in this chapter.) More important, by 1997, the problem of arbitrary taxation had evolved into outright demands from government officials for bribes, which was the leading concern reflected in the 1997 survey.

References

Bai, Chong-en, David D. Li, Yingyi Qian, and Yijiang Wang. "Limiting State Predation Through Anonymous Banking: A Theory with Evidence from China." Working paper, Centre for Economic Policy Research. London, 2000.

Chang, Chun, and Yijiang Wang. "The Nature of the Township-Village Enterprise." *Journal of Comparative Economics*, December 1994, *19*(3), 434–52.

Che, Jiahua, and Yingyi Qian. "Insecure Property Rights and Government Ownership of Firms." *Quarterly Journal of Economics*, May 1998, *113*(2), 467–96.

Fan, Gang. "*Shui lai gei zhong xiao qi ye dai kuan?*" [Who Will Lend to Medium and Small Enterprises?]. *Zhu Jiang Jing Ji*, 1999, 7, 6–7.

International Financial Corporation: *China Private Enterprise Study: A Draft Report*. Beijing: International Financial Corporation, 2000.

Jiang, Leyi. "*Guangdong fei gong you jing ji de xian zhuang he fa zhan qu shi (shang)*" [The Current Status and Trend of Development of Guangdong's Non-Nonstate Economy, Part I]. *Guangdong Fa Zhan Dao Bao* [*Guangdong Development Report*], 1999, *3*, 11–18.

Li, David D. "A Theory of Ambiguous Property Rights in Transition Economies: The Case of the Chinese Non-Nonstate Sector." *Journal of Comparative Economics*, August 1996, *23*(1), 1–19.

———. "Government Control vs. Insider Control in State Enterprises in Transition." Hong Kong University of Science and Technology, 1998. Mimeographed.

Li, Shuhe, and Weiying Zhang. "*Kung zhi quan sun shi de bu ke bu chang xing yu guo yon qi ye jiang bing zhong de chang quan zhang ai.*" [The Non-Noncompensatability of Control Rights and Obstacles to Mergers of State Enterprises]. In Zhang Chuguang (ed.), *Zhong guo jing ji xu, 1998* [*Economics in China, 1998*]. Shanghai: Shanghai People's Publisher, 2000.

Qing, Hui. "*Shi zhi luo kou kan xiang qi: Qinghua da xue xiang zheng qi ye zhuan zhi bao gao zhi yan jiu (xia)*" [TVEs at the Crossroad: Studies of Reform of TVEs by Tsinghua University, Part II]. *Gaige* [*Reform*], 1998, *1*.

State Development Research Center. Almanac of China's Economy. *Beijing: China Economic Yearbook Publisher, published annually.*

State Statistical Bureau. *China Statistical Yearbook.* Beijing: State Statistical Publishing House, published annually.

———. *China TVE Statistical Yearbook.* Beijing: State Statistical Publishing House, published annually.

Weitzman, Martin L., and Chenggang Xu. "Chinese Township-Village Enterprises as Vaguely Defined Cooperatives." *Journal of Comparative Economics*, April 1994, *18*(2), 121–45.

Zhang, Houyi, and Lizhi Ming. *Zhongguo siying qiye fazhan baogao* [*A Report on China's Private Enterprises*]. Beijing: Shehui Kexue Wenxian Chuban She [Social Science Archive Publishing House], 1999.

5

The More Law, the More . . . ?

Measuring Legal Reform in the People's Republic of China

William P. Alford

The more laws and orders are made prominent
The more thieves and robbers there will be.
Laozi, *Dao-de-jing*, v. 57

The challenge of addressing the course of legal reform in the People's Republic of China (PRC) over the past two decades for an audience of persons deeply learned about China and especially its economy, but not necessarily steeped in its law, is an inviting, if daunting, one. It provides an opportunity to step back and consider more fundamental questions than are typically raised in intramural exchanges between legal specialists who, even though their particular positions may differ, share a frame of reference. At the same time, it also requires that one take account of the increasing tendency of leading economists and others outside the law to hinge important elements of their arguments on what are essentially legal concepts (such as property rights, contracts, and the rule of law itself). As such, it holds the prospect not only of enriching consideration of Chinese reform within and beyond the law but also of pushing us to think in theoretical terms about possible linkages between law, economic development, and society more broadly.

This chapter has three sections. The first provides a brief review of the course of state-led legal development during the reform period. The second endeavors to identify and consider questions that one would ideally hope to address in order to reach a full and balanced assessment of the degree of success of Chinese law reform. And the third suggests directions for further research that might enable us to address more thoroughly the questions raised in part two and reflect sensibly on possible priorities for further legal development in China.

Legal Development During the Reform Period

As befits a nation possessed of five thousand years of history and almost a quarter of all persons now alive, China thinks big—and the project of post–Cultural Revolution legal development is no exception. Whether one looks to the substantive law concerning economic matters, legal institutions and processes, or the personnel needed to staff this infrastructure, the Chinese state's efforts over the past two decades to build a legal framework for an increasingly marketized economy are, at least quantitatively, of historic proportions, irrespective of which nation's or civilization's experience one might choose as a measure. Those efforts, to be sure, have been much chronicled but warrant at least brief recounting here as a foundation for the more qualitative discussion that follows.[1]

A, if not the, centerpiece of the PRC's post–Cultural Revolution program of law reform has been the development of a body of substantive law intended to help facilitate the transformation from an economy that was principally planned to one more hospitable to market endeavor. Twenty years ago, the overwhelming cast of the PRC's relatively modest body of legislation and regulation, at both the national and subnational levels, was criminal and administrative. China's scant measures addressing contract law were more accurately thought of as providing the means to cement relationships determined by the state, rather than party volition; lawful forms of property were limited to those defined as state or collective; and substantive measures addressing foreign economic activity, such as the Joint Venture Law of 1979, were few in number and open-ended in nature.

Through a concerted program of legal development—supported in important respects both financially and intellectually by a host of external agencies including the World Bank, the Asian Development Bank, the United Nations Development Programme, the European Union, the Ford Foundation, and other actors both public and private—the government of the PRC has promulgated since that time a framework of increasingly market-oriented substantive law at the national level while also allowing subnational units of government to develop further rules, provided they are consistent with national enactments.[2] Simple contract provisions aimed principally at recording state-directed transactions gave way in the 1980s to a set of broad principles (articulated as part of an overarching set of general principles of the civil law), coupled with a series of sector-specific rules that still paid considerable homage to state-led endeavor. These were supplanted, in turn, in 1999 by a unified and comprehensive law (encompassing more than four hundred articles) that strives to effect a balance between party autonomy and state imperative. Formal legal protection for a variety of types of property (including real property, securities, and intellectual property) and modes of economic organization (including corporations enjoying limited liability and partnerships) have blossomed, leading to constitutional amendments and the recent launching of efforts to produce a national law on property that would set forth broad, crosscutting principles. Foreign business is now the subject of an increasingly elaborate legal framework concerning matters ranging from equity joint ventures to technology transfer to taxation, among many others.[3] And the government has put in place an array of other measures, some directly related to economic affairs (including laws dealing with matters such as accounting, bankruptcy, consumer protection, labor, and a national budget) and others providing needed underpinnings for further marketization (including provisions concerning administrative regularity, corruption, and social security). Although volume is hardly a proxy for quality or impact, Chinese authorities report with pride that more than thirty-seven thousand laws, regulations, and legal measures have been issued over these two decades (Qiushi, 1998).

Attention, of course, has not been confined to the substantive law. Legal institutions were virtually in shambles as the Cultural Revolution came to a close, with, for instance, the Ministry of Justice closed, the procuracy (a Soviet-style prosecutor's office) eliminated, and local governments replaced by revolutionary committees, while even those entities nominally left standing, such as the National People's Congress (NPC), the Bureau of Legislative Affairs of the State Council, and the Supreme People's Court, were relatively modest operations, both formally and practically.

Over the intervening two decades, the PRC government has sought to inject new life into the organs of state charged with making, administering, and applying the law. The 1982 constitution elaborated the powers of the supreme organ of state, the NPC, by authorizing it (either directly or through its Standing Committee) to amend the constitution, enact national legislation, interpret legislation, and oversee both the administrative arm of national government and subnational units of government to ensure that their enactments were in conformity with the constitution and national measures (Cai, 1992). Toward that end, the constitution authorized the NPC to establish specialized committees (now numbering eight), which have been among the factors in the NPC's developing an increasingly professionalized staff.[4] Throughout the same period, the highest organ of national administration, the State Council, has endeavored, pursuant both to its constitutionally derived powers and a 1985 NPC Standing Committee resolution authorizing the making of provisional regulations concerning economic reform, to build its own rule-making expertise (both through its Bureau of Legislative Affairs and more generally) while also continuing to oversee the application of those rules (Corne, 1997). And in perhaps the largest institutional departure from the prereform era, the PRC's judiciary has expanded throughout the entire nation via a four-part court system, running from the district level through the Supreme People's Court in Beijing, which body has since 1981 been authorized to issue judicial interpretations (*sifa jieshi*) of points of law arising in the course of its adjudicative work (Liu, 1997; Finder, 1993).

As it has created these institutions, the PRC has also enacted legislation designed to structure their processes and staff them properly. Beijing is now in its
second generation of reform era civil and criminal procedure laws, with each
defining a more distinct role for judicial and other actors (attorneys in the former case, the police, procuracy, and defense bar in the latter) than was true previously. The 1989 Administrative Litigation Law and subsequent legislation concerning administrative punishments, state compensation for persons harmed by
unlawful administrative acts, administrative review, and administrative procedure
more generally suggest at least the possibility of using law to bound administrative discretion (Pei, 1997; Lubman, 1998). And China's law on legislation (*lifa fa*),
recently promulgated after years of debate, aspires to clarify the respective roles
and responsibilities of a variety of institutional actors at both the national and
subnational levels (Xinhua News Agency, 2000).

These efforts have been complemented on the personnel front by both legislation designed to provide further definition for the pertinent professionals and
the associated specialized training. In the former regard, the PRC has within the
past five years alone promulgated new measures concerning judges, lawyers, civil
servants, and other personnel while also bringing to over three hundred the number of universities and other institutions offering legal training (a larger number
than in the United States). Consequently, China today has close to 300,000 judicial personnel (including 130,000 judges), some 175,00 lawyers (with plans to
grow to 300,000 by 2010, which would make it the world's second-largest bar
in absolute terms), 160,000 prosecutors, an increasingly professionalized staff of
some 2,000 at the NPC, and a periodic mandate that civil servants heed the example of President Jiang Zemin, Premier Zhu Rongji, and other senior national
leaders by acquainting themselves with law through lectures or other means
(Qiushi, 1998; Luo, 1998; Alford, 1995a; Xinhua News Agency, 1999a).

Assessing the Success of China's Law Reform

The PRC leadership's decision to devote substantial resources to legal development seems premised on the notion that such development correlates with overall economic development. Laws, legal institutions, and legal personnel of the
type described earlier in this chapter are seen as having the potential to foster
economic growth and to attract foreign involvement in the economy and are to
be encouraged for those reasons, among others.

This is, of course, hardly a new thought. Max Weber compensated for many
a sociological error (as, for example, in his accounts of Chinese life) by explaining how legal rationality spurred the development of capitalist societies by facilitating the predictability he indicates business so prizes (Rheinstein, 1954).
Douglass North (1990) earned the Nobel Prize by pushing this line of thought
further in demonstrating how relative clarity in and security of property rights,

spawned in important part through formal legal institutions, had been a prime factor in the rise of major Western economies. Andrei Shleifer won the Bates Prize in part through further refinements of this core notion that suggest why common law regimes are generally more conducive to the accumulation of capital and the ensuing economic development than their civil law counterparts, particularly in the Francophone world (though he and his coauthors seem not to have controlled for the impact on productivity of excessive consumption of pâté de foie gras, Roquefort, and champagne, let alone Jerry Lewis films) (La Porta et al., 1998). And the leading multilateral development banks, the G-7 and EU governments, prestigious foundations, the deans (including my own) of the more prominent American law schools, and a bevy of very talented economists and other social scientists seem convinced that "the establishment of the rule of law," as typically exemplified in major measure through the further elaboration of formal legal institutions, is perhaps "the biggest challenge for China to complete its market transition" (Qian, 1999, p. 42).

So, who am I, especially as a law professor who for some two decades been enmeshed in the process of legal development in the PRC, to take issue with such wisdom? Without being flip or nihilistic, it seems that there is a utility in being the skunk at this particular garden party, if for no other reason than to push beyond the "feel good" rhetoric of advocacy of the rule of law (about which few, other than stray colleagues of mine at the Harvard Law School, have anything but praise) in order to examine the impact that the legal developments described earlier in this chapter are having in China, ascertain what within the vast black box labeled "law" might warrant accentuation, and speculate about the broader societal circumstances that might be conducive to further, desirable growth in law. If this has a strong normative ring, that is because assessments of the current course of law reform to date and attempts to set priorities for its future, even if focused chiefly on law's impact on economic performance, are, perforce, grounded ultimately in a normative framework, as will be elaborated shortly.

A departure point for such an inquiry is to remind ourselves that the link between formal legal institutions (here broadly defined as North would) and economic development even in the advanced economies of the United States and Europe is hardly beyond contention, especially if one is endeavoring to speak comprehensively (as opposed to seeking to correlate fairly specific changes in particular laws with comparably specific economic outcomes, as, for example, in measuring the impact of an extension of the copyright term on the value of a copyright). North's claim that a relative clarity and fixity of property rights has been central to economic development in the West has been construed by many as showing that developing countries (and foreign donors) desirous of growth should be devoting prime attention and resources to their formal legal system, yet North himself is quite clear that other factors, such as "informal constraints," matter, even if we "need to know much more about culturally derived norms of behavior and how they interact with formal rules to get better answers" (North, 1990, p. 140). At the broadest of levels, I remain somewhat uneasy in the face of statements that would definitively attribute overall economic growth to formal legality or even the rule of law, as distinct from political institutions in general, political culture, a free media, a self-confident and assertive populace, a vibrant civil society beyond political institutions, religion, or other factors, for we lack a controlled experiment that could effectively parse such variables in an irrefutable manner (Singapore notwithstanding).

Turning to the law, even looking only at economically advanced Western nations, presumably we need to ascertain more precisely what the motive forces are. Is what matters most particular substantive laws (such as those that limit liability and so make possible the corporate form, as many would assert)? Or could it be procedural regularity (or perhaps the perception thereof), as distinct from the content of any given set of laws? Or might it be the presence, self-interest, or ideology of a class of professional judges and lawyers? Or is it a belief in the system's legitimacy (Tyler, 1990)? Is it rather some combination of all of these? And how in such a calculus would we account for what some economists, social scientists, and others suggest may be the baleful effects of law and lawyers (Magee, Brock, and Young, 1989; Epstein, 1995; Shleifer & Vishny, 1999)?

Remaining with the developed West, the inquiry, of course, cannot stop with the formal law itself. In effect demonstrating the soundness of North's intuition, there is a range of top-flight scholars such as Macaulay (1963), Greif (1996), and Ellickson (1991) whose work suggests that it is only through careful study of the interplay of formal legal institutions with other, more informal norms and processes that we can begin to understand the power, as well as the limits, of legality and to appreciate that some of that very power may manifest itself in ways quite different from those intended by the people who drafted or developed said formal legal institutions. Indeed, in practice, these very institutions themselves may be rather distinct from what we had assumed, as suggested, for example, by Herbert Kritzer's (1990) book arguing that in many civil matters, American lawyers are appreciably more akin to "brokers" than professionals.

Finally, throughout all this, we would not want to lose sight of the impact of time on our analysis. One suspects that writing, especially emanating from Washington, about the centrality of the rule of law to economic development might have presented Chinese reformers with somewhat less of an air of inevitability had it been produced during the double-digit inflation and unemployment of the late Carter and early Reagan years, the savings and loan crisis of the mid-1980s, the stock market crash of 1987, or the recession of 1991 that cost President Bush reelection (all events transpiring during the PRC's reform era). Or, to take another illustration closer both in time and locale to this inquiry, the World Bank in a celebrated 1993 study suggested that the insulation of high-level bureaucrats from politics may have been an important cause of the so–called East Asian economic miracle, which notion would seem potentially in tension with the current emphasis on the rule of law. And there is always the question of just what is the time frame within which one is reasonably to expect legal change to produce economic growth.

As we turn our attention outward, even if only to the economically advanced nations of East Asia, the concerns I have just expressed may become yet more daunting. To begin with, if our goal is to assess the impact of legal institutions on economic development, what are the germane institutions? Does Japan have a very modest number of lawyers relative to other industrialized societies (which would seem to be the case if we confine our consideration to *bengoshi,* or individuals authorized by the state to represent clients in court)? Are the proportions somewhat more comparable, at least as concerns the civil law jurisdictions of western Europe (which would seem to be the case if we include tax and patent specialists, judicial scriveners, and others licensed by the state to perform functions akin to those performed by counsel elsewhere)? Or does it, to be perverse for the moment, enjoy (or suffer from) a greater proportion of legally trained persons in the work place than even the United States (which would be the case if one focused on graduates of law departments)? But even if we take the seemingly easiest alternative and focus only on *bengoshi* (as the closest equivalent to lawyers as we in the United States know them), is the equivalence necessarily close enough to capture the very features for which we may be testing, as *bengoshi,* for example, have until quite recently had only an extremely modest role in business planning and an almost negligible role in government service and within corporate hierarchies, as compared with their North American counterparts?

To take another issue that at least some scholars would need to resolve at a fairly early stage in the inquiry, how are we to classify the legal systems of jurisdictions such as Japan, Korea, and Taiwan? The recent work of Shleifer and colleagues on the relationship of law and finance turns on the very question of the relative efficacy of common law and what they term French, German, and Scandinavian civil law systems in promoting capital markets. Japan, Korea, and Taiwan, we are informed, are "German civil law countries" for purposes of this study (La Porta et al., 1998). Yet in each of these jurisdictions, much of the very substantive law of corporate governance on which they are focused is derived quite explicitly and with little alteration from American models. In addition, before pigeonholing Japan as a German civil law country, one might want to take account of such further legal data potentially relevant to an assessment of Japanese law enforcement as two thousand years of Japanese legal history and the presence of a constitution and other legal enactments beyond the corporate governance area bearing a distinct American imprint.[5] And of course, it may well be that what Shleifer would describe as the Germanness of Japan's capital markets and associated legal infrastructure may have a good deal less to do with the power of the German example than with more fundamental decisions of an economic and political nature. Facetiousness aside, the point here is to illustrate the need for caution as we consider what even much acclaimed work presents as the link between law and development.

Shleifer's study also suggests other respects in which caution may be warranted even in thinking about societies such as Japan, Korea, and Taiwan that have already attained a high level of economic development (and in which, therefore, it would be easier to track the impact of law than on a society at a far earlier stage of development such as the PRC—whose scholars, incidentally, typically describe it as being a civil law state). Is it prudent, for example, to rely so heavily on assessments generated by international business consultants (such as Business International Corporation) about such crucial matters as "efficiency of the judicial system," the "rule of law," and "corruption"? Are international consultants (even if they use domestic sources to gather some of their data) an accurate proxy for domestic economic actors, be they state, corporate, or other? Would international business have access to or be as willing as domestic actors (given the constraints of the U.S. Foreign Corrupt Practices Act and comparable legislation in a growing number of other OECD countries) to use extralegal methods to address certain matters (one thinks, for instance, of rumored alliances of *yakuza* and certain Japanese businesses or of the massive underground economy existing on the small island of Taiwan about which Jane Kaufman Winn [1994] has written so well)? Might not the excessive confidence that foreign business has displayed at earlier times about the robustness of the Japanese and Korean economies suggest that we would wish now to approach such assessments with a good deal of humility (Vogel, 1979)?[6]

The very question of timing suggests yet another caveat as we ponder what the examples of Japan, Korea, and Taiwan may have to tell us about the link between law and economic development. Each of these societies became a developed economy far more rapidly than the United States, Britain, France, Germany, the Scandinavian nations, or other prime actors in Shleifer's sampling and managed to do so with formal legal institutions, by virtually all accounts, playing an appreciably smaller role than was the case in North America or Europe. And growth in each, arguably, has slowed appreciably with the introduction and increasing reliance on certain types of formal legality. Obviously, a great many factors could be cited in explanation of both the rapid rise of East Asian economies (including borrowings of technologies and institutional forms generated in the West) and the troubles that they have encountered in the 1990s (including an insufficient embrace of more arm's-length, rule-oriented ways of doing business), but the point is that it is not necessarily waggish to think that large questions remain unresolved, even among China's developed neighbors, as to the link between law and development.

So what, then, about China? As with so much else, the sheer size, diversity, and complexity of China, together with the relative lack of transparency about many matters pertinent to an assessment of the law there and the uncertainty that continues to shroud at least some available statistics, suggest that we will face the types of challenges encountered elsewhere, and more, as we turn our attention to the PRC.

Linking Law Reform to Economic Development

For starters, the effort to measure the impact of law on economic development in China should endeavor to take a comprehensive view. Far too much of the writing concerned with current or prospective links between law and economic development in China has focused on presumed positive outcomes (such as increases in rates of foreign investment or overall growth in the economy), but would it not be equally relevant to include in the equation baleful consequences of the same? At the most obvious level, in the case of China, it would seem, for example, that one ought to offset against the figures for foreign direct investment those monies unlawfully sent overseas and perhaps also those funds diverted into the underground economy—for in their own way, they speak to the effectiveness of the new legal system. In August 1999, for instance, PRC Auditor General Li Jinhua announced that public funds totaling more than 117 billion RMB yuan (more than U.S.$14 billion) had been misused in the first six months of 1999 alone—a sum greater than the amount of that year's special government spending package designed to stimulate the economy—and some observers have suggested that money held in illegal offshore public accounts may total as much as U.S.$6 billion and that tens of billions of yuan in customs revenue have been lost by virtue of illegal imports said to run as high as U.S.$30 billion a year (Becker, 1999b). Moreover, the possibility exists that these figures may understate the case, given, for instance, the considerable gap between World Bank and Chinese government estimates of lawful net capital outflow ($72 billion versus $16 billion for 1998) (Becker, 1999a).

An argument might be made that one may also wish to add on to the scale externalities, both positive and negative, that can be credibly linked to such economic gains as enhanced foreign investment or a more open, market-oriented economy. For example, a World Bank report titled *Clean Water, Blue Skies* suggests that urban air pollution results in some 178,000 premature deaths annually, which, when taken with other "hospital and emergency room visits, lost work days and the debilitating effects of chronic bronchitis are estimated at more than $20 billion a year" in the cities alone (World Bank, 1997, p. 23). Arguably, if one is to "credit" China's emerging legal regime for drawing in foreign direct investment and spurring growth, one might also wish to "debit" that regime for that part of the aforementioned damage that could reasonably be attributed to the inability of China's growing body of environmental law to curb such problems, particularly if generated by foreign-invested plants.[7] And a similar point might even be made regarding the sharp increase in crime (criminal cases were, according to the Supreme People's Court, up more than 9 percent in 1998; Han, 1999; Xiao, 1999b) and particularly the rapid proliferation of economic crimes of a type largely unknown during the decade that preceded the reform period, with, for instance, the courts dealing with 17,612 cases involving alleged violations of the law by its own personnel (principally concerning corruption and other economic crimes; Xiao 1999a) in 1998 and many more such matters (running into the hundreds of thousand) having been dealt with through Party disciplinary mechanisms (Luo, 1996).

Another, more subtle "externality" of China's growing legalization may be its impact on at least some of the "informal constraints" that may in the past have been vehicles for the resolution of disputes (whether themselves directly related to the economy or not) and the building of trust of the type that helps foster the social stability and legitimacy on which sound economies rest. In making this point, we need, of course, to be careful neither to fall victim to the tendency to romanticize such practices nor to assume that even absent the rapid development of the formal legal system, the more "traditional" of these ways would necessarily be able to retain their vitality in an increasingly urbanized, industrialized, and internationalized China. Nonetheless, a fair ledger sheet on current law reform ought to try to take account of the ways in which the elaboration of the formal legal system is, both by design and unwittingly, eroding less formal institutions and customs. This may be most apparent with respect to the falling off of mediation that has accompanied the rise in litigation (to the point that in 1997, the number of disputes litigated was roughly equivalent to the number mediated—for perhaps the first time in the history of the Chinese mainland; *Zhongguo Sifa Xingzheng Nianjian*, 1998), but it is also having an impact on the letters and visit (*xinfang*) process of citizen complaint (which has long historical antecedents). Some might contend that this shift simply reflects a voluntary movement by people with problems toward a more effective mode of dispute resolution. There is, however, more to it, with the state diverting resources from informal toward formal processes and advancing the position of attorneys relative to that of "legal workers" (*falu gongzuozhe*) who, like the barefoot doctors of the 1960s, provided crude but readily available services in the countryside—raising the as yet unexplored question of whether there has been a constricting of the access of poorer peoples (especially in rural areas) to dispute resolution even as options become more abundant for the more affluent (Liebman, 1999).

Corrections to the way in which the link between law and development is typically considered also need to be made at the input as well as the output stage. Much has been made of the fact that China has of late been the world's largest recipient of foreign direct investment (other than the United States), and some attention has also been focused on estimates that approximately 60 percent of such investment comes from overseas Chinese (including PRC Chinese routing money through Hong Kong and other overseas Chinese communities in an effort to enjoy various tax exemptions reserved for foreign investment; Wei, 1997).

Relatively little consideration, however, has been given in the developmental community to the ways in which this datum regarding the provenance of incoming FDI may require a scaling-down of the assumption that a stronger legal regime will perforce enhance the PRC's capacity to attract foreign capital. For one thing, research on such investment suggests that overseas Chinese investors are appreciably less interested in formal legal protections than major corporate investors from the G-7 nations, in part because of the greater availability to them of informal networks and in part because of a considerable skepticism on their part about the effectiveness of the PRC's legal system (Wei, 1997; Huang, 1998). Indeed, my own research has unearthed anecdotal data suggesting that some overseas Chinese endeavored to conduct business in the PRC precisely because they believed that it had a weaker legal regime with respect to intellectual property, labor law, and many other matters than surrounding jurisdictions (such as Taiwan and Hong Kong) and that this has evoked resentment among some PRC nationals both for the condescension it is seen as representing and for its impact on the already difficult task of building respect for legality in China.[8]

In fairness, we ought not necessarily to take at full face value the assertions of other foreign investors, many of whom may not be overseas Chinese, about how dearly they desire the rule of law in China. Consider the data, gleaned by Daniel Rosen (1999) from extensive interviews, which suggest that some foreign managers, for all their rhetoric about the need for more law, are not above resorting to extralegal measures. Or think about the late-1990s multibillion-dollar collapse of the Guangdong International Trust and Investment Corporation (GITIC). When Chinese authorities refused to bail out investors on the grounds that GITIC was a distinct corporate entity for which the state was not financially responsible, a number of Western and Japanese investors conveniently urged China to overlook such niceties, arguing that had they thought China might invoke GITIC's limited liability, they would have invested less (or sought a higher return).[9] Also, to the extent that investment figures may include sizable PRC funds unlawfully laundered abroad to take advantage of incentives for foreign money, one would want to think twice before using it as evidence of the formal legal system's performing its stated functions ("An Alchemist's Downfall," 2000).

The issue of the strength of PRC legal processes raises yet another delicate question that presumably needs to be addressed as we weigh the impact of law reform on economic development. As indicated earlier, the sociologist Herbert Kritzer has argued that in many instances, it may be more accurate to think of American lawyers as brokers than as professionals—which suggests to me the possibility that at least in some instances, we may want to consider their contribution to economic development as rooted in relationships, influence peddling, common sense, business acumen, and the like as much as in anything peculiar to the law (although the quasi-monopolistic power their licensed identity as lawyers provides should not be ignored; Kritzer, 1990). Without wishing to demean the Chinese bar, my own research on elite PRC business lawyers suggests that the phenomenon Kritzer discusses may even be appreciably more the case in China, given the novelty of so much of the legal system, the lower levels of training (relative to the American system) of most people working in it, historically rooted notions of *guanxi* (connections), and the difficulty of enforcing ethical and other constraints on wayward attorneys (Alford, 1995a, 2003). If true, viewed benignly, this suggests that we might need to attribute some of the economic gains typically associated with growing legalization more to brokering (perhaps even of a very "traditional" *guanxi* peddling type, albeit in a new venue) rather than to the law or legal analysis. But in the spirit of Laozi, there is also a less benign reading, emerging from my interviewing of elite lawyers, to the effect that the proliferation of laws and lawyers may actually in some instances be degrading the quality of state administration by providing a plethora of opportunities for corruption (or, if one subscribes more to Richard Epstein than Laozi, by generating a good deal of unnecessary and economically unproductive work; Epstein, 1995). A comparable point with respect to institutional design more generally is nicely made by Melanie Manion (1996).

The point of raising such matters has been to begin to sketch what might go into a comprehensive metric for evaluating the relationship between Chinese legal and economic reform and not to denigrate the Chinese project of post–Cultural Revolution legal development, for that effort poses a number of excruciatingly difficult dilemmas. I shall now examine two of the most important of these dilemmas.

Dilemmas in Legal Reform

The first concerns the viability of top-down, as opposed to socially generated, legal reform. In some senses, this is obviously a false dichotomy. Any type of formal or positivist legal change, by definition, involves action by legislatures, the executive, the judiciary, or other state actors and even in highly democratic states may well reflect a disproportionate influence of elites beyond the state structure. Furthermore, change of the magnitude pursued in China over the past two decades (in terms of economic and social liberalization) could not have commenced without the leadership's endorsement; may well entail a fairly strong, ongoing steadying state hand during a period of enormous and wrenching transition; and as a practical matter is unlikely to proceed much further if the powers that be feel threatened by it. And those of us whose experience lies chiefly in the United States need to be mindful that in most civil law states (and indeed some other common law jurisdictions), citizens enjoy somewhat less capacity to initiate formal legal change than is, at least in theory, the case here.[10]

These caveats notwithstanding, however, if our assessment is to be responsible, we need to inquire as to the extent to which one can reasonably expect that heavily top-down development will generate a legal framework sufficiently reflective of and responsive to the needs of merchants and the citizenry more generally. For some years now, multilateral financial institutions, multinational corporations, and developmental economists have tended to urge states with appreciably more liberal economies than China's to temper their inclinations to rely on a centralized direction of development so that they might better accommodate the interests and initiative of merchants and others in civil society (see, for instance, Shleifer & Vishny, 1999). And yet when it comes to China, whose leaders, however savvy, have had no direct experience working in a market economy and whose civil society continues to have very considerable difficulty either in influencing the direction of public policy or in asserting its own independence from the state, the international development community seems to have a pervasive faith in the willingness and capacity of Chinese political and bureaucratic authorities to act in a more disinterested manner to advance the values of the market than economic analysis typically assumes is the case for their counterparts in more liberal societies.

Experience from the first two decades of Chinese law reform suggests some of the costs of this mode of legal development. First, the single most important actor in the nation in terms of its capacity to shape the economy, the Communist Party, has seen fit to exempt itself, formally and informally, from the constraints of the legal system, as exemplified by the fact that it is not covered by the Administrative Litigation Law (which, though not insignificant, has received a good deal more credit than it deserves as a means of citizen empowerment)[11] and the further fact that individuals (particularly of consequence) forming and carrying out economic policy are far more likely to be subject to Party than legal discipline and, when subject to law, are far more likely to receive substantially lighter punishment than ordinary citizens for comparable offenses (Luo, 1996; Manion, 1998). At a minimum, this cannot help but send a message to the general public that contradicts the bountiful official rhetoric about relying on law to govern the nation and so complicate the task of building support for and faith in China's emerging legal system, not to mention trust more generally in the new institutions of a market economy at this formative stage in their development. Even more problematic, in undercutting the transparency, predictability, and accountability that are believed to be among the principal benefits to be derived from legal development, this would seem to exacerbate the temptation of cadres (local as well as national) and businesspeople (foreign as well as domestic) to resort to extralegal or even illegal means to advance their economic and other interests.

Given that the Party has exempted itself from the formal legal system, it is somewhat ironic that it continues to dominate the apparatus of that system. Knowledgeable observers suggest that virtually all significant legal personnel are

Party members or have been closely vetted by the Party prior to assuming office. This is particularly the case with regard to the judiciary. At the very highest levels, the previous president of the Supreme People's Court served simultaneously for many years as head of the Party's committee on legal and disciplinary affairs. At more mundane strata, loyalty to the Party remains a crucial criterion, if not the most important, in the selection of new judges,[12] while sitting judges are extolled as models for their devotion to the Party (He, 1995).

The indelible link between the Party and the judiciary would seem to raise serious questions about the latter's independence in matters having implications for the former, including those concerning economic affairs, even as we remember that under the constitution, it is the individual court (e.g., the Haidian district court) rather than the individual judge that is said to be independent (*Constitution of the PRC,* 1982, art. 126). (Nor, incidentally, should we forget that the institutional, rather than individual, nature of judicial independence is itself another consequence of Party design.) Scholars such as Donald Clarke (1997) of the University of Washington and Anthony Dicks (1996) of the School of Oriental and African Studies of the University of London suggest quite interestingly that the judiciary's lack of independence may be a prime reason that the courts have experienced such difficulty in securing enforcement of their judgments in civil and commercial matters, particularly vis-à-vis other government actors who, it is said, do not tend to see the courts as imbued with any special qualities or aura but rather as one among many bureaucratic actors and not an especially noteworthy one at that.[13] And anecdotal data I have gleaned suggest a considerable degree of unease among lawyers, both Chinese and foreign, about the prospect of litigation involving state-owned enterprises or other actors with powerful links to the Party (Alford, 2003).

On the other hand, as the situation of the judiciary illustrates, there are no easy answers. A judiciary composed to a significant degree of people not affiliated with the Party might be more irrelevant in the contemporary Chinese context than is now the case. Apart from issues of links to the Party, the endowing of individual judges with independence in a manner akin to that of their common law counterparts assumes a higher level of training and experience than is generally the norm among lower-level PRC judges and also a willingness of the center to see power further and less predictably dispersed. Given problems of local courts favoring local actors, such a move is not without potentially troubling consequences of its own. Indeed, in yet another irony, some serious observers suggest that the Chinese judiciary will not improve substantially until the central government takes a far more active role vis-à-vis the judiciary (which, though national in name, follows subnational geographical units in its organization and source of financing; O'Neill, 1999).

The aforementioned top-down quality is also mirrored in the substance of Chinese law itself. This is perhaps most significantly borne out by the constitution of the PRC, which is limited to a statement of the state's structure and as-pirations (among which are the rights it wishes to bestow on the populace) and does not itself provide any basis or means by which citizens might, through law, vindicate such rights or otherwise protect economic or other interests vis-à-vis the state (Liu, 1997). Stated differently, citizens are unable directly to invoke the constitution to protect the interests in property that that document acknowl-edges or otherwise shield themselves against unwarranted state or Party action but must instead premise any relief they might seek on further, specific legisla-tion, assuming it is available. Beyond the constitution, many of the central legal pillars of China's move toward the market—such as its new unified contract law, its intellectual property laws, and its laws concerning the Internet—strike that balance in a manner tilted appreciably more toward state interest relative to the autonomy of nonstate economic actors than is the norm in most major market economies. (On intellectual property law, see Alford, 1995b.) Again, however, there are no easy answers here. Even among the G-7 nations, the way in which this balance is struck differs considerably. And in case of the PRC, the afore-mentioned tilt could be said to reflect such goals as establishing a reasonable pace for economic transition, fostering a market intended ultimately to be national in scope, and protecting consumers and other citizens who might have difficulty in doing so themselves.

As challenging as the foregoing may be, China's post–Cultural Revolution project of legal development raises a second and in some respects even more daunting set of challenges that go beyond issues of the power of the Party or cen-ter to the very character of law itself anywhere. How is China to balance stabil-ity with flexibility, uniformity with difference, and a recognition of the need for law to transcend instrumentalism with a very real need to deploy it instrumen-tally? And what is the relation of whatever type of law may be needed to un-derlying values and institutions?

There is, to be sure, no single definition of the rule of law (which is, in fact, part of its attraction as a rallying cry for some politicians worldwide), but there seems a fairly broad consensus that at its heart is the belief that the law must tran-scend any particular politics, policies, and persons and apply in a predictable and evenhanded way to all.[14] That ideal, however, is somewhat in tension with the dictates of any society, especially, it might be argued, during times of consider-able transition. It seems naive, as some scholars have done, to call on China to refrain from using law "instrumentally" when the nation's needs are great and perhaps the chief rationale and source of ongoing support for law lies in its per-ceived capacity to help transform the nation economically and otherwise, but where ought the line to be drawn and how? Predictability is to be prized, but does that require that China eschew its practice of experimenting with a vari-ety of solutions to particular problems through what are termed provisional or temporary (*zanxing*) legal measures that draw on different foreign models or

have application during particular phases of economic development? Is this phenomenon a major impediment to developing the rule of law, as most foreign
scholars suggest, or an ingeniously Chinese innovation, as Ji Weidong (1992) has
argued, that in the longer run may facilitate a more stable legal order by enabling
China to customize its legal regime, rather than take foreign-generated models
lock, stock, and barrel?[15] And an analogous point might be made regarding uniformity. The PRC is, by its own statement, a unitary national state rather than
a federal entity, and yet, even leaving aside the situation of Hong Kong and the
other special administrative regions, there has been an explosion of lawmaking
subnationally. Ought we to understand this as a clever and necessary functional
equivalent to federalism (which cannot be addressed directly for political reasons)
or an indication of a chaotic legal regime, lacking the clear hierarchy of legal
norms so essential to a fair and ordered society?

Lurking behind all of these questions is a no less difficult conundrum posed
by China's use of foreign models as a relative latecomer to market-oriented legal development. To what degree will China's reliance on such models either require or result in its embracing the values and institutions with which they are
associated in their originating societies? To pose this question is not to exaggerate China's choices in a falsely dichotomous fashion by assuming that it will either wish or be able fully to emulate or to reject such values and institutions. Nor
is it to ignore the long history of adoption and adaptation of foreign legal forms
both in the West and throughout Sino-centric East Asia (Watson, 1974; Bodde
and Morris, 1967). Rather, the point is that if one believes that law and society
are linked (or, as North would put it, that the operation of formal constraints is
shaped by that of informal constraints and vice versa), both those endeavoring
to shape Chinese legal development and those who would write about it need
to confront the implications of a program marked by considerable use of foreign models as they weigh its performance and ponder its future direction. Can
we reasonably expect that legal measures taken with little change from G-7 states
will perform in China as they have in the very different institutional and cultural
milieu from which they came (Pistor and Wellons, 1999)? If, on the other hand,
such forms are substantially modified to suit Chinese circumstances, in a manner
analogous to Qian Yingyi's argument with respect to international "best practices" in economics, is there a danger that crucial features will be lost (Qian,
2000)? And given China's practice of drawing elements from many different settings (as, for example, in its reliance on a Soviet-style civil law model for its judiciary but an increasingly American model for its bar), how well will the different pieces mesh? My own research, for instance, suggests that the divergent
conceptions of the relative roles of judge and lawyer emanating from these different models are a significant cause of the very high level of tension one finds
between the PRC bench and bar (Alford, 2003; Xia, 1995).

Discussion of foreign models for Chinese law reform surfaces the question of the position of foreign donors and advisers, even if we are mindful of avoiding the common pitfall of exaggerating our impact on Chinese processes. Particularly of late, foreign sources have provided considerable financial support for legal development in the PRC (although it totals far less than 1 percent of all developmental assistance provided China). Among the most noteworthy of such efforts have been those of the European Union (with some U.S.$20 million to be dispensed), the World Bank (which has devoted well over U.S.$8 million to such programs), the United Nations Development Programme (which has spent millions on legislative drafting; Seidman, Seidman, and Payne, 1997), the Asian Development Bank (which has been providing legal assistance in a variety of forms), assorted national governments (led by the Scandinavians, Germans, and Canadians), various major foundations (Ford having spent close to U.S.$10 million since 1982), and other actors. Nor is money all. Many of the aforementioned organizations have imparted ideas as well, both through the provision of technical legal assistance and through the examples they set via their own work in and with China. And they have been joined in that regard by universities, think tanks, businesses, law firms, and a host of others.[16]

Assessing this foreign contribution is virtually as complex as evaluating Chinese law reform itself (in part because it is so closely intertwined with the question of how the PRC has sought to generate and use foreign support). We need at the outset to recognize that the vast bulk of such assistance emanating from international organizations, multilateral developmental entities, and even foreign governments and foundations has tended to flow through and be directed toward actors that are either a part of the state or closely affiliated therewith. There are many reasons why this is quite understandable. To some degree, law, by definition, involves the building of public institutions. Developmental agencies are bound by agreements, formal or otherwise, to work through particular official Chinese intermediaries (as, after all, their assistance often comes in the form of loans to the PRC government), while their charters typically preclude intervention in political affairs. And in any event, there is surely a far greater need among official or officially blessed PRC actors than there are foreign assistance funds available. Nonetheless, as scholars, we ought not to take this approach as given but should instead be probing its implications.

We need to be mindful that the foregoing approach may as a practical matter reinforce bureaucratic actors and formal constraints, relative to the private economy and civil society more generally, when the stated purpose of the endeavor, at least judging from the rhetoric of both the PRC government and the multilateral development agencies, is to facilitate movement toward a more liberal economy. Accustomed as state and Party authorities have been to permeating economy and society, it seems somewhat hopeful to structure developmental initiatives on the assumption that such authorities will refrain from seeking to use the ensuing infusions of cash and technical assistance to buttress their position rather than to cultivate forces in society that may eventually compete for resources and power. Some state agencies have seized on legal reform as a means to justify their continuation at a time of transition and have accordingly been busy churning out a plethora of legal enactments that may not have been in the broad interest of the economy or society (Manion 1996). Indeed, at its worst, there are indications that some regulatory authorities and courts have developed regulations or encouraged litigation as a means of generating their own institutional (or even personal) revenues, legitimately or otherwise—as the central government has recognized in various anticorruption campaigns that have led to tens of thousands of Party disciplinary matters and thousands of criminal actions concerning corruption in 1998 alone (Luo, 1996; Xiao, 1999a; Xinhua News Agency, 1999b).

Alternatives to the overwhelmingly statist orientation of developmental assistance for law in China are obviously not without potential problems of their own (concerning, among other things, possible or perceived encroachments on state sovereignty and the legitimacy of unofficial organizations). Nonetheless, one cannot help but wonder whether espoused goals of legal development such as economic development or the cultivation of greater trust—and perhaps even legal development itself—might not be further advanced were law thought of more in its social context and resources and attention allocated accordingly. Dasgupta and Wheeler (1996) have shown, for example, that holding other variables constant, a 1 percent increase in literacy in China is likely to yield a 2 percent increase in the use of the letters and visits (*xinfang*) process to register complaints concerning the environment, and Shi Tianjian (1997) has documented the continuing interest even of Beijing residents in this traditionally rooted mode of seeking redress for injustice. Amartya Sen (1994) has made a powerful case, based principally on the Indian state of Kerala, for the proposition that increased literacy and workplace opportunity for women are more effective in lowering birthrates than laws or policies of a coercive nature. One could well imagine that increased support for education (be it primary, secondary, or tertiary and general or focused on civics), nongovernmental organizations, and unofficial media, to give but a few illustrations, might yield very substantial benefits with regard to law and the ends that law is supposed to achieve.

This general point about indirection has more specific analogues with respect to both substantive legal questions and issues of legal institutions. On the substantive side, the predominant attention of foreign donors, especially among the developmental agencies, has been on what is loosely called economic law. It could well be, however, that the goal of promoting greater confidence in the legal and economic institutions of a marketizing economy might be advanced less by another complex provision on securities or copyright and more by anticorruption measures that were understood to cover everyone, rather than stopping at mid-level officials or persons in higher position (such as former Beijing Mayor

Chen Xitong) who, anecdotal evidence suggests, may be viewed as having been selected for punishment (deservingly, to be sure) chiefly for having lost the latest power struggle (Berlozi, 1998).[17]

On the institutional front, the argument might be made that foreign donors have been too inclined to focus resources and attention on such avowedly legal apparatus as the courts and offices doing the technical drafting of laws. This is not to deny their obvious importance but rather to urge that we remember, for example, that courts occupy a somewhat different role in China than the United States. Their decisions in civil matters lack precedential value (and so do not bind subsequent courts). Their decisions in administrative matters have, until the recent passage of the Administrative Reconsideration Law (on which "the jury is still out"), had the potential to declare unlawful only specific administrative actions (rather than a pattern of behavior or the underlying regulation itself). And their decisions in criminal matters rarely result in determinations of innocence (with conviction rates typically running between 98 and 99.5 percent). It might well be that concentrating on providing citizens with more meaningful opportunities for substantive input into the lawmaking process (for which improvements in technical legal drafting are not a substitute) and with greater access to principled and transparent administrative decision making might be of appreciably greater consequence in the promotion of the rule of law in China.[18]

Implicit in the approach advanced by the vast majority of foreign donors is the notion that law can be detached from politics and perhaps even from society. While this posture is understandable given the difficulties that might ensue from acknowledging any such linkage and China's unfortunate recent history in which politics played all too prominent a role in legal and other affairs, it carries considerable risks. Perhaps the most significant is that it may serve to shroud the difficult choices inherent in any serious program of law reform. Although they are often presented in neutral or technical terms, matters such as the independence of the judiciary or the content of laws concerning property involve the allocation of power within the government and between state and society (as we should know from our own experience), as well, of course, as the Party. Undue obliqueness about what is involved in such decisions, however well intended, may serve to reinforce instrumentalist conceptions of law among Chinese leaders and thereby divert their attention from concerns that will need to be addressed for even the more technical measures to flourish. By definition, this would seem to work against greater engagement of the Chinese citizenry on issues of consequence at a time when popular support seems crucial to the success of the law reform effort.[19] And it has the potential to place donors in the awkward position of advocating particular legal reforms without fully disclosing to aid recipients what they believe may be important implications of the assistance being provided, including its potentially transformative impact on the polity.

Foreign involvement in Chinese legal development is not, of course, limited to multilateral institutions and foundations and we therefore ought also to be mindful of the impact of other actors, including governments, business, legal practitioners, and academe. Many among these latter actors have, for example, in recent years had a great deal to say about the promotion of the rule of law in China. Without being unduly cynical, assessment in this area would need to move beyond the rhetorical to an examination of behavior. It may be, for instance, that the American government's much touted (but as yet largely unfunded) rule-of-law initiative is better understood as having as much to do with domestic American politics as with Chinese reform (in the sense of finding common ground for the business and human rights communities that have been divided over China policy; Alford, 2000). As Daniel Rosen's (1999) fine study of foreign enterprises in China suggests, notwithstanding what may be quite sincere expressions of concern about the need for greater legality, many expatriate managers indicate that they are not adverse to employing extralegal measures. And one might ask whether foreign business's enormous enthusiasm for arbitration in China, though quite understandable in view of the quality of Chinese courts, represents an embrace of what is, in effect, a system of private justice for wealthy enterprises and a concomitant lack of commitment to public institutions that presumably have an essential role to play if the rule of law is to be achieved in and for Chinese society.

Directions for Further Research

As we turn our attention to possible research that might be of interest to parties who may be involved in the future of Chinese law reform, the good news is that there is a vast array of topics worthy of the attention of serious scholars. That, unfortunately, also happens to be the bad news. Stated differently, notwithstanding noteworthy work by the teams led by the late Gong Xiangrui (1993) and Xia Yong (1995) in China and such individual scholars as Fang Liufang (1999), He Weifang (1998), Liang Zhiping (1997), Donald Clarke (1997), and Pitman Potter (1994), there is far too little writing that examines the types of questions posed throughout this chapter. And there are very substantial reasons for this, including the sheer complexity of separating different explanatory elements sufficiently to construct verifiable hypotheses, the uncertain reliability of at least some major categories of officially promulgated data,[20] the practical difficulties of gathering alternative data (Xinhua News Agency, 1999c), the sensitivity of parts of the exercise,[21] and the need to be cross-disciplinary not only in a formal methodological sense but also in one's appreciation of the biases of one's own discipline and the multiple readings that might be given to the course of legal development in the societies against which China is inevitably, if implicitly, being measured.

The prime area in which research needs to be focused is the interplay between formal and informal norms. As I suggested earlier, Chinese authorities, foreign donors, and most scholars seem to be proceeding on the assumption that the growth of formal legal institutions, formal rules, and formal legal personnel is synonymous with the promotion of greater respect for legality, which will in turn foster further economic development (and perhaps other desirable goals such as a more just society). We need to move beyond such assumptions to consider the impact that this burgeoning of the formal is having on both existing and emerging norms of a less formal sort. For example, it is virtually universally assumed, at least among persons working on Chinese legal development, that the rapid expansion of the Chinese bar has been a boon for legality. But is this necessarily so? As suggested earlier, my research on elite, internationally oriented business practitioners in Beijing (who typically have a higher level of legal education and more exposure to international norms than the vast majority of Chinese lawyers) is not necessarily encouraging. It suggests that at least some such lawyers may be exacerbating problems of corruption among the judiciary and officialdom (Alford, 2003), while there is evidence that in its drive to build a legal profession, the Chinese state may be displacing China's paraprofessional "barefoot lawyers" and weakening more traditional, less formal methods of dispute resolution such as mediation (Liebman, 1999). Moreover, my research further suggests that in exploring such issues, we need to examine what it is that lawyers are actually doing (as distinct from assuming that actors bearing the same name in different settings are carrying out the same set of activities in the same manner) and who, in addition to lawyers, benefits from such endeavor. We ought not, for example, simply take the increase in cases filed as incontrovertible proof of a popular commitment to the legal system and evidence of justice being done, as there are suggestions that some judges have been soliciting cases so that their courts, which do not receive adequate government funding, might secure additional court filing fees (Fang, 1999). The point here is to surface questions that will undoubtedly be difficult to answer and to suggest that at a minimum we examine them with care prior to concluding that increasing the number of lawyers is a warranted expenditure or that the present prevalent conception of what lawyers are, how they should be trained, and how they should be regulated is sound and will promote further reform, be it in the law or for society more broadly.

Optimally, if circumstances permit, such research ought to go still further, utilizing the rich example that China provides to delve seriously into the more general question of why law matters to economic growth in a manner akin to that Jean Oi and Andrew Walder (1999) have successfully deployed in a recent work that weighs broad theory concerning the centrality of property rights in light of the Chinese experience. For all the difficulties in conducting research discussed earlier in this chapter, China does present a highly attractive opportunity to test the received wisdom concerning the interplay of legal and economic development, given that although it has a long history of informal (and some formal) institutions that appear to have been facilitative of a market-oriented economy, the sharp break engendered by the early years of the PRC, culminating in the Cultural Revolution, enables us to trace from a fairly precise starting point both its contemporary move toward marketization and its program of legal development. Moreover, the fact that we have a fairly comprehensive chronicle of the particular foreign provenance of much of China's program of law reform and broad agreement as to its largely top-down character suggests the possibility of undertaking research designed to test out assumptions regarding the relationship of law to underlying values and institutions and the significance of popular involvement that explicitly or otherwise inform theoretical writing about legal development. And if we were sufficiently adventuresome, we might even think about bringing the Chinese case together with work in social psychology that suggests that the elaboration of formal, external constraints may result in a weakening of individual moral resolve (Deci and Ryan, 1985; Eisenberger and Cameron, 1996; Jolls, Sunstein, and Thaler, 1998). Perhaps from such inquiries we might in time reach a fuller understanding of what it was Laozi was endeavoring to convey in his cautionary adage concerning the law.

Notes

1. For general overviews of the first fifty years of PRC legal development, see Chen (1999), Lubman (1999), Potter (1999), and Alford (1999). Wang Liming's four-volume collection of essays (1998) touches on most major civil and commercial law developments of the post–Cultural Revolution period.

2. The challenge of developing a clear hierarchy of legal norms is thoughtfully treated in Keller (1994).

3. For an overview of legal protections for foreign investors, written for prospective investors, see Cohen and Lange (1997).

4. I discuss the role of one such committee (concerned with Environment and Natural Resources) in Alford and Liebman (2001).

5. To be sure, Shleifer and company note in a single line that "after World War II, the American occupying army 'Americanized' some Japanese laws, particularly in the company law area, although their basic German-civil-law structure remained"(La Porta et al., 1998, p. 1119).

6. Robert Barro (1997, p. 27) suggests that "although these data are subjective . . . the willingness of customers to pay substantial fees for this information is perhaps some testament to their validity." Presumably, at a minimum, one would want to know how such vendors performed; how they were valued in the market over a sustained period of time, including downturns; and who their customers were.

7. Arguably, the United Nations Development Programme's impressive *China Human*

Development Report (1999), produced under the leadership of Wu Jinglian, represents an important step toward generating a metric that would capture both the benefits and costs of development.

8. This is based on interviews with PRC lawyers and businesspersons conducted in Hangzhou and in Cambridge, Massachusetts, in 1996.

9. This argument has a disingenuous quality to it, as some sophisticated foreign lenders had acted on the basis of nonbinding "comfort letters" rather than formal bank guarantees. Similarly, we ought not to read concerns currently expressed in OECD states about corruption too far back into history as, after all, bribes paid to foreign officials to secure business abroad were tax-deductible in Germany until quite recently.

10. We ought, for instance, to remain mindful of the argument of Marc Galanter (1974), among others, as to how judge-made law may come to favor repeat players—which typically are corporations or wealthy individuals.

11. Actions can only be brought under the Administrative Litigation Law (ALL) against governmental entities. Attempts to ground actions against the Party on this law have been rejected by the courts as lacking a legal basis (Alford, 1993). The number of cases brought under the ALL since its promulgation in 1990 through the end of 1998 was less than three hundred thousand, with well over half of them having come during the last two of these years. Early research suggests that citizens prevail in approximately 20 percent of the cases that proceed to judgment. While this clearly represents an advance from earlier days in which citizens lacked such a legal remedy, before according the ALL the rather lavish praise it has received, one would want to know a great deal more about the level of officials against whom cases are brought, the merits of particular cases, the success citizens have had in enforcing those judgments received, and actions brought pursuant to this law by state agencies against citizens. There are indications that the law has overwhelmingly been directed against local officials (which would seem consistent with the fact that the ALL is designed to address individual actions, rather than broad patterns of official behavior or major state policy). To be sure, the newly enacted Administrative Reconsideration Law, at least in theory, does empower citizens to challenge certain general rules, rather than particular instances of their administrative application. For a particularly thoughtful examination of administrative law issues in China in general, see Lubman (1998).

12. Claims about the Party's role in the judiciary are, by their nature, difficult to prove. I base these statements on discussions conducted between 1993 and 1999 with several noted Chinese legal experts, many with substantial experience working in government or with the judiciary.

13. Indeed, problems with enforcing judgments reached such proportions—with close to a million unenforced through the middle of 1999—that Chinese authorities recently launched a massive nationwide campaign directed at this, with particular attention to governmental agencies that have ignored judgments (Ni, 1999).

14. For an enormously thoughtful article on competing definitions of the idea of the rule of law, see Ohnesorge (2003).

15. In a sense, this position is similar to Qian Yingyi's call with respect to economics for the development of "adaptive institutions" that would enable China to adapt, rather than simply adopt, international "best practices" (although neither Ji nor other advocates of it reference Qian; Qian, 1999). I discuss this position with respect to law later in this chapter and in Alford (2000).

16. U.S. foreign legal assistance is thoroughly and thoughtfully treated in de Lisle (1999).

17. Some foreign observers, such as law and economics scholar Richard Posner

(1998), have suggested that developing nations such as China would be better advised, at least in the immediate future, to concentrate their efforts in law on developing a few clear substantive rules regarding property and contract and a relatively simple, judicial, arbitral, or other enforcement apparatus. The establishment of "an extensive system of civil liberties" and a more elaborate judiciary, suggests Posner, absorb human and other resources that a developing society can ill afford to lose from more productive economic activity. As I suggest elsewhere (Alford, 2000), even if one were to accord economic development the centrality that Posner does, this is a flawed argument. It is questionable whether a few clear rules regarding property and contracts are sufficient to undergird the type of transformation that nations such as China are undertaking and to satisfy the international business community (which is likely, in their absence, to require a higher risk premium). Moreover, Posner and others of similar mind seem to neglect the ways in which independent media and autonomous nongovernmental organizations may facilitate economic growth (by, among other things, ensuring that unfavorable economic news is generally available and exposing corruption and mismanagement).

18. Hearings, it should be noted, have been held in some instances at both the national level (as with regard to the Water Pollution Prevention and Control Act) and the provincial level (in Guangdong).

19. This proposition is borne out, at least in a preliminary fashion, by research that I have been conducting with colleagues, American and Chinese, from a variety of disciplines on the popular understanding of and behavior toward the environment (Alford et al., 2002). Notwithstanding considerable state effort, the populace we studied seems only in a limited way to have understood and embraced official messages (conveyed through campaigns, law, education, and politics) about the environment.

20. Official statistics, at least regarding law, warrant intense scrutiny. For example, the pertinent official yearbooks not only indicate court appearances by lawyers but also specify such additional data as the number of contracts negotiated by lawyers, the amounts at stake in such negotiations, and the number of times lawyers provided legal advice to clients—even as the Chinese government indicates that it does not know how many of its citizens are undergoing "reeducation through labor." Nor do such official sources regarding lawyers indicate how they have dealt with the challenges to the accurate gathering of such data posed by lawyers' (and clients') incentive to underreport in order to avoid legal (and extralegal) exactions (Alford, 2003).

21. The Chinese government has of late indicated that it wishes to exercise a high degree of oversight regarding survey research, especially when foreigners are involved. There are indications that some surveys need to be vetted by state authorities prior to being administered (Xinhua News Agency, 1999c). In this context, it is questionable whether one could (or would be well advised to) poll merchants or citizens more generally as to their views on the Communist Party's willingness to observe the law or similar topics.

References

"An Alchemist's Downfall." 2000. *Economist*, June 3, p. 42.

Alford, William, P. 1993. "Double-Edged Swords Cut Both Ways: Law and Legitimacy in the People's Republic of China." *Daedalus*, 122(2), 45–70.

————. 1995a. "Tasselled Loafers for Barefoot Lawyers: Transformation and Tension in the World of Chinese Legal Workers." *China Quarterly*, 141, 22–39.

————. 1995b. *To Steal a Book Is an Elegant Offense: Intellectual Property Law in Chinese Civilization*. Stanford, Calif.: Stanford University Press.

————. 1999. "A Second Great Wall? China's Post-Cultural Revolution Project of Legal Construction." *Cultural Dynamics*, 11, 193–213.

————. 2000. "Exporting 'The Pursuit of Happiness.'" *Harvard Law Review*, 113, 1677–1713.

————. 2003. "Of Lawyers Lost and Found: Searching for Legal Professionalism in the People's Republic of China." In Arthur Rosett, Lucie Cheng, and Margaret Woo, eds., *East Asian Law: Universal Norms and Local Cultures*. London: RoutledgeCurzon.

Alford, William P., and Benjamin L. Liebman. 2001. "Dirty Air, Clear Processes: The Struggle over Air Pollution Law in the People's Republic of China." *Hastings Law Journal*, 52, 703–48.

Alford, William P., Robert P. Weller, Leslyn Hall, Karen R. Polenske, Yuanyuan Shen, and David Zweig. 2002. "The Human Dimensions of Pollution Policy Implementation: Air Quality in Rural China." *Journal of Contemporary China*, 11, 495–513.

Barro, Robert J. 1997. *Determinants of Economic Growth: A Cross-Country Empirical Study*. Cambridge, Mass.: MIT Press.

Becker, Jasper. 1999a. "Capital Flight May Threaten to Undermine Mainland." *South China Morning Post,* August 11, 1999, p. 8.

————. 1999b. "Money Burns as the Party Fiddles." *South China Morning Post*, August 21, 1999, p. 15.

Berlozi, Antoaneta. 1998. "'Catching Big Fish' Impresses Few." *Inter Press Service*, August 9, 1998.

Bodde, Derk, and Clarence Morris. 1967. *Law in Imperial China*. Cambridge, Mass.: Harvard University Press.

Cai, Dingjian. 1992. *Zhongguo Renda Zhidu* [The Chinese National People's Congress System]. Beijing: *Shehui Kexue Wenxian Chubanshe* [Social Science Publishing House].

Chen, Albert. 1999. *An Introduction to the Legal System of the People's Republic of China*, 2nd ed. Hong Kong: Butterworth.

Clarke, Donald. 1997. "State Council Notice Nullifies Statutory Right of Creditors." *Ease Asian Executive Reports*, 19(4), 9–15.

Cohen, Jerome A., and John E. Lange. 1997. "The Chinese Legal System: A Primer for Investors." *New York Law School Journal of International and Comparative Law,* 17, 345.

Constitution of the PRC. 1982. Beijing: Xinhua News Agency.

Corne, Peter H. 1997. *Foreign Investment in China: The Administrative Legal System*. Hong Kong: Hong Kong University Press.

Dasgupta, Susmita, and David Wheeler. 1996. *Citizen Complaints as Environmental Indicators: Evidence from China*. Washington, D.C.: World Bank.

Deci, Edward, and Richard Ryan. 1985. *Intrinsic Motivation and Self-Determination in Human Behavior*. New York: Plenum Press.

de Lisle, Jacques. 1999. "Lex Americana? United States Legal Assistance, American Legal Models, and Legal Change in the Post-Communist World and Beyond." *University of Pennsylvania Journal of International Economic Law,* 20, 179–308.

Dicks, Anthony. 1996. "Compartmentalized Law and Judicial Restraint: An Inductive View of Some Jurisdictional Barriers to Reform." In Stanley B. Lubman, ed., *China's Legal Reforms*. Oxford: Oxford University Press.

Eisenberger, Robert, and Judy Cameron. 1996. "Detrimental Effects of Reward: Reality or Myth." *American Psychologist*, 51, 1153–66.

Ellickson, Robert C. 1991. *Order Without Law: How Neighbors Settle Disputes.* Cambridge, Mass.: Harvard University Press.

Epstein, Richard. 1995. *Simple Rules for a Complex World.* Cambridge, Mass.: Harvard University Press.

Fang, Liufang. 1999. *"Minshi Susong Shoufei Gao"* [A Study of Fees in Civil Proceedings]. *Zhongguo Shehui Kexue* [Social Science in China], 117, 130–53.

Finder, Susan. 1993. "The Supreme People's Court of the People's Republic of China." *Journal of Chinese Law,* 7, 145–224.

Galanter, Marc. 1974. "Why the 'Haves' Come Out Ahead." *Law and Society Review,* 9, 95.

Gong, Xiangrui, ed. 1993. *Fazhi de Lixiangyu Xianshhi* [The Ideal and Reality of the Rule of Law]. Beijing. *Zhongguo Zhengfa Daxue Chubanshe* [China University of Politics and Law Publishing House].

Greif, Avner. 1996. "Contracting, Enforcement, and Efficiency: Economics Beyond the Law." In Michael Bruno and Boris Pleskovic, eds., *Annual World Bank Conference on Development Economics, 1996.* Washington, D.C.: World Bank.

Han Zhubin. 1999. "Zuigao Renmin Jianchayuan Gongzuo Baogao" [The Work Report of the Supreme People's Procuracy]. *Renmin Daibiao Dahui Gongbao* [Gazette of the National People's Congress] 2, 193–205.

He Weifang. 1995. "Tongguo Sifa Shehui Zhengyi: Dui Zhongguo Faguan Xianzhuang de Yige Toushi" [The Realization of Social Justice Through Judicature: A Look at the Current Situation of Chinese Judges]. In Xia Yong, ed., Zou Xiang Quanli de Shidai: Zhongguo Gongmin Quanli Fazhan Yanjiu [Toward a Time of Rights: A Perspective of the Development of Civil Rights in China]. Beijing: Zhongguo Zhengfa Daxue Chubanshe [China University of Politics and Law Publishing House].

———. 1998. *Sifa de Linian yu Zhidu* [The Concept and System of the Judiciary]. Beijing: *Zhongguo Zhengfa Daxue Chubanshe* [China University of Politics and Law Publishing House].

Huang, Yasheng. 1998. *FDI in China: An Asian Perspective.* Hong Kong: Chinese University Press.

Ji, Weidong. 1992. "On Reflective Mechanism of Law Trial Implementation in China." In Hans Leser and Tamotsu Isomura, eds., *Wege zum Japanischen Recht: Festschrift für Zentaro Kitagawa* [The Way of Japanese Law: A Festschrfit for Zentaro Kitagawa]. Berlin: Duncker & Humbolt.

Jolls, Christine, Cass R. Sunstein, and Richard Thaler. 1998. "A Behavioral Approach to Law and Economics." *Stanford Law Review,* 50, 1471.

Keller, P. 1994. "Sources of Order in Chinese Law." *American Journal of Comparative Law,* 42, 711–59.

Kritzer, Herbert M. 1990. *The Justice Broker.* New York: Oxford University Press.

La Porta, Rafael, Florencio Lopez de Silanes, Andrei Shleifer, and Robert W. Vishny. 1998. "Law and Finance." *Journal of Political Economy,* 106, 1113–55.

Liang Zhiping. 1997. *Liang Zhiping Zixuanji* [Selected Writings of Liang Zhiping]. Guilin: *Guangxi Shifan Daxue Chubanshe* [Guangxi National University Publishing House].

Liebman, Benjamin L. 1999. "Legal Aid and Public Interest Law in China." *Texas International Law Journal,* 34, 211–86.

Liu Nanping. 1997. *Opinions of the Supreme People's Court: Judicial Interpretation in China.* Hong Kong: Sweet & Maxwell.

Lubman, Stanley B. 1998. "Chinese Administrative Law and the Challenges of Chinese Law Reform." Unpublished manuscript.

————. 1999. *Bird in the Cage: Legal Reform in China After Mao.* Stanford, Calif.: Stanford University Press.

Luo, Bing. 1996. "*Mijian Xielu Zhongguo Zuzhi Fulan*" [Secret Document Exposes Decay in Communist Party Organization]. *Cheng Ming* [Controversy], 225, 6–8.

Luo Qizhi. 1998. "Autonomy, Qualifications, and Professionalism of the PRC Bar." *Columbia Journal of Asian Law*, 12, 1–38.

Macaulay, Stewart. 1963. "Non-Contractual Relations in Business: A Preliminary Study." *American Sociological Review*, 28, 55–67.

Magee, Stephen P., William A. Brock, and Leslie Young. 1989. "The Invisible Foot and the Waste of Nations: Lawyers as Negative Externalities." In *Black Hole Tariffs and Endogenous Policy Theory: Political Economy in General Equilibrium.* New York: Cambridge University Press.

Manion, Melanie. 1996. "Corruption by Design: Bribery in Chinese Enterprise Licensing." *Journal of Law, Economics, and Organization*, 12(1), 167–95.

————. 1998. "Issues in Corruption Control in China." *Issues and Studies*, 34(9), 1–21.

Ni, Siyi. 1999. "*Zhongguo Gedi Kaizhan Zhifa Xuanchuan Huodong*" [Law Enforcement Activity Publicized Throughout China]. *People's Daily*, overseas ed., August 17, 1999, p. 8.

North, Douglass C. 1990. *Institutions, Institutional Change and Economic Performance.* Cambridge: Cambridge University Press.

Ohnesorge, John K. M. 2003. "The Rule of Law, Economic Development, and the Developmental States of Northeast Asia." In Christoph Antons, ed., *Law and Development in East and Southeast Asia.* London: RoutledgeCurzon.

Oi, Jean C., and Andrew G. Walder, eds. 1999. *Property Rights and Economic Reform in China.* Stanford, Calif.: Stanford University Press.

O'Neill, Mark. 1999. "Beijing Pressed for Removal of Local-Authority Power over Courts." *South China Morning Post*, January 14, 1999, p. 4.

Pei Minxin. 1997. "Citizens v. Mandarins: Administrative Litigation in China." *China Quarterly*, 152, 832–62.

Pistor, Katharina, and Philip A. Wellons. 1999. *The Role of Law and Legal Institutions in Asian Economic Development, 1960–1995.* Oxford: Oxford University Press.

Posner, Richard A. 1998. "Creating a Legal Framework for Economic Development." *World Bank Research Observer*, 13, 1–11.

Potter, Pitman B. 1994. "Socialist Legality and Legal Culture in Shanghai: A Survey of the *Getihu*." *Canadian Journal of Law and Society*, 9, 41–72.

————. 1999. "The Chinese Legal System: Continuing Commitment to the Primacy of Power." *China Quarterly*, 159, 673–83.

Qian, Yingyi. 2000. "The Institutional Foundations of China's Market Transition." In Boris Pleskovic and Joseph Stiglitz, eds., *Proceedings of the World Bank's Annual Conference on Developmental Economics, 1999.* Washington, D.C.: World Bank.

Qiushi. 1998. "China: 20 Years of Legal System Developments." Original in Chinese published December 1, 1998, translated in *FBIS*, January 16, 1999.

Rheinstein, Max, ed. 1954. *Max Weber on Law in Economy and Society.* Cambridge, Mass.: Harvard University Press.

Rosen, Daniel H. 1999. *Behind the Open Door: Foreign Enterprises in the Chinese Marketplace.* Washington, D.C.: Institute for International Economics.

Seidman, Ann, Robert B. Seidman, and Janice Payne, eds., 1997. *Legislative Drafting for Market Reform: Some Lessons from China.* London: St. Martin's Press.

Sen, Amartya. 1994. "Population: Delusion and Reality." *New York Review of Books*, September 22, 1994, pp. 62–72.

Shi, Tianjian. 1997. *Political Participation in Beijing*. Cambridge, Mass.: Harvard University Press.

Shleifer, Andrei, and Robert W. Vishny. 1999. *The Grabbing Hand: Government Pathologies and Their Cures*. Cambridge, Mass.: Harvard University Press.

Tyler, Tom R. 1990. *Why People Obey the Law*. New Haven, Conn.: Yale University Press.

United Nations Development Programme, China. 1999. *The China Human Development Report*. New York: Oxford University Press.

Vogel, Ezra F. 1979. *Japan as Number One*. Cambridge, Mass.: Harvard University Press.

Wang, Liming. 1998. *Minshangfa Yanjiu* [Research on Civil and Commercial Law]. Beijing: *Falu Chubanshe* [Law Publishing House].

Watson, Alan. 1974. *Legal Transplants: An Approach to Comparative Law*. Charlottesville: University of Virginia.

Wei, Shang-jin. 1997. *How Taxing Is Corruption on International Investors?* NBER Working Paper No. 6030. Cambridge, Mass.: National Bureau of Economic Research.

Winn, Jane Kaufman. 1994. "Relational Practices and the Marginalization of Law: Informal Financial Practices of Small Businesses in Taiwan." *Law and Society Review*, 28, 193–232.

World Bank. 1993. *The East Asian Miracle*. New York: Oxford University Press.

———. 1997. *Clean Water, Blue Skies*. Washington, D.C.: World Bank.

Xia Lu. 1995. "*Shei Lai Baohu Zhongguo Lushi?*" [Who Will Protect China's Lawyers?]. *Zhongguo Lushi* [China Lawyer], December 5, 1995, pp. 3–5.

Xia Yong, ed. 1995. *Zou Xiang Quanli de Shidai: Zhongguo Gongmin Quanli Fazhan Yanjiu* [Toward a Time of Rights: A Perspective on the Development of Civil Rights in China]. Beijing: *Zhongguo Zhengfa Daxue Chubanshe* [China University of Politics and Law Publishing House].

Xiao Yang. 1999a. "*Jianjue Qingchu Sifa Renyuan Fubai, Nuli Weihu Sifa Gongzheng*" [Resolutely Eliminate Corruption Among Judicial Personnel, Energetically Protect Judicial Fairness]. Report issued in Beijing, January 29.

———. 1999b. "*Zuigao Renmin Fayuan Gongzuo Baogao*" [The Work Report of the Supreme People's Court]. Report issued in Beijing, January 29.

Xinhua News Agency. 1999a. "President Jiang Zemin Urges Stronger Rural Legal Infrastructure." Press release in English, June 11.

———. 1999b. "Legislators Say They Will Fight Judicial Corruption." Press release in English. August 26.

———. 1999c. "*Zhongguo Jiang Dui Shewai Shehui Diaocha Huodong Jinxing Shenpi*" [China's Movement Toward an Approval Process Regarding Foreign Social Science Surveys]. Press release, August 1.

———. 2000. "Legislation Law: Another Milestone in China's Legal Construction." Press release in English, March 13.

Zhongguo Sifa Xingzheng Nianjian [Yearbook of Judicial Administration]. 1998. Beijing: Yearbook Publishing Co.

Part III

TOWARD GREATER ECONOMIC INTEGRATION

6

Trade Policy, Structural Change, and China's Trade Growth

William Martin, Betina Dimaranan, Thomas W. Hertel, and Elena Ianchovichina

Since the beginning of the reform era in China, the growth in the volume and importance of trade for China and its trading partners has been extraordinary. Part of the growth has flowed from policy reforms that have directly helped to open the Chinese economy—and to stimulate economic growth that has in turn stimulated growth and change in trade patterns. Major changes in trade policy are likely to take place in the near future as China makes the adjustments required by the World Trade Organization (WTO) for accession and as the Chinese economy adjusts to the post-WTO trading environment. Understanding these changes will be important for the design of policies to take advantage of the opportunities created by these changes and to ensure that difficulties are anticipated and dealt with.

The primary purpose of this chapter is to provide some information on likely developments in China's trade sector during the critical first decade of the new century. We see these changes as likely driven by two major forces—changes in trade policies and underlying changes in the Chinese economy that can be expected to alter the level and composition of output. These underlying structural changes include changes in the rate of growth of the population and workforce, changes in the rate of capital accumulation, and changes in the rate at which human capital and skills are acquired.

Both changes in trade policies and the underlying changes in the structure of the Chinese economy and those of its trading partners involve complex general equilibrium interactions. To capture these in a simple, intuitive manner, we use a variant of the Global Trade Analysis Project (GTAP) global general equilibrium model designed to take into account the duty exemptions provided on inputs used in the production of exports. The trade policy reforms undertaken to date and those being discussed in the WTO negotiations involve different degrees of liberalization in different sectors and cannot be analyzed as a simple uniform liberalization of all sectors. Similarly, the pressures for structural change arising from rapid accumulation of capital and human capital create potential for differential rates of growth in different sectors that will have important implications for the composition and direction of trade.

In this chapter, first we consider some of the developments in the growth of China's international trade. We then consider developments in China's trade policies. Finally, we discuss the approach used to project future developments in China's trade and present some key results from the analysis.

Key Developments in China's Trade Sector

In the early 1970s, China's economy was extremely isolated from the world economy. The share of exports of goods and nonfactor services in GDP was below 3 percent in 1970, compared to 14 percent for the world as a whole in that year. Over the next twenty-five years, China's openness increased dramatically, reaching 23 percent in 1997. China's export share was actually higher than the world average in 1994—an extraordinary outcome for such a large economy. Up to 1987, the increase in China's export share was almost continuous, but since then, it has varied considerably in response to a range of economic shocks, including exchange rate changes and variations in domestic and foreign demand. There was a sharp decline in the export share in 1997, in large part because of the Asian economic crisis.

The rapid increase in China's openness and the accompanying rapid growth in the Chinese economy have resulted in a very rapid increase in China's share of world exports. As is evident from Figure 6.1, China's share of total world exports has more than tripled since 1982, rising to exceed 3 percent in 1998.

Evaluating whether the increase in China's exports is due to domestic growth or to greater openness is less straightforward than these figures would suggest. This is because of the dramatic changes in relative prices brought about by the devaluations of the official rate of the *renminbi* (RMB) yuan during the 1980s and early 1990s. As the currency was brought from a controlled and highly over-valued rate during the 1980s, the measured value of trade rose relative to domestic nontraded goods, contributing part of the apparent increase in openness observed in Figures 6.2 and 6.3. Another important contributing factor to the apparent increase in openness has been the very substantial use made of duty exemptions for specific purposes in China's trade regime. While these exemptions, of which the most important by far has been exemptions for inputs used in the production of exports, are a form of partial liberalization (Gruen 1999), they tend to favor assembly-type operations that contribute more to gross exports and imports than to engagement of domestic resources in trade-related activities. Further, there is a serious concern that such concessions will reduce the political pressure for reductions in tariffs on intermediate inputs from exporting firms (see Cadot, de Melo, and Olarreaga, 2003).

FIGURE 6.1
China's Share of World Exports

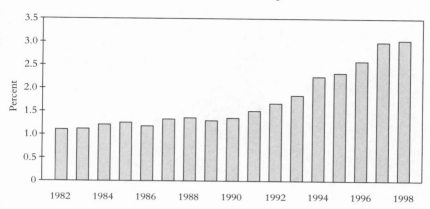

SOURCE: World Bank, World Development Indicators.

FIGURE 6.2
The Share of Exports of Goods and Nonfactor Services in GDP

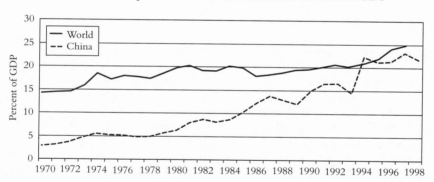

SOURCE: World Bank, World Development Indicators.

If we remove the valuation effects by examining changes in output at constant prices, the apparent increase in openness seems to disappear. Between 1982 and 1997, China's share of world output at constant prices rose by a factor of 2.85, very close to the increase of 2.7 times in its share of world exports. This use of constant price measures understates the importance of increasing openness in the Chinese economy, where the price of nontraded goods was greatly over-stated before the real devaluations that took place during the reform era.

Another important feature of the evolution of China's trade has been a very

FIGURE 6.3

Changes in the Composition of Exports from China

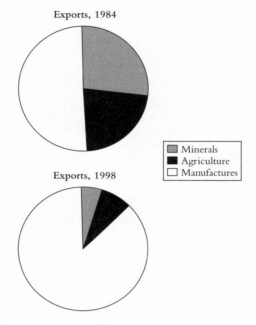

SOURCE: World Bank, World Development Indicators.

rapid change in the composition of its exports. In 1984, manufactures made up barely half of China's merchandise exports, minerals accounted for a quarter, and agricultural products the remainder. By 1998, manufactures comprised 87 percent of exports, and agricultural and mineral exports had declined to 7.7 and 4.8 percent, respectively. Such a large change in the composition of output is primarily due to the heavy investments in physical and human capital that allowed China to quickly alter the structure of its production and export mix. This increase in reliance on manufactures exports is not unique to China. Hertel and Martin (1999) found that the share of manufactures in the exports of the average developing country has risen from around 30 percent in the early 1980s to around 75 percent.[1] However, China's nearly 90 percent reliance on manufactures exports is particularly high.

China's Trade Policies

China's trade regime still retains many features that date from the prereform era. Understanding this regime and the evolution of trade policy is essential to gain insights about the sources of resistance to further changes. We begin with a short description of the prereform system and trace the evolution of the current system through the reform era.

The Prereform Chinese Trade Regime

The prereform Chinese trade regime was dominated by ten to sixteen foreign trade corporations (FTCs) with effective monopolies in the import and export of their specified ranges of products (Lardy, 1991). Planned import volumes were determined by the projected difference between domestic demand and supply for particular goods, with export levels being determined by the planners at levels necessary to finance the planned level of imports. The product ranges of the FTCs paralleled those of the industrial ministries responsible for production, and both were, in principle, under the overall control of the State Planning Commission and the State Economic Commission.

Under the prereform Chinese system, commodity prices were set without regard to scarcity or cost and were intended to serve only an accounting function. Further, the exchange rate was very substantially overvalued, creating a general disincentive to export and an artificial incentive to import. Thus it was not possible to use estimates of commodity markups to determine whether FTCs were creating trade barriers. Many producer goods had low prices that would have made exports artificially profitable and made necessary imports of some needed goods unprofitable. An explicit objective of the FTCs was to create a filter between producers and foreign markets that would counteract the artificial incentives created by the pricing system.[2]

An interesting feature of the prereform Chinese trade regime was the limited importance of conventional trade policy instruments such as tariffs, quotas, and licenses. Price-based measures such as tariffs were obviously unimportant since the planning system was based on quantity decisions rather than behavioral responses to prices. There was little need for quotas or licenses since the quantities to be imported could be controlled by the relevant monopoly trading corporations. As Lardy (1991) notes, the introduction of licensing actually reflected a liberalization of China's trade regime.

A major World Bank study (1988) of China's foreign trade regime highlighted the many disadvantages and costs of China's prereform trade regime, many of the features of which were still present in the mid-1980s. The filter between China and the world market created by the state trading monopolies was a particular focus of concern because of the resulting lack of information about the needs of export markets, as well as a lack of competition from imports, both of which generated substantial inefficiencies. The rigid foreign exchange system was another major cause for concern because it created a need for inefficient, bureaucratic allocation of foreign exchange.

Reform of China's Trade Regime

Reform of China's trade regime had four major dimensions: increasing the number and type of enterprises eligible to trade in particular commodities, developing the indirect trade policy instruments that were absent or unimportant under the planning system, reducing and ultimately removing exchange rate distortion, and reforming prices so that they could play a role in guiding resource allocation. These reforms of the trading system were inextricably linked with reforms of the enterprise sector to replace central planning of output with indirect regulation through market-determined prices. These reforms were undertaken incrementally, with feedback from each reform taken into account in designing the next stage of the reform—an approach colorfully described as "crossing the river by feeling the stones"—rather than proceeding according to a comprehensive overall plan for reform.

A central feature of the reforms was the decentralization of foreign trade rights beyond the handful of centrally controlled foreign trade corporations. This was not done according to the usual negative-list approach, whereby enterprises can trade in any good except those subject to restricted trading rights. Rather, the combination of a negative list for commodities and a positive list for trading firms was introduced. A negative-list approach is used to reserve specific commodities for trading by specified enterprises. Firms wishing to trade in other products are required to be on a positive list of firms with trading rights for those particular goods. The reform process gradually increased both the number of firms allowed to trade and the number of different types of firms eligible for trading rights.

The number of FTCs with trading rights was progressively expanded, with trading rights provided to branches of the FTCs controlled by the central government and to those controlled by regions and localities. Since 1984, these trading enterprises have been legally independent economic entities (Kueh, 1987), and state-owned trading enterprises of this type now appear to operate very strongly along commercial lines (Rozelle et al., 1996). Firms located in the special economic zones, and joint ventures between domestic and foreign firms were also allowed the right to trade their own products relatively early during the reform process. At a later stage, large producing firms began to gain direct foreign trade rights. The process of decentralizing trade was gradual, but the trend was very consistent, with commodities being progressively removed from export and import planning controls. Indeed, by 1992, these plans covered only a comparatively small number of products (World Bank, 1994; Yin, 1996), and they have since been abolished.

An important feature of the reforms was the introduction of special arrangements for processing trade. Imports of intermediate inputs for use in the production of exports were almost completely liberalized, as were capital goods inputs for use in joint ventures with foreign enterprises. As a result of this free trade in inputs used in the production of exports, this category of imports came to represent a very large share of total imports, accounting for almost half of total imports in 1996.

Import and export licensing measures were introduced in 1980 to replace the controls imposed under the previous trade monopoly (Lardy, 1991). The coverage of licensing was initially small but increased sharply as more and more trade was removed from the planning process. Lardy (1991) notes that licensing covered two-thirds of China's imports in 1988. Since then, the coverage of licensing has fallen dramatically.

The primary transitional device used to reduce and ultimately remove the distortions in both commodity prices and exchange rates was the multitier pricing system. Under the two-tier pricing system for commodities, the plan price continued to operate for the quantity of the commodity that producers were contracted to supply. However, to stimulate output, producers were allowed to supply additional output at a secondary market price. When plan prices are below market prices, this system can, in the short run, allow revenue to be generated in a nondistorting manner (Sicular, 1988; Byrd, 1989). The revenues raised were frequently redistributed to consumers within the same market. This was the case for grains, where consumers were supplied with fixed rations of grain at below-market prices. The two-tier system for foreign exchange involved an overvalued official exchange rate and a depreciated secondary-market rate. This distorted trade by discouraging both exports and imports (see Martin, 1993; World Bank, 1994). Over time, the share of foreign exchange receipts that exporters could retain for sale on the secondary market was raised, lowering the gap between the rates received by exporters and paid by importers and reducing the extent of the distortion. The exchange rate was unified in 1994, removing this distortion.

The importance of market prices relative to plan prices increased very rapidly as the reforms progressed, as is evident from Table 6.1. The share of retail com-

TABLE 6.1

Share of Goods Sold at State-Fixed Prices, 1978–93
(percent)

Year	Retail Commodities	Agricultural Goods	Capital and Industrial Goods★
1978	97	94	100
1992	10	15	20
1993	5	10	15
1994	7	17	16
1995	9	17	16

NOTE: ★Capital goods up to 1993 and all industrial goods thereafter. The two were essentially the same in the only overlap year, 1993.
SOURCES: Lardy (1995) up to 1993; Richard Garbaccio (personal communication) from 1994.

modities sold at fixed prices declined from 97 percent in 1978 to only 5 percent in 1993. Even for agricultural goods, where state pricing of some basic commodities such as grains remains important, only 10 percent of total sales were at state-administered prices in 1993. However, in a significant reversal of the trend toward liberalization, the share of goods subject to state pricing increased substantially between 1993 and 1995, although this share remained much lower than it had been prior to the early 1990s.[3]

Types and Numbers of Trading Firms

The positive-list system for allocating trading rights in China would potentially allow direct control of imports if the numbers of trading enterprises were small and if these enterprises were subject to a single supervisory body. However, the Ministry of Foreign Trade and Economic Cooperation (MOFTEC) reports that roughly nine thousand foreign trade corporations are active with very broad trading rights (MOFTEC, personal communication, June 1999). Of these, around one hundred are owned by the central government, and the remainder are owned by provincial and local governments. In addition to these FTCs, several other types of firms have trading rights, as may be seen from Table 6.2.

The firms in the first row of Table 6.2 are the FTCs with trading rights for a range of commodities. The other enterprise types in the table typically have trading rights only for their own inputs and outputs. The enumeration of firms in Table 6.2 is based on the enterprise identification codes on individual customs declarations. These numbers may differ substantially from the numbers of firms officially granted trading rights. MOFTEC (personal communication, June 1999) reported that only 8,000 FTCs had trading rights in 1994, even though the ITC reported 9,400 firms active in importing. It appears that the

TABLE 6.2

Contribution of Different Firms to China's Trade, 1994

	Exporting		Importing	
	Number of Firms	Share of Exports (percent)	Number of Firms	Share of Imports (percent)
Foreign trade corporations	9,400	53	8,700	44
State-owned enterprises	7,800	17	3,600	8
Joint ventures	30,000	19	64,800	34
Foreign-owned firms	9,730	9	23,239	12
Collectives and private enterprises	1,060	1	1,828	1
Other	520	0.2	5,378	1
Total	58,500	100	107,545	100

NOTE: Some numbers may not add because of rounding.
SOURCE: International Trade Centre (1996), p. 22.

larger number of firms reported on the customs declarations results from subsidiary firms' use of the trading rights granted to their parent firms. According to MOFTEC, the number of FTCs has increased dramatically since 1994. In October 1997, the number of FTCs with trading rights had increased to 15,000. Since then, there has been some relaxation of trading rights for larger state-owned enterprises (SOEs), and over one hundred private firms have been given trading rights for their own products.

While trading enterprises are typically subject to restrictions on the range of products that they may trade, the constraints imposed on the business scope of most FTCs appear to be quite liberal. While joint ventures and foreign-owned enterprises are subject to tighter restrictions on the scope of the products they trade, the sheer number of these enterprises means that many are likely to be active for most important product groups. As a consequence, consumers and producers wishing to purchase imports or sell exports will typically have a range of enterprises through which they can undertake these transactions.

Naughton (1996) notes that SOEs accounted for a relatively large share of the trade subject to ordinary customs duties (as distinct from preferential regimes such as imports for processing). In 1996, ordinary customs trade accounted for only 28 percent of imports (Economic Information and Agency, 1997), and SOEs of one form or another accounted for 79 percent of this trade. However, these SOEs include a very wide range of firm types, including state trading monopolies, FTCs administered by the central government, FTCs administered by provinces and municipalities, SOEs with direct trading rights for their own products, and wholesale and retail trading firms. Except for cases where there are restrictions on trading rights, the very large numbers of potential importers within and outside the ranks of the SOEs seem likely to create a relatively competitive trading environment.

Despite the large number of trading firms overall, there are two broad groups of commodities for which the number of firms entitled to engage in trade is tightly restricted. One of these groups is subject to state trading, and the other is subject to designated trading. The state trading system applies to a relatively small number of commodities that are believed to be of particular importance for the people's livelihood and national economic development—not surprisingly, many of these commodities are agricultural products or agricultural inputs such as fertilizer. The system of designated trading applies to a range of other important commodities. The 70 tariff lines subject to state trading on the import side are drawn from the commodity groups set out in Table 6.3, as are the 115 tariff lines covered by state trading on the export side. The 229 tariff lines subject to designated trading are primarily importables.

The products subject to state trading are typically handled by one or a few foreign trade corporations, making direct control of the quantities imported and exported relatively practical. The system of coordination and control used for

TABLE 6.3

Products Covered by State Trading and Designated Trading

	Imports	Exports
State trading	Grain, vegetable oils, sugar, tobacco, crude oil, refined oil, chemical fertilizer, cotton	Tea, maize, soybeans, tungsten, coal, crude oil, refined oil, silk, unbleached silk, cotton, antimony
Designated trading	Rubber, timber, plywood, wool, acrylics, steel and steel products	Rubber, timber, plywood, wool, acrylics, steel and steel products

SOURCE: Government of China (1997).

major state-traded commodities such as grains and fertilizer appears to follow the basic lines used under the traditional planning system. Estimates of the gap between supply and demand are made up to eighteen months in advance of the actual trade's taking place, and there appears to be considerable reluctance to adjust the quantity targets in responses to developments such as unanticipated shocks to domestic supply or demand. Recent empirical research concludes that rather than helping stabilize domestic grain prices, this inflexible system contributes substantially to the volatility of domestic grain prices (World Bank, 1997a). Carter, Chen, and Rozelle (1998) identified many of the classic features of the traditional monopoly trading system in the grain trade—a barrier between buyers and suppliers, poor quality matching, and unpredictable timing of deliveries. In addition, they found many of the features of poorly operating markets, particularly concerns that traders are using their superior information to take advantage of buyers in China.

While state trading can be legal under the provisions of the WTO, there appears to be a strong case for the reform of these state-trading monopolies, given the serious concerns about the performance of this approach to trade administration.

Nontariff Barriers

The coverage of state trading and designated trading is shown, together with other nontariff barriers (NTBs) affecting China's import trade, in Table 6.4. The table indicates that state trading and designated trading accounted for 11 and 7 percent, respectively, of total imports and made up over half of the total trade coverage of NTBs in China. Clearly, the regime used for state trading and designated trading is an important special feature of the Chinese trade regime but very much a minority part of the overall system rather than the dominant part. The heavy reliance on state trading for major agricultural trade has, however, raised concerns about the transparency of China's agricultural trade regime (see Dixit and Josling, 1997).

The average protective impact of the complete set of NTBs presented in Table 6.3 was estimated to be equivalent to a 9.3 percent ad valorem tariff (World

Bank, 1997b). This evaluation was undertaken using information on the tariff equivalents of these NTBs obtained from the Unirule Institute study prepared for the Institute of International Economics (Zhang, Zhang, and Wan, 1998) and from price comparisons drawn from the International Comparisons Project. Even though the coverage of the information available was incomplete, it did provide some initial basis for evaluation. Products imported under the state trading categories accounted for only 0.7 percentage points of this total protection. On this basis, it appears that state trading of imports has been a very minor restriction on trade in the recent past.

One additional feature of China's trade regime is a system of automatic import registration (AIR) that has covered wool, tobacco, and cotton, as well as important nonagricultural commodities such as oil, steel, copper, nonferrous metals, and polyester. There is considerable overlap between this system and other trade measures, with some of these commodities also covered by state trading, some by designated trading, and some by quotas and licenses. This system has not been listed as a NTB and has typically been justified as purely for statistical monitoring. However, some officials also appear to see it as a way to ensure that imports are not brought in when there is "insufficient" market demand or as a means to induce purchasers to buy local products that the State Economic and Trade Commission (SETC) judges to be adequate substitutes for the imported good. Clearly, any such use of market demand criteria for approving requests for AIR would qualify this as a serious NTB.

TABLE 6.4

Share of Imports Protected by NTBs in 1996, Using 1992 Trade Weights

(percent)

	State Trading	Designated Trading	London Convention	Import Licenses	Import Quotas	Price Tendering	All
Rice	100.0	0.0	0.0	100.0	0.0	0.0	100.0
Wheat	100.0	0.0	0.0	100.0	0.0	0.0	100.0
Coarse grains	0.0	0.0	0.0	0.0	0.0	0.0	0.0
Nongrain crops	50.0	22.9	0.0	72.9	72.9	0.0	72.9
Livestock	0.0	72.7	0.0	72.7	72.7	0.0	72.7
Meat and milk	0.0	0.0	0.0	0.0	0.0	0.0	0.0
Other food products	37.2	0.0	0.0	32.9	31.7	0.0	38.4
Natural resources	46.6	12.8	0.0	0.0	0.0	0.0	59.5
Textiles	0.3	5.7	0.0	12.7	12.7	0.0	12.7
Wearing apparel	0.0	0.0	0.0	0.0	0.0	0.0	0.0
Light manufactures	0.0	9.3	0.0	0.0	0.0	0.0	9.3
Transport equipment	0.0	0.0	0.0	35.8	35.8	6.6	42.4
Machinery and equipment	0.0	0.0	0.0	9.2	9.2	20.4	26.8
Basic heavy manufactures	18.7	16.2	0.3	23.5	22.7	0.0	37.7
Services	0.0	0.0	0.0	0.0	0.0	0.0	0.0
Share of total	11.0	7.3	0.1	18.5	16.3	7.4	32.5

SOURCE: World Bank (1997c).

Over the course of the 1990s, China made substantial progress in reducing the number of NTBs in its trade regime. Nicholas Lardy (personal communication) estimates that the number of products subject to quotas and licenses fell from 1,247 tariff lines in 1992 to 261 in 1999. China committed to refrain from introducing new NTBs or increasing the coverage of existing NTBs during the negotiations for WTO accession. Organizational changes in the Chinese government during 1998 resulted in some changes in the administration of particular measures. One important change was the removal of some of the major state trading firms owned by the central government from the control of MOFTEC and the ministries responsible for particular industries.

Tariff Barriers

The pace of tariff reform begun in the early 1990s has been sustained in recent years. A significant tariff reform was implemented in October 1997, reducing average tariffs significantly below 20 percent, and a more limited reform in January 1999 focused on timber products. Some basic data on trends in average tariff rates are given in Table 6.5, where simple averages, as well as trade-weighted averages, are reported for broad groups of merchandise trade.

The progressive reductions in tariffs from 1992 to 1998 have reduced average tariffs by more than half. For the manufactures sector, the reductions have been greater than average. The fact that these reductions have been phased in means that the reductions required for WTO membership will be much less abrupt than would otherwise have been the case. Another important feature of the reforms has been a substantial reduction in the dispersion of tariff rates—with the standard deviation of tariffs falling from 32.1 percent in 1992 to 13.1 percent in 1998. This reduction in the dispersion of tariffs can be expected to greatly reduce the costs of protection. Bach, Martin, and Stevens (1996) found that reductions in the variance of tariffs associated with China implementing its (then) proposed WTO accession package accounted for a large share of the benefits.

TABLE 6.5

Changes in Average Tariff Rates in China, 1992–98

(percent)

	All Merchandise		Primary Products		Manufactures	
	Simple	Weighted	Simple	Weighted	Simple	Weighted
1992	42.9	40.6	36.2	22.3	44.9	46.5
1993	39.9	38.4	33.3	20.9	41.8	44.0
1994	36.3	35.5	32.1	19.6	37.6	40.6
1996	23.6	22.6	25.4	20.0	23.1	23.2
1997	17.6	18.2	17.9	20.0	17.5	17.8
1998	17.5	18.7	17.9	20.0	17.4	18.5

SOURCE: World Bank (1999), p. 340.

An important feature of China's tariff reforms has been the inclusion of very important exemptions for processing trade and for foreign investment. According to Chinese customs authorities, 75 percent of imports entered either duty-free or subject to reduced duties. The exempt and reduced categories (1998 import exempt shares) were as follows:

Processing trade (50 percent, exempted)
Initial investment of joint ventures (10 percent, exempted)
Bonded warehouse imports (5 percent, exempted)
Other exempted or reduced (10 percent, exempted or reduced)

These figures suggest that only around 25 percent of imports in 1998 entered as ordinary trade, subject to normal customs duties. The presence of these exemptions contributes substantially to the oft-remarked divergence between the weighted average tariff rate and the average tariff collection rate in China. In 1998, the collection rate for customs duties was only 2.7 percent. If the average tariff rates on exempted and nonexempted goods were the same, the average collection rate should have been on the order of 4.7 percent. Since ordinary trade items are likely to be subject to higher tariff rates, on average, the unexplained shortfall in customs tariffs is probably larger than these numbers would suggest.

An important development in customs administration in 1999 was an anti-smuggling campaign, which appears to have reduced smuggling from Hong Kong considerably. In 1997, it was reported that China's recorded imports from Hong Kong were 10 percent less than Hong Kong's recorded exports. During the first five months of 1999, China's recorded imports were 5 percent above Hong Kong's exports. The success of this antismuggling campaign appears to have been sufficient to suggest caution in interpreting China's overall trade statistics over this period.

China's heavy reliance on exemptions for goods used in the production of exports as a way to stimulate its export production has clearly encouraged development of export processing industries that rely heavily on imported intermediate goods. In many respects, this is a good thing, since global manufacturing production is increasingly moving toward production sharing, where the production chain is broken up into many small links, and each of these links is located wherever comparative advantage is greatest (see Ng and Yeats, 1999). However, the reliance on high protective barriers and deep exemptions, rather than more comprehensive liberalization, has the disadvantage of discriminating against industries that rely more heavily on domestic value added, rather than imported intermediate inputs. The continued presence of high tariffs on goods used indirectly in the production of exports also raises the price of locally produced goods that embody traded goods. Furthermore, the protection raises the price of nontraded goods (the so-called real exchange rate effect)—an effect that discriminates against exports that embody significant amounts of domestic value added. The end result is an export mix, like China's current export mix, that depends heavily on processing sector exports with relatively little domestic value added.

This problem can be overcome by more comprehensive liberalization. With lower tariffs, the costs of domestic inputs to exporters will fall. This can in turn be expected to result in a shift toward reliance on exports that embody a greater amount of domestic value added. Clearly, this would be a favorable development, building appropriately on the export base developed during the period of partial liberalization. However, it is likely to require substantial adjustments in the pattern of China's exports and hence could be threatened by foreign protection measures, such as antidumping measures, that tend to resist changes in trade patterns.

China's WTO Accession

At the time of writing, the final details of China's WTO accession package were confidential. However, the November 1999 bilateral agreement between China and the United States and the May 2000 agreement with the European Union formed the basis for the final agreement. Accordingly, we drew on these agreements, on which a substantial amount of information was available.

WTO entry required China to bring its rules into line with WTO norms in a wide range of areas. Perhaps the most important of these stipulations are those on nondiscrimination between suppliers in accordance with the most favored nation principle and the abolition of most nontariff barriers. However, WTO rules require much more, including the implementation of intellectual property regimes consistent with the Agreement on Trade-Related Aspects of Intellectual Property Rights (TRIPS), customs valuation procedures consistent with the agreement on customs valuation, and safeguards procedures and standards and phytosanitary restrictions consistent with GATT rules.

The Protocol of Accession also includes important stipulations designed to increase the transparency of China's trade regime and provide for judicial review of administrative decisions. It specifies procedures for judicial review of administrative actions, requires the phasing out of the general restrictions on trading rights, requires elimination of multitier pricing systems, and requires China's SOEs to make purchasing and sales decisions based solely on commercial considerations. Unfortunately, the agreement also includes transitional procedures that will make it easier for China's trading partners to impose product-specific protective barriers during the transition period, when China's trade mix is likely to need to adjust sharply in response to liberalization. The criterion for imposing product-specific safeguards is market disruption, which the U.S. House of Representatives (2000, sec. 421) defined to occur when increased imports are a significant cause of material injury.

As a result of WTO accession, China will move strongly toward a trade regime based on tariffs. Quotas, licenses, and designated trading will all be phased out. State trading is to remain on most of the commodities listed in Table 6.3, although it will be subject to WTO rules after accession. State trading monopolies on imports of soybean oil, crude oil, oil products, and fertilizer and on exports of raw silk, however, are to be abolished.

In addition, China will make specific commitments to reduce protection for merchandise and services. The office of the United States Trade Representative (1999) reported that China committed to bind all agricultural and industrial tariffs. The simple average tariff on manufactures is to be reduced to 9.44 percent—a substantial reduction from the 17.4 percent reported in Table 6.5 for 1998. The simple average tariff for agriculture is reported to be 17 percent—broadly in line with the 1998 estimate in Table 6.5 for all primary products. China will also commit not to use agricultural export subsidies. In subsequent bilateral negotiations with the European Union, China committed to additional tariff reductions on a number of products, including butter, olives, textiles, leather, spirits, and a range of machinery.

The reductions in tariff protection for manufactures will clearly be an important liberalization step for China. Those reductions are to be phased in over the period to 2005, with a limited number of exceptions. The Multi-Fiber Agreement (MFA) quotas, which sharply restrict China's exports of textile and clothing products, are also to be phased out by 2005 and textile-specific safeguards introduced under the accession agreement by 2008. The transition period allows some time for investors to anticipate the changes in competitiveness in the Chinese economy. Because these commitments are given greatly enhanced credibility by being bound under the WTO, investors should be able to make plans with much less uncertainty about the trade regime than has been the case in the past.

In agriculture, the main impact of the WTO commitments is likely to operate through the subsequent reductions in uncertainty about agricultural trade policies. While state trading will be retained for some important commodities, the WTO's rules on state trading impose significant disciplines on the protection that state-trading enterprises (STEs) can provide (Davey, 1998). In particular, they require importing STEs to meet market demand, and they limit STEs' ability to restrict imports if the domestic price would consistently exceed the agreed tariff binding.

The disciplines on agricultural protection may become extremely important if comparative advantage continues to shift against agriculture in China. In the absence of WTO disciplines, China would almost certainly have followed the general East Asian pattern of sharply rising agricultural protection (Anderson and Hayami, 1986). As is evident from Table 6.6, most of the tariff bindings negotiated with China are very low by East Asian standards and may turn out to

TABLE 6.6

Final Tariff Bindings on Selected Agricultural Products

(percent)

Commodity	Uruguay Round Final Binding	Likely Final Binding
Almonds	30	10
Apples	40	10
Barley	91	9
Beef	40	12
Citrus	52	12
Grapes	40	13
Pork, frozen cuts	40	12
Poultry, frozen cuts	40	12
Soybeans	114	3
Wheat, maize, rice	114	65
Wine	135	14

SOURCES: World Trade Organization (1994b); Chen (1999); United States Trade Representative (1999); Carter and Huang (1998); European Union (2000).

save China from developing an extremely inefficient and high-cost agricultural sector. Another important feature of Table 6.6 is the comparison of the bindings in the current proposal with those that China had offered in the Uruguay Round—illustrating how far China has been willing to come.

The agricultural trade regime includes a range of tariff rate quotas that provide for lower tariffs on specified quantities of imports. These commitments provide for specified shares of the tariff rate quotas to be allocated to foreign-owned private firms. The main economic effect of this is to provide rent transfers, rather than to liberalize, although it does have an advantage in providing greater transparency in domestic pricing, thereby making it easier to detect violations of the rules governing state trading entities.

China has also made important commitments on services under GATT, including comprehensive commitments on distribution and tourism, and commitments on telecommunications, insurance, banking, construction, professional services, and audiovisual services. The commitments on distribution are particularly important because of the transparency they create and because they preclude the emergence of de facto import barriers through controls on distribution.

It is clear that China's accession to the WTO will require a very large number of reforms both in legislation and in the way that business is conducted. The need for reform will be particularly acute in areas such as the financial sector and telecommunications, where substantial reforms in the regulatory structure, as well as international trade policies, are likely to be required. Agricultural policy will be unable to take the inward-looking approach that has characterized agricultural policy in other East Asian "miracle" economies. Some relief from adjustment pressures may be found by using WTO negotiations to reduce the disproportionately high barriers that face China's agricultural exports. Measures such as increased educational opportunities and greater labor mobility, which facilitate movement of rural workers, will probably be the most powerful, and necessary, policy measures for dealing with these problems in the longer term. In industry, sectors such as automobiles will require massive restructuring to allow the development of a modern, efficient sector.

Growth, Structural Change, and Liberalization

China's economy continues to grow relatively rapidly, and this growth, if sustained over the coming decade, will cause substantial changes in the composition of output. In addition, the liberalization associated with WTO accession is likely to have important implications for the structure of output and the orientation of production between domestic and international markets.

To obtain some assessment of the likely changes in the structure of China's foreign trade, we have used the GTAP Version 4 model of the global economy (Hertel, 1997; http://www.gtap.org), modified by Ianchovichina and Martin (2001) to reflect the tariff exemptions on intermediate inputs used in producing exports in China. We use the modified version of the GTAP to provide both a baseline scenario in which China does not enter the WTO and a companion scenario under which China and Taiwan both enter the WTO. Both scenarios broadly replicate World Bank projections for overall output growth in each region and use projections of factor input growth and a residually determined level of total factor productivity growth to ensure consistency between the two. For most countries and regions in the model, projection rates were based on tariffs applied in the model's base year of 1995,[5] but for China, the 1997 tariff rates were used.

Because the available projections suggest that the growth of factor endowments in high-growth regions such as East Asia will be highly unbalanced, the structure of output can be expected to change quite sharply as a result of Rybczynski effects. These pressures for change are in addition to those resulting from Engel effects in consumption, which are incorporated in the model through nonhomothetic preferences in the model's consumer demand systems. Simulations have been performed over the period from the model's benchmark year of 1995 to 2005. While this provides only a short "forecast," it does provide an indication of the pressures for change operating over longer or shorter periods of interest.

Under the baseline scenario, tariff rates on all industrial products are held constant, and the MFA quotas are projected to grow at the rates determined in each country's agreements. Tariff rates on agricultural products are also held constant, in line with the move to tariffication in the Uruguay Round. Since the MFA quota growth rates for WTO members are subject to acceleration and eventual elimination (World Trade Organization, 1994a), while those for nonmembers

TABLE 6.7

Cumulative Percentage Growth Rates, 1995–2005

(annual rate of change in parentheses)

Regions	Population	Unskilled Labor	Skilled Labor	Capital	Manufacturing TFP*
North America	11	14	39	63	low
	(1.05)	(1.29)	(3.33)	(4.98)	
Western Europe	1	0	29	30	medium
	(0.10)	(0.03)	(2.60)	(2.70)	
Australia/New Zealand	10	11	66	38	low
	(0.97)	(1.09)	(5.20)	(3.29)	
Japan	2	−3	32	29	low
	(0.20)	(−0.29)	(2.83)	(2.59)	
China	9	12	43	174	medium
	(0.83)	(1.17)	(3.66)	(10.62)	
Taiwan	8	13	51	102	high
	(0.73)	(1.21)	(4.18)	(7.28)	
Other newly industrialized countries (NICs)	9	8	66	71	low
	(0.84)	(0.73)	(5.18)	(5.54)	
Indonesia	14	21	79	21	low
	(1.31)	(1.96)	(6.00)	(1.96)	
Other Southeast Asia	19	26	79	38	low
	(1.73)	(2.36)	(6.00)	(3.30)	
India	17	23	73	85	medium
	(1.59)	(2.11)	(5.65)	(6.36)	
Other South Asia	23	33	77	56	medium
	(2.10)	(2.92)	(5.87)	(4.52)	
Brazil	13	22	70	25	low
	(1.26)	(2.04)	(5.46)	(2.22)	
Other Latin America	18	23	89	25	low
	(1.63)	(2.11)	(6.55)	(2.22)	
Turkey	15	22	104	66	low
	(1.44)	(2.02)	(7.41)	(5.19)	
Other Middle East and North Africa	27	37	109	15	low
	(2.43)	(3.17)	(7.64)	(1.37)	
Economies in transition	3	6	69	30	low
	(0.27)	(0.60)	(5.37)	(2.70)	
South African Customs Union	23	29	64	15	low
	(2.06)	(2.59)	(5.06)	(1.43)	
Other sub-Saharan Africa	33	37	88	19	medium
	(2.87)	(3.19)	(6.50)	(1.78)	
Rest of world	18	21	83	88	low
	(1.65)	(1.90)	(6.22)	(6.51)	

NOTE: * The low, medium, and high growth assumptions for total factor productivity (TFP) in manufacturing correspond to annual growth rates of 0.1 percent, 1.0 percent, and 2.0 percent, respectively.

(including China had accession not occurred) are not, China's low MFA quota growth rates would have become an increasing burden in the absence of WTO accession.

The actual projections used are presented in Table 6.7. These projections were generated by combining historical and forecast data from the World Bank. Projections for population and unskilled labor were obtained by cumulating the average growth rates between 1995 and the projected 2005 data. The skilled labor projections were based on forecasts of growth in the stock of tertiary-educated labor in each developing country (Ahuja and Filmer, 1995), along with projected growth rates of skilled labor in developed countries from the World Bank. They provide an indication of changes in the stock of individuals qualified for employment as professional and technical workers. Growth rates of physical capital were projected using investment profiles over the 1995–2005 period, coupled with estimates of initial (1995) capital stocks and depreciation rates.

As is evident from Table 6.7, the rate of growth in the workforce in China is projected to slightly outpace the growth of the population over the projection period, although not greatly, because much of the demographic dividend (Bloom and Williamson, 1998) resulting from the sharp decline in the Chinese birthrate has now passed. Most important for the growth and structure of the economy are the very high projected growth rates for skilled labor and for physical capital. This augmentation of physical and human capital can be expected to have profound implications for growth and structural change. There is some uncertainty regarding the estimated growth rate for skilled workers, and this element of the projection may require revisiting.

The details of bilateral accession offers in the WTO accession process are generally treated as confidential, and the latest offer available to us at the time the simulations were conducted was that presented to the Accession Working Party in April 1998. This offer was intended to bring the simple average tariff on industrial products down to 10.8 percent, as distinct from the 9.4 percent reportedly involved in the April 1999 offer to the United States (United States Trade Representative, 1999). Subsequent analysis (Ianchovichina and Martin, 2001, 2003) confirms that this offer provides a reasonable indication of the order of magnitude and the pattern of liberalization resulting from accession. It is assumed that there are no reductions in applied agricultural tariff rates resulting from WTO accession because the WTO offer does not generally appear to require such reductions from currently applied rates. This assumption probably greatly understates the benefits of the agreement because it seems unlikely that agricultural protection in China would remain constant in the absence of WTO disciplines. Our estimates of the consequences of accession are also modified to some degree because we omit the consequences of liberalization in the services sector and of stronger rules.

The tariff rates for China used in the baseline and in the case of WTO accession are given in Table 6.8. The numbers presented in the table highlight the substantial nature of the offer for industrial products. Protection to textiles and apparel products falls dramatically, as does protection to automobiles and electronics. The sharp decline in protection for electronics is undoubtedly related to China's agreement to implement the Information Technology Agreement as

TABLE 6.8

*Weighted Average Tariffs in China with and Without
WTO Accession*

(percent)

	Baseline	With Accession
Foodgrains	0.00	0.00
Feedgrains	6.03	6.03
Oilseeds	4.16	4.16
Meat and livestock	10.14	10.14
Dairy	26.74	26.74
Other agriculture	22.09	22.09
Other food	27.68	27.68
Beverages and tobacco	123.50	123.50
Extractive industries	3.59	1.65
Textiles	57.10	9.64
Wearing apparel	75.99	16.15
Wood and paper	21.57	9.38
Petrochemicals	20.17	12.81
Metals	17.52	8.57
Automobiles	129.07	29.63
Electronics	21.69	6.03
Other manufactures	23.53	11.11

part of its accession package. The actual reduction in protection for the automotive sector is even larger than is suggested by these tariff results, since quota protection for this sector is also to be phased out. Overall, the reduction package appears to be an important step toward developing a much more efficient and competitive industrial sector, particularly given some of the largest reductions in protection are in the most highly protected industrial sectors.

The implications of the baseline growth scenario and the liberalization scenario for China's share of world output and export markets are shown in Table 6.9. These results provide the basis for a number of interesting conclusions. The first is the rapid growth in China's share of world output and exports, even in the absence of WTO accession. Without accession, China's share of world output is projected to increase from 3.4 to 5.3 percent over the decade, while its share of exports rises to 4.8 percent. Although accession has almost no impact on China's share of aggregate world output, it has a large impact on its share of trade. With accession, China's share of world export markets rises to 6.3 percent and of world import markets to 6.4 percent.

At the sectoral level, the most important impact of accession is on China's share of world apparel output. This share rises dramatically because of the lifting of the burdens imposed by the MFA quotas on China's exports and by China's protection on the cost structure of the industry. China's share of world export markets for apparel also increases dramatically, to over 45 percent, for the same reason. Imports of textiles increase substantially because of the input demand from the apparel industry. A number of relatively high-tech sectors, such as automobiles and electronics, also experience very substantial increases in their export shares under the accession scenario as their costs are reduced following the liberalization. These results are very much affected by the presence of tariff exemptions on intermediate inputs in the database. In an earlier version of this chapter, where the same analysis was performed using the standard GTAP model, which does not incorporate this feature, the estimated liberalization of China's trade was much greater, and China's final share of world apparel exports was over 60 percent.

On the import side, China becomes a much bigger market for its trading partners following accession to the WTO. The increases in import market share are particularly large in agriculture, even though protection of that sector has been assumed to remain constant. This increase in the importance of agricul-

TABLE 6.9

Output, Exports, and Imports as a Share of the World Economy

(percent)

	Output			Exports			Imports		
		2005			2005			2005	
	1995	Without Accession	With Accession	1995	Without Accession	With Accession	1995	Without Accession	With Accession
Foodgrains	14.29	19.59	19.86	0.30	0.06	0.05	6.45	16.35	17.08
Feedgrains	8.33	10.55	10.63	0.72	0.12	0.11	3.20	9.18	9.73
Oilseeds	5.13	6.22	6.35	4.05	0.76	0.66	1.15	3.94	4.20
Meat and livestock	6.70	11.62	12.09	3.51	0.51	0.43	2.02	8.88	9.94
Dairy	0.75	1.34	1.44	0.08	0.03	0.02	0.17	0.61	0.67
Other agriculture	10.58	15.65	15.90	2.32	0.36	0.31	2.74	9.62	10.32
Other food	2.27	3.15	3.17	2.61	1.21	1.17	3.10	6.39	6.48
Beverages and tobacco	4.89	7.02	7.05	2.42	1.03	1.03	0.89	1.29	1.25
Extractive industries	8.07	12.29	11.95	1.69	0.12	0.14	1.55	9.09	8.68
Textiles	10.79	13.88	13.54	8.43	8.84	10.15	13.35	17.96	25.38
Wearing apparel	7.02	8.84	19.09	19.58	18.54	45.14	1.04	1.09	3.72
Wood and paper	2.41	3.67	3.45	2.19	2.59	2.85	2.57	3.86	4.44
Petrochemicals	5.00	7.57	7.26	2.56	3.06	3.29	4.02	5.76	6.00
Metals	5.45	8.99	8.04	3.38	5.47	6.09	4.23	5.77	6.48
Automobiles	1.91	3.76	0.93	0.13	0.69	1.62	1.95	1.81	5.32
Electronics	2.63	4.53	4.60	4.97	7.79	9.11	3.57	5.25	5.65
Other manufactures	6.40	10.41	9.81	5.49	8.05	9.17	4.23	5.89	7.06
Utilities	2.69	3.90	3.82	5.82	6.70	7.24	1.20	1.73	1.54
Trade and transport	2.55	3.73	3.70	1.70	2.79	2.93	2.03	2.41	2.27
Construction	3.29	6.22	6.13	0.00	0.00	0.00	1.82	2.81	2.74
Business and finance	0.89	1.34	1.32	1.92	2.50	2.58	1.49	1.95	1.88
Government services	1.58	2.37	2.36	1.01	0.62	0.62	0.72	1.31	1.26
Total	3.38	5.26	5.17	3.71	4.78	6.34	3.36	5.34	6.36

tural imports reflects the strong shift in comparative advantage away from agriculture implied by the baseline growth scenario and is close to an inevitable consequence of successful economic development. Note that in all of the agricultural commodities, the underlying pattern of strong economic growth and factor accumulation is what leads to the decline in export share and the increase in import share; China's output share is also expanding. The robust growth in output reduces the need for concern about food self-sufficiency, and the fast growth in per capita incomes underlying the scenario means that the food security of most people—the ability of the poor to afford sufficient food (Sen, 1983)—is likely to improve greatly, although attention must be given to possible adverse impacts on particular groups, as is emphasized by Chen and Ravallion (2003).

The exact numbers given in the table should not be taken too literally, since the world is a much more complex place than we are able to represent in an economic model. However, the results do provide useful insights into some of the powerful forces for structural change that are likely to operate during the next few years. The importance of liberalization for export market share is an important insight, as is the importance of growth and structural change for the decline in China's comparative advantage in agriculture. The importance of the MFA quotas in suppressing development of China's textile and clothing industries is also highlighted.

Conclusions

Since the late 1970s, China's production and trade patterns have changed dramatically. China's share of world output and trade has grown substantially in response both to trade reforms and liberalization and to productivity growth in the domestic economy. The composition of its export basket has also changed radically, with agricultural and mineral exports declining steeply and the share of manufactures in total merchandise exports rising to over 87 percent.

The trade policy regime has been transformed, moving from a system based on a handful of centralized product monopolies to a quite decentralized system involving hundreds of thousands of trading firms. Tariff rates have fallen by more than half since 1992, and a further substantial reduction has been offered in the context of the ongoing WTO negotiations. Virtually all remaining NTBs are to be phased out in the context of WTO accession, with the remaining exception being state trading on a range of (mainly agricultural) products subject to a form of state trading that currently differs little in principle from the thoroughly discredited monopoly state-trading system of the prereform era. Following WTO accession, these state-trading firms now face stronger rules and increased competition. Although the state-trading system appears to be legal under the WTO, maintaining it is likely to continue to be an inefficient and costly policy.

To get some idea of the likely patterns of growth in China's trading system, we used the GTAP model of the global economy, modified to account for tariff exemptions for exports in China, to project forward the structure of the world economy and countries' trade patterns. The projections took into account changes in factor endowments that influence the structure of the world market and the implications of China's accession to the WTO.

The projections suggest that China's share of the world economy will increase substantially by 2005. Its share of world exports could have been expected to in-crease—from 3.7 percent in 1995 to 4.8 percent in 2005 even in the absence of WTO accession. China's export growth is extremely sensitive to the extent of liberalization, with its share of world export markets rising to 6.3 percent fol-lowing accession. There are likely to be substantial and rapid changes in the structure of China's production and exports as China implements the WTO ac-cords. The trade policies of China's trading partners will need to adjust to these substantial changes and also to take advantage of the market opportunities cre-ated in areas ranging from agriculture to telecommunications.

Notes

1. Because the focus of the Hertel and Martin (1999) study was on the WTO nego-tiations, a relatively inclusive definition of a developing country was used: any country that claims to be a developing country is considered to be one.

2. The intent was originally to insulate the economy from the harmful irrationalities of world market prices (World Bank, 1988).

3. The following goods were subject to state pricing in 1997: grain, edible oil, cot-ton, tobacco, compressed tea, timber, crude oil, natural gas, gasoline, kerosene, diesel oil, heavy oil, urea, polyethylene sheeting, steel for locomotives and rolling stock, aircraft and aircraft engines, edible salt, pharmaceuticals, and silk cocoons.

4. By contrast, WTO safeguards under Article 19 require that serious injury to do-mestic firms be demonstrated.

5. In some cases, 1995 tariffs are unavailable and tariffs for the nearest available year were used.

References

Ahuja, V., and Filmer, D. 1995. *Educational attainment in developing countries: New estimates and projections disaggregated by gender.* Policy Research Working Paper 1489. Washing-ton, D.C.: World Bank.

Anderson, K., and Hayami, Y. 1986. *The political economy of agricultural protection: East Asia in international perspective.* Sydney, Australia: Allen & Unwin.

Bach, C., Martin, W., and Stevens, J. 1996. China and the WTO: Tariff offers, exemptions and welfare implications. *Weltwirtschaftliches Archiv,* 132(3), 409–31.

Bloom, D., and Williamson, J. G. 1998. Demographic transitions and economic miracles in emerging Asia. *World Bank Economic Review,* 12(3), 419–56.

Byrd, W. 1989. The impact of the two-tier plan/market system in Chinese industry. *Journal of Comparative Economics,* 11, 295–308.

Cadot, O., de Melo, J., and Olarreaga, M. 2003. Can duty drawbacks have a protectionist bias? Evidence from Mercosur. *Journal of International Economics,* 591, 161–82.

Carter, C., Chen, J., and Rozelle, S. 1998. *China's state trading in grains: An institutional overview.* Unpublished manuscript, University of California at Davis.

Carter, C., and Huang, J. 1998. *China's agricultural trade: Patterns and prospects.* Unpublished manuscript, University of California-Davis.

Chen, S., and Ravallion, M. 2003. Household welfare impacts of WTO accession. In D. Bhattasali, S. Li, and W. Martin, eds., *Impacts and policy implications of WTO accession for China.* Washington, D.C.: World Bank. Available from http://www/worldbank.org/trade.

Chen, X. 1999. *The WTO and the Sino-U.S. agricultural agreement.* Symposium on the WTO and the Chinese economy sponsored by the State Information Center, Beijing, May 22–23.

Davey, W. 1998. Article XVII GATT: An overview. In T. Cottier and P. Mavroidis, eds., *State trading in the twenty-first century.* Ann Arbor: University of Michigan Press.

Dixit, P., and Josling, T. 1997. *State trading in agriculture: A background paper.* Paper presented at the Economic Research Service seminar, U.S. Department of Agriculture, Washington, D.C.

Economic Information and Agency. 1997. *China's customs statistics monthly, December 1996.* Hong Kong: Economic Information and Agency.

European Union. 2000. *The Sino-EU agreement on China's accession to the WTO: results of the bilateral negotiations.* Available from http://europa.eu.int/comm/trade/bilateral/china/wto.htm.

Gruen, N. 1999. Towards a more general approach to trade liberalization. *Economic Record,* 75, 385–96.

Hertel, T. W. 1997. *Global trade analysis: Modeling and applications.* Cambridge: Cambridge University Press. Available from http://www.worldbank.org/trade.

Hertel, T. W., and Martin, W. 1999. Liberalising agriculture and manufactures in a millennium round: Implications for developing countries. *World Economy,* 23, 455–69.

Ianchovichina, E., and Martin, W. 2001. Trade liberalization in China's accession to the WTO. *Journal of Economic Integration,* 16(4), 421–45.

Ianchovichina, E., and Martin, W. 2003. Economic impacts of China's accession to the WTO. In D. Bhattasali, S. Li, and W. Martin, eds., *Impacts and policy implications of WTO accession for China.* Washington, D.C.: World Bank. Available from http://www/worldbank. org/trade.

International Trade Centre. 1996. *Survey of China's foreign trade.* Geneva: International Trade Centre.

Kueh, Y. 1987. Economic decentralization and foreign trade expansion in China. In J. Chai and C. K. Leung, eds., *China's Economic Reforms.* Hong Kong: University of Hong Kong.

Lardy, N. R. 1991. *Foreign trade and economic reform in China, 1978–1990.* Cambridge: Cambridge University Press.

————. 1995. The role of foreign trade and investment in China's economic transformation. *China Quarterly*, 144, 1065–82.

Martin, W. 1993. Modeling the post-reform Chinese economy. *Journal of Policy Modeling*, 15, 545–79.

Naughton, B. 1996. *China: From export promotion to an open economy?* San Diego: University of California.

Ng, F., and Yeats, A. 1999. *Production sharing in East Asia: Who does what for whom, and why?* Policy Research Working Paper No. 2197. Washington, D.C.: World Bank.

Rozelle, S., Park, A., Huang, J., and Hehui, J. 1996. *Bureaucrat to entrepreneur: The changing role of the state in China's transitional commodity economy.* Stanford, Calif.: Stanford University. Mimeographed.

Sen, A. K. 1983. *Poverty and famines: An essay on entitlement and deprivation.* Oxford: Clarendon Press.

Sicular, T. 1988. Plan and market in China's agricultural commerce. *Journal of Political Economy*, 96, pp. 383–87.

United States. House of Representatives. 2000. *An act to authorize extension of nondiscriminatory treatment to the People's Republic of China and to establish a framework for relations between the United States and the People's Republic of China.* H.R. 4444. Washington, D.C.: U.S. House of Representatives.

United States Trade Representative. 1999. Statement of Ambassador Charlene Barshevsky regarding broad market access gains resulting from China WTO negotiations. Press release, Washington, D.C., April 8.

World Bank. 1988. *China: External trade and capital.* Washington, D.C.: World Bank.

————. 1994. *China: Foreign trade reform.* Washington, D.C.: World Bank.

————. 1997a. *China: Long-term food security.* Washington, D.C.: World Bank.

————. 1997b. *China engaged: Integration with the world economy.* Washington, D.C.: World Bank.

————. 1999. *World development indicators.* Washington, D.C.: World Bank.

World Trade Organization. 1994a. *The results of the Uruguay Round of multilateral trade negotiations.* Geneva: World Trade Organization.

————. 1994b. *Uruguay Round of multilateral trade negotiations: Legal instruments embodying the results of the Uruguay Round of multilateral trade negotiations*, vol. 4. Geneva: World Trade Organization

Yin, X. 1996. China's trade policy reforms and their impact on industry. In D. Wall, J. Boke, and X. Yin, eds., *China's opening door.* London: Royal Institute of International Affairs.

Zhang, S., Zhang, Y., and Wan, Z. 1998. *Measuring the costs of protection in China.* Washington, D.C.: Institute for International Economics / Unirule Institute.

7

Sizing Up Foreign Direct Investment in China and India

Shang-jin Wei

Many developing countries made a remarkable transformation from being hostile to foreign direct investment (FDI) in the 1960s and 1970s to eagerly seeking it in the 1980s and 1990s. A celebrated example is China, which had virtually no foreign investment in the 1970s but now is a major host country of FDI. This chapter focuses on the magnitude of inward FDI into China and draws lessons that may be relevant for other developing countries. In particular, it considers the importance of the various dimensions of the business environment (including taxes, corruption, and regulatory burden) in determining the volume of inward FDI and whether an improvement in the business environment could increase FDI into China in a quantitatively significant way.

The economic consequences of inward FDI have been discussed elsewhere. For example, studies by Lardy (1992, 1994) and Wei (1996) have shown that foreign-invested firms have contributed significantly to China's impressive export expansion and overall economic growth. Indeed, as the Chinese economy slowed down due to the late-1990s Asian economic crisis, the Chinese government worried intensely about the consequence of a possible decline in the inward FDI into China.

China's leaders (and its people) are convinced that inward FDI can and does play an important role in their aspiration for sustained, rapid economic growth. To attract more FDI, China offers supranational treatment to foreign firms in a variety of ways (e.g., tax and nontax incentives that may be unavailable to domestic firms). By some measures, China's FDI policy is spectacularly successful. According to officially reported data on FDI into China (State Statistical Bureau, 1999), China for the past few years has been the largest developing-country host of FDI and the second-largest host in the world (after the United States). In fact, the figures on China's inward FDI look so impressive that some observers call China "the world's strongest magnet for overseas investment,"[1] or use the phrase

"China fever" to describe the inflow of FDI into the country.[2] If China has already been the "strongest magnet," is there much scope for its inward FDI to increase significantly?

India makes an interesting comparator for China. It is, of course, a latecomer on the stage. Its "open door" policy, beginning in 1991, has brought in more FDI, but its total FDI is still less than one-tenth that of China. The Indian government has been actively looking for ways to increase its inward FDI, including mimicking China in offering supernational treatment to foreign firms.

China and India do share some common features. Both countries are perceived to have relatively high levels of bureaucratic corruption. For example, a subjective corruption index promulgated in the *Global Competitiveness Report* (World Economic Forum, 1997) on a scale where 7 is the most corrupt rated China and India as 4.1 and 5.1, respectively (see Table 7.1). (In comparison, Singapore was rated 1.6.) Both China and India also have a Byzantine maze of bureaucratic red tape. According to a World Bank (1997) worldwide survey of firms, on a 1–7 scale where 7 indicates the highest regulatory burden, China and India received ratings of 4.6 and 5.1, respectively. (In comparison, Singapore's bureaucratic burden received a score of 2.1.)

TABLE 7.1

Business Environment in Selected Countries, 1990s

Host Country	GDP Per Capita	Growth	Corporate Tax	Corruption	Capital Control	Domestic Financial Repression
China	**631**	**0.47**	**30**	**4.1**	**11**	**6.01**
Colombia	2092	0.17	35	5.1	10	3.41
France	26692	0.03	33	2.6	4	2.91
Germany	29869	0.05	45	2	2	1.95
Hong Kong	23054	0.22	16.5	1.8	0	2.65
India	**413**	**0.18**	**40**	**5.1**	**12**	**4.45**
Indonesia	1105	0.30	30	5.5	9	3.87
Japan	42295	0.06	37.5	2.2	3	3.64
Korea	10728	0.28	30	4.3	10	4.27
Malaysia	4488	0.33	30	4	11	4.15
Mexico	3245	0.14	34	4.4	8	3.56
Philippines	1092	0.06	35	5.5	9	2.58
Russia	2271	−0.43	38	5.3	10	4.37
Singapore	29894	0.33	26	1.6	1	2.96
Taiwan	12861	0.26	25	3.3	.	2.84
Thailand	2957	0.33	30	5.5	9	4.83
United Kingdom	19263	0.04	24	1.5	1	2.5
United States	27471	0.08	35	1.9	3	2.16

NOTES:
1. GDP per capita data are from 1996; growth is for 1990–94, weighted growth from 1991–94 for Germany.
2. Domestic financial repression measured by interest rate control; source Global Competitiveness Report (97).
SOURCES: World Bank; World Economic Forum (1997).

Using data on U.S. outward FDI, Hines (1995) shows that American firms tend to invest less in more corrupt countries. He interpreted this as a consequence of the U.S. Foreign Corrupt Practice Act, which until 1999 had made the United States the only source country in the world that penalized its firms for bribing foreign government officials. Using a matrix of bilateral FDI from fourteen source countries to forty-one host countries, Wei (1997, 2001) shows that countries rated as more corrupt receive less FDI from all major source countries, not just from the United States.

This chapter aims to achieve several objectives. First, it investigates the importance of various dimensions of the business environment in attracting foreign direct investment. Second, it examines whether China's apparently impressive numbers on inward FDI make it an exceptional host. Third, it assesses the potential for China (or India) to increase the volume of inward FDI significantly if it can improve its business environment.

The chapter demonstrates that corruption and red tape are significant deterrents to FDI. Moreover, China is not an exception. On the contrary, as far as FDI from the major source countries is concerned, China is a significant underachiever as a host relative to its potential. While offering further tax benefits would raise China's or India's inward FDI only marginally, reducing red tape and corruption to a level comparable to Singapore could more than double FDI in these nations.

Using data from the United Nations Council of Trade and Development (UNCTAD), I fitted a linear regression on direct investment during 1987–90 from the world's five largest source countries to a number of host countries and compared China's actual reception of FDI with its potential as predicted by the regression (Wei, 1996). Based on that methodology, I found that FDI into China was significantly below its potential, in both the economic and the statistical sense.

A number of factors could explain that finding. First, given that China's opening up to foreign investment started relatively late (from 1980) and that the Tiananmen Square incident temporarily diminished FDI in 1989–90, 1987–90 may not be a good period to judge China's appeal as a host country. FDI in China has grown exponentially recently. For example, total FDI in China in 1997 was 1,200 percent more than that in 1990 (see Table 7.2). Second, the econometric specification was perhaps oversimplified. This could bias the result to exaggerate the potential amount of FDI that China could receive. Third, while my earlier work examined the host country size, level of development, and relationship with the source country as determinants of FDI, it neglected the importance of the business environment, particularly the extent of corrupt practice by government officials in the host country. This chapter seeks to advance our understanding of FDI into China in a number ways. I use more recent data with more

TABLE 7.2

*Realized Foreign Direct Investment
in China and India*

Annual Flows, 1980–2000
(billions of U.S. dollars)

Year	China	India
1980	0.15	0.01
1981	0.38	0.01
1982	0.41	0.07
1983	0.64	0.06
1984	1.26	0.06
1985	1.66	0.16
1986	1.88	0.21
1987	2.31	0.18
1988	3.19	0.29
1989	3.39	0.35
1990	3.49	0.10
1991	4.37	0.14
1992	11.01	0.26
1993	27.52	0.57
1994	33.77	0.95
1995	37.52	1.93
1996	41.73	2.42
1997	45.26	3.05
1998	45.46	3.00

SOURCES: United Nations; China State Statistics Bureau; China
Ministry of Foreign Trade; World Bank; Reserve Bank of India.

source countries (drawing on the bilateral stock of direct investment up to 1996
from the OECD). I employ fixed-effects, random-effects, and Tobit regressions
to check for robustness of the results. And I explicitly examine whether corruption and red tape have deterred FDI.

Evolution of China and India as Hosts of FDI

The Overall Picture

The transformation of China from a country with virtually no foreign investment
before 1979 to "the world's strongest magnet for overseas investment" is remarkable and has been well documented. To say that before 1979 China viewed foreign investors with suspicion is an understatement. The Chinese government was
downright hostile to private enterprises, including, if not especially, foreign-
owned private enterprises. Under Deng Xiaoping, the promulgation of the 1979
Law on Chinese-Foreign Equity Joint Ventures, together with the establishment
of four special economic zones, formally signaled the adoption of an "open door"
policy by the central government.

Consistent with the Chinese preferences for cautious reforms, the welcome mat for foreign direct investment was extended gradually at first. In the beginning, only equity joint ventures or contractual joint ventures were allowed. Wholly owned foreign firms were prohibited. Foreign exchange use was tightly regulated, and firms desiring to import raw materials, in principle, had to earn foreign exchange directly (at a time when no open market existed). There was a tight export performance requirement with, sometimes, 100 percent of the firm's output to be exported. In each of these areas, restrictions have been relaxed over time. For example, by now the annual value of inflow to establish wholly owned foreign firms (U.S.$16.5 billion in 1998) has exceeded that of contractual joint ventures (U.S.$9.3 billion in 1998) and is close to that of the equity joint ventures (U.S.$18.8 billion in 1998; Ministry of Foreign Trade and Economic Cooperation, 1999).

Table 7.3 shows the evolution of all the major laws and regulations promulgated by the Chinese and Indian central governments affecting FDI. Three things are worth noting. First, in terms of the starting date of the reform, China was a decade ahead of India.[3] Second, on several occasions over the past two decades, the Chinese government promulgated laws and regulations specifically designed to attract investment from overseas Chinese, particularly those in Hong Kong, Taiwan, and Macao. Third, China offers supernational treatment to foreign firms. For example, foreign firms typically receive an exemption of income tax for the first two profitable years followed by three additional years of 50 percent tax reduction. Such benefits are withheld from domestic Chinese firms.

In Chinese statistics, two notions of FDI are used: the contractual amount and the realized value. The contractual amount is the amount that investors plan to invest over a specified period at the time they apply for approval to invest. The actual or realized value is not bound by the contractual amount and is typically much smaller. Because the ability of local officials to attract foreign investment is often used by their superiors as an indicator of performance, government officials have an incentive to encourage foreign investors to overstate the (not legally binding) contractual amount. For this reason, all data on FDI in this chapter refer only to the realized values.

Table 7.2 shows the realized flow of FDI into China and India every year from 1980 to 1999. Until very recently, for China the growth has been truly exponential: the total inward FDI flow was a mere $640 million in 1983. It grew to $3.19 billion in 1988, to $33.77 billion in 1994, and to more than $45 billion in 1997 and 1998. The inflow of FDI did less well in 1999 and 2000 due to the East Asian crisis (and the slow adjustment of China's domestic economy). Every year since 1995, China received more foreign direct investment than any other country except the United States.

Foreign direct investment may be in the form of joint ventures, contractual

TABLE 7.3

Evolution of Laws and Regulations on FDI in China and India

	China	India
1979	Law on Chinese-foreign equity joint ventures.	
1986	Law on foreign capital enterprises: China permits foreign enterprises, other foreign economic organizations, and individuals to set up enterprises with foreign capital in China and protects the lawful rights and interests of such enterprises.	
1988	Law on Chinese-foreign contractual joint ventures.	
1990	Interim provisions for the duration of Chinese-foreign equity joint ventures. Regulations of the state council for encouraging investment from overseas Chinese and compatriots from Hong Kong and Macao. Regulations for contracted operation of Chinese-foreign equity joint ventures. Rules for the implementation of the law on foreign-capital enterprises.	
1991	Rules for the implementation of the income tax law for enterprises with foreign investment and foreign enterprises. Income tax law for enterprises with foreign investment and foreign enterprises.	Automatic approval for projects with foreign equity participation up to 51 percent in thirty-five high-priority sectors. All other proposals up to US$171 million and 100 percent equity approved by Foreign Investment Promotion Board (FIPB) or Secretariat of Industrial Approvals (SIA) on a case-by-case basis. Proposals for investment in excess of the above amount to be approved by the Cabinet Committee on Foreign Investment. Automatic approval of foreign technology agreements up to a lump-sum payment of US$2 million net of taxes with a 5 percent royalty on domestic sales and 8 percent for exports. Foreign investment up to 100 percent permitted in approved domestic venture capital funds/companies, with FIPB approval and for establishing asset management companies.

(continued)

TABLE 7.3
(*continued*)

China	India
	Liberalization of the Foreign Exchange Regulation Act reduced list of industries requiring industrial licensing.
	Dilution of MRTP reduction in the number of industries reserved for the public sector.
	Liberalization of imports and reduction in tariffs.
	Convertibility of the rupee on current account.
	Opening up of the capital market to foreign investors.
1994	Law of the People's Republic of China to protect and encourage investment of Taiwan compatriots and to promote the economic development on both sides of the Straits.
	Regulations on labor management in enterprises involving overseas investment to protect the legitimate rights and interests of both foreign-invested enterprises and the employees working in these enterprises and to establish, maintain, and develop stable and harmonious work relationships between the enterprises and their staffs.
1995	Detailed rules for the implementation of the law on Chinese-foreign cooperative joint ventures.
	Provisional regulations on the establishment of foreign-funded joint stock limited liability companies: foreign companies, enterprises, and other economic entities or individuals are allowed to jointly set up foreign-funded joint stock limited liability companies in China jointly with Chinese companies, enterprises, and other economic entities or individuals, under the principle of mutual benefit.
	Provisional regulations on investment companies established by foreign investors: foreign investors are permitted to establish investment companies in China in accordance with relevant Chinese laws and regulations concerning foreign investment.

(continued)

Provisions on the establishment of foreign-funded construction enterprises to meet the needs of opening up, strengthening the management of foreign-funded construction enterprises, and safeguarding the order of the construction market.

Implementation measures for the administration on import by foreign-funded enterprises.

Catalog for the guidance of foreign investment industries recognizing encouraged projects for foreign investment.

Interim provisions on guidance for foreign investment to guide foreign investment, adapt foreign investment to China's national economic and social development programs, and adequately protect the legal rights and interests of investors.

Rules on the approval and control of resident representative offices of foreign enterprises: foreign enterprises, when applying to set up resident representative offices within the territory of the People's Republic of China, must have the approval of the MOFTEC or its empowered foreign trade and economic cooperation commissions.

Detailed Rules on the Implementation of the Law on Sino-Foreign Joint Cooperative Ventures

Urgent Notice on Issues Relating to Current Examination and Approval of Enterprises with Foreign Investment.

1996

Regulations on the examination and approval of foreign-funded enterprises serving as agents for international cargo transport to standardize the work to examine and approve foreign-funded enterprises serving as agents for international cargo transport, and in accordance with state laws and regulations concerning foreign-funded enterprises and the provisions of China on the management of international cargo transport agency business.

Procedures to ensure the smooth progress of the process of liquidation of the foreign-funded enterprises (FFEs), protect the rights and interests of the creditors and investors, and safeguard the social and economic order related to the liquidation.

TABLE 7.3
(continued)

China	India
Circular of the State Council Concerning the Extension of the Limits of Power Vested with the Inland Provinces, Autonomous Regions, Cities Separately Listed in the State Plan and the Departments Concerned Under the State Council in Examining and Approving Direct Foreign Investment Projects Provisional Measures on the Establishment of Sino-Foreign Joint Venture Trading Companies on a Pilot Basis.	
Regulations concerning the examination and approval of international freight-forwarding agencies with foreign investment for standardizing the examination and approval of international freight-forwarding agencies with foreign investment.	
1998 Preferential taxation policies for FDI including exemptions from tariffs and import value-added tax for imports of capital goods by foreign-funded high-tech projects and 50 percent reduction of tariffs and import value-added tax for imports of capital goods by sectors where foreign investment is encouraged.	Indian companies no longer require prior clearances from the Reserve Bank of India for inward remittances of foreign exchange or for the issuance of shares to foreign investors.

SOURCES:
1. Information on rules, regulations, and laws for China is from the Ministry of Foreign Trade and Economic Cooperation (MOFTEC) (http://www.moftec.gov.cn/moftec/official/html/laws_and_regulations/foreign_investment.html).
2. Information on rules, regulations, and laws for India is from
http://www.docuweb.ca/India/news/9612.html#S0135
http://www.linktochina.com/Invest/indexinvest.html
http://strategis.ic.gc.ca/SSG/da90887e.html (U.S. Department of Commerce)

joint ventures, wholly owned foreign firms, or joint exploration arrangements (mainly for offshore oil). Joint ventures are by far the dominant form of FDI and account for roughly half of all FDI throughout the sample. Investment in the form of foreign wholly owned firms is catching up fast, growing by 400 percent cumulatively in 1992–96, compared to the 279 percent growth rate for all FDI in the same period.

Sources of FDI

Foreign direct investment into China comes from a very unusual assortment of countries. According to the United Nations, the world's five most important sources of direct investment outflows during 1990–95 were the United States, Japan, Germany, the United Kingdom, and France. Collectively, they accounted for over 70 percent of all direct investment from developed countries.

Yet if one looks at who invests in China (see Table 7.4), one finds that Hong Kong is the dominant direct investor in China. Hong Kong's annual inflow accounts for a half or more of the total FDI into China for each year from 1990 to 1997. Hong Kong's dominance tends to be more important in earlier years. So if one looks at the stock of FDI, Hong Kong's share is close to 60 percent. Japan and the United States are the second- and third-largest investors in China (the relative ranking may switch between the two, depending on the year). However, each typically invests less than a quarter of what Hong Kong invests. Britain, France, and Germany also are important source countries, but their investments lag distantly behind that of Hong Kong and sometimes also behind those of Singapore and Macao.

One may question whether Hong Kong's investment in mainland China should be counted as foreign direct investment. This is particularly so since July 1, 1997, when Britain formally returned the territory to China. Under these circumstances, one should probably now treat investment coming from Hong Kong as quasi-foreign.[4]

Part of the reported FDI from Hong Kong is in fact capital that originated in China and returned to the mainland disguised as Hong Kong investment (what is sometimes called "round-tripping" capital) to take advantage of tax, tariff, and other benefits accorded to foreign-invested firms. Chinese official estimates put round-tripping capital at 15 percent of the total FDI from Hong Kong (Huang, 1998). Such capital is best described as "false foreign direct investment." Using the 15 percent estimate, false foreign investment was on the order of U.S.$3 billion in 1997, or over 6 percent of the total FDI flow into China.

To summarize, if one excludes the false foreign and quasi-foreign direct investment in China, "true" FDI would be 50 percent smaller in terms of flows in recent years and 60 percent smaller in terms of accumulated stocks.

TABLE 7.4

Sources of Foreign Direct Investment in China

(flow data in millions of U.S. dollars)

Country	1990	1991	1992	1993	1994	1995	1996	1997
Hong Kong	1,880.00	2,405.25	7,507.07	17,274.75	19,665.44	20,060.37	20,677.32	20,632.00
Japan	503.38	532.50	709.83	1,324.10	2,075.29	3,108.46	3,679.35	4,326.47
U.S.A.	455.99	323.20	511.05	2,063.12	2,490.80	3,083.01	3,443.33	3,239.15
Germany	64.25	161.12	88.57	56.25	258.99	386.35	518.31	992.63
Macao	33.42	81.62	202.00	586.50	509.37	439.82	580.39	394.55
Singapore	50.43	58.21	122.31	490.04	1,179.61	1,851.22	2,243.56	2,606.41
U.K.	13.33	35.39	38.33	220.51	688.84	914.14	1,300.73	1,857.56
Italy	4.10	28.21	20.69	99.89	206.16	263.31	166.94	215.04
Thailand	6.72	19.62	83.03	233.18	234.87	288.24	323.31	194.00
Australia	24.87	14.91	35.03	109.96	188.26	232.99	193.92	313.74
Switzerland	1.48	12.31	29.14	41.02	70.54	63.53	187.61	215.67
Canada	8.04	10.76	58.24	136.88	216.05	257.02	337.93	344.12
France	21.06	9.88	44.93	141.41	192.04	287.02	423.75	474.65
Bermuda	0.00	8.00	0.29	18.53	50.74	109.14	86.12	104.89
Netherlands	15.98	6.67	28.41	84.00	111.05	114.11	125.11	413.80
Norway	2.23	6.05	5.06	1.34	2.31	1.53	26.79	6.46
Philippines	1.67	5.85	16.28	122.50	140.40	105.78	55.51	155.63
Panama	6.76	3.56	8.19	14.84	18.30	15.66	15.47	7.547
Ireland	0.00	2.50	1.00	1.50	0.00	0.99	10.03	0.3
Indonesia	1.00	2.18	20.17	65.75	115.70	111.63	93.54	79.98
Malaysia	0.64	1.96	24.67	91.42	200.99	259.00	459.95	381.83
Total	3,487.11	4,366.34	11,007.51	27,514.95	33,766.50	37,520.53	41,725.52	45,257.04

SOURCE: China Ministry of Foreign Trade and Economic Cooperation.

China as a Host of Direct Investment from the Major Source Countries

I now turn to examining whether China is an underachiever as a host of investment from the world's major source countries and whether corruption has deterred foreign investment. Let me first explain the data and the specifications of the statistical framework before presenting and discussing the results.

Data

Foreign Direct Investment

I focus on the bilateral stock of foreign direct investment from seventeen major source countries to forty-two host countries. To minimize the influence of year-to-year variations in the data, I use the three-year average over 1994–96. The data come from the OECD bilateral FDI database covering outward FDI by destination, based on reports by individual source countries, including the United States, Japan, Germany, the United Kingdom, France, Italy, and Norway. The number of host countries is constrained by the availability of data on corruption and taxes.

The data set "relies on a database developed by the OECD Directorate for Financial, Fiscal and Enterprise Affairs for comprehensive statistics on international direct investment. Data collection is based on a joint OECD/EUROSTAT questionnaire" (Organization for Economic Cooperation and Development, 1998, p. 9). The raw data typically come from source countries' national statistical offices or central banks. Efforts were made by the OECD to improve the comparability of the data across countries "based on the recommendation of the *IMF Balance of Payments Manual*, Fifth Edition, and the *OECD Benchmark Definition of Foreign Direct Investment*, Third Edition." Despite these efforts, there are still questions about comparability of FDI definitions across reporting countries. The most notable reason for a lack of comparability is that reinvested earnings are counted as part of FDI by some source countries (which is conceptually correct) but not by others (OECD, 1998, p. 9).[5]

As a digression, it is useful to compare FDI into China as reported by the Chinese against that reported by the investing country. Table 7.5 presents such a comparison (of annual flows) for 1990–97. A striking feature is the sometimes quite large discrepancies in the bilateral FDI from the two reporting sources. For example, in 1996 and 1997, the Chinese source claims to have received FDI inflows from the United States on the order of U.S.$3.4 billion and $3.2 billion, respectively. The Americans (based on a survey of U.S. firms by the U.S. Commerce Department) report only $0.9 billion and $1.2 billion, respectively, in those years. The estimates differ by a multiple of 3. Generally speaking, the Chinese-reported inflows were much greater than the source countries' own reporting for FDI from the United Kingdom, France, Australia, and Italy as well.

The notable exceptions are FDI from Japan and Germany, where the re-

TABLE 7.5

Foreign Direct Investment Flow into China: Chinese versus Source Country Statistics (U.S. $ millions)

Country	1990	1991	1992	1993	1994	1995	1996	1997
U.S.A.								
(OECD report)	30	40	74	556	1,232	261	941	1,217[P]
(Chinese report)	455.99	323.20	511.05	2,063.12	2,490.80	3,083.01	3,443.33	3,239.15
Japan								
(OECD report)	349	579	1,070	1,691	2,565	3,834	2,599/	—
(Chinese report)	503.38	532.50	709.83	1,324.10	2,075.29	3,108.46	3,679.35	4,326.47
Germany								
(OECD report)	—	75.86	144	64.88	304.11	437.39	763.33	723.53
(Chinese report)	64.25	161.12	88.57	56.25	258.99	386.35	518.31	922.63
U.K.								
(OECD report)	—	31.80	30.24	31.11	12.5	83.7	351.67	—
(Chinese report)	13.33	35.39	38.33	220.51	688.84	914.14	1,300.73	1,857.56
France								
(OECD report)	-2.14	89.38	53.75	85.66	113.54	141.43	250.98	226.38
(Chinese report)	21.06	9.88	44.93	141.41	192.04	287.02	423.75	474.65
Australia								
(OECD report)	—	—	—	10.83	38.84	24.59	—	—
(Chinese report)	24.87	14.91	35.03	109.96	188.26	232.99	—	—
Italy								
(OECD report)	—	—	19.48	2.55	20.46	31.31	88.14	115.69
(Chinese report)	4.10	28.21	20.69	99.89	206.16	263.31	166.94	215.04
Netherlands								
(OECD report)	—	6.32	-31.11	-15.79	184.44	105.63	294.12	—
(Chinese report)	15.98	6.67	28.41	84.00	111.05	114.11	125.11	413.80
Switzerland								
(OECD report)	—	—	—	21.33	120	285	306.67	164.67
(Chinese report)	1.48	12.31	29.14	41.02	70.54	63.53	187.61	215.67

SOURCES: Organization for Economic Cooperation and Development (1998); China Statistical Bureau; China Ministry of Foreign Trade.

ported numbers from the two sources were comparable. However, it is worth noting that the Japanese reported number refers to the approval values of FDI rather than actual realized values. Since the former is generally much bigger than the latter, it is quite possible that the Chinese reported FDI from Japan is still greater than the real amount coming from Japan. German-reported German investment in China is based on an annual stock survey of German firms. In Germany, a reporting obligation exists if a resident holds more than 20 percent of the shares or voting rights in a foreign enterprise. Hence a German–Chinese joint venture in which the German share is less than a fifth would not be reported in the German data but would be reported in the Chinese data.

There are several reasons why the Chinese data may be overstated. Some are related to bureaucrats' incentive to exaggerate their ability to attract FDI and foreign investors' incentive to exaggerate the amount of investment in order to report lower taxable incomes. But there are also plausible reasons why the OECD numbers may be understated: for example, reinvested dividends may not be accurately counted. Given that the Chinese reported annual *inflows* were often bigger than the entire *stock* as reported by the source countries in the same years, it seems likely that the Chinese figures contain much fat.

Whatever the pluses and minuses, in the interest of using a consistent database, all of the subsequent regressions are run using the OECD data. I will, however, discuss the implications of measurement errors on the interpretation of the statistical results.

Other Measures

By its very nature, corruption is difficult, if not impossible, to measure objectively. Researchers have relied on corruption perception indexes based on surveys of experts or firms. For example, the Business International (BI) index, based on surveys conducted during 1980–83, asked the expert or consultant to rank a country according to "the degree to which business transactions involve corruption or questionable payments." Mauro (1995) and Wei (2000) used it to examine the relationship between economic growth and corruption and between FDI and corruption. Unfortunately, the BI index does not cover China in its sample.

The *corruption* measure that I use in this chapter is a perception index based on a survey of 2,827 firms in fifty-eight countries conducted by the World Economic Forum in 1996 for its *Global Competitiveness Report, 1997* (GCR97). Question 8.02 in the survey asks the respondent to rank the level of corruption in his or her country on a scale of 1 to 7, according to the extent of "irregular, additional payments connected with imports and exports permits, business licenses, exchange controls, tax assessments, police protection or loan applications." The corruption rating used in this chapter is based on the country averages of individual responses. (The original rating is such that a low number implies high corruption. I have transformed the number so that the higher number means more corruption: the new rating is defined as 8 minus the original rating.)

Regulatory burden is based on the GCR97 survey question (Question 2.02) that asks the respondents to rank the "pervasiveness" of "administrative regulations that constrain business." Again, in the original rating, a lower number means more pervasive regulatory burden. With a transformation, the rating used in this chapter is 8 minus the original rating.

Capital controls are derived by adding up to twelve possible restrictions on capital account transactions as identified at the back of the International Monetary Fund's 1997 *Annual Report on Exchange Arrangements and Exchange Restrictions*. A possible hypothesis is that foreign exchange control is an impediment to the movement of capital that makes it less attractive for foreign director investors to invest.

Interest rate control is meant to be a measure of the degree of domestic financial repression. It is similarly based on a GCR97 survey question that asks the respondents the degree to which "deposit and lending interest rates in your country are freely determined by the market." I have transformed the index so that the new value equals 8 minus the original value. One hypothesis is that financial repression could promote FDI by *lowering* the cost of capital. An opposite hypothesis is that financial repression is often associated with the rationing of credit (and denial of cheap domestic credits to foreign investors). So it may discourage FDI by *raising* the cost of capital for foreign investors.

For the host countries' *tax rates*, I use the marginal corporate income tax (the top bracket), which also appear in the *World Competitiveness Report* (World Economic Forum, 1997). The *GDP* data come from the International Monetary Fund's *International Financial Statistics Yearbook* (1998). In a few cases where GDP data are unavailable, GNP data are substituted. The *wage* data are from the International Labor Organization (1995).

The *distance* data measure the "great circle distance" between the economic centers in source-host pairs. The dummy on *linguistic tie* takes the value of one if the source and host countries share a common language, and zero otherwise.[6]

Econometric Specification

I perform three different specifications. I start with a fixed-effects regression that includes separate dummies for all source countries:

$$\text{Log(FDI}_{jk}) = \beta + X_{jk}\Gamma + e_{jk}$$

where β denotes the source country fixed effects, Γ is a vector of parameters, and X_{jk} is a vector of determinants of bilateral FDI. For example, we start with four control variables:

$X_{jk} = [\log(\text{GDP}_k), \log(\text{GDP}_k/\text{population}_k), \log(\text{distance}_{jk}), \text{linguistic tie}_{jk}]$

Later on, I add other control variables including country k's marginal corporate income tax rate (in the highest bracket), its (perceived) level of corruption, and its regulatory burden. Finally, e_{jk} is assumed to be an independently and identically normally distributed variable with a zero mean.

This specification assumes that the error terms are uncorrelated with each other. If a particular characteristic of the host country that is a relevant determinant of FDI is missing from the specification, it would induce a host-country-specific component of the error term leading to correlated errors across observations for the same host country. As a second specification, I also implement a random-effects regression that assumes a host-specific error term:

$$\text{Log(FDI}_{jk}) = \beta + X_{jk}\Gamma + u_k + e_{jk}$$

where u_k is a host-specific normal variate with zero mean, e_{jk} is the same as before (i.i.d. across all observations), and the two terms are uncorrelated with each other.

Some host countries receive no direct investment from certain source countries. A potential drawback of the previous specifications is that observations of zero FDI are dropped by this specification. Therefore, I also implement a Tobit version of the fixed-effects regression:

$$\begin{aligned}\text{Log(FDI}_{jk} + A) &= \text{fixed effects} + X_{jk}\Gamma + e_{jk} \text{ if FDI}_{jk} > 0 \\ &= \ln(A) \qquad\qquad\qquad\quad \text{if otherwise}\end{aligned}$$

where A is a constant (set to 0.1 in the reported tables, although alternative values would not make a difference qualitatively), u is an i.i.d. normal variate with mean zero and variance σ^2. In this specification, if $X\Gamma + u$ exceeds a threshold value, $\ln(A)$, source country j accumulates a positive stock of investment in host country; otherwise, the realized foreign investment is zero (and the desired level could be negative).

Regression Results and Interpretation

Basic Findings

The first three columns in Table 7.6 implement a fixed-effects, a random-effects, and the Tobit regression on the benchmark specification. Aside from the source country dummies, the list of regressors include marginal tax rate; host country's GDP and per capita GDP, both in logarithmic form;[7] log distance between the economic centers of the source and host countries; a dummy if the source and the host share a common linguistic tie and a historical colonial tie; and

TABLE 7.6

China as a Host for FDI Compared to Its Potential

(dependent variable: log of FDI stock[1])

	Fixed[2] Effects OLS	Fixed[2] Effects Tobit	Random[3] Effects	Fixed Effects OLS	Fixed Effects Tobit	Random Effects
China	—	—	—	−1.021**	−1.070**	−1.522*
				(0.461)	(0.543)	(0.821)
India	—	—	—	−1.018**	−1.421**	−1.184#
				(0.472)	(0.548)	(0.803)
Log (GDP)[4]	0.829**	0.961**	0.909**	0.885**	1.023**	0.978**
	(0.052)	(0.060)	(0.084)	(0.056)	(0.064)	(0.092)
Log (per capita GDP)[4]	0.209**	0.144**	0.134#	0.095	0.010	0.000
	(0.056)	(0.065)	(0.092)	(0.070)	(0.080)	(0.113)
Log (distance)	−0.654**	−0.835**	−0.930**	−0.692**	−0.876**	−0.961**
	(0.072)	(0.084)	(0.076)	(0.073)	(0.085)	(0.076)
Linguistic tie	1.609**	1.910**	1.091**	1.626**	1.938**	1.068**
	(0.220)	(0.258)	(0.202)	(0.220)	(0.258)	(0.201)
Lagged growth rate	0.536#	0.981**	1.297**	0.844**	1.306**	1.674**
	(0.368)	(0.430)	(0.582)	(0.388)	(0.451)	(0.625)
Corporate tax rate	−0.037**	−0.029**	−0.036**	−0.038**	−0.028**	−0.037**
	(0.009)	(0.010)	(0.014)	(0.009)	(0.010)	(0.015)
Number of observations	580	620	580	580	620	580
R[2]†	0.72	0.26	0.72	0.72	0.26	0.73

NOTES:

**5 percent significant, *10 percent significant, #15 percent significant. Standard errors in parentheses.

[1] Average, 1994–96.

[2] $Y(i,j) = a(i) + BX(i,j) + e(i,j)$, where i is source index and j is host index.

All regressions include a source country dummy. Not reported to save space.

[3] $Y(i,j) =$ source dummy $+ BX(i,j) + e(i,j)$

[4] Average, 1994–96.

†Adjusted R^2 for fixed effects, overall R^2 for random effect, and pseudo R^2 for tobit.

the lagged growth rate of the economy. The last three columns of Table 7.6 replicate these regressions with the addition of two dummies for China and India as host countries, respectively.

The coefficient on the tax rate is negative and statistically significant, indicating high taxes tend to discourage foreign investment. The coefficient on log(GDP) is positive, significant, but less than 1, suggesting that larger economies receive more FDI, although the increment in FDI is less than proportional to the increment in country size. The coefficient on log(distance) is negative but significant. That on the linguistic dummy is positive, significant, and quantitatively large.

The key variables of interest are the dummies for China and India as host countries for FDI from the major source countries. The coefficients on both variables are −1.02, and statistically significant at the 5 percent level. In other words, controlling for this list of regressors, China, like India, is a significant underachiever as a host of FDI. The quantitative effect is large. Taking the point

TABLE 7.7

Adding Public Policies and Public Institutions

(dependent variable: log of FDI stock[1])

	Fixed Effect[2] OLS	Fixed Effect[2] Tobit	Random Effect[3]	Fixed Effect OLS	Fixed Effect Tobit	Random Effect
China	—	—	—	−1.314**	−1.660**	−1.458#
				(0.508)	(0.593)	(0.894)
India	—	—	—	−1.567**	−2.034**	−1.580**
				(0.458)	(0.528)	(0.786)
Log (GDP)[4]	1.022**	1.155**	1.108**	1.086**	1.230**	1.169**
	(0.059)	(0.068)	(0.094)	(0.061)	(0.069)	(0.100)
Log (per capita GDP)[4]	−0.043	−0.140	−0.037	−0.282**	−0.441**	−0.257
	(0.100)	(0.115)	(0.159)	(0.118)	(0.136)	(0.190)
Log (distance)	−0.780**	−0.950**	−1.003**	−0.812**	−0.985**	−1.021**
	(0.077)	(0.089)	(0.078)	(0.076)	(0.088)	(0.078)
Linguistic tie	1.313**	1.592**	0.994**	1.305**	1.579**	0.979**
	(0.219)	(0.256)	(0.204)	(0.219)	(0.254)	(0.203)
Lagged growth rate	0.446	0.693#	1.008*	0.763**	1.083**	1.327**
	(0.373)	(0.433)	(0.611)	(0.382)	(0.442)	(0.645)
Corporate tax rate	−0.028**	−0.018*	−0.028*	−0.027**	−0.017*	−0.027*
	(0.009)	(0.010)	(0.015)	(0.009)	(0.010)	(0.015)
Corruption	−0.050	−0.058	−0.031	−0.146*	−0.174*	−0.112
	(0.081)	(0.094)	(0.128)	(0.087)	(0.099)	(0.138)
Regulatory burden	−0.302**	−0.374**	−0.283#	−0.317**	−0.395**	−0.315#
	(0.113)	(0.131)	(0.189)	(0.112)	(0.129)	(0.195)
Capital controls	0.008	−0.029	0.017	−0.006	−0.048#	0.005
	(0.027)	(0.031)	(0.043)	(0.027)	(0.031)	(0.045)
Interest rate control	−0.391**	−0.289**	−0.457**	−0.309**	−0.186#	−0.367**
	(0.102)	(0.118)	(0.167)	(0.111)	(0.128)	(0.187)
OECD	−0.647**	−0.771**	−0.894**	−0.594**	−0.694**	−0.810**
	(0.190)	(0.219)	(0.294)	(0.189)	(0.218)	(0.305)
Number of observations	570	608	570	570	608	570
R²[†]	0.75	0.28	0.76	0.75	0.28	0.76

NOTES:

**5 percent significant, *10 percent significant, #15 percent significant. Standard errors in parentheses.

[1] Average, 1994–96.

[2] $Y(i,j) = a(i) + BX(i,j) + e(i,j)$, where i is source index and j is host index.

All regressions include a source country dummy. Not reported to save space.

[3] $Y(i,j)$ = source dummy + $BX(i,j) + e(i,j)$

[4] Average, 1994–96.

[†] Adjusted R^2 for fixed effects, overall R^2 for random effect, and pseudo R^2 for tobit.

estimates on the China dummy and the tax variable literally, one needs to raise the tax rate by 30 percentage points (= 1.02/0.037) to reduce the inward FDI as much as to explain the negative coefficient on the China (and India) dummy.

Corruption and Other Measures of Public Institutions

In Table 7.7, we add a set of variables measuring the quality of public institutions. The new variables are corruption, regulatory burden, capital controls, and the extent of domestic financial market repression (interest rate control). The relative quantitative effect of corruption on FDI is also significant. A one-step worsening in the GCR97 corruption rating would be equivalent to raising the marginal tax rate by 5 percentage points. An increase in the host country corruption rating from the Singapore level (GCR97 index = 1.6) to the China level (GCR97 index = 4.1) has the same effect on inward FDI as raising the tax rate by 12.5 percentage points (= 2.5 × 5). In other words, the (perceived) corruption in China is likely to have significantly discouraged foreign direct investment.

Flow of FDI

As we noted earlier, the welcome mat from the Chinese government for FDI was extended gradually. As well, China (and India) started with an extraordinarily low level of FDI in the early 1980s. This raises the possibility that China is a supermagnet for FDI as far as recent *annual flows* are concerned, even if its *stock* of inward FDI remains low.

Such an argument may be invalid, as twenty years of liberalization seems long enough. Nevertheless, in Table 7.8, I replicate the key regressions in Table 7.7 for a dependent variable based on FDI inflow. There are three noteworthy results. First, both the China and India dummies continue to be negative, implying that China underperforms relative to its potential, even if one only looks at the inflows. Second, the gap between actual and potential FDI is much bigger for India than for China. Third, corruption and the regulatory burden continue to affect inflows of FDI negatively in most regressions, although relative to their (increased) standard errors, the effect is not always statistically significant.

The Hong Kong Connection

It is often remarked that Hong Kong is a mecca for foreign direct investment. It seems possible that partly because the investors from the major source countries loathe the corruption and red tape situation on the mainland, they invest heavily in Hong Kong as a stepping-stone to or substitute for investing in China itself. Indeed, part of the Hong Kong investment in China may have been made on behalf of investors from the major source countries.

To see if the Hong Kong connection helps solve the puzzle of China's underachievement, I redefine all the FDI into Hong Kong from the major source countries as part of the FDI into China from the same source countries and eliminate Hong Kong as a separate host in the regressions. Furthermore, I do not upgrade the business environment of the Chinese economy toward that of Hong Kong (e.g., reducing the rating on corruption and regulatory burden, which would have raised the potential amount of FDI and hence the gap between the actual and potential FDI). It is important to bear in mind that this is an overadjustment since a substantial part of FDI into Hong Kong is truly des-

TABLE 7.8

Inflow of FDI

(dependent variable: log of FDI flow[1])

	Fixed Effect[2] OLS	Fixed Effect[2] Tobit	Random Effect[3]	Fixed Effect OLS	Fixed Effect Tobit	Random Effect
China	—	—	—	−1.325#	−1.636#	−0.949
				(0.830)	(0.993)	(1.310)
India	—	—	—	−2.068★★	−2.400★★	−1.715#
				(0.680)	(0.813)	(1.120)
Log (GDP)[4]	0.791★★	0.951★★	0.870★★	0.851★★	1.017★★	0.925★★
	(0.083)	(0.097)	(0.142)	(0.084)	(0.099)	(0.150)
Log (per capita GDP)[4]	−0.026	−0.235	−0.067	−0.373★	−0.646★★	−0.298
	(0.160)	(0.188)	(0.244)	(0.204)	(0.240)	(0.303)
Log (distance)	−0.865★★	−0.955★★	−0.868★★	−0.876★★	−0.965★★	−0.872★★
	(0.100)	(0.118)	(0.102)	(0.099)	(0.116)	(0.102)
Linguistic tie	0.897★★	1.017★★	0.828★★	0.964★★	1.080★★	0.841★★
	(0.273)	(0.321)	(0.263)	(0.273)	(0.321)	(0.264)
Lagged growth	1.044	1.986★★	1.196	1.150	2.102★★	1.325
	(0.840)	(0.998)	(1.371)	(0.830)	(0.984)	(1.397)
Corporate tax rate	−0.020★	−0.026★	−0.031#	−0.020★	−0.025★	−0.030#
	(0.011)	(0.014)	(0.020)	(0.011)	(0.013)	(0.021)
Corruption	−0.061	0.060	0.009	−0.227#	−0.139	−0.077
	(0.128)	(0.151)	(0.199)	(0.145)	(0.172)	(0.218)
Regulatory burden	−0.234#	−0.342★	−0.230	−0.169	−0.265	−0.226
	(0.160)	(0.190)	(0.282)	(0.159)	(0.189)	(0.288)
Capital controls	0.027	−0.032	0.016	−0.001	−0.067	0.001
	(0.041)	(0.048)	(0.064)	(0.042)	(0.049)	(0.067)
Interest rate control	−0.242★	−0.349★★	−0.311	−0.178	−0.264	−0.268
	(0.147)	(0.174)	(0.244)	(0.159)	(0.189)	(0.274)
OECD	−0.728★★	−0.607★	−0.687#	−0.747★★	−0.622★	−0.663#
	(0.288)	(0.338)	(0.426)	(0.284)	(0.332)	(0.433)
Number of observations	267	274	267	267	274	267
R[2]†	0.66	0.21	0.69	0.67	0.22	0.70

NOTES:

★★5 percent significant, ★10 percent significant, #15 percent significant. Standard errors in parentheses.

[1] Average, 1990–95.

[2] $Y(i,j) = a(i) + BX(i,j) + e(i,j)$, where i is source index and j is host index. All regressions include a source country dummy. Not reported to save space.

[3] $Y(i,j) = $ source dummy $ + BX(i,j) + e(i,j)$

[4] Average, 1990–95.

† Adjusted R^2 for fixed effects, overall R^2 for random effect, and pseudo R^2 for tobit.

tined for Hong Kong. Nonetheless, it is interesting to see if such a draconian adjustment could turn the China dummy from a significant negative to zero.

The results are reported in Tables 7.9 (stocks) and 7.10 (flows). As it turns out, the coefficient on the Hong Kong dummy is now indifferent from zero but continues to be negative. This experiment is highly arbitrary. It serves nevertheless to demonstrate that the gap between the actual FDI into China and the

TABLE 7.9

Hong Kong Connection for FDI Stock

(dependent variable: log of FDI stock[1])

	Fixed Effects[2] OLS	Fixed Effects[2] Tobit	Random Effects[3]
China	0.087	−0.650	−0.056
	(0.518)	(0.604)	(0.917)
India	−1.542★★	−2.018★★	−1.567★
	(0.461)	(0.538)	(0.803)
Log (GDP)[4]	1.087★★	1.233★★	1.173★★
	(0.061)	(0.071)	(0.102)
Log (per capita GDP)[4]	−0.287★★	−0.442★★	−0.261
	(0.119)	(0.138)	(0.193)
Log (distance)	−0.818★★	−0.971★★	−1.039★★
	(0.077)	(0.090)	(0.079)
Linguistic tie	1.239★★	1.554★★	0.882★★
	(0.224)	(0.263)	(0.208)
Lagged growth rate	0.742★	1.039★★	1.348★★
	(0.387)	(0.452)	(0.661)
Corporate tax rate	−0.029★★	−0.018★	−0.028★
	(0.009)	(0.010)	(0.016)
Corruption	−0.147★	−0.179★	−0.115
	(0.087)	(0.101)	(0.140)
Regulatory burden	−0.328★★	−0.409★★	−0.316#
	(0.115)	(0.134)	(0.203)
Capital controls	−0.010	−0.051#	0.005
	(0.028)	(0.033)	(0.048)
Interest rate control	−0.299★★	−0.174	−0.367★
	(0.113)	(0.132)	(0.194)
OECD	−0.623★★	−0.705★★	−0.830★★
	(0.194)	(0.227)	(0.320)
Number of observations	555	593	555
R^2[†]	0.75	0.28	0.76

NOTES:

★★5 percent significant, ★10 percent significant, #15 percent significant. Standard errors in parentheses.

[1] Average, 1994–96.

[2] $Y(i,j) = a(i) + BX(i,j) + e(i,j)$, where i is source index and j is host index. All regressions include a source country dummy. Not reported to save space.

[3] $Y(i,j)$ = source dummy + $BX(i,j) + e(i,j)$

[4] Average, 1994–96.

[†] Adjusted R^2 for fixed effects, overall R^2 for random effect, and pseudo R^2 for tobit.

potential amount as defined by these regressions is enormous. Furthermore, while the existence of Hong Kong may have helped China attract FDI from the major source countries, it does not fully compensate for corruption, regulatory burden, and other elements of the Chinese environment that have discouraged FDI.

TABLE 7.10

Hong Kong Connection for FDI Flow

(dependent variable: log of FDI flow[1])

	Fixed Effect[2] OLS	Fixed Effect[2] Tobit	Random Effect[3]	Fixed Effect OLS	Fixed Effect Tobit	Random Effect
China	−0.615	−0.678	−0.345	−0.339	−0.672	0.024
	(0.705)	(0.745)	(1.029)	(0.828)	(0.992)	(1.327)
India	−0.971★	−1.041★	−0.758	−2.058★★	−2.416★★	−1.696#
	(0.588)	(0.621)	(0.878)	(0.677)	(0.810)	(1.132)
Log (FDI1990)	0.487★★	0.495★★	0.498★★	—	—	—
	(0.051)	(0.054)	(0.053)			
Log (GDP)[4]	0.263★★	0.298★★	0.286★★	0.855★★	1.021★★	0.936★★
	(0.094)	(0.100)	(0.134)	(0.084)	(0.098)	(0.151)
Log (per capita GDP)[4]	−0.223	−0.442★★	−0.202	−0.376★	−0.657★★	−0.305
	(0.174)	(0.181)	(0.241)	(0.203)	(0.239)	(0.305)
Log (distance)	−0.480★★	−0.438★★	−0.446★★	−0.883★★	−0.961★★	−0.889★★
	(0.095)	(0.100)	(0.099)	(0.099)	(0.116)	(0.102)
Linguistic tie	0.221	0.009	0.203	0.856★★	0.957★★	0.682★★
	(0.245)	(0.258)	(0.236)	(0.277)	(0.325)	(0.266)
Lagged growth	−0.314	−0.203	−0.358	1.183	2.056★★	1.320
	(0.738)	(0.779)	(1.113)	(0.835)	(0.993)	(1.425)
Corporate tax rate	−0.005	−0.010	−0.010	−0.021★	−0.026★	−0.031#
	(0.010)	(0.010)	(0.016)	(0.011)	(0.014)	(0.021)
Corruption	−0.220★	−0.196#	−0.105	−0.239★	−0.161	−0.094
	(0.124)	(0.131)	(0.173)	(0.145)	(0.172)	(0.220)
Administrative regulations	−0.122	−0.144	−0.194	−0.190	−0.277#	−0.246
	(0.138)	(0.146)	(0.227)	(0.161)	(0.191)	(0.297)
Capital controls	0.053	0.016	0.052	−0.008	−0.072	−0.003
	(0.037)	(0.039)	(0.055)	(0.043)	(0.051)	(0.071)
Interest rate control	0.159	0.062	0.111	−0.155	−0.242	−0.250
	(0.142)	(0.149)	(0.219)	(0.160)	(0.190)	(0.280)
OECD	−0.008	0.217	0.171	−0.808★★	−0.662★	−0.725#
	(0.264)	(0.277)	(0.363)	(0.289)	(0.339)	(0.445)
Number of observations	252	253	252	259	266	259
R²†	0.75	0.30	0.77	0.68	0.23	0.70

NOTE:

★★5 percent significant, ★10 percent significant, #15 percent significant. Standard errors in parentheses.

[1] Average, 1990−95.

[2] $Y(i,j) = a(i) + BX(i,j) + e(i,j)$, where i is source index and j is host index.
All regressions include a source country dummy. Not reported to save space.

[3] $Y(i,j)$ = source dummy + $BX(i,j) + e(i,j)$

[4] Average, 1990−95.

† Adjusted R^2 for fixed effects, overall R^2 for random effect, and pseudo R^2 for tobit.

Concluding Remarks

Although the absolute values of FDI into China in recent years look impressive, the aggregate situation masks the unusual composition of source countries. A significant fraction (maybe 15 percent) of Hong Kong's investment in China could be round-tripping mainland capital in disguise. This should be counted as false foreign direct investment and should be deleted from the statistics on FDI into China.

The remaining part of Hong Kong investment in China should be regarded as quasi-foreign direct investment, for Hong Kong has always been a special extension of China even under British rule and since July 1, 1997, has legally been part of China. Taking out these two parts would reduce the annual flows of FDI into China in recent years by half and the stock by 60 percent.

A comparison of FDI into China reported by the official host source with that reported by the investing countries generally reveals a big discrepancy. The amount of inward FDI from the United States, the United Kingdom, France, and other countries as claimed by China is often two to three times larger than what is reported by the corresponding investing countries. One possible explanation is that the official Chinese statistics on FDI contain serious fat.

Using cross-national data on bilateral stocks of FDI from the seventeen most important source countries, one can estimate the potential amount of inward FDI for a host country such as China as a function of its economic and policy characteristics. Compared with the model-predicted potential, China is found to be a significant underachiever as a host of FDI from the major source countries. The gap is huge. There is evidence to suggest that China's relatively high corruption and regulatory burden discourage FDI by a significant amount.

If we take the point estimates literally, the high corruption and regulatory burden have discouraged far more FDI than generous tax provisions have helped attract. A positive way to read the same message would be this: China and India have not exhausted their potential as hosts for foreign investment. For the sake of concreteness, I perform a "thought experiment" on how much China and India's inward FDI might increase if they could improve their business environments by reducing their respective corruption and regulatory burden to the same levels as in Singapore.

Reducing corruption to the Singapore level means a reduction in the corruption ratings by 2.5 and 3.5 for China and India, respectively (see Table 7.11). Similarly, reducing regulatory burden to the Singapore level means a drop in the corresponding ratings by 2.5 and 3.12 for China and India, respectively. Taking the fixed-effects (linear) regression as the benchmark, the coefficients on corruption and red tape are -0.146 and -0.317, respectively. Therefore, for China, reducing these variables to the Singapore levels would imply an increase in log(FDI) by 1.158. In other words, the new hypothetical level of FDI into China would be more than twice the current level. Similar calculation implies that FDI into India, if it reduces its corruption and regulatory burden to Singapore levels, would be almost 3½ times current flows.

Of course, the calculation here is meant to be illustrative. Reducing corruption and eliminating excessive regulation is much more easily said than done.[8] In addition, China and, to a much lesser extent, India have received large vol-

TABLE 7.11

Increment in FDI as a Result of Reducing Corruption and Red Tape

	China	India
"Experiment"		
Reducing corruption to Singapore level	$4.1 - 1.6 = 2.5$	$5.1 - 1.6 = 3.5$
Reducing regulatory burden to Singapore level	$4.58 - 2.08 = 2.5$	$5.1 - 2.08 = 3.12$
"Outcome"		
Increment in log(FDI)	$2.5 \times 0.146 + 2.5 \times 0.317$ $= 1.158$	$3.5 \times 0.146 + 3.12 \times 0.317$ $= 1.50$
Percentage increase in FDI [FDI(new)/FDI(current) − 1]	$\exp\{1.158\} - 1 = 218$	$\exp\{1.50\} - 1 = 348$

NOTES:
1. FDI(new) is the hypothetical new level of FDI if the country could manage to reduce corruption and red tape to the corresponding Singapore levels.
2. Calculations are based on the fixed-effects linear regression in Table 7.8 in which the point estimates on corruption and red tape are -0.146 and -0.317, respectively.

umes of FDI. Increments in FDI for these economies in response to a given improvement in public governance would probably be less than for a smaller host country.[9] Nonetheless, the illustrative calculation suggests the possibility that both China and particularly India could increase their inward FDI dramatically if they were to improve their business environment significantly.

Notes

1. *Economist*, March 1, 1997, p. 38.
2. P. T. Bangserg, *Journal of Commerce*, December 27, 1996, p. 3A.
3. By contrast, when the Indian government decided to open up in 1991, it chose to liberalize more quickly than China.
4. A portion of the Hong Kong investment may be disguised Taiwanese investment made to avoid political inconvenience with the Taiwanese government. If one adopts the view that Taiwan and China belong to the same country, which is the official position of the two governments on both sides of Taiwan Strait, then this part of investment should also be treated as quasi-foreign. Another portion of the Hong Kong investment may in fact be investment from the world's major source countries such as the United States and the United Kingdom. This portion is not likely to be substantial. We will return to this topic later in the chapter.
5. For details, see the "Technical Notes" for each source country at the end of the OECD yearbook (1998).
6. Both sets of data were used in Frankel, Stein, and Wei (1995) and are available from http://www.nber.org/~wei.

7. One may prefer to include log(GDP) and log(GDP per capita) instead. The coefficients on these two variables would be a linear combination of the two coefficients on log(GDP) and log(Population).

8. For a survey on the determinants of corruption, see Wei (2000), section 3. For a practical entry point to an anticorruption strategy, see Wei (1999).

9. Conversely, reducing corruption and regulatory burden would probably also lead to an improvement in the provision of infrastructure and to faster growth (Mauro, 1995), which could in turn indirectly increase inward FDI.

References

Frankel, Jeffrey, Ernesto Stein, and Shang-jin Wei. 1995. "Trading Blocs and the Americas: The Natural, the Unnatural, and the Supernatural." *Journal of Development Economics*, 47, 61–95.

Hines, James. 1995. *Forbidden Payment: Foreign Bribery and American Business After 1977.* NBER Working Paper No. 5266. Cambridge, Mass.: National Bureau of Economic Research.

Huang, Yasheng. 1998. *Foreign Direct Investment in China*. Singapore: National University of Singapore Press.

International Labor Organization. 1995. *International Labor Yearbook*. Geneva: International Labor Organization.

International Monetary Fund. 1997. *Annual Report on Exchange Arrangements and Exchange Restrictions, 1997*. Washington, D.C.: International Monetary Fund.

International Monetary Fund. 1998. *International Financial Statistics Yearbook, 1998*. Washington, D.C.: International Monetary Fund.

Lardy, Nicholas R. 1992. *Foreign Trade and Economic Reform in China, 1978–1990*. Cambridge: Cambridge University Press.

———. 1994. *China in the World Economy*. Washington, D.C.: Institute for International Economics.

Mauro, Paolo. 1995. "Corruption and Growth." *Quarterly Journal of Economics*, 110, 681–712.

Ministry of Foreign Trade and Economic Cooperation. 1999. *Almanac of China's Foreign Economic Relations and Trade, 1999–2000*. Beijing: China Foreign Economic Relations and Trade Publishing House.

Organization for Economic Cooperation and Development. 1998. *International Direct Investment Statistics Yearbook*. Paris: Organization for Economic Cooperation and Development.

State Statistical Bureau. 1999. *China Statistical Yearbook, 1999*. Beijing: State Statistical Publishing House.

Wei, Shang-jin. 1996. "Foreign Direct Investment in China: Source and Consequences." In Takatoshi Ito and Anne O. Krueger, eds., *Financial Deregulation and Integration in East Asia*, pp. 77–102. Chicago: University of Chicago Press.

———. 1997. *Why Is Corruption So Much More Taxing than Taxes? Arbitrariness Kills.* NBER Working Paper No. 6255. Cambridge, Mass.: National Bureau of Economic Research.

———. 1999. "Special Governance Zones: A Practical Entry Point to a Winnable Anti-Corruption Strategy." Paper presented at the Ninth International Anti-Corruption

Conference, Durban, South Africa, October 10–15. Revised version available from http://www.brook.edu/views/papers/wei/20000924.htm.

———. 2000. "How Taxing Is Corruption on International Investors?" *Review of Economics and Statistics*, 82, 1–11.

———. 2001. "Corruption in Economic Development: Grease or Sand?" *Economic Survey of Europe*, 2, 101–12.

World Bank. 1997. *World Development Report, 1997*. Washington, D.C.: World Bank.

World Economic Forum. 1997. *Global Competitiveness Report, 1997*, Geneva: World Economic Forum.

8

How Much Can Regional Integration Do to Unify China's Markets?

Barry Naughton

How integrated is China's national market today? How much can regional integration do in the future to expand China's market? These basic economic questions take on particular importance in the Chinese context. China's enormous size means that its integration into the world economy cannot be as smooth as that of earlier, smaller, export-oriented developing economies. In recent years, the repeated failure to resolve issues related to China's WTO accession at the bargaining table throws into question the ability of the existing world economic order to smoothly accommodate China's emergence. It is therefore conceivable that in its future economic development China might have to rely more on the expansion of its internal market than has been the case in the recent past. In addition, China's geographic expanse and rugged topography mean there are significant physical barriers to interregional trade. Under such conditions, one would normally expect that economic development should involve a steady integration of heretofore relatively independent economies and increasing exploitation of regional specialization and gains from trade. However, numerous analysts have argued that China's economy today is underspecialized and that interregional trade is below optimum levels. Some have even argued that China's provinces are becoming *less* integrated and are devolving into separate protected regional economies. These arguments imply substantial gains from eliminating interregional barriers and expanding trade.

In this chapter, I first examine current conditions of interprovincial trade. I exploit a new data set to show that interprovincial trade in 1992 was, in fact, large. Such comparative data as are available should convince us that China has the basic characteristics of a single country, rather than of an international trading union. Moreover, comparisons with 1987 data show that interprovincial trade was growing more rapidly than either provincial GDP or foreign trade between 1987 and 1992, meaning that national economic integration was increasing. Finally, examination of the commodity composition of interprovincial trade reveals that trade is dominated by intraindustry trade in manufactures (final goods) rather than intermediate inputs. Two-way trade of similar goods (within broad categories) is consistent with competition among producers in different regions.

Having discarded the view that China's provinces are relatively autarkic units linked by weak trade flows, I proceed to discuss current conditions with regard to interprovincial trade and integration and project future trends. I exploit the difference, familiar in the economic geography literature, between intermediate and final goods. Based on this distinction, I argue that we can profitably think of China's challenge as consisting of two types of integration. The first consists of building adequate infrastructure to permit adequate transport of bulky, energy-intensive commodities and fuels at reasonable cost. The second consists of creating a unified competitive marketplace in which enterprises can exploit productivity differentials and comparative advantage so that the economy as a whole can reap gains from trade. Progress has been made in both areas, but much more needs to be done. Current changes in the economy, however, have enormous implications for both types of integration. As these recent changes are very imperfectly understood, we need to monitor current developments closely. The chapter closes with some suggestions for future research and opens with some discussion of the existing literature.

Review of the Literature

The literature on the Chinese spatial economy is vast. Most of it examines regional disparities, especially the coast–inland gap. However, a significant strand of the literature argues that China's regional economies are insufficiently specialized, national economic integration is low, and potential gains from increased specialization and a deeper division of labor may be large. Moreover, there are indications that provincial economies are becoming more similar. Together, these observations have led some authors to conclude not only that potential gains to further integration are large but also that movement may be in the opposite direction, such that losses from lack of specialization may be increasing. I am skeptical of such claims. There are problems with the data and even more serious problems with the interpretation of what data are available.

There are three main strands in this literature. The first strand is descriptive, providing evidence of policy and management decisions made at the local level that interfere with interprovincial trade. During the mid-1980s, various examples such as the "wool war" and the "silk war" were cited, in which local governments tried to retain low-priced raw materials within their own locality in order to favor local manufacturers (Watson et al., 1989; Wedeman, 2003). Parallel with these struggles over low-priced raw materials were efforts to prevent inflows of manufacturing goods with high markups. More broadly, a literature developed in both Chinese and English on the extensive power of local governments, and their attempts to maintain protective barriers around local industries (Shen and Dai, 1990). There are also stories of semiofficial tolls and police and customs checks. However, these descriptive accounts rely on anecdotes, and many were tied to specific circumstances, including price controls that were for the most part abandoned in the 1990s.

The second strand uses fragmentary data on interprovincial transfers. Kumar (1994) pointed to the declining ratio of interprovincial transfers by state-owned commercial organs to provincial GDP and argued that this indicated that interprovincial trade was declining in relative terms. This argument suffered from the problem, which Kumar acknowledged, that state-owned commerce was itself a declining proportion of total trade since the economy was "growing out of the plan" as nonstate merchants took an increasing share of economic activity. No statistics have been available for the forms of interprovincial trade that were increasing, and so conclusions on trends for overall trade remained nearly impossible to reach with any confidence. The need for better data was simply made more evident.

The third strand of the literature has been most influential. This is the argument that provincial economic structures are similar and becoming more similar. This argument has been made in many different forms and is relatively robust through the early 1990s. Economic structure tends to become more similar whether one is examining structure of GDP, structure of manufacturing output, or per capita output of main products (Li Boxi, 1995; Young, 1996, 1999; Development Research Center, 1997). However, these trends are stronger in the 1980s than in the 1990s. The Development Research Center (1997, pp. 12–13) finds that in a comparison of provincial manufacturing output structure between 1987 and 1994, only six provinces show a trend toward convergence and twenty-three show a trend toward divergence. The year 1992 appears to have been a turning point.

The main problem with arguments based on structure of production, however, is the lack of a theoretical yardstick with which to evaluate changes. Structural change in all Chinese provinces has been driven primarily by ongoing rapid industrialization. All Chinese provinces have experienced significant increases in industry's share of GDP, except for the three independent municipalities of Beijing, Tianjin, and Shanghai. These municipalities, of course, had by far the highest share of industry in GDP on the eve of reform. As development has proceeded, all three municipalities have moved into the phase of tertiary sector development and experienced reductions in industry's share of GDP. This contributes to a kind of measured "convergence," but hardly one that should be considered ominous. Moreover, all economies experience certain kinds of regional structural convergence at different levels of economic development. Most economists accept that the United States is an integrated national economy that progressed from a set of regional economies to an integrated economy between the nineteenth and twentieth centuries. But Kim (1995) shows that the manufacturing structure of the American states or regions converged slightly between 1860 and 1878, then diverged dramatically through 1914 and remained relatively divergent until the 1930s before beginning a prolonged and sustained process of renewed convergence. By 1987, state manufacturing sectors were more similar than they had ever been. Which of these phases would be the most appropriate for China to emulate?

Furthermore, changes in production structure in China during the reform era sometimes reflect movement away from inappropriate patterns of regional specialization imposed under the planned economy. Central planners built electronics, machinery, and armament factories in interior China, while fostering textile industry development in Shanghai and other advanced coastal regions. Since reform, many inland high-tech industries have collapsed, while all three municipalities have moved dramatically out of textiles. Such changes may also contribute to measured convergence as dissimilar regions abandon inappropriate or outmoded patterns of regional specialization. Reversal of inefficient patterns of specialization may enhance efficiency but look like convergence.

In spite of these complexities, some analysts have drawn extreme conclusions from data on production structure. Young (1996, 1999) argues that China has devolved into "a fragmented internal market with fiefdoms controlled by local officials." He further argues that improved transport capacity, combined with declining transport intensity of GDP, supports his view that local market protectionism is behind the trend toward structural similarity. (Young also examines some price data and agricultural yields.) Others use the same data on declining transport intensity to argue that gains from trade are being forgone (Kumar, 1994). In fact, it is extremely difficult to make robust conclusions about interregional trade, cooperation, and competition from structural data alone.

Interprovincial Trade

The simplest and most logical first step in studying regional integration in China would be to directly examine data on interprovincial flows. In fact, there are some previously unexploited data of this sort available that enable us to measure commodity flows among China's provinces for occasional benchmark years. Before I present these data, I should acknowledge that regional integration includes more than trading commodities, and a full consideration should include integration of markets for services as well as an assessment of factor market development and the degree of mobility of capital and labor. It is impossible to do this in the compass of this chapter and, I would argue, probably impossible to do so at all given the current state of our understanding of the Chinese economy.

It is undoubtedly true that the service sector—particularly that of relatively more sophisticated business services of the kind most likely to be provided across regions—is underdeveloped in China in terms of both the quality of services available and the degree of interregional service provision. Partly as a result, interprovincial capital mobility is probably relatively modest. As is more widely appreciated, labor has only recently begun to move across provincial boundaries in search of higher income, and nobody argues that a single integrated national market for labor is yet in sight. Other types of integration are therefore likely to lag behind commodity market integration. Moreover, these other types of integration present special challenges to the collection of data. Even in the most sophisticated economies, measuring cross-regional provision of services is difficult.[1] Therefore, it is appropriate to limit the scope of this chapter to commodity market integration. Even in the discussion of commodity markets, some of the following discussion will be devoted to establishing what ought to be the most basic facts. In service markets and capital market integration, existing data do not even allow us to outline these basic facts with any confidence.

The new data exploited in this chapter are the provincial input-output (I-O) tables compiled by most of China's provinces. Provincial I-O tables have been put together at five-year intervals, so provincial I-O tables should exist for 1982, 1987, 1992, 1997, and 2002 (an additional national table was published for 1995). The provincial tables are not published and are considered sensitive for commercial and national security reasons. However, my Chinese colleagues and I have obtained access to the final-demand columns of twenty-seven provincial-level I-O tables for 1992. Two of these provinces list only net outflows and are thus not useful for studying interprovincial trade. Ten provinces separate inflows and outflows into domestic and foreign sectors. I have combined these data with provincial import and export data from the General Administration of Customs, for all provinces, which also serve as a check on the foreign trade data from the ten provinces presenting these data separately. Together, this information provides meaningful domestic and foreign trade data for twenty-five provincial-level units for 1992. In addition, Zhou Zhenhua (1996) performs a similar exercise using data from the 1987 provincial I-O tables. This provides a basis for examining trends between 1987 and 1992.

Details of data sources and manipulation are provided in the appendix to this chapter, but a few notes on the compilation of these tables are in order. Compilation of the provincial input-output tables involves an enormous amount of data collection and data handling. Existing data from State Statistical Bureau or ministerial sources provide only about 70 percent of the data required to build up the tables; the remainder are collected directly by provincial statistical personnel. Compilers break industrial sectors down into main products, visit factories, and interview sales personnel. Often production and sales by township and village enterprises have to be separately estimated and added to the data routinely collected for state-sector and urban enterprises. On the basis of these

TABLE 8.1

Domestic and Foreign Trade Ratios, 1992

(percent of provincial GDP, twenty-five provinces)

		(Adjusted)
Total Outflows	70	
Domestic outflows	49	
Exports	20	
Total Inflows	68	
Domestic inflows	53	(48)
Imports	15	(21)

newly collected data, input–output table compilers estimate flows of inputs and outputs by main product, collecting data on over one hundred products for the larger industrial sectors. Inputs are easier to collect since factories maintain relatively complete records on inputs, but outputs must also be allocated to intermediate and final uses and to within-province and outside-province destinations. The product-by-product estimates are then reaggregated into sectoral data in value terms, providing estimates of the value of products (Zhang and Li, 1985. pp. 79–98, esp. pp. 95–97 on interprovincial flows; Zhang Shouyi, 1992. For updated information, unfortunately not including a discussion of interprovincial flows, see National Accounts Division, 1997b.) The data collection phase takes over a year, and an additional nine months is required to compile them into the first draft of a provincial table.

Table 8.1 summarizes the basic data. Interprovincial trade is large, both relative to GDP and relative to foreign trade. The picture of Chinese provinces as relatively autarkic units, separated from each other, though perhaps open to foreign trade, is clearly false. The column of adjusted figures for inflows in Table 8.1 reflects the fact that the provincial foreign trade data from Customs do not capture all flows: whereas 95 percent of exports are covered, only 74 percent of imports are captured. The omitted imports appear to consist of commodities imported by central government foreign trade corporations and distributed through national networks. If provincial statisticians recorded all those imports as domestic inflows, it would be appropriate to adjust inflows as shown, which would make them essentially identical to outflows. Domestic trade is about 2½ times as important as foreign trade.

It is also possible to examine the same data from the standpoint of individual provinces, which is done in Figures 8.1 and 8.2. In both figures, provinces are ranked from left to right by share of domestic inflows in GDP. By this standard, Jilin is the province most open to domestic trade, followed by Tianjin, Jiangsu, Shanghai, and Hebei. Yunnan and Fujian are the two provinces least open to domestic trade, although the result for Fujian is sensitive to the procedure used to combine the two data sources.[2] There are two provinces for which foreign trade is more important than domestic interprovincial trade. It will come as no sur-

FIGURE 8.1

Outflows and Exports, Twenty-Five Provinces

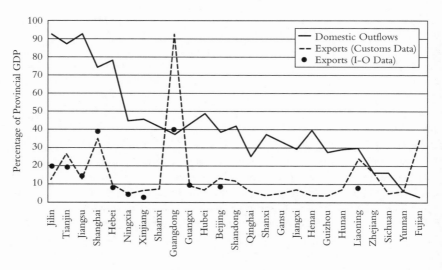

prise that these two are Guangdong and Fujian, designated more than two decades ago as the pioneers of China's opening and long recognized as the core of a "China Circle" region extending across international boundaries and including Hong Kong and Taiwan (Naughton, 1997). Guangdong has an average level of domestic trade dependence, combined with a very high dependence on foreign trade; Fujian has a low domestic trade dependence, combined with moderate openness to foreign trade. Clearly, Guangdong's extremely high level of foreign trade dependence is a reflection of Hong Kong's proximity: many transactions within the metropolitan Hong Kong region cross an international border and are considered "foreign trade" for both Guangdong and Hong Kong. Fujian is very open to trade and investment but lacks a metropolitan area in such close proximity. Figures 8.1 and 8.2 show the export and import data from the Customs Administration (lower solid line), as well as the data provided in the I-O tables for eleven provinces. The figures are close, except in the case of Guangdong. Guangdong statisticians have long handled "export processing" trade by recording only the "processing fees" earned, rather than the full value of imported inputs and processed exports. The Customs Administration follows opposite procedures, which explains the discrepancy.[3]

If Guangdong and Fujian are subtracted from the totals, due to their distinctively different pattern of integration with foreign trade, the remaining twenty-three provinces still show a high degree of openness. When the sample is restricted to those twenty-three provinces, the export ratio declines by 8 percentage

FIGURE 8.2

Inflows and Imports, Twenty-Five Provinces

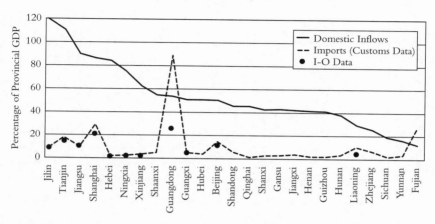

TABLE 8.2

Interprovincial Trade, 1987 and 1992

(percent of provincial GDP, twenty-three provinces)

	1987	1992
Gross outflows	52	69
Gross inflows	53	68
1992 values (1987 = 100)		
Nominal provincial GDP (twenty-three provinces)		229
Nominal gross outflows (twenty-three provinces)		305
Nominal gross inflows (twenty-three provinces)		296
National export growth		
E = Swap rate		250
E = Official posted rate		319
National import growth		
E = Swap rate		216
E = Official posted rate		276

points to 12 percent, but the domestic outflow ratio *increases* from 49 to 51 percent. Total outflows for these provinces equal 63 percent of GDP, and domestic outflows are more than four times as important as exports. Similar results hold on the import side.

Is interprovincial trade growing rapidly? With existing data it is possible to make only a simple comparison between two benchmark years, 1987 and 1992. Table 8.2 shows the contrast between results that can be derived by assessing the data with identical methodologies for 1987 and 1992 for twenty-three provinces. The summary data for 1992 differ slightly from those given in Table 8.1

FIGURE 8.3

Total Provincial Outflows, 1987 and 1992

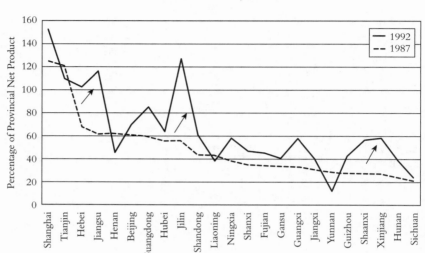

for three reasons: (1) the sample of provinces is different, lacking two observations; (2) foreign trade is not separated out, because of inadequate coverage of provincial trade flows by the Customs data in the earlier year; and (3) inflows and outflows include small amounts of services, primarily transport and commerce. These changes were made to track the available 1987 summary data as closely as possible. Judging from the figures resulting from this methodology, provincial trade was increasing rapidly between 1987 and 1992. Total outflows (to other provinces and abroad) increased from 52 to 69 percent of provincial GDP, and total inflows increased from 53 to 68 percent.

These are dramatic increases. Could it be that they were driven primarily by increases in foreign trade? Unfortunately, provincial-level trade data are inadequate to replicate the calculations made for 1992; but Table 8.2 shows the aggregate growth of total Chinese trade. Those numbers show that foreign trade has been growing at about the same rate as gross outflows and could not account for a disproportionate share of the increase. Indeed, if we value imports and exports at swap market exchange rates (which is preferable, as a more accurate evaluation of import procurement costs and export sales prices), the growth of foreign trade is slower than that of total interprovincial flows.

Figures 8.3 and 8.4 compare total outflows and inflows between 1987 and 1992 for the twenty-three provinces with comparable data. In absolute volume, inflows and outflows in all provinces increased rapidly, with a minority of provinces recording a decline in the proportion of GDP accounted for by outflows

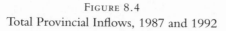

FIGURE 8.4

Total Provincial Inflows, 1987 and 1992

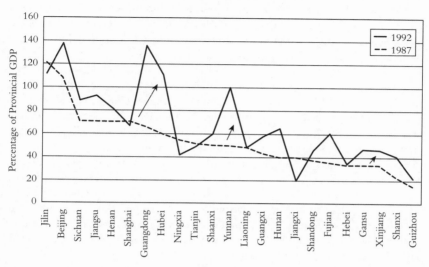

or inflows: four recorded decreased proportional outflows and six decreased proportional inflows. The stragglers seem plausible and may reflect real problems: only Tianjin and Liaoning experienced reductions in the shares of both outflows and inflows. Both these provinces are old industrial bases struggling with serious economic problems and an unfavorable northern location. Two provinces experienced large changes that are difficult to interpret: Yunnan experienced a large increase in inflows and a large decline in outflows; while Jilin experienced a large increase in outflows and a small decline in inflows. For both these provinces, transfers are dominated by a single industry (cigarettes in Yunnan, automobiles in Jilin), which may account for some of the volatility. Jiangxi suffered a large drop in inflows that is unexplained, and Shanghai experienced a slight drop in inflows. Overall, the exceptions seem to "prove the rule": regional integration is moderate to high and increasing for the period we can measure.

The numbers for interprovincial trade cited here certainly seem substantial. Can we say anything more definite about these numbers, perhaps in a comparative perspective? Data on interregional trade within nations in general are rather scarce: the United States does not collect data on interstate trade, for instance. However, a recent strand of trade literature finds that national borders still have a big impact on trade flows. For example, Canada is one of the few countries that collect data on interprovincial sales. McCallum (1995) reports that 44 percent of goods shipped stay within the original province, 23 percent go to other provinces in Canada, 24 percent to the United States, and 9 percent go to the rest of the world (1988 figures). Most strikingly, McCallum finds that Canadian producers are twenty times as likely to ship a product to a Canadian customer as to a U.S. customer, even after distance and market size are accounted for. (Engel and Rogers, 1996, confirm these results.) The results reflect the fact that Canada is actually closer to the United States than it is to itself. Surprisingly, Wolf (1997), studying the United States, finds that in addition to a "home country" effect, there is also a "home state" effect, making businesses about four times as likely to ship a product within state even after distance and market size are accounted for.[4] Chinese provinces are much bigger than American states by population and are separated by more significant geographic barriers. Certainly, we should expect Chinese interprovincial flows to be substantially larger than flows between national entities in Chinese geographic space.

Clearly, these are no simple comparisons because there is no geographic entity similar to China. We can compare the Chinese data, however, with data on international trade among countries within a larger entity that has some geographic unity. For example, exports within the European Union amounted to 12.4 percent of GDP in 1980, inching upward to 13.6 percent in 1990. Another potential comparison is with ASEAN: the exports of Singapore, Malaysia, Thailand, Indonesia, and the Philippines to each other and to other ASEAN members amounted to 13 percent of their GDP in 1997. Chinese interprovincial trade is about four times larger, in relation to GDP, than is international trade within either of these multinational regions.[5]

Such comparisons do not prove that China is a tightly integrated economic space, but they do indicate that China looks somewhat more like a national economy with regions that trade with each other rather than a collection of national economies engaging in foreign trade. National borders still matter. Intra-EU trade is held back by language barriers, currency risk (now greatly reduced by the euro), and regulatory barriers, factors that are less present in China. Conversely, transportation infrastructure is far better in the EU. Finally, the share of services in EU GDP surpasses 60 percent (versus only 34 percent in China in 1992), and trade in services is excluded from our measures. Excluding the tertiary sector from GDP in both the EU and China permits a further comparison. Intra-EU trade is about 34 percent of value added in goods-producing sectors; interprovincial transfers in China in 1992 are 75 percent of value added in goods-producing sectors. Clearly, China's provinces do not stand out as autarkic economic units.

In addition, interprovincial trade seems to be significant for virtually all provinces, regardless of income level or geographic location. There is enormous variation in the degree to which individual provinces are involved in *foreign* as well as domestic trade. As has been widely recognized, coastal provinces, and Guangdong in particular, are at least an order of magnitude more open to foreign trade than inland provinces. Given this differential, it would be alarming if we found that interprovincial trade was small as a share of output for inland provinces, since they would have no alternative means to exploit local comparative advantages. But the data clearly show that this is not the case. Indeed, the average of the fourteen inland provinces for which we have good data is that domestic inflows were 43 percent of GDP and outflows 55 percent, only slightly lower than the average of the eleven coastal provinces, at 58 percent for inflows and 63 percent for outflows.

More striking is the large net flows, particularly for inland provinces. Part of this is explained by the fact that some imports are treated as domestic inflows (and conversely, virtually all provinces have apparent export surpluses on the foreign trade account). When domestic and foreign trade are combined, the average inland province has a 10 percent of GDP surplus of inflows over outflows, while the average coastal province has a 1.5 percent of GDP surplus of outflows. Most of the inland inflow surplus can be attributed to four provinces with huge net inflows: Xinjiang, with 40 percent; Ningxia, with 34 percent; Qinghai, with 19 percent; and Jilin, with 15 percent of GDP. These inflow surpluses correspond to transfer payments from the central government, predominantly through the government budget. This should be a caution, since these beneficiaries of government largesse may simply be "welfare-dependent" rather than specimens of healthy integration. When those beneficiaries are excluded, the other ten inland provinces have an average net inflow of just under 3 percent of GDP.

Commodity Composition

Having established that China's provinces are not autarkic economies but are rather deeply involved in interprovincial trade, let us now push the analysis further in a number of directions. First, let us consider differences between types of commodities. Oversimplifying, we can consider a distinction between intermediate goods—usually bulk commodities—and final manufactured goods with individualized characteristics. Generally speaking, we expect to find two regularities. Bulk commodities should be engaged primarily in one-way flows. Since the commodities have identical characteristics, we would not expect to see two-way flows of a given commodity (assuming we have divided the commodity classification finely enough). Interindustry trade would dominate total trade in these commodities.[6] By contrast, final goods have individualized characteristics, and there should be significant two-way flows as consumers seek goods with the attributes they want. Two-way flows of commodities within a single industrial sector—known as intraindustry trade (IIT)—will be most common when commodities incorporate a bundle of characteristics that can vary in many dimensions, and this is more likely to be true of final than intermediate goods. (I define IIT, as is conventional, as occurring when a province both imports and exports goods in a given industrial sector.)

Second, early in the development process, we would expect to see more interindustry trade, for two reasons. First, suppose that the initial "sprouts" of industrialization occur in localized areas where there are specific mineral resources or locational advantages that encourage the earliest, most difficult phases of industrialization. We would expect initial industrialization to be quite specialized, and early modern producers (mines or factories) would be large relative to their local communities. Moreover, much initial manufacturing would be simple processing of raw materials, especially in agriculture. Thus we would expect to see substantial interindustry trade and, in particular, substantial exchange of manufactures for raw materials. Such trade should dominate total trade. Subsequently, as industries diversify and become more sophisticated, the proportion of intraindustry trade should increase. This is partly because of the simple fact of greater diversity of local economies, partly because more output would involve more sophisticated stages of processing, and partly because higher-income consumers would be more concerned about the specific attributes of the goods they are purchasing. Indeed, as Baldwin and Martin (1999) have pointed out, we observe exactly this trend in world trade. During the first wave of globalization (1880–1914), world trade was dominated by the exchange of manufactures for raw materials (especially between industrialized and agrarian economies) and by the exchange of consumer goods for capital goods (between industrialized economies at different levels of development). Subsequently, during the more recent second wave of globalization, total world trade is dominated by intraindustry trade, in which similar economies exchange essentially similar goods with slightly different attributes.

Such a distinction is surely of interest in the current discussion of market integration in China, because the problems—and therefore the data of interest—differ substantially between the two categories of goods. For raw materials, we are concerned that different regional economies have adequate access to energy, minerals, metal products, and cement, such that bottlenecks of supply or transportation do not retard development. These goods are bulky and heavy. Energy (for the production and transport of these goods) and transportation are the key issues. National integration is a meaningful concept, but the realization of the concept is to have sufficient capacity in transportation and energy production and adequate efficiency in the production of energy and transport services to ensure the predominantly one-way flows of these goods to the manufacturing centers that concentrate demand. Let us call this "integration A." It is not at all the case that for flows of bulk commodities, more is better; quite the contrary: if production of goods and services can increase while using less of these material inputs, that is all to the good. This is particularly relevant in examining transition economies, because we know that the socialist economies operated with strikingly high material intensities. Toward the end of its days, the Soviet Union produced more steel, oil, and chemical fertilizer than any other economy, but it converted these inputs into final goods with breathtaking inefficiency. If, for example, China manages to grow while shipping less coal among regions, this should not be taken as a reduction in specialization but rather as an improvement in economic performance.

By contrast, trade in manufactured goods correlates well with national integration in the sense of a unified, competitive market in which consumers can choose among competing goods from different regions, of essentially similar type but with different attributes. Intraindustry trade in manufactures should be a good index of this type of national economic integration, which we can call "integration B" or competitive market integration. Once again, this issue might be particularly sensitive in transition economies. We know that manufacturing centers such as Shanghai paid high tax rates, corresponding to net uncompensated transfers on the provincial "capital account." Correspondingly, there must have been a large apparent "trade surplus" on the current account, consisting of manufactured goods. If these large one-way flows are reduced, due to declining taxes, growth of diversified industries in other regions, or changes in the structure of Shanghai industry—or all of these combined—should we identify this with a reduction in exploitation of regional comparative advantage and a decline in the level of national economic integration? Not necessarily.

Table 8.3 shows that Chinese interprovincial trade is dominated by intra-

TABLE 8.3

Characteristics of Goods in Interprovincial Trade

(percent)

	Share of Total Domestic Outflows	Intraindustry Trade Share of Total Trade	Domestic Outflows/ Final Use
Chemicals, rubber, plastic	12.7	70.3	8.5
Machinery	9.8	63.4	43.9
Food products	9.4	67.5	63.1
Agriculture	8.9	56.2	42.5
Textiles	8.7	62.8	7.2
Transport machinery	8.4	56.2	36.3
Metallurgy	8.3	55.4	0.8
Building materials	5.0	49.0	10.9
Electric machinery	4.7	39.8	23.5
Electronics	3.6	50.4	41.8
Metal products	3.2	50.1	12.7
Coal mining	3.2	33.5	11.6
Garments	3.0	50.4	66.2
Paper, toys, handicrafts	2.9	59.2	16.9
Petroleum refining	1.6	36.7	3.7
Petroleum	1.5	35.2	0.0
Other industry	1.4	44.0	5.4
Mineral mining	0.9	37.0	9.8
Ferrous mining	0.8	36.7	0.0
Instruments	0.8	61.8	18.0
Coking and coal gas	0.5	35.9	35.2
Lumber and furniture	0.4	32.0	28.3
Electricity	0.3	15.4	16.6

industry trade. The table shows interprovincial trade broken down into the twenty-three sectors used in the 1992 (and 1995) I-O tables. The definition of intraindustry trade (column 2) is standard, taking two-way flows within a given sector as a percentage of total flows of commodities in that sector. The sectors are highly aggregated—slightly more aggregated than a standard "two-digit" classification—and thus overstate the degree of intraindustry trade to some extent. Nevertheless, it is clear that the bulk of provincial outflows consist of products from sectors with differentiated output, high rates of intraindustry trade, and a relatively high share of final uses (consumption and fixed investment) in total domestic uses (column 3). Here, share of final use is the national average, taken from the 1995 national I-O table (National Accounts Division, 1997a).[7] Because of the high degree of aggregation, we can't really tell that provinces are exchanging goods with similar attributes, only that provinces are exchanging goods within broadly similar categories. But the data are good enough to show that interprovincial flows are certainly not dominated by one-way transfers of raw materials, such as we might expect to see under a central planning regime or perhaps at an early stage of economic development. At least China's interprovincial flows are not inconsistent with a hypothesis of an integrated national market with competition among producers located in different provinces. Moreover, when we examine trends in interprovincial trade by *value*, we are primarily examining trends with respect to manufactured goods.

Bulk Goods and Materials

When we examine trends in interprovincial trade by *volume* or *weight*, we are primarily examining trends with respect to intermediate goods. If we do not adequately differentiate between intermediates and final products, we are in danger of misunderstanding other data about the Chinese economy. Figure 8.5 shows that according to official Chinese data, the energy intensity and transport intensity of the Chinese economy have both declined dramatically since 1980. To be sure, the figure overstates the magnitude of decline because it uses official Chinese data that overstate the growth of real GDP. But it is important to recognize that the underlying phenomena appear in the data even with fairly radical revisions of GDP growth. If real GDP growth is reduced by 2 percentage points every year from 1980 through 1998—which is near the upper range of the consensus critique of Chinese GDP figures—energy intensity still declines significantly. Taking a unit of energy consumed per unit of real GDP produced in 1980 as 100, energy usage declines to 57 in 1998 under adjusted GDP growth (instead of 41 if official data are used), and transport intensity declines to 80 (instead of 57). Under any reasonable set of assumptions, the Chinese economy has dramatically reduced the amount of energy required for a given output value.

In fact, it would be astonishing if this were not true. In the early 1980s, there were virtually no commodities in the Chinese civilian economy that had high

FIGURE 8.5

Energy and Transport Intensity of GDP

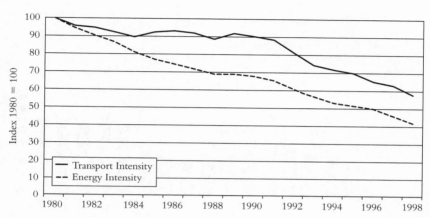

value per weight. The economy displayed the pathologies of both a centrally planned economy and an underdeveloped economy. There has been a vast change in the economy since then. Reduction in the share of bulk, low-value commodities in the economy improves the energy and transport efficiency of the economy. Consider these points from Rong et al. (1997, p. 49):

> The inadequacy of the national transport system remains the major barrier to greater regional integration. . . . Coal alone accounts for two-fifths of the overall railway ton/km freight task. . . . Apart from coal, the other main freight flows are of grain and iron and steel (each 8 percent of the railway ton/km task). . . . The main transport problem . . . is the serious shortage of railway capacity, largely because of the priority given to coal, building materials, and other bulk freight. Space for non-priority freight has to be booked weeks in advance and there is no certainty as to when consignments will reach their destination.

Although coal, grain, and iron and steel account for well over half of railroad freight task, they make up at most 10 or 15 percent of the value of interprovincial trade. At one point, the need to ensure shipments of these bulk commodities obstructed the development of shipments of high-value commodities. However, that is unlikely to be the case today, except in individual areas of China. During the 1990s, China made a major investment effort to upgrade its transportation and communications infrastructure. This included substantial upgrading of the railroad infrastructure (double-tracking, conversion to electric and diesel engines, etc.) as well as construction of major new interprovincial express highways and fiber-optic backbones for communication. Figure 8.6 shows the increase in investment effort in infrastructure that became evident in 1993.

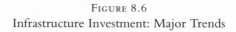

FIGURE 8.6

Infrastructure Investment: Major Trends

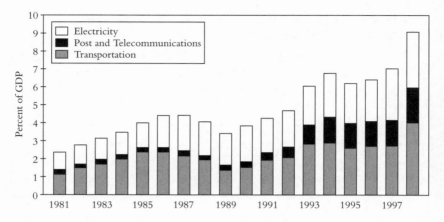

Since 1993, annual investment in physical infrastructure has consistently been above 6 percent of GDP.

The combination of improving availability of transport and declining transport intensity of GDP almost certainly reflects an underlying shift in the structure of the economy. The overall materials intensity and energy intensity of the economy are declining. This trend is strongly supported by the data on energy consumption. The result is less pressure on transport infrastructure and more room for interregional exchange of higher-value commodities. In a broad sense, then, the data on transport infrastructure and transport intensity should reassure us that the physical bottlenecks are unlikely to be a major obstacle to regional integration (contra Rong et al. 1997). We have already seen that manufactured final goods make up a large proportion of the value of interprovincial shipments. Neither "integration A" nor "integration B" seems to be at crisis levels.

Provincial Policies That Restrain Trade

Thus far we have focused on data that encourage us to view China essentially as a normal developing economy. Interprovincial trade is substantial and increasingly consists of manufactured goods; an intensive investment effort is easing transport bottlenecks and lowering the effective cost of transport and communications. At the same time, there are clearly institutional features of the Chinese economy that retard the growth of regional specialization and interfere with national integration. At the heart of these institutional features is the continuing role of local governments as owners and managers of a significant part of the local economic base. Local government ownership is significant because local officials have complex objectives that extend beyond the normal economic activities of the enterprise: local officials have interests in sustaining employment and maximizing tax revenues and nontax benefits. In addition, local officials have a number of strategic objectives: positioning themselves to obtain rents and central government subsidies and preserving firms that may serve as suppliers or customers to other strategic firms. Because local officials also have significant regulatory powers over both production and trade, it is not surprising to find that on occasion they use their diverse portfolio of powers to protect local firms and obstruct competition from firms outside their locality.

The Institute of Industrial Economics (1998, p. 294) describes the situation not long ago:

In recent years, as reform and opening have developed in greater depth, regional protectionism has been reduced but not eliminated. For example, some local governments have used administrative, economic, or legal measures to protect their local beer or chemical fertilizer industries, creating obstacles for competing products from outside. Some localities turn a blind eye to substandard or defective products sold by their firms while at the same time intentionally creating problems with commercial registration, health inspections, or technical certification for top-quality products from outside. Some local governments encourage discriminatory treatment in access to bank credit between local or outside firms, and some even go so far as to forbid bank loans to outside firms. In commercial disputes, some local courts blatantly favor local firms.

This description rings true. Local governments don't blockade their borders or impose tariffs. But their pervasive influence over the local regulatory apparatus enables them to impose significant nontariff barriers to outside firms that can significantly increase the costs of trade and cross-border investment.

This description suggests that the key problems with respect to interregional trade are the same as the key problems with respect to further economic reform more broadly defined. To understand current and future trends with respect to interregional trade, we need to examine the benefits and costs to local governments of protecting local economies. Until recently, local governments have had very strong incentives to intervene in local economies and substantial means to do so. Through the early 1990s, these incentives were shaped by the disproportions between "basic" raw materials sectors (intermediate goods, in our terminology) and "processing" sectors (manufactured final goods, in our terminology). A long-term pricing policy kept the relative price of most raw materials low, and a development strategy encouraged energy- and material-intensive sectors such that bottlenecks remained pervasive. Under these circumstances, government intervention was repeatedly justified: governments *ought* to intervene in intermediate goods industries to ease bottlenecks, and governments *wanted* to intervene in processing industries because it established a claim on scare, cheap materials and provided a source of revenues. Local protectionism—including the various "wool wars" and other anecdotal incidents—flourished under this environment.

After the mid-1990s, though, this economic environment began to change. Economic reform reduced demand for intermediates, and supply increased. The industrial policy of 1990, which had focused overwhelmingly on energy, steel, and other "basic industries," was set aside as unnecessary. But planners then took a page from the plan book of Japanese industrial policy and set out to identify a new list of priority "pillar" industries. Pillar industries were expected to have high income elasticities, significant technological (learning-by-doing) content, and spillover effects in economic development. Local governments were encouraged to carry out their own planning exercises. In this case, the expectations of industrial policy very much corresponded to the economic interests of local officials, who felt they were being invited to stake out territory on the ground floor of the most profitable industries of today and tomorrow. Not surprisingly, they responded enthusiastically.

As Table 8.4 shows, at least nineteen (out of thirty) provinces selected automobiles as a priority industry; and nearly as many provinces selected other favorite industries. As the right two columns of the table also show, these desires were translated into investment decisions that sharply increased the new capacity under construction. The result has been something just short of disastrous, with massive overcapacity in a range of "pillar industries." Today, however, these incentives are weaker, in part because of the results of past policies. The shift toward pervasive oversupply in many markets, accompanied by fierce competition and falling prices, has made many local governments acutely aware of the costs of being stuck with uncompetitive capacity. During 1998, responsibility over industrial policy was transferred from the State Planning Commission to the State Economic and Trade Commission, which has much more regard for market conditions and more interest in the current economic health of existing enterprises. A notable reduction has occurred in the extent to which sectors and firms are designated for priority support by national policymakers ahead of marketplace signals (Ma and Lu, 1999). These changes mean that the benefits to local governments of engaging in active industrial policy are being reduced.

At the same time, one of the most important forces constraining local governments and tipping them toward market intervention is also being reduced. This is the need to defend employment levels. Since 1996, the imperative to protect local employment levels has been dramatically reduced. Widespread layoffs in state-owned firms have followed. Between 1992 and the end of 1998, the state-owned enterprise workforce has declined by twenty-one million people, almost a third; the urban collective enterprise workforce has declined by sixteen million, also more than a third. Although ten million of these workers have been absorbed into joint stock and limited liability corporations, some of which are merely public firms with converted administrations, the net reduction in the

TABLE 8.4

Provincial Priority Industries Selected for the Ninth Five-Year Plan

	Auto	Electronic	Petro-Chemical	Machinery	Metallurgy	Building Materials	New Capacity Under Construction (thousand units)	
							Automobile	Motorcycle
Beijing	2	1		3	5		120	
Tianjin	1	2			4		100	
Hebei	3	5		3	6	7		
Shanxi				2	1	4	11	
Inner Mongolia	4				3			
Liaoning		3	1	4	2		53	
Jilin	1		2	5			274	
Heilongjiang	1	4						
Shanghai	1	2	5	3,4	5		120	
Jiangsu	4	2	3	1			194	1,200
Zhejiang		2		1		7	21	200
Anhui	1	4	2			3	173	10
Fujian			1	2		4	26	120
Jiangxi	2	1	4	3		8	51	50
Shandong	3	2	1				103	700
Henan	1		3	2		4	337	
Hubei	1	2			3	5	293	275
Hunan	2				1	3	3	307
Guangdong	1	4	2			3	3	450
Guangxi	3			4	2	5	97	100
Hainan	2		1			7	50	
Sichuan	6	5		4	1	7	105	5
Guizhou	4				2	7	90	
Yunnan					3		60	
Tibet						5		
Shaanxi		2		1			23	
Gansu			1	3		2	3	
Qinghai			3		4			
Ningxia					1			
Xinjiang			2			6		
Totals	19	15	14	15	15	17	2,017	3,837

SOURCE: Lu Dadao and Xue Fengxuan (1997, pp. 62 and 84).

size of the public enterprise workforce has been very substantial. Local governments no longer need prove that they can protect public employment levels; some, indeed, are even under pressure from above to cut workers. This reduces one of the incentives for active market interventions. The benefits to local protectionism have thus been reduced. Nevertheless, as long as local governments own and regulate firms, there will be incentives to restrain trade.

At the same time, it has become more costly for local governments to attempt to countermand market outcomes. Recourse to bank loans and tax exemptions to prop up local firms has become more difficult. Premier Zhu Rongji has imposed a harder budget constraint on the state banking system, and reorganization of the commercial banking system has broken the tight link between local government officials and local bank branches. Consistent stress from the central government on the need to increase budgetary revenues has made it incrementally more difficult to prop up local firms through tax exemptions or hidden subsidies.

Enterprise-Level Changes

Changes at the enterprise level are also combining to make local government intervention more costly. Notably, enterprise reforms that may be inadequate to fundamentally change the incentive environment of the enterprise itself may have a positive impact on local government incentives. The clearest example is the conversion of state firms to joint stock companies with majority or complete ownership by government agencies. As a model of enterprise reform, such a conversion is likely to have limited impact. But such an organizational change does tend to break the nexus between local government and enterprise. Because equity control can be exercised by extralocal governments or even by enterprises in other regions, this model facilitates the diversification of the local economic base and its separation from local government stewardship. Indeed, there has been a wave of takeovers of local by outside firms in recent years, seen as a favored way for local governments to shed responsibility for troubled firms with minimum adverse impact. Successful producers of consumer durables, for example, have in many instances taken over local firms to their expand market reach.

In a related fashion, recent years have seen a dramatic diversification in the channels through which goods reach their final consumers. For years, state–run commercial enterprises (or material supply firms for producer goods) ran wholesale networks, firmly positioning themselves between producers and consumers. Even as the apparatus of planning was dismantled, state wholesalers were able to exploit their strategic position to control many commodity flows and extract profits (and rents). They also provided local governments with a convenient channel to exercise influence over trade. Conversely, Chinese distribution channels were widely recognized as one of the least efficient parts of the entire economic system.[8] These arrangements are now crumbling. By 1996, state material supply enterprises were transacting only a sixth of producer goods sales. Production firms were creating their own sales networks, relying on their own subsidiaries or, increasingly, on designated agents. Producers of consumption goods were experiencing a related diversification, with distribution networks, wholesale markets, and increasingly active retailers expanding upstream into distribution. Former profits of state-owned commerce were eroding (Institute of Industrial Economics, 1998). Clearly, this means that local governments are losing an important instrument for intervening in interregional trade.

It seems clear that the systemic characteristics I have described—local government sponsorship of specific firms, subsidies and protection to less efficient firms, and so on—have been substantially reduced in strength in recent years. Under the pressure of a macroeconomic downturn and an unprecedented level of capacity expansion, competition has intensified. The combination of increased competition, reduced resources available for implicit and explicit subsidies, and an ideological green light for restructuring, bankruptcy, and privatization (at least of small firms) appears to have led to a rapid growth of consolidation and restructuring. However, we know relatively little about the pace of restructuring in the aggregate. A crucial question is the extent to which inefficient, surplus capacity is being shut down.

In two troubled sectors, textiles and coal mining, the government has taken an aggressive role in shutting down excess capacity. During 1998, a total of 5.12 million spindles were decommissioned, and 660,000 textile workers were laid off—both numbers "above targets." Similarly, during 1998–99, extensive efforts were made to shut down small and often dangerous and polluting coal mines, the output of which is no longer needed (Ma and Lu, 1999). These efforts certainly seem consistent with the rapid reduction in the public enterprise labor force. We know that there have been substantial changes in the number of firms in business, indicating substantial birth and death of firms. For example, in 1998, 40,000 nonfinancial state-owned enterprises went out of business, and 16,000 new ones were set up. The result was a 24,000 net decrease in state firms, to 238,000 total at year-end. On a more specific note, the number of breweries declined from 740 in 1996 to 500 in 1998, indicating an industry undergoing rapid consolidation (She, 1999; Chen, 1999). There are numerous indirect indications that rapid restructuring is taking place.

It is inconceivable that changes of this magnitude could not have implications for regional specialization. More rapid restructuring, and particularly a willingness to shut down less efficient producers in different regions, could contribute to a greatly accelerated process of national integration. Nonetheless, there is still much we do not know about the current restructuring. We do not know its overall magnitude. For example, what proportion of laid-off workers come from firms that are shut down, and what proportion correspond to firms that are being slimmed down in an attempt to keep them in business? We do not know the extent to which ongoing restructuring is truly market-driven and to what extent government is driving it, as in the case of the consolidation of the coal industry. We may hypothesize that a process of restructuring is under way that we expect to lead to rapid increases in national integration. However, the evidence is not yet sufficient to justify whether this hypothetical process is in fact truly happening or whether it will be sustained through the coming years.

Conclusion

There is a great deal we don't know about interprovincial trade and specialization and national integration in China. One strand of future work would ideally focus on measuring and analyzing interprovincial trade. Although data sets are in short supply, creative exploitation of existing data may provide some interesting avenues of approach. The 1995 and subsequent input-output tables should provide substantial insight into the process of regional change. Data sets based on shipments might be useful, as Wolf (1997) showed for U.S. data. In essence, all the interesting questions that trade economists have been examining with respect to international trade can be reexamined in the Chinese context, with potentially fruitful results. An important substrand of this work will be to examine interregional flows from the standpoint of services. It appears that finance, trade, and transport in particular are growing rapidly in their role in the national economy, but we have almost no clear quantitative understanding of these processes.

Second, regional growth models seem a potentially important area for future research. Economic geography has been a source of excitement in economics lately, and China should provide a fertile source of empirical data and new hypotheses. The work is difficult, though: Chinese price data in particular need to be carefully handled if they are to produce meaningful results. One essential finding of nearly all careful empirical work has been that there are large, enduring productivity differentials favoring coastal provinces in a wide range of production sectors. We need a better understanding of the sources of such differentials. We also need to understand and anticipate the consequences of such findings, if they are confirmed by future research. Enduring productivity differentials and a more integrated national economy imply that shifts of output and income toward the coastal areas can be continued for another couple of decades. That implies that Chinese economic geography will be dramatically reshaped in coming years, with labor and capital migrating eastward and creating productive new agglomerations along the Chinese coast.

Third, and finally, topics related to regional integration cannot be separated from an understanding of the ongoing process of enterprise reform, privatization, and marketization in the Chinese economy. Despite the enormous progress that has been made since 1978, these processes have by no means run their course. This means that although serious problems still lie ahead, the potential productivity gains that might be reaped relatively soon are still enormous. Probably, it will be possible for China to reap most of these gains from an ongoing reform process, especially one that responds to WTO membership and further radical opening to the outside world. But momentum must be maintained, as a slowdown of domestic initiatives would mean a huge cost in terms of forgone output and failed developmental initiatives.

We know enough about Chinese interprovincial trade to know that it is an important topic for future research. Overly simple characterizations of Chinese provinces as quasi-autarkic protected economies simply don't fit the facts. Instead, important flows of materials link these different regions. It is worthwhile to understand the content and determinants of these flows. Moreover, it is clear that the system still imposes unnecessary costs and limitations on interregional flows. Removing those barriers will provide an additional source of growth and improved productivity to the Chinese economy. A better understanding of the issues would give us a better grasp of the magnitude of the potential benefits to growth from great integration.

Appendix

The provincial input-output tables provide a superb source that allows us to get much closer to the information we actually need on interprovincial flows. However, the provincial tables appear to vary substantially in quality and reliability. It is clear from visual inspection of the input-output tables that (1) provinces follow somewhat different procedures for collecting information and compiling tables, so inconsistencies may exist when provinces are compiled; (2) the quality of collected data varies substantially; and (3) there may be conceptual errors in the way some provinces have collected or recorded data. Clearly, one should be cautious in relying too heavily on these tables for specific points. Yet if the tables provide strong and unambiguous evidence for any general point, they are far to be preferred over indirect inference from other data sources, which suffer from both data presentation inconsistencies and theoretical problems with the inferences used to formulate observations about interregional integration.

For 1992, I had access to the final demand columns for twenty-seven provincial input-output tables (missing are Tibet and Inner Mongolia; also, Hainan and Chongqing, which now have provincial status, are included with Guangdong and Sichuan, respectively). Unfortunately, the full tables are considered sensitive information (perhaps for both national security and commercial reasons) and require formal government approval to be released; I have not seen the full provincial tables. Two provinces (Anhui and Heilongjiang) have only net outflows, so they are not usable for studying interregional integration. Therefore, useful information exists for twenty-five provinces. Ten of these tables break the outflow and inflow columns into domestic outflows and exports. These, not surprisingly, tend to be the provinces for which foreign trade is most important—Guangdong, Shanghai, Beijing, Liaoning, and Jiangsu—or those in which potential for increased foreign trade appear significant—Xinjiang, Guangxi, Ningxia, Hebei, and Jilin.

For provincial (foreign trade) exports and imports, I have used a series from the General Administration of Customs, published in China's *Latest Economic*

Statistics, February 1993, pp. 16–26. Note that 1992 was a year in which China's statistical collection system for foreign trade was in transition. From 1993 onward, we have complete data from the Customs Administration, breaking down exports and imports into provincial totals both by location of the ultimate producing and purchasing enterprise and by location of the enterprise that carried out the export or import transaction. The data for 1992 are available only for location of the enterprise that carried out the export or import transaction and cover 95 percent of exports but only 74 percent of imports. The coverage of imports is more incomplete because trade by China's large, centrally controlled foreign trading companies (FTCs) are not included in the provincial figures, and these large central-government FTCs mainly serve to import bulk commodities (grain, fertilizer, etc.) and feed them into the domestic distribution network. From the standpoint of the province, they are probably indistinguishable from domestic inflows. Without adjustment, then, the data set understates the importance of foreign trade imports in total provincial inflows. However, we know the average magnitude of understatement in our total because we have figures for total imports and exports. The averages are used in the adjusted figures reported in Table 8.1. Provincial exports are understated by 5 percent: this is insignificant in our context, and I have not imposed an additional adjustment on the data for exports.

The data set has a second shortcoming that may somewhat affect the allocation of flows to specific provinces: it is classified by location of the exporter or importer rather than the ultimate producer. This may explain one of the anomalies in the data, the considerably larger exports from Liaoning reported by Customs than by the I-O table, reflecting the exportation from Liaoning of oil or other products produced farther north. At one time, the distinction between producer and exporter was important, but gradually most provinces have gained control of their own export companies, and the difference for most provinces is not large. By inspecting data for the following year, 1993, we can see that only two provinces—Shanxi and Heilongjiang—produce significantly more exports than they transact (coal and oil, respectively). These caveats are not large enough to affect our conclusions.

In all cases, I have used the Customs data to measure foreign trade imports and exports. For the fifteen provinces that do not break down inflows and outflows into domestic and foreign components, I have simply subtracted Customs imports and exports from total inflows and outflows. For the ten provinces that do break down inflows and outflows into domestic and foreign components, I have substituted the Customs imports and exports for the I-O table imports and exports but retained the I-O figures for domestic inflows and outflows. For Guangdong, where it matters the most, this is clearly the correct procedure. The figures in the I-O table correspond to the figures Guangdong province collected and published at that time on foreign trade. "Processing trade," under which materials enter the province from Hong Kong duty-free, are processed for a fee, and then reexported, are recorded only to the value of processing fees (in the same way that *maquiladora* trade in Mexico was originally counted). Since Guangdong procedures are consistent, and are consistent with their reported value of domestic outflows, it would clearly be improper to adjusted domestic flows to reconcile the total with the much larger Customs figures for exports and imports. For Fujian, however, where no breakdown is provided in the I-O tables, a similar problem might mean that I have underestimated Fujian's domestic inflows and outflows.

The foreign trade data are collected and reported in U.S. dollars. I have converted to Chinese currency units at the swap rate prevailing in 1992 (6.2 RMB yuan to the dollar) rather than the official exchange rate. The swap rate probably reflects domestic costs and selling prices more accurately than the official posted rate. Moreover, using the swap rate yields a larger total value of foreign trade. Since this value is subtracted from total flows for fifteen provinces, a higher value of foreign trade is unfavorable to my general argument that domestic trade is relatively large and important.

In addition, I have used a similar data set from Zhou Zhenhua (1996, pp. 131–37), which contains essentially the same information for 1987, based on the 1987 provincial I-O tables. I do not have specific information on how Zhou has manipulated the data, but he provides a list of twenty-five provinces with their domestic inflows and outflows and imports and exports expressed as a share of provincial GDP. His import and export data can be checked with other foreign trade data, and they correspond closely in the overwhelming majority of provinces to a set of export and import figures provided by provincial trading bodies. This gives some confidence that his methodology is essentially the same as mine, which is reinforced by the underlying nature of the I-O tables. However, while his use of the foreign trade data increases confidence in methodological compatibility, the data he uses are too incomplete to be useful. In particular, the import data cover only one-quarter of total imports, and the export data cover only four-fifths of exports. Therefore, some of Zhou's inferences are unreliable. There are two provinces for which we have 1992 data but no 1987 data (Zhejiang and Qinghai) and two provinces for which we have 1987 but no usable 1992 data (Inner Mongolia and Heilongjiang). The omitted provinces may slightly bias our results, since Qinghai, Inner Mongolia, and Heilongjiang are relatively slow-growing provinces with lots of problems; Zhejiang, on the other hand, has grown extremely rapidly since 1978. Combining the two data sets gives comparable data for twenty-three provinces in 1987 and 1992.

Notes

1. The input-output tables do provide some data on services, including extraprovincial supply of services, but the data are fragmentary and difficulty to interpret and have not been used in this analysis.

2. It may seem surprising that Jilin is so open to interprovincial trade, but Jilin contains China's largest truck producer, and in fact interprovincial flows are dominated by transportation machinery, so this may be the explanation. Fujian is very open to foreign trade but is geographically quite separated from the remainder of China by rugged mountains and unreliable transport connections. This may explain the surprisingly low level of intraprovincial trade recorded.

3. In the case of the ten provinces that break out foreign trade from domestic outflows and inflows, Figure 8.1 uses the estimate of domestic trade from the I-O table, combined with estimates of imports and exports from Customs. In the case of provinces that do not separate foreign and domestic trade, the Customs figures are subtracted from total outflows or inflows. In the case of Fujian, this procedure would underestimate domestic trade if processing trade is calculated in the same fashion as it is in Guangdong.

4. Wolf (1997) uses a data set based on rail, truck, air, and water shipments. The Chinese data are not based on shipments but rather on estimates of sources, uses, and destinations (although statisticians occasionally consult transportation data as a secondary reference). Consequently, no direct, simple comparison is possible, only an observation on roughly comparable orders of magnitude.

5. The two multinational regions are very different with respect to the amount of trade they carry on outside their region. Intra-EU trade is more than half of total trade by EU member nations. By contrast, the ASEAN-5 countries export 40 percent of GDP to outside ASEAN. Indeed, the ASEAN countries are open to foreign trade but trade little with each other; a similar generalization cannot be applied to China.

6. This would be especially true early in the industrialization process. Later on, more differentiated intermediate goods would develop, in a process that has been hypothesized to be one of the forces that gives impetus to continuing economic development.

7. The commodity data include domestic outflows from the ten provinces that separate domestic and foreign outflows plus total outflows from the fifteen provinces that do not separate outflows. Provinces separating domestic and foreign flows include Guangdong, Shanghai, and Liaoning, the three largest exporters in 1992, which account for half of total exports. Remaining included exports are therefore a very small proportion of total outflows. Share of final uses is from the 1995 I-O tables.

8. This inefficiency also attracted interest from foreign firms and made WTO-related market access provisions particularly controversial.

References

Baldwin, R. E., and P. Martin. 1999. *Two Waves of Globalization: Superficial Similarities, Fundamental Differences.* Cambridge, Massachusetts, National Bureau of Economic Research.

Chen, Z. 1999. "Trouble Now Brewing for Domestic Beer Sector." *China Daily,* September 26, p. 3.

Development Research Center. 1997. *Zhongguo Kuashiji Quyu Xietiao Fazhan Zhanlue [A Cross-Century Coordinated Development Strategy for China's Regions].* Beijing: *Jingji Kexue Chubanshe* [Economic Science Publishing Company].

Engel, C., and J. H. Rogers. 1996. "How Wide Is the Border?" *American Economic Review,* 86, 1112–25.

Institute of Industrial Economics. 1998. *Zhongguo Gongye Fazhan Baogao [China's Industrial Development Report].* Beijing: *Jingji Guanli Chubanshe* [Economic Management Publishing Company].

Kim, S. 1995. "Expansion of Markets and the Geographic Distribution of Economic Activities: Trends in the U.S. Regional Manufacturing Structure, 1860–1987." *Quarterly Journal of Economics,* 110, 881–908.

Kumar, A. 1994. "Economic Reform and the Internal Division of Labour in China: Production, Trade and Marketing," pp. 99–130. In D. Goodman and G. Segal, eds., *China Deconstructs: Politics, Trade and Regionalism.* London: Routledge.

Li Boxi. 1995. *Diqu Zhengce yu Xietiao Fazhan [Regional Policy and Coordinated Development].* Beijing: *Zhongguo Caizheng Jingji Chubanshe* [China Financial Economics Publishing Company].

Lu Dadao and Xue Fengxuan. 1997. *1997 Zhongguo Chuyu Fazhan Baogao [China Regional Development Report, 1997].* Beijing: *Shangwu Yinshuguan* [Commercial Press].

Ma Hong and Baifa Lu. 1999. *Zhongguo Hongguan Jingji Zhengce Baogao [Report on China's Macroeconomic Policy].* Beijing: *Zhongguo Caizheng Jingji Chubanshe* [China Financial Economics Publishing Company].

McCallum, J. 1995. "National Borders Matter: Canada-U.S. Regional Trade Patterns." *American Economic Review,* 85, 615–23.

National Accounts Division. 1997a. *Zhongguo Touru Chanchu Biao 1995 [China Input-Output Table, 1995].* Beijing: *Zhongguo Tongji* [China Statistics Press].

National Accounts Division. 1997b. *Zhongguo Touru Chanchu Biao (Yanchangbiao) Bianzhi Fangfa [Methodology for Compilation of the China Input-Output Table (Extended Version)].* Beijing: *Zhongguo Tongji* [China Statistics Press].

Naughton, B., ed. 1997. *The China Circle: Economics and Technology in the PRC, Taiwan, and Hong Kong.* Washington, D.C.: Brookings Institution.

Rong, C., et al. 1997. "Linking the Regions: A Continuing Challenge." In G. Linge, ed., *China's New Spatial Economy: Heading Towards 2020,* pp. 46–71. Hong Kong: Oxford University Press.

She Shui. 1999. "China's Total State Assets Published." *China Economic News,* September 13, p. 1.

Shen, L., and Y. Dai. 1990. *"Woguo 'Zhuhou Jingji' de Xingcheng jiqi Biduan he Genyuan"* [The Formation of China's Fiefdom Economy and Its Defects and Origin]. *Jingji Yanjiu [Economic Research],* 1990(3), 12–16.

Watson, A., et al. 1989. "Who Won the 'Wool War'?: A Case Study of Rural Product Marketing in China." *China Quarterly,* 118, 213–41.

Wedeman, A. H. 2003. *From Mao to Market: Rent Seeking, Local Protectionism, and Marketization in China.* New York: Cambridge University Press.

Wolf, H. C. 1997. *Patterns of Intra- and Interstate Trade.* Cambridge, Mass.: National Bureau of Economic Research.

Young, A. 1996. *The Razor's Edge: Distortions, Incremental Reform, and the Theory of the Second Best in the People's Republic of China.* Boston: Boston University Press.

———. 1999. *The Razor's Edge: Distortions and Incremental Reform in the People's Republic of China.* Paper presented at the Fifth Nobel Symposium in Economics: The Economics of Transition, Stockholm.

Zhang Sai and Li Qiang. 1985. *Touru Chanchu Diqu Biao Bianzhi Fangfa* [*Methodology for Compilation of Regional Input-Output Tables*]. Taiyuan: *Shanxi Renmin Chubanshe* [Shanxi People's Press].

Zhang Shouyi. 1992. "The Development of Input-Output Technique in Our County." In Li Qiang, ed., *Dangdai Zhonngguo Touru Chanchu Yingyong yu Fazhan* [*The Use and Development of Input-Output in Contemporary China*], pp. 16–25. Beijing: *Zhongguo Tongji* [China Statistics Press].

Zhou Zhenhua. 1996. *Diqu Fazhan* [Regional Development]. Shanghai: *Shanghai Renmin Chubanshe* [Shanghai People's Press].

Part IV

SHARING RISING INCOMES

9

China's War on Poverty

Scott Rozelle, Linxiu Zhang, and Jikun Huang

Few observers deny that China has made remarkable progress in its war on poverty since the launching of economic reform in the late 1970s. According to official Chinese and international statistics, during the two decades of reform, more than 200 million Chinese rural residents escaped poverty (World Bank, 1999). The incidence of rural poverty has fallen equally fast.

But while most agree with the scope of the drop in poverty, the reasons for the decline in the rural poor are less understood. Understanding the determinants of success in poverty alleviation and the growth of the economy in poor rural areas is important beyond its academic interest since there are from 50 to 120 million people living below the nation's poverty line. Is the reduction in poverty due more to the growth of the rest of the economy and the success that poor areas have enjoyed in linking themselves to China's robust economy? Or should credit be given to the nation's poverty program? In assessing the record of poverty investments, other questions arise: Have the nation's poverty investments been targeted effectively? Have funds that have been invested positively affected growth? Answers to these questions are important in designing policies to alleviate China's remaining poverty.

In this chapter, we will attempt to answer some of these questions as a way of providing information to policymakers that can help guide their future decisions affecting poverty alleviation. To meet this overall goal, we will pursue several specific objectives. First, we briefly describe China's policies for poor areas and examine how China's leaders have invested the funds of one of the developing world's largest poverty alleviation programs. Second, we seek to provide a detailed examination of the record on poverty alleviation. Finally, we attempt to assess how much of the decline in poverty is from the nation's poverty policy, centering our attention on issues of targeting and program growth effects.

To narrow the focus of such an ambitious set of objectives and to reduce the amount of data needed to examine some of these questions, we necessarily restrict the scope of our analysis. For example, we focus primarily on rural poverty. Although urban poverty is a new and perhaps increasing phenomenon, it is still small relative to rural poverty in terms of both head count and severity. In this chapter, we also focus primarily on the plight of the poor in China's officially designated poor areas. In the analytical part of the chapter, we examine how well China's leaders choose the counties for inclusion in the national poverty program, but to the extent that there are poor individuals or families in nonpoor counties, it is difficult with China's data to study this aspect of poverty. Fortunately, many people inside and outside of China who have worked extensively in poor areas believe that most of China's poor indeed live in officially designated poor areas (Piazza and Liang, 1997). We also examine poverty mainly on the basis of an income metric. While there is not a one-to-one correspondence between income and other measures of human welfare, Wang and Zhang (1999) and the World Bank (1999) show that there is a fairly high degree of correlation between areas with low income and those that do poorly on measures such as illiteracy and infant mortality.

Finally, in some cases, we restrict our attention to specific provinces and study poverty mostly with more aggregate data at the county level. Specifically, for examining targeting and the determinants of growth, we use data from two poor provinces in western China, Sichuan and Shaanxi. Looking at only a subset of China's poor regions necessarily means that idiosyncratic, province-specific policies and economic traits of the two provinces should be considered before extending the findings to the rest of China. But Sichuan and Shaanxi are large and diverse provinces, with a combined population of about 180 million people, and their territories include vast areas of mountains and drought-prone plains that typify the poor regions of China. The World Bank's recent poverty report (1999) identifies the depth of poverty in these areas as particularly severe. To this extent, we can consider the results drawn from these two provinces as representative.

Moreover, although there are some rich studies that use household data (e.g., Ravallion, 1999), the data only go through the late 1980s. Since the data were collected without regard to China's poverty policies, nothing is known about the participation of the households in any of the poverty programs, greatly restricting the ability to draw any conclusions about the effectiveness of policy. Our aggregate data provide longer time series and allow us to match performance indicators with participation in the policy program.

Poor Area Policy

Even though the Chinese leadership had not formulated an explicit national policy on poverty alleviation prior to 1986, the rural poor already received some special attention. With little to lose given the marginal contribution of poor areas to the overall economy, reformers permitted communes in poor areas to decollectivize earlier than in other areas (as early as the late 1970s). The central government was already subsidizing poor areas, both through direct budgetary transfers (Park et al., 1996) and through subsidized grain sales and other assistance to farmers in need (Park, Rozelle, and Cai, 1994). With fiscal decentralization and increasing scarcity of budgetary resources, however, these forms of support were reduced over time.[1] Market reforms led to widespread increases in production specialization, yields, and income (Weersink and Rozelle, 1997). These changes helped many escape poverty, especially people in central and coastal China, who had been hurt most by grain-first policies because they lived in areas not well suited for grain production (Lardy, 1983).

In the mid-1980s, leaders decided that redressing poverty of resource-poor households living in remote, isolated regions required more than favorable macroeconomic conditions and decentralized decision making (State Council, 1989a–1989e). A special poverty alleviation task force, the Leading Group for Economic Development in Poor Areas would oversee the new war on poverty. The task force would focus its efforts on counties that would be officially designated as "poor." National and provincial leaders would allocate resources from their budgets and direct banks to make loans to poor areas from special funds set up for poverty alleviation.

Poor Area Selection

When the government decided to set up a large-scale poverty alleviation plan in 1986, a standard was necessary to determine which counties would receive specially allocated funds (Park et al., 1998). The Leading Group initially adopted a mixed set of poverty lines to choose poor counties. The basic standard for selecting nationally designated poor counties was net income per capita below 150 RMB yuan in constant 1985 prices. However, a higher poverty line was applied to counties in old revolutionary base areas and counties with large minority populations. For some counties in important revolutionary base areas and for several minority counties in Inner Mongolia, Xinjiang, and Qinghai, the poverty line was raised to as high as 300 yuan. Three hundred poor counties were chosen to be supported by national poverty programs based on these standards, which used 1985 State Statistical Bureau data. In 1988, 37 pastoral counties were added (Tong et al., 1994). Some 370 additional counties were also designated for provincial government support in 1986. By 1988, the Leading Group and its provincial counterparts were running a program targeting 698 counties, about a third of China's counties.

In the 1980s, aside from those in counties under special military administration, most of China's poor lived among the more than 200 million residents who resided in officially designated poor counties (Piazza and Liang, 1997). These poor counties were distributed across twenty-three of China's provinces, but 78 percent of them were concentrated to the west of a north-south line that runs through the central mountainous parts of the country from Heilongjiang, Gansu, and Inner Mongolia in the north to Guangxi and Yunnan in the south. The remaining "poor" counties, generally better off among all poor counties, were located in less contiguous islands of poverty in the hills of eastern and southeastern China.

Poor counties in the first wave of officially designated counties were normally characterized as being poorly endowed by geographic location (remote and mountainous) and at a disadvantage in terms of agricultural resources (such as soil, rainfall, and climate; Tong et al., 1994). Many of these areas suffer from severe ecological damage such as deforestation and erosion (Li, 1994). Poor counties also tend to have more variable yields (Weersink and Rozelle, 1997). Partly as a result of these poor natural conditions and partly as a result of poverty itself, farmers in poor areas suffer from below-average irrigation facilities, fertilizer use, and general infrastructure (Tong et al., 1994). Poor counties in the 1980s were still highly subsistent in their grain needs and in net terms often needed to procure grain to meet household demand (Piazza and Liang, 1997). Participation in nonfarm labor markets in the 1980s lagged far behind the national average (Rozelle et al., 1999).

These official poverty lines were soon criticized by both researchers and local officials (Park et al., 1998). First, there was no explanation for why 150 yuan was chosen as the basic poverty line. Second, the line was not uniform. Political criteria played an important role in county selection. Third, because incomes in poor, agriculturally dominated areas are influenced by weather, using income data from one year may not reflect the average income levels of different counties. Finally, there was also nearly no adjustment in the late 1980s or early 1990s (except for the addition of three counties in Hainan province). The Leading Group had no set way to graduate those counties that developed rapidly or to support those that fell into poverty during the first years of implementation.

In response to these complaints and in preparation for the new push to eliminate poverty in the mid-1990s (called the 8–7 plan), the Leading Group asked the State Statistical Bureau to calculate a new poverty line based on nutritional criteria (Park and Wang, 2001). With these new criteria, national officials made their first (and so far only) sweeping adjustment to the designation of poor counties in 1994 (Piazza and Liang, 1997). The distinction between national and provincial was eliminated. And despite the large reduction in poverty counts, the number of nationally supported poor counties was established at 592. Park, Wang, and Wu (1998) provide a detailed province-by-province listing of the new poverty counties.

TABLE 9.1

National Government's Investment in China's Poor Areas by Program, 1986–97

(100 million yuan)

Year	Subsidized Credit		Food for Work		Development Fund		Total	
	Nominal	Actual	Nominal	Actual	Nominal	Actual	Nominal	Actual
1986	23	22	8	7	10	9	41	39
1987	23	21	8	7	10	9	41	37
1988	29	22	2	2	10	8	41	31
1989	30	19	2	1	10	6	42	27
1990	30	18	7	4	10	6	47	28
1991	35	21	38	23	10	6	83	49
1992	41	23	36	20	10	6	67	49
1993	35	17	51	25	11	5	87	48
1994	45	18	61	25	11	4	117	47
1995	48	17	61	11	9	3	118	30
1996	57	18	31	10	13	4	101	32
1997	87	28	31	10	28	9	146	45
Total	483	244	336	145	142	75	931	462

NOTE: All numbers in real 1985 prices.
SOURCE: Zhang, Huang, and Rozelle (2003).

Investment Programs

After 1986, the government aimed a major set of investments at increasing income growth in poor areas (see Table 9.1). Between 1986 and 1997, the government invested over 96 billion yuan through its main poverty alleviation loan, Food for Work, and grants programs (columns 1, 3, and 5). Nominal investments in poor areas increased in every year except 1992 and 1996 (column 7). In real terms (after adjusting for the impact of inflation), however, the picture is still impressive, although the trend is worrisome. In real 1985 yuan, total expenditures have reached 46 billion (column 8). After increasing steadily between 1986 and 1990, however, real expenditures in poor areas have fallen (when comparing, for example, the years 1990–92 to the years 1995–97).

Linking the nation's investment of poverty funds to poverty alleviation and economic growth, however, is not easy because of the sharp differences among different poverty investment programs and changes in the way that the investments have been made. We next examine the way that the national poverty alleviation program has managed its investment programs, focusing on its evolving strategy, and then shifting our attention to the sources and uses of funds from different subprograms.

Early Programs: Grants and Loans to Households

In 1986, the State Council formed the interministerial Leading Group for Economic Development in Poor Areas at the national level to administer a new investment program allocating 4 billion yuan per year to 300 nationally designated poor counties. Provincial governments also designated additional poor counties to receive provincial support. By 1988, some 698 counties received public help through these programs. Poor Area Development Offices (PADOs) were established at the provincial and county levels to administer funds from both national and provincial sources.

China's multilevel poverty alleviation network was funded by grants and loans approved by the State Council.[2] In the first years, most funds came from programs such as *laoshao bianqiong diqu daikuan* (subsidized credit for supporting old revolutionary bases, minority areas, and remote areas) and *bu fada diqu fazhan zijin* (development capital funds [DCF] for supporting underdeveloped areas). As the real value of grants declined due to inflation (the nominal level of funding for DCF remained largely unchanged from 1986 to 1993), new subsidized loan programs became the main form of poverty investment. In its initial years, local PADOs controlled most of the loan portfolios (Li and Li, 1992). Agricultural banks, which disbursed and collected the loans, exercised little decision-making authority according to interviews with PADO and banking officials.

Policies during 1986–1988 stressed that funds should be allocated directly to poor households to support agricultural production and other income-generating projects (State Council, 1989a–1989e; World Bank, 1992). Program rules often required local poverty officials to allocate up to 80 percent of their funds for agricultural loans to households (Li and Li, 1992).

After these first few years of implementation, poor area policies came under closer scrutiny. There was a general perception that much of the assistance was not spurring growth but was being used to support consumption directly (State Council, 1989a–1989e). As is typical for formal subsidized loan programs, loan repayment rates were low. Estimates of timely repayment on subsidized poverty loans range from 30 to 65 percent (Park et al., 1998). The main problem, as described in an important policy document, was that the long-term development of "social productive forces" in poor areas was being neglected (Zhou, 1988; State Council, 1989a–1989e). Even after four years of targeted programs, there were still over 100 million rural poor in 1989. Interestingly, these conclusions were drawn on the basis of limited data and observation. No systematic, large-scale evaluation of China's poverty program was ever conducted.

Policy Reform: Targeting Development Projects

By the late 1980s, the widespread belief that economic growth in poor areas had stagnated led to a major policy shift. New directives ordered local officials to turn their attention away from poverty alleviation through direct transfers to households in favor of projects that would better promote economic development (State Council, 1989a). The new measures encouraged officials in poor areas to redirect loans from households toward "economic entities" (*jingji shiti*) that could better coordinate activities requiring new technology, greater input use, and marketing support (State Council, 1989a). In recognition of the need for local governments to generate fiscal revenues, local officials were allowed to allocate more funds to enterprises. A new poverty loan program was established to support county state-owned enterprises. The Food for Work program to support basic infrastructure construction, which had previously focused on roads and drinking water, was expanded to include infrastructure projects in agriculture designed to help spur long-term productivity increases (Zhu and Jiang, 1994).

Local officials welcomed these changes. By the end of the 1980s, fiscal decentralization, which tied budgetary expenditures more closely to local revenues, had created a budgetary crisis in nearly all poor counties (Park et al., 1996). This created a strong incentive for local officials in poor areas to invest in revenue-producing enterprises rather than other growth-oriented activities or to divert earmarked investment funds to meet fixed expenditure obligations such as wage payments to government cadres (Wu, 1994; Park et al., 1996). Investment funds and loans were commonly channeled to county-run enterprises regardless of the investment's projected rates of return; the infusion of cash allowed government officials to transfer funds to the county budget (through fees and remittances or tax payments) or to shift fiscal burdens to enterprises (such as for hosting guests or paying travel costs).

Banking reforms in the late 1980s also affected the allocation of investment funds. Reforms made bankers more responsible for their profits and losses (Park and Rozelle, 1998; Li and Li, 1992). In response, bank managers began to assert more influence on loan decisions, including subsidized poverty loans. Conflicts arose between bank managers and PADO officials over proposed projects. Given the excess demand for low interest loans, bankers also began to target borrowers with less risky projects or larger projects that made loans less costly to administer (Du, 1994). As is common in rural settings, banks sought to ration out the poor, who have fewer assets, demand small loans with high transaction costs, and face greater uncertainty over crop yields (Carter, 1988). Thus the poverty policy shift in emphasis from household to enterprise and from agriculture to industry was reinforced by changing incentives caused by fiscal and banking reforms.

Shifts in the 1990s

There was a growing consensus among some of those interested in poverty work that by the mid-1990s, the subsidized credit directed at *jingji shiti* for integrated agricultural and rural development had not met any of its goals. Repayment rates on loans did not increase markedly. In one interview with banking officials in northern Shaanxi, we were told that repayment rates of subsidized loans in the northernmost prefecture of the province were less than 40 percent. A provincial leading group project officer in Sichuan revealed that only about 25 percent of the loans to *jingji shiti* were ever repaid in full, and partial repayments were made on only slightly more than 50 percent.

The effectiveness in stimulating local development of subsidized poverty loans also became increasingly suspect. Fieldwork frequently uncovered cases in which, in pursuit of scale economies, farmers were forced into collective projects that they preferred to avoid. In other cases, loans were taken out by *jingji shiti* managers for projects that were inappropriate for the local economy—projects that often ended in failure and unpaid debts. Loans were often diverted into economic entities that had political and fiscal importance (Park et al., 1996). (Later in this chapter, we describe the results of a study that measured the ineffectiveness of loans to counties and townships and the greater impact on growth of loans to farm households.)

But the largest problem of lending to economic entities may be that there is less effort to direct the funding to poor households. Many of the loans were given to township and village enterprises (TVEs) or county-owned enterprises, which increased the local revenue base for local governments but did not greatly benefit poor households (Wu, 1994). Wu's work shows that few poor farmers in investment sites get access to loans at all and that when they do obtain loans, they receive much smaller ones than their nonpoor counterparts. The failures of the program in reaching the poor were criticized by researchers and some local leaders. At a national work conference on poverty in September 1996, the Chinese government decided to return the focus of lending to providing direct loans to poor households.

Sources and Uses of Poverty Funds

In the face of China's fiscal crisis in poor areas (as illustrated by the declining amount of investment in these areas; see Figure 9.1) and the need for outside assistance, the importance of investments channeled into poor counties is undeniable. Such investments, which enter poor county balance sheets as earmarked subsidies, supplement funds used directly in infrastructure development. Besides adding to fiscal resources, because of better monitoring, loans are often more likely actually to be invested and are subject to less outright diversion. We shall use the experience of Shaanxi province in the earlier years of the poverty alleviation program and that of Sichuan province in the 1990s to examine how poor areas have raised and used poor area funds.

Shaanxi Province in the Late 1980s and Early 1990s

Shaanxi province is typical of the agricultural provinces in China's interior. Growth in output and income was very high in the early 1980s. After the mid-

FIGURE 9.1

Investment-to-Wage Spending Ratio in Shaanxi, 1982–92

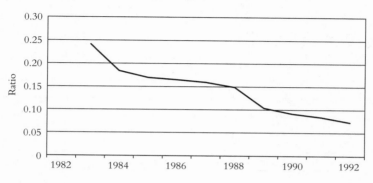

SOURCE: Park et al. (1996).

1980s, real per capita income growth slowed, rising by only 1.3 percent per year between 1986 and 1991 (State Statistical Bureau, 1987–1993). Over 55 percent of the gross value of rural social product came from agriculture in the early 1990s, about average for noncoastal provinces but much higher than in rapidly developing coastal provinces. Starting in the mid-1980s, the province's industrial output increased by more than 10 percent every year except 1989 (a recession year). Industrial output started from a low base and was concentrated around several urban centers. In most outlying regions, rural industry is underdeveloped, producing labor-intensive products with simple technologies.

Of the ninety-five counties in Shaanxi in 1992, poverty officials had designated thirty-four as "national poor counties" and twelve as "provincial poor counties." Data for a sample of forty-three poor counties that received targeted investment funds in 1992 were provided to us. The study counties are located in the Loess Plateau region in Yulin and Yanan prefectures (northern Shaanxi), Shangluo prefecture in the Qinling Mountains south of Xian (southern Shaanxi), and a set of "other" poor counties scattered throughout the province.

Sources of Poverty Funds

During the first three years of the poverty program, the total amount of poverty alleviation funds more than tripled in real terms, rising from 4.5 yuan per capita in 1986 to 14 yuan per capita in 1988 (see panel A of Figure 9.2).[3] Nearly 65 percent of the poverty funds in the first year came from the DCF, a grant fund administered by PADOs in each county (see panel B). When the national subsidized loan program began in 1987, however, agricultural loans rose to 7.5 yuan per capita, surpassing the funds available from the DCF, which fell in real terms.

FIGURE 9.2

Poverty Alleviation Investment Per Capita and Proportion of Investment
by Source in Forty-Three Sample Counties in Shaanxi, 1986–91

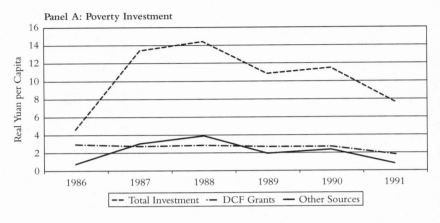

Panel A: Poverty Investment

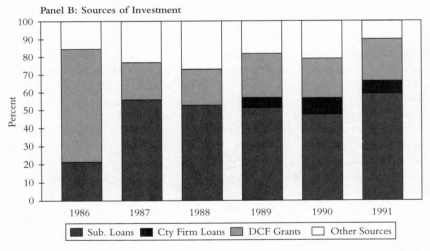

Panel B: Sources of Investment

NOTE: DCF stands for development capital funds.
SOURCE: Shaanxi Poor Areas Development Office.

Subsidized loans accounted for more than 50 percent of poverty funds in 1987
before falling to 45 percent in 1990.

While the aggregate funds available for poverty alleviation remained fairly constant in nominal terms between 1988 and 1992, inflation eroded the real level of
funding (see panel A of Figure 9.2). Except for a small rise in 1990, total real

funding fell, dipping to 7.5 yuan per capita in 1991, about half of the 1988 level and only slightly above the level of the first year of the program. The real value of DCF funds fell continuously after 1988. Interviews with finance bureau officials revealed that at about this time, many of the funds originally distributed as grants began to be loaned out instead.

The change in the composition of loan sources reflects other policy changes in the late 1980s. As described earlier, to help local governments expand their revenue bases and keep them from diverting loans earmarked for households, a special loan fund targeted at county state-owned enterprises (SOEs) was created in 1989.

The sources of funds differed only slightly in northern and southern Shaanxi. Being old revolutionary base areas, Yulin and Yanan prefectures received a higher fraction of their funds from budgetary grants administered through the DCF program. Southern Shaanxi counties, the site of many third-front industrial concerns, received significantly more earmarked funds for county enterprise development.

Uses of Poverty Funds

There is no direct correlation between the sources of poverty funds and the sector in which they are ultimately used. Money from subsidized loan programs, DCF, and other sources can be used for activities in any sector. Even when national rules govern expenditure (e.g., in the late 1980s, guidelines set by the Leading Group stated that agricultural households should receive 80 percent of subsidized loans; Li and Li, 1992), local leaders still have discretion over the use of investment monies, as seen by the varied pattern of fund use (see Figure 9.3). Local and national policy changes, however, did affect the pattern of investment. In the first years of the program, agricultural loans and grants to households rose faster than those of other categories (see panel A of Figure 9.3). In response to poverty policy reforms, funds targeted at agricultural households fell beginning in the late 1980s (although the proportion of agricultural loans remained around 40 percent; see panel B).

Officials also used poverty alleviation funds for industrial projects in the early years, even though national guidelines made it difficult to do so. In the first years of the program, loans and grants to TVEs were about equal to those to county-run firms and exceeded those to other nonagricultural uses. Although many county enterprises lost money and as a group never contributed more than 11 percent of poor county output value, the amount of funds devoted to county enterprises did not fall like those for TVEs and agricultural production. This was due in large part to the new county enterprise subsidized loan program. The fraction of poverty funds spent on county-run SOEs increased from 15 percent in 1986 to more than 25 percent in 1990 (and rose to 30 percent in 1992).

FIGURE 9.3

Poverty Alleviation Investment Per Capita and Proportion of Investment
by Users in Forty-Three Sample Counties in Shaanxi, 1986–90

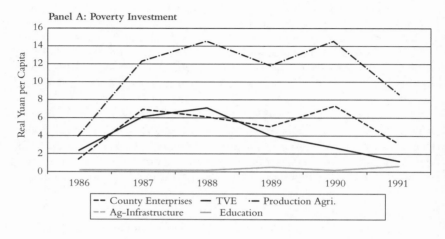

Panel A: Poverty Investment

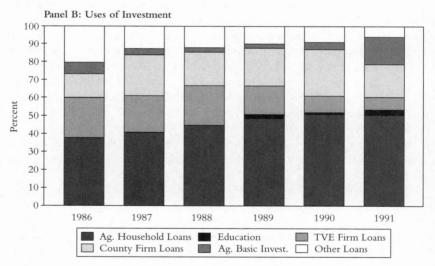

Panel B: Uses of Investment

SOURCE: Shaanxi Poor Areas Development Office.

FIGURE 9.4
Total Provincial Poverty Investment in Sichuan, 1991–95

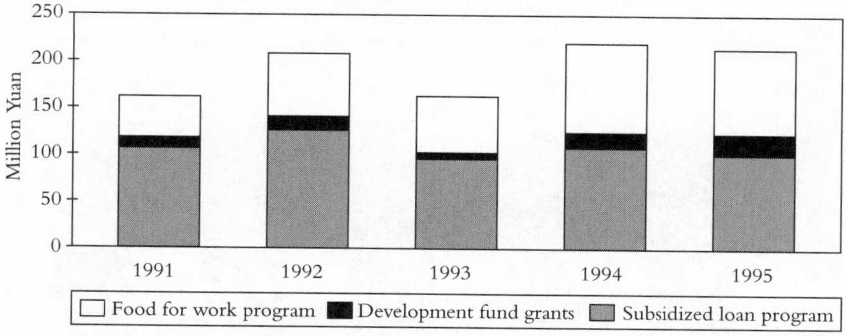

SOURCE: Shaanxi Poor Areas Development Office.

Sichuan Province in the 1990s

With data on all three sources of poverty funds (see Figure 9.4)—Food for Work, development grants, and subsidized loans—the profile of Sichuan's funding in the 1990s parallels that of the nation (compare with data from Table 9.1). In the early 1990s, funding came primarily from subsidized loans (more than 100 million yuan in 1991). Funds allocated through the national FFW program were the second largest, about 45 million yuan, a level larger than grants, which were less than 10 million yuan. The level of grant funding to Sichuan is lower than to many other provinces because few of Sichuan's poor counties are designated minority counties and even fewer are in designated revolutionary base regions.

By the mid-1990s, the level of poverty funding from all three sources rose slightly in aggregate real terms, and the composition changed (see Figure 9.4). The success of FFW programs induced officials to increase the proportion of funding through these channels (see Figure 9.5). Following the national government's push to eliminate poverty through its 8–7 plans, development grants almost doubled in real terms between 1991 and 1995 but still contributed only a small percentage of the province's total poor area investments. Subsidized loans remained almost constant in real terms. Even though the national government had advertised the large increases in support, apparently funding increases just barely kept up with the high rates of inflation that affected China in the mid-1990s.

Our data show the targeted nature of the different programs and how increases in funding of one program have affected the total amounts invested into specific activities. Almost all subsidized loans in China in the early 1990s went

FIGURE 9.5

Provincial Investment of Total Poverty Funds,
by Target Sector, in Sichuan, 1991–93

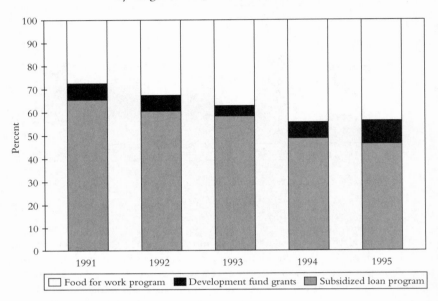

SOURCE: Shaanxi Poor Areas Development Office.

for investments into industrial production, and Figure 9.6 shows that over 90 percent of poor area fund investments in Sichuan's industry come from the targeted loan program. Unlike a number of other provinces in the 1980s (e.g., Shaanxi, as noted earlier), a large share of subsidized loans also was allocated to agricultural infrastructure investment (see Figure 9.7). Whereas loan investments to industry slightly exceeded agricultural infrastructure in 1991–93, the two uses together took up nearly 90 percent of the total loan amount (see Figures 9.4, 9.6, and 9.7).

Food for Work funding, in contrast, went mainly to support investments in transportation and drinking water improvements (see Figures 9.8 and 9.9). More than 90 percent of investments in roads and more than 80 percent of investments in drinking water and other infrastructure projects came from the FFW program. If this trend continued through the mid-1990s (investment fund use data for 1994 and 1995 were unfortunately unavailable), the rise in importance of FFW funding may be leading a new push for the nation's investment into roads and other basic infrastructure.

FIGURE 9.6
Total Provincial Poverty Investments in Industry,
by Program in Sichuan, 1991–93

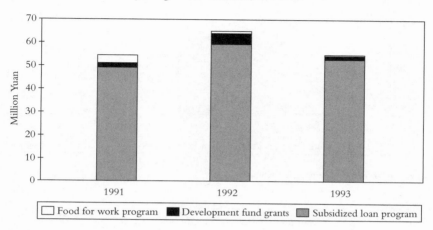

SOURCE: Shaanxi Poor Areas Development Office.

FIGURE 9.7
Total Provincial Investments in Agricultural Infrastructure,
by Program in Sichuan, 1991–93

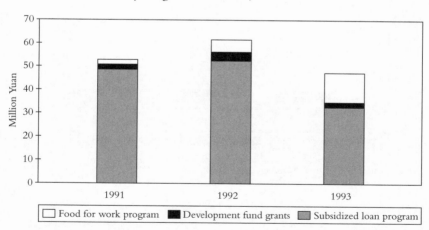

SOURCE: Shaanxi Poor Areas Development Office.

Figure 9.8
Total Provincial Poverty Investments in Transportation Infrastructure,
by Program in Sichuan, 1991–93

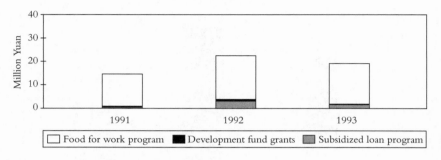

source: Shaanxi Poor Areas Development Office.

Figure 9.9
Total Provincial Poverty Investments in Other Sectors,
by Program in Sichuan, 1991–93

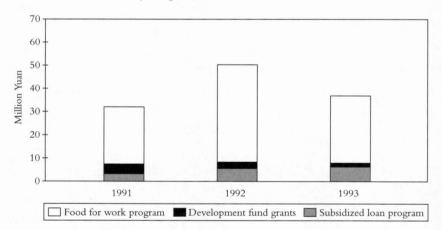

source: Shaanxi Poor Areas Development Office.

The Record on Poverty Alleviation

The official poverty lines in China are currently calculated by the State Statistical Bureau (SSB) based on its own household survey data and a nutrition standard set at a daily intake of 2,100 kcal and a food bundle recommended by the Chinese Nutrition Association. However, careful measurement of poverty is a

relatively recent phenomenon. One of the characteristics of China's poverty statistics over the reform period is that different poverty lines have been used at different times.[4] The official poverty lines, according to the World Bank's calculations, are lower than the international level set at U.S.$1 per day (in PPP terms).

Estimated using China's own poverty lines, China's rural poor decreased dramatically from 260 million in 1978 to 128 million in 1984 (see Table 9.2). After
slowing in the late 1980s, the rapid fall in the poverty head count continued in
the 1990s, declining to 42 million in 1998. The incidence of rural poverty (defined as rural poor divided by rural population) also decreased sharply during the
reforms. The incidence of poverty fell from 32.9 percent in 1978 to 15.1 percent
in 1984 and then to 4.6 percent in 1998.

Different levels but similar trends are found using international standards (in
the 1990s, the only years for which these measures are available). Poverty estimates based on U.S.$1 per day (in PPP terms) developed by the World Bank in-
dicate substantially greater numbers of absolute poor in China in all years (see
columns 4 and 5 of Table 9.2). Despite the differences, the trend of both head
count and incidence measures confirm the remarkable decline in poverty during the 1990s.

TABLE 9.2

Estimates of the Number of Poor in Rural China, 1984–98

Year	Official Government Estimates			International Standards ($1/day)	
	Poverty Line (current yuan/ year)	Number of Rural Poor (million)	Share of Rural Population (percent)	Number of Rural Poor (million)	Share of Rural Population (percent)
1978	—	260	32.9	—	—
1980	—	218	27.6	—	—
1982	—	140	17.5	—	—
1984	200	128	15.1	—	—
1985	206	125	14.8	—	—
1986	213	131	15.5	—	—
1987	227	122	14.3	—	—
1988	236	96	11.1	—	—
1989	259	106	12.1	—	—
1990	300	85	9.5	280	31.3
1991	304	94	10.4	287	31.7
1992	317	80	8.8	274	30.1
1993	350	75	8.2	266	29.1
1994	440	70	7.6	237	25.9
1995	530	65	7.1	200	21.8
1996	580	58	6.3	138	15.0
1997	640	50	5.4	124	13.5
1998	635	42	4.6	—	—

SOURCES: Poverty data for 1978–82 from World Bank (1992). Data from 1984 to 1998 are from
World Bank (1999) and Wang and Zhang (1999).

Economic Linkages or Policy?

Given an impressive record of poverty alleviation, the natural question to ask is, how much of the reduction is a by-product of growth in the overall (rural) economy, and how much can be reliably attributed to poverty programs?

In fact, the rural economy and almost all of its subsectors have grown quite fast, although at different rates during different periods (see Table 9.3). During the prereform period, per capita income growth rates increased by only 0.6 percent per year from a very low level, and the growth of agricultural and key crops barely kept up with population growth (column 1). After the launching of the reforms, however, income growth and the rise in almost every sector of the rural economy soared (column 2). Although growth slowed markedly after 1984 (column 3), it remained positive throughout. The pace of the rise in incomes has fluctuated dramatically, ranging from only 1 percent per year between 1985 and 1991 to almost 5 percent per year between 1991 and 1996. Obviously, robust economic growth helps reduce poverty, as long as the gains are reasonably distributed.

But during this time of rapid growth, poverty investments have also risen. As noted earlier, the government has taken a keen interest in trying to solve the nation's poverty problem. Before 1986, special grant funds and initiatives to spur growth were pushed in poor areas (Tong et al., 1994). Since 1986, nearly 100 billion yuan (in nominal terms) have been allocated to poverty alleviation (as indicated in Table 9.1). What impact have these expenditures had, independent of economic growth?

A strong case can be made for the importance of the linkages to the rest of the economy and the minimal effect of poverty policy by examining the results of a *simple* regression that looks at the relationship between falling poverty inci-

TABLE 9.3

Annual Real Growth Rates of Key Sectors in China's Rural Economy, 1970–95

(percent)

	Prereform Period	Reform Period	
	1970–78	1978–84	1984–95
Per capita real income	0.6	19.1	3.2
Agricultural value added	2.7	7.1	4.0
Agricultural gross value	2.3	7.5	5.6
Cropping	2.0	7.1	3.8
Grain	2.8	4.7	1.7
Rice	2.45	4.5	0.6
Wheat	7.0	7.9	1.9
Cotton	−0.4	7.2	−0.3
Oil crop	2.1	14.9	4.4

SOURCE: Huang and Rozelle (1998).

dence (PI) and economic growth (Y) and poverty incidence and poverty investments (PF) (t-statistics are in parentheses):

$$PI = 65 + 2,515/Y - 10 \times \ln(Y) + 0.7 \times \ln(PF) \tag{1}$$
$$(2.37) \qquad (2.60) \qquad (0.39)$$
$$R^2 = 0.98$$
$$PI = 69 + 2,453/Y - 11 \times \ln(Y) \tag{2}$$
$$(2.40) \qquad (2.78)$$
$$R^2 = 0.98$$

The coefficients on the growth variables (Y, specified to allow for decreasing marginal impacts of growth on poverty reduction) show that as growth has occurred, poverty has fallen sharply (although the reduction in poverty incidence per percentage point of economic growth is smaller over time). In contrast, the statistical analysis finds no significant relationship between poverty incidence and poverty investment. In fact, the R^2 statistic, although quite high at 0.98, does not change when poverty investments are included (equation 1) or omitted (equation 2).

Although the simplistic nature of the analysis precludes us from drawing any firm conclusions, it does aid us in specifying several hypotheses that our subsequent analysis can examine more carefully. Economic growth appears to be one of the major determinants of poverty alleviation. Poverty investment has been ineffective. As the poverty levels fall, it is becoming more difficult to lift the remaining poor out of poverty by relying solely on economic growth. We next examine these issues in greater depth.

Impact of China's Investments in Poor Areas: Targeting Success and Growth Effects

Here we seek answers to two questions: How good have China's poverty programs been at targeting the poor? And what has been the impact of China's poverty programs in stimulating growth? County-level data from Sichuan will be used to examine the effectiveness of targeting, and the analysis will focus exclusively on how well the Leading Group selected designated poor area counties. The Sichuan data and an additional county-level data set from Shaanxi will be used to examine the determinants of growth.

Targeting

In 1986, the national and provincial Leading Groups designated seventeen Sichuan counties as national poor counties and twenty-four as provincial poor counties. In 1994, after the announcement of the 8–7 plan, Sichuan's Leading Group announced that twenty-one of the original poor counties would graduate

TABLE 9.4

Gross Per Capita Income (deflated) in Sichuan Counties, Grouped by Income Levels and Poverty Designation, 1985–95

(yuan)

	n	1985	1986	1987	1988	1989	1990	1991	1992	1993	1994	1995
All counties	177	384	425	457	473	441	435	489	536	639	778	822
National designated poor, 1986	17	251	273	280	298	287	301	335	359	358	393	436
Provincially designated poor, 1986	24	284	313	331	344	324	327	357	386	390	450	497
All designated poor, 1986	41	272	298	312	326	310	317	349	376	378	426	470
Poor, not designated, 1986	53	297	320	338	353	302	303	322	333	330	358	377
Very poor, not designated in 1986	26	266	282	301	316	273	271	289	303	306	327	343
The poorest twenty counties in 1986	20	220	239	251	268	252	258	289	309	316	348	374
The poorest ten counties in 1986	10	217	228	239	248	235	240	271	284	295	328	367
Designated poor in 1994	38	255	288	295	303	271	267	292	308	302	324	347
Designated poor in 1986 but not in 1994	20	300	325	343	357	334	338	368	398	406	468	522
Designated poor in 1994 but not in 1986	17	272	311	315	315	254	234	247	252	242	245	250
Designated poor in both years	21	241	269	279	294	284	295	329	353	350	387	426
Poor, not designated, 1994	56	336	360	373	374	324	326	392	342	353	337	344
Very poor, not designated, 1994	40	343	359	369	368	311	311	324	330	307	303	319
Not poor, 1994	83	476	531	587	617	572	587	646	766	1,011	1,297	1,382
Not poor, 1986	83	497	556	605	622	569	579	667	748	963	1,216	1,291

SOURCE: China Ministry of Agriculture.

FIGURE 9.10

Gross Per Capita Income in Sichuan's Poor and Nonpoor Counties, 1985–95

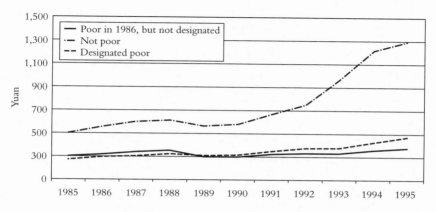

SOURCE: Shaanxi Statistical Bureau.

from that status and that seventeen new counties would be added. To examine the issue of targeting, our strategy will be to compare the income levels of these different groups in terms of their 1985 income levels, the criterion that was originally used to make the poor county designations. Two measures of income—total county income divided by county population ("gross per capita income") and net per capita income—are used for the analysis. Although both measures come from the provincial year-end reporting system and are not based on survey data, there is no a priori reason to favor one measure over the other. However, the higher correlation between gross per capita income at the provincial level and SSB-reported income statistics (which are not available for each county over time) leads us to put more stock in the results of the gross income figures. In addition, since leaders consider net per capita income statistics more direct measures of a county's economic performance, analysts in China sometimes fear that political pressure compromises the accuracy of reporting.

When compared with the provincial average and the average of nonpoor counties, nationally and provincially designated counties are poor in terms of 1985 gross per capita income levels (see Table 9.4 and Figure 9.10). Gross per capita income in the seventeen national poor counties was 251 yuan per capita in 1985, and that of the twenty-four provincial ones was 284 yuan (rows 2 and 3 of the table). The average of these provinces was significantly less than the provincial average (384 yuan per capita—top row) and even further below the average income of the eighty-three counties we count as "not poor" (497 yuan per capita—bottom row). Counties are counted as "not poor" if they are not nationally or provincially designated poor counties and are not "nondesignated" poor, which we define as counties that have incomes lower than the richest of the

TABLE 9.5

Net Per Capita Income (deflated) in Sichuan Counties, Grouped by Income Levels and Poverty Designation, 1985–95

(yuan)

	n	1985	1986	1987	1988	1989	1990	1991	1992	1993	1994	1995
All counties	177	271	293	304	298	262	255	275	283	270	274	286
National designated poor, 1986	17	165	179	182	186	182	191	213	223	213	214	226
Provincially designated poor, 1986	24	182	199	206	208	195	197	213	221	206	214	226
All designated poor, 1986	41	175	191	196	199	190	194	213	222	209	214	230
Poor, not designated, 1986	53	196	214	219	219	193	194	207	218	208	215	223
Very poor, not designated in 1986	26	185	204	206	207	182	183	199	210	205	211	216
The poorest twenty counties in 1986	20	145	155	159	161	158	166	190	202	196	198	220
The poorest ten counties in 1986	10	142	146	149	151	155	165	192	206	204	202	221
Designated poor in 1994	38	192	214	216	218	191	184	201	207	195	192	203
Designated poor in 1986 but not in 1994	20	192	207	213	217	201	204	219	227	211	218	229
Designated poor in 1994 but not in 1986	17	234	261	262	262	206	183	193	195	181	171	167
Designated poor in both years	21	159	176	179	182	178	185	208	217	207	210	232
Poor, not designated, 1994	56	246	265	268	263	228	220	234	238	218	212	223
Very poor, not designated, 1994	40	242	259	260	251	220	211	224	227	204	193	204
Not poor, 1994	83	323	353	369	357	319	312	336	349	342	355	372
Not poor, 1986	83	338	428	384	363	324	311	334	346	333	340	356

SOURCE: China Ministry of Agriculture.

FIGURE 9.11

Net Per Capita Income in Sichuan's Poor and Nonpoor Counties, 1985–95

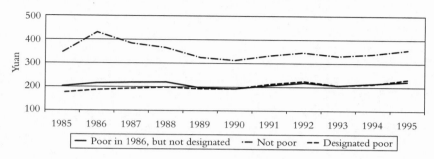

SOURCE: Shaanxi Statistical Bureau.

TABLE 9.6

Income Levels and Program Designation of Sichuan Province's Poorest Counties

(counties ranked as poorest on the basis of income per capita)

Category	Number	Income Per Capita, 1986 (yuan)	Income Per Capita, 1995 (yuan)
The Poorest Twenty Counties			
Nationally designated poor	8	237	454
Provincially designated poor	6	243	384
Not designated poor	6	237	257
The Poorest Ten Counties			
Nationally designated poor	4	224	442
Provincially designated poor	2	230	448
Not designated poor	4	230	251

NOTES: Program is China's 1986 national and provincial poverty program. Rankings were different in China's 1993 poverty program revisions.

poor counties. Nationally and provincially poor counties also have significantly lower reported net income per capita levels (166 and 182 yuan, respectively) than the provincial average (271 yuan) and nonpoor counties (338 yuan; see Table 9.5 and Figure 9.11). Interestingly, the average poor county in Sichuan had an income that exceeded the 150 yuan minimum income standard set by the Leading Group as the primary criterion for inclusion as a national poor county.

Targeting was good but imperfect. Although the counties that became part of the national and provincial poverty program in 1986 were indeed poor and clearly below average, a number of counties that were equally poor or poorer were excluded. Gross income per capita of fifty-three counties in Sichuan (297 yuan) was lower than that of the "least poor" poor county ("Poor, not designated"—row 5 of Table 9.4), and the income of twenty-six counties (266 yuan) was below the income of the nationally designated poor counties at the 75th

TABLE 9.7

Results from Growth Regressions on County-Level Per Capita Incomes

	Dependent Variable: Log Gross Per Capita Income						Dependent Variable: Log Net Per Capita Income					
Year Variable	0.0352 (7.76)	0.0534 (10.6)	0.0534 (10.5)	0.0534 (10.6)	0.0384 (7.8)	0.0418 (8.77)	−0.006 (2.21)	−0.0186 (6.72)	−0.0186 (−6.63)	−0.0186 (6.65)	−0.0181 (6.57)	−0.0089 (3.2)
Interaction Dummies												
Ten poorest counties		−0.356 (5.06)						0.0241 (5.25)				
All poor counties			−0.033 (4.76)						0.0308 −6.97			
Poor, not designated in 1986				−.0512 (6.4)						0.0207 (3.5)		
Very poor, not designated in 1986					−0.0292 (2.6)						0.0249 (3.66)	
Nationally designated poor, 1986				−0.004 (0.366)	0.011 (0.797)					0.0479 (6.4)	0.0474 (6.24)	
Provincially designated poor, 1986				−0.012 (1.157)	0.003 (0.238)					0.0312 (4.8)	0.0307 (4.64)	
Designated poor in 1994, but not 1986						−0.072 (5.39)						−0.0406 (5.21)
Designated poor in 1986						0.0025 (0.27)						0.0284 (5.19)
N	1,573	1,573	1,573	1,573	1,573	1,573	1,748	1,748	1,748	1,748	1,748	1,748
R^2	0.037	0.456	0.442	0.453	0.304	0.289	0.003	0.427	0.41	.415	0.389	0.35

NOTES: The absolute values of t-statistics are in parentheses. Coefficients on intercepts and intercept dummies are not reported.

percentile ("Very poor, not designated"—row 6 of the table). In addition, of the twenty poorest counties in Sichuan in 1985, six were not chosen to be part of the national poverty program, and four of the ten poorest were not selected (see Table 9.6). Clearly, there appear to be grounds for complaints by local officials from these nondesignated poor counties who believed that they had been unfairly passed over in the selection process in 1986.

Although not an excuse for poor targeting, given the ultimate goal of poverty alleviation, local officials and national policymakers do point out that concerns for efficient use of scarce poverty funds may also have led to the exclusion of the poorest of the poor. Poverty officials are evaluated in no small part on the basis of concrete targets for the numbers of people lifted out of poverty, as well as on other indicators related to the improvements that poverty investments have made. With limited funds, officials who must invest in poor areas still have an incentive in some cases to direct the funds to the better-off poor areas. With better locational advantages and often with better human and natural resources, project costs can be lower and the expected success rate higher. For example, Food for Work project officials told us in interviews that they almost always initially concentrate their road construction investments on areas in the immediate neighborhood of the county seat or on intertownship routes. The returns to such roads are much greater on average. They know that the per-kilometer cost of road building to reach the poorest of the poor villages is so high that it would use up the entire budget and benefit only a relatively small number of people. World Bank officials also admit that local officials who guarantee loans to villages and households insist on investing in the better-off areas in order to minimize the possibility of default. The record of targeting is consistent with such a decision-making rule.

In 1994, the government's efforts to retarget poverty funds did reach some, but not all, of the nondesignated poor counties that had been missed in the earlier round (see Table 9.4). Counties that were removed from the rolls (i.e., graduating counties) had an average income of 300 yuan per capita in 1985 (twice the national standard) and had average income levels of 406 yuan per capita in 1993 (the year of the reorganization—see row 11 in the table). In 1994, the graduating counties were replaced by newly designated poor counties, which had had lower income levels in 1986 (272 yuan) and much lower income levels (than both the graduating counties and their original levels) in 1993 (242 yuan—see row 12). The newly designated poor counties were apparently chosen not only for their low income levels but also for their poor performance during the late 1980s and early 1990s. There was still considerable leeway in designation in 1993, as fifty-six counties still had income levels lower than the richest "poor" county, and income levels of forty counties still fell below the 75th percentile (rows 14 and 15).

Impact on Growth

The impact of participation in the national or provincial poverty program on the rise in income levels can be seen in the simplest terms (not holding other factors constant) by examining plots of income levels over time of Sichuan's designated poor (using the 1986 designations, unless otherwise noted), nondesignated poor, and not poor (see Figures 9.10 and 9.11). Using both gross and net income per capita measures, designated or program counties started lower in 1985 and ended higher than nondesignated poor counties. Growth of real gross per capita income in program counties was clearly positive and exceeded the very small rise for nonprogram poor counties. Income (gross) increases of poor program counties, however, did not keep up with increases in the nonpoor counties.

To examine the statistical significance of the differences in the growth rates among subgroupings of counties, we regress the log of gross and net per capita income on a series of year and group dummy variables (making the coefficient on the year variable the baseline growth rate and the coefficients on the year and group dummy interaction terms the difference in the growth rates from the baseline; see Table 9.7). These initial growth impact results support the hypothesis that program participation increased growth in poor counties. The coefficients on the year variable in the first six columns show that there were positive growth rates in gross income per capita during the study period (1985–95). The insignificant signs on the dummy variables for nationally and provincially designated poor counties (rows 6 and 7) show that growth rates of poor program counties were statistically indistinguishable from nonpoor counties, a result that was originally noted (though not rigorously proven) by Tong et al. (1994) for all poor counties in the late 1980s and by Rozelle (1996) for poor provinces. The negative and significant signs on the nondesignated poor and nondesignated very poor variables in rows 4 and 5 show that the poor counties that were not included in the program had significantly slower growth. The magnitude of the coefficients means that growth in these nonprogram counties was between 0 and 1 percent. (When examining the net per capita regressions, program and nonprogram poor grew faster than the average county in the province, but the larger coefficients on the program county variables mean that program counties grew faster than nondesignated counties.) The growth regression also demonstrates that the 1994 reorganization included counties that had grown significantly more slowly than the average county (rows 8 and 9).

Determinants of Growth

Explaining Growth in Sichuan Province

A series of regressions explaining the growth and level of income in Sichuan are included to identify the determinants of growth in all counties in Sichuan and to examine the impact of China's poverty programs, holding other factors con-

TABLE 9.8

Ordinary Least Squares Regression Explaining Income Levels and Growth in Sichuan Province, 1990–95[a]

	Dependent Variable			
	Growth in Total Income[b]	Total Income[c]	Gross Per Capita Income[d]	Net Per Capita Income[d]
Year	0.0346	4,809	64.6	4.55
	(9.06)	(2.12)	(4.75)	(2.6)
Endowments and Economic Structure				
Rural labor force	−0.0496	−1,512	657.7	−2.84
	(3.0)	(6.33)	(2.28)	(0.078)
Sown area	0.029	332.6	−82.3	−13.7
	(0.280)	(3.39)	(4.4)	(5.73)
TVE labor force	0.033	10,004	2,828	414.7
	(2.99)	(11.3)	(11.4)	(13.4)
Cash crop sown area	0.0713	933.4	366	57.97
	(3.43)	(2.64)	(4.55)	(5.66)
Investments				
Infrastructure expenditures	−0.00001	−9.80	0.2358	0.121
	(1.15)	(−1.08)	(0.109)	(0.423)
Agricultural expenditures	0.00003	−3.62	3.79	0.243
	(2.19)	(−0.414)	(1.90)	(0.940)
Health and education expenditures	0.000001	20.4	−1.847	−0.333
	(2.06)	(5.8)	(2.66)	(3.82)
Electrification	0.00002	−4.0	2.5	−0.243
	(1.83)	(−0.479)	(0.747)	(0.552)
Performance of Poor Counties				
Poor, not designated in 1986	−0.0456	−39,363	−329.8	−93.8
	(4.21)	(6.175)	(8.09)	(16.0)
Designated poor in 1986	−0.0295	−51,303	−372.2	−95.3
	(2.54)	(7.37)	(8.52)	(17.8)
Per capita income (lagged one year)	0.000025			
	(3.076)			
N	859	1,028	854	1,023
R^2	0.33	0.535	0.38	0.468

NOTES: [a]Regressing ordinary least squares estimators. Coefficients on constants are not reported and absolute values of t-stats are in parentheses.
[b]Dependent variable, endowment, and structure variables are in logged growth form.
[c]Variables are in absolute levels.
[d]Variables are in per capita form.

stant (see Table 9.8). Three different specifications using gross county income (columns 1 to 3) and one using net per capita income (column 4) as the dependent variables are presented (definitions of the variables are in footnotes to the table). Growth rates and income levels are regressed on sets of independent variables representing resource endowments and the economic structure of the county, investments (by type) made through the fiscal system (which include some but not all of poor area investments), and program participation. County-level data for the analysis come from the SSB. Six years of data (1990–96) are used for 177 Sichuan counties, providing 859 observations when explaining year-to-year growth (column 1) and 1,028 observations when explaining income levels (column 2). In the year-to-year growth equation (column 1), endowment and structural variables are also in year-to-year form. Right-hand side investment and endowment variables are lagged one period to help avoid endogeneity problems.

The growth models performed quite well in terms of goodness-of-fit measures and performance of endowment and economic structure variables. The adjusted R^2 values range from 0.33 to 0.535, fairly high for such short time series. The positive coefficients on the year variable mean that the economies were growing quite fast (3.46 percent per year) during the reform era. Certainly, these growth rates are partly due to the impact of reform and general market development and partly due to technological developments (Lin, 1992; Huang and Rozelle, 1996). Increases in endowments and economic activities that create linkages with the rest of the economy, such as the nonfarm labor force and cash cropping, augment growth in all four of the aggregate growth, income level, and per capita income equations. Holding labor market activity and high-value agriculture constant, however, further increases in population (rural labor force) and grain-cultivated area generally hold down income increases and growth.

In the most traditional specification (column 1), investments in agriculture, health and education, and electrification positively affect growth, though the effects on growth of some investments (e.g., those in "other" infrastructure projects) are not readily apparent. The positive impact of these investments should convince policymakers who support the development of poverty projects to continue to emphasize these investments. The weak effect of infrastructure investment may be caused by aggregating the effect of transportation investments (which should be expected to have strong growth effects) with other investments, such as terracing, which, when done poorly, have only small impacts on agricultural output and growth and may even be detrimental to growth because the heavy labor investment required has a high opportunity cost for farmers (Li, 1994). Health and education investments also have particularly strong growth-inducing effects on overall income levels. For every dollar invested in health and education, there is a twentyfold return. The investment variables have mixed results in the per capita calculations, curiously showing a negative impact of per capita spending on health and education on per capita incomes. It may be that lagging the independent variables fails to control for all of the endogeneity. Poor areas that are growing more slowly may require higher health and education expenditures—because it may cost more to deliver even a marginal service (because of negative scale economies or the poor initial level of the social service).

The main finding of the growth regressions is that the poverty program does increase growth, or, more accurately, keeps growth rates of designated poor counties from falling, as do growth rates of nondesignated poor counties (compared to nonpoor counties—see Table 9.8, column 1). The negative sign on the coefficient of the designated poor variable means that after accounting for endowments, structure, and beginning levels of income, poor program counties grow more slowly than nonpoor counties (2.95 percent per year less). However, this lower growth rate was still above that of the poor counties outside the 1986 program, which experienced growth rates 4.56 percent slower. From this point of view, without considering the higher (presumably, although they could be lower) fiscal investments that came with being part of the national or provincial poverty alleviation program (since budgetary investments are held constant), poor program counties maintained higher growth rates than nonprogram poor counties. These higher rates could be due either to more effective use of poverty investments that go through the fiscal system (which might occur if they are better designed or monitored by county PADOs than by officials in counties without PADOs) or to FFW or other poor area programs that do not show up in fiscal investments.

Growth in Shaanxi Province's Poor Counties

Growth regressions examining the impact of use of poverty investments on agriculture, rural industry, and state-owned enterprise growth are in Rozelle et al. (1998). The study employs a unique data set to examine the sources, uses, and effectiveness of targeted poverty investments in forty-three poor counties of Shaanxi Province during 1986–91. The overall goal of the study is to understand China's poverty alleviation policy, trace changes over time, assess the motives for the changes, and evaluate the effectiveness of the various strategies pursued. For this sample of Shaanxi (nationally and provincially) poor area counties, targeted investment funds allocated directly to households for agricultural activity have a significant positive effect on growth, while investments in township and village enterprises or county state-owned enterprises do not have a discernible effect on growth. Investments in agricultural infrastructure do not positively affect growth rates in agricultural output, suggesting that other types of basic investments (e.g., roads and education) should receive higher priority. These results suggest that the program's initial emphasis on household lending was most appropriate for furthering economic growth in poor areas.

To the extent that these results can be generalized to the whole of China, the change in poverty alleviation strategy and the preference to allocate scarce resources to revenue-generating (if not growth-enhancing) enterprises has a clear rationale. In particular, the dwindling fiscal resources in poor areas have forced local leaders to pursue every possible source of funds to finance public expenditures and fulfill mandatory government functions. A viable local government surely plays an important role in the process of economic development, both in promoting growth and in pursuing equity concerns. The lack of discernible impacts of industrial investments on growth in part reflects the failure to solve the fiscal problems that have emerged in poor areas; this increases the incentives to distort resource allocation decisions. This linkage suggests that addressing the fundamental problems in the fiscal system could lead to a more effective poverty investment program.

In summary, our results generally show that markets and appropriate investments matter for growth in all counties, rich and poor, and that, *ceteris paribus*, the poverty program aids the growth process in poor counties. Investments centered on agriculture and those that get into the hands of farmers have positive growth impacts. Projects that create an economic environment that can foster entrepreneurship and labor movement, such as increasing human capital, also affect growth. The weak correlation between growth and infrastructure merits closer examination with better, more disaggregated data. Most important of all, the impact of poverty investments is not always strongly significant and positive. There may be ways to invest with much greater effectiveness.

Conclusions: Promoting Efficient Resource Allocation in China's Poor Areas

Here we look in greater detail at a number of important issues surrounding the efficient use of specific resources in poor areas, an important issue especially in the face of scarce investment resources. When funds are available, officials who want to have an effect on poverty need to make good investments. Lessons for making efficient investments emerge from different types of widespread failures and successes frequently encountered in China. In particular, we will show cases where projects failed because they were ill-designed, imposed on farmers who did not understand the technology or have the requisite skills, or allocated to enterprises that had close political connections to the government and were preyed on by fiscally starved government authorities. We will then look at several cases of successful investments, focusing on successful schemes that directed funds straight into the hands of farmers while providing concomitant extension and other support, were designed to take account of the interests of stakeholders in the area, and focused on channeling investment funds without diversion by local fiscal authorities.

Problems in Delivering Effective Poor Area Investments

Project Design

When projects are carried out with inferior designs and inappropriate mixes of investment inputs, they can result in little change, in effect, wasting the investment effort. Li (1994) illustrates the importance of a well-designed project by examining the results of projects undertaken during a two-phase prefecturewide terracing project in Shanxi province.

In one phase, the government used World Food Programme support to develop high-quality terraces according to design plans created by the local agricultural technical college. Large-scale equipment and local labor combined to create deep, straight-cut terraces with reconditioned soil in each terrace bed. In the other phase, local leaders mobilized local laborers with little or no capital support (for dynamite or grading equipment). At the most, township leaders rubberstamped the hastily prepared work plan of village officials. The difference in the impact of the project in meeting the goal of the two projects—increased grain output—shows the importance of good design.

To test whether or not traditional terraces were worth investing in, Li (1994) collected data on inputs and outputs from different types of terraces and upland plots of farmers and added three dummy variables—high-quality terraces; locally designed, traditional terraces; and unimproved, moderately sloped land—to a traditional production function. The base land type (against which the coefficients of the land type variables are tested) was "very steep" slope land—implying that all dummy variables should be positive but that the better the land, the larger the coefficient. When compared to the baseline land type, the positive and significant coefficients on all of the variables in all of the equations demonstrate that using less steep land or terracing does lead to increased land productivity. However, in none of the cropping equations do traditional terraces outperform moderately sloped land (the most typical place where traditional terraces are built). The size and significance are almost the same. In other words, in terms of increased production (the stated purpose of building terraces), there is almost no increase in yields over land on which crops were initially grown. The problem, according to Li (1994), is that narrowly terraced slopes do not improve the soil (and by disturbing it may decrease productivity) and do not help in water runoff retention (in the way that well-designed terraces do). Farmers best reflected their view of spending the time and effort under the direction of local leaders to create the traditional terrace: "We work; we do not get paid; we cannot make other money; and we do not see our land get any better" (interview in Henan province, 1997).

Involuntarily Drafting Unwilling and Untrained Project Participants

One of the most prevalent complaints of farmers in poor areas with poverty alleviation investment funds is that they were given no choice of activities and often were forced to participate even when they had inadequate time, resources, or know-how to undertake the projects. For example, during a field visit to a Hebei province poor county in 1997, the poor area alleviation office had disbursed a 700,000-yuan loan for livestock production to a local state-owned meatpacking enterprise. The enterprise manager described how the project mainly focused on trying to break into a new but risky export market for frozen rabbit meat. The official in charge of the project chose ten project villages and signed contracts with the village leader for each farmer in the village to receive four rabbits, part of the caging facilities, and a first batch of feed in exchange for assuming responsibility for a 100-yuan debt. The village leader also required each farmer in the village to put up the rest of the investment for cages (50 yuan), a down payment on additional feed, and a veterinarian service contract. Although the farmers in this area had never raised rabbits, participants claim that the rabbits and cages arrived one day with no explanation. Village leaders had to explain how to begin animal care.

Unsurprisingly in light of such little preparation, the production of rabbits did not proceed very smoothly and created a great deal of frustration among the participants. Almost all the animals died before being sold. According to the contract, the dead animals could be returned to the project manager, and if it was determined that they had died of unavoidable causes, the farmer would be reimbursed part of the investment. But no one ever carried out these reimbursements. There was no one to talk to who would collect or receive the dead carcasses. Almost every farm household in one project village lost its entire investment and was unable even to return the cage. Some farmers even gave in to bankers' demands to repay the loan. Others related that when they refused repayment, they were threatened with never again being able to borrow from the local bank.

Project officials did not accept blame, were not punished, and actually received funding for a second phase that ended up going to a nonpoor set of villages. Project officials blamed the poor education levels of the farmers—and told bank officials from whom they borrowed the money that the responsibility for repayment should reside with the local PADO, which had forced the meat-packing plant to loan to the poorer villages. After investigating the matter, and over objections by the local PADO, bank officials, who administer poverty loans, distributed the second installment of the loan to the company, which lent it to a smaller set of richer villages.

Loans Made on Noneconomic Grounds

Although a great fraction of poverty grants and subsidized loans went to township-run (and county-run) factories in the late 1980s and early 1990s (Rozelle et al., 1998), Jin (1994) demonstrates that the economic performance of township enterprises fell short of that of village and private enterprises. Jin's analysis shows that the probability of creating a loss-making firm at the township levels is much greater than that for village enterprises. The ratio of losses to profits is only 0.14 for village enterprises but 0.56 for township enterprises in poor areas. (Poor area firms in both categories also performed less well than their rich area counterparts.) The rate of return on capital was also much lower for township-run firms.

When closely examining the poor performance of local-state run enterprises, many reasons for the ineffectiveness of an industry-based strategy for poor area development can be identified. Township leaders lay claim to poverty alleviation loan funds even if their record is poor compared to villages and households. Access to low-interest loans was essential in founding enterprises and creating a revenue source, if they had any hope of achieving expenditure and other poverty alleviation goals. In a broader context, it is not surprising that government officials have been unable to generate high returns to their investments in local state-run enterprises. The experience of project managers in the World Bank's poverty project is that there is no reason to expect that leaders should be able to choose winners in local economies where firms have little natural comparative advantage relative to other, more developed areas of China. There are few infrastructure resources, human or physical, on which successful industrial development can be built.

Success in Delivering Effective Poor Area Investments

Household-Based Schemes, Increased Welfare, and Increased Confidence

When households are given funds, provided with extension assistance, subjected to tight monitoring on their repayment, and offered participation in a sympathetic, supportive group, not only is there a very rapid increase in the household economic status, but the increased empowerment of farmers, especially women in rural areas, is readily noticeable. In a recent trip to Yilong County, the site of a UNDP-sponsored microcredit project, we observed the result of three years of project intervention. Under the direction of Madame Xiaojun Gao, the Yilong microcredit project has flourished as the project mangers have kept tight discipline on their staff, insisted on a participatory approach to lending and collection, and pursued a farmer-first strategy.

Not only has there been a large increase in confidence and well-being among program participants, but the descriptive results of a pretest survey (which we commissioned) comparing the economic status of participants and nonparticipants show that project households have fared well. Their average asset holdings increased by 25 percent in 2½ years. Many households that have received loans have focused more attention on higher-return activities instead of subsistence crop production. And repayment rates have been almost 100 percent, ensuring that the capital can be re-lent.

Avoiding Diversion

One very common problem of poor area investment management is that loans and grant funds are often diverted to other uses before they can reach the local agency in charge of investment. In a study of Food for Work projects in Guizhou and Sichuan provinces, Zhu and Jiang (1994) found that only through creative investment fund management, primarily dependent on keeping investment funds out of the fiscal system, could large investments be effectively made in remote rural areas. The manager of FFW projects in the late 1980s and early

1990s (the State Planning Commission, or SPC) sold whatever materials it was allocated on the open market and used the funds to purchase cement, steel, and large equipment on its own initiative. These in-kind construction project investments were given to local companies and leaders under the close supervision of the local SPC. Official policy only allowed investment in roads and drinking water, two types of projects that are easily monitored (especially when there are no other projects ongoing).

In their analysis, Zhu and Jiang (1994) showed that there were significant and real gains in incomes in the places that participated in FFW projects. The returns were also greater in terms of investment in roads in poorer areas. Unfortunately, after the mid-1990s, this formula for successful investment has been abandoned in poor areas, as PADOs were offered more resources (i.e., control of the FFW funds) in return for a greater effort in alleviating poverty.

A New Strategy for Poverty Alleviation

When confronting poverty in the twenty-first century, one is left with some basic questions that must be answered before deciding on a new strategy. To the extent that China's poverty policy and general economic development push have been successful over the past two decades, is it the right strategy to help the remaining farming households out of poverty? What are the factors that link economic development to poverty reduction? How can the current policy framework begin to address the pockets of poverty outside of the designated poverty areas and in urban areas?

The most important thing to realize is that even with the successes to date, there are still up to 100 million rural absolute poor. And much of the remaining poverty is both extreme and subject to severe natural constraints. As we have seen, in the past, the wide incidence of poverty made it possible to achieve substantial reductions in poverty through general economic growth, establishing linkages through labor and commodity markets and through programs that were more broadly targeted. At present, however, most rural poor are concentrated in resource-deficient areas and comprise entire communities located primarily in upland sections of the interior provinces of northern, northwestern, and southwestern China. Although these poor have access to land, their soil is of such poor quality that it is impossible to achieve subsistence, and so they, of all farming communities when it comes to survival, are reliant on markets and outside sources of income. However, it is these poorest households that are typically most disadvantaged by high dependency ratios, ill health, poor human capital, and living in such isolation that they have little information on market opportunities. Minority peoples and peoples with disabilities account for a highly disproportionate share of the rural poor. Poverty also exacerbates societywide problems of lower rates of female participation in education, higher relative female infant mortality rates, and higher rates of maternal mortality. Available evidence suggests that the severity of the remaining poverty worsened somewhat during the 1990s. A recent World Bank report on poverty (1999) shows that the squared poverty gap index increased during the 1990s and in 1998 remained considerably greater than in 1990.

Hence the old strategy based on providing the poor with capital for creating their own economic activities or building them bridges to the rest of the economy (with road projects) may not work as well and perhaps not at all. Since the educational, health, and nutritional status of the remaining absolute poor is deplorable, the new strategy must address these issues. This is not a problem that lends itself to an immediate solution. As many as half of the boys in many of China's poorest villages and, especially in some minority areas, nearly all of the girls do not attend school and will not achieve literacy. The World Bank (1999) reports that infant mortality rates and maternal mortality ratios in very poor counties exceed 10 percent and 0.3 percent. respectively, levels that are up to twice the national average. Many individuals still suffer from chronic nutrition and disease problems. The traditional programmatic focus on hardware construction in search of immediate poverty alleviation must be replaced by a more patient effort that will invest in rural education, health, and welfare.

That is not to say that traditional investment programs are not needed or that linkages to the rest of the economy are unimportant. Indeed, they may ultimately be more important. There is still a need for agricultural development and for programs that move people out of the most uninhabitable environments. During the time that rural education and other human capital enhancement programs are being run, the standard of living of those remaining in rural areas can be made less dreadful with appropriate investment programs in irrigation, drinking water, roads, communication, and other rural development projects. But the regions where the poorest of the poor live are most relatively abundantly endowed with labor, and poverty alleviation will require most of all an investment in that factor, providing it with the skills to enable it to participate in the activities of the rest of economy.

Other challenges also remain, especially dealing with rising poverty in pockets outside of poor areas and in urban areas. Policies that facilitate the care of those without traditional support, such as a functioning family unit, which serves as the safety net for most rural residents, need to be adequately established and funded. Creating pension and health care for China's working class in rural and urban areas will be critical for avoiding the worst of the urban blight that has plagued so many other nations. Little is known about these problems, and China's leaders should support work to monitor these problems and begin to explore alternative policies for dealing with them before they become too widespread.

Notes

1. Park et al. (1996) describe greater fiscal self-reliance among poor counties. In 1993, the state eliminated national subsidies on resold grain.

2. In this chapter, we are primarily concerned with the policies of the Leading Group. The State Council also funds a large food for work (FFW) program aimed at the construction of roads and drinking water delivery projects. Analysis of this program is beyond the scope of this chapter, and the interested reader should see Zhu and Jiang (1994). Total funding on combating poverty (including FFW, subsidized loans, and budgetary grants) expanded very rapidly in the 1990s, from 4.6 billion RMB yuan in 1990 to 10.8 billion RMB yuan in 1996 (Park, Wang, and Wu, 1998).

3. All values in this section are deflated to 1986 yuan using the provincial consumer price index.

4. The poverty line was 100 yuan per year in 1978, 200 yuan per year in 1984, 300 yuan per year in 1990, 530 yuan per year in 1995, and 635 yuan per year in 1998.

References

Carter, M. R. (1988). "Equilibrium Credit Rationing with Small Farm Agriculture." *Journal of Development Economics*, 28, 83–103.

Du Xiaoshan. (1994). "Improving Access to Rural Credit for Poor Households: Experimenting with a Chinese-Style Grameen Bank." In *Promoting Economic Development in China's Poor Areas: A Collection of Policy Briefs*, ed. Albert Park and Scott Rozelle. Beijing: China Poverty Research Association.

Huang, Jikun, and Scott Rozelle. (1996). "Technological Change: Rediscovery of the Engine of Productivity Growth in China's Rural Economy." *Journal of Development Economics*, 49, 337–69.

————. (1998). *Decomposing the Productivity Growth of Agriculture in China's Reform Economy*. Working Paper, Center for Chinese Agricultural Policy, Beijing.

Jin Hehui. (1994). "Rural Enterprise Development in Undeveloped Areas: Productivity Gaps and Investment Strategies." In *Promoting Economic Development in China's Poor Areas: A Collection of Policy Briefs*, ed. Albert Park and Scott Rozelle. Beijing: China Poverty Research Association.

Lardy, Nicholas R. (1983). *Agriculture in China's Modern Economic Development*. Cambridge: Cambridge University Press.

Li Jianguang and Li Guo. (1992). *The Use of Poverty Alleviation Funds and Economic Development in China's Poor Areas*. Working Paper, Food Research Institute, Stanford University, Stanford, Calif.

Li Zhou. (1994). "Adjusting Agricultural Production Practices in Econologically Sensitive Regions." In *Promoting Economic Development in China's Poor Areas: A Collection of Policy Briefs*, ed. Albert Park and Scott Rozelle. Beijing: China Poverty Research Association.

Lin, Justin. (1992). "Hybrid Rice Innovation in China: A Study of Market Demand–Induced Technological Innovation in a Centrally Planned Economy." *Review of Economics and Statistics*, 74, 14–20.

Park, Albert, and Scott Rozelle. (1998). "Reforming State-Market Relations in Rural China." *Economics of Transition*, 6, 461–80.

Park, Albert, Scott Rozelle, and Cai Fung. (1994). "China's Grain Policy Reforms: Implications for Equity, Stabilization, and Efficiency." *China Economic Review*, 5, 15–34.

Park, Albert, Scott Rozelle, Christine Wong, and Ren Changqing. (1996). "Distributional Consequences of Fiscal Reform on China's Poor Areas." *China Quarterly*, 147, 1001–32.

Park, Albert, and Sangui Wang. (2001). "China's Poverty Statistics." *China Economic Review*, 12, 384–98.

Park, Albert, Sangui Wang, and Guobao Wu. (1998). *Regional Poverty Targeting in China*. Working Paper, Department of Economics, University of Michigan, Ann Arbor.

Piazza, Alan, and Echo H. Liang. (1997, May). "The State of Poverty in China: Its Causes and Remedies." Paper presented at the conference titled Social Consequences of Economic Reform in China, Harvard University.

Ravallion, Martin. (1999). "China's Lagging Poor Areas." *American Economic Review*, 89, 301–5.

Rozelle, Scott. (1996). "Stagnation Without Equity: Changing Patterns of Income and Inequality in China's Post-Reform Rural Economy." *China Journal*, 35, 63–96.

Rozelle, Scott, Guo Li, Minggao Shen, Amelia Hughart, and John Giles. (1999). "Leaving China's Farms: Survey Results of New Paths and Remaining Hurdles to Rural Migration." *China Quarterly*, 158, 367–93.

Rozelle, Scott, Albert Park, Vince Benziger, and Changqing Ren. (1998). "Targeting Poverty Investments and Economic Growth in China." *World Development*, 26, 2137–51.

State Council. (1989a). "*Guowuyuan Pinkun Diqu Jingji Kaifa Lingdao Xiaozu Diyici Qiautihuiyi Jiyao*" [Summary of the First Meeting of the Leading Group for the Economic Development of Poor Areas of State Council]. In *Pinkun Diqu Jingji Kaifa Wenjian Huibian* [*Collection of Documents on Economic Development in Poor Areas*], p. 29. Beijing: People's Press.

———. (1989b). "*Guowuyuan Pinkun Diqu Jingji Kaifa Lingdao Xiaozu Dierci Qiautihuiyi Jiyao*" [Summary of the Second Meeting of the Leading Group for the Economic Development of Poor Areas of State Council]. In *Pinkun Diqu Jingji Kaifa Wenjian Huibian* [*Collection of Documents on Economic Development in Poor Areas*], p. 37. Beijing: People's Press.

———. (1989c). "*Guowuyuan Pinkun Diqu Jingji Kaifa Lingdao Xiaozu Disici Qiautihuiyi Jiyao*" [Summary of the Fourth Meeting of the Leading Group for the Economic Development of Poor Areas of State Council]. In *Pinkun Diqu Jingji Kaifa Wenjian Huibian* [*Collection of Documents on Economic Development in Poor Areas*], p. 48. Beijing: People's Press.

———. (1989d). "*Guowuyuan Pinkun Diqu Jingji Kaifa Lingdao Xiaozu Diqici Qiautihuiyi Jiyao*" [Summary of the Seventh Meeting of the Leading Group for the Economic Development of Poor Areas of State Council]. *Jingji Kaifa Luntan* (*Forum of Economic Development*), 2, 60.

———. (1989e). "*Guanyu Jiushi Niandai Jinyibu Jiaqiang Fupin Kaifa Gongzuo De Qingshi*" [A Proposal on the Strength of Poverty Alleviation in 1990s]. In *Pinkun Diqu Jingji Kaifa Wenjian Huibian* [*Collection of Documents on Economic Development in Poor Areas*], p. 37. Beijing: People's Press.

State Statistical Bureau. (1987–1996, published annually). *China Statistical Yearbook*. Beijing: State Statistical Publishing House.

Tong Zhong, Scott Rozelle, Bruce Stone, Jiang Dehua, Chen Jiyuan, and Xu Zhikang. (1994). "China's Experience with Market Reform for Commercialization of Agriculture in Poor Areas." In *Agricultural Commercialization, Economic Development, and Nutrition*, ed. Joaquim von Braun and Eileen Kennedy, pp. 119–40. Baltimore: Johns Hopkins Press.

Wang, Sangui, and Linxiu Zhang. (1999). "Report on Poverty Alleviation in China for Common Country Assessment (CCA)." Report to UNPD Task Force Group on Poverty, Beijing.

Weersink, Alfons, and Scott Rozelle. (1997). "Market Reforms, Market Development, and Agricultural Production in China." *Agricultural Economics,* 17, 95–114.

World Bank. (1992). *China: Strategy for Reducing Poverty in the 1990s.* Washington, D.C.: World Bank.

———. (1999). *Poverty Sector Report: China.* Washington, D.C.: World Bank.

Wu Guobao. (1994). "Goal Conflicts in Poor Areas: Growth, Budget Solvency, and Poverty Alleviation." In *Promoting Economic Development in China's Poor Areas: A Collection of Policy Briefs*, ed. Albert Park and Scott Rozelle. Beijing: China Poverty Research Association.

Zhang, Linxiu, Jikun Huang, and Scott Rozelle. (2003). "China's War on Poverty: Assessing Targeting and the Growth Impacts of Poverty Programs." *Chinese Journal of Economic and Business Statistics.*

Zhou Binbin. (1988). "Fupin Zhengce Tiaozheng Zhong De Jige Wenti" [Some Topics on Poverty Alleviation Policy Adjustment]. Jingji Kaifa Luntan (Forum of Economic Development), 1, 2.

Zhu Ling and Jiang Zhongyi. (1994). "Public Work and Poverty Alleviation" In *Promoting Economic Development in China's Poor Areas: A Collection of Policy Briefs*, ed. Albert Park and Scott Rozelle. Beijing: China Poverty Research Association.

10

Social Welfare in China in the Context of Three Transitions

Athar Hussain

Social welfare is taken here in its broad sense, protecting a population from deprivation and developing that population's capabilities. A few simple questions underlie the discussion here:

- How free is the Chinese population from the threat of destitution?
- What are the arrangements for income maintenance in contingencies such as old age and unemployment, and how effective are they?
- Does the population have access to adequate medical care in cases of illness, and how far has China succeeded in abolishing the incidence of preventable illnesses?
- What are the major impediments in the implementation of social security reforms aimed at replacing the inherited system?

In terms of the current level of human development indicators, China stands out among low-income economies (China is a low-income economy in terms of per capita GNP, if not PPP statistics), as it resembles middle-income economies in welfare indicators. Its population enjoys a comparatively high life expectancy of sixty-nine years and low infant mortality rate of thirty-eight per thousand live births, and its adult illiteracy rate (including the semiliterate) of 15.8 percent is among the lowest in low-income economies (World Bank, 1999). Compared to other populous developing economies, the percentage of the population living in poverty is low (World Bank, 1992).

China's outstanding record in human development, however, is losing its luster. Over the reform period since 1978, improvements in indicators of human development have not been as sustained and dramatic as growth in per capita income, which underscores the point that rapid economic growth alone is not sufficient for a sustained reduction in deprivation. A concerted policy is also necessary. Following a sharp drop in the population in absolute poverty from 33 percent to 12 percent between 1978 and 1985, progress in reducing poverty has since been slow (World Bank, 1992). Urban poverty, previously rare, has been rising. The downward trend in the mortality rate of children under age five (the preferred indicator of child health), in evidence until the early 1980s, seems to have slowed to a halt or even risen in some of the poorer provinces (World Bank, 1996a).

Looking ahead to 2020, the appropriate comparators for China are no longer low- but middle-income economies whose ranks it would be joining over the next several years. In health indicators and educational attainment, China lags behind a number of Asian countries. Its under-five mortality rate of forty-seven per thousand live births is higher than those in Malaysia, Thailand, and Sri Lanka and several times those in Hong Kong, South Korea, and Singapore (United Nations Development Programme, 1999). The incidence of preventable diseases such as viral hepatitis is high. The average length of schooling is significantly shorter, and the dropout rate before the completion of basic nine-year schooling is higher than in Malaysia, Thailand, or Sri Lanka, let alone South Korea. The percentage of secondary (including vocational) school graduates entering higher education is a mere 20 percent (State Statistical Bureau, 1999e), which is very low even compared to low-income Asian countries. What these gaps suggest is that without a concerted effort in improving child and maternal health and raising the educational level of its population, China would in the near future begin look like a laggard among East and Southeast Asian economies.

The purpose of this chapter is to provide an overview of various social welfare programs in urban and rural areas in a wider context of socioeconomic changes. First, I will discusses the three transitions China has been undergoing over the past two decades or so. I then analyze the arrangements for income maintenance in urban areas, including old-age pensions, unemployment insurance, and poverty relief in rural areas. Next, I briefly outline the rural social security system before focusing on healthcare and health insurance, and I conclude with some observations. The emphasis is on the current situation and the likely trend of changes in the near future, which are taken to be the years between now and 2020.

Three Transitions

Social welfare in present-day China is shaped by the three transitions it has been undergoing over the past twenty or so years:

- The demographic transition
- The process of economic development
- The transition from a command to a market economy

The first refers to the transition from a demographic regime of high fertility and low life expectancy to one of low fertility and high life expectancy with a non-rising population. From the viewpoint of social welfare, its most important feature is the changing age structure, not a deceleration in population growth. The second transition (termed "economic development") consists of an outflow of labor from farming and, associated with it, a shift from self-employment to wage employment and population migration. For the present purposes, the salient features of the third transition are, first, a change in the terms of employment in the state sector and its falling employment share and, second, the hiatus between the erosion of enterprise-based social welfare and the establishment of a government-managed "socialized system."

Demographic Transition

The Chinese population was around 1.25 billion in 1998, around a fifth of the world total, and growing by around 1 percent a year (State Statistical Bureau, 1999c). This is similar to the rate in the United States, half that of India, and a third lower than the average rate of 1.5 percent in middle-income economies (World Bank, 1999). By international standards, the process of the demographic transition in China has been exceptionally rapid, with associated changes in the age structure of the population crowded into a much shorter period than elsewhere (Feeney, 1996). The fertility rate is already down to 1.5 children per woman (State Statistical Bureau, 1999c). Under current trends, the population is expected to stabilize around a grand total of 1.5 billion by the year 2040, some 252 million more than in 1998 (see State Statistical Bureau, 1999c). Given the asymptotic growth pattern, most of this increase will take place in the next twenty to twenty-five years and will be accompanied by a radical change in the age structure of the population, which is brought out by a comparison of the population profile in 1998 and 2020 (see Table 10.1).

Compared with the 1998 population composition, in 2020 there will be 23 million fewer children, 106 million more elderly people, and 111 million more working-age adults. The rise in the ratio of the elderly to the total popu-

TABLE 10.1
Population Profile, 1998 and 2020

	1998	2020
Total population	1,248,100,000	1,441,980,000
Population of children[1]	24.2%	19.3%
(Dependency)[2]	(35.2%)	(27.9%)
Population of the elderly[3]	7.2%	11.4%
(Dependency)	(10.5%)	(16.5%)
Total dependency[3]	45.7%	44.3%

NOTES: The age division here follows the convention in demographic literature.
[1] Aged 0–14.
[2] Following the convention in demography, the denominator of the dependency ratio is the population aged 15–64.
[3] Aged 65+.
SOURCES: State Statistical Bureau (1999c and 1999d).

lation and working–age adults, on which much of the discussion in China tends to be focused, will be accompanied by a fall in the ratio of children. The net result will be a fall in the crude dependency ratio (i.e., unadjusted for the labor participation rate of working–age adults and the differing needs of various age groups).

An exclusive focus on the ratio of the elderly as the index of the burden of old–age support is misleading, for two reasons. First, it concentrates on the adverse side and neglects the huge economic bonus provided by a declining ratio of children. Accruing first, the benefit will continue to outweigh the cost until 2020, if not later (for a similar argument in relation to the United States, see Cutler et al., 1990). Moreover, the cost associated with the rise in the ratio of the elderly relative to working–age adults is mitigated by the fact that China is, and will for sometime remain, a surplus–labor economy. Following Sen (1984), this is taken to mean that the withdrawal of a substantial percentage of working–age adults from the labor force, which is what the rise in the ratio of the elderly means, would have no or little effect on the burden of supporting the dependent population. The implication is that China has more time to adjust to the aging population than is generally believed. China's old–age pension system is beset with major problems, but these are due far more to internal systemic design faults than to the process of aging associated with the demographic transition. Second, the ratio of the elderly gives a distorted picture of the geographic distribution of the burden of supporting the elderly population. In terms of the ratio of the elderly alone, compared to the interior provinces, the coastal provinces carry a higher burden of supporting the elderly population. But most of these tend to have a lower ratio of children to the population because of their lower fertility rates. As a result, the total dependency ratio, including both children and the elderly, is generally lower in richer coastal areas than in the poorer interior provinces. To give two examples: Shanghai, with the highest per capita income, has the highest ratio of the elderly of all provinces. Guizhou, the poorest province in terms of per capita income, has a low ratio of the elderly but a higher total dependency ratio than that of Shanghai, 39 compared to 38. 3 (State Statistical Bureau, 1998c). To explore the full ramifications of the demographic transition for social welfare, it is necessary to go beyond the crude dependency ratio and examine changes in the composition of various age groups. These are divided here into the "dependent" (or nonactive) population (children and the elderly) and working–age adults, which we discuss in turn.

Composition of the Dependent Population

The composition of the dependent population matters for two reasons. First, the respective needs of children and the elderly differ, a feature that is captured by equivalence scales (see, for example, Cutler et al., 1990; Deaton, 1997). Second and more important for the present purpose, the pattern of financial support of children is different from that of the elderly. Thus with the dependency ratio held constant, a shift in the composition of the dependent population away from children toward the elderly, as has been happening in China, has significant distributive implications. Much of the financial cost and personal care of children falls on households. But a large part of their cost of education is met from public resources, although over the reform period, the cost borne by parents has risen steadily. Currently, financial support for the elderly population is split between households and society (which in China means the government and work units), with the former carrying the main burden. Taking sixty as the benchmark retirement age,[1] only 35.9 million (20 percent) of the 178.1 million aged over sixty receive pensions, and all but a small percentage of these are in urban areas. The remaining 80 percent are mostly rural residents dependent on their children, predominantly sons, for financial support. There are now collective (community) pension schemes in rural areas, but these are still in the development stage and cover only part subsistence.

Taking the current arrangements for old-age support as givens, the government, enterprises, and families will all feel the financial impact of the rising elderly population. In urban areas, the cost will fall mainly on work units (including their employees) and the government. For the latter, with all else held constant, it will be offset by the declining ratio of children, though not necessarily completely. State-owned units (including government and public organizations), which already carry a heavy burden of old-age pensions, will be most adversely affected by the trend, as they will receive none of the dividends from the falling ratio of children. Currently, around 77 percent of retirees are former state sector employees (State Statistical Bureau, 1999b), and this percentage will rise over the next two decades because of the higher median age of the state-sector labor force compared to that of the nonstate sector. Given the high percentage of the urban elderly population receiving old-age pensions, urban households would feel the financial impact of the rising elderly population largely in the form of higher taxes (including social security contributions) rather than in the form of providing direct financial support for elderly parents. In contrast, rural households would feel the economic impact of the changing age structure largely through expenditure on children and elderly relatives. With the development and extension of rural collective pension schemes, a part of the cost will be shifted to the community or the local government and show up as contributions to the pension schemes or local taxes.

Focusing on the elderly, the distributive implications of old-age financial support through pensions (on a pay-as-you-go basis) and by families are very different. Leaving aside the cost borne by work units, support through pensions distributes the burden across all households regardless of their age composition. In contrast, old-age support by families concentrates the burden on a proportion of households, those with dependent elderly relatives. As increasingly realized in China, the current heavy reliance on the family for old-age support goes against the grain of the demographic trend and socioeconomic changes. Because

TABLE 10.2

Age Structure of Working-Age Adults, 1982 and 1998

Age Group	1982	1998
Aged 15–29 (millions)	47.3% (292)	36.3% (311)
Aged 30–64 (millions)	52.7% (325)	63.7% (546)

SOURCES: State Statistical Bureau (1982 and 1999d).

of the birth control policy, which in many localities means one child per couple, the future cohorts of the elderly will have fewer children to depend on than the present cohort has. An extreme example, which is often cited in China, is a future hypothetical family consisting of two earners and five dependants: a working couple (both single children themselves), their single child, and their four elderly parents. Thus a crucial issue for China is the progressive replacement of family financial support with old-age pensions.

Age Structure of Working-Age Adults

The age structure of working-age adults matters because age, either on its own or as a correlate of features such as educational attainment and experience, is a central consideration in hiring decisions. Having started in the late 1960s, the demographic transition has begun to have a significant impact on the age structure of China's working-age population, with important implications for social welfare. To show this, Table 10.2 compares the age structure of working age adults in 1982, when the effect of fertility decline from the late 1960s had yet to feed through to the population of working-age adults, and in 1998. The latter includes birth cohorts (aged fifteen to twenty-nine) that were affected by the fertility transition and received most, if not all, of their education in the reform period since 1979, benefiting from the revival of the educational system after the Cultural Revolution.

The change in the age structure over the sixteen years is striking. The percentage of younger working-age adults (aged fifteen to twenty-nine) has dropped by 11 percentage points. In absolute terms, only 19 million (7.9 percent) of the 240 million rise in the numbers of working-age adults is in the fifteen-to-twenty-nine age group, and the remaining 221 million (92.1 percent) is in the thirty-to-sixty-four age group. One straightforward implication of the change in the age structure of the labor force is a reduction in the problem of finding jobs for school leavers, which would diminish still further as the effect of the fertility decline feeds through to the labor force.

Added to this, the change has implications for the age structure of the unemployed, whose numbers have risen sharply in recent years. As a benchmark, if all unemployed persons have an identical chance of finding a job, the time spent unemployed will be the same for all age groups. But as in other economies, the spell of unemployment tends to be longer in China for older than for younger workers. The available evidence strongly suggests that older workers (men over forty and women over thirty-five) have less chance of finding another job than younger workers do. The problem of unemployment among older workers in China is compounded by their much lower educational attainment compared to younger workers. Because of the adverse impact of the Cultural Revolution (1966–78) on secondary and higher education, a large proportion of birth cohorts from 1953 to 1963 (aged thirty-five to forty-five) missed out entirely on postprimary education and occupational training. In contrast, the post-1970 birth cohorts (aged twenty-eight or under in 1998) have largely escaped the deleterious effect of the Cultural Revolution. The implication is that China faces a serious problem of long-term unemployment due to the combination of the negative effects of the Cultural Revolution on education and training and of the impact of the demographic transition on the age structure. Further the problem of unemployment among older workers is likely to get worse over the next ten to fifteen years because of a rising trend in the median age of the labor force driven by the falling size of cohorts entering the labor force.

Economic Development

The salient aspects of economic development with implications for social welfare are the following:

- The shift of labor out of farming into industry and services
- The changeover from self-employment to wage employment
- Labor migration and associated population migration

Part and parcel of economic development, these are not unique to China but take on particular forms and have special consequences in the Chinese context. The three are correlated but not perfectly. To run through their broad social welfare implications, the division of the labor force between farming and non-farming activities determines the relative impact of weather fluctuations on personal incomes and assets. With 46.6 percent of the labor force still engaged in farming (State Statistical Bureau, 1999a), natural disasters loom large in China as a major cause of deprivation. In the past few years, much of social protection in rural areas has been concerned with the alleviation of devastation caused by summer floods.

The division between wage employment and self-employment is of special relevance for social security because two of its principal components, old-age pensions and unemployment benefits, have traditionally been tied closely to wage employment (Atkinson, 1991), as indeed they are in China. Compared to income from self-employment, especially when in kind, wages provide an easily verifiable standard for defining benefits and a convenient tax handle for financing social security schemes. The implication is that a shift from self-employment to wage employment widens the scope for the application of a mandatory social insurance scheme with entitlement to benefits tied to the contribution record. Labor and population migration is pertinent to social welfare because, first, it is associated with a change in the composition of households and hence the pattern of sharing of incomes and, second, migrants often do not have the same access to employment, housing, public services, and social security schemes as locals do. This second aspect has a special resonance in the Chinese context because of restrictions on migration and the associated disadvantageous status of migrants.

Compared with other populous developing economies, China presents two anomalies with respect to the distribution of the population and labor force that have repercussions on the social security system. The most striking of these is the wide discrepancy between the percentage of the population with the official designation "nonagricultural" (*fei nongye*) and the percentage of the labor force engaged in nonfarming activities. According to the household registration system, a mere 32.2 percent of the population is classified as "nonagricultural," and the corresponding percentage of the labor force designated as urban is 29.6 percent (State Statistical Bureau, 1998c, 1999b). This falls well short of the percentage of the labor force actually employed in services and industry, which is 53.4 percent (State Statistical Bureau, 199a, 1999b). Reckoned in terms of the household registration designation "nonagricultural," the urbanization rate in China is not only, as widely noted, exceptionally low by international standards but also at odds with its GNP share of agriculture of only 18.4 percent. But reckoned in terms of the percentage of the labor force and, correlatively, the population actually dependent on farming as the principal income source, the Chinese urbanization rate of more than 50 percent is neither low by international standards nor at odds with its GNP composition. This estimate of the urban population also fits in with the spatial definition of "urban" in terms of the population in high-density settlements with a preponderant share of nonfarming activities in local GNP, say, at least 85 percent. In terms of this definition, the urban population exceeds half of the total (for details, see Hussain, 2003). This estimate still errs on the low side because it excludes most of the migrant population, defined as those residing and working in cities and towns for more than six months—the threshold used in the 1990 population census to distinguish migrants from short-term visitors. Including them would add another 4 to 5 percent to the total.

What implications follow from the observation that the actual urbanization rate exceeds the official rate of 32.2 percent by 20 percentage points or more? One implication is that social welfare issues correlated with urbanization, such as housing and unemployment, affect a majority rather than, as official statistics would suggest, less than a third of the Chinese population. Second and more important for present purposes, given that the official rural poverty line of 635 yuan per year is around a third of the commonly used urban poverty line of 2,000 yuan per year, the incidence of poverty is substantially higher than that implied by the commonly used estimate of the urbanization rate. This observa-

tion is especially pertinent to rural counties in the immediate vicinity of the urban districts of large cities that are often comparatively rich by rural standards
but relatively poor by urban standards.

The other anomaly is presented by the sectoral distribution of the labor force
in China, which was even more marked at the outset of economic reforms. The
employment share of 49.8 percent in the primary sector (of which farming accounts for 46.6 percentage points) is similar to that in low-income or low-
middle-income economies. But the employment share of the secondary sector
in China (23.5 percent) is comparatively high, and that of the tertiary sector
(services) is comparatively low (26.7 percent). The period since 1978 marks a
break from the prereform period in two respects: first, a marked acceleration in
the transfer of labor out of farming, and second, a steady shift of labor toward
services in the nonfarming sector. From 1978 to 1998, the share of labor in farming (or more accurately, in the primary sector) has dropped by 21 percentage
points, more than twice as rapidly as the mere 13 percent drop in the twenty-
six years from 1952 to 1978 (State Statistical Bureau, 1999b). A side effect of the
single-minded emphasis on industrialization and bias against services in the prereform period was to put brakes on the transfer of labor out of farming, thus
dampening the rise in per capita income.

The period since 1978 has also seen a steady shift of nonfarm employment
toward services: its share in total employment has more than doubled, from 12.2
to 26.7 percent. Contrasted with this, in the prereform period, the share of
services fluctuated and was in 1978 less than 3 percentage points higher than that
1952. In those twenty-six years, all but a small proportion of the labor outflow
from agriculture was toward industry. Looking forward to 2020, what would
the sectoral labor distribution look like, and what might its social welfare implications be? Assuming that the sectoral distribution of employment up to 2020
follows the same pattern of change as it has since 1990, the share of the labor
force in agriculture would fall at an annual rate of around 1.4 percentage points,
and the shares of industry and services would rise by 0.3 and 1.1 percentage
points per year, respectively. The result would be services with the largest share,
followed by industry and agriculture, an exact reversal of the order in 1978 (see
Table 10.3).

TABLE 10.3

Sectoral Distribution of Labor Force

(percent)

Sectors	1998	2000
Primary (almost all farming)	49.8	16.7
Secondary (industry except for mining)	23.5	31.5
Tertiary (services)	26.7	51.8

SOURCE: State Statistical Bureau (1998a).

By 2020, the sectoral distribution of the labor force in China would be very similar to that in present-day South Korea. Relevant to the discussion here, in what particular respects would the working lives of the people in 2020 and contingencies they face be different from those of the present-day population? Given the long shadow of the rural-urban distinction on the life trajectory of individuals and the contingencies they face, the answer is that they will be different for the rural and for the urban populations. At present, 70 percent of the rural labor force is self-employed in farming combined with some sideline activity and for the most part residing in the place of birth (State Statistical Bureau, 1999a). The remaining 30 percent employed in town and village enterprises (TVEs) retains strong links with agriculture. Their households have each a plot of land, which is worked on by some family members. Unlike their urban counterparts, they have no old-age pensions, unemployment benefits, or, in most cases, health insurance; the land allotted to them is supposed to be the substitute for these. Most members of the present-day urban labor force have worked for the same unit (predominantly, the state sector) since entering the labor market and have had until recently little or no experience of unemployment.

By 2020 — and most likely earlier — an overwhelming majority of the labor force will be wage-employed on a terminable contract in either industry or services with (likely) little or no direct family link to farming. A middle-aged member of the labor force would have experienced several job changes, including adapting to different occupations, interspersed with spells of unemployment and also a change in the place of residence since entering the labor force, most likely from a village to a town or a city. This individual will also face the prospect of retirement at some age and may have only one child. The purpose of this contrast is to bring into relief the changes with ramifications for social security. These are

- The shift from self-employment to wage employment
- The prospect of unemployment
- Migration and increased labor mobility
- Retirement at a particular age

The current legal and administrative framework and the social security system implicitly assume life trajectories and contingencies for individuals that are increasingly at variance with reality. The designation "formally employed" (*zhigong ren*) is reserved for the urban labor force and does not apply to the rural labor force despite the fact that 30 percent (91.6 million) of them are wage-employed in TVEs (State Statistical Bureau, 1999a). Neither labor insurance nor many of the labor laws apply to wage employees in rural areas who are regarded as "self-employed," nor are they counted as unemployed when laid off or entitled to a retirement pension. Moreover, though migrant labor ("floating population") currently totals 50 to 70 million (depending on the estimate) — 7 to

10 percent of the labor force—labor migration is still treated largely as a temporary episode rather than as a permanent phenomenon. As elsewhere, migration in China is driven by the gap between urban and rural incomes, which has been widening since the mid-1980s. Rural migrants are allowed to take up temporary or casual employment in cities but not allowed to settle permanently without permission, which is hard to obtain in large cities, though not any longer for towns and medium-sized cities. Migration, although it contributes to an increase in income in rural areas, has implications for social security. Not being allowed to settle permanently, a large percentage of migrants do not have permanent housing, lack full access to public amenities, and are largely excluded from urban social security. Provisions for portability of the old-age pensions and unemployment insurance either do not exist or are rudimentary.

Both the growth in wage employment in rural areas and rural out-migration, though massive, remain yet to be incorporated in the Chinese social security system, which is still based on the anachronistic assumptions that rural labor is self-employed in farming and is immobile. Government policy is only slowly beginning to recognize labor migration as an irreversible feature of economic development. A tangible policy change is the emphasis on the proliferation and development of medium and small towns and a loosening of restrictions on immigration into them.

Transition to a Market Economy

Economic reforms have brought in their train a rapid and sustained growth rate and an unprecedented rise in living standards, but they also have had a profound impact on the working-life history of individuals and on the contingencies they face. Even though the Chinese economy has managed to skip the downward part of the J-curve of the transition from a command to a market economy, in the fields of employment and social welfare it is undergoing changes similar to those in transitional economies of eastern Europe. In the present context, of special importance are the following:

- Growing incompatibility between the traditional social welfare responsibilities of enterprises and their economic role
- The increasing replacement of permanent employment with terminable employment and rising numbers of layoffs
- The rapid growth of nonstate enterprises (particularly private ones) with sparse social security coverage
- Widening inequality in the distribution of personal incomes

Taking these in turn, historically, Chinese state enterprises have operated as semiclosed communities, more akin to the army than to firms in market economies (Walder, 1986). In addition to producing goods or services for sale, they have also provided, either free or at low prices, a wide range of services to their current and retired employees and often their families as well. Prominent among these have been housing, outpatient and in large enterprises also inpatient medical care, schooling for children, and in some cases even public utilities. The cash wage has traditionally been just one component of a package with an array of benefits in kind (see Hu, 1996). The extended social role of Chinese state enterprises has traditionally bound most members of the urban labor force to their respective work units (*danwei*) for not merely their working lives but also retirement. This bond is increasingly perceived as a major barrier in the restructuring of state enterprises, including the closure of the ones with little or no chance of survival in a market economy. Confronted with a dramatic worsening of financial position in recent years, many state enterprises are forced to default on their social obligations, such as pensions to their retirees, and to lay off their employees in large numbers. As a result, the urban labor force no longer perceives employment in a state enterprise as a secure guarantee of income for life complemented with generous benefits in kind. It offers, in Chinese parlance, neither an "iron rice bowl" nor an "iron chair."

Dating from the prereform period, the social role of state enterprises was originally embedded in an economic and political structure with three salient features:

- Integration of the government budget with enterprise budgets and the profitability of the state sector as a whole
- A combination of low wages with overemployment and lifetime employment
- The work unit as the primary locus of political organization and social control

The integration of enterprise and government budgets spread the financing of social responsibilities across all enterprises and insulated employment and wages in cash and kind from an enterprise's financial performance. Labor recruitment in state and urban collective enterprises and government organizations was geared less toward meeting the labor demand and more toward preventing the emergence of unemployment in urban areas. As it were, the labor supply created its own demand, and this had two consequences. First, the work–unit–based social provision covered a large majority of the urban population. In 1978, fully 78.3 percent of the urban labor force was employed in state enterprises and government organizations, and the rest was employed in collective enterprises, which tended to emulate the state sector.

Second, because of the large excess of job seekers relative to vacancies in urban areas, most work units had more employees than they needed. State enterprises have been the mainstay of the urban social welfare system. Preempted by the extensive social role of work units, government provision of social services has tended to be sparse. Thus a paradoxical feature of the Chinese urban economy has been the combination of extensive social security benefits with a rudimentary capacity of the government to manage and administer social security

schemes. If government agencies have performed many of the managerial functions, such as making output and investment decisions, enterprises have in turn
provided what in developed market economies governments or civil organizations do. Thus whereas economic decision making was centralized in government departments, decisions concerning social services and collective goods were
dispersed across many enterprises. Broadly, economic reforms are reversing this
pattern by decentralizing economic decision making to enterprises and centralizing (termed "socializing" in China) the social security system in the newly established Ministry of Labor and Social Security and its territorial counterparts.
The first type of reform preceded the second, which began only a few years ago
and, as we shall see, is far from completed.

The economic reforms and ensuing fallout have gradually cut the ground from
underneath the social role of the state sector and call into question its rationale.
Three aspects are particularly relevant in this regard:

- The separation of enterprise budgets from the government budget
- The weakening of centralized wage determination and the granting to the
  enterprise management of discretion over wage determination
- The introduction of employment on terminable contracts and, in the past few
  years, a sharp rise in the numbers of layoffs (*xiagang*, literally, "standing-down")

Each of these has been necessary to raise the efficiency of state enterprises, and
each in a particular way raises problems for continuing with their social role. The
separation of enterprise budgets from those of territorial governments, among
the first measures of economic reform, converted social provisions by enterprises from a joint financial liability of the state sector into individual enterprise
liabilities, akin to "mandated employer benefits" (for a discussion of such benefits, see Kingson and Schulz, 1997). Such benefits create a special problem in a
transitional economy such as China's, given that state enterprises were not established with reference to their future financial viability and are not selected for
survival in a market economy. The change introduced a tension between the extended social role of enterprises and their transformation into market-oriented
organizations. Strict adherence to financial autonomy threatened to cut the
ground from underneath the urban social welfare system and many social services. Conversely, subsidies to insolvent enterprises blunted, if not negated, the
main aim of reforms. Since 1978, the Chinese government has tried to deal with
this dilemma through ad hoc compromises. Insolvent enterprises have been kept
afloat, though disadvantaged in various ways. A major effect of these compromises has been to widen variation in the range and level of welfare and social
provision by enterprises depending on their financial position. The marked deterioration in the financial position of the state sector in recent years due to
competition (both internal and from imports) and a shift in the share of value
added going to wages (see Hussain and Zhuang, 1998) has made subsidization of

losses increasingly untenable, pushing the enterprise-based social welfare system to the brink of collapse.

Besides, two developments in the state sector have diminished the large overlap that previously existed between enterprise-based and urban social welfare and provision. First, the percentage of state sector employees on short-term terminable contracts has risen from a mere 7 percent in 1986, when it was generalized to all new recruits, to 51.6 percent in 1997 (State Statistical Bureau, 1998b). Second, a significant percentage of those who are formally "permanently employed" or have yet to come to the end of their employment contracts are "laid off" (*xiagang*). These receive a living allowance in lieu of wages conditional on signing a contract that fixes a time limit to links with the work unit (usually three years). The number of laid-off employees from the state sector at the end of 1998 totaled around 8.8 million, 9.8 percent of the employees in the state sector (State Statistical Bureau, 1999b). The spread of contract employment and the increasing frequency of separations from work units in various forms imply that the long-term attachment to work units that has underpinned their social welfare role no longer holds for a majority of the urban labor force. The share of the state sector in urban employment has declined, not just relatively but since 1995 also absolutely. The percentage of urban employees in the sector has dropped from 78.4 percent in 1978 to 43.8 percent in 1998 (State Statistical Bureau, 1999b).

Social Security System

The Chinese social security system has two central features (for a detailed discussion, see Hussain, 1993). First, it consists of two separate subsystems, urban and rural (discussed later in this chapter), with different organizations and benefits—a common feature. Second, until the reform over the past few years (to be discussed shortly), the urban system was segmented according to the ownership status of the work unit (state versus nonstate), which it still is in practice. Both features are anomalous carryovers from the prereform period. Employees of the government and state-owned enterprises (SOEs), almost all in urban areas, have traditionally benefited from subsidized housing and comprehensive labor insurance, providing disability and old-age pensions, maternity and sickness benefits, medical care, and since 1986, unemployment benefits as well. Traditionally, there has also been a parallel, but less generous, labor insurance for urban collective enterprises.

Recent Reforms in Urban Social Security

As generally recognized in China, work-unit-based social welfare, encompassing subsidized housing and labor insurance, is no longer sustainable. After a period of piecemeal reforms to stop the system from collapsing and a number of localized experiments, the State Council has over the past few years promulgated regulations to institute an urban social security system to replace the inherited work-unit-based system. The salient changes can be summarized in the following five items:

1. Extending social security schemes, previously confined to state and urban collective sector employees, to all urban wage-employed workers regardless of the ownership status of the work unit but not to wage employees in rural counties
2. Centralizing the oversight and administration of social security schemes in the Ministry of Labor (renamed Ministry of Labor and Social Security) and its territorial subsidiaries—provincial and municipal Labor and Social Security Bureaus (LSSBs) and gradually transferring the management and administration of social security schemes from work units to them
3. Replacing the financing of social security by work units alone with joint financing by employers, employees, and the government; introduction of employee contributions accompanied by individual accounts for old–age pensions and (yet to be implemented) health insurance; at some future date, upgrading the financing of social security schemes from the municipal to the provincial level so as to ensure adequate risk pooling
4. Reappraisal of entitlements and their formalization
5. Introduction of the social relief scheme for urban households falling below the poverty line

What are the implications of these reforms, and are the reforms sufficient to institute a viable social security system that protects the urban population from various risks? To answer this multipart question, we examine each of the five items in turn.

Item 1 has been long overdue, necessitated by a steady decline in the share of the state and urban collective sector in urban employment. Some cities, such as Shanghai, have had a unified scheme covering all urban wage employees for some years. Item 2 lays the foundation for the administration of an integrated social security system. It ends the split responsibility within the government. Previously, labor insurance for government employees came under the Central Ministry of Personnel, while that for enterprise employees was the responsibility of the Ministry of Labor. Health insurance was supervised by the Ministry of Public Health. The centralization of oversight in one government agency makes possible the integration of hitherto disparate social security schemes. In principle, the reform also relieves work units of the burden of administering social security schemes, which has risen sharply in recent years with the rise in the number of pensioners. However, it would take some years before work units are fully divested of their social welfare responsibilities. Because of a heavy reliance on work-unit-based social welfare in the past, municipal governments have a limited capacity to administer social security schemes, an impediment that is often overlooked by the central government and observers. My own fieldwork in Liaoning and Sichuan in 1999 suggests that it would take municipal governments a number of years before they are in a position to administer social security schemes.

Items 3 and 4 are complementary, both aimed at putting urban social security on a sound financial footing. In terms of economic theory, it should make no difference whether the employer or the employee pays social security contributions. But assuming imperfect omniscience, in practice, employee contributions serve to make the costs visible to the covered labor force and thus facilitate a revision of benefits so as to contain rising costs, which is one of the main problems Chinese urban social security system faces. Further, given rising urban unemployment and the pressure on enterprises to contain costs, employee contributions are compensated by a rise in wages only partially or not at all. The introduction of individual accounts for old-age pensions and in future for health insurance, which is inspired by the example of Singapore, serves two purposes. The first and immediately more important one is to lower resistance to the introduction of employee contributions against the historical background of the financing of labor insurance by work units alone. Second, compared to the usual practice in pooled systems, individual accounts institute a tighter link between the contribution record and benefits and thus limit the extent of redistribution between the covered population and also facilitate a reappraisal of benefits. But one has to observe that individual accounts make huge demands on administrative capacity, which is of special importance in the Chinese context. In particular, the introduction of individual accounts for health insurance, as envisaged in China, raises formidable operational problems because in such an account, payins and payouts run concurrently rather than separated in time, as they are in an old-age pension account. The evidence on the ground suggests that the health insurance scheme as now conceived is nonviable and would need design changes.

The introduction of a government contribution toward urban social security, rather than being a novelty, simply formalizes what has implicitly been the case. Municipal governments have long subsidized old-age pensions and health care expenditure of loss-making enterprises in their charge. There is also a fiscal justification for a government contribution in that it partially spreads the cost of urban social security across the whole of the tax base rather than concentrating it all on the payroll tax, which is a tax and is already high in China. The principal problem in the government financing of urban social security is that it takes place at the level of municipal governments. The fiscal capacity of municipal governments in China varies very widely, and there is at present no regular system of fiscal transfers across municipal governments within a province, let alone across provinces. As a result, municipal governments, caught in the pincers of an eroding tax base due to the poor financial performance of local enterprises, on the one hand, and a rising expenditure on social security benefits, on the other, find it very difficult to meet their statutory obligations. Consequently, although urban social security schemes are supposed to be fairly uniform, the coverage of the schemes and the level of benefits vary widely across cities. The pooling of social security contributions and expenditure at the provincial level is the professed policy aim, but most provinces do not have a road map for the province-wide integration of social security schemes.

Item 5 is an innovation in response to the rising numbers of the urban poor, currently estimated to be 13 million, 3.3 percent, or 5.4 percent of the urban population, depending on its definition (see Hussain, 2003). The urban social relief covers all urban residents (excluding migrants) instead of employees only and is noncontributory. The scheme is financed from the municipal budget, assisted by transfers from the Ministry of Finance for poor municipalities. It is means-tested on the basis of household income and is operated not by the Ministry of Labor and Social Security but by the Ministry of Civil Affairs, which has traditionally been responsible for poverty relief in urban areas. The national poverty line is 2,000 yuan per person per year for urban areas, compared to 635 yuan for rural areas. But the national urban poverty line is notional, used for the head count of urban residents living in poverty but not for targeting relief to the urban poor. For the practical purposes of providing social relief or assistance to poor households, each municipality determines its own poverty line, which varies widely as exemplified by the following:

Shenzhen (special economic zone): 3,828 yuan per year
Xiamen, Beijing: 3,120 yuan per year
Yinchuan (Ningxia): 1,716 yuan per year

The wide range of local poverty lines is due far more to variations in the fiscal capacity of cities than to that in price levels. As recognized by the Ministry of Civil Affairs, poverty lines in poorer cities fall below the lowest acceptable subsistence level and are no more than the level needed to prevent severe hardship.

Labor Insurance

We turn now to a brief discussion of the three principal schemes of labor insurance:

- Old-age pensions
- Unemployment insurance
- Health care insurance

The first and the third date from the 1950s, when labor insurance was introduced. The second dates from 1986. Its absence in the past reflected partly the ideological assumption that unemployment was a characteristic of capitalist economies and partly the nation's employment and recruitment policies. Employment was for life, and the government carried responsibility for finding employment for the urban labor force, features rendered obsolete by the economic reforms.

In addition to these three schemes, there are also disability and maternity benefit schemes, which are comparatively small.

The three listed schemes differ in magnitude, organization, and the problems they face. In terms of expenditure, the old-age pension scheme is by a wide margin the largest, followed by health insurance, the cost of which has risen sharply in recent years. For the most part, its management still rests in the hands of work units, which are also responsible for its financing, in the first instance at least despite the recent reforms. Whereas the pension costs of the employees of state-owned and collective enterprises have been pooled for some years, health care insurance is in the middle of a major transition to a municipal system. Since its inception in 1986, unemployment insurance has been managed not by work units but by provincial or municipal labor bureaus and financed by a payroll tax. In terms of management and financing, the scheme has served as the model for the reform of other schemes.

With recent reforms, all schemes are now financed by payroll taxes split between employers and employees, with the government acting as the residual source. But each scheme is still financed by a separate tax. A unified payroll tax covering all social security schemes has been proposed but not promulgated. Further, default on social security contributions is reported to be substantial. As a result, the social security schemes do not cover all urban wage employees as they are supposed to do. In the aggregate, the social insurance contributions exceed current expenditures (State Statistical Bureau, 1999b). But the financial surplus on social insurance does not convey an accurate picture because "contributions" include payments into individual old-age pension accounts of current employees and "expenditures" on some major items, such as medical expenditures on noncatastrophic illnesses. Appropriately calculated, the social insurance account is in deficit. But the principal problem is not the deficit in the aggregate because government expenditure on social security remains comparatively small. Rather, the main problem is the discrepancy between the deficit across cities and their fiscal capacity.

Old-Age Pensions

The old-age pension system is in the midst of a major transition from the inherited system to a new system, a transition that will take several decades to complete. The inherited system applies to the 35.9 million existing pensioners and would continue to apply to those retiring over the next thirty or so years. Under the system, pensions are a percentage of the last "basic wage" (excluding bonuses) in employment, and pensioners also have their health care costs covered by their former work unit, although this will change with the switchover to municipal health care insurance. Pensions are based on a national schedule, ranging from 75 to 100 percent of the basic wage, and depend on the number of years of employment and the date of recruitment. The ratio of average pension to the average wage of urban employees is 79.8 percent—83.1 percent in the state sector (State Statistical Bureau, 1999b). The replacement rates in China, although they have fallen, are exceptionally high by international standards. But in assessing the replacement rate, it is important to keep two considerations in view. First, because of a low average wage, a significant proportion of pensioners receive pensions lower than the local poverty line. A significant percentage of recipients or urban poverty relief are pensioners. Second and more important, default by work units on pension payment has been widespread in recent years. Thus pensions that are generous in principle can be niggardly in practice.

The management of old-age pensions still rests predominantly with work units. They keep records of the parameters relevant to determining pensions, disburse pensions of their former employees, and are also responsible for their personal care. This highly decentralized system raises two sets of problems: first, its viability and efficiency, and second, the scope for abuse of the system. The system worked reasonably well when the number of pensioners was small, but it is now under strain and will become increasingly cumbersome as the number of pensioners rises relative to the labor force. The disappearance of enterprises due to the rising tide of mergers and bankruptcies compounds the problem. Further, the keeping of records of employment and wages by enterprises makes it easier for them to abuse the system and makes it more difficult for the authorities to prevent abuses.

Currently, pensions are financed on what is generally termed a pay-as-you-go basis. Employee contributions toward pensions, which were rare only a few years ago, have become a general norm, but their rates vary across cities. The current pension costs are pooled, and a recent government regulation has abolished separate pools for state and collective work units and for particular industries such as the railways and the electricity industry. But separate pools continue to exist by default because the administrative structure for the operation of a unified pool is not in place. Enterprises participating in a pooling scheme devote a set percentage of their wage bill to pensions, which varies across localities. But since it is not the pool but the work unit that disburses pensions, the pooling arrangement works by an ex post redistribution that introduces a huge uncertainty in the payment of pensions. Enterprises spending more than the percentage claim the difference, and conversely, those spending less pay the difference into the pool. But the pooling arrangements work far from smoothly. Contributions to the pension pools are not based in law, and compliance rates have been significantly less than full (World Bank, 1996b) and in recent years have dropped sharply. Further, because of ex post redistribution, pools do not provide a solution to the nonpayment of pensions by enterprises in the first place, which has been a serious problem for some years.

Under the new system that is being phased in, the one-tier system is replaced with a two-tier system. The first tier is supposed to provide a basic pension to ensure a minimum living standard regardless of earnings in employment but conditional on a certain number of years of contribution, which is usual in old-age pensions systems. The first tier is supposed to be financed entirely by employer and government contributions, with the government acting as the residual risk bearer. The second tier is supposed to be earnings-related and based on individual accounts. It is to be financed entirely from employer and employee contributions, with no government contribution except via tax expenditure. The new system is modeled on the system in use in a large number of economies and combines the "defined benefit" and "defined contribution" systems (for a discussion, see Diamond, 1994). It is important to distinguish between short- and long-term effects of the new system. The immediate effect is no more than to introduce employee contributions toward pensions. The process of establishing individual accounts has just begun and will take a number of years to complete. Unlike the old system, the operation of individual accounts is premised on information on the earnings and contributions of each individual over the whole of the person's working life. The introduction of individual accounts also opens the issue of setting up notional accounts for those who are well into their working lives and thus do not have a sufficient number of working years left before retirement to accumulate enough for an earnings-related second tier. As yet, there is no national framework for assigning notional credit to such accounts. Currently, all accounts are largely notional in the sense that in most cities, contributions by employers and employees are mostly used to finance current pension expenditures. The implication is that until an alternative source for financing pension liabilities over the next three to four decades is found, the new system will remain inoperative.

The new scheme lays the foundation for a better system for the future. But apart from introducing the employee contribution, it has no bearing on the following issues, which the Chinese old-age pensions system will be facing over the next two to three decades:

- Timely payment of pensions
- Establishment of a government structure for the collection of contributions and disbursement of pensions
- Implementation of provincewide pooling of contributions and expenditures, which is the professed policy aim
- Partial funding of future liabilities so as to smooth the impact of the rising number of pensioners
- Financing the health care expenditures of retirees under the municipal health care insurance scheme

Unemployment Insurance

Initially restricted to employees in state enterprises, participation in unemployment insurance (UI) is now mandatory for wage employees in urban districts, including those in small private enterprises. However, the actual coverage of the scheme falls well short of 100 percent because of problems in collecting contributions from smaller nonstate enterprises. In 1998, UI covered 43 percent of all urban employees, compared to 39 percent in 1997 (State Statistical Bureau, 1998a, 1999b). Despite the rise, the rate remains comparatively low, limiting the importance of UI as an income maintenance mechanism in the face of raising urban unemployment. A potentially serious problem is the rapidly falling employment share of the state and urban collective sector, with a high coverage rate of 76.8 percent, and the rising employment share of the remaining sector (dominated by private enterprises), with a derisory coverage rate of 4.6 percent. The implication is that without a substantial extension of UI coverage in the private sector, the effectiveness of UI as an income maintenance scheme will steadily diminish. This leads to the related question of the percentage of the urban unemployed receiving UI benefits. The percentage of "registered unemployed" receiving UI benefits in 1998 was 27.7 percent (State Statistical Bureau, 1999b). The percentage with respect to the "actually unemployed" would be much lower. As in other economies, people not entitled to UI have little or no incentive to register.

Previously linked to wages in employment, the unemployment benefit (UB) is now set at a flat rate that ranges from 60 to 70 percent of the minimum wage, which is fixed by the local government and may vary between districts in the same city. The percentage varies with the locality and reflects its financial position. Workers dismissed for misconduct may receive a reduced benefit or none at all, depending on the gravity of the offense. Coverage for health care costs varies. In some localities, recipients receive another 10 percent of the minimum wage for medical care; in others, the incurred cost in excess of a fixed amount is split between the recipient and the insurance fund. Currently, there is no separate housing allowance, which may have to be introduced in the future as rents rise with the commercialization of housing. The maximum duration of benefit is two years, which is comparatively long by international standards. Each year's contribution yields entitlement to three months' benefit. Unemployed workers who have exhausted their benefit entitlement can apply for means-tested, urban social relief.

UI is financed by a payroll tax of 3 percent, with employers paying two-thirds and employees the remainder. Until June 1998, the rate was only 1 percent and paid entirely by employers. Until a few years ago, the UI fund tended to be in surplus and was used for a variety of purposes, some with no relation to unemployment. In response to reports of mismanagement and misuse, the Ministry of Finance has tightened control over the use of UI funds. Territorial governments are forbidden to charge any administration costs to social security funds. The rise in the contribution rate was prompted by a sharp increase in registered unemployment and layoffs and reports of widespread default on UB and on living allowances to laid-off employees. As well as raising funds, this rise introduced two important principles that have implications for the financial sustainability of the system: first, a relation between total cost and the contribution rate, and second, shifting a part of the cost to employees without compensation. The second has become the norm for all social security schemes and is equivalent to a personal income tax because it is not shifted back to employers.

On the basis of evidence gleaned during fieldwork in China's Northeast, the unemployment insurance account is now in deficit in most cities in the region. The deficit has to be covered from the municipal budget. The amount of deficit and its ratio to the municipal budget varies from city to city. Residual financing from the municipal budget is in keeping with the government policy of splitting the social security costs among employees. A further rise in payroll taxes for unemployment insurance would reduce the deficit but at the likely cost of reducing coverage. The current financing system is under stress in particular cities, and its financial sustainability over the medium to long run would depend crucially on the level of the territorial government at which social security accounts are balanced and deficits are financed. The present arrangement, with each city responsible for covering the deficit on social security schemes within its jurisdiction, is too decentralized for long-term sustainability, as it does not provide for sufficient risk pooling. There is as yet no regular framework for spreading the financial burden of UI and other social security schemes across cities. The need for such a framework will grow in importance as the number of claimants relative to contributors rises with the transfer of laid-off employers from enterprises to UI. The central government policy is to raise the level of financing to the province, but there is as yet no national framework for putting the policy into practice. A crucial precondition for the institution of any financial integration of social security schemes in a province is the establishment of a provincewide database with details of contributions and expenditures cross-classified by various levels of subprovincial government, which most provinces lack at present.

Drawing on international experience, the Chinese unemployment insurance scheme is not marred by any obvious design flaws, though there would seem to be scope for improvement through changes in specific details. On the benefit side, the flat-rate payment is low enough to preserve an ample incentive for benefit recipients to take up employment at the minimum wage rate and to constitute a disincentive for a worker to give up a job for the unemployment benefit. These issues loom large in discussion of UI in developed market economies but do not seem to be important in the Chinese context, at least as yet. Is the benefit adequate to prevent severe hardship? The answer is mixed. The unemployment benefit is widely seen as no more than a basic income for an individual. Unadjusted for household size or income, it is insufficient to prevent severe hardship in households with no earners. This is officially recognized in that benefit recipients are eligible for newly introduced social relief on the grounds of poverty.

The implication is that UB is too low to leave any room for reducing expenditure by cutting the benefit. The maximum benefit duration of two years seems long by international standards. But as yet the provision has had little purchase because very few workers qualify for the maximum duration, which requires eight years of uninterrupted contributions. The scheme started only in 1986, and until 2000, a large majority of UB recipients consisted of workers previously employed on short-term contracts of less than eight years. Almost all the unemployed workers with a long record of employment were until then regarded as "laid-off" employees and thus entitled to a "living allowance" from their work units instead of unemployment benefits. This has changed because of the policy to gradually phase out the category of "laid-off employees" by the end of 2003 or 2004, depending on the locality. As a consequence, since the beginning of 2000, there has been a rise in the number of beneficiaries entitled to UB for two years. Thus there is a growing need to assess the maximum duration of UB. But to avoid economic hardship, such an assessment has to be done in conjunction with special measures for unemployed workers with low chances of reemployment.

Accounting for 61.6 percent of the unemployed urban workers (counted according to the International Labor Organization definition), the laid-off employees form, as it were, the submerged bulk of the urban unemployment iceberg. As they are formally still employed, they are outside the UI umbrella. They receive a living allowance that is a percentage of the local minimum wage, not from labor and social security departments but from their enterprises, which are also responsible for their retraining and reemployment. "Laid-off worker" is a transitional category due for abolition no later than the end of 2004. The remaining laid-off workers will, from then on, be treated as unemployed workers. The numbers of laid-off employees shifting from their former work units to unemployment will rise even before the abolition because after two years, laid-off workers still without a job have to transfer to unemployment insurance. Laid-off workers transferring to UI are entitled to benefits for up to two years, depending on their employment history.

The abolition of the "laid-off workers" category, which is crucial for divesting enterprises of their social welfare responsibilities, has far-reaching administrative and financial implications for UI. It will imply a transfer of functions from work units to labor and social security departments, perhaps tripling their workload. It will also mean increased expenditures on UB without any rise in contributions because, like unemployed workers, laid-off employees are not liable for UI contributions. The abolition will amount to a partial transfer of the cost of supporting laid-off employees from enterprises to the municipal budget, but only a part because the UI fund and the municipal budget already cover up to two-thirds of the cost. Except in cities with strained budgets, the administrative implications of the phase-out are more serious than its financial implications.

Rural Social Security

In contrast to the elaborate social security benefits enjoyed by most of the urban population, social security provisions in rural areas are sparse and highly variable. Labor insurance does not apply to town and village enterprises, despite the fact that they employ 125.4 million workers, compared to 90.6 million in the state sector (State Statistical Bureau, 1999b). The rural social security system consists of special assistance to officially designated "poor counties," means-tested social relief to destitute persons and households, and disaster relief. In addition, there are also locally organized and financed partial old-age pensions. Rural medical care now largely takes the form of fee-for-service care, although some localities have cooperative health insurance (discussed later in this chapter). The sparseness of social provisions in rural areas would suggest that China's success in preventing deprivation in rural areas is due far more to households' having opportunities for earning a living either through farming and nonfarming activities than to social security schemes.

The pronounced urban bias in social security provisions is not exclusive to China; it is found in many developing economies. Though highly inequitable, to a degree it is unavoidable, given serious problems in designing and financing social insurance schemes for the self-employed and informally employed even in developed economies. The main problem in China lies with the anachronistic administrative distinction between the urban and the rural population, which regards the rural labor force as self-employed. This assumption has been rendered obsolete with the rapid growth of TVEs, which in 1998 employed more people than the state sector. The present administrative distinction between the urban and rural population is particularly anomalous in the case of the labor force in the rural counties in the vicinity of large cities, where a majority of the labor force may be wage-employed in nonfarming activities.

The extension of labor insurance to rural wage employees is desirable in principle, and a number of cities have already extended selected schemes to rural counties within municipal boundaries. But this extension raises two sets of issues: administration and equity. Municipal Labor and Social Security Bureaus that are now supposed to be responsible for labor insurance are still being established. Even after they are established, it will take them a number of years to fully assume the functions that work units currently perform in the administration of labor insurance for the urban labor force. Turning to equity, in the case of old-age pensions, by far the largest component of labor insurance, at least for the period needed to qualify for the basic pension (fifteen years), rural wage employees would be making contributions but receiving no benefits. Given that in most cities, contributions are used to finance current pension expenditures and not accumulated, rural wage employees would for some time be financing the pensions of retired urban workers, predominantly former state sector employees. This does not pose a problem in a mature system, but it does in a system that is undergoing a fundamental transformation and is still far from financially secure. The widespread default on payment of pensions of existing retirees inspires little confidence among rural employees that they would receive their due pensions when they come to retire. The implication is that there is little justification for extending labor insurance, with its existing administrative structure and make-shift financing pattern, to rural wage employees.

Health Status and Health Care

Health Status

There are three aspects of the health status of the population that deserve attention, leading to concerted policies for their reversal: first, the slow improvement or retrogression in child health over the reform period; second, the persistence of wide interprovincial variations; and third, a significant and in some cases even rising incidence of easily preventable infectious and parasitic diseases, especially in rural areas.

One indicator of health status is causes of death, which vary between rural and urban China (see Table 10.4) and following the usual convention, consist of three groups:

1. Communicable, maternal, prenatal, and nutritional conditions
2. Noncommunicable diseases
3. Injuries and toxicosis

Emblematic of poverty and lack of adequate health care, the first group of diseases claims virtually all of its victims in developing countries. But contrary to the usual presumption, noncommunicable diseases are neither diseases of afflu-

TABLE 10.4

Causes of Death in Urban and Rural China

(percent)

	Urban Areas	Rural Areas
Communicable, maternal, prenatal, and nutritional conditions	20.2	35.2
Noncommunicable diseases	72.9	52.6
Injuries and toxicosis	6.8	12.2

NOTE: The classification is not precise and should be taken as illustrative of the broad pattern.
SOURCE: State Statistical Bureau (1999d), pp. 740–741.

ence nor necessarily those of old age. In urban China, these diseases account for almost three-quarters of deaths, 3½ times as many as group 1 diseases. Among people aged thirty to forty-four, these diseases are responsible for 57 percent of male deaths and 60 percent of female deaths (Harvard Institute of Public Health, 1996). In contrast to urban areas, the pattern of the causes of death in rural China is similar to that in low-income economies. Thus China, like other developing economies, is burdened with both communicable and noncommunicable diseases.

With the death pattern akin to that in middle-income economies, urban China is in the middle stages of the "epidemiological transition" from the prevalence of deaths from group 1 to group 2 diseases as the main causes of deaths. But rural China is still in the initial stage. Communicable diseases still take a substantial and avoidable death toll. Their incidence is much higher than suggested by their rank in causes of death in rural and in urban areas. A survey in Sichuan revealed that as many as 40 percent of infectious ailments in rural areas go unreported (Chen, 1989).

Looking forward over the coming decades, how would the disease pattern change, and what implications would this have for health care? Already the biggest killer, noncommunicable diseases would further rise in importance as the main cause of deaths, as would their incidence, especially among the elderly population. The pattern of death causes in urban areas, if not in rural areas, will approach that in developed economies. The speed of elimination of infectious diseases will depend crucially on the implementation of the existing plan for their elimination (People's Republic of China, 1994). Moreover, the narrowing of the gap between rural and urban areas will depend on extending access to health care by raising the health insurance coverage in rural areas and reducing inequality in health care provision. The growing importance of noncommunicable diseases suggests the need for campaigns for a healthier lifestyle and an additional tax on tobacco, a major cause of such diseases. With the aging of the population, the need for long-term care will rise.

Health Care Provision

Consisting of three loosely connected strands, two large and one nascent, China's health care system disposes of a large infrastructure and employs a huge number of people. There are 314,097 health establishments and 4.4 million medical personnel, including doctors of both Western and Chinese medicine, nurses, and paramedics (State Statistical Bureau, 1999e). Most of the two million doctors are employees of either public health departments or work units; the proportion of the self-employed (private practitioners) is small but growing. At the core of the health care system are 67,081 hospitals (including small clinics) with 2.9 million beds. These vary widely in size and services provided; around 50,000 of them are rural (located in townships and villages, excluding those in county seats).

Hospitals also provide outpatient care, even in cases of minor ailments, and specialized outpatient facilities are rudimentary and tend to offer low-quality medical care.

There are three separate health care networks, loosely connected and each fairly decentralized. One is public, the second is "occupational," and the third is private. The distinctions between them lie in the supervising agency, the source of funding, and their clientele. The largest is the public health network, which performs the dual function of serving government employees and also the population at large and covers both rural and urban areas. It is not free at the point of service and only partially subsidized by the government. Generally, public hospitals receive all but a small percentage of their income from user charges. The tight government control of charges for basic medical treatment, which takes up most doctors' time, provides a huge incentive to doctors to demand side payments and for hospitals to branch out into high-tech treatments, the prices of which are uncontrolled. The network is public in the restricted sense that its staff consists of employees of departments of public health from the central down to the county level. As state enterprises, public hospitals are graded according to the territorial division of the government. Thus a large city may have central, provincial, municipal, and urban district hospitals. Allied to the urban public network is the rural network of clinics and hospitals run by townships (the lowest government tier in rural areas) and villages (a communal rather than a governmental unit), which cover a large proportion of townships and villages, but as yet not all. Except in some regions, their staffs are not employees of public health departments.

The occupational network is run by state-owned enterprises and larger collectives, the armed forces, prisons, and a range of other institutions. It is mainly urban and extensive, encompassing a disparate range of facilities, each serving a restricted category of patients, to whom it is for the most part free at the point of service. The network is mainly financed by "work units," and their staffs are not employees of public health departments but of the parent unit. With the trend toward divesting enterprises of their social facilities, larger enterprise hospitals market their services, and some of them are far more profitable than their parent enterprises.

The third is the private medical service, which is more prevalent in rural than in urban areas. Unlike their peers, private practitioners are not employees but self-employed. Their proliferation is a post-1978 development prompted in rural areas by the collapse of cooperative health insurance and in urban areas by the rise in the number of people without health insurance. Aside from curative services, there are three networks of preventive and early diagnostic services. These include the Epidemiological Prevention Services, Maternal and Child Health Service, and Family Planning Service, which receive budgets from provincial and county governments. But increasingly, they have come to depend on fee-for-service arrangements, which has had a deleterious effect on preventive and early diagnostic services in some rural areas. Operating relatively independently of each other, these networks provide overlapping services, which suggests some scope for raising efficiency through administrative coordination and consolidation.

Medical Provision in Rural Areas

Two features distinguish medical provision in rural areas from that in urban areas: it is sparser and more variable from locality to locality. There still remain many villages without any medical facility, notwithstanding the plan to have a clinic in most villages by 2000 (People's Republic of China, 1994). A three-tiered medical network serves the 69.6 percent of the population classified as rural. The first tier consists of around 40,000 village health stations or clinics staffed by 733,315 medical personnel (State Statistical Bureau, 1999a). These include "village doctors," who evolved from the original "barefoot doctors" of the pre-reform period. They are the first port of call for rural inhabitants needing primary medical care, and they channel patients to township health centers or hospitals. They engage in medical practice either full time or part time, as a sideline to farming. Except in a few localities where "rural cooperative health insurance" survives or has been reintroduced, they charge a fee for their service and also receive a markup (typically about 15 percent) on prescriptions, which provides an incentive to overprescribe drugs—an incentive that pervades the Chinese health care system.

The second tier consists of 9,600 rural health hospitals and hospitals at the rural township level (the lowest government tier). These operate on fee-for-service basis, but a part of their costs is covered by the rural local government. The extent of subsidies varies widely, depending on local revenue. Richer localities with developed TVEs tend to have better facilities than poorer ones. The first two tiers are local and are not an integral part of the public health network, though they are supervised by county health bureaus. The top tier of the system is made up of county hospitals, with one million beds; these dovetail into city hospitals with around two million beds. The county hospitals are usually the last point of referral for rural patients, since few can afford the services of large specialized city hospitals. The urban–rural gap in health care provision is wide, and it has widened. Since 1985, the number of hospital beds and medical personnel (doctors, nurses, and paramedics) has been rising in urban areas but falling in rural areas (State Statistical Bureau, 1999e). A part of the decline in hospital beds in rural areas is due to the consolidation of facilities in urban hospitals, which are more intensively used than rural hospitals. But because for most rural inhabitants, county hospitals are the medical facilities of last resort, the reduction in the number of hospital beds in rural areas represents a reduction in accessible medical facilities for a part of the rural population.

Health Care Financing: Sources and Uses

Currently, China devotes around 4 percent of GNP to health care, up from 3 percent in 1978 and comparatively high for a low-income country. The reported percentage would be higher still but for comprehensive government price controls on medical treatment and drugs and may be an underestimate due to the underreporting of out-of-pocket expenses and the exclusion of under-the-table payments to doctors. Extrapolating from international trends, this percentage will rise, driven by two factors: the aging of the population and the rising cost per treatment as a result of rising wages of medical personnel and increasing non-labor cost.

Turning to sources of health care expenditure, their importance derives from their implication for the distribution of the demand for medical care and its cost. For example, under financing on a fee-for-service basis (without any insurance), the burden falls entirely on patients and is distributed according to medical care dispensed. This usually means that a proportion of those struck with illness either purchase medical treatment at the cost of slipping into poverty or cut down and forgo treatment but pay the price in ill health and a higher risk of avoidable death. Either choice creates a vicious circle between inadequate medical care and poverty. Fee-for-service care is particularly inequitable when it is confined primarily to the relatively poor section of the population, as it is in China. Most of the population with health insurance coverage (albeit now eroded) is urban, and all but a small proportion of the rural population is subject to fee-for-service arrangements. Financing through insurance (commercial or non-profit) by spreading the burden widely over the covered population rather than just patients loosens the link between payment and medical care. An inevitable consequence of health insurance is a higher demand for and expenditure on medical care. A part of this increase is justified and fits in with the social purpose of health insurance: to provide medical care to those who need it but are forced to forgo it under the fee-for-service arrangement. But there is also a part that is wasteful arising from moral hazard. However, the main problem is that it is not easy to distinguish between a justified increase in demand and moral hazard.

The three main sources of financing for health care in China are government subsidies, the health insurance schemes, and individuals' out-of-pocket payments. Over the reform period, the first two have diminished in importance, shifting a greater burden of financing to the third. Government financing for health is provided in two forms: as subsidies on curative and preventive services for the population at large (here termed "spending from the budget") and as reimbursements under the Government Health Insurance Service (GIS). Grouping the latter with the other employee health insurance scheme (labor insurance), the composition of health financing in selected years of the reform period is shown in Table 10.5.

TABLE 10.5

Sources of Health Financing

(percent)

	1978	1986	1993
Government budget[1]	28	32	14
Insurance schemes[2]	30	33	36
Rural insurance schemes	20	5	2
Out of pocket[3]	20	26	42
Others	2	4	6
Health expenditure, as a percentage of GDP	3.0	3.2	3.8

NOTES:
[1] Excludes insurance expenses for government employees.
[2] Includes the insurance schemes for government employees (GIS) and labor insurance (LI).
[3] Includes user fees, copayments, and fee-for-service plans.
SOURCE: World Bank (1996a).

Out-of-pocket expenses cover a variety of payments by individuals, with different distributive implications. These include "full" fee-for-service care, copayments, and registration fees (which fall entirely on those receiving treatment), on the one hand, and individual contributions toward insurance (which falls on all those covered under the scheme). The latter is common only in rural cooperative schemes and still rare in the occupational schemes covering the urban population. With the implementation of the planned municipal scheme, individual contributions will become a universal feature of health insurance. In the fifteen years from 1978 to 1993, the composition of health expenditures underwent a major change, with a highly adverse implication for the distribution of medical expenditures by income groups and between the ill and the healthy. In the eight years from 1978 to 1986, the principal change consisted of a huge reduction in the share of rural cooperative insurance schemes and a significant rise in the share of out-of-pocket expenses due mainly to the shift to fee-for-service plans in rural areas.

The following seven years saw a change as major as that in the preceding period, but this time it consisted largely of a shift of expenditure from the government budget to the pockets of urban as well as rural patients. The share of out-of-pocket expenses is likely to be an underestimate because it excludes under-the-table or side payments to medical personnel, which are improper or illegal and therefore go unreported. Circumstantial evidence suggests that these have risen in importance.

Health Insurance Schemes

Compared to other developing economies in Asia, in China, a high proportion of the population has been covered by some form of health insurance (as yet) mostly noncontributory in urban areas and contributory in rural areas. Given its high rate of growth and its long experience with health insurance, China has the potential to extend health insurance coverage to a large majority of the population in the near future. This will involve the replacement of the inherited health insurance in urban areas, which has seriously eroded with the worsening financial position of state enterprises, and the institution of cooperative health insurance in rural areas.

Following the trial experiments in two cities (Zhenjiang and Jiujiang) and then in another fifty-seven, the central government decided to replace occupational health insurance schemes with municipal schemes. The principal features of the new municipal schemes, introduction of which began in 2000, include the following:

- Joint financing by employers, employees, and the municipal government
- Individual medical accounts to cover "small" expenses, financed by employee contributions
- A social fund to cover "major" expenses, financed by a portion of employer contributions and the municipal government
- A cap on the expenses covered by the social fund

The details of the scheme vary from city to city and have undergone revisions.

From the point of view of insurance, the new scheme has three major features. First, the scheme covers only a part of the urban population: wage employees paying in contributions, pensioners, and recipients of unemployment benefits. The insurance status of those on urban poverty relief is unclear, and dependants are not covered. Second, the coverage of "small" expenses depends crucially on the accumulated funds in the personal account. The implication is that whereas younger employees, with a low incidence of illnesses, pay little or nothing from their own pockets, older employees, especially those with chronic ailments, would be covering "small" expenses themselves. Third, because of the cap on reimbursement from the social fund, the scheme leaves most catastrophic illnesses uncovered. The cap is set at a fixed multiple of the yearly salary of the individual, not the average. The implication is that the extent of the cover varies inversely with the income of the individual. In principle, employees are expected to take out commercial insurance to cover catastrophic illnesses, but that is voluntary, not mandatory.

This introduces a serious potential problem of adverse selection. Because younger employees face a small risk of catastrophic illnesses, they have little or no incentive to purchase commercial health insurance, whereas older workers, who face a higher risk, have the incentive to do so. Moreover, employees with a high wage, with more extensive coverage under the mandatory scheme, have less incentive to purchase supplementary commercial insurance than low-wage employees have. Currently, municipalities maintain a relief fund to cover the cost of major medical expenses of patients without means. But there is as yet no regular system of financing these funds. Richer cities tend to have large funds, and poorer cities, small funds. In many cities, the relief fund is exhausted well before the end of the financial year. Finally, as pointed out earlier, the operation of individual medical accounts raises massive operational problems.

Rural cooperative health insurance developed as an offshoot of collective agriculture. A part of collective income went into the establishment and running of health stations (cooperative medical care clinics) at the brigade (village) level. These were staffed by local inhabitants with elementary medical training on top of primary education, known as "barefoot doctors" (now termed "rural doctors"). They were paid by the collectives on the remuneration system used to pay farmers. The system was financed partly by the collective and partly by prepayments and copayments. The system received a boost during the Cultural Revolutionary period and by the mid-1970s covered around nine villages in ten.

The decollectivization of the rural economy unraveled the cooperative health insurance schemes with which it was intertwined. Their collapse was due to three factors: first, the disappearance of the administrative underlay of the schemes; second, a decline in collective funds, which subsidized the schemes; and third, the erosion of cooperative ideology. The scheme inherited from the prereform period suffered from major defects. The quality of service varied widely and involved coercion. But it served an important function of bringing medical care, albeit rudimentary, to villages. A notable step toward a revival of rural cooperative health insurance schemes was the Sichuan Rural Health Experiment. This experimental scheme was organized in 1989–90 and covered a sample of twenty-six villages and 40,443 individuals. A wide range of cooperative health insurance schemes are now in place in rural areas, but most of these are in relatively prosperous areas. A major component of the health policy announced in 1997 is the introduction of cooperative health insurance schemes in all villages. As these schemes have to be initiated and funded locally, well-governed and prosperous localities are likely to take the lead.

Conclusion

To conclude, I would like to provide answers to two questions:

- What are the immediate priorities in social security reforms?
- Of what would a sustainable social security system for China consist?

Priorities in Social Security Reform

Given the urban-rural segmentation in social security provision in China, the immediate priorities are different in rural and urban areas. Rural areas are unaffected by the collapse of the inherited social security system, which did not apply to them. The principal task there is establishing income maintenance schemes and health care insurance almost from scratch. In urban areas, priorities are set by the unraveling of the work–unit–based social security system, on the one hand, and the growing problem of poverty. State and urban collective enterprises that have been the mainstay of social welfare in urban China are increasingly unable to carry on with their traditional social welfare role. Since the middle of the 1990s, they have been undergoing a stringent market selection, which is mirrored in the social security field as inordinate delays in the payment of pensions and the reimbursement of health care expenses or outright default in some cases. This has contributed strongly to the upward trend in urban poverty in recent years. The other is the steady rise in urban unemployment, including layoffs that are not regarded as unemployment in official statistics.

Thanks to a series of reforms in recent years, the blueprint of the alternative to work–unit–based social security in urban areas is almost completed, though still far from implemented. The major impediments in its implementation are administrative and financial. Given the long history of reliance on work units to administer the labor insurance schemes for their employees (and indirectly for most of the urban population), municipal governments lack the administrative structure that is needed for a socialized (government-managed) social security system. Municipal Labor And Social Security Bureaus that are to function as social security agencies are still in the process of being established in many cities. Thus one immediate priority is to speed up the establishment of LSSBs.

The other immediate priority is the reform of social security financing. In urban areas, all contributory schemes, including old-age pensions, health care insurance, and unemployment benefits, are now financed jointly by employer and employee contributions, with the government acting as the residual source. This arrangement is common throughout the world and in principle provides the foundations for a financially sustainable system. But the current financing system as it operates suffers from several serious defects. First, contributions are collected separately for each of the five schemes. There is a proposal to transform disparate contributions into one composite social security tax (split between employers and employees) that is collected together with other taxes, which would simplify collection and also help raise the compliance rate. Second, with the proposed social security law still under discussion, social security contributions lack a legal backing and have a lower priority in claims on enterprise resources than taxes do.

Third and most important, the budgeting of social security revenues and expenditures is highly decentralized. The budgetary units are 226 or so cities (excluding rural county seats), and deficits generally have to be covered from municipal budgets. As yet, there is no settled procedure for fiscal redistribution across cities. This highly decentralized budgeting weakens the financial foundation of the urban social security system because the balance between contributions and expenditures varies widely across cities, and so do their finances. Cities are generally too small a budgetary unit to ensure sufficient risk pooling to ensure sustainability. A pooling of social security contributions and expenditures at the provincial level is the professed policy aim and would seem to be an urgent priority in the case of old-age pensions, which is by far the largest scheme in terms of expenditures. In most cases, this would be sufficient to put the urban social security system on a sound financial footing. Many of the Chinese provinces are as populous as sizable foreign countries. The upgrading of the level of budgeting from cities to provinces can take a number of forms, ranging from a full integration to compensatory transfers within a decentralized system. It raises important issues of the appropriate degree of decentralization in administration and of how to deal with the incentive to "free-ride" arising from the pooling of expenditures and contributions. A national pooling of social security contributions and expenditures seems to be infeasible. It would also be inequitable, in that under the present financing arrangements, poorer provinces would be making transfers to richer provinces because the latter tend to have a higher ratio of pensioners to contributors than do the former.

Turning to priorities in rural areas, poverty has fallen since the beginning of reforms in 1979—sharply until the mid-1980s and in fits and starts since then. The success in reducing extreme rural poverty is making the traditional approach to poverty alleviation obsolete. Thus far, poverty relief in rural areas has been mainly focused on relief from natural disasters and assistance to counties officially designated as poor. Natural disaster relief will continue to remain important, but assistance to poor counties suffers from blind spots. Many of the counties designated as poor are no longer poor. More important, poor households and individuals are distributed over the whole of rural China; they are not confined to designated rural counties. Geographic targeting is appropriate when poverty is primarily associated with causes affecting the whole locality, such as poverty of natural resources, but not when causes are particular to individuals or households. A major lacuna in China's rural antipoverty policy is the absence of an effective system for dealing with household and individual poverty in the midst of prosperity. The existing schemes deal with a very restricted category of people, such as the elderly without a family, and are highly variable from locality to locality. Instead what is needed is "rural poverty relief," on the same line as the recently introduced scheme in urban areas, which is targeted at individuals and households below the poverty line and covers all urban residents. An essential precondition for such a scheme is a system of intergovernmental transfers because the fiscal position of rural counties and township varies even more widely than that of cities.

A combined social security system for urban and rural areas, although desirable, is infeasible in the immediate future for financial and administrative reasons. So too is a substantial narrowing of the gap in coverage and the range of benefits. The tax system these require is decades in the future. The current official position that the urban and the rural systems have to be reformed separately is therefore realistic. The problem is the low priority given to reform in rural areas. Given the growth of wage employment, social security reform in rural areas requires the institution of parallel labor insurance financed by employer and employee contributions, at least in larger rural enterprises. Rural areas have an advantage over urban areas in starting with a blank slate; they are not handicapped by an overhang of problems left by an inherited system, such as financing unfunded pension liabilities.

Turning to priorities with respect to particular social security schemes, the new two-tiered old-age pension scheme and the unemployment insurance schemes are not marred by faulty design. They follow principles tested and tried in many countries. Nevertheless, these schemes, especially old-age pensions, suffer from some serious problems. The most serious of these consists of inordinate delays in the payment of pensions to a significant percentage of current retirees. A permanent solution is premised on the development of a social security administration and the institution of a system of fiscal transfers across cities, at least within the same province. Without these, the financing of unfunded old-age pensions liabilities of future retirees, which has been a major focus of multilateral and bilateral assistance to the Chinese social security system, makes little sense. The other pressing issue is the institution of effective health care insurance. The work-unit-based health care insurance in urban areas has almost collapsed, and most of the rural localities have no health insurance system. Problems in establishing an effective health care insurance system are far more formidable than those in the case of old-age pensions. These concern not only financing but also cost control and an overhaul of the health care delivery system. Further, unlike old-age pensions and unemployment, the proposed municipal health care insurance system in urban areas is still in a formative phase. The proposal in its current form suffers from serious design faults. It fails to provide insurance against catastrophic illnesses when it is most needed, lacks an effective mechanism to control rising costs, and is costly to administer.

A Sustainable Social Security System for China

The numerous problems besetting Chinese social security schemes raise the fundamental question of the kind of social security system a developing economy such as China's can sustain. The question has a special resonance in the Chinese context because the work-unit-based provision of social welfare in urban China has traditionally been more extensive and generous than in other developing economies. Here it is important to emphasize that the inherited system has already undergone a massive pruning and an alternative system is in place, albeit not fully operational. The question of a sustainable system, therefore, is pertinent only in the context of the reformed system that is taking shape. Sustainability is premised on two sets of considerations: administrative capacity to operate social security schemes and financial viability.

To appraise the reformed system, we divide the schemes under two headings:

social insurance and social assistance (the "social safety net"). The principal differences between the two types of schemes lie in the method of financing and
qualifications for receiving benefits. Social insurance schemes are contributory,
and benefits are consequently limited to individuals who have made the requisite contributions. In the Chinese context, the five labor insurance schemes fall
under this category. In principle, social insurance schemes can be self-financing,
like commercial schemes. But in practice, they are only partially self-financing
because of the social consideration of ensuring wide coverage. Thus one issue
in the assessment of such schemes is the percentage of cost financed through
general taxes, which I will analyze shortly with respect to the labor insurance
schemes. In contrast to social insurance, social assistance schemes are noncontributory, and the entitlement to assistance depends on need and is not tied
to the record of employment or contribution. In the Chinese context, such
schemes includes the newly introduced urban poverty relief scheme, disaster relief, and assistance to poor rural localities, and a likely addition in the near future is a rural poverty relief scheme similar to the one for urban areas. Apart from
the first, all the rest apply to a limited segment of the population, and in terms
of expenditures, social assistance schemes trail social insurance schemes by a
wide margin. Viewed in these terms, it becomes clear that the social security system that is taking shape is neither open-ended nor prima facie unsustainable.
There are problems with particular schemes, but as I outline next, these can be
addressed through feasible reforms.

Social insurance consists of five schemes that cover major contingencies of life:
old-age pensions, unemployment benefits, health care insurance, disability benefits, and maternity benefits. Though currently restricted to the urban labor force,
the schemes provide the basis for developing a nationwide social insurance system covering a substantial percentage of the labor force. A central issue in assessing the financial sustainability of these schemes as currently organized is their
financial burden, of which there are two indicators: the ratio of their cost to the
wage bill and the balance between contributions and outlays on these schemes
and hence their claim on general tax revenue. Focusing on the state sector, the
sector with the highest burden, the ratio of expenditures on social insurance and
also on additional welfare facilities to the total wage bill is 40.3 percent (State
Statistical Bureau, 1999b). This is high but not an outlier by international standards. Further, the average ratio for all employees covered by labor insurance is
5 percentage points lower. These expenditures do not include housing subsidies,
but they are not relevant because they are not a part of social insurance and are
being phased out. The provision of housing to employees is no longer mandatory, and the existing housing stock is being privatized.

Turning to the current balance between contributions and outlays, the balance is positive on the five social insurance schemes taken together (State Statistical Bureau, 1999b). Taken individually, the old-age pension scheme is the only

one in deficit. Thus in the aggregate, social insurance does not require any supplementary funds from the government budget. As the social insurance budget
is compiled at the highly disaggregated level of 226 cities, the surplus at the national level goes together with unsustainable deficits in numerous cities, a problem that can be addressed by upgrading the level of budgeting to provinces. Besides, the deficit on old-age pensions is more serious than it appears because
contributions also include payments into individual accounts that should be accumulated rather than used to finance current pensions.

The issue of financial sustainability in the immediate future principally concerns old-age pensions and health care insurance. The new city-based health
care insurance scheme, still in a formative stage, does not yet lend itself to evaluation. Turning to old-age pensions, the problem is largely in the state sector
and is caused by pay-as-you-go financing with a very short-term planning horizon. Currently, 77.4 percent of retirees are from the state sector, and this percentage is likely to rise in the near future. The ratio of retirees to contributors
in the state sector, which was already high, has risen sharply over the past few
years owing to a huge labor retrenchment. In the three years from 1995 to 1998,
the total employment in the sector dropped by 22 million (or 20 percent), and
the downward trend looks likely to continue for some time. One less employee
means one less contributor but the same or a larger number of pensioners because older state sector employees may be allowed to retire early instead of being laid off. The implication is that the financial sustainability of the old-age
pension scheme, as currently financed, depends crucially on extending its coverage of the nonstate sector so as to raise the number of contributors without
adding to the numbers of pensioners in the short-run. The possible sources of
new contributors are foreign-invested and private enterprises in urban areas and
rural enterprises.

But the extension of the old-age pension scheme even in urban areas faces
two closely related problems. The first is the operational one of collecting contributions from small enterprises with a rapidly rising share of urban employment. The second is the doubtful credibility of the promise of a pension in the
distant future in return for contributions over the near future, which is what the
extension of the scheme to nonstate sector employees involves. Given the widespread delays and defaults on the payment of pensions to current retirees, this
promise does not inspire confidence. The implication is that the possibilities of
financing the rising cost of old-age pensions in the short to medium term by
extending the coverage of the scheme or by raising the contribution rate are
limited. A partial financing of pension costs by the government is necessary to
ensure the sustainability of the old-age pension scheme. There are various proposals concerning the possible sources of finance. One is to use assets in state
ownership, such as enterprises and land, for funding the pension liabilities of the
state sector. The other is to use general tax revenues.

The foregoing discussion leads to the general question: Is social insurance covering old-age and disability pension, unemployment benefits, and health care sustainable in the long run for a low-income economy such as China's? Tied to wages, the benefits provided by these schemes are austere, and entitlement is confined to those with a contribution record. In design, the reformed old-age pension scheme announced in 1995 with its two components (a subsistence allowance and a funded supplement tied to contributions) is sustainable. The problem the old-age pension scheme faces is caused by the overhang of pension liabilities left behind by the old system, which was characterized by the absence of any forward financial planning. The pension overhang impedes the new two-tiered scheme from functioning because current contributions are entirely used up covering current pension payments, leaving no accumulation of reserves to fund the earnings-related component as provided by the new scheme.

This points to the fundamental problem: it is simply infeasible to use payroll contributions both to finance the overhang of unfunded pension liabilities and to fund the earnings-related component of the new scheme. The contribution rate this requires is too high to be enforceable. To give an idea, in the state sector, the current pension payment in 1998 came to around 25 percent of total earnings in the sector (State Statistical Bureau, 1999b). The new pension scheme envisages a contribution rate of 11 percent of total earnings to fund the earnings-related component. The two together come to 36 percent of total earnings, which is already 16 percentage points higher than the guidance ceiling of 20 percent laid down by the State Council. The policy implication is that the sustainability of old-age pensions over time requires a separation of the funded component of the new pension schemes from the unfunded pension liabilities left behind by the old system and the financing of the latter from sources other than payroll contributions.

Turning to social assistance schemes, including urban poverty and natural disaster relief and various poverty alleviation schemes in rural areas, these raise two major issues: their total cost and their effectiveness in preventing deprivation. The total cost of these schemes is small relative to the total budgetary expenditure, which covers only a part of government expenditures. For example, in 1999, the urban poverty relief scheme assisted 2.9 million, 22 percent of the estimated 13 million or so urban residents below the poverty line, at the total cost of 2 billion yuan (just over 0.2 percent of total government budgetary expenditures). Assuming that average cost per assisted person remains constant, the total cost of the scheme for full coverage would come to around 1 percent of the total government budgetary expenditures. All government expenditures on social security and various relief schemes (including those in rural areas) in 1999 came to around 4.1 percent of the total. The conclusion is that government expenditures on social security, over and above contributions to labor insurance, in China is on the low rather than the high side.

Turning to effectiveness in preventing deprivation, the existing social assistance schemes suffer from blind spots and fail to reach a significant percentage of individuals who under the prevailing criteria qualify for assistance. This raises the question, Can China afford a universal poverty relief scheme on the lines of the urban poverty relief scheme? A universal scheme would not add greatly to the cost because the rural population is already covered by a number of anti-poverty schemes. A broad-based scheme is likely to be more cost-effective than the current geographically targeted schemes.

What would a social security package for China that is both financially sustainable and also provides an acceptable degree of insurance against deprivation and contingencies look like? A universal income maintenance scheme, on the lines of the newly introduced urban poverty relief scheme, is not only necessary but also appears to be financially sustainable. Given sufficient risk pooling through compensatory transfers between government tiers and a separate financing of the overhang of unfunded pension liabilities, contributory schemes covering old-age and disability pension, health care, and unemployment also appear to be feasible. The universal income maintenance scheme and contributory schemes are complementary. The former is needed to cover the gap left by the latter, and the latter, in turn, serves to keep in check the number of claimants in the former.

Note

1. The current official retirement age in China is low by international standards, ranging between fifty and sixty. The actual retirement age is a distribution rather than a number, and the choice of sixty as the benchmark retirement age does not affect the argument here.

References

Atkinson, A. B. (1991). *Social Insurance*. Welfare State Programme Discussion Paper No. 65. London: London School of Economics.

Chen, G. C. (1989). *Medicine in Rural China*. Berkeley: University of California Press.

Cutler, D. M., Poterba, J. M., Sheiner, L. M., and Summers, L. H. (1990). *An Aging Society: Opportunity or Challenge?* Washington, D.C.: Brookings Institution.

Deaton, A. (1997). *The Analysis of Household Surveys*. Baltimore: Johns Hopkins University Press.

Diamond, P. (1994). "Pension Reform in a Transition Economy: Notes on Poland and Chile." In O. J. Blanchard, K. A. Froot, and J. D. Sachs (eds.), *The Transition in Eastern Europe*, vol. 2. Washington, D.C.: National Bureau of Economic Research.

Feeney, G. (1996). "Fertility in China: Past, Present, Prospects." In W. Lutz (ed.), *The Future Population of the World: What Can We Assume Today?* London: Earthscan.

Harvard Institute of Public Health. (1996). *Global Burden of Disease.* Cambridge, Mass.: Harvard Institute of Public Health, World Bank, and World Health Organization.

Hu, Xiaoyi. (1996). "Reducing State-Owned Enterprises' Social Burdens and Establishing a Social Insurance System." In H. G. Broadman (ed.), *Policy Options for Reform of Chinese State-Owned Enterprises.* Washington, D.C.: World Bank.

Hussain, A. (1993). *Reform of the Chinese Social Security System.* China Programme Discussion Paper No. 27. London: London School of Economics.

———. (2003). "Urban Poverty in China: Measurement, Patterns and Policies." In *Focus Programme on Socio-Economic Security.* Geneva: International Labor Organization. Available at http://www/ilo.org/ses

Hussain, A., and Zhuang, J. (1998). "Enterprise Taxation and Transition to a Market Economy." In J. S. Brean (ed.), *Taxation in Modern China.* London: Routledge.

Kingson, E. R., and Schulz, J. H. (1997). *Social Security in the 21st Century.* Oxford: Oxford University Press.

People's Republic of China. (1994). *China's Agenda 21: White Paper on China's Population, Environment, and Development in the 21st Century.* Beijing: Government Printing Office.

Sen, A. K (1984). "Peasants and Dualism with or Without Surplus Labor." In A. K. Sen, *Resources, Values and Development.* Oxford: Blackwell.

State Statistical Bureau. (1982). *1982 Population Census of China (Results of Computer Tabulation).* Beijing: State Statistical Publishing House.

———. (1998a). *China Labor Statistical Yearbook, 1998.* Beijing: State Statistical Publishing House.

———. (1998b). *China Statistical Yearbook, 1998.* Beijing: State Statistical Publishing House.

———. (1998c). *China Urban Yearbook, 1998.* Beijing: State Statistical Publishing House.

———. (1999a). *China Agricultural Yearbook, 1999.* Beijing: State Statistical Publishing House.

———. (1999b). *China Labor Statistical Yearbook, 1998.* Beijing: State Statistical Publishing House.

———. (1999c). *China Population Yearbook, 1999.* Beijing: State Statistical Publishing House.

———. (1999d). *China's Population, 1999.* Beijing: State Statistical Publishing House.

———. (1999e). *China Statistical Yearbook, 1999.* Beijing: State Statistical Publishing House.

United Nations Development Programme. (1999). *Human Development Report, 1996.* New York: United Nations.

Walder, A. G (1986). *Communist Neo-Traditionalism: Work and Authority in Chinese Industry.* Berkeley: University of California Press.

World Bank. (1992). *China: Strategies for Reducing Poverty in the 1990s.* Washington, D.C.: World Bank.

———. (1996a). *China: Issues and Options in Health Financing.* Washington, D.C.: World Bank.

———. (1996b). *China: Pension System Reform.* Washington, D.C.: World Bank.

———. (1999). *World Development Report, 1999.* Washington, D.C.: World Bank.

11

Housing Reform in Urban China

Jeffrey S. Zax

April 2000 marked the approximate twentieth anniversary of housing reform in China. Twenty years earlier, a speech by Deng Xiaoping initiated the discussion of alternative organizational approaches to the socialized provision of urban Chinese housing. The intervening years saw experimentation in individual urban areas, a substantial expenditure of energy on the part of national policymaking bodies, and remarkable levels of housing production. In this chapter, I review the history of urban housing policy reform. I then examine original evidence regarding changes in the quality of the urban Chinese housing stock and the extent to which that stock has become commodified.

At the same time, the government has remained the owner of most urban housing, government housing expenditures have continued to increase, and deplorable housing conditions remain unacceptably common. Construction costs have exceeded any conceivable notion of affordability throughout the reform period. Moreover, policy seems to be driven by a mistaken commitment to quantitative housing goals, the false impression that urban housing is "scarce," and the unsupported belief that "subsidized" occupants should "pay" for ownership rights.

The next portion of the chapter analyzes the reasons why significant commercial owner occupancy has failed to materialize, considers levels of urban housing investment from an economic perspective, and discusses potential policies for the conversion of the urban housing stock to private ownership.

These issues have been foremost in policy discussions. However, reform will have to confront several others as it evolves. Consequently, the chapter goes on to explore land allocation and pricing, property rights, mortgage financing, informal housing, and property taxation and identifies areas where reforms might be beneficial.

The Evolution of Urban Housing and Urban Housing Reform

Urban Chinese housing reform has already been the subject of a large literature. I shall summarize the experience of the past twenty years as reflected therein. Most of the material here appears in several or even many of the referenced articles. Many of the citations therefore indicate representative rather than unique discussions.

The Urban Chinese Housing Stock

The physical characteristics of the urban Chinese housing stock are for the most part undocumented (Hamer and van Steekelenburg, 1999). However, estimates of urban floor areas omitting "corridors, kitchens, toilets or bathrooms" (Dwyer, 1986, p. 484) are plentiful. This measure, labeled "living space," yielded approximately 67 square feet per urban resident with the advent of the People's Republic in 1949.

However, it apparently declined to as low as 32 square feet during the next decade (Dwyer, 1986, p. 484) and recovered only to 45 square feet per capita by 1978 (Wang, 1991, p. 104). Moreover, housing conditions varied dramatically despite nominal commitments to equity in allocations (Dwyer, 1986). At this point, "the extreme shortage of residential accommodations in China's cities [had] already reached crisis proportions and [was] widely acknowledged by Chinese citizens to be one of the most explosive social issues facing their society today" (Lalkaka, 1984, p. 64; see also Taubman, 1984, and Lee, 1998).

The perception of shortage was unquestionably fueled by the prevailing regime for urban housing finance. Rents for urban housing were negligible (Lee, 1988), both to support the conception of housing as a welfare good (Lalkaka, 1984) and to enable low wages that formed the foundation of the urban labor-management regime (Chen and Gao, 1993b; Zhou and Logan, 1996). At these rent levels, excess demand was inevitable.

Regardless, expressions of excess demand were interpreted as indications that the aggregate quantity supplied was actually deficient, rather than that the rationing mechanism had failed. This created enormous pressure for increased government investment in urban housing (Taubman, 1984). In consequence, explicit government expenditures implied nominal subsidies of 49.64 yuan per worker in 1978, the equivalent of 6.7 percent of the value of average total worker compensation (Wang, 1991, pp. 112–13).

Noteworthy increases in housing supply occurred during the ensuing years. As a consequence of massive government expenditures, reported per capita living space attained levels of 56 square feet in 1985, 72 square feet in 1990, and 87 square feet in 1995 (State Statistical Bureau, 1996, tab. 9-1).

However, the perception of shortage remained largely unaffected (Gu and

Colwell, 1997). Derisory rents continued to encourage exaggerated housing de-mands. In the mid-1980s, actual rents comprised barely 1 percent of urban house-hold expenditures (Tong and Hays, 1996) and "6.5 per cent of the full-cost rent" (Chiu, 1996b, p. 562).

Consequently, the role of subsidies in urban housing finance was, if anything, expanded. As recently as 1997, "nearly 80% of the [urban] population was liv-ing in state-owned housing" (Hui and Wong, 1999, p. 141). The attendant an-nual housing subsidy grew to 429 yuan per urban worker in 1988, or 15 percent of worker compensation (Wang, 1991, pp. 112–13). It rose to 1,960 yuan per urban household, or "59.6% of households' total welfare subsidization" in 1997 (Hui and Wong, 1999, p. 141).

Nevertheless, inequities apparently became more pronounced. In 1986, 18 percent of urban residents had less than 43 square feet of living space (Tong and Hays, 1996); the World Bank (1992) reported this proportion to be 30 percent. "In spite of increasing average space, the number of households facing difficul-ties increased, from approximately one-fourth in 1985–1986 to one-third of the total in 1991" (Tong and Hays, 1996, p. 629).[1]

The Evolution of Housing Reform

For the most part, rural housing in China has been financed by individual house-holds. Chinese housing reform is therefore an urban process (Wang, 1991). It was originally motivated by the perception that urban housing was in short sup-ply and that much of what was available was substandard. It was further en-couraged by anticipations that population growth would exacerbate these con-ditions and that future government resources would be insufficient to ameliorate them (Fong, 1989b; Chaichian, 1991).

Reform became a national issue with Deng's April 1980 address, in which he advocated private ownership through sales of state-owned housing and private housing production, increased rents with compensating wage increases for low-paid workers, and profit-oriented state housing production (Barlow and Renaud, 1989; Tong and Hays, 1996). This address both initiated the reform process and, intentionally or not, identified all of the policy options that have been raised since.

Subsidized housing sales, the first option to be tested, actually began slightly before Deng's speech and remained the principal reform policy through 1985 (Shaw, 1997). A number of experimental subsidy programs arose with variations in payment terms and the extent and sources of subsidies (Zhou and Logan, 1996). The most celebrated of these required equal payments from the buyer, the buyer's work unit, and the government (Wang and Murie, 1996). These ex-periments failed to generate much enthusiasm for housing purchases. Subsidies were huge, and subsidized purchase prices remained far in excess of most fam-ilies' resources and far in excess of the subsidized rents that characterized the alternative source of housing provision (Barlow and Renaud, 1989; Tong and Hays, 1996).

Marked by the State Council's creation of the Housing Reform Steering Group in February 1986 (Wang and Murie, 1996), reform emphasis shifted to reductions in rent subsidies with accompanying wage increases (Shaw, 1997).[2] This emphasis was relatively short-lived. Wage changes mandated by housing reform conflicted with the wage requirements of the prevailing labor management system.

In 1988, the Chinese National People's Congress passed legislation clarifying private property rights (Lai, 1998; Dowall, 1993). The central government also convened the first national housing reform conference (Wang and Murie, 1996). These initiatives led to renewed attempts at subsidizing private housing ownership (Tong and Hays, 1996; Wang and Murie, 1996 Shaw, 1997).

Subsequent reform initiatives have continued to explore strategies to increase the owner-occupied share of urban housing and to increase rental payments in the remainder. The second national housing reform conference in 1991 "confirmed earlier objectives and policies" (Tong and Hays, 1996, p. 641). However, it also attempted to bring an end to the pattern of sporadic experimentation by issuing a resolution that "required all urban authorities to carry out housing reform" (Wang and Murie, 1996, p. 980).[3]

The national scope of urban housing reform was reaffirmed by its inclusion in the Ten-Year Scheme of Economic and Social Development (1991–2000) and the eighth Five-Year Plan (1991–95) (Shaw, 1997). "The ultimate goal was to ensure that all households have their own housing" (p. 206, quoting the Leading Group for Housing Reform). The principal mode of possession was to be ownership (Hui and Wong, 1999). According to the State Council's "Opinions Concerning an All-Around Promotion of Housing Reforms in Cities and Towns" of 1991, this was to be achieved by encouraging through policy and subsidy the purchase of older publicly owned housing units by their current tenants and the sale of new units to members of the sponsoring work units (Bian et al., 1997).

In 1994, additional policies stipulated three-part pricing for housing based on purchaser income. Market prices were to be required for buyers with high incomes or to purchase units above state standards for space. Subsidies were to be targeted toward owner-aspirants with lower incomes (Tong and Hays, 1996; Wang and Murie, 1996). At the same time, the central government issued several documents warning against excessive subsidies (Wang and Murie, 1996). Moreover, subsidized purchasers were to receive only limited resale rights, in part to prevent arbitrage between the subsidized and unsubsidized markets (Hamer and van Steekelenburg, 1999).

As an additional spur to ownership, the Chinese government introduced forced savings programs for housing purchases in 1991. In general, these savings were to consist of parallel mandatory contributions of 5 percent of wages from both the worker and the work unit (Bian et al., 1997). In some work units, to-tal contributions reached a quarter of wages (Cheung and Nadelson, 1991).

The consistent theme in rent reforms has been to reduce the accounting deficit between rents and costs (Wang, 1991). The first step in achieving this was to set rents to cover continuing costs of operating dwelling units (Bian et al., 1997; Shaw, 1997).[4] Subsequent rent increases were to cover financial obliga-tions as well (Bian et al., 1997). At this point, originally scheduled to occur in 2000, rents were expected to consume approximately 15 percent of household income (Wang and Murie, 1996; Lai, 1998). Eventually, they are to cover all economic costs including profit (Bian et al., 1997).

The reforms of 1991 also envisioned the creation of new "economic entities" for the purpose of managing residential real estate (Bian et al., 1997). What be-came "real estate development corporations" were to relieve work units of their responsibilities regarding the management of worker dwelling units (Dowall, 1993; Soileau, 1995; Chiu, 1996b) and to introduce elements of market disci-pline to the housing sector (Wu, 1996). Initially, they were merely additional manifestations of the government, but recently their activities have become more commercial (Lai, 1998).

Finally, reform initiatives have tentatively addressed the question of private housing finance. The People's Construction Bank of China no longer has a mo-nopoly in the mortgage market. Moreover, the possibility of profit has begun to attract commercial financing from other banks, private domestic and foreign in-vestors, and the ubiquitous work units (Lai, 1998).

The Goals of Housing Reform

Despite the energies devoted to housing reform, ultimate goals remain some-what opaque. Clearly, "commoditization" is among them (Dowall, 1993; Tong and Hays, 1996; Lai, 1998). This implies some movement away from subsidies and toward "economic" and even "market" pricing (Tong and Hays, 1996). Whether this is an ideological imperative in its own right or simply a tactic de-signed to relieve the government and work units of what they feel to be oner-ous housing responsibilities (Tong and Hays, 1996) by transferring those re-sponsibilities to occupants (Cheung and Nadelson, 1991) is an open question.

Equity is also a concern (Fong, 1989a; Tong and Hays, 1996). In an ideologi-cally striking reversal, commoditized allocation systems have apparently come to be regarded as better guarantors of equity than those of the work units. The latter have failed even the rudimentary test of horizontal equity, providing roughly similar treatment for similar households. More concretely, subsidies are to be targeted more precisely on the needy (Tong and Hays, 1996).

The Chinese urban housing system vigorously pursues quantitative targets. Regardless of the commitment to decentralization implicit in the goal of com-moditization, the government originally set a goal of approximately 86 square feet of living space per urban resident by 2000 (Song, 1992). This was accomplished ahead of schedule (Hamer and van Steekelenberg, 1999)—tellingly, the only reform goal to achieve that distinction. As of the ninth Five-Year Plan, beginning in 1996, the goal for 2000 was increased to 97 square feet (Song, Chu, and Cao, 1999).

Some Evidence Regarding Recent Changes

I draw my analysis in this section from the two urban waves of the China Household Income Project (CHIP) surveys, recording household and housing characteristics in 1988 and 1995. The first covered 8,996 urban households in ten provinces: Anhui, Beijing, Gansu, Guangdong, Henan, Hubei, Jiangsu, Liaoning, Shanxi, and Yunnan.[5] The second survey covered 6,080 households located in the same ten provinces.[6]

Structural Housing Conditions

As measured in the CHIP data, many structural aspects of urban Chinese housing improved between 1988 and 1995. Consistent with the aggregate evidence cited earlier in the chapter, Table 11.1 reports that average total housing area increased by almost 17 percent. As a consequence of declining household size, square footage per household member increased by even more—31 percent. Assuming that each square foot of total housing area corresponds to 0.75 square feet of living area (Tolley, 1989), living area per person exceeded government standards in both years.

Table 11.2 demonstrates that Chinese urban dwelling units experienced impressive improvements along many other structural dimensions between 1988 and 1995. The proportions of dwelling units reporting no sanitary facilities or no means of heating both fell by approximately 11 percentage points. The proportion reporting no telephone fell by nearly 40 percentage points. Finally, the proportion relying on coal for heat fell by almost 30 percentage points, approximately equal to the increase in the proportion relying on some form of gas.[7]

TABLE 11.1

Dwelling Unit Size in 1988 and 1995

	1988	1995	Change (percent)
Households reporting	8,926	6,073	—
Average total household area (sq.f.)	443	520	16.9
	(23.6)	(28.8)	(22.0)
Household area per household member (sq.f.)	132	174	31.2
	(7.48)	(11.3)	(50.8)

NOTE: Standard deviations are in parentheses.

TABLE 11.2

Other Housing Characteristics in 1988 and 1995

	1988	1995
Households reporting type of sanitary facilities	8,950	6,074
No sanitary facilities (percent)	36.3	25.1
Households reporting type of heating equipment	8,955	6,021
No means of heating (percent)	57.1	46.5
Households reporting type of fuel	8,949	6,079
Coal (percent)	53.9	24.5
Bottled or piped gas (percent)	42.2	69.0
Households reporting availability of telephones	8,849	6,053
No telephone (percent)	96.6	57.4

TABLE 11.3

Tenure Type in 1988 and 1995

(percent)

Tenure Type	1988	1995
Rental units		
Publicly owned house	84.5	58.3
Public housing owned by work unit	—	46.9
Other public housing	—	11.5
Rented private house	1.71	0.81
Owner-occupied units		
Inherited old private house	6.84	4.34
Private house built by household	6.52	7.11
Private house bought since rent reform	0.44	28.7
Other	—	0.72
Observations	8,953	6,080

NOTES: The 1988 survey combined both "public housing owned by work unit" and "other public housing" in the single category "publicly owned housing." The 1988 survey did not include a category for "other."

Tenure

Table 11.3 makes evident that an enormous transformation in tenure occurred between 1988 and 1995.[8] In the former year, less than 1 percent of all dwelling units had been purchased. In the latter, this subsector represented more than a quarter of all urban Chinese housing.

Nearly all of this increase was attributable to a corresponding reduction in the proportion of publicly owned housing. However, inherited private housing also became less frequent. In addition, the private rental sector, already small in 1988, almost vanished by 1995.[9]

In terms of reform, the increase in owner occupancy is great progress. However, the scarcity of private rental dwellings is not. This subsector is potentially the most flexible source of housing supply. It often contains a broader variety of structure types than the ownership sector, especially among dwellings offering lower levels of housing services. It usually offers smaller transaction costs, as well. With restricted rental supply, labor market mobility will be substantially impeded.

Rental Housing and Housing Reform

Table 11.4 presents average rent and subsidy measures for 1988 and 1995. Rents in 1988 are consistent with our earlier discussion. On average, they represented less than 1 percent of household income. Furthermore, average housing subsidies exceeded average rents. Consistent with the intent of reform, rents in 1995 were higher than in 1988 in both absolute terms and relative to income. Subsidy levels in 1995 were also greater, reflecting the policy of matching rent increases with wage supplements. The net changes between the two years were small: households went from a small average surplus of subsidies over rents to a small average deficit. Table 11.5 demonstrates that actual rents in 1995 were still far below estimated market rents. Average estimates of market rents among tenants of publicly owned housing were more than ten times average actual rents. Even in the private rental sector, where market forces might have been expected to be most effective, average expected market rents were nearly triple actual rents.[10]

Across all three subsectors, 2,526 renters reported both positive current rents and positive expected market rents. This subsample confirms the comparisons. On average, current rents in this subsample were 30.8 yuan per month. Average expected market rents were 386 yuan per month, or more than twelve times av-

TABLE 11.4

Monthly Rents and Housing Subsidies in 1988 and 1995

	Publicly Owned		Rented Privately		Owned Privately	
	Number	Average	Number	Average	Number	Average
1988						
Total household income (yuan)	7,565	508	153	561	1,235	490
Monthly rent						
Amount (yuan)	7,228	3.87	129	11.9	1,235	0.27
Share of household income						
(percent)		0.8		2.6		0.1
Sum of individual monthly						
housing subsidies (yuan)	4,979	6.71	93	7.58	718	6.6
1995						
Total household income (yuan)	2,848	1,230	696	1,140	49	1,113
Monthly rent						
Amount (yuan)	2,850	27.3	697	25.5	49	64.2
Share of household income						
(percent)		2.7		2.9		7.2
Sum of individual monthly						
housing subsidies (yuan)	607	19.1	166	12.5	15	13.4

TABLE 11.5

Actual and Estimated Market Monthly Rents in 1995

	Owned by Work Unit	Other Public Housing	Rented Privately
Actual monthly rent			
Number of households reporting positive monthly rent	2,598	652	44
Average monthly rent (yuan)	30	27	72
Estimated monthly market rent			
Number of households reporting positive monthly rent	2,140	513	25
Average monthly rent (yuan)	385	366	203
	(513)	(445)	(305)
Maximum monthly rent (yuan)	8,000	5,000	1,500

NOTES: Standard deviations are given in parentheses. Averages and standard deviations for estimated market rent omit observations reporting zero estimated rent.

TABLE 11.6

Correlations Between Estimated Market Rents and Actual Rents in 1995

	Number	Correlation	*p*-Value
Public housing			
Owned by work unit	2,018	.061	0.0061
Other public housing	486	.058	0.20
Private rented house	22	−.093	0.68

NOTE: Includes only observations with positive values for actual and expected market rents.

erage current rents. Among these households, almost all (2,449) reported that their actual rents were less than expected market rents. Differences between averages of this magnitude imply that market rates actually obtained in very few instances. Some semblance of market incentives might persist, however, if actual rates were roughly proportional to expected market rates. Table 11.6 demonstrates that to the contrary, actual and estimated market rents were essentially unrelated.

Approximately 80 percent of the 2,504 households in public housing tabulated in Table 11.6 inhabited dwelling units owned by the work unit of some household member. Among them, the correlation between actual and expected market rents was .06. This correlation is statistically significant because of the large sample but is substantively negligible. Among households in other public housing, the correlation between actual and expected market rents was .06, again negligible and here insignificant. Finally, 22 households in private rental housing also report actual and expected market rents. Among them, the correlation between the two was −0.09.

In sum, Tables 11.5 and 11.6 demonstrate that the urban rental sector of 1995 was essentially unreformed. Most of this housing remained in government ownership. Although rents had increased since 1988 more quickly than incomes, they barely exceeded subsidies and remained at a fraction of expected market rates. Furthermore, these expected rates were essentially uncorrelated with actual rent charges.

Owner-Occupied Housing and Housing Reform

Table 11.7 describes housing finance for the three subsectors of urban owner-occupants, of which purchased housing is the principal focus of housing reform. The evidence in Table 11.7 suggests that reform has had few effects, apart from changes in nominal tenure status (Zhou and Logan, 1996). The purchased-housing subsector, at the very least, consists of households that have actually engaged in transactions. Of households in this subsector, 97.2 percent reported purchase prices and 97.5 percent reported the terms of their purchase. However, less than 5 percent of these latter households claim to have paid the market price for their dwelling unit.[11] Instead, 91.5 percent of these households purchased their dwelling units on preferential terms. Table 11.7 indicates the extent of these preferences. The average purchase price was 10,556 yuan, whereas the average estimated market value was more than four times as much, 44,603 yuan.

Comparisons among only the 1,439 households reporting both positive purchase prices and positive estimated market values for owned dwellings reinforce these inferences. Of them, 1,295, or 9 in 10, reported purchase prices below market value. The average purchase price in this subsample was 10,831 yuan. Average market value was 44,753 yuan, or slightly more than four times larger than average purchase prices.[12]

Moreover, the correlation between purchase prices and estimated market

TABLE 11.7
Housing Finance for Owner-Occupied Housing in 1995

	Inherited Private House		Self-Built Private House		Purchased Private House	
	Number	Average	Number	Average	Number	Average
Total household monthly income (yuan)	264	1,097	432	1,058	1,744	1,287
Market value (yuan)	209	48,329	388	62,119	1,451	44,603
Percentage of annual total household income		368		527		305
Housing debt (yuan)	11	7,991	52	12,546	244	7,804
Percentage of annual total household income		74		96		63
Purchase price (yuan)	8	10,688	30	16,011	1,695	10,556
Percentage of annual total household income		89		189		83
Terms of house purchase	9		30		1,701	
Percentage purchased at market price		33.3		63.3		4.8
Percentage purchased at preferential price		55.6		30		91.5

NOTE: Averages include only observations with positive values.

TABLE 11.8

Correlations Between Estimated Market Values and Estimated Market Rents in 1995

	Number	Correlation	*p*-Value
Purchased private house	1,332	.10	0.0002
Purchased at preferential price	1,219	.08	0.0051
Purchase at unreported terms	10	.57	0.088
Purchased at market price	64	.78	0.0001
Purchased at other price	39	.55	0.0003
Self-built private house	334	.69	0.0001
Inherited old private house	194	.77	0.0001

NOTE: Each correlation includes only observations with positive values for both of the relevant variables.

value in this subsample, while significant at the 1 percent level, was only .19. As in the rental sector, estimated market values here were not only much greater than actual purchase prices but were largely unrelated to them. This suggests that even in the subsector of purchased private housing, very few transactions actually took place under marketlike conditions.

The concept of market value itself appears to be unclear to households owning purchased private housing. In principle, a dwelling unit's estimated market value should be the capitalized value of its expected stream of future housing services. A competitive housing market should equate rents to the instantaneous value of this stream. The value of the capital in the housing unit and the value of the stream of services produced by that unit should therefore be closely related.

According to Table 11.8, some 1,332 households with purchased private housing reported both an estimate of the capital value of their dwelling unit and an estimate of the market rent that their unit could command. These households represent more than three-quarters of those in this subsector. Among them, the correlation between these two estimates of market value is only .10, statistically significant but surprisingly low.[13] But the source of this surprise is, perhaps, not a surprise. Of these 1,332 households, 1,219, or more than 90 percent, reported that they purchased their dwelling unit on preferential terms. The correlation between their estimates of market value and market rent was only .08.

In other words, households that bought their dwelling units on preferential terms constituted the vast majority of Chinese urban owner-occupants in 1995. These households had no experience with true market conditions in housing transactions. Furthermore, they had no consistent understanding of what those conditions might entail. While these households were clearly outside the traditional government-owned housing sector, the preferential nature of their housing purchases implies that they were still within a part of the housing sector where administrative imperatives supersede market forces.[14] In contrast, the households in every other owner-occupied subsector had expectations of market valuations that revealed much greater internal consistency.

The evidence here implies that the allocation of inherited and self-built homes may take place largely outside of government controls and with a reasonable understanding of how market forces operate. However, these subsectors cannot represent the future of owner-occupied housing. Under any effective reform, most ownership changes would take place through housing purchases. As of 1995, only a very small proportion of these transactions had taken place under anything like market conditions. Few participants in the remaining transactions were able to imagine what such conditions might mean.

Why Can't China Sell Its Urban Housing at "Market" Prices?

One of the most compelling results of the foregoing examination is the virtually universal use of preferential prices among home purchasers. Two explanations are possible for the virtual absence of owner occupancy at "market" prices. First, almost trivially, prices construed as representing "market" value may exceed what nearly all households are willing to pay. Second, subsidized owner occupancy is so widely available that the unsubsidized alternative may only be attractive to those with housing demands well beyond what subsidized housing can provide. There is evidence to suggest that both explanations may be valid. I will examine them in order and conclude with a discussion of current policy initiatives aimed at improving the "affordability" of urban housing.

What Are "Market" Prices?

The comparison between housing prices and willingness to pay must first confront a bewildering array of possible "prices" (Zhou and Logan, 1996). Under the prevailing multilevel subsidy scheme, different households can pay different prices for the same unit. The "standard price" is the most heavily subsidized. It has evolved from "building costs and land compensation costs" (Wang and Murie, 1996, p. 978) to "three years' total salaries of a couple . . . . plus 80 per cent of housing savings" (p. 984). In its later incarnation, it is intended to be available only to the poorest potential purchasers.

Middle-income purchasers have recently become subject to a price that "should cover seven cost elements: the costs of land acquisition and compensation, pre-construction costs (survey, design), building, neighbourhood public facilities, management, interest on loans, and tax" (Wang and Murie, 1996, p. 983). Market prices apparently now apply to "units exceeding state space standards," which cover "all expenses, taxes, and profits for the transaction and the construction of the unit" (Tong and Hays, 1996, p. 649). They also appear to apply to "high-income families . . . . defined as those who can afford to purchase a two-bedroom apartment from the market on 5–6 times annual family income" (Wang and Murie, 1996, p. 983).[15]

These definitions demonstrate two important points. First, price concepts have evolved over time. Whether price quotations from different historical times are comparable in any meaningful sense is an open question. Second, even the most recent reforms have left quoted prices partly dependent on purchaser income. A third point emphasizes, should that be necessary, the limitations of existing price information. As I will discuss later in this chapter, land use rights have often been conveyed at discounted or zero prices. "Site values can average 25 to 50 percent of the cost of housing in cities throughout the world," notes Tolley (1989, p. 106). Thus "the failure to include site values contributes to a serious misestimation of the cost of housing" (p. 107).

In other words, the true economic cost of urban Chinese housing is revealed imperfectly, if at all, by any of the quoted prices. As I will discuss later, this poses a daunting challenge to any attempt to evaluate whether the Chinese economy allocates an appropriate level of resources to urban housing. However, urban Chinese incomes are also distorted, as discussed earlier. Therefore, the comparison of quoted prices to observed incomes is a reasonable way to simulate the immediate partial equilibrium problem of an individual household's attempts to optimize its housing consumption.

Is Urban Housing Affordable?

The existing literature on Chinese urban housing contains many references to housing costs and prices. The interpretations of these references are problematic, as virtually all sources ignore the ambiguities associated with these terms.[16] Nevertheless, a review of these references is instructive. Among the earliest, Taubman (1984) asserts that construction costs per square meter nearly tripled between 1957 and 1984, during the first wave of housing reform. Table 11.9 demonstrates that estimates of construction costs per square meter have increased con-

TABLE 11.9

Estimates of Housing Construction Costs

Approximate Year of Estimate	Source	Estimated Cost Per Square Meter (yuan)
1978	Badcock (1986, 167)	89
1980	Lalkaka (1984, 71)	113
1981	Lalkaka (1984, 71)	128
1981	Lalkaka (1984, 71)	100–170
1981	Wang and Murie (1996, 974)	120–150
1981	Song, Chu, and Cao (1999, 546)	150
1984	Badcock (1986, 167)	160
1985	Tolley (1989, 11)	200
1987	Kim (1987, 222)	300
1989	Fong (1989b, 34)	300–600
1989	Tolley (1989, 102)	900–2,000
1991	Wang and Murie (1996, 980)	750
1991	Chaichian (1991, 134)	1,700
1994	Dowall (1994, 1505)	1,974

TABLE 11.10

Estimates of Subsidized and Market Housing Sale Prices

Approximate Year of Estimate	Source	Estimated Cost Per Square Meter (yuan)
Prices of subsidized housing		
1983	Bian, Logan, Lu, Pan, and Guan (1997, 240)	250
1992	World Bank (1992, 73)	521–800
1994	Wang and Murie (1996, 984)	567
1998	Hui and Wong (1999, 147)	3,000–3,500
Market prices of commodity housing		
1991	Chaichian (1991, 134)	1,000
1991	Chen (1996, 1084)	1,500
1991	Cheung and Nadelson (1991, 42)	2,000–2,200
1991	Tong and Hays (1996, 649)	3,000
1994	Wang and Murie (1996, 984)	3,000–6,000
1995	Song, Chu, and Cao (1999, 546)	1,710
1995	Leaf (1995, 153)	7,000
1998	Hui and Wong (1999, 147)	4,400

tinually throughout the reform period. They doubled between 1978 and 1985, doubled again by 1989, and might have doubled again by 1994.

Table 11.10 demonstrates that subsidized sale prices have, if anything, increased even more rapidly. However, "market" prices for commodity housing appear to have outstripped both subsidized prices and construction costs. They may have increased by a factor of 4 during the decade of the 1990s alone.

These statistics, though alarming, understate the increase in costs and prices per dwelling unit. Minimum standards for dwelling unit sizes have also increased regularly throughout the reform period (World Bank, 1992). In 1983, a "median-quality apartment" consisted of 430 square feet (Bian et al., 1997, p. 240). Around 1991, a "modest apartment" covered about 590 to 650 square feet (Chaichian, 1991, p. 134), consistent with statements that in the early 1990s, apartments of 600 square feet were considered typical (World Bank, 1992; Wang and Murie, 1996).[17]

The consequence has been that new housing costs have been well beyond any notion of "affordability." Table 11.11 presents a collection of comparisons between average housing costs or prices and average incomes. These comparisons usually do not specify whether they are comparing construction costs, total costs, subsidized prices, or market prices to earnings or income. Despite the ambiguities, they demonstrate conclusively that new housing has been unaffordable to the vast majority of urban Chinese households by any conventional standard throughout the entire reform period (World Bank, 1992; Chen and Gao, 1993b). In only two of the twelve comparisons of Table 11.11 do the estimated ratios of housing costs to incomes fall below 10. In contrast, the World Bank (1992, pp. 13–14) estimates that these ratios range from 1.8 to 5.5 in developed

TABLE 11.11

Comparisons Between Housing Costs or Prices and Average Incomes

Approximate Year of Estimate	Source	Estimated Ratio of Housing Cost to Income
1981	Wang and Murie (1996, 974)	10–20
1983	Bian, Logan, Lu, Pan, and Guan (1997, 240)	12
1985	Kim (1987, 222)	40–71
1988	Kim (1990, 112–13)	22–83
1991	Cheung and Nadelson (1991, 41)	6
1991	Chaichian (1991, 134)	15–55
1991	Chiu (1996b, 573)	27–41
1992	World Bank (1992, 13)	8–20
1995	Song, Chu, and Cao (1999, 546)	20
1996	Zhou and Logan (1996, 416)	20
1996	Chiu (1996b, 578)	11
1998	Hui and Wong (1999, 147)	13–25

countries and from 2.5 to 6.0 in developing countries. Song et al. (1999, p. 546) attest to "the international norm of a 5:1 ratio." In this context, it can be no surprise that few urban Chinese have purchased commodity housing at market prices.[18]

Why Is Urban Housing So Expensive?

Inefficiencies in the construction industry are inevitably among the explanations for high housing costs (Badcock, 1986; Chen, 1996; Wu, 1996). They would certainly cause elevated housing prices for any type of unit. However, they cannot explain the persistent compulsion to produce housing units that are simply unaffordable. This compulsion appears to derive, instead, from a tradition of housing policy based on noneconomic criteria. The alleged "suppression" of housing investment during prereform times was driven by an ideological preference for heavy industry (Lim and Lee, 1990) rather than a plausible economic strategy designed to maximize national wealth.

Although housing reform was motivated in part by a belief that improved housing would contribute to productivity, the reform movement defined housing first as "special consumption goods ensuring a decent quality of life" (Lim and Lee, 1990, p. 484). Planners and urban administrators adopted "improved space standards as a basic goal" without "any serious debate on standards in China" (Dwyer, 1986, p. 485).[19]

Trained planners are in short supply, and what training occurs is largely in engineering (Chu and Kwok, 1990). Consequently, planners lack both the tools and the inclination to consider the economic implications of housing policies (World Bank, 1992; Dowall, 1993). Their influence helps sustain the continued reliance on noneconomic criteria in the formulation of those policies.[20]

The influence of planning standards has led to a system of housing provision that is almost exclusively quantity-driven: "Discussions with housing planners and government officials across China reveal a preoccupation with the per capita living and constructed area" (Dowall, 1994, p. 1507). As such, "success" is defined in terms of increasing housing quantities with little regard for other considerations (World Bank, 1992).

The obsession with housing quantities leads to planning standards that are extravagant at the development and metropolitan levels, as well as at the level of the individual dwelling unit. These standards increasingly require multistory construction, despite higher costs per square foot (Taubman, 1984; Kirkby, 1988; World Bank, 1992). Nevertheless, they stipulate ultimate residential densities in new housing projects that are well below international standards (Badcock, 1986; Dowall, 1993; World Bank, 1992).[21] Moreover, the commitment to low residential densities in central cities can lead to master plans that, paradoxically, dictate the highest densities where the resource cost of land is lowest, at the metropolitan periphery (World Bank, 1992).

The apparent dominance of the quantity-driven engineering perspective is responsible for a number of other deadweight losses. Regulations and practices impose inefficient uniformity on dwelling units and inefficient spatial relationships between dwelling units and the public spaces in new developments (World Bank, 1992; Chen, 1993). The losses here derive less from increases in housing offer prices then to attendant reductions in bid prices.[22]

The dominant perspective also discourages alternative sources of housing supply that might be more efficient. At its most general level, housing policy has been supportive of "self-help" or "own-built" housing since Deng's 1980 speech. However, the planning system is largely hostile to it (Wu, 1996). In addition, the system of land allocation has little sympathy for claims to land use rights for this purpose (Wu, 1996). Similarly, old housing is usually demolished rather than rehabilitated (Taubman, 1984), even though these and own-built dwellings often meet resident needs more effectively (Chen, 1993; Zax, 1997) and rehabilitation is often less expensive than new construction (Taubman, 1984; Tolley, 1989).

Although planning standards mandate excessive housing costs, these costs are elevated further by a second element of the Chinese system of urban housing provision. Supply prices for new housing incorporate not only construction costs but also many other charges. Some of them represent alleged resource costs of necessary public infrastructure (Dowall, 1994; Li, 1997). However, many appear to be transfers. "Infrastructure charges" often do not fund infrastructure (Dowall, 1993). When they do, the funded facilities often do not serve the funding development (Dowall, 1994). Title taxes in Beijing, for example, are 6 percent of the sale price, approximately equal, on average, to average household annual income (Song et al., 1999), far in excess of any conceivable cost of registration.[23]

Prices for new housing in redevelopments also include explicit transfers to tenants in predecessor dwelling units. These households are typically entitled to relocation and living expenses during development (Tolley, 1989) as well as dwelling units in the new structures (Dowall, 1993). With housing standards that require continual improvements in housing quality, these households obtain new housing that is often far superior to their old homes (Dowall, 1993, 1994) in return simply for their rights to habitation at that location. The implicit value of these rights is substantial. The value of a compensatory housing unit may be more than double that of its existing housing equivalent previously consumed (Dowall, 1994). The aggregate cost of compensatory housing, when capitalized into the sale price for the remaining new dwelling units, is typically at least as great as the actual construction costs for those units and often greater (Dowall, 1993).

In sum, excessive planning minimums, payments to upgrade inadequate infrastructure, and transfers all contribute to high housing prices. The inefficiencies associated with planning standards are simply deadweight losses. In contrast, transfers to local governments and to prior tenants at the development location are redistributive but potentially efficient, given the array of implicit property rights on which they are based.

However, transfers may be badly inefficient if this array of rights is inconsistent with social welfare. For example, local governments interfere with the pursuit of improved housing conditions when they use exactions to appropriate rents from new housing developments. Moreover, the capitalization of these transfers into purchase prices creates the possibility of substantial changes in capital values if future policies alter the underlying property rights.

Why Are the Alternatives to Home Ownership So Attractive?

The disparity between housing costs and incomes would be more than sufficient, on its own, to discourage all but a few households from aspiring to commoditized owner occupancy. Unfortunately, this disincentive is compounded by the continuing availability of subsidized alternative housing sources. These alternatives arise as a consequence of continuing distortions in the urban Chinese labor market. They not only present a formidable challenge to the success of housing reform, but they are also beyond the reach of housing policy alone.

Prior to and during the early years of reform, most urban Chinese housing was financed by the government but allocated to families through work units. This system was rife with inequities, both between work units (Lalkaka, 1984; Whyte and Parish, 1984; Badcock, 1986; Walder, 1992; Wu, 1996; Logan, Bian, and Bian, 1999) and within work units (Fong, 1989a; Chu and Kwok, 1990; Walder, 1991; World Bank, 1992; and Bian et al., 1997). Moreover, its principal advantage, the reinforcement of prohibited labor market mobility with residential immobility, increasingly became a liability as reform progressed in other sectors of the Chinese economy. As a consequence, the World Bank (1992, p. 54) asserts that "thorough going reform must cut the umbilical cord binding the worker to the employer."

However, during the past decade, the government has been more interested in reducing the nominal burden of housing expenditures on its budget. In the absence of affordable commodity housing, new entrants to the labor market have continued to rely on their work units for housing, In consequence, work units must now finance housing as well as allocate it (Wu, 1996). Work units have therefore become more rather than less engaged in the urban housing sector (Bian et al., 1997). Overall, they own 60 percent to 70 percent of urban housing (Wu, 1996; Bian et al., 1997) and house "the overwhelming majority of people" (Wang and Murie, 1966, p. 981).

Chinese practice has been to set urban wages that are "highly socialized" (Zhou and Logan, 1996, p. 418). Cash wages have been low, but workers have also received many consumption items, such as housing, directly from their work units (Wu, 1996). Although identical increases in wages and in prices paid to work units for consumption items would not alter worker welfare, the government apparently fears that such a policy would damage work unit finances and lead to commodity price inflation (Wu, 1996).[24] Therefore, the "low-wage policy" continues in force, at least in the state-owned sector.

Consequently, work units continue to provide housing but are constrained from raising cash wages. These facts have led to the inference that cash rents for work unit housing must also be kept low (see, e.g., Cheung and Nadelson, 1991; Chen and Gao, 1993b; Zhou and Logan, 1996). They are noticeably lower, as a proportion of income, than in other developing countries (Chaichian, 1991; Tong and Hays, 1996) and much lower, by the same standard, than in industrialized market economies (Chen and Gao, 1993b).[25] Holding income constant allows continued occupation of rental housing at these rental rates naturally to dominate unsubsidized housing purchases (Lalkaka, 1984; Chu and Kwok, 1990; Kim, 1990; Chen, 1996; Tong and Hays, 1996; Wang and Murie, 1996). Available methods of financing home purchases make this comparison all the more compelling: subsidized sales often require complete payments in a relatively few years (Wang and Murie, 1996). Mortgages are rare, short-term, and usually available only to individuals with personal funds equal to the loan amount (Zhou and Logan, 1996).[26]

What Has Been Done to Improve Affordability?

The Chinese government has recognized the affordability problem (Lai, 1998) and experimented with a number of policies to deal with it. Foremost among them, as noted earlier, is discounted housing sales. In return for the discount, these sales convey only limited property rights. In particular, the sponsoring work unit has the right to repurchase and typically owns a share of any capital gains (Tong and Hays, 1996). Obviously, this policy fails fully to disentangle housing consumption from employment and provides occupants with only partial maintenance incentives.

More promising, if much more limited, experiments address the issues underlying the affordability problem. As discussed earlier, the government has imposed a forced saving program on the demand side. At 10 percent of annual income, the typical accumulation rate, these funds require a substantial sacrifice of current purchasing power. Nevertheless, they will take many years to noticeably close the affordability gap.

On the supply side, Shenzhen has tried to encourage the production of what it terms "small-sized" dwelling units (Chiu, 1996b). More generally, as discussed earlier, the government has tried to vest production responsibilities in quasi-independent property development companies, in the hope that profit incentives will lead to greater construction efficiencies (Soileau, 1995). However, thoughtful analyses of the underlying problem are scarce (Hamer and van Steekelenburg, 1999).

These initiatives demonstrate the government's limited awareness of the affordability problem. Their narrow scope confirms that the problem is not yet solved. Until it is, sales of commodity housing are certain to be disappointing.

Why Has China Built So Much Urban Housing?

An economy that aspires to obtain the efficiencies associated with market transactions should be alert to the signals those transactions provide. Given the manifest impossibility of recouping, at least on an accounting basis, the apparent investments, China's continued enthusiasm for the construction of urban housing is puzzling. Most of this enthusiasm appears to reflect unreconstructed elements of the prereform system.

The first relevant element is the difference between nominal and true economic costs. Apart from the confusion regarding prevailing quoted prices, the true opportunity costs of the resources devoted to housing are obscured by the entire Chinese system of administered and semiadministered prices. If true housing costs are unknown, investment levels are likely to be mistaken (Tolley, 1989).[27] The second relevant element is the heritage of policies based on noneconomic criteria. The quantity-driven goals of the housing policy process have a legitimacy that dominates those that might be derived from considerations of economic efficiency. Investment has been further justified by apparent excess demand, even though subsidized prices must be primarily responsible. There has been no attempt to explore whether shortages, in any economic sense, actually exist (see, e.g., Dowall, 1994).

Consequently, China's urban housing stock appears to be better than that of other countries at a similar stage of economic development (Lalkaka, 1984; Chaichian, 1991). Chaichian concludes that "the housing conditions in urban China were much better than in other developing countries in 1976" (p. 137), even though that was during the period in which living space per urban Chinese resident reached its Communist-era minimum. Chinese goals for per capita living space in the early reform period were equal to or greater than those set in Singapore and Hong Kong, both of which were at much more advanced stages of development (Dwyer, 1986). Actual "living space per resident" in urban China now exceeds that in Hong Kong (Hamer and van Steekelenburg, 1999).

It is precisely this evidence of "success" that suggests China's investment in urban housing stock has been too large, rather than too small. The experience of other countries at China's stage of development indicates that some of the resources China has devoted to improving its urban housing standards would yield greater increases in welfare if diverted to other uses. The inadequacy of maintenance practices (see, e.g., World Bank, 1992), while partly attributable to moral hazard derived from uncertain property rights, is also an indication that at prevailing implicit prices, the optimal level of housing services is much less than that for which the housing capital stock has been designed. Wang (1991, p. 116) concludes, "We may well say that there is overconsumption of housing among China's urban dwellers."[28]

Most important, there is abundant evidence that urban Chinese commodity housing has been in excess supply for most of the reform period. Large stocks of unsold housing are reported for 1987–1992 by the World Bank (1992), for 1988 by Chen and Gao (1993b), for 1988–1994 by Chiu (1996a), for 1991–1993 by Chen (1996), for 1994 by Wang and Murie (1996), for 1994–1995 by Song et al. (1999), for 1997 by Lai (1998), and more recently by Hui and Wong (1999). In other words, the one sector where housing prices are most likely to reflect true values appears to be plagued with a perpetual surplus rather than a shortage.

In sum, it appears likely that the housing conditions that stimulated China's elevated levels of urban housing investment did not represent "shortages," given China's level of economic development. The few available market-related signals have been consistent with this inference. However, this evidence has been overridden by China's ideological commitment to quantitative urban housing goals.

Why Doesn't China Just Give Its Urban Housing Away?

The urban housing accounts of the government display a persistent, troubling deficit (Soileau, 1995; Wu, 1996). One of the principal motivations for urban housing reform was a desire to reduce that deficit (Wu, 1996). Ironically, the dramatic increase in investment during the reform period, coupled with the persistent excess of construction costs and maintenance expenses over purchase prices and rents, has increased it instead:

The urban housing system is like a one-way ticket, operating on a track from the government to individuals. The state cannot recoup its investment to produce new housing.

Furthermore, the state has increasing annual expenditures just to keep existing public units operating. . . . The more the state invests in housing, the more revenue it loses. . . . As new units are completed, new subsidies must be added. In sum, state investment in housing has become nothing less than throwing money into a bottomless pit. (Tong and Hays, 1996, pp. 637–38)

The simplest way to stop the growth in these deficits would be to stop investing in new housing and abandon the existing stock: "The current operation of public housing loses money in all the PCPEs [previously Communist planned economies]. Giving such assets away would increase government revenues even if no taxes on private-housing returns or capital were collected" (Buckley, 1996, p. 39).

In China, the government could legitimately aspire to more. The willingness of many households to purchase restricted property rights at prices that are positive, if well below replacement costs (Chen, 1996), demonstrates that urban housing is not without value.[29] Sales at these prices would achieve the goal of "commoditization" and recover at least some of the costs sunk in the existing stock. Chen (1996) has recommended this policy. However, accelerated privatization through reduced sale prices has not been seriously considered. I shall examine potential obstacles to its adoption.

Who Owes Whom?

The perception that the government's urban housing accounts are in deficit is reinforced by an analogous perception regarding the housing accounts of work units (World Bank, 1992; Soileau, 1995; Wu, 1996). One goal of economic reform in general is to reduce such deficits in order to improve government finances and to prepare work units for more market-oriented environments. Moreover, these deficits create the perception that the recipients of government and work unit housing are subsidized.[30] The reduction or elimination of subsidies is another goal of economic reform. Finally, the government has an independent aspiration to recover the replacement costs of housing (Tong and Hays, 1996; Bian et al., 1997).

Adherence to these three goals could sustain government resistance to privatization at further reduced prices. However, the third of these goals is unattainable, and the perceptions on which the other two are based are unverified, overstated, and perhaps false. The aspiration to recover replacement costs is fantastical. The economic value of urban housing is far below replacement costs (Tolley, 1989). Even if they were equal, replacement costs cannot be extracted from Chinese urban incomes.

The perception that households receive housing subsidies relies on the discrepancy between measured housing payments and the measured costs of housing provision. However, the exchange of housing between the government and work units, on the supply side, and households, on the demand side, is only one of many exchanges in which these entities participate. In particular, households supply labor at wages that have been deliberately suppressed. The "surplus" almost surely accrued by the government and work units on this labor account implies that any net subsidy received by households is smaller than the explicit deficit in the housing accounts. It is possible that there is none at all. Without a clear demonstration to the contrary, there is no substantive support for the claim that either reform or efficiency requires additional extractions from the household sector in support of urban housing.

Similarly, the perception that the government and work units suffer losses through their involvement in the housing sector relies on measured deficits in their housing accounts. However, these deficits have no discernible economic interpretation. In China, as in other previously Communist planned economies, most of the revenue for the housing sector must come from implicit taxes on labor imposed through the low-wage system, taxes implicit in the system for allocating land and construction rights, and the retention of any implicit capital gains on the existing housing stock. Similarly, the majority of government housing expenditures probably occur as indirect subsidies through the allocation of land rights and as continued state support of the construction industry in particular and state-owned enterprises in general.[31]

In consequence, accounting deficits are not informative regarding the true fiscal position of either the government or the work units with respect to the urban housing sector. Therefore, these positions are mysteries. In the absence of evidence that true deficits actually exist, the argument that revenues from housing sales are essential to close the deficits can have only superficial appeal.

The question of who has actually "paid" for Chinese urban housing remains not only unanswered but also essentially unasked. The sector has indisputably absorbed real resources that came from elsewhere in the Chinese economy, but their exact sources are unknown.[32] Similarly, it has returned payments to the rest of the economy, but their destinations have not been identified. It is impossible, therefore, to perform the accounting that would identify whether any sector or entity has actually contributed resources in excess of compensation received. It might be appropriate to retain public ownership of urban housing while this accounting takes place. However, there is no indication that this is on the policy agenda. It is inappropriate to retain public ownership on the unsupported assertion that such an accounting exists and verifies that the government and work units need and are entitled to claim additional household resources.

Housing Inequality

Although the question of whether investments in the urban housing sector have caused net intersectoral transfers remains open, there is substantial evidence that the allocation of urban housing has created interhousehold inequities, as discussed earlier. The Chinese government apparently has no policy to deal with horizontal inequities. Chinese policy toward vertical inequities emphasizes giving "priority to finding new housing for those who are in the worst circumstances" (Bian et al., 1997, p. 226) and includes subsidies that are declining in income.

However, many continuing housing policies are probably heightening inequities. For example, increasing national standards for average living space per capita failed to target households in substandard dwelling units. To the contrary, they have encouraged the production of oversized luxury dwelling units because these units have disproportionate impacts on national averages. Under socialized housing provision, differences in political access and influence led to differences in the quality and quantity of housing available to different work units. Reform has typically not altered the relevant political configurations (Wu, 1996; Bian et al., 1997). Increased reliance on work units for housing provision has therefore magnified differences in the housing to which they have access (Wu, 1996).

Perhaps as a result, the government apparently now believes that inequities can best be addressed in the context of commoditization (Lai, 1998). Not surprisingly, this belief has yet to be vindicated. Commodity housing is designed for, and apparently oversupplied to, the wealthiest households (Chu and Kwok, 1990; Lai, 1998). Current policy also exacerbates inequalities between households already allocated housing and those entering the urban housing market for the first time. It has no provisions for new arrivals (Lai, 1998), who must presumably rely on low priorities in work unit allocation schemes or commodity housing. Attempts to focus commoditization on new construction force new households to confront market prices for housing while preserving the prereform housing arrangements of older households (Tong and Hays, 1996).

Any attempt to address horizontal inequities would probably threaten many households with the loss of their current abode.[33] Accelerated privatization would probably have to ratify these inequities instead. However, the current policy regime does the same, as will attempts to raise housing prices slowly in the hope of eventually converging to market levels (Buckley, 1996).

Accelerated privatization has several advantages over these alternatives. It would quickly divest the government and work units of depreciating, loss-making housing assets. It would release most of the urban housing stock for market transactions. The consequent market disciplines might encourage greater efficiencies not only for resale transactions but also for new construction. Last, it would create the possibility of addressing horizontal inequities through capital gains taxation on subsequent sales.

What Else Is There to Worry About?

Sustainable housing commoditization will require further institutional reform. Land use rights must be clarified and priced appropriately. The aggregate of all property rights inhering in a dwelling unit must be similarly clarified and provided with appropriate protection. Effective, or at least abundant, mortgage financing is unlikely to appear until these issues and several others are addressed. Activity in the informal housing sector should be examined, to inform progress in the formal sector if not to serve as an important alternative. Finally, property taxation requires rationalization. I shall examine these issues in turn.

Land Use Rights

Urban land ownership remains vested in the Chinese government. In principal, it uses two methods to convey land use rights to developments. Those adopted through the state planning process receive these rights at little or no cost. "Commercial" developments must purchase these same rights (Zhu, 1994). This second method accounts for the conveyance of rights to only a very small proportion of urban land (Zhu, 1994; Tong and Hays, 1996; Yeh and Wu, 1996). In practice, the extent of subsidization varies widely across the remaining transactions (Zhou and Logan, 1996).

As with housing itself, subsidies applied to land use rights inevitably encourage excess demand and hoarding (Zhu, 1994; Tong and Hays, 1996; Zhou and Logan, 1996). In this case, the problem is exacerbated because legal, if ill-defined, opportunities for resale exist (Zhou and Logan, 1996). Consequently, the government transfers massive unrealized surpluses to the holders of subsidized land use rights (Zhu, 1994; Zhou and Logan, 1996; Li, 1997).[34] Nevertheless, the government remains committed to subsidized conveyance.[35]

This commitment presents a challenge to the entire process of urban housing reform. Reform is entirely a response to perceptions of resource misallocations: between the housing and other sectors, between the government and work units, between work units and households, and among households themselves. However, misallocations cannot be truly remedied unless they can be accurately identified.

That requires prices that convey meaningful information regarding opportunity costs. In the case of urban housing, these costs depend heavily on those associated with land use (Tolley, 1989). If the value of land use rights remains unknown, perceptions of misallocations will remain.

Property Rights

To be priced accurately, land use rights need to be defined clearly. This is a demanding task in urban China, because legal rights can vary across parcels and transactions (Fong, 1989a; Tolley, 1989; Zhou and Logan, 1996). Different and potentially separable rights inhere to structures and to the land on which they stand (Fong, 1989b; Soileau, 1995). Moreover, bureaucratic and institutional practices can often create substantial discrepancies between juridical and effective rights (Soileau, 1995; Zhou and Logan, 1996).

In particular, "owner occupancy" subsumes a wide variety of property right configurations. For example, an owner's actual right to occupancy is not absolute, because it can be superseded by the rights of existing tenants (Badcock, 1986; Tolley, 1989; Chen, 1996). As noted earlier, rights of resale depend on the degree to which ownership has been subsidized (Chen, 1996), as well as the extent to which land lease transfers in the secondary market are permitted (Yeh and Wu, 1996; Huang and Hua, 1995).[36]

Whatever rights currently exist may change as the role of urban planning agencies continues to evolve. In practice, the allocation of land use rights to individual projects and uses has been largely independent of urban master plans (Yeh and Wu, 1996; Yeh and Wu, 1999). These plans have had little authority because zoning regulations do not exist (Yeh and Wu, 1996, 1999). However, attempts to introduce zoning and to increase planning authority further through parcel-specific "development control" (Yeh and Wu, 1996, 1999), if successful, will substantially reduce the autonomy of residential property owners.[37]

Formally, the exercise of residential property rights requires the registration of ownership (Huang and Hua, 1995; Soileau, 1995). For example, registration is a legal prerequisite for mortgages in China (Randolph and Jianbo, 1999:). Failure to register may invalidate transactions or the rights conveyed thereby (Huang and Hua, 1995; Soileau, 1995; Randolph and Jianbo, 1999). The State Land Administration Bureau, directly under the State Council, supervises a system of land administration departments whose purpose is to maintain the necessary records (Huang and Hua, 1995). In practice, however, uncertainties in the registration process compound those inherent in the underlying rights. They begin with parcel definitions, which are unclear because of "inaccurate and out-of-date cadastres" (Dowall, 1993, p. 191). Inadequate registration systems in most cities make procedures idiosyncratic (Soileau, 1995). Bureaucrats exploit these idiosyncrasies to their own advantages, further impeding registration procedures (Soileau, 1995).[38]

Uncertainties persist subsequent to the transaction. "Consultation, conciliation, administrative mediation, arbitration and litigation" are recognized methods for resolving real estate disputes (Huang and Hua, 1995, p. 615). In practice, however, "property rights laws are still subject to veto both by actors in possession of property and their supervisors" (Soileau, 1995, p. 342; see also Zhou and Logan, 1996; Yeh and Wu, 1999). Judicial inadequacies and politicization compete with legal rectitude in determining court judgments, which are difficult to enforce in any case (Soileau, 1995).

The precarious nature of rights in real estate is not entirely inconsistent with government policies. In broad terms, those policies intend to convey greater and more secure property rights to private actors (Soileau, 1995). However, "privatization is not really their goal. Rather, it is the value-driven use and exchange through commoditization and marketization of housing that is the goal of policy reform. The P.R.C. is attempting to prove, with some success, that this is possible without fully alienating ownership in public property" (p. 359). Consequently, regulations defining property rights "also clarify the government's continuing willingness to burden these rights in order to maintain administrative and fiscal control over housing rights use, transfer, price, and profits" (p. 372). To the extent that the exercise of this control requires the capacity for arbitrary enforcement, it will continue to conflict with economic development. Development requires secure property rights, which can only arise under more consistent registration and enforcement procedures.

Mortgage Financing

Mortgage financing of real property transactions has a long history in China, which continued under the People's Republic even prior to the introduction of a supporting legal framework (Soileau, 1995). However, mortgages have been rare (Hui and Wong, 1999). Mortgage financing is now an important element in the government's conception of urban housing reform (Soileau, 1995; Wang and Murie, 1966; Lee, 1998; Randolph and Jianbo, 1999), and mortgage rights and procedures are now becoming codified accordingly (Soileau, 1995). In general, regulations seem to be more favorable to lenders than to borrowers (Randolph and Jianbo, 1999). This may represent an attempt to invite financial institutions into a market that they have hitherto avoided (Barlow and Renaud, 1989; Chu and Kwok, 1990). However, any institutions that accept this invitation will confront many additional issues.

Mortgage relationships in urban China are complicated because of the nature of real estate ownership. Structures can be owned by nongovernment entities and are mortgageable. The land on which they stand is not mortgageable because the government owns it. However, the land use rights assigned to structures are mortgageable, under appropriate conditions (Huang and Hua, 1995). Moreover, land use rights and structures require two separate mortgage instruments (Randolph and Jianbo, 1999). In general, the two are to be exchanged together, as a consolidated transaction (Huang and Hua, 1995). They may become separated, however, in part because different elements of a real estate development are mortgageable at different stages in the development process (Soileau, 1995).

The subtleties of ownership are problematic for property valuation, which is already difficult enough, partly because very few professional appraisers exist (Chen, 1996). As noted, little information is available regarding true market value. In any case, it is typically ignored by valuation practices (World Bank, 1992). In this context, useful valuation of properties that embody a multiplicity of mortgageable rights presents a substantial challenge.

This challenge cannot be completely avoided because commercial mortgage banking typically requires reliable property valuations (Soileau, 1995).[39] In their absence, lenders in China have relied on additional guarantees rather than the underlying assets (Hamer and van Steekelenburg, 1999; Randolph and Jianbo, 1999).[40] These may be provided by employers (World Bank, 1992) or developers (Randolph and Jianbo, 1999). While they may form the basis of a workable system of mortgage financing (Buckley, 1996), this system would be much more effective if the housing stock itself could provide the principal collateral.

If a mortgage can be agreed on, supporting regulations confer several distinctive rights on lenders. Their very existence removes some of the prior uncertainty that usually worked to the borrower's advantage (Lee, 1998). When the mortgage is on a commercial property, lenders are apparently entitled to receive lease payments directly from property lessees, without the intermediation of the property owner (Randolph and Jianbo, 1999). Creditors can also prevent the resale of a property on which they hold a lien, even if it is not in default (Randolph and Jianbo, 1999).

However, creditors are vulnerable in other dimensions of the mortgage transaction. Multiple mortgages create not only the aforementioned risk that the security is overburdened but the risk that priorities will be confused or ignored. In principle, registration records contain the necessary history of encumbrances (Lee, 1998; Randolph and Jianbo, 1999). However, as noted, these records are suspect, and registry agencies bear no responsibility for omissions (Randolph and Jianbo, 1999). This vulnerability becomes acute in the event of default, which may be a substantial risk in an environment where housing has previously had negligible marginal cost and eviction risk. (Randolph and Jianbo, 1999). If default occurs, creditors may find, to their cost, that many other entities have claims on the residential assets at issue.

Government organs may have substantial rights in the event of foreclosure. In principle, they retain the rights to any land use not explicit in the authorization for the defaulting property. These restrictions, if enforced, may reduce the value of the secured property (Randolph and Jianbo, 1999). In some cases, mortgagees of defaulting state-owned industrial enterprises have claims only on the assets that remain after fulfilling that enterprise's social welfare responsibilities and converting the underlying land use right (Randolph and Jianbo, 1999).[41] The rights of work units to repurchase housing units sold to workers at subsidized prices presumably also retain some force if those workers default on mortgages obtained elsewhere, though the literature appears to be silent on this point.

Nongovernment entities may also have competing claims. Tenants have preemptive purchase rights to the property that they rent. The status of these rights in the event of foreclosure is uncertain (Randolph and Jianbo, 1999). Lessees also have rights to tenancy that may persist in foreclosure (Randolph and Jianbo, 1999). Apartment owners may have ill-defined and potentially competing claims to the public spaces in their buildings or developments (Soileau, 1995).

Foreclosure procedures introduce additional hazards.[42] Although problems with these procedures are well known (World Bank, 1992), they have not yet been resolved (Randolph and Jianbo, 1999). The law discourages litigation in favor of other forms of negotiation or mediation (Lee, 1998). Courts are unfamiliar with their responsibilities in mortgage transactions (Randolph and Jianbo, 1999) and short of the resources necessary to undertake them (Soileau, 1995).[43]

Moreover, judges are locally funded and appointed (Randolph and Jianbo, 1999). They may be reluctant or even unwilling to enforce a foreclosure judgment sought by a creditor from elsewhere against a local resident (Lee, 1998; Randolph and Jianbo, 1999). Finally, corruption can sustain shocking breaches of creditor rights (Lee, 1998).

In sum, mortgage banking is likely to remain an exotic undertaking in urban China for some time to come. Apart from the problems of affordability discussed earlier in the chapter, legal property definitions, registration procedures, the status of competing claims, and the foreclosure process are all far too uncertain to support commodity mortgages. Progress on any of these individual issues will require major efforts. In consequence, mature mortgage markets are likely to be among the last accomplishments of urban housing reform.

Informal Housing

I noted earlier that the formal housing sector ignores or obstructs informal or "self-help" housing, despite official policy support. Nevertheless, there are examples of entire communities consisting of housing of this type. Leaf (1995) describes the example of Zhejiangcun, adjacent to the Beijing metropolitan area. In this community, housing is almost surely unsubsidized. Moreover, land use rights are apparently obtained at uncontrolled prices from the agricultural households that hold them. The dwelling units are small, but they appear to be well built and affordable.

This seems a remarkable achievement. Zhejiangcun's success appears to demonstrate the efficiency of truly market-driven development, as well as the inefficiency of government design standards. Dwelling units here are smaller than the state standard and apparently built to higher than standard residential densities without the assistance of multistory construction (Leaf, 1995).

Government policy has apparently failed to engage the experience of this community and others like it. To the contrary, nothing systematic is known about this subsector of the housing market, perhaps because the government is reluctant to acknowledge its presence and accomplishments (Leaf, 1995). Partly for this reason, developments of this type are unlikely to make large contributions to the aggregate urban housing stock in the near future. However, they may provide an essential experiment in the effectiveness of alternatives to housing types specified by state design standards. Moreover, they may be very valuable in helping equate housing supplies with the demands of households that have no or weak claims to allocated housing (Zax, 1997).

Property Taxation

Property taxation has been an element of fiscal policy throughout Chinese history. The People's Republic has continued this tradition (Li, 1989) since its inception. However, tax policy with regard to real estate continues to evolve and has changed substantially during the reform period (Li, 1989; Huang and Hua, 1995); currently, several taxes may apply to real estate transactions.[44] Fees appear to be proportional to sales price, rather than fixed, and can apparently amount to more than one-third of the total cost of the transaction (Song et al., 1999). This amount may include the "house property tax," which is apparently also proportional to sale price (Huang and Hua, 1995).

A complicated array of charges applies to the land use rights conveyed in any transaction. Apparently, the government charges housing purchasers for the as-signment of land use rights for a period of fifty to seventy years. These charges account for an additional one-fifth of total sales price (Song et al., 1999).[45] There also appears to be a "house property contract tax" levied perhaps as a surtax on these charges (Huang and Hua, 1995). Capital gains taxes evidently apply to transactions in land use rights alone (Huang and Hua, 1995; Soileau, 1995). Their intent appears to be to discourage speculation (Lai, 1998). It is possible for these taxes to be waived if residential construction takes place (Huang and Hua, 1995).

Dwelling units may also be subject to periodic taxes. As with transactions taxes, separate instruments apply to structures and land use rights (Li, 1989; Huang and Hua, 1995; Song et al., 1999).[46] Broad exemptions appear to be available, for all urban residences, according to Song et al. (1999), or for all nonbusiness properties or properties owned by the government and armed forces, according to Li (1989).[47] Under some conditions, subsidized housing purchases have also received temporary exemptions (Wang and Murie, 1996).

In sum, the contemporary property taxation regime seems complicated and haphazard. In particular, the multiplicity of taxes attached to charges for land use rights, which themselves provide government revenues, seem ripe for rational-ization. Song et al. (1999) suggest a number of reforms, including reducing the range of exemptions and consolidating different tax instruments.

However, as in other dimensions of the urban housing issue, the immediate imperative would be to identify the true resource flows engendered by the cur-rent system. Nothing is apparently known regarding the incidence of any indi-vidual tax instrument. The net effects of the entire system are unquestionably a mystery,[48] a mystery compounded by the fact that the relationship between tax payments and services actually delivered to residences and residents has not even been raised in the literature. If the former exceed the value of latter, as com-plaints about the magnitude of taxes might imply (Song et al., 1999), then the urban public finance system is transferring resources to other parts of the econ-omy. Whether this is true or not is another component of the problem raised earlier, the question of the true fiscal position of the government sector as a whole with respect to the urban housing sector.

Were these mysteries resolved, the property tax system might be employed to address three difficult issues arising elsewhere in the urban housing sector. First, in the absence of long-term financing, capital constraints compound the basic affordability problem. Given the apparent size of government exactions on real estate transactions, this problem could be substantially ameliorated if these exactions were restructured as periodic payments rather than extracted as a lump sum (Hamer and van Steekelenburg, 1999; Song et al., 1999).

Second, any process that achieves substantial increases in the extent of and rights accruing to urban owner occupancy is also likely to leave substantial inequities. Appropriately designed property taxes might reduce them to some degree (Song et al., 1999). For example, the burden of property taxation could be inversely proportional to the degree of subsidy in the original purchase. Some degree of progressive property taxation, increasing with the value of the dwelling unit, might compensate for some of the arbitrariness in work units' housing assignments. Capital gains taxes on housing sales that yield a profit might be similarly useful.

Third, commercial land use rights conveyed at below-market prices will cause additional inequities in the future. Recipients will presumably expect to retain the surpluses so obtained when they sell their rights on the secondary market. Continued and perhaps reconfigured taxes on capital gains accruing to land use rights may also be necessary to distribute these surpluses acceptably (Li, 1997; Lai, 1998).[49]

Conclusion

China's urban housing stock has improved dramatically over the past twenty years. As a result, China's urban housing problem, from a policy perspective, has worsened. There appears to have been almost no new construction that is economically sensible. Each new unit of housing seems to widen the gap between what households are willing to pay and what construction costs.

The accounting consequences are inevitable. Government and work unit housing accounts display increasing expenditures and deficits. Moreover, the allocation of each new unit confers a huge surplus on the recipient household. That household then joins the many others who will resist reform if it threatens their windfall.

This process will never provide vertical equity. However, that has never been a feature of the urban housing system, despite representations to the contrary. The true indictment is that it does nothing to ameliorate horizontal inequity. As always, if two households with identical wealth have dwelling units of different quality, it is almost surely because the occupant of the better home had more influence with the providing work unit or that work unit had more influence with organs of government.

In this sense, China's administered and semiadministered housing allocation system has truly been less effective than a market system would have been at attaining its own stated objectives. With housing allocated by open bids, differences in housing consumption among otherwise identical households would be attributable to differences in choice. Successful commoditization is also the only way to reconcile construction costs with willingness to pay.

The obvious difficulty is in achieving "success." Many of the obstacles are administrative: eliminating them requires more sensible housing regulations, more reliable systems of property registration, more complete and trustworthy definitions of property rights, a more transparent regime for the allocation of land use rights, and more consistent enforcement. All of these requirements are essentially public goods. Their provision is appropriately the responsibility of the government. They offer the government an important opportunity to make an undeniably positive contribution to social welfare.

Naturally, the other obstacles are political. The most important is the existing distribution of economic rents, or surpluses, through the housing system. Residents who enjoy such surpluses can be assumed to be well placed to defend them, simply on the evidence that they were placed sufficiently well to receive them in the first place. Similarly, individuals originally denied access to these surpluses are unlikely now to have the power to confiscate them. Therefore, any proposed reform that immediately threatens the existing distribution is almost surely doomed.

This implies that commoditization and horizontal equity cannot be achieved simultaneously. Horizontal equity cannot precede commoditization either, because it is politically infeasible and because commoditization is necessary to identify the distribution of surpluses. Therefore, commoditization must be the primary policy goal of current urban housing reform.

The best way to achieve this goal is through accelerated privatization. Current residents should receive title to their dwelling units. In return, they should contribute whatever balance has accrued in their provident funds. In addition, some administrative procedure or bidding mechanism that might extract at least some of any excess of each household's true bid prices over these funds would be helpful. However, privatization should not be delayed in the vain hope of discovering a procedure that would reveal these prices in their entirety.

Commoditization alone will simply validate the existing distribution of housing surpluses. Postcommoditization policy will need to address redistribution explicitly. Three sources may provide revenues for this purpose. Proceeds from provident funds and other privatization revenues will be available almost immediately. The government will realize additional revenues from sales of land use rights at proper prices.

Finally, equity will require a substantial and long-lasting capital gains tax on real estate transactions between nongovernmental entities. The comparison between sale prices and privatization revenues would be a reliable estimate of the surpluses associated with the original occupancy grant. Progressive taxation of these surpluses at time of resale would be the least provocative means of extracting them. The ensuing revenues, over time, could be used to slowly rectify the inequities from which they arose.

A program such as this would differ substantially from the government's current approach to existing housing, and its appeal lies in the evident failure of that approach. By contrast, the government's position with regard to new housing is more promising. Marketized provision by real estate development corporations that are at least semiprivatized is clearly the appropriate direction. There appear to be two reasons why these corporations do not yet provide affordable housing. The first is that the demand for affordable housing at market prices is greatly diminished by the availability of subsidized alternatives. The second is that government regulations appear to prohibit the construction of units that might be affordable.

Commoditization as proposed here would abolish subsidized alternatives. The government also has the authority to abolish the second problem, as it is the source. Housing regulations that are appropriate for China's level of economic development are absolutely essential for further rationalization. Any attempt to continue providing housing at unaffordable construction costs dooms China to perpetual subsidies, imbalances, and inequities in its urban housing sector.

Notes

1. "Families with housing difficulties" consist of homeless families and those with more than two generations or more than one family in the same dwelling unit. Pudney and Wang (1995, p. 149) conclude that "public housing is not the powerful egalitarian influence that is often assumed."

2. In practice, these experiments had contradictory equity intentions. According to Barlow and Renaud (1989, p. 84): "Housing should no longer be allocated according to rank, but rents should be higher for apartments of more space." At the same time, "subsidies should reflect the wage of the employee; those with higher wages should receive a higher subsidy."

3. Local governments have had considerable autonomy in the implementation of national reform policies (Dowall, 1993; Tong and Hays, 1996; Zhou and Logan, 1996).

4. There is some definitional ambiguity. For example, maintenance, management, and depreciation are "standard costs" in Bian et al. (1997). They define standard costs plus mortgage interest and property tax payments as the "semicommodity" level of rents. However, Shaw (1997) includes all five cost items in "standard rent."

5. This survey is described in Khan et al. (1992). It was funded by the Ford Foundation and conducted with extraordinary care under difficult circumstances by economists at the Institute of Economics, Chinese Academy of Social Sciences, led by Zhao Renwai and Li Shi. Western economists led by Keith Griffin and Carl Riskin assisted. This survey and the rural companion survey are available from the Inter-University Consortium for Political and Social Research (IUCPSR) as data set 9836.

6. The second wave of the CHIP surveys also included Sichuan province, omitted

from this analysis. It was funded by the Ford Foundation and the Asia Development Bank and conducted under the primary supervision of Li Shi and Carl Riskin. It is available from the IUCPSR as study number 3012.

7. No noteworthy changes occurred in the proportions of dwelling units with kitchen or sanitary facilities. Conditions as revealed in Table 11.2 were somewhat better than described in Tong and Hays (1996).

8. Official sources apparently contain no information on this issue (Hamer and van Steekelenburg, 1999).

9. Chen (1996) agrees that the private rental market is negligible. Table 11.3 indicates that approximately 40 percent of urban households were owner-occupants of some sort in 1995. This is substantially greater than the estimated private ownership in 1991 of 30.2 percent in Chen (1996, tab. 2). Differences in years and geographic coverage may be partly responsible. In addition, Chen's estimate is apparently the ratio of estimated living area in private ownership to that in all urban housing.

10. The similarity of average estimated market rents in dwelling units owned by work units and by other public entities is somewhat surprising, given the presumption that "tenants of municipal housing have inferior conditions to tenants of state work–unit housing" (Wu, 1996, p. 1621). Average estimated market rents here exceed, by an order of magnitude, the imputations of Pudney and Wang (1995, tab. 4) for cities in Liaoning and Sichuan provinces. Clearly, the expectations of urban Chinese households in 1995 and the imputations of Pudney and Wang, based on a hedonic regression for housing in Cartgena, Colombia, differ dramatically. According to Wang and Murie (1996), the motivation behind rent reforms was to cover a greater proportion of housing supply costs rather than necessarily to introduce complete market pricing. The discrepancy between actual rents and estimated market rents of Table 11.5 may therefore reflect reform objectives. Unfortunately, the surveys examined here do not provide any information about the supply cost of housing.

11. The 1995 survey contained a question that asked if "the purchase price was: (1) market price, (2) preferential price, (3) other." This result is consistent with the World Bank (1992) and Zhou and Logan (1995).

12. Wang and Murie (1996, p. 983) state that "new policies were introduced in 1994 to stop the sale of existing public–sector housing at low prices." Table 11.7 demonstrates both that this policy was aimed at the vast majority of housing sales in urban China and that if implemented, it had not had time to make any noticeable impact by 1995. The standard sale price set by these policies of 31,752 yuan for an apartment of just over 600 square feet (Wang and Murie, 1996, p. 984) was well above the average purchase prices in this table, though below estimated market prices.

13. The average ratio of estimated market value to estimated market monthly rent is 54.8. According to Chen (1996), if this ratio prevailed, owner occupancy would be the preferred option for most households.

14. Among households that purchased their dwelling, 1,512 reported both purchase price and estimated market rent. The correlation between these two is only .06, with a p-value of .03. Moreover, average purchase prices were only 18.5 times greater than average estimated market rents. Following Chen (1996), this implies that subsidized purchases would be an overwhelmingly dominant choice, in comparison to renting at market rates.

15. Zhou and Logan (1996, pp. 410–11) describe examples of two additional and more bizarre pricing procedures. The first is "arbitrary pricing," which "depends on policy rather than on the market." The second is "comparative pricing," where prices in "other market-oriented economies in Chinese-speaking Asia, such as Hong Kong, Taiwan and Singapore, provide pricing standards."

16. Furthermore, few writers indicate whether costs per square feet apply to total area, living area, or some other definition of dwelling unit space.

17. Shenzhen in the late 1980s defined apartments of less than about 750 square feet as "small-sized" (Chiu, 1996b, p. 566). Shaw (1997, p. 210) points out that "an apartment of 50 m^2 [538 square feet] is far beyond the official standard. The state goal for the year 2000 is that each urban resident have 8 m^2 [86 square feet] of living space. The average size of urban households was 3.43 persons in 1991." This is an example of the inflation that occurs in quantity-driven objectives when economic considerations are ignored.

18. Ratios of housing costs to household income in urban China would be lower than those in Table 11.11 because most households contain multiple earners. However, estimated ratios in other countries are also unadjusted for multiple earners per household. Therefore, Chinese ratios would surely remain extreme by international standards if this adjustment were applied universally. The ratios of estimated market value to household income in Table 11.7 are much lower than those of Table 11.11. The income measure here includes many items of nonpecuniary compensation that are typically omitted from official income statistics. In addition, true economic values are certainly less than replacement values (Tolley, 1989). This may be reflected in "estimated market values" that are lower than the costs or prices employed in Table 11.11.

19. Increasing incomes may have led to legitimate expectations of improved housing (Fong, 1989b). However, they cannot be blamed for expectations that new housing standards would perpetually exceed affordable levels.

20. This reliance has led to policies that reverse the role of housing "prices." In many cases, quoted prices are now supposed to be a simple function of income (Chiu, 1996b; Wang and Murie, 1996). In other words, they represent housing demand alone. This reduces, if not eliminates, the information regarding housing supply, in terms of resource or opportunity costs, that prices ordinarily embody. The suppression of this information cannot be in the service of improved economic efficiency.

21. Densities are further diluted by the land allocation system, discussed later in the chapter, which encourages urban land hoarding (Tong and Hays, 1996).

22. "The market 'bid' price for housing units built in the last three to five years falls below the cost of construction" (World Bank, 1992, p. 11). New construction that "is of higher quality than is consistent with demand conditions" (Tolley, 1989, p. 3) is partly responsible.

23. Song, Chu, and Cao (1999) describe the array of charges imposed on real estate transactions as excessive. However, the true net government impact is impossible to evaluate because, if nothing else, it provides many developments with land use allocations that are subsidized to an unknown degree. I return to this point later in the chapter.

24. It is certainly possible, if not likely, that consumption patterns subsequent to monetization of in-kind benefits would differ, perhaps greatly, from those imposed by the composition of those benefits.

25. Nominal rents are typically much less than the cost of ongoing maintenance (Kirkby, 1988). The disparity between rents and resource costs is much greater (Fong, 1989a; World Bank, 1992; Chen and Gao, 1993a).

26. Since 1998, mortgage financing is much more readily available, in particular from the four large commercial banks.

27. Tolley (1989) suggests that true costs may be less than quoted prices; Pudney and Wang (1995) take the opposite position.

28. Buckley (1996) doubts that the prereform state of disequilibrium in previously centrally planned economies "is generally one of shortage" (p. 29).

29. It also demonstrates that the value of the expected future stream of housing services from these assets exceeds the expected future maintenance costs. This implies

that rent increases are possible, though again, not to the point of recapturing replacement costs.

30. Hamer and van Seekelenberg (1999, p. 97) suggest that "the highly politicized issue of burden-sharing . . . is enough to end the search for new solutions" to urban housing problems.

31. Buckley (1996) makes these points and cites the example of Poland, where measured net implicit transfers out of the housing sector are larger than net explicit government housing expenditures.

32. The excess of replacement costs over the economic value of urban housing indicates that this sector has wasted some of these resources. It is possible that urban housing is financed, at least in part, from the transfers that accrue to urban China from rural sectors (Khan et al., 1992).

33. Pudney and Wang (1995) assert that inequities in imputed housing consumption are approximately proportional to income and therefore largely vertical in origin. Anecdotal evidence and note 8 suggest that these imputations may be unreliable. However, if their conclusion is reliable, continuing discontent (Bian et al., 1997) may simply reflect discomfort with the novelty of the income-based distinctions that inevitably arise in marketized economies.

34. The central government, which owns urban land, and local governments, which administer it, are in conflict regarding the distribution of any surpluses that are retained by the government sector (Li, 1997).

35. This commitment is apparently based on several misconceptions. The government justifies price controls as a response to the perception of "an acute undersupply of land" (Li, 1997, p. 332), when this perception is almost surely the consequence of this policy. It regards exaggerated demand for subsidized land use rights as indicators of desirable development activity (Li, 1997), rather than of misallocated resources. Finally, it fails to recognize these subsidies as the source of market prices for land use rights that are excessively high and volatile. The supply of these rights to the commercial market is small and unpredictable because entities with development interests apply bureaucratic and political influence to divert them to subsidized allocation (Zhu, 1994). This encourages the purchase of commercial land use rights for speculative rather than substantive purposes (Zhou and Logan, 1996).

36. The question of mortgageability will be addressed later in this chapter.

37. Owner occupants in urban peripheries may be especially at risk for unexpected changes in property rights. In principle, collectively owned land on urban peripheries should be converted to state ownership prior to development (Huang and Hua, 1995). In practice, "spontaneous conversion" prevails, with attendant confusion regarding the status of property rights (Yeh and Wu, 1999).

38. Reliable registration procedures compromise reform goals as well as individual rights. For example, commodity mortgage banking is impossible without standardized registration (Buckley, 1996; Soileau, 1995). Registration is also important to local governments because it "is a major point at which local governments extract value from property rights transactions" (Soileau, 1995, p. 368).

39. For example, Chinese law permits multiple mortgages on a property if their aggregate value does not exceed that of the property itself. This limitation is almost impossible to enforce in the absence of standardized valuations (Lee, 1998).

40. China's financial industry still has only a limited capability to examine credit histories and assess creditworthiness.

41. The government has exclusive claim on the land use rights associated with any property allocated through the planning system. However, it now permits transfers of these rights, in the event of foreclosure, for a fee (Randolph and Jianbo, 1999).

42. Weak "postcontract governance" discourages mortgage supply "in most developing countries" (Buckley, 1996, p. 3).

43. For example, if a mortgagor in default conveys the collateral to an unsecured creditor prior to foreclosure proceedings, courts may not enforce the mortgagee's claim to it (Lee, 1998). This raises the possibility of collaboration between debtors and unsecured creditors at the mortgagee's expense.

44. The discussion in this section is tentative because the English language literature on this subject is ambiguous and inconsistent.

45. The literature is silent as to whether the government retains this fee in its entirety if the purchaser leaves the property prior to the expiration of this period.

46. No source discusses the methods by which structure values are determined.

47. Li (1989) does not address whether this includes residences owned by state-owned work units.

48. Analysis of this issue is currently so rudimentary that Song et al. (1999) repeatedly refer to "incidence" when they mean "nominal responsibility."

49. While these taxes might "deter investment interests," (Li, 1997, p. 333), it is efficient to do so when the investments in question depend for their profits on the surpluses attached to underpriced land use rights.

References

Badcock, Blair. (1986). Land and housing policy in Chinese urban development, 1976–86. *Planning Perspectives*, 1(2), 147–70.

Barlow, Melinda, and Bertrand Renaud. (1989). Housing reforms and commercialization of urban housing in China. *Review of Urban and Regional Development Studies*, 1(1), 81–84.

Bian, Yanjie, John R. Logan, Hanlong Lu, Yunkang Pan, and Ying Guan. (1997). Work units and housing reform in two Chinese cities. In Lu Xiaobo and Elizabeth J. Perry, eds., *Danwei: The changing Chinese workplace in historical and comparative perspective*, pp. 223–50. Armonk, N.Y.: Sharpe.

Buckley, Robert M. (1996). *Housing finance in developing countries*. New York: St. Martin's Press.

Chaichian, Mohammad A. (1991). Urban public housing in China: The case of Tianjin. *Habitat International*, 15(1–2), 127–140.

Chen, Aimin. (1996). China's urban housing reform: Price-rent ratio and market equilibrium. *Urban Studies*, 33(7), 1077–92.

Chen, Ke. (1993). Process and product: A comparative study of state and traditional housing in China. *Habitat International*, 17(3), 101–114.

Chen, Xiangming, and Xiaoyuan Gao. (1993a). China's urban housing development in the shift from redistribution to decentralization. *Social Problems*, 40(2), 266–83.

———. (1993b). Urban economic reform and public-housing investment in China. *Urban Affairs Quarterly*, 29(1), 117–45.

Cheung, Tai Ming, and Robert Nadelson. (1991). A home of your own. *Far Eastern Economic Review*, August, pp. 40–42.

Chiu, Rebecca L. H. (1996a). Housing. In Y. M. Yeung and Sung Yun-wing, eds., *Shanghai: Transformation and modernization under China's open policy*, pp. 341–74. Hong Kong: Chinese University Press.

————. (1996b). Housing affordability in Shenzhen Special Economic Zone: A forerunner of China's housing reform. *Housing Studies*, 11(4), 561–80.

Chu, David K. Y., and R. Yin-Wang Kwok. (1990). China. In Willem van Vliet, ed., *International Handbook of Housing Policies and Practices*, pp. 641–70. New York: Greenwood Press.

Dowall, David E. (1993). Establishing urban land markets in the People's Republic of China. *Journal of the American Planning Association*, 58(2), 182–92.

————. (1994). Urban residential redevelopment in the People's Republic of China. *Urban Studies*, 31(9), 1497–1516.

Dwyer, D. J. (1986). Urban housing and planning in China. *Transactions: Institute of British Geographers*, 11(4), 479–89.

Fong, Peter K. W. (1989a). The commercialisation of housing in a socialist state: An attempt to solve China's urban housing problem. *Planning Quarterly*, 13(4), 32–36.

————. (1989b). Housing reforms in China. *Habitat International*, 13(4), 29–41.

Gu, Yanxiang Anthony, and Peter F. Colwell. (1997). Housing rent and occupational rank in Beijing and Shenyang, People's Republic of China. *Journal of Property Research*, 14(2), 133–43.

Hamer, Andrew Marshall, and Ester van Steekelenburg. (1999). Urban housing in mainland China: A new chapter. *Review of Urban and Regional Development Studies*, 11(2), 91–99.

Huang, Yao Liang, and Xie Zhao Hua. (1995). An overview of China's real estate law. *John Marshall Law Review*, 28(3), 593–617.

Hui, Eddie Chi Man, and Francis Kwan Wah Wong. (1999). Housing reform in Guangzhou and Shenzhen, China. *Review of Urban and Regional Development Studies*, 11(2), 141–52.

Khan, Azizur Rahman, Keith Griffin, Carl Riskin, and Zhao Renwei. (1992). Household income and its distribution in China. *China Quarterly*, 132, 1029–61.

Kim, Joochul. (1987). China's current housing issues and policies. *Journal of the American Planning Association*, 53(2), 220–25.

————. (1990). Housing development and reforms in China. In Gil Shidlo, ed., *Housing policy in developing countries*, pp. 104–20. New York: Routledge.

Kirkby, Richard. (1988). Urban housing policy after Mao. In Stephan Feuchtwang, Athar Hussain, and Thierry Pairault, eds., *Transforming China's economy in the eighties: Vol. 1. The rural sector, welfare, and employment*, pp. 227–44. Boulder, Colo.: Westview Press.

Lai, Ok-Kwok. (1998). Governance and the housing question in a transitional economy: The political economy of housing policy in China reconsidered. *Habitat International*, 22(3), 231–43.

Lalkaka, Dinyar. (1984). Urban housing in China. *Habitat International*, 8(1), 63–73.

Leaf, Michael. (1995). Inner city redevelopment in China: Implications for the city of Beijing. *Cities*, 12(3), 149–62.

Lee, Brian Y. (1998). Taking mortgage interests in real property under the guarantee law of the People's Republic of China. *Hastings International and Comparative Law Journal*, 21(2), 539–63.

Li, Jinyan. (1989). China's tax system: An evaluation. *Denver Journal of International Law and Policy*, 17(3), 527–80.

Li, Ling Hin. (1997). The political economy of the privatisation of the land market in Shanghai. *Urban Studies*, 34(2), 321–35.

Lim, G. C., and M. H. Lee. (1990). Political ideology and housing policy in modern China. *Environment and Planning C: Government and Policy*, 8(4), 477–87.

Logan, John R., Yanjie Bian, and Fuqin Bian. (1999). Housing inequality in urban China in the 1990s. *International Journal of Urban and Regional Research*, 23(1), 7–25.

Pudney, Stephen, and Limin Wang. (1995). Housing reform in urban China: Efficiency, distribution and the implications for social security. *Economica*, 62(246), 141–59.

Randolph, Patrick A., Jr., and Lou Jianbo. (1999). Chinese real estate mortgage law. *Pacific Rim Law and Policy Journal*, 8(3), 515–80.

Shaw, Victor N. (1997). Urban housing reform in China. *Habitat International*, 21(2), 199–212.

Soileau, William D. (1995). Past is present: Urban real property rights and housing reform in the People's Republic of China. *Pacific Rim Law and Policy Journal*, 3(2), 299–387.

Song, Shufeng. (1992). Policy issues involving housing commercialization in the People's Republic of China. *Socio-Economic Planning Sciences*, 26(3), 213–22.

Song, Shufeng, George S.-F. Chu, and Rongquing Cao. (1999). Real estate tax in urban China. *Contemporary Economic Policy*, 17(4), 540–51.

State Statistical Bureau. (1996). *China statistical yearbook, 1996*. Beijing: China Statistical Publishing House.

Taubman, Wolfgang. (1984). Problems of urban housing in China. In Chi-Keung Leung and Joseph C. H. Chai, eds., *Development and Distribution in China*, pp. 173–212. Center of Asian Studies Occasional Papers and Monographs No. 61. Hong Kong: University of Hong Kong.

Tolley, George S. (1989). An economic analysis of Chinese housing reform. Working paper, University of Chicago.

Tong, Zhong Yi, and R. Allen Hays. (1996). The transformation of the urban housing system in China. *Urban Affairs Review*, 31(5), 625–58.

Walder, Andrew G. (1991). Workers, managers and the state: The reform era and the political crisis of 1989. *China Quarterly*, 127, 467–92.

———. (1992). Property rights and stratification in socialist redistributive economies. *American Sociological Review*, 57(4), 524–39.

Wang, Ya Ping, and Alan Murie. (1996). The process of commercialisation of urban housing in China. *Urban Studies*, 33(6), 971–89.

Wang, Yukun. (1991). The size of housing subsidies in China. *Review of Urban and Regional Development Studies*, 3(1), 103–16.

Whyte, Martin K., and William L. Parish. (1984). *Urban life in contemporary China*. Chicago: University of Chicago Press.

World Bank. (1992). *China: Implementation options for urban housing reform*. Washington, D.C.: World Bank.

Wu, Fulong. (1996). Changes in the structure of public housing provision in urban China. *Urban Studies*, 33(9), 1601–27.

Yeh, Anthony Gar-On, and Fulong Wu. (1996). The new land development process and urban development in Chinese cities. *International Journal of Urban and Regional Research*, 20(2), 330–53.

———. (1999). The transformation of the urban planning system in China from a centrally planned to a transitional economy. *Progress in Planning*, 51(3), 167–252.

Zax, Jeffrey S. (1997). Latent demand for urban housing in the People's Republic of China. *Journal of Urban Economics*, 42(3), 377–401.

Zhou, Min, and John R. Logan. (1996). Market transition and the commoditization of housing in urban China. *International Journal of Urban and Regional Research*, 20(3), 400–21.

Zhu, Jieming. (1994). Changing land policy and its impact on local growth: The experience of the Shenzhen Special Economic Zone, China, in the 1980s. *Urban Studies*, 31(10), 1611–23.

Part V

SUSTAINING POLICY REFORM

12

Can China Grow and Safeguard Its Environment?

The Case of Industrial Pollution

David Wheeler, Hua Wang, and Susmita Dasgupta

China's industrial growth has been extremely rapid during the period of economic reform. In the 1990s, the output of China's ten million industrial enterprises increased by more than 15 percent annually. Industry is also China's largest productive sector, accounting for 47 percent of its gross domestic product and employing 17 percent of the country's total labor force. As a source of rapidly expanding income, Chinese industry has provided one of the strongest forces lifting many millions of people from poverty.

Unfortunately, serious environmental damage has accompanied this rapid growth. Many of China's waterways are close to biological death from excessive discharge of organic pollutants. In many urban areas, atmospheric concentrations of pollutants such as suspended particulates and sulfur dioxide routinely exceed World Health Organization safety standards by very large margins. As a result, hundreds of thousands of people are dying or becoming seriously ill from pollution-related respiratory diseases each year.

There can be no doubt that Chinese industry is a primary source of this problem. China's State Environmental Protection Agency (SEPA) estimates that industrial pollution accounts for over 70 percent of the national total: 70 percent for wastewater, including organic water pollution (COD, or chemical oxygen demand); 72 percent for sulfur dioxide (SO_2) emissions; 75 percent for flue dust (a major component of suspended particulates); and 87 percent for solid wastes. Many polluting industries are located in densely populated metropolitan areas where emissions exposure causes particularly serious damage to human health and economic activity.

China's pollution control agencies are aware of these problems and have responded with stricter enforcement of regulatory standards for water pollutants. As a result, many industrial enterprises have reduced emissions through the adoption of end-of-pipe equipment, process changes, and materials recycling. Since

FIGURE 12.1

SO$_2$ Emissions and Atmospheric Concentration in Chinese Cities, 1991–93

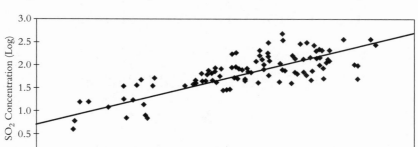

1987, provinces that have tightened enforcement have witnessed a substantial decline in the water pollution intensity, or pollution per unit of output, of factories under regulatory supervision.[1] Emissions intensity for some water pollutants has declined so rapidly that total emissions have fallen despite rapid industrial growth.

Unfortunately, the same cannot be said for industrial air pollution. The evidence shows that some regulatory incentives for air pollution control have actually weakened since 1987. Industrial discharges continue at very high levels, seriously contaminating the atmosphere of many cities. Figure 12.1 shows the strong relationship between emissions of SO$_2$ and atmospheric concentrations in fifty-three Chinese cities during 1991–1993.

As we will show in this chapter, market reforms have been another important source of change in environmental performance. The reforms have shifted production away from state-owned enterprises (SOEs) and toward larger plants. With these changes have come substantial increases in productive efficiency and decreases in the cost of abating pollution, both important sources of declining pollution intensity. These two factors may have had as great an impact on industrial pollution as changes in direct regulation.

Although the general trend is positive, there remain great regional disparities in industry's environmental performance. In provinces with stricter regulation and a strong commitment to economic reform, many industrial facilities have already shown the way to a cleaner future. However, the legacy of the past remains strikingly apparent in thousands of highly polluting plants. With industry expected to maintain rapid growth during the next twenty years, a steep decline in pollution intensity will be necessary just to keep emissions constant.

The consequences of current pollution are tragically apparent in public health

FIGURE 12.2
Projected Deaths from Air Pollution, 1997–2020

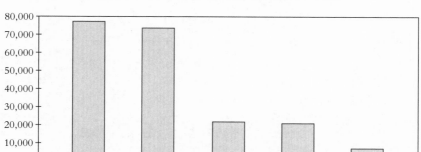

statistics for polluted areas. As we will show, the best available evidence suggests that approximately four thousand people suffer premature death from pollution-related respiratory illness each year in Chongqing, four thousand in Beijing, and one thousand in both Shanghai and Shenyang.[2] If current trends persist, we project large cumulative losses in human life through 2020. Figure 12.2 illustrates the grim stakes: Beijing could lose nearly eighty thousand people; Chongqing, seventy thousand; and other major cities could suffer losses in the tens of thousands.

In light of other pressing needs, how strongly should China respond to this challenge? Environmental improvements are desirable, but pollution abatement uses valuable economic resources, and there may be other, less costly health interventions that will save lives. Nevertheless, after a careful assessment of the benefits and costs, we will argue that stricter regulation of air emissions in heavily polluted areas is a very cost-effective option for public health improvement.

We will also highlight the beneficial effect of recent economic reforms on public health through their impact on industrial pollution intensity. Other compelling arguments for continued modernization of China's economy are bolstered by its clear environmental benefits.

Economic Reform, Regulation, and Pollution Reduction Since 1987

The Basic Economics of Industrial Pollution Control

Figure 12.2 reveals great variation in pollution-related mortality across China's urban areas. As Figure 12.3 suggests, however, the differences in pollution are not primarily due to differences in the *scale* of industrial activity. Rather, they reflect differences in *pollution intensity*, or pollution per unit of output: Since the late

FIGURE 12.3
Provincial Pollution Intensities

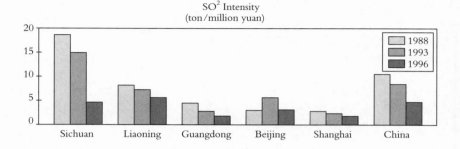

SO^2 Intensity
(ton/million yuan)

1980s, industry has been generally "dirtiest" in Sichuan and "cleanest" in Shanghai; Liaoning has had more pollution-intensive industry than Guangdong and Beijing. Figure 12.3 focuses on differences in SO_2 intensities, but the patterns for other air and water pollutants are very similar.

Figure 12.3 also reveals some remarkable changes in a very short period: Pollution intensity has fallen sharply since 1988, with particularly strong and consistent reductions in Guangdong and Sichuan.[3]

Key Factors for Improved Environmental Performance

What can account for such variations? Our recent research has shown that several factors play important roles in factory managers' abatement decisions, including regulations, plant and industry characteristics, and pressure applied by neighboring communities (Hettige et al., 1996; Pargal and Wheeler, 1996). By assessing penalties for noncompliance, regulators raise the "price of polluting" and provide economic incentives for lowering emissions. However, the degree of response to these incentives varies widely by industry sector, type of ownership, and scale of operations. There is also strong evidence that local communities exert independent influence on abatement decisions through various forms of "informal" pressure on plant managers (e.g., political leaders, community leaders, and the media). Richer and better-educated communities seem to operate quite effectively through such informal means.

Regulation

In China, national, provincial, and local pollution control agencies can affect factory-level emissions by enforcing the existing emissions standards, pollution levies, and other regulatory instruments. Penalties for noncompliance raise the price of polluting for factories and lead to increased pollution control activity. However, our own research in China and other Asian countries has shown that the impact of regulation is mediated by the consistency and strictness of enforcement (Hartman, Huq, and Wheeler, 1997; Wang and Wheeler, 1996). Pollution abatement incurs costs, so the interest of plant managers in emissions control is highly dependent on the likelihood that the authorities will detect noncompliance. This, in turn, depends on the monitoring and inspection resources made available to local regulators. Even if noncompliance is detected, the degree of management responsiveness depends largely on the size of the legally specified penalties and the proportion actually collected by the authorities.

The SEPA's own reports suggest that consistency and strictness of enforcement have varied greatly across China's provinces (Dasgupta, Huq, and Wheeler, 1997). Figure 12.4 provides evidence on two comparable measures of regulatory strictness: actual collections of pollution levy assessments (or "effective levies") per unit of excess (above-standard) discharge of wastewater and per unit of discharge for air pollutants. Comparison with Figure 12.3 reveals a roughly inverse relationship between ranking on pollution intensity and ranking on effec-

FIGURE 12.4
Provincial Pollution Levies

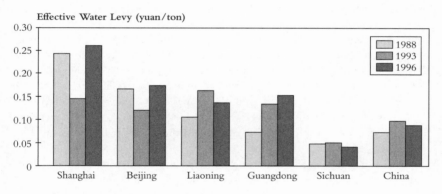

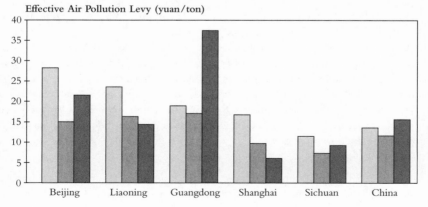

tive levies. Beijing has the highest effective levies and is among the lowest in pollution intensity; the converse is true for Sichuan. In both cases, Liaoning is intermediate. Effective water and air levies have sharply increased in Guangdong, the most rapidly growing area. Notably, Shanghai does not conform to the general pattern. Its effective air pollution levy seems entirely out of line, both with its effective water pollution levy and its status as the area with lowest pollution intensity.

Our research has shown that these variations in effective levies have had significant effects on the pollution intensity of production across China's provinces. Each 1 percent increase in the effective water pollution levy (from increased levels of legally defined penalties or tightened enforcement) leads to an approximately 0.8 percent decrease in COD pollution intensity (COD per unit of output). Each 1 percent increase in the effective air discharge levy leads to decreases of approximately 0.3 percent in SO_2 intensity. For the two components of suspended particulates, industrial smoke and dust, reductions in emissions intensity are 0.8 percent and 0.4 percent, respectively, when the effective air levy is raised by 1 percent. Clearly, regulation makes a significant difference, and equally clearly, China's provincial regulators have pursued quite different regulatory policies.[4]

Why do regulators behave so differently? Our research suggests that two broad sets of factors influence regulatory enforcement policy (Afsah, Laplante, and Wheeler, 1996). Local regulators are apparently responsive to *economic factors* that influence total damage assessment. These include the local pollution load, the size of the exposed population, and local income per capita. However, effective levies are also affected by differential *community capacity to enforce*, which depends on average education, available information, and the power to bargain with local industry.

Our results also suggest that regulators respond to citizen complaints, the incidence of which varies widely across provinces (Dasgupta and Wheeler, 1996). Complaints per capita are most strongly related to average education levels: areas with high illiteracy are notably "silent" because uneducated citizens are less likely to be aware of environmental problems and less willing to confront the authorities. Provincial total suspended particulates (TSP) pollution also has significant effects on the incidence of complaints. Figure 12.5 illustrates the implications of the educational and income effects for our five provinces. The incidence of complaints is positively associated with effective air and water pollution levies and negatively associated with actual pollution intensity. Our evidence suggests that this kind of citizen feedback is a powerful independent force for environmental improvement.

Plant and Industry Characteristics

Our research has identified three variables in this category that contribute significantly to pollution intensity in a particular region. The first, not surpris-

FIGURE 12.5
Provincial Differences in Citizen Environmental Complaints

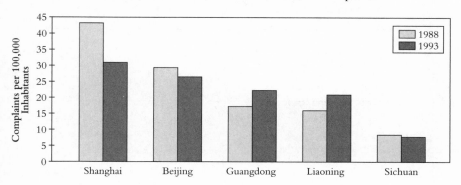

ingly, is the sectoral composition of industry. Some industrial processes generate large volumes of harmful pollutants; others do not. Some sectors also face substantially higher abatement costs, increasing the resistance to pollution control in cost-sensitive enterprises.

Scale of operation is also an important determinant of pollution intensity. In part, this is because end-of-pipe pollution abatement has very significant economies of scale. Large plants have lower unit costs of abatement and respond more readily to regulatory incentives. They also tend to be more technically efficient, since their size permits spreading overhead costs for skilled personnel across many units of production.

Our research also suggests that state-owned enterprises are substantially more pollution-intensive than other plants in China. The basic cause is apparently lower operating efficiency, which affects both abatement costs and the generation of waste residuals in production. Recent research in Asian mixed economies has suggested that SOEs' insulation from regulation is another contributing factor (Pargal and Wheeler, 1996; Hartman et al., 1997). However, our analysis of enforcement practices in China finds the converse to be true there: SOEs experience more, not less, rigorous enforcement (Dasgupta, Huq, and Wheeler, 1997). Their greater pollution intensity in China therefore seems attributable to efficiency effects alone.

Comparative Significance of Pollution Intensity Factors

Figures 12.6 and 12.7 summarize the results of our econometric analysis of provincial differences in water and air pollution intensity.[5] The intensity factors displayed in the figures are based on beta coefficients, which measure the direction and relative importance of explanatory variables in a multivariate relationship. For both water (COD) and air (SO_2) pollution intensity, the share of production in large plants is the most significant factor in reducing intensity.[6] Its

FIGURE 12.6
COD Intensity Factors: Effect and Significance

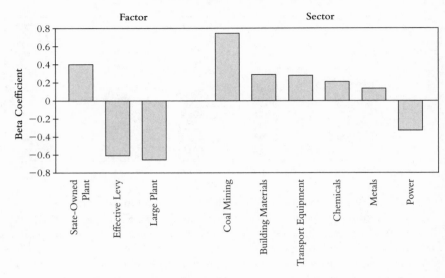

FIGURE 12.7
SO$_2$ Intensity Factors: Effect and Significance

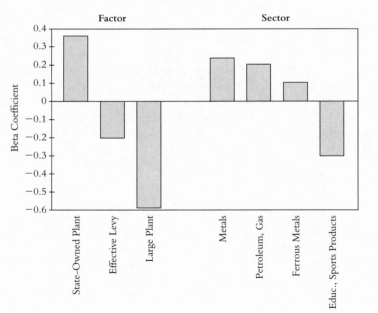

beta-coefficient measure (approximately −0.6) is essentially the same in the two cases. The share of production in state-owned plants has large weight as a contributor to pollution intensity, with a beta measure of approximately 0.4 in both cases. The economic incentive for pollution abatement provided by the pollution levy is also important, although apparently more so for COD pollution. The beta coefficient for the effective water levy is approximately −0.6, while it is −0.2 for the effective levy on air pollutant discharges.

Among sectors, the major contributors to higher intensity vary by pollutant.[7] For COD pollution, the significant "dirty" sectors are coal mining, building materials, transport equipment, chemicals, and metals. In the case of air pollutants, metals, petroleum and gas, and ferrous metals are exceptionally "dirty" for SO_2, and furniture, metals, electrical equipment, textiles, paper, and ferrous metals for TSP.

The Reform Experience Since 1987

China's economic reforms since 1987 have focused on increasing the role of price signals in the economy, reducing constraints on enterprise expansion (and contraction), reducing the role of SOEs, and reducing trade protection. The results have included extremely rapid industrial growth and major changes in economic structure. The reforms have also had a major impact on industrial pollution, because they have affected the sectoral composition of output, the size distribution of Chinese factories, their ownership, and their sensitivity to economic incentives provided by the pollution levies.

Our sample of five provinces and China as a whole reveals a clear and consistent pattern of increase in plant scale during the period 1988–97 that is most pronounced for Shanghai (see Figure 12.8). Our analysis has shown that this in-

FIGURE 12.8
Output Share of Large Plants

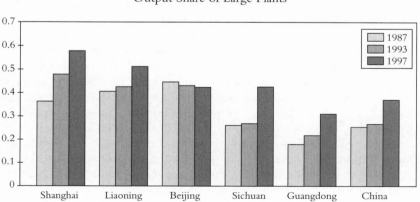

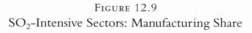

FIGURE 12.9
SO$_2$-Intensive Sectors: Manufacturing Share

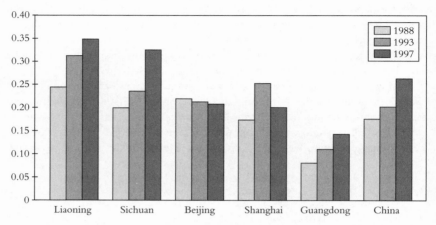

NOTE: The SO$_2$-intensive sectors are power, building materials, ferrous and nonferrous metals, paper, chemicals, and mining.

crease in scale has been accompanied by a substantial decline in pollution intensity.[8] There has also been a large decline in the output share from SOEs during the reform period, most notably in Shanghai and Guangdong. Our econometric results suggest that the decline in SOE share has been accompanied by a significant decline in pollution intensity.

The impact of sectoral change on "dirty" sectors has been mixed. Whereas there has been little change for water polluters, Figure 12.9 shows that the share for air polluters has risen markedly.

Trade Liberalization

China has opened its frontiers to more trade as the economic reforms have proceeded. From an analytical perspective, the impact of trade liberalization on the environment could be either positive or negative. Positive effects include enhanced production efficiency in export-oriented enterprises and more rapid absorption of newer, cleaner technologies from OECD sources.[9] On the other hand, China's comparative advantage could be in pollution-intensive industries because it has weaker environmental regulation and lower-cost heavy raw materials than many of its trading partners. We have checked for this possibility by analyzing recent trends for the five most heavily polluting industry sectors: chemicals, pulp and paper, nonferrous metals, ferrous metals, and nonmetallic minerals (principally cement).[10] Using production and trade data for China and its trading partners, we have developed three indices of change in pollution intensity.

The first is the proportion of China's total industrial output produced by these five sectors during the era of reform. Figure 12.10 provides the evidence: From 1977 to 1992, the output share of the five "dirty" sectors trended downward. Within the period, rapid decline in the early 1980s was succeeded by an increase in the late 1980s and a leveling off in the early 1990s. There is no evidence of any long-run shift toward a pollution-intensive industry structure.

Our second index is the trend in net imports (imports minus exports) of products from the five heavily polluting sectors. If China's comparative advantage is really in pollution-intensive industries, then the era of trade liberalization should be witnessing a shift toward net exports of their products. In fact, Figure 12.11 shows that the opposite has occurred: Real net imports of these products have trended strongly upward since 1987.

Finally, we have used the available data to calculate China's consumption-production ratio for the output of the five dirty sectors. If China's comparative advantage lies in "dirty" production, two things should be true. First, this ratio

FIGURE 12.10

Trend in the Output Share of the Five Dirtiest Industrial Sectors, 1977–92

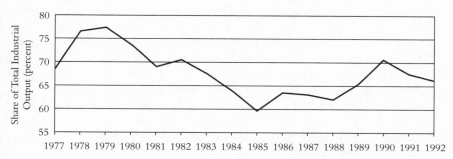

FIGURE 12.11

Trend in Net Imports from Pollution-Intensive Industries, 1987–94

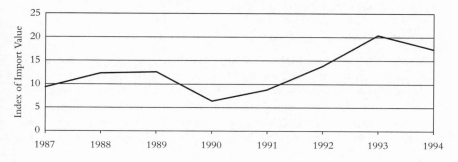

FIGURE 12.12

Consumption-Production Ratio of Polluting Products, 1987–92

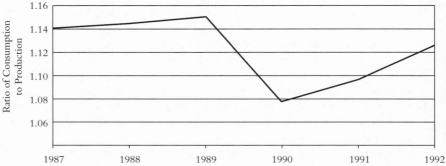

should be less than 1, since China should be a net exporter of pollution-intensive goods. Second, the ratio should fall over time because production for export should increase faster than production for domestic consumption. The evidence in Figure 12.12 is mixed but is not generally consistent with the hypothesis that China's comparative advantage is in pollution-intensive production. The series has a modest downward trend for the period since 1987. However, the consumption-production ratio has remained well above 1 throughout the period. This supports the story in Figure 12.11: China has been and remains a net *importer* of pollution-intensive goods from its trading partners.

Overall, the evidence seems clear. China's revealed comparative advantage in the era of trade liberalization has been in non-pollution-intensive goods. Of course, all industries have experienced rapid growth in recent years, including pollution-intensive ones. Their cleaner counterparts have simply grown faster, both in the domestic sphere and in China's international trade. The comparative advantage effect of trade liberalization has therefore reinforced its positive impact on efficiency and absorption of clean technology. For China, increasing openness seems to have had a generally "clean" impact on the sectoral composition of industrial output.

Regulation, Pollution Abatement, and Industrial Migration

Our research has identified the effective pollution levy as a powerful instrument for inducing emissions reduction by Chinese industry (see Wang and Wheeler, 1996; Dasgupta, Wang, and Wheeler, 1997). Pollution intensity is significantly lower in provinces with higher effective levies, and it is falling in provinces where the levies are rising. However, China's recent history suggests that commitment to stricter regulation has been mixed at best. Despite clearly damaging levels of air pollution revealed by Figure 12.6, real effective air pollution levies have actually fallen since 1987 in all of our focal provinces except Guangdong. The decline is particularly striking in Liaoning and Shanghai. Real effective water pollution levies have also fallen in these cities, while they have risen sharply in Liaoning and Guangdong (and more modestly in Sichuan).

The Impact of Regulation

Industrial air and water pollution intensity have declined in all five provinces, but at very different rates. To interpret these variations, it is useful to combine the evidence on air and water levies in Figure 12.4. For both air and water pollution, declining real levies in Beijing and Shanghai have produced incentives for increased pollution intensity. The observed declines in intensity are therefore attributable to countervailing shifts in scale, ownership, and sectoral composition induced by the economic reforms. For air pollution intensity, the same conclusion follows for Liaoning, Guangdong, and Sichuan: the decline is due to the structural impact of reform, because the air pollution levy has actually fallen in real terms. In the case of water pollution, on the other hand, there has been a sharp drop in intensity in these three provinces because the two factors have reinforced one another: effective water pollution levies have risen substantially, and the structural impact of reforms has been strongly pollution-reducing.

Migration of "Dirty" Sectors Within China?

Earlier we established that trade reforms have not had a "dirty" sector bias. However, it is at least possible that internal differences in regulatory strictness could have induced a relocation of "dirty" industries within China. Despite the evident trend toward equalization of the effective levy in the eastern provinces, Figure 12.4 includes differences as great as 3:1 in levy rates. Lucas (1996) has investigated whether such differences have induced faster growth of pollution-intensive sectors in provinces with laxer regulation. His results suggest that differential levies are not significant as location factors, so there has apparently been no regulation-induced migration of "dirty" sectors within China. Lucas's results are similar to those of researchers on OECD economies, who have concluded that regulation-induced differences in abatement costs are small relative to other cost factors that determine regional patterns of industrial location.

Economic Reform and the Cost of Abatement

In recent econometric research, we have used plant-level data from SEPA to develop detailed estimates of abatement costs for air and water emissions by Chinese industry (Dasgupta, Huq, Wheeler, and Zhang, 1996; Dasgupta, Wang, and Wheeler, 1997). Our results show that marginal abatement costs (MAC) vary greatly by sector, scale, abatement rate, ownership, and pollutant. The impact of these variables on marginal cost is dramatically illustrated by a few comparisons. Holding other factors constant, MAC ratios can vary as much as 20:1 between large and small facilities, 45:1 across sectors, 13:1 between 10 percent and 90 percent abatement, 5:1 between SOEs and non-SOEs, and 4:1 across pollutants.

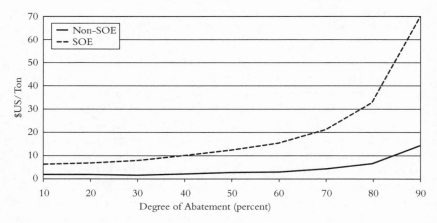

FIGURE 12.13
Particulate Marginal Abatement Costs: Large Plants

FIGURE 12.14
Particulate Marginal Abatement Costs: Small Plants

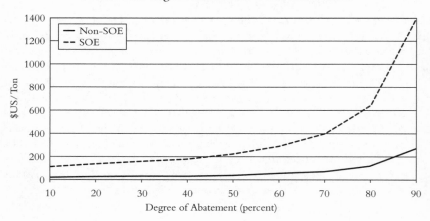

The range of potential variation is suggested by the comparative MAC schedules in Figures 12.13 and 12.14. In the case of particulates, MAC for large non–
SOE plants is barely above $10 per ton at 90 percent abatement. By contrast,
large SOE facilities reach the same MAC at 40 percent abatement and increase
to $70 per ton at 90 percent. For small plants, MACs for particulates increase by
an order of magnitude in both cases: to over $200 per ton for non–SOEs and
$1,400 per ton for SOEs. Similar relative results hold for SO$_2$, but the MAC
schedules shift upward by half an order of magnitude. At 90 percent abatement,

MACs are approximately $50 per ton for large non–SOE plants, $280 per ton for large SOEs, $1,000 per ton for small non–SOEs, and $5,500 per ton for small SOEs.

These dramatic differences highlight the beneficial impact of economic reform on China's prospects for industrial pollution control. As an increasing share of industrial production moves toward large non–SOE plants, the marginal cost of abatement for the industrial system is falling significantly. Our results suggest that the marginal cost of abatement is now substantially lower (in real terms) than it was in 1987.

The Role of Local Communities

During the era of reform, incomes have risen rapidly across China and literacy rates have continued to improve. Our research on regulation in China suggests that these developments have also had a significant effect on industrial water pollution. As local communities become wealthier and better educated, three forces for declining pollution intensity are strengthened. First, increased community income and education push the water levy rates upward as provincial regulators adjust their enforcement policy to improved conditions and higher valuation of environmental benefits. Second, feedback through citizen's environmental complaints increases, with amplifying effects on enforcement. Finally, rising income and education strengthen "informal regulation" as communities with more resources and greater interest in environmental protection increase pressure for abatement through a variety of political and social channels.

Although the link between socioeconomic development and effective water pollution levies seems clear, we have found no equivalent empirical relationship between development and effective air pollution levies. This is unfortunate, because the evidence suggests that air pollution, not water pollution, is the major source of damage to human health in China. In fact, our evidence shows that real air pollution levies have been declining all over China during a period of rapid growth and otherwise progressive change. The implication is clear and sobering: nothing in the Chinese system will automatically guarantee stricter regulation of air pollution as the economy advances. If current trends continue, many thousands of lives will be lost to air pollution in China's industrial centers.

To summarize, several factors have strongly affected industry's environmental performance in China in recent years. For China's environmental regulators, important policy options are identified by the direct impact of regulation on emissions and the use of public environmental information to bolster informal regulation by local communities. National and provincial economic reforms also have a major impact on polluters' behavior and abatement costs, through their effects on sectoral growth rates, plant ownership, and scale of operations. Finally, more general economic development policies influence industry's environmental performance in the long run by increasing community incomes, education levels, and bargaining power. These feed back into regulation, both formally (through citizen complaints and the enforcement policy of regulators) and informally (through increased pressure on plants from local communities).

Designing Future Pollution Scenarios

The Past as Prelude

Our review of recent Chinese experience with industrial pollution shows that significant progress in abatement is possible. In cases where regulatory incentives to abate have complemented the progressive impact of economic reforms, there have been rapid declines in the pollution intensity of production—so rapid, in fact, that total water pollution loads from regulated industries have actually fallen.[11] But in many cases, particularly for hazardous air pollution, the recent trend in regulatory incentives has been the contrary: effective levies have declined significantly, producing an inducement to higher pollution intensity that has offset much of the impact of the reforms. Furthermore, the reforms themselves will inevitably run their course: increases in the output shares of large and non–SOE factories are naturally self-limiting. Although the reforms have certainly bought time for China, the future spotlight must shift to the prospects for tighter regulation. If abatement incentives are not adjusted, industrial pollution intensities, pollution loads, and contamination of the ambient environment will almost certainly increase. Given China's current industrial growth rate, the consequences for public health could be severe. Here we use our econometric results to project the consequences of alternative policy strategies for China's environmental future.

Projecting the Pollution Impact of Alternative Policies

China affords a unique opportunity for projection of alternative futures because for many parts of China, the future already exists. China's provinces and major urban areas exhibit great disparity in the present strictness of environmental regulation, the share of production in large enterprises, and the degree of state ownership of industry. Shanghai, for example, has a high proportion of production in large facilities, a low proportion in state enterprises, a high (though, unfortunately, falling) degree of regulatory strictness, and as a result, low levels of pollution intensity per unit of industrial output. Sichuan's statistics are the converse in most cases.

For much of China, it will be many years before current conditions in Shanghai are replicated. Thus although we cannot predict the future path of technological progress with any accuracy, we can develop conservative projections for much of China based on actual conditions in the more advanced provinces. And even among the latter, there is sufficient diversity of characteristics to permit use of econometrically estimated relationships to approximate the consequences of moving toward leading-edge status in the dimensions that matter most for pollution intensity.

China's second advantage is its wealth of data. Large databases made available to us by SEPA have enabled us to base our entire forecasting exercise on the econometric analyses summarized in this chapter. To our knowledge, this has not previously been possible, in China or any other country. We have used the SEPA databases in three related studies: (1) the determinants of industrial air and water pollution intensity, (2) the impact of air emissions on atmospheric pollutant concentrations, and (3) the cost of pollution abatement. For our air pollution scenarios, we have completed the forecasting exercise by joining our estimates to the empirical findings of Xu et al. (1994) on the health impact of air pollution.

Projecting Pollution Damage

Emissions Intensities and Loads

Our analysis begins with projections of industrial pollution loads, which are based on our econometric studies of variations in pollution intensity for COD, SO_2, and TSP. Figures 12.6 and 12.7 summarize the significant intensity factors: the effective pollution levy, large-plant share of output, SOE share of output, and the shares of exceptionally "clean" and "dirty" sectors. Assuming that the economic reforms will continue, we have extrapolated from recent trends in these variables to project their future paths.

We treat the effective pollution levy as a policy variable in three scenarios: (1) holding the air and water pollution levies constant at their 1993 levels, which would represent regress for water but progress for air (in light of the decline since 1987); (2) an annual increase of 5 percent a year, which would approximately reflect the recent national trend for water pollution levy rates and a considerable reversal of trend for air pollution; (3) an annual increase in 10 percent a year, representing a much stronger commitment to pollution control.[12]

We combine these three levy scenarios with projected changes in sector, output scale, and ownership to generate projected paths for industrial COD, SO_2, and TSP intensity for China as a whole and for the major cities in our five focal provinces: Beijing, Shanghai, Shenyang (Liaoning), Guangzhou (Guangdong), and Chongqing (formerly in Sichuan). These are combined with exogenously projected changes in total industrial output to produce estimates of future air and water pollution loads.[13]

Ambient Concentration

We use the econometric results illustrated in Figure 12.1 to project the consequences of changing air pollution loads for ambient concentrations of SO_2 (see Dasgupta, Wang, and Wheeler, 1997). Controlling for precipitation, the estimated elasticity that links load to concentration is approximately 0.51. A 1 percent increase in SO_2 emissions density (or emissions per unit area) in a particular city increases its atmospheric concentration by 0.51 percent. We use this elasticity and the projected air emissions change in each city to project future atmospheric concentrations. We have been unable to replicate the exercise for suspended particulates or water pollution because supporting data are unavailable.

Health Damage

The next link in the analytical chain requires estimation of the change in mortality that is induced by a change in atmospheric SO_2 concentration. For this exercise, we rely on empirical studies in Beijing and Shenyang by Xu et al. (1994). They have estimated "dose-response" relationships linking atmospheric concentrations of TSP and SO_2 to respiratory disease in the two cities. They find the strongest relationship between mortality and ambient SO_2 concentration, but with high variability: mortality responds much more strongly to SO_2 concentration change in Beijing than in Shenyang. For these two cities, we have projected health risks using the dose-response parameters estimated by Xu's team. For the other three cities, we have used the average of the two parameter values. In each case, we have estimated mortality risks from projected atmospheric SO_2 concentrations and combined the risk estimates with projected city populations to forecast changes in mortality from respiratory illness.

Our projections focus on SO_2 concentrations because Xu's study shows that they are highly correlated with damage from respiratory disease. Recent scientific evidence provides some insight into the nature of this relationship. Sulfur dioxide and other oxides of sulfur combine with oxygen to form sulfates and with water vapor to form aerosols of sulfurous and sulfuric acid. These acid mists can irritate the respiratory systems of humans and animals. Therefore, a high concentration of SO_2 can affect breathing and may aggravate existing respiratory and cardiovascular disease. Sensitive populations include asthmatics, individuals with bronchitis or emphysema, children, and the elderly.

The second and probably more significant effect of SO_2 is traceable to the impact of fine particulates on mortality and morbidity. A review of evidence by the U.S. Environmental Protection Agency (2000) suggests that fine particulates are the source of the worst health damage from air pollution. In the case of China, there is reason to believe that 30 to 40 percent of fine particulates are in the form of sulfates from SO_2 emissions.

While Xu's results and the available data have led us to focus on SO_2, we also recognize the potential contribution of TSP to atmospheric concentrations of fine particulates (FP). For Beijing and Shenyang, we interpret Xu's weak results for TSP to mean that measured total suspended particulates in those cities do not have a substantial FP component. Nevertheless, we recognize that this may not be true in other cases. Therefore, our policy scenarios include projections for industrial TSP emissions, both for China as a whole and for our five cities.

Projecting Abatement Costs

Abatement costs are projected from our econometric analyses of Chinese factory data for several air and water pollutants. The major determinants are pollutant type, industry sector, ownership, scale of abatement activity (related to the volume of discharge), pollutant concentration in the waste stream, and the degree of abatement (or percent reduction in pollutant concentration). At the city level, we use our results to project incremental costs for degrees of abatement ranging from 10 percent to 90 percent.

Data on fine particulate emissions are unavailable, so we have used SO_2 as a proxy because SO_2 emissions have a significant FP content. However, SO_2 reduction is considerably more expensive than abatement of particulates. To avoid severe bias in our cost-benefit assessment, we therefore consider the costs of air pollution abatement for both SO_2 and particulates. We recognize that our analysis understates the benefits of direct removal of fine particulates, since these represent only a part of total volume for SO_2. In any case, our results provide an extremely strong cost-benefit rationale for air pollution abatement.

Policy Choices and Environmental Consequences: Scenarios for Five Cities

Decisions on the pace of economic reform and local environmental regulation have significantly affected the pollution intensity of industrial production in China. Because they reflect much of China's regional variety, our five cities provide a good focus for exploring the past results of these policies and their implications for future environmental conditions. To provide overall perspective, we also include projected pollution intensities and loads for China as a whole.

Trends in Pollution Intensity Factors

In the first stage of the analysis, we use recent trends to project future levels of nonregulatory determinants of pollution intensity (pollution per unit of output) for COD, SO_2, and TSP. At the national level, we project the share of COD-intensive sectors to remain constant at 20 percent between 1994 and 2020, the share for SO_2-intensive sectors to drop from 6.6 percent to 4.7 percent, and the TSP-intensive share to increase very slightly, from 32 percent to 32.8 percent. The projected result is increasing diversity in the structure of regional production. All pollution-intensive sectors have a rising output share in Beijing and a falling share in Guangdong. Liaoning has rising SO_2- and TSP-intensive shares but a falling share for COD-intensive production. The pattern in Shanghai and Sichuan is mixed, with rising COD- and TSP-intensive shares but a falling SO_2-intensive share. Although these impacts are unintentional, they are part of "business as usual" under the reform. On this margin, provinces with a rising share of pollution-intensive output will carry a heavier regulatory burden than those with a falling share. The environmental impact of changing shares is reflected in our projections.[14]

Recent trends suggest less diversity in the movement toward concentration of production in large plants. Shares in all five cities are trending upward at about the same rate, so the projected distribution across provinces in 2020 has a spread similar to the current one. Cities in the northeast group (Beijing, Shanghai, Shenyang) are tightly clustered around one path, Guangzhou and Chongqing around another. For China as a whole, the large-plant share increases from 30 percent to 58 percent during 1988–2020. Across provinces, the minimum large-plant share rises from 22 percent to 49 percent (Guangdong), while the maximum increases from 48 percent to 70 percent (Beijing). Although they forecast large changes, our projections are mostly within the range of current experience.

For state ownership, the projections show a continued sharp decline at the national level but a more mixed experience across provinces. Extrapolation from recent trends yields a projected national decline in SOE share from 58 percent to 43 percent during 1988–2020. Beijing, Shanghai, and Chongqing experience a similar decline in SOE share: from around 70 percent in 1988 to around 40 percent in 2020. Guangzhou preserves its status as a strong non-SOE "outlier," declining from an already low SOE share of 45 percent in 1988 to around 15 percent in 2020. Shenyang, on the other hand, had an actual *increase* in SOE share during 1988–1994. Although we do not expect this to continue, we have no evidence to support a projection of declining SOE share in Shenyang. We therefore assume that it will remain stable at its current level—perhaps overly conservative, but consistent with our approach for other cities.

Industrial Production

Total discharge of a pollutant is the product of pollution intensity (or pollution per unit of output) and output. Obviously, projected output scale is a critical predictor of future pollution problems. China's overall industrial growth rate has been among the highest in the world, and we forecast that it will slacken somewhat in the first decade of the twenty-first century. Again, an analysis of regional trends reveals considerable diversity within China. Shanghai's industrial economy is already huge, and its economy is shifting rapidly toward the service sector at the margin. Extrapolating from the trend during 1988–1994, we project a 4.1 percent annual growth rate for Shanghai's industry through 2020—an overall increase of about 180 percent during the forecasting period. Guangdong has a projected industrial growth rate of 5.7 percent and an overall increase of 320 percent. Beijing and Liaoning are intermediate, with annual growth rates near 5 percent and overall increases of around 250 percent. The contrast between the coastal regions and the interior is evident in Sichuan's trend output growth. Although our projection (3.5 percent annual, 150 percent overall) would be respectable for many economies, it is clearly lagging by comparison with the coastal provinces.

Of course, these simple extrapolations cannot fully anticipate the dynamics of regional change during the coming decades. It is entirely possible that congestion and rising factor costs in the coastal region will reduce its comparative advantage for industrial location, leading to a shift toward interior locations. However, agglomeration economies are powerful, and the coastal region is China's entrepôt for international trade. On balance, extrapolations from recent trends seem to yield reasonable predictions.

Economic Reform and Environmental Regulation: Possible Futures

Prospects for "Win-Win": Economic Reform Without Stricter Regulation

China's economic reforms have generated powerful forces for reduced pollution intensity in manufacturing. The consolidation of production in large plants has lowered pollution intensity because unit abatement costs and generation of waste residuals are lower in large facilities. Non-SOE factories have absorbed a growing share of industrial output, producing further reductions in pollution intensity from efficiency gains. Our econometric analysis suggests that these factors have accounted for much of the decline in air and water pollution intensity across China's provinces since 1987. The experience of regulation has been more mixed: Higher air and water pollution levies have significantly reduced pollution intensity, but real effective air levies have actually fallen in four focal provinces since 1987, and the water levies have fallen in Beijing and Shanghai.

The results have been equally mixed. In Guangdong, where increases in the water levy have reinforced the impact of reform (including a decline in the share of COD-intensive sectors), there has been a very sharp decline in water pollution intensity. In Beijing, by contrast, the effective air pollution levy has fallen substantially while the share of SO_2- and TSP-intensive sectors has risen. These changes have partly counteracted the impact of the reforms, and industrial SO_2 and TSP intensities have declined modestly while production scale has risen rapidly.

What will happen in the future if the reforms continue but regulation isn't tightened? To explore this possibility, we have combined our econometrically estimated intensity equations for COD, SO_2, and TSP with projected changes in pollution intensity factors (sector, scale, ownership) while holding air and water pollution levies at 1993 levels for each province. This is equivalent to projecting the environmental consequences of continued economic reform alone, with no contribution from stricter regulation. We term this the "win-win" scenario because economic reform is already presumed to be beneficial on other grounds. Its impact on pollution intensity provides a net environmental gain without any cost explicitly incurred for pollution control.

FIGURE 12.15
COD Loads in Three Scenarios

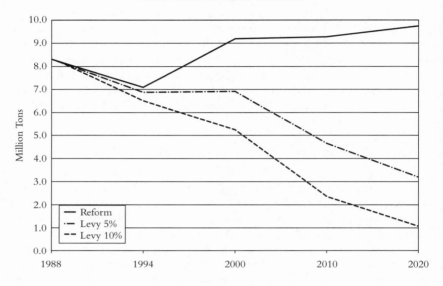

Tightening Regulation: Two Scenarios

Tightening regulation will provide explicit incentives to reduce pollution intensity, which will complement the impact of economic reform. To explore the implications of different strategies, we have developed two scenarios. In the first, air and water pollution levies are both increased by 5 percent annually. This leads to a fourfold increase in the real levy by 2020. The second scenario increases levies by 10 percent annually, leading to a thirteenfold increase by 2020.

Water Pollution

Comparative forecasts for total COD load are presented for China as a whole in Figure 12.15. The projected impact of continued reform alone (the "win-win" scenario) is remarkable. For China, total COD emissions from industry are projected to rise only modestly, from 8.3 million tons annually to 9.8 million tons, during a period of rapid industrial growth. In three of the five cities—Shanghai, Guangzhou, and Shenyang—projected changes in sectoral composition, scale, and ownership are sufficient to maintain or reduce total COD loads. For two cities—Beijing and Chongqing—COD discharges increase, but at a far slower rate than industrial output.

Our first (5 percent) levy scenario reflects a continuation of recent trends in water pollution regulation. The results for China are very encouraging: a projected reduction from 8.3 million tons to 3.3 million tons. In the five cities, a fourfold increase in the effective levy (coupled with the reforms) induces a COD load reduction of 66 percent. This amounts to over 120,000 tons annually in Shanghai alone. The imposition of a 10 percent annual increase in the levy leads to a fall in emissions from 8.3 million tons to 1.1 million tons nationally and 88 percent reductions for the five cities: 160,000 tons annually in Shanghai, 145,000 in Beijing; 60,000 in Chongqing, 55,000 in Guangzhou, and 21,000 in Shenyang.

All three scenarios lead us to an optimistic view of the potential for solving China's industrial water pollution problem, at least in the case of COD. The best available evidence suggests that total COD loads will increase only modestly as economic reform proceeds, even if regulations are not tightened. Moreover, the projected results of higher pollution levies are quite striking. We project that a 10 percent annual increase in the levy through 2020 would eliminate most of the COD emissions from regulated factories in China.

Air Pollution

For TSP and SO_2, we project national and city emissions using the same approach:

- We use projected pollution levies and shares of large plants, SOEs, and "dirty" sectors and "clean" sectors to project national and provincial pollution intensities. We assume that provincial intensities are the same as the pollution intensities of our focal cities (not an unreasonable assumption, since these cities are the main industrial centers of their provinces and in two cases—Beijing and Shanghai—are identical to the provinces).[15]
- To estimate city emissions, we multiply projected provincial industrial output by the city's share of provincial industrial output in 1993. Thus we assume (again, not unreasonably) that the growth of industry in the province's main industrial city will be identical to the growth of industry in the province.
- To obtain total projected TSP and SO_2 loads for China and the five cities, we multiply projected pollution intensities by projected industrial outputs.

For SO_2, the available information permits us to go several steps further:

- We calculate SO_2 concentration in each city's atmosphere by adjusting the previous year's concentration at 0.51 times the rate of change of the estimated pollution load. This reflects the econometric result illustrated in Figure 12.1.
- We substitute the estimated concentration into the dose-response function estimated by Xu et al. (1994) to obtain the probability of individual mortality from SO_2 pollution in a particular city. To benchmark our estimates, we make the conservative assumption that SO_2 concentrations below 30 $\mu g/m^3$ are not harmful.[16]
- We multiply the individual mortality probability by the city's projected population to obtain the estimated number of deaths from SO_2 pollution.

FIGURE 12.16
Industrial SO₂ Loads in China

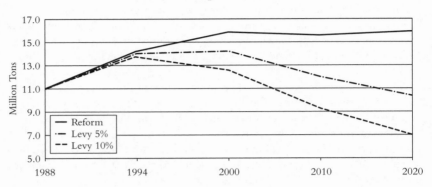

Our results on emissions are somewhat different for TSP and SO₂, reflecting the underlying differences in their econometrically estimated response elasticities. In the pure reform ("win–win") scenario, continued decline in the air pollution intensity of industrial production is not enough to offset industrial growth: Total projected SO₂ emissions rise from 14.2 million tons in 1994 to 15.7 million tons in 2020 (see Figure 12.16); TSP emissions rise from 16.1 million tons to 17.1 million tons. In the two levy-increase scenarios, however, sharp improvements are projected at the national level. A 5 percent annual increase in the levy induces reductions of SO₂ and TSP emissions to 10.3 and 7.5 million tons, respectively. When the increase is raised to 10 percent annually, emissions fall to 6.9 and 3.6 million tons, respectively. Thus the 10 percent annual levy increase is sufficient to eliminate half of SO₂ emissions and three-fourths of TSP emissions by 2020.

For the pure reform case, we find that changes in scale, ownership, and sectoral composition induce considerable reductions in pollution intensity. However, these are generally insufficient to prevent further deterioration in ambient air quality because of large increases in the scale of industrial production. Across cities, only Chongqing experiences a slight improvement in the pure reform scenario, and its air quality remains terrible. Otherwise, conditions deteriorate substantially. Beijing's SO₂ concentration rises from 117 μg/m³ in 1993 to 159 in 2020; projected annual deaths from pollution-related respiratory disease increase from 3,400 to 6,400. Shanghai's air quality deteriorates from 50 to 59 μg/m³; and annual deaths rise from 700 to 1,300. Shenyang's air quality deteriorates dramatically, from 131 to 217 μg/m³, and projected annual deaths rise from 800 to 1,500. Guangzhou's SO₂ concentration deteriorates from 47 to 54 μg/m³; deaths increase from 200 to 300. Finally, Chongqing's slight improvement in air quality (from 270 to 264 μg/m³) produces slightly lower mortality risk for a significantly larger population, and projected deaths rise from 4,100 to 5,000.

A 5 percent annual increase in the effective air pollution levy significantly improves on the pure reform outcome in all five cities. For Guangzhou and Chongqing, air quality in 2020 is substantially better than the 1993 level. Shanghai maintains roughly constant air quality, while there is slower deterioration in Beijing and Shenyang. Finally, we trace the projected impact of a 10 percent annual increase in the levy. This is sufficient for rough maintenance of the 1993 status quo in Shenyang and Beijing, while Shanghai, Guangzhou, and Chongqing experience strong improvements in air quality.

As Table 12.1 shows, the projected impact of levy increases on annual deaths is quite impressive in all five cities. For the 10 percent levy increase, projected deaths in 2020 fall by 67 percent in Guangzhou, 50 percent in Shenyang, 47 percent in Beijing, 36 percent in Shanghai, and 31 percent in Chongqing.

The full results of strengthened regulation are portrayed in Figure 12.17. To produce these estimates, we have calculated the cumulative projected annual deaths from 1997 to 2020 in the three scenarios. Net lives saved in the two increased-levy scenarios are calculated by subtracting cumulative deaths from

TABLE 12.1

Projected Annual Deaths from Industrial SO$_2$ Pollution

	Reform	Levy 5 Percent	Levy 10 Percent	Percent Decrease for Levy 10 Percent
Beijing	4,500	3,200	2,400	47
Chongqing	3,200	2,600	2,200	31
Shenyang	1,200	900	600	50
Shanghai	1,100	700	700	36
Guangzhou	300	200	100	67

NOTE: Estimated deaths in the text discussion are for total SO$_2$ pollution and are therefore higher than the estimates in this table.

FIGURE 12.17

Lives Saved by SO$_2$ Regulation, 1997–2020

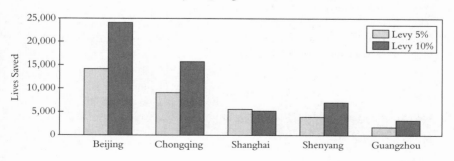

FIGURE 12.18
Total Deaths from Industrial Air Pollution, 1997–2020

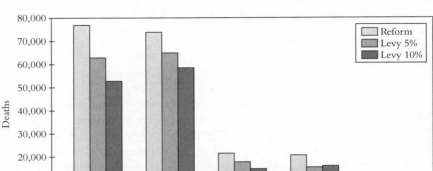

cumulative deaths in the pure reform case. The lifesaving value of the levy emerges clearly in this illustration. Beijing, for example, saves about 14,000 lives with a 5 percent annual increase and 24,000 lives with a 10 percent increase. Chongqing saves 9,000 and 16,000 lives, respectively, and lifesaving in the other cities is also counted in the thousands.

Finally, we should note that pollution-related deaths remain at high levels even in the strict regulation scenario. Figure 12.18 displays the prospects. Faced with industrial output increases in the range of 150 to 300 percent by 2020, our focal cities face very heavy loss of life even with greatly increased regulation of pollution. The cases of Beijing and Chongqing are particularly grim, with total deaths above 70,000 in the pure reform scenarios and dropping into the 50,000–60,000 range with the 10 percent annual levy increase. Chongqing loses more than 50,000 people in all the scenarios, Shenyang and Shanghai more than 10,000.

In view of these projected losses, it is appropriate to pose the question: Can further abatement possibly be too costly to justify the loss of so many lives? This seems hard to believe on the face of it, since many Chinese cities are moving toward decent public health standards in other domains. We turn next to the assessment of benefits and costs: How much air pollution in China's urban centers would it be socially worthwhile to abate?

Is Stricter Regulation Worthwhile?

Certainly, lifesaving through air pollution reduction is a laudable objective. But China remains a poor country with many basic needs unmet for hundreds of millions of citizens. Public investment in health facilities and education can also yield major health benefits, and direct investment in productive capital can improve health by increasing incomes. An appropriate welfare analysis of air pollution abatement must therefore consider its costs as well as its benefits.

Our econometric results show that the cost of abating China's industrial pollution rises steadily at the margin with degree of abatement. At some level of abatement, further pollution reduction may no longer be warranted because the same resources could be used for other investments with greater lifesaving potential. Using two cases to illustrate our approach, we address this issue with a systematic assessment of abatement benefits and costs.

Case 1: Beijing

Abatement Benefits

Beijing had a population of about 11,120,000 in 1993; the pollution-related mortality rate was about 0.611 percent; total deaths were about 68,000; and total SO_2 emissions were about 366,000 tons (of which 204,000 were from industry). From this base, a decrease of 1,000 tons in SO_2 emissions decreases total emissions by $(1/366 \times 100)$ percent. Our econometric results imply an associated decrease of $(0.51 \times \frac{1}{366} \times 100)$ percent in Beijing's ambient SO_2 concentration. Applying the Beijing dose-response result of Xu et al. (1994) to the new concentration, we obtain an estimated saving of 10.4 lives per year. Dividing both elements by 10 yields a useful round number for policy discussion: *one life saved per 100 tons abated annually.* This is actually a very conservative estimate of potential abatement benefits, since it ignores the likelihood that abating SO_2 has significantly lower lifesaving impact per ton than direct abatement of fine particulates (including, of course, those in the sulfates associated with SO_2 emissions).

How should lifesaving be valued for comparison with abatement costs? A useful benchmark is provided by the average wage of a worker in Beijing, which is approximately $800 (6,526 yuan) per year. A baseline estimate of the loss to society when one worker dies from respiratory disease is the present discounted value of the annual wage over a working lifetime. For Beijing, this is approximately $8,000 in present-value terms at a 10 percent discount rate.[17] We should stress that it is a very partial index of loss, for two main reasons. First, it takes no account of pain and suffering. Second, it focuses exclusively on mortality, although very large losses are also associated with working days lost to nonfatal respiratory disease. It is a tiny figure when compared with statistical life values commonly employed in the OECD countries.[18]

Abatement Costs

In China, we observe extreme variations in marginal abatement cost by pollutant, sector, size class, ownership, and degree of abatement. It clearly makes little sense to talk about abatement costs in a general way. For this illustrative case, we have estimated marginal abatement cost schedules for Beijing by combining our econometric MAC equation with current sectoral and ownership information

TABLE 12.2

Industrial SO₂ Abatement in Five Cities

	SO$_2$ Produced (tons)	SO$_2$ Emitted (tons)	Abatement (percent)
Shenyang	196,100	144,700	26.2
Shanghai	393,700	356,700	9.4
Chongqing	544,800	494,800	9.2
Guangzhou	165,100	151,500	8.2
Beijing	208,900	203,700	2.5

for that city. Large plants are a major source of air pollution in Beijing, so the MAC numbers for large facilities are particularly interesting. We begin with the more expensive option, SO_2 abatement. Our results show that the MAC curve for 100 tons of SO_2 abatement by large plants in Beijing varies from about $2,900 at 15 percent abatement to $27,000 at 85 percent.[19] The MAC curve for large plants crosses the $8,000 incremental benefit line at around 60 percent abatement; by implication, the MAC curve for non–SOE large plants would cross the incremental benefit line at a much higher abatement level. The MAC schedule for small facilities crosses the incremental benefit line at around 15 percent abatement.

For particulates, the numbers are much more attractive: MAC scarcely rises above $500 for 100 tons abated, even at 85 percent abatement for small plants. Costs are substantially less for large facilities. MAC estimates for our other four cities differ somewhat but have the same order of magnitude. A useful contrast is provided by SEPA's current estimates of actual abatement in the five cities, displayed in Table 12.2.

According to SEPA, Beijing's current abatement rate for industrial SO_2 is 2.5 percent. For a conservative cost-benefit assessment, we adopt the lowest rate of abatement—15 percent—that has been included in our exercise. At that rate, we estimate the incremental cost of 100 tons of SO_2 abatement to be $2,860. Taking this to be the incremental cost of saving a life, we use our estimated incremental lifesaving benefit ($8,000) to calculate a social rate of return to abatement of approximately 180 percent.

We should stress that this estimated rate of return, while clearly attractive, is extremely conservative as a guide to the lifesaving value of air pollution abatement in Beijing. For a large non-SOE plant, our econometric results imply a MAC of $332 for 100 tons of SO_2 abated when the abatement rate is 10 percent. The equivalent figure for 100 tons of particulates abated is around $120. If (as seems likely, given an overall abatement rate of 2.5 percent) there are large non-SOE plants in Beijing that are abating at less than 10 percent, then failure to enforce greater abatement is equivalent to valuing a Beijing worker's life at less than $500. Continued inaction means ignoring a public investment, the social rate of return of which is likely to be in excess of 3,000 percent! We believe that the opportunities for such high returns may be quite rare in China's urban health sector.

We conclude that it would make extremely good economic sense to tighten air pollution control in Beijing. Our abatement cost estimates show that it would also be sensible to focus on particulate emissions from large facilities.

Case 2: Zhengzhou

Our results for Beijing do not necessarily yield appropriate conclusions for other urban areas in China. First, our cost analysis reflects only microeconometric evidence on marginal abatement costs for end-of-pipe treatment. These almost certainly overstate overall MAC because process changes often provide the least-cost abatement opportunities for industrial facilities. Second, Beijing is not a representative Chinese city for environmental analysis. It is extremely large and considerably more polluted than the average large urban area in China.

Our second case is designed to address both of these problems. For the abatement cost analysis, we use our cross-provincial econometric results on pollution intensities because they incorporate all abatement options available to Chinese factories. Our focal city is Zhengzhou, the capital of Henan province, which we have chosen because its population, income, and air pollution level are representative for China's large cities.[20] Zhengzhou's industry pours approximately 45,000 tons of SO_2 into the atmosphere every year, contributing to an ambient SO_2 concentration of 90 $\mu g/m^3$. At this level of air pollution, Xu's dose-response function predicts that over 400 people are dying annually from SO_2-related pollution. Thousands more are undoubtedly suffering from serious respiratory illness.

Because Zhengzhou is a representative large city, we use it to develop an estimate of the optimum air pollution levy for urban China. The optimum levy should be set at the point where the incremental benefit of abatement is equal to its incremental cost. To identify this point, we simulate pollution control alternatives by reducing Zhengzhou's SO_2 emissions in 10 percent increments until 90 percent abatement is reached. We follow the method used for Beijing to estimate reductions in atmospheric SO_2 concentration and mortality from respiratory disease. We value mortality reductions at $8,000 per "statistical life," yielding the marginal benefit schedule in Figure 12.19.

To estimate the marginal cost schedule, we turn to our cross-provincial econometric results for the SO_2 intensity of industrial production. The levy response elasticity in this equation (which is always estimated with the appropriate sign and high statistical significance) registers the overall result when enterprise managers weigh incremental levy payments for pollution against the incremental cost of abatement. At the equilibrium level of pollution intensity, the effective levy rate should be just equal to the incremental cost of abatement for

FIGURE 12.19
Additional SO$_2$ Abatement in Zhengzhou: Marginal Benefits and Costs

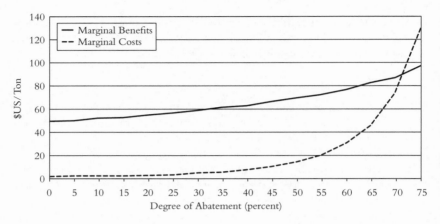

industry as a whole, whether the abatement is achieved by process change or by installation of end-of-pipe treatment. Solving the estimated SO$_2$ intensity equation "in reverse" for the effective levy rate (or, in equilibrium, the incremental cost of abatement), we obtain an expression for incremental abatement cost as a function of industrial SO$_2$ intensity. We have plotted this MAC schedule in Figure 12.19.

The Optimum Air Pollution Levy in Zhengzhou

Our results suggest that air pollution control in Zhengzhou should be far stricter. At the city's current atmospheric SO$_2$ concentration, abating a ton of SO$_2$ will save about 0.63 percent of a "statistical life," yielding a benefit of approximately $50. By contrast, we estimate the incremental cost of abating one ton at the current emissions level (represented by the zero point in Figure 12.19) to be approximately $1.70. Clearly, there is huge social "profit" to be made by abating more pollution. As the graph shows, additional abatement remains socially profitable at the margin until about 73 percent of current emissions are eliminated. The levy that will induce this reduction is about $90 per ton, at the intersection of the marginal benefit and cost curves. This is our estimate of the *optimum industrial air pollution levy* for Zhengzhou, since a lower levy would leave socially profitable abatement opportunities unexploited and a higher levy would impose an abatement cost higher than the social gain from further pollution reduction.

Implications for China

According to our results, the current levy in Zhengzhou makes sense only if China's policymakers value the life of an average urban resident at approximately

$270 ($1.70/0.00625). This figure seems tragically low when compared to the loss of a life, with the associated pain, suffering, and elimination of a lifetime's contribution to China's economic output. Even our suggested statistical life value of $8,000 is a very conservative number, which only takes account of economic output forgone. But to meet even this conservative standard, *our result suggests that the air pollution levy should be increased more than fiftyfold in Zhengzhou*—and by implication in the rest of urban China. The optimum rate—$90 per ton— is not exceptionally high by industrial economy standards (e.g., $130 per ton for tradable SO_2 permits in the United States in 1995, an emissions charge of $72 per ton in Poland in 1993 and $29 per ton in France in 1992). However, China is much poorer than any of these countries. The optimum levy for Zhengzhou (and by implication for the rest of urban China) is so high because current air pollution is so bad—arguably the worst in the world.

Revenue Implications

The purpose of the levy is to reduce pollution, but it generates public revenue as well. If Zhengzhou's environmental regulators increased the air pollution levy to $90 per ton, the city's annual revenue from air pollution charges would be approximately $1.1 million ($90 per ton × 12,500 tons after the 73 percent reduction). For all of China's large cities, scaling up the Zhengzhou result for a charge of $90 per ton yields a revenue estimate of approximately $250 million— a substantial sum, but only a small fraction of the levy's value as a lifesaving policy tool.

Keys to the Future

Our analysis suggests that well-designed policies can substantially improve China's urban environment and that the associated costs are well worth incurring. We can summarize the keys to effective policy in the following propositions:

- *Continued economic reform is necessary to preserve past environmental gains.* Our research has demonstrated the powerful impact of the reforms on the air and water pollution intensity of Chinese industry. Reform-induced changes in sectoral composition, ownership, and scale of production have been sufficient to compensate for much of the increase in scale of output during the reform period. Our projections show that continuation of the reforms can have similar mitigating effects in the coming decades. Rapid industrial growth without further changes in ownership and production scale would produce far greater pollution loads than those contemplated in this study.
- *Pollution levy reform would be a very cost-effective investment in public health.* In this chapter, we focus on the consequences of strengthening the pollution levy system. Our results suggest that a much higher air pollution levy would save lives very cost-effectively in urban China. However, we would also recom-

mend certain changes in the design of the levy system. Water pollution levies are assessed only on "above-standard" discharges, making emissions "free" for polluters until the standards are reached. The air pollution levy is assessed on the total volume of air pollutants, but it is not fully adjusted for individual pollutants according to relative risk. For both air and water emissions, it would be sensible to consider adoption of a complete charge system that would be targeted on specific pollutants and assessed on all units of pollution. Research on the water pollution levy (Dasgupta, Huq, Wheeler, and Zhang, 1996) has demonstrated that a revised system could be considerably more cost-effective.

- *Enforcement should be targeted on low-cost sources.* The cost analysis in this chapter shows why targeting is a good idea: large polluters are easier to monitor and have far lower unit abatement costs. The key to cost-effective reduction of industrial pollution in China's cities is targeted enforcement of higher abatement standards for large facilities.

- *Township and village industrial enterprises should be fully integrated into the regulatory system.* Our results show that stronger regulation has produced significant reduction of industrial pollution in China. However, many TVIEs remain outside the current sphere of regulation. Pollution from TVIEs is a "dark star" on China's horizon: It is growing rapidly, but information currently available is insufficient to judge the consequences. Inclusion of major TVIE pollution sources should be a priority for China's regulators during the coming decade.

- *Rapid development will promote stricter pollution control.* In the long run, this may be the most important factor of all. Recent research has shown that the strength of regulation in China's provinces is heavily affected by their levels of social and economic development. Poor communities with low education levels are far less able to promote their environmental interests than their more highly developed counterparts. Ultimately, China's environmental interests will be best served by rapid economic development, coupled with concerted efforts to inform and empower poorer communities. In this context, greater commitment to public environmental information should make a very valuable contribution.

Conclusions

China's industrial growth in the era of reform is a remarkable success story, but it has been clouded by serious pollution damage. Hundreds of thousands of people are suffering premature death or serious respiratory illness from exposure to industrial air pollution. Many of China's waterways are seriously contaminated by industrial discharges, rendering them largely unfit for direct human use. However, China's own experience during the past decade shows that this damage can be substantially reduced at modest cost. Much potential damage has been avoided already, through the impact of China's economic reform policies on industry and the specific effect of stricter regulation in some polluted areas. Together, these policies have lowered industry's pollution intensity sufficiently to reduce organic water pollution in many areas and to curb the growth of air pollution in the face of rapid industrial growth.

Despite this encouraging progress, a conservative assessment of the benefits and costs of further air pollution abatement suggests that much higher levels of particulate and SO_2 emissions control are warranted in China's polluted cities. For our analysis, we developed three scenarios that projected pollution damage under varying assumptions about future policies. Even if regulation is not tightened further, we find that continued economic reform should have a powerful effect on pollution intensity. Organic water pollution will stabilize in many areas and actually decline in some. Air pollution will continue growing in most areas, but at a much slower pace than industrial output.

However, our projections also highlight the unnecessarily high cost of regulatory inaction. If economic reform is not supplemented by tighter regulation, most of China's waterways will remain heavily polluted and many thousands of people will die or suffer serious respiratory damage from air pollution. Continuing recent movement toward tighter regulation for water pollution will result in sharp improvements; adopting an economically feasible policy of much stricter regulation will restore the health of many waterways. In the case of air pollution, the stakes are even higher because regulatory enforcement has apparently weakened in many areas in recent years. Reversal of this trend will save many lives at extremely modest cost. Adoption of SEPA's recommendation for a tenfold increase in the air pollution levy would produce a major turnaround in most cities, and our results suggest that even SEPA's recommendation is very conservative. For a representative Chinese city, Zhengzhou, we find that a fiftyfold increase in the levy appears warranted from an economic perspective.

Finally, our microeconomic analysis of abatement alternatives has highlighted the cost-effectiveness of a pollution control policy targeted on large sources of particulate and SO_2 emissions. Abatement of particulates from large non-SOE plants is so cheap that even an extremely conservative economic analysis affirms the benefits of very high abatement levels. Our analysis suggests that high social rates of return can be obtained from regulation that induces at least 70 percent abatement of SO_2 and even greater abatement of particulates from large urban industrial facilities. At present, lax regulation of such facilities is causing so much health damage that reform seems imperative. Inaction amounts to valuing a Chinese worker's life at less than U.S.$500, a tragically low figure by any standard.

In this chapter, we have focused on China's industrial pollution problems. Our analysis suggests that stricter pollution regulation would yield a high social rate of return. We recognize, however, that other environmental problems may warrant high priority as well. Topics that might particularly benefit from detailed analytical work include natural resource degradation, agricultural pollution, and solid waste generation. As in the case of industrial pollution, future policy research will benefit substantially from China's impressive investment in environmental, social, and economic data.

Notes

1. It is important to note that this does not include many township and village industrial enterprises (TVIEs), which are often highly polluting and account for a major share of China's industrial production.

2. These estimates are based on the dose-response relation established for atmospheric SO_2 in Beijing and Shenyang by Xu et. al. (1994). This relation is combined with monitoring data on SO_2 concentrations to produce estimated individual probabilities of premature mortality by city. City-specific probabilities are multiplied by current population estimates to produce estimated annual deaths.

3. Again, it is important to point out that TVIEs are not included in the analyses.

4. Detailed econometric results are presented in Dasgupta, Wang, and Wheeler (1997).

5. For a detailed presentation of the econometric work discussed in this chapter, see Dasgupta, Wang, and Wheeler (1997).

6. The results for smoke and dust intensity, the two components of TSP intensity, are similar to those for SO_2.

7. These sectors are identified by multivariate analysis, in which exceptionally "clean" or "dirty" sectors are those that depart significantly from average pollution intensities after accounting for the effects of the levy, scale, and ownership.

8. These results are representative of changes in China as a whole. See Wang and Wheeler (1996) for an analysis of changes in industrial water pollution across all of China's provinces.

9. Huq, Martin, and Wheeler (1993) have found that more open developing economies absorb clean technologies in metals and paper production much more rapidly than their less open counterparts.

10. See Hettige et al. (1995) and Mani and Wheeler (1998) for detailed information on pollution intensities by sector.

11. It is less clear that overall loads from industry have fallen, because much production in rapidly growing TVIEs is apparently not covered by the traditional regulatory system. The evidence for TVIEs is extremely scanty, and research on the environmental performance of TVIEs is clearly a top priority for future work.

12. SEPA has recommended a tenfold increase in the air pollution levy rate, which would be in the same range as our 10 percent annual increase scenario.

13. We assume that growth rates of pollution loads for the five cities are the same as the projected rates for their provinces. For Beijing and Shanghai, this is a tautology. The assumption seems quite reasonable in the other cases, since the three cities are the primary industrial regions of their respective provinces.

14. As previously noted, the "pollution-intensive" sectors in this analysis are the sectors with large "dirty" or "clean" residual effects after size, ownership, and provincial pollution levies are accounted for.

15. Since the calculations were made, Chongqing has also achieved provincial status independent of Sichuan.

16. Note that 30 $\mu g/m^3$ is the tightest SO_2 standard in the world, maintained in Canada, Switzerland, and Poland. By contrast, the World Health Organization standard is 60, China's standard is 50, and the U.S. standard is 80.

17. This estimate implicitly assumes that the actual discount rate in China is higher and that the increment is equal to the expected growth rate in real wages for a currently employed worker.

18. For comparison, it is not uncommon to see public policy decisions in the United States reflect "statistical life" values of several million dollars.

19. We should note that this MAC curve is an average that reflects the distribution of production between SOE and non-SOE plants in Beijing. As we have seen, the MAC schedule for non-SOE plants is always far lower than the SOE schedule. A targeted regulatory strategy could, of course, exploit this difference to capture the largest returns from stricter enforcement for the least-cost plants.

20. Zhengzhou's 1993 population was 1.8 million; its average industrial wage was 3,350 yuan per year.

References

Afsah, Shakeb, Benoit Laplante, and David Wheeler. *Controlling Industrial Pollution: A New Paradigm.* Policy Research Department Working Paper, November 1996. Washington, D.C.: World Bank.

Dasgupta, Susmita, Mainul Huq, and David Wheeler. *Bending the Rules: Determinants of Discretionary Pollution Control in China.* Policy Research Department Working Paper, January 1997. Washington, D.C.: World Bank.

Dasgupta, Susmita, Mainul Huq, David Wheeler, and C. H. Zhang. *Water Pollution Abatement by Chinese Industry: Cost Estimates and Policy Implications.* Policy Research Department Working Paper, August 1996. Washington, D.C.: World Bank.

Dasgupta, Susmita, Hua Wang, and David Wheeler. *Surviving Success: Policy Reform and the Future of Industrial Pollution in China.* Development Research Group Working Paper, November 1997. Washington, D.C.: World Bank.

Dasgupta, Susmita, and David Wheeler. *Citizen Complaints as Environmental Indicators: Evidence from China.* Policy Research Department Working Paper, December 1996. Washington, D.C.: World Bank.

Hartman, Raymond, Mainul Huq, and David Wheeler. *Why Paper Mills Clean Up: Survey Evidence from Four Asian Countries.* Policy Research Department Working Paper, December 1997. Washington, D.C.: World Bank.

Hettige, Mala, Mainul Huq, Sheoli Pargal, and David Wheeler. "Determinants of Pollution Abatement in Developing Countries: Evidence from South and Southeast Asia." *World Development*, December 1996, 24(12), 1891–1904.

Hettige, Mala, Paul Martin, Manjula Singh, and David Wheeler. *IPPS: The Industrial Pollution Projection System.* Policy Research Department Working Paper, February 1995. Washington, D.C.: World Bank.

Huq, Mainul, Paul Martin, and David Wheeler. "Process Change, Economic Policy, and Industrial Pollution: Cross-Country Evidence from the Wood Pulp and Steel Industries." Paper presented at the annual meetings of the American Economic Association, Anaheim, Calif., January 1993.

Lucas, Robert. *Environmental Regulation and the Location of Polluting Industry in China.* Policy Research Department, 1996. Washington, D.C.: World Bank. Mimeographed.

Mani, Muthukumara, and David Wheeler. "In Search of Pollution Havens? Dirty Industry in the World Economy, 1960–1995." *Journal of Environment and Development,* September 1998, 7(3), 215–47.

Pargal, Sheoli, and David Wheeler. "Informal Regulation of Industrial Pollution in Developing Countries: Evidence from Indonesia." *Journal of Political Economy,* December 1996, 6, 1314–27.

U.S. Environmental Protection Agency. *Latest Findings on National Air Quality: 1999 Status and Trends.* EPA Document No. EPA-454/F-00-002, August 2000. Washington, D.C.: U.S. Environmental Protection Agency.

Wang, Hua, and David Wheeler. *Pricing Industrial Pollution in China: An Econometric Analysis of the Levy System.* Policy Research Department Working Paper, September 1996. Washington, D.C.: World Bank.

Xu, Xiping, Jun Gao, Douglas W. Dockery, and Yude Chen. "Air Pollution and Daily Mortality in Residential Areas of Beijing, China." *Archives of Environmental Health,* July-August 1994, 49(4), 216–22.

13

The Political Economy of China's
Rural–Urban Divide

Dennis Tao Yang and Cai Fang

Governments in most developing countries have adopted policies that discriminate against agriculture. Interventions take a variety of forms, including the pricing and distribution of agricultural commodities and inputs, and fiscal and credit policies that favor the industrial sector. Governments also use indirect instruments, such as trade regimes and exchange rate policies, that often amplify the discriminatory impacts against the countryside. The results of a large body of research indicate that these interventions introduce distortions in the economic systems, cause large income transfers away from the rural sector, and ultimately lead to slower agricultural and overall economic growth.[1]

Although urban bias is virtually universal in the process of economic development, there are primarily two competing analytical paradigms for explaining policy formation. One theory, associated primarily with the work of Michael Lipton (1977) and Robert Bates (1981), finds answers in the political structure of those countries, arguing that agriculture is disfavored in development because urban groups are politically powerful.[2] The second theory emphasizes the development strategy of the modernizing elites who, as evidence shows, believe that industry is the catalyst for rapid growth and that taxing agriculture provides the much needed financial support for industrialization.[3] Despite the clarity of views at the conceptual level, empirical assessment of these two hypotheses is difficult because of an identification problem. The coexistence of political activities of urban groups and the belief of the modernizing elites in industrialization complicates the measurement of the two causes, making it hard to separate the individual effects of the causes on policy formation. As a consequence, the explanatory power of the two hypotheses remains largely untested.

This chapter has two main purposes. First, we document the extent of China's rural-urban inequality for periods both before and after the initiation of reforms, and we investigate the institutions and policies that have been responsible for the disparity. Second, through a case study on China, we assess the relevance of the two existing explanations for the formation of urban bias. China's experience is unique because the period under consideration spans two episodes of distinct economic and political circumstances. During the centrally planned period before 1978, China had tight economic and political controls in a hierarchical system in which pressure groups and voter voices were largely absent, contrasting with norms found in many other developing countries. In the postreform era, China has corrected the heavy-industry-oriented development strategy and relaxed political controls, creating an environment that is responsive to the pressures of interest groups. These regime changes provide special opportunities for isolating the influence of industrial development strategy on policy formation in the first period and for examining the impact of political pressures on government behavior in the second. The findings from this social experiment will provide insights into the determinants of urban bias for China in particular as well as general implications for the political economy of policy formation.

We shall first estimate the extent of China's urban bias by examining the differences in per capita income and consumption expenditures between the rural and urban sectors. Data indicate that during the centrally planned period, the gap was large but stable. Since the reforms, the inequality has exhibited a cyclical pattern of declines in the initial years followed by a period of increases and then by renewed declines. For the entire period, China's disparity has been larger than the disparity in most other countries. We then analyze policy measures and institutions that have been responsible for the high level of disparity as well as its changes over time. We find that some policy instruments are unique to China, including direct restrictions on labor mobility and large-scale income transfers to the state-owned enterprises (SOEs). The government has increasingly used direct transfers to protect the income of urban dwellers since the inception of economic reforms.

Next, we investigate economic and political factors that have influenced the making of urban-biased policies. We find that the sharp sectoral divide in the planning episode was a result of industrial development strategy, but since the reforms, the politically powerful urban population has pressured the government for fast income growth through various transfer programs. The central government has continued an urban bias to preserve regime stability and political legitimacy. Our analysis indicates that while the urban coalition may pressure the state for favors, political activities are not a necessary condition for the existence of urban bias. The pursuit of industrial development strategy alone can result in a rural–urban divide. Finally, we discuss the feasibility of policy reforms. We suggest that improvements in factor markets are strategically important for bridging China's rural–urban gulf, which will enable China to tap its potential for sustained economic growth.

The Rural-Urban Gap

The impact of discriminatory policies on the welfare of rural and urban dwellers can be assessed in several ways. One approach is to examine closely each of the specific policy interventions, quantify various policy measures, and estimate their direct impact on income transfers across the groups of agents in the two sectors. The total effects of the policies can be aggregated from the individual programs. This is the primary approach taken by the series of World Bank studies that assessed the effects of agricultural pricing policies. More specifically, for instance, to examine the distributional consequences of a particular program, such as a price ceiling for an agricultural commodity, one could first estimate the demand and supply schedules for this commodity and then proceed to assess the welfare consequences to producer and consumer groups. If the program under consideration is related to an exportable or importable product, the difference in the domestic and the world market price would serve as a measure of the extent of the distortion.[4] Although these methods are appropriate tools for assessing agricultural pricing programs, it is difficult to apply them to China for several reasons. First, for a long period, China did not have well-functioning agricultural commodity markets, which rendered the estimation of demand and supply schedules virtually impossible. Second, many governmental interventions went beyond the standard measures in agricultural pricing so that the usual tools of welfare analysis are not directly applicable. Finally, because China's institutions and policies have changed dramatically over time, it would be difficult, if not impossible, to trace all the specific policies and to aggregate their effects.

In what follows, we use an alternative approach that focuses on the outcomes of the discriminatory policies by examining the disparities in per capita consumption and incomes across urban and rural regions. This approach rests on a simple premise: despite the complexity in measures of intervention and complicated channels of policy effects, sector-biased policies would eventually lead to differences in consumption expenditures and incomes across the sectors, which are directly observable and easily measurable. Therefore, if the consumption and earnings for comparable labor differ greatly between urban and rural areas, that would indicate the severity of the effects of policies and institutions on sectoral segmentation.

However, we should be cautious in making rural-urban comparisons in consumption and incomes. First, labor quality, including schooling, training, and experience, has to be adjusted when considering earnings in rural and urban areas. Second, the comparison should be made in real, not monetary, terms. Third, any differences in the cost of living between urban and rural areas should be taken into account. Furthermore, the comparison should also reflect differences in the provision of subsidized public services, such as health care and housing, across

the sectors. At the empirical level, it is difficult to adjust for all these factors because usually some information is unavailable. Here we will first compare rural-
urban per capita consumption expenditures. Then we will use information from
the State Statistical Bureau (SSB) to examine intersectoral income differences
and compare them with the trends in consumption expenditures. We will make
attempts to adjust for the values of social welfare provision in urban regions and
the differential inflation rates across rural and urban areas. Unfortunately, we
were unable to adjust for differences in labor quality and the cost of living due
to a lack of information. However, our analyses will cover an extended period
so that if the intersectoral differences in the two sets of factors stayed stable over
time, there would be only a time-invariant, fixed-effect bias. Consequently, our
assessment on the *changes* in the rural-urban divide would not suffer from the
two potential biases.

Table 13.1 presents per capita consumption expenditures and their ratios for
rural and urban residents between 1952 and 1997. The consumption figures are
in nominal prices, taken from various volumes of the *Statistical Yearbook of China*
(State Statistical Bureau, 1990–98b) corresponding to the national average, separate statistics for rural and urban levels, and the ratio of expenditures for the
two sectors. However, because the two regions can have varying consumer price
indices over time, one should deflate sector-specific consumption levels by the
corresponding price deflator. The real ratio column reports the consumption
ratios in real terms since 1978, reflecting the fact that the SSB started collecting
sector-specific price indices in that year. Therefore, the best series of consumption ratios that are available to us are the nominal ratios for the period 1952–77,
continued with the ratios in real terms for the period 1978–97. Given the fact
that the government set and rarely changed the prices for a large bundle of commodities during the centrally planned period, consumer prices were stable before 1978. Therefore, the nominal consumption ratios for that period should not
deviate much from the ratio in real terms.[5] This series on rural-urban consumption ratios reveals long-term patterns of change. Inequality between rural and urban regions was high but stable during the centrally planned regime. However,
since the reforms, the level of disparity has exhibited marked cyclical changes:
the declines in initial years were followed by a period of increases and then by
recurring declines. Throughout the period, the per capita consumption in urban areas has been about two to three times higher than the level in rural areas.

More specifically, the data suggest four distinct periods: (1) 1952–77, the
centrally planned period, in which the consumption ratio fluctuated within a
narrow range around 2.5, except for the two years during the Great Leap famine (1959–60), when the ratio reached 3.2; (2) 1978–85, the initial period
of economic reforms, in which the ratio dropped from 2.9 to 1.9, its lowest
point; (3) 1986–93, a period in which the ratio slowly climbed to 2.7, almost

TABLE 13.1

Per Capita Consumption of Rural and Urban Residents 1952–97

(nominal yuan per year)

Year	Consumption			Rural to Urban Ratio	
	National Average	Rural Residents	Urban Residents	Ratio (Nominal)	Ratio (Real)
1952	76	62	149	2.4	—
1953	87	69	181	2.6	—
1954	89	70	183	2.6	—
1955	94	76	188	2.5	—
1956	99	78	197	2.5	—
1957	102	79	205	2.6	—
1958	105	83	195	2.4	—
1959	96	65	206	3.2	—
1960	102	68	214	3.2	—
1961	114	82	225	2.8	—
1962	117	88	226	2.6	—
1963	116	89	222	2.5	—
1964	120	95	234	2.5	—
1965	125	100	237	2.4	—
1966	132	106	244	2.3	—
1967	136	110	251	2.3	—
1968	132	106	250	2.4	—
1969	134	108	255	2.4	—
1970	140	114	260	2.3	—
1971	142	116	267	2.3	—
1972	147	116	295	2.6	—
1973	155	123	306	2.5	—
1974	155	123	313	2.6	—
1975	158	124	324	2.6	—
1976	161	125	340	2.7	—
1977	165	124	360	2.9	—
1978	175	132	383	2.9	2.9
1979	197	152	406	2.7	2.6
1980	227	173	468	2.7	2.5
1981	249	194	487	2.5	2.3
1982	267	212	500	2.4	2.1
1983	289	234	531	2.3	2.0
1984	329	266	599	2.3	2.0
1986	451	353	850	2.4	2.0
1987	513	393	997	2.5	2.0
1988	643	480	1,288	2.7	2.1
1989	700	518	1,404	2.7	2.2
1990	803	571	1,686	3.0	2.4
1991	896	621	1,925	3.1	2.5
1992	1,070	718	2,356	3.3	2.5
1993	1,331	855	3,027	3.5	2.7
1995	2,311	1,479	5,044	3.4	2.6
1996	2,677	1,756	5,620	3.2	2.4
1997	2,936	1,930	6,048	3.1	2.3

NOTE: There are minor inconsistencies in the consumption values reported in different volumes of the *State Statistical Yearbook*. Moreover, the format of reporting differs across the years.
SOURCES: State Statistical Bureau (1990–98b).

as high as at the start of the reforms; and (4) 1994–97, marked again by consistent declines. These results represent more accurate and extended consumption patterns than those documented by Yang and Zhou (1999), who analyzed the ratios in nominal terms, and their last year of coverage was 1992. In doing so, they indicated a V-shaped change for 1978–92, which contrasts with the cycles just documented that have reduced amplitudes, a result of expressing the ratios in real terms.

Although relative consumption expenditure is indicative of the comparative welfare between rural and urban dwellers, it does not reflect real purchasing power because savings are omitted. For this reason, incomes are usually better indicators of rural-urban disparity. To calculate household incomes in China, one must be aware of the institutions that determine the sources of earnings. In cities, wages represent only a fraction of total income, which also includes welfare provisions such as housing, health services, in-kind transfers, and various price subsidies. But the *Urban Household Survey* does not contain many of these nonwage earnings. In contrast, earnings in the *Rural Household Survey* are more inclusive. They contain labor market incomes from agricultural and nonagricultural sources, value added from self-employed activities, transfer incomes including remittances, and asset earnings. Because of those differences in earning sources and survey coverage, the sectoral incomes inferred from the household surveys are not readily comparable. Researchers at the SSB (Zhang et al., 1994) made an effort to construct comparable incomes for rural and urban households. Supplementing the household surveys with information on urban nonwage earnings, their study was capable of dealing with the institutional ambiguities that affect the estimation of full incomes.

Based on the methods suggested by Zhang and his collaborators, Table 13.2 presents total per capita disposable income and its components for urban residents between 1978 and 1997.[6] We divide total income into two broad categories, wages and nonwage earnings, where the latter consists of housing subsidies, various welfare and health care services, and in-kind compensation. Although nonwage incomes are not recorded in the *Urban Household Surveys*, aggregate measures are available at city levels (Ministry of Labor, 1990–98). We use aggregate information for computing per-worker allocations of nonwage compensation to obtain estimates for the "hidden earnings." The figures in Table 13.2 show that nonwage earnings accounted for a large share of urban disposable income (about 24 percent in 1978), and despite a steady decline, they still accounted for about 15 percent of total income in 1997. These nonwage benefits were provided by specific institutions to their employees with urban registration and therefore were unavailable to rural migrants working temporarily in cities. Later we will discuss these urban welfare provisions as barriers to permanent rural-to-urban migration.

Table 13.3 reports urban and rural per capita total incomes and their ratios de-

TABLE 13.2

Total Per Capita Disposable Income and Its Components for Urban Residents

(nominal yuan per year)

Year	Wage Income	Welfare, Medical Subsidies	Housing Subsidies	In-Kind Subsidies (5 percent wage income)	Total Income
1978	343	31	63	17	454
1979	412	35	65	21	532
1980	478	39	73	24	613
1981	498	40	73	25	636
1982	538	44	73	27	682
1983	572	49	74	29	723
1984	661	55	78	33	827
1985	739	64	89	37	929
1986	900	82	99	45	1,125
1987	1,002	94	104	50	1,251
1988	1,181	123	113	59	1,477
1989	1,376	141	120	69	1,705
1990	1,510	167	145	76	1,898
1991	1,701	192	159	85	2,137
1992	2,027	211	167	101	2,505
1993	2,577	252	197	129	3,155
1994	3,496	243	253	175	4,166
1995	4,283	274	292	214	5,064
1996	4,839	297	312	242	5,690
1997	5,160	308	306	258	6,032

SOURCES: State Statistical Bureau (1988–98); Ministry of Labor (1990–98).

flated by sector-specific price indices. While urban income has been adjusted for nonwage components, rural income is full earnings based on the original *Rural Household Surveys*. Our coverage starts with 1978 because it was the first year when the SSB reported income by sector. Those figures on the ratio of urban to rural earnings confirm the cyclical patterns found earlier for relative consumption expenditures in the postreform era: the rural-urban gap first declined in the initial years of reforms, reaching the lowest level of 1.93 in 1985, but then increased steadily to 2.6 in 1993, after which followed another period of decline.

To summarize the findings on rural-urban gaps in consumption and incomes and to visualize their changes over time, we have plotted the series for consumption and income ratios in Figure 13.1. Several noticeable features emerge immediately. One is that estimating these ratios based on real prices has a smoothing effect on the trend that is exhibited by nominal ratios. Another is that the real sectoral disparities displayed in terms of consumption and incomes share remarkably similar patterns for the period after 1978. Moreover, the broad picture indicates that marked cyclical movements in the postreform era have replaced a high yet steady level of disparity in the prereform period.

TABLE 13.3

Real Per Capita Total Income for Rural and Urban Residents

(nominal yuan per year)

Year	Urban Per Capita Income	Rural Per Capita Income	Ratio of Urban to Rural Income
1978	454	134	3.4
1979	523	160	3.3
1980	560	190	3.0
1981	567	219	2.6
1982	597	261	2.3
1983	620	296	2.1
1984	690	330	2.1
1985	692	358	1.9
1986	784	360	2.2
1987	801	369	2.2
1988	783	370	2.1
1989	778	343	2.3
1990	855	374	2.3
1991	916	378	2.4
1992	989	399	2.5
1993	1,073	413	2.6
1994	1,133	443	2.6
1995	1,179	487	2.4
1996	1,217	551	2.2
1997	1,252	584	2.1

SOURCES: State Statistical Bureau (1988–98).

FIGURE 13.1

Ratio of Urban to Rural Consumption and Income

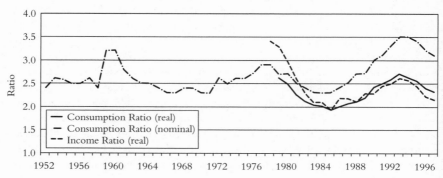

As noted earlier, large disparities in consumption and income between rural and urban regions are the results of government policies that discriminate against agriculture. Consequently, the magnitude of China's inequality relative to other countries may indicate the relative extent of discrimination in China. Table 13.4 presents the ratio of nonagricultural to agricultural incomes for a standard worker

TABLE 13.4

The Ratio of Nonagricultural Income to Agricultural Income:
An International Comparison

(U.S. dollars)

Country	Income per Capita (1995)	Ratio 1985	Ratio 1990	Ratio 1995
Switzerland	36,320	1.25	1.25	1.26
Denmark	26,390	1.50	1.59	—
Netherlands	20,850	1.16	1.12	1.11
Canada	20,290	0.76	0.77	—
U.K.	18,150	1.15	1.14	1.16
Australia	17,790	1.46	1.50	—
Singapore	17,440	—	2.08	—
Israel	13,720	1.69	1.66	1.85
Cyprus	10,300	1.31	1.34	1.29
Bahrain	8,130	—	1.69	1.72
Seychelles	6,020	1.46	1.22	1.19
Belarus	3,210	1.11	1.06	1.34
Hungary	3,170	1.23	1.40	1.66
Botswana	2,980	4.08	3.09	3.02
Mauritius	2,860	0.92	1.08	1.09
Turkey	2,850	—	0.99	1.39
Russia	2,750	1.05	1.01	—
Ukraine	2,430	1.09	—	—
Fiji	2,090	1.44	1.22	—
Slovakia	2,070	0.99	0.97	—
Costa Rica	2,020	1.75	1.83	1.59
Poland	1,940	1.01	1.09	1.19
Kazakhstan	1,740	0.96	0.91	1.01
Lithuania	1,730	1.01	1.03	1.30
Paraguay	1,390	2.04	2.68	2.01
Bulgaria	1,360	1.16	0.88	2.01
Peru	1,350	—	—	—
Moldova	1,350	1.09	0.99	1.03
Swaziland	1,190	0.82	—	—
Romania	1,190	1.04	0.94	1.22
Egypt	660	1.28	1.62	1.56
Sri Lanka	550	1.73	1.55	1.51
Ghana	450	1.32	1.43	—
Kenya	330	3.18	2.86	—
Burundi	210	1.76	—	—
Malawi	190	3.76	4.33	—

SOURCES: World Bank (1995); International Labor Office (1995).

for thirty-six countries. The ratios for the majority of the countries are below 1.5, contrasting sharply with the range for China, which generally fluctuates between 2 and 3. More specifically, in 1985, there were only four countries for which average urban earnings were more than twice average rural earnings. There were five countries in 1990 and three in 1995 that had ratios of 2 or more. Although caution is required in making cross-country comparisons, these figures suggest that China's rural-urban gap has been very large indeed.[7]

Determinants of the Disparities

If governments do not intervene in output and factor markets across rural and urban regions, the allocation of capital and labor would tend to adjust to equalize wages and capital returns in a spatial equilibrium context. Large sectoral differentials in earnings for comparable labor generally imply the existence of interventions by governments and are indicators of misallocation of labor. Government interventions can take a variety of forms: they can be located in the output market, as in the case of suppression of agricultural prices and imposition of export taxes; they can reflect regulations in the factor markets, such as credit allocations or restrictions on labor mobility; and they can take the form of direct transfers across urban and rural groups. Moreover, the choice of these policy instruments is often influenced by the general economic policies of the government. Consequently, major changes in policies over time, such as a revision of the development strategy or implementations of certain economic reforms, are often associated with changes in the policy instruments that influence the rural-urban disparity.

We will now analyze the policies and institutions employed by the Chinese government in each of the four periods specified earlier. We will attempt to identify the major economic plans of the government in each of the periods and determine how they translated into the corresponding policy measures and institutions that directly affected the rural-urban gap. Thus we will try to offer consistent explanations for the observed patterns of disparity and their changes over time.

Period One (1952–1978): Episode of Central Planning

During this period, the central government formed and pursued the development strategy that promoted heavy industries, which became the root of China's rural-urban divide.[8] This strategy aimed at achieving rapid industrialization by extracting agricultural surplus for capital accumulation in industries and for supporting urban-based subsidies. The main enforcement mechanisms were a trinity of institutions: the unified procurement and unified sale of agricultural commodities, the people's communes, and the household registration system. This strategy resulted in massive distortions in the factor market with an excessive concentration of capital in urban areas and of labor in rural areas.[9]

Prior to the reforms in 1978, urban workers' productivity and earnings far exceeded those of their rural counterparts. Shortly after the founding of the People's Republic, the state acquired agricultural products at prices lower than those in the commodity markets. When the purchases became increasingly difficult in 1953, the state initiated the unified purchase and sale system, which was completed in 1958. Under this system, the government monopolized the whole process of production and procurement of agricultural commodities in rural areas and at the same time controlled the distribution of food and other agricultural products through rationing in the cities. Because this system lowered the cost of living in urban regions, the government had to implement corresponding policies to control intersectoral labor movements.

At that time, the people's communes were already established, and they became effective institutions for carrying out the government's economic as well as administrative plans. Because the control of labor flows was a key link for implementing the development strategy, a formal household registration system was established in the late 1950s that in effect designated the legal place of residency and work for the entire population. A rural registration status would restrict a family and its future generations to living in the countryside. This package of policies and institutions enabled the state effectively to suppress agricultural prices and to tightly control the mobility of productive factors, especially labor. The results were highly distorted output and input markets that favored urban dwellers. As Table 13.1 illustrates, the urban-rural consumption ratios stayed at a high level between 2.3 to 2.9 for the entire period except for the two years during the Great Leap Forward famine. These ratios indicate a stable level of urban bias that resulted from the set of government interventions associated with the development strategy.

It is instructive to take a closer look at the two crisis years of the Great Leap Forward during which the level of urban bias jumped to 3.2. In 1959, China's total grain output suddenly dropped by 15 percent and, in the following two years, food supplies reached only about 70 percent of the 1958 level. During this period, massive hunger and starvation prevailed in China, resulting in twenty to thirty million excess deaths, mostly in rural regions. This disaster is one of the worst catastrophes in human history. According to Lin and Yang (2000), a primary cause of the tragic deaths was the food entitlement originating from policies biased in favor of urban residents, who were given the legal right to food through the rationing system. The peasants, as food producers, were burdened with coercive quotas and were entitled only to the residual food. Therefore, when the nation experienced dramatic food shortages, the peasants were more likely to suffer from the famine. This tragic event is captured by the consumption data in Table 13.1 that indicate the extent to which urban bias increased during the course of adversity.

Period Two (1979–1985): Initial Years of Reforms

The foregoing discussions suggest that the trinity of urban-biased institutions introduced distortions in the Chinese economic system. Therefore, along with reforms that began removing certain elements of the inefficient system, we would expect a decline in the rural-urban gap. That is what happened in this period.

Broad changes in rural policy began at the end of 1978. The first reform was the introduction of the Household Responsibility System (HRS), under which farm household members became the residual claimants of their marginal effort, thus solving the long-standing incentive problems associated with the egalitarian compensation rules created in the commune system. The remarkable success of the HRS led to such sweeping institutional changes that by the end of 1983, virtually all farmers operated as individual cultivators and entrepreneurs. In 1984, the people's commune system was officially abolished and replaced with local county and township governments.

Parallel with the introduction of the HRS, the government also engaged in profound price reforms. Effective in 1979, the state dramatically increased the weighted average agricultural procurement prices by 22.1 percent, which immediately induced the farmers to use more inputs and to supply more agricultural output. Since then, price reforms have continued, narrowing the gap between the procurement and market prices.

The third element of the market-oriented reforms was to enhance the role of the markets in guiding household decisions. One aspect was the liberalization of trade in commodities that was previously monopolized by the government. A system of dual-track pricing replaced price setting. Factor markets also emerged during this period, where some limited mobility of labor and capital began both within and outside the rural sector. Particular forms of mobility included long-distance transportation and trade in farm products by farmers, flows of capital and labor from agricultural to nonagricultural activities within rural regions, and mobility of labor from rural areas to small towns and even to cities. The renewed role of the households as independent decision makers made all these market developments possible.

This package of market-oriented reforms generated remarkable growth in farm household earnings. Rural real per capita income nearly tripled in eight years, rising from 133.6 yuan in 1978 to 357.9 yuan in 1985 (see Table 13.3), due primarily to the adoption of the HRS and increases in agricultural prices (see McMillan, Whalley, and Zhu, 1989, and Lin, 1992). Although further reforms continued to raise farm household earnings in later periods, the income effects were the most dramatic in these initial years.

In contrast, the pace of urban reforms in this period was slower than that of rural reforms. The initial urban reforms also started in the late 1970s, when state-owned enterprises reintroduced work bonuses and the government experimented with various ways to delegate autonomy to enterprises. Reforms in the financial relationships between the state and enterprises also proceeded gradually through the experiments of replacing the old system of profit submissions with the retention of partial profits by enterprises. This was followed by experiments of profit contracting and taxation on profits. But these various urban reforms had much less immediate impact on enterprise profitability. Consequently, the sequencing of rural versus urban reforms resulted in sharp declines in the urban-rural disparity. The real urban-rural ratios of income and consumption fell from 3.4 and 2.9, respectively, in 1978 to 1.9 in 1985, both reaching their lowest levels for the entire two decades.

Period Three (1986–1993): Urban Reforms and Redistribution

After having accomplished remarkable success in rural reforms, the central government announced a series of plans in 1984 and 1985 that aimed to speed up the urban economic reforms. As a result, the growth in urban incomes quickened. During this period, reforms in the urban sector were concentrated in three areas: the broadening of various SOE reforms, the introduction of redistributive programs associated with the allocation of investment credits, and the unfolding of regional development policies that gave priorities to coastal regions. All these reform measures tended to raise urban incomes relative to the rural sector.

Reforms in the financial relationships between the state and its enterprises continued, including the forms of "delegating autonomy and profit retentions" that embodied various practices, including "replacing tax for profit" and "replacing bank loan for direct investments" (*bo gai dai*), and the contract responsibility system. These reforms provided incentives to both managers and workers (e.g., Grove et al., 1995), and allowed enterprises to retain growing shares of profits, making it possible both to increase wages and to create more incentives to raise wages.

Although SOEs generally improved their performance because of better incentives and competitive pressure from nonstate firms (e.g., Jefferson, Rawski, and Zheng, 1996), large monetary transfers from the state to the SOEs occurred during this period of reforms. Enterprises performing well managed to retain higher shares of profits through negotiations with the government industrial bureaus, and SOEs performing poorly continued to survive on government subsidies and bank loans, which they used to cover losses and to pay wages to redundant workers. Despite the start of banking reforms in the mid-1980s, the state banks were still required to provide loans to SOEs through the administrative credit plans (Brandt and Zhu, 2000). At the same time, because inflation became rampant in the late 1980s and early 1990s, the state also allocated large direct inflation subsidies to all urban workers through the central budget. These various programs protected the standard of living for city dwellers. Figure 13.2 shows that the SOEs' wage growth relative to their output growth continued to increase throughout the reform period, indicating that the government made large income transfers to the state sector.[10]

In the same period, China's regional development policies also tilted toward favoring the eastern coastal regions, where more than 70 percent of China's urban population resided. Starting in the mid-1980s, the central government formulated development strategies and implemented policies that explicitly favored the eastern regions, moving the center of gravity of economic reforms and de-

FIGURE 13.2

Changes in Relative Agricultural Price and Relative SOE Wage Growth

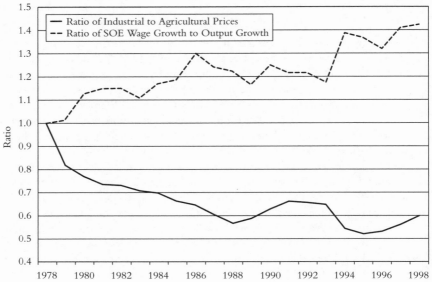

velopment eastward.[11] First, the government opened four coastal cities as special economic zones and followed by opening fourteen more cities in the coastal areas. In the late 1980s, the government gradually extended these special policies to all coastal areas but focused on coastal cities. This policy orientation is known as the "coastal area development strategy." In the meantime, township and village enterprises (TVEs) in the coastal regions started making remarkable progress and becoming a driving force in China's economy. Favorable policies for the coastal regions contributed to a divergence of economic growth and income growth between regions. This widening regional gap increased the rural–urban disparity because of the heavy concentration of urban populations in the eastern, coastal regions.

Not all the changes in this period moved against the farmers' welfare. Rural labor mobility continued to rise over the period. Because of a slowing down in TVEs' ability to absorb rural labor, more rural workers moved to cities to seek temporary jobs. However, there still existed various institutional constraints, such as the household registration system and related employment regulations, which reduced labor mobility and strongly constrained population migration. Urban residents continued to receive welfare privileges, such as housing, health and insurance services, child care, education, and pensions, which were largely unavailable to rural migrants. These systemic biases in welfare provision prevented rural families from migrating permanently into cities, thus maintaining the wedge between urban and rural earnings.

In sum, the net effects of the changes enlarged the real rural-urban income and consumption gaps from 1.9 in 1985 to 2.6 and 2.7, respectively, in 1993, their highest levels since the start of reforms in 1978.

Period 4 (1994–1997): Renewed Declines

The steady declines of the rural-urban gap after 1993 were due to the effects of a combination of factors: the pursuit of balanced regional growth, sustained gains in rural labor mobility, further reductions in discriminatory agricultural pricing, and the deterioration of urban employment conditions. Clearly, regional growth policies have become more balanced. In 1993, the central government began raising the priority given to the opening and development of more regions in the central and western parts of China. This initiative was known as "the over-all open-up strategy in coastal areas, on river sides, and along border areas." Beyond the original four special economic zones and fourteen open cities, local governments, with approval from the center, have experimented with many other regional efforts to speed up reforms and the opening process. Table 13.5 tracks the progression of these efforts to extend reform into the central and western regions. Because these new initiatives penetrated inner and rural regions, they had the effects of raising relative rural earnings.

Rural labor mobility has continued to improve in this period, partly because

TABLE 13.5

Regional Development Policies and Their Geographical Coverage

Steps of Reforms	Content of Reforms (official names)	Number of Cities and Counties Included in the East	Number of Cities and Counties Included in Central and Western China
(1)	Special economic zones	23	—
(2)	Open-up coastal cities	14	—
(3)	Coastal economic open-up zones	260	—
(4)	Open-up cities along rivers	—	6
(5)	Open-up capital cities	2	16
(6)	Open-up cities and towns on borders	—	13
(7)	Economic and technological development zones	26	4
(8)	Bonded zones	13	—
(9)	Economic cooperation border zones	2	11
(10)	Development zones for high and new technological industries	29	23
(11)	National tourism and recuperation zones	10	1
(12)	Local government designated economic development zones	All places	All places

SOURCE: State Council (1994).

the enlarged income gap has provided a strong "pull force" and partly because some stringent rules of household registration have been relaxed. For instance, those who invest or contribute above a certain amount of money in cities may receive special household registrations. With the development of small towns, a series of policy changes have been made to approve urban registration with special circumstances, such as awarding urban status for children who plan to live with one of the parents, for spouses separated for a long time, and for the elderly who need to live with children in cities. The removal of rationing and the reforms in urban welfare provisions have also made it more feasible for rural labor migrants to make a living in the cities.[12]

The increase in agricultural prices has continued. In fact, the relative price level of agricultural products has reached an all-time peak in PRC history. Measured by producer subsidy equivalence, agriculture policy has been moving from taxation toward protection. Agricultural taxation on both direct and indirect sources experienced an enormous drop, from 88 percent of agricultural output value in 1988 to less than 3 percent in 1994 (Garnaut, Cai, and Huang, 1996).

In the meantime, urban unemployment has become increasingly serious with the progression of industrial structural reforms, combined with further employment reforms and overcapacity in production. In recent years, unemployment rates have risen sharply, and many more enterprises have been unable to pay wages because of the corporatization process of SOEs, the adjustment of industrial structure, and operation below capacity for many SOEs. It has been estimated that the urban unemployment rate is higher than 6.9 percent and that the proportion of laid-off workers is 5 percent (State Statistical Bureau, 1997b), which accounts for a high share of total unemployment.[13]

Several factors have contributed to the high unemployment rate. First, a mild depression of the macroeconomy due to the lack of aggregate demand is a major cause. Second, many sectors have lost their comparative advantage and competitiveness in the process of adjusting industrial structure. Many inefficient firms and industries survived during the centrally planned period but are now subject to fierce competition from abroad and from the nonstate sector. This process inevitably leads to structural and frictional unemployment in a transition period. Third, the recent reforms of SOEs have converted redundant workers into unemployed or laid-off workers, making the unemployment issue apparent. The interaction of these three factors has resulted in high unemployment.

Despite the progress of economic reforms and the recent decline in the income gap between rural and urban residents, there are still many policies in place that act against the interests of the farm population. The regulations on labor mobility, for instance, remain biased. Local employment policies still give high priority to employment of the registered urban population. An example of this practice is local labor bureaus' rewarding employers who hire locals instead of outside workers.

Although the rural-urban gap has diminished in recent years, whether the trend will continue depends on the orientation of the government's overall policy. It is very likely that the decline in urban welfare will induce new regulations to block rural workers from taking jobs in cities in order to reduce competition for urban employment.[14] The interactions of pressure groups with the government and the reasons behind the choices of various government policies are issues of political economy to which we now turn.

Policy Formation: Development Strategy or Political Pressure?

We have documented the changing patterns of China's rural-urban disparity and have examined the specific policies and institutions that determined the level and the cycles of the sectoral gap. Now we cast the Chinese case into a more general analysis of the political economy of government interventions. China's experience is worthy of investigation because the period under consideration spans two eras of distinct economic and political regimes, providing a special opportunity for studying government behaviors. In particular, we attempt to address the following questions: what are the similarities and differences between China's policy instruments and the choices of other developing countries, and are there policy instruments unique to a centrally planned system and to a reforming economy? Why has China's urban bias persisted over the two periods? Has the package of policy measures changed over the two periods? From this case study on China, what can we conclude on the determinants of policy formation: does urban bias result from pursuing development strategy or from succumbing to political pressures? The answers to these questions will be useful in understanding China's urban bias as well as the policy choices confronting other developing countries.

We start our analysis with China's adoption of its heavy-industry-oriented development strategy. Upon the founding of the People's Republic in 1949, the Chinese government inherited a war-torn agrarian economy in which nine out of every ten people resided in rural areas and industry generated only one-eighth of the national income. At that time, a developed heavy-industry sector was sought as a symbol of the nation's power and economic achievement. Like government leaders in many other newly independent developing countries, Chinese leaders were motivated to accelerate the development of heavy industries. After China's involvement in the Korean War in 1950, with its resulting embargo by Western nations, catching up with the industrialized powers also became a matter of national security. In addition, the Soviet Union's successful record of building the nation in the 1930s while the Great Depression devastated the Western market economies gave the Chinese leadership both the inspiration and the precedent to adopt a heavy-industry-oriented development strategy. Therefore, in 1952, after a short period of recovery from wartime destruction, the Chinese government made heavy industry the priority sector for economic development. The goal was to build the country's capacity to produce capital goods and military materials as rapidly as possible.

Historical evidence therefore suggests that the formation of China's development strategy was not an outcome of political pressures from the urban interest groups. It came from the desire of the new Chinese government to catch up with industrial nations and reflected their belief that the industrial strategy was the best way to accomplish their goals.

Additional evidence also supports the view that during this period, there was limited scope for pressure groups to influence the government in choosing its development strategies and policies. When the People's Republic came into existence, the central government was politically powerful because of its leadership in winning the civil war. Its administrative framework and decision-making process inherited the basic elements of the military structure, where commands were effectively carried out via a top-down hierarchy. In contrast with the experience of most other developing countries, there were no pressure groups or voter blocs pressing the government to make policy. Because the Communist Party formed a powerful political coalition consisting of workers and peasants as core members, the state did not need to succumb to pressures from other interest groups. Throughout this period, the nation experienced no organized or significant political opposition to the industrial development strategy. Of course, different opinions on policy implementation existed within the power structure of the central government, but those debates were concentrated on microlevel incentive issues.[15] All of this circumstantial evidence suggests that industrialization captured the collective desires of the entire nation.

To implement its strategy, China adopted a set of policy instruments commonly seen in other developing countries. Scissors prices for agricultural commodities were the main tools to transfer resources away from agriculture. These interventions were supplemented with direct taxation and net saving outflows. According to Li (1993), the government transferred a total of 543 billion yuan of surplus away from agriculture through suppressed agricultural prices between 1955 and 1985. The net transfer through taxation and saving outflows amounted to 149.6 billion yuan. The government's squeeze on agriculture was also reflected in its fiscal and credit policies. As Figure 13.3 shows, the shares of government expenditures and loans to agriculture have always been much below the share of agriculture's contribution to GNP, indicating systematically biased investments against the rural sector.

The most unique aspects of China's policy instruments under central planning were the coercive interventions in the factor markets, particularly for labor. The forms and the extent of the interventions that were employed in China have rarely been seen in other developing countries. As described earlier, the key in-

FIGURE 13.3

Shares of Government Expenditures and Loans to Agriculture

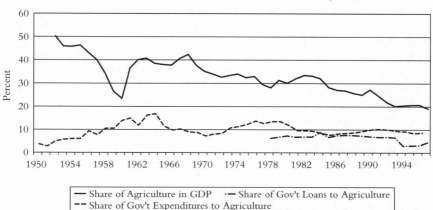

stitution was the household registration system, which designated the legal place of residence and work for the entire population, and a companion institution was the provision of welfare exclusively to households of urban registration status. These institutions played a key role in China's rural-urban divide. They are also crucial in understanding the effects of economic reforms on income distribution and the strategic areas for further reforms.

Did the heavy-industry-oriented development strategy accomplish its goals? At a stage where capital was the bottleneck in developing heavy industry, those resource flows helped China achieve its objective of building up an industrial base. Judging from China's sector composition, the traditional economic system reached its intended goal of accelerating the development of heavy industry. In the entire prereform period, heavy industry received the lion's share of the state's investments. As a result, the output value of heavy industry in the combined total output value of agriculture and industry grew from 15 percent in 1952 to about 40 percent in the 1970s (State Statistical Bureau, 1989b). However, China paid a high price for the achievement. Apart from inefficiency caused by (1) low allocative efficiency, due to the deviation of the industrial structure from a pattern that might have emerged from the comparative advantages of the economy, and (2) low technical efficiency, resulting from managers' and workers' low incentives to work (Lin et al., 1996), the rural-urban income gap became extraordinarily large. This taught China's leaders that the prevailing economic theories and practices in China would not accelerate overall development and well-being. To develop the economy, it was imperative to reform fundamental aspects of the economic system and the related, traditional strategy.

What general implications can be drawn from the Chinese experience? We have shown that during this period, China's urban bias was a result of pursuing a heavy-industry-oriented development strategy in the absence of political pressure groups. Development strategy alone was the decisive factor behind the rural-urban income gap. In light of the general analysis on the formation of urban bias, we have shown that the existence of pressure groups is not a necessary condition—and for China, not even an important condition—for urban-biased policies. This result lends support to the findings of the celebrated World Bank project (Krueger et al., 1992). With changing circumstances, however, pressure groups can be an important force behind the urban-biased policies. Support for this statement will be presented shortly, but we first need to explain why the government decided to amend its industrial development strategy in the late 1970s.

Although it was long recognized that the institutions and policies associated with the development strategy were inefficient, the timing of the reforms depended largely on a sequence of political and economic events. First, the pursuit of the heavy-industry-oriented development strategy failed to achieve the desired outcomes. Under this strategy, per capita income did not grow rapidly, and the gap between China and the developed countries widened. With serious shortages in the supply of food and other daily necessities, several hundred million peasants lived under the threat of starvation. After the Cultural Revolution, the national economy was on the verge of collapse. Second, while China struggled, neighboring economies, especially the astonishing four Little Dragons that originally had the same prospects for growth as China, developed rapidly. China fell further behind those economies. Third, when the new leadership came to power after disposing of the Gang of Four—the handpicked successors of Chairman Mao—the leaders hoped drastically to increase people's standards of living in order to strengthen their own political legitimacy. Fourth, because the weaknesses of the old strategy were apparent, the political and economic opportunity costs of giving up the traditional economic system became very small. Last, because of the death of Mao and the ensuing change in leadership, the methods of decision making had to change accordingly. New leaders could not make decisions as forcefully as Mao, and they had to make decisions collectively. As a result, they were more responsive to people's voices. Because of all these changes, the new government started reforming the old system.

Out of the economic reforms, a new political system emerged. In this system, people's voices and opinions began having much more influence on decision making. At the same time, the environment began allowing the existence of interest groups. The previously powerful coalition consisting of farmers and urban workers began to split because institutional reforms affected the two groups differently. Moreover, the collapse of the communes introduced a new governance system in rural areas, while political reforms also took place in urban areas. These changes resulted in a new situation in which people could, to a certain extent, influence the election of policymakers. China therefore began to have organized political activities and moved toward becoming a society more like those of other developing countries.

As we documented earlier, the profound impact of rural reforms on farm earnings resulted in a significant narrowing of the rural–urban gap in the initial years of the reforms. However, the gap did not continue to decline after 1985 but instead rose consistently until the early 1990s.

Why has China's urban bias persisted into the period of economic reforms? The short answer is that urban residents pressured the government to protect their relative welfare. Compared with rural residents, urban dwellers were the beneficiaries of the prereform system. In the initial period of reforms, urban residents suffered no direct losses because of the Household Responsibility System, which simply improved farmers' incentives while the central budget covered most fiscal costs of raising agricultural prices. When steady increases in agricultural prices began to raise urban costs of living and lower the urban people's relative economic income and welfare, urban residents reacted by putting political pressure on the government and fighting for a greater share in the fruits of economic reforms. Because the primary concern of the government was regime survival, and also because it realized that economic and political stability were a precondition for further reforms, the state naturally responded to pressure from the urban group. Consequently, we observed a cycle in which reforms first lowered the relative welfare of the urban dwellers, who then pressed the government for policy adjustments, which in turn led to income redistribution in their direction.

An example of interactions between the government and the city groups lies in the programs of urban price subsidies. As documented, a substantial increase of agricultural procurement prices occurred in 1979. To compensate for the potential drop in urban real income, the government immediately implemented a large increase in price subsidies for the urban population. In 1978, the government spent only 1.1 billion yuan of fiscal resources on price subsidies. In 1979, the subsidies jumped to 7.9 billion to compensate for the increase in agricultural prices. In 1985, a meat subsidy was initiated at the same time as meat prices were liberalized. Government total price subsidies increased to 26.2 billion yuan in 1985 and in 1998 reached a peak of 71.2 billion, 7.6 percent of the government's total budget.[16]

The government's balancing actions to placate the urban interest groups were typified by the events surrounding the political chaos in 1989. In 1988, inflation of 18.5 percent was unleashed by a series of price liberalizations and the announcement of further price reforms early in that year. This led to serious political unrest in 1989, primarily due to the erosion of living standards. In fact, this political event was not simply a student demonstration but a movement with the participation of urban residents who voiced their dissatisfaction over their losses from reforms.

Although the government settled the chaos by resorting to military force, the state made subsequent compromises to please the urban sector with revised economic policies. The government blamed rural industries for competing for raw materials with the SOEs and for producing low-quality products and tightened its controls over rural industrial firms. The total number of TVEs was reduced in two consecutive years (1989 and 1990); total employment decreased accordingly, and real output dropped by 3.7 percent in 1989. During the same period, the SOEs continued to increase in number, total employment, and real output value. During the same period, the central government also tightened employment policies restricting rural workers' access to work in cities.

Government responses to interest group pressures were also manifested in the large subsidies and financial transfers to SOEs. With the progression of reforms, many inefficient SOEs were under pressure to lay off workers and were unable to support wage growth. However, unemployment and deterioration of living standards were very costly in political and social terms. Succumbing to pressures from urban residents, the government adopted policies to protect workers in the state sector in order to avoid political risks. Initially, the state provided direct subsidies to enterprises that suffered financial losses. When reforms ended the budgetary relationship between the government and SOEs, the government turned to state banks to allocate credit to enterprises with poor performance. The total monetary value of these transfers has been large, and they continued throughout the reform period (see note 10).

What general implications can we draw from China during its period of economic reforms? Ample evidence has suggested that during changing political and economic circumstances, pressure groups can, and indeed have, become a determining factor in the formation of urban-biased policies in China. We must point out, however, that the institutions and policies inherited from the centrally planned system, particularly those imposing distortions in the labor and capital markets, have not yet been completely removed from the economy. These remaining institutional barriers and interest group pressures have jointly determined the level of the rural-urban disparity and its cyclical changes over time.

Finally, we note that the central government has used several new policy instruments in the postreform era. We have observed the declining importance of such traditional measures as suppressed agricultural prices. As Figure 13.2 shows, the ratio of industrial to agricultural prices has continued to decline since the inception of reforms in 1978, evidence consistent with the fact that the index measure of the degree of price discrimination against agriculture has fallen almost to zero. In the meantime, however, other policy instruments have gained importance with reforms. The most important ones include budgetary or credit allocations to inefficient SOEs, such direct income transfers to urban dwellers as inflation subsidies, and discriminatory employment policies that restrict labor flows into cities. Identifying these policy instruments represents the first constructive step in designing reforms to remove the existing distortions.

Bridging the Rural-Urban Gulf

The most compelling reason for eliminating the rural–urban income gap is to improve economic efficiency. The disparity between the two sectors is both a potential source of social and political instability and an important indicator of economic inefficiency. The cost of urban–biased interventions lies in the inefficiency of misallocating labor and other factors of production across the sectors, and these interventions may impede China's sustained growth in the long run. Although policies that favor urban residents may be needed in the short run to overcome the opposition of interest groups to economic reforms, the long-term objective of the government should be to promote the development of competitive factor markets, which implies the elimination of urban–biased institutions and policies.

We can illustrate the productivity gains from improving labor market efficiency. A fact well documented by economists is that when the income gap between rural and urban sectors is large, labor movements to cities or capital investments to rural regions may have immediate productivity effects. For China, this statement is not a hypothesis but a proven fact of past growth. Several studies have estimated that the labor movements from the low-productivity sector (agriculture) to higher-productivity sectors (say, industry) were a major source of economic growth in China in the postreform period. The contribution of labor mobility to total GDP growth rate ranges from 16 percent to 20 percent.[17]

Our earlier analysis pointed to two sets of factors that have caused the existing rural–urban income gap. The first set is various interventions in the factor markets, which lead to distorted labor and capital concentrations across rural and urban regions. One such intervention is the restriction of labor mobility, where governments, especially those at the municipal level, continue to suppress rural labor migration to reduce competition for local workers. Another major intervention is the government's control over credit, which leads to allocations of capital that are biased against the rural sector. These two practices are inherited from the centrally planned regime. They have remained major obstacles to China's long-term growth.

The second set of factors is the government's use of direct transfer programs (e.g., price subsidies) to favor the urban sector. This type of intervention was nonexistent in the prereform period. It is an outgrowth of the dilemma that has confronted the Chinese government during reforms: its desire to improve the efficiency of the factor markets requires reforms (say, greater rural labor mobility) that could erode urban welfare (a more competitive urban labor market). To escape the dilemma, the government has increasingly used direct transfers to protect urban income. This policy tool, unlike the employment policies and capital allocations, does not introduce direct distortions in the optimal allocation of productive inputs, but it may introduce inefficiency through other, indirect channels such as the negative effects of inflation.

There is little doubt that economic efficiency requires the removal of the various interventions noted here. However, as our analysis suggests, the government will not simply do so because it gives high priority to distributional considerations in order to preserve regime stability and political legitimacy. Therefore, given the government's short-run desires to protect urban interests, the more relevant question for policy reform is, what are the government's policy options? What should be the priorities for further reforms?

Our analysis suggests that China's policy reform should aim to improve the functioning of factor markets. In addition to the direct income gains that would be realized by the owners of the resources, this direction of reforms supports the government's objective of achieving political stability. This is so, in particular, because improvements in factor market efficiency will lead to faster growth, thus creating "a bigger pie." If needed, the government would have command over more resources to accomplish direct income transfers in order to win political support and to push forward economic reforms.

To continue intervening in the allocation of capital by providing more credit to inefficient SOEs just to sustain jobs is a great mistake. This is because the practice will further undermine factor market efficiency. Similarly, the government should gradually relax the existing restrictions on labor mobility, which would allow workers to pursue better employment opportunities and hence higher earnings. A concern is that both of these actions may cause a redistribution of income away from urban dwellers, resulting in political instability. In refuting this concern, we emphasize that the improved allocation of capital and labor may create real efficiency gains that will improve the government's budgetary situation, for instance, through higher tax revenues. If the government has to offset a reduction in welfare for urban workers, it would have more resources with which to do so. This package of policy reforms would satisfy the government's short-term political needs while allowing it to pursue its long-term goals of improving factor market efficiency.

Urban residents have been protected by a variety of institutions and policies that are associated with the centrally planned system. The fact that urban labor has faced fierce competition in employment from rural workers during reforms reflects the government's past mistakes in pursuing heavy-industry-oriented development strategy. How and when city dwellers' privileges should be removed involves efficiency, equity, and political considerations. Indeed, it is a political economy question. However, by economic criteria alone, there can be no doubt that Chinese economic reforms should aim quickly to restore allocative efficiency.

Notes

1. A series of research projects organized by the World Bank, including the well-known study by Krueger, Schiff, and Valdes (1991–1992), have analyzed the agricultural pricing policies in developing countries. This project covered eighteen countries and a wide range of issues, including the history of agricultural price interventions in each country, policy instruments implemented, estimates of the effects of both direct and indirect interventions on agricultural prices, the distribution of income among various groups, and the evolution of the country's pricing policies.

2. As articulated by Lipton (1977, p. 13), "The rural sector contains most of the poverty and most of the low-cost sources of potential advance; but the urban sector contains most of the articulateness, organization, and power. So the urban classes have been able to win most of the rounds of the struggle with the countryside." Bates (1981) advanced the analysis by examining the political basis for the selection of agricultural policies: the states in Africa have successfully divided up the countryside into supporters (through subsidies and projects) and opponents (through various forms of taxation). Moreover, Bates attributed the powerlessness of the peasantry to high communication costs for collective actions because they are geographically dispersed and the products of individual farmers account for only small shares of agricultural output, which introduces the free-rider problem.

3. As Krueger et al. (1991–92) summarized the World Bank project based on studying agricultural pricing policies in eighteen countries: "There was a strong consensus among the modernizing elite that raising living standards and achieving economic development were major social objectives. That consensus translated, however, into the view that industry was to be highly encouraged. . . . It was further believed that most of agriculture represented 'backwardness,' that agricultural output is unresponsive to incentives, and that, therefore, agriculture could be discriminated against in order to raise a surplus for industry without larger economic costs. . . . This set of ideas, or rationales, for policy was supported, or at least not seriously challenged, by the state of economic knowledge at that time" (vol. 5, p. 129).

4. See Tolley, Thomas, and Wong (1982) and Krueger et al. (1991–1992) for the analytical frameworks and applications to estimate the impact of various pricing policies.

5. The original data sources for these consumption expenditures are the Urban Household Survey and the Rural Household Survey administered by the SSB, which has collected data annually since 1952. These surveys consist of large, national random samples and contain diary information on an exhaustive set of consumption items. State Statistical Bureau (1985–95a) contains the questionnaires and detailed descriptions of the survey designs.

6. The analysis presented by Zhang and his collaborators covered only the period between 1980 and 1992. We have extended the analysis to the missing periods, 1978–79 and 1993–97.

7. Studies have shown that the large rural–urban income gap has contributed significantly to regional income inequality in China (Fleisher and Chen, 1997; Yang, 1999; Kanbur and Zhang, 1999; Yao and Zhang, 2001).

8. See Rawski (1979), Perkins and Yusuf (1984), Riskin (1987), Putterman (1993), Lin, Cai, and Zhou (1996), and World Bank (1997b) for the origin and development of China's rural-urban divide.

9. In 1978, the urban sector employed 95 million workers, while the rural sector had a labor force of approximately 306 million. In contrast, the total value of fixed assets in the state-owned enterprises (primarily urban) counted for 449 billion yuan, while the value of the fixed assets in agriculture was only about 95 billion yuan (State Statistical Bureau, 1993b; Perkins and Yusuf, 1984). These numbers indicate a capital-labor ratio of 4,726 yuan per urban worker and a ratio of 310 yuan per rural worker. The capital concentration in the urban sector is more than fifteen times of the rural sector.

10. Brandt and Zhu (2000) computed a series of net cash flows between the government and the SOEs for the period between 1981 and 1993. Their estimates show that initially in 1981, SOEs contributed revenues to the government amounting to 14.0 percent of GNP. But this percentage fell over time and turned negative by 1985, and in 1993, the SOEs received net cash inflows from the state equal to 3.4 percent of GNP. Their estimates provide convincing evidence of the government's net income transfers to the state sector in the late 1980s and the early 1990s.

11. China's central regions played a leading role in the first phase of the reforms. For instance, the HRS was initiated from poor provinces, such as Anhui and Sichuan. Sichuan also took the lead in experimenting with fiscal decentralization, which, among other things, allowed enterprises to retain part of their profits. Consequently, provinces in the central part of China benefited relatively more in that phase of the reforms.

12. It should be noted that there are still serious institutional barriers to rural labor mobility. For instance, under the current responsibility system, Chinese farm households have land-use rights but not alienation rights. If rural families leave agriculture permanently, they have to return the land to local authorities and consequently give up a stream of future land earnings (Yang, 1997). The migration cost imposed by the land arrangement discourages out-migration from agriculture and drives a wedge between sectoral earnings.

13. The number of urban unemployed is the sum of three types of worker: first-time job seekers, workers who lost a previous job and are seeking a new job, and those who are waiting to be transferred to another work unit because production has been suspended at their enterprise.

14. Currently, governments at all levels are taking measures to reduce urban unemployment, which results in the adoption of policies that effectively reduce competition from rural migrant workers. Viewing migrants as competitive rivals to their native workers, local governments have issued a series of discriminatory policies that include (1) charging various fees to increase the costs for rural laborers to migrate into cities, (2) penalizing urban enterprises from hiring migrant workers for certain jobs, and (3) inducing enterprises to use local unemployed workers instead of migrant workers by imposing penalties or giving out rewards.

15. For instance, there was support among government officials at all levels for a system called *sanzi yibao*, which encouraged the practice of private plots, free trade, self-responsibility for profits and losses, and the allocation of responsibility land to individual households. These were various activities created spontaneously by peasants to avoid government controls. At the state level, Liu Shaoqi, the then-president of the PRC, explicitly advocated those forms of incentives. But his focus had been on providing more freedom to peasants for the production and distribution of their products. The development strategy was not a point of debate.

16. These subsidies were targeted in several areas: to price increases in grain, cotton, and edible oil (79.4 percent of the 1998 total), to curbing price increases (4.0 percent), to increases in meat prices (3.7 percent), and other price subsidies (13.0 percent).

17. The World Bank (1997a) estimates that labor mobility contributed 1.5 percentage points to the average annual GDP growth rate of 9.4 percent over the period 1978–95. Cai and Wang (1999) provide a higher estimate, suggesting a 1.62 percentage point contribution to the 8.01 percent of annual GDP growth rate in the past reform years. Johnson (1999) argues that over the next three decades, if the barriers to migration are gradually removed and rural and urban wages are nearly equalized for individuals with similar levels of human capital, the intersectoral labor transfers could annually contribute as much as 2 or 3 percentage points to annual economic growth.

References

Bates, Robert. (1981). *Markets and States in Tropical Africa*. Berkeley: University of California Press.

Brandt, Loren, and Xiaodong Zhu. (2000). "Redistribution in a Decentralizing Economy: Growth and Inflation in China Under Reforms." *Journal of Political Economy*, 108(2), 422–39.

Cai, Fang, and Dewen Wang. (1999). "Sustainability and Labor Contribution of Economic Growth in China." *Journal of Economic Research*, 10(October), 62–68.

Fleisher, Belton, and Jian Chen. (1997). "The Coast-Noncoast Income Gap, Productivity, and Regional Economic Policy in China." *Journal of Comparative Economics*, 25(2), 220–36.

Garnaut, Ross, Fang Cai, and Yiping Huang. (1996). "Turning Point in China? Agricultural Development." In Ross Garnaut, Guo Shutian, and Ma Guonan, eds., *The Third Revolution in the Chinese Countryside*. New York: Cambridge University Press.

Grove, Theodore, Yongmiao Hong, John McMillan, and Barry Naughton. (1995). "China's Evolving Managerial Labor Market." *Journal of Political Economy*, 103(4), 873–93.

International Labor Office. (1995). *Yearbook of Labor Statistics, 1995*. Geneva: International Labor Office.

Jefferson, Gary, Thomas Rawski, and Yuxin Zheng. (1996). "Chinese Industrial Productivity: Trends, Measurement Issues, and Recent Developments." *Journal of Comparative Economics*, 23(2), 146–80.

Johnson, D. Gale. (1999). "Agricultural Adjustment in China: The Taiwan Experience and Its Implications." Office of Agricultural Economics Research, University of Chicago.

Kanbur, Ravi, and Xiaobao Zhang. (1999). "Which Regional Inequality? The Evolution of Rural-Urban and Inland-Coastal Inequality in China from 1983 to 1995." *Journal of Comparative Economics*, 27(4), 686–701.

Krueger, Anne, Maurice Schiff, and Alberto Valdes, eds. (1991–92). *The Political Economy of Agricultural Pricing Policy*, 5 vols. Baltimore: Johns Hopkins University Press.

Li, Wei. (1993). *Agricultural Surplus and Accumulation of Industrialization* [in Chinese]. Kunming, China: Yunnan People's Press.

Lin, Justin Yifu. (1992). "Rural Reforms and Agricultural Productivity Growth in China." *American Economic Review*, 82(1), 34–51.

Lin, Justin Yifu, Fang Cai, and Li Zhou. (1996). *The China Miracle: Development Strategy and Economic Reform*. Hong Kong: Chinese University Press.

Lin, Justin Yifu, and Dennis Tao Yang. (2000). "Food Availability, Entitlement and the Chinese Famine of 1959–61." *Economic Journal*, 110(1), 136–58.

Lipton, Michael. (1977). *Why Poor People Stay Poor: Urban Bias in World Development*. Cambridge, Mass.: Harvard University Press.

McMillan, J., J. Whalley, and L. Zhu. (1989). "The Impact of China's Economic Reform on Agricultural Productivity Growth." *Journal of Political Economy*, 97(4), 781–807.

Ministry of Labor. (1990–98, published annually). *Statistical Yearbook of Wages and Labor of China* [in Chinese]. Beijing: State Statistical Publishing House.

National Population Sampling Survey Office. (1997). *Tabulation of National One Per Cent of Population Sampling Survey, 1995*. Beijing: State Statistical Publishing House.

Oi, Jean C. (1993). "Reform and Urban Bias in China." *Journal of Development Studies*, 29(4), 129–48.

Perkins, Dwight, and Shahid Yusuf. (1984). *Rural Development in China*. Baltimore: John's Hopkins University Press.

Putterman, Louis. (1993). *Continuity and Change in China's Rural Development: Collective and Reform Eras in Perspective*. New York: Oxford University Press.

Rawski, Thomas. (1979). *Economic Growth and Employment in China*. New York: Oxford University Press.

Riskin, Carl. (1987). *China's Political Economy: The Quest for Development Since 1949*. Hong Kong: Oxford University Press.

State Council. (1994). *Yearbook on Special Economic Zones and Economic Opening Areas in China*. Beijing: Reform Publishing House.

State Statistical Bureau. (1985–95a). *The Plan for Urban Household Survey and the Plan for Rural Household Survey*. Beijing: State Statistical Publisher.

———. (1987–98b; published annually). *Statistical Yearbook of China*. Beijing: State Statistical Publishing House.

Tolley, George S., Vinod Thomas, and Chung Ming Wong. (1982). *Agricultural Pricing Policies and the Developing Countries*. Baltimore: Johns Hopkins University Press.

World Bank. (1995). *World Bank Data and Text*. CD-ROM. Washington, D.C.: World Bank.

———. (1997a). *China 2020: Development Challenges in the New Century*. Washington, D.C.: World Bank.

———. (1997b). *China 2020: Sharing Rising Incomes*. Washington, D.C.: World Bank.

Yang, Dennis Tao. (1997). "China's Land Arrangements and Rural Labor Mobility." *China Economic Review*, 18(2), 101–15.

———. (1999). "Urban-Biased Policies and Rising Income Inequality in China." *American Economic Review*, 89(2), 306–10.

Yang, Dennis Tao, and Hou Zhou. (1999). "Rural-Urban Disparity and Sectoral Labor Allocation in China." *Journal of Development Studies*, 35(3), 105–33.

Yao, Shujie, and Zongyi Zhang. (2001). "On Regional Inequality and Diverging Clubs: A Case Study of Contemporary China." *Journal of Comparative Economics*, 29(3), 466–84.

Zhang, Xinmin, et al. (1994). "Analysis of Rural-Urban Income Disparity." Manuscript, State Statistical Bureau.

14

What Will Make Chinese Agriculture More Productive?

Jikun Huang, Justin Y. Lin, and Scott Rozelle

The international community has long recognized China's effort to produce enough food to feed its growing population. Tremendous progress has been achieved in agricultural productivity growth, farmer's income, and poverty alleviation during the reform period. China's experience demonstrates the importance of institutional change, technological development, price and market liberalization, and rural development in improving food security and agricultural productivity in a nation with limited land and other natural resources (Lin, 1998).

Policies successful in the past, however, do not guarantee future agricultural productivity growth. While most recent studies have led to a consensus that the increases in China's grain imports will not starve the world, China still faces an enormous challenge to supply its growing population with high-quality, reasonably priced food and steadily raise rural income (World Bank, 1997). Agricultural productivity growth will determine whether China has the ability to feed itself in the future because rapid industrialization and urbanization will lead to competition for resources between agricultural and nonagricultural sectors.

Several key questions arise for policymakers when they address the challenge of how to sustain agriculture's productivity growth, achieve food security, and increase farm incomes, especially as China faces a difficult process of agricultural trade liberalization (Huang and Chen, 1999; Cheng, 1998). What will be the future sources of agriculture growth in China? What major constraints and challenges will China's agriculture face? How important will be the role of technology, given its past contribution? How will trade liberalization affect China's agricultural production and the national food security? What are the policy implications of the changes in the economy that will result from the trade liberalization? In general, how can China formulate effective policies to achieve sustainable growth of agriculture supply and productivity in the decades ahead?

The overall goal of this chapter is to begin to provide some answers to these questions, a complicated matter given that China is undergoing a number of radical changes: transition from a planned to a market economy, global integration, urbanization, a shift of comparative advantage from agriculture to other sectors, and diversification of diet. To meet this goal, we emphasize a more circumscribed set of objectives. Our chapter first reviews China's development strategies and the reforms that it has pursued to achieve its current level of food security, a central goal of China's agricultural policy, and to raise agricultural productivity and farm income. Next we evaluate the effects that the strategies and reforms have had on agricultural production. Finally, we seek to identify constraints and challenges that China will face and to analyze the scope for further agricultural and rural reforms.

Although we are interested in farm sector productivity and rural incomes in general, most of this chapter focuses on a narrower set of issues, especially the role of technology in China's food economy. Rural development in China is a complicated process and will require good policies beyond the government's management of agricultural technology. Land management, fiscal and financial policy, and a host of other issues are equally important. In fact, in a recent conference on land tenure in Beijing, D. Gale Johnson convincingly argued that land reform is essential to promote economic modernization of both the rural farm and nonfarm sectors. We agree. Unfortunately, space limitations preclude us from giving more emphasis to these issues here.

Agricultural Development in the Reform Economy

Role of Agriculture in the Economy

Since China's leadership initiated the economic reforms in 1978, the economy has grown steadily. The annual growth rate of China's GDP averaged around 9.5 percent between 1979 and 1995 (see Table 14.1). China's foreign trade has expanded even more rapidly than its overall economic growth, except during the last period shown, 1996–98. Even when the Asian financial crisis plagued the region in the late 1990s, China's economy continued to grow, albeit at a somewhat more moderate rate than during the precrisis period.[1] China's GDP grew at 7.8 percent in 1998, 7.1 percent in 1999, and 8.0 percent in 2000. From a technological point of view, China's economy has the potential to maintain a dynamic GDP growth rate of 8 to 10 percent annually in the coming decades (Lin, Shen, and Zhao, 1996).

Successive transformations of China's reform economy have been rooted in rapid growth of the agricultural sector. However, agriculture's contribution to national economic development, in terms of gross value added, employment, capital accumulation, urban welfare, and foreign exchange earnings, has been de-

TABLE 14.1

Annual Growth Rates of China's Economy, 1970–98

(percent)

	Prereform Period 1970–78	Reform Period		
		1979–84	1985–95	1996–98
Gross domestic product	4.9	8.5	9.7	8.7
Agriculture	2.7	7.1	4.0	4.0
Industry	6.8	8.2	12.8	10.7
Service	N.A.	11.6	9.7	7.9
Foreign trade	20.5	14.3	15.2	5.0
Import	21.7	12.7	13.4	10.8
Export	19.4	15.9	17.2	2.0
Population	1.8	1.4	1.4	1.0
GDP per capita	3.1	7.1	8.3	7.7

NOTES: GDP in 1970–78 is the growth rate of national income. Growth rates are computed using the regression method. GDP growth rates refer to the value in real terms.
SOURCES: State Statistical Bureau, *China Statistical Yearbook,* various issues.

clining. Agriculture contributed 40 percent of GDP in 1970 but less than 20 percent by the mid-1990s (see Table 14.2). Agriculture employed 81 percent of labor in 1970 but only 50 percent in 1998. Within the agricultural sector, cropping is the dominant activity, contributing 82 percent of the gross value of agricultural output in 1970. By 1998, however, its share fell to only 56 percent. The shares of livestock and aquatic output more than doubled during the same period (see Table 14.2).

The declining role of agriculture in international trade is particularly striking. The share of primary (mainly agricultural) products in total exports was 50 percent in 1980 (see Table 14.2). By the mid-1990s, the share was less than 15 percent. The share of food exports to total exports fell from 17 percent in 1980 to only 6 percent in 1998. Food imports fell from 15 percent to 3 percent in the same period.

The declining importance of agriculture, particularly the cropping subsector, in the economy is historically common to all developing economies. Since China is densely populated and its average farm size is barely an acre, population growth and limited land resources should be expected to shift China's comparative advantage from such land-intensive economic activities as traditional row crops to labor-intensive activities in agriculture, manufacturing, and other industrial activities (Anderson, 1990).

Agricultural Production Growth

Agricultural production growth is one of the main accomplishments of China's development and national food security policies. Production growth rates have

TABLE 14.2

Changes in the Structure of China's Economy, 1970–97

(percent)

	1970	1980	1985	1990	1995	1998
Share in GDP						
Agriculture	40	30	28	27	20	18
Industry	46	49	43	42	49	49
Services	13	21	29	31	31	33
Share in agricultural output						
Farming (crop)	82	76	69	65	58	56
Forestry	2	4	5	4	4	3
Livestock	14	18	22	26	30	31
Fishery	2	2	4	5	8	10
Share in employment						
Agriculture	81	69	62	60	52	50
Industry	10	18	21	21	23	23
Services	9	13	17	19	25	27
Share in export						
Primary products	N.A.	50	51	26	14	11
Foods	N.A.	17	14	11	7	6
Share in import						
Primary products	N.A.	35	13	19	18	16
Foods	N.A.	15	4	6	5	3
Share of rural population	83	81	76	72	71	70

SOURCES: State Statistical Bureau, *China Statistical Yearbook,* various issues; and *China Rural Statistical Yearbook,* various issues.

outpaced population growth since the early 1950s, with the exception of the famine years of the late 1950s and early 1960s. Even between 1970 and 1978, when much of the economy was reeling from the effects of the Cultural Revolution, grain production grew at 2.8 percent annually (see Table 14.3). Oil crop production grew 2.1 percent annually and fruit and meat output by 6.6 and 4.4 percent, respectively.

Decollectivization, price increases, and the relaxation of marketing restrictions on most agricultural products fueled China's food economy takeoff (1978 to 1984). Grain production increased 4.7 percent annually, and fruit output rose 7.2 percent (see Table 14.3). Oil crop, livestock, and aquatic production all grew spectacularly, expanding annually in real value terms by 14.9 percent, 9.0 percent, and 7.9 percent, respectively.

After the efficiency gains of the shift to the Household Responsibility System were exhausted by the mid-1980s, however, agricultural production decelerated (see Table 14.3). The decline was most pronounced for grains and oil crops, sectors in which prices and markets were still highly regulated. Growth rates of other crops, livestock, poultry, and fishery products have remained steady or increased during the reform period in response to rising demand and market and price liberalization.

Earlier studies demonstrate that a number of factors contributed simultaneously to agricultural growth during the reform period, in both its early and late stages. The earliest empirical efforts focused on the contributions of reform policies (McMillan, Whalley, and Zhu, 1989; Fan, 1991; Lin, 1992). These studies conclude that increased productivity was primarily a result of institutional innovations, particularly the rural Household Responsibility System, which restored the primacy of the individual household in place of the collective production team system as the basic unit of production and management in rural China.

Recent studies show that technological change has become the primary engine of agricultural growth since the completion of the Household Responsibility System reform in 1984 (Huang and Rozelle, 1996; Huang, Rozelle, and Rosegrant, 1999; Fan and Pardey, 1997). The results also indicate that reforms beyond decollectivization have high potential to affect agricultural growth. Price policy has had a sharp influence on the growth of both grain and cash crops during the postreform period. Favorable output-to- input price ratios contributed to rapid growth in the early 1980s. However, the new market force is a two-edged sword. The deterioration of China's price ratio, caused by gradually falling output prices and rapidly rising input prices, was one cause of the agricultural production slow-

TABLE 14.3

Annual Growth Rate of Agricultural Economy by Sector and Selected Agricultural Commodity, 1970–97

(percent)

	Prereform Period 1970–78	Reform Period		
		1979–84	1985–95	1996–97
Agricultural output value	2.3	7.5	5.6	7.4
Crop	2.0	7.1	3.8	6.2
Forestry	6.2	8.8	3.9	4.5
Livestock	3.3	9.0	9.1	7.9
Fishery	5.0	7.9	13.7	12.7
Grain production	2.8	4.7	1.7	2.9
Rice	2.5	4.5	0.6	4.1
Wheat	7.0	7.9	1.9	9.8
Maize	7.0	3.7	4.7	−3.5
Soybean	−1.9	5.1	2.9	2.4
Cash crops				
Oil crops	2.1	14.9	4.4	−2.1
Cotton	−0.4	7.2	−0.3	−1.7
Fruits	6.6	7.2	12.7	9.9
Red meats	4.4	9.1	8.8	11.2
Pork	4.2	9.2	7.9	10.2

NOTES: Growth rates are computed using regression method. Growth rates of individual and groups of commodities are based on production data; sectoral growth rates refer to value added in real terms.
SOURCES: State Statistical Bureau, *Statistical Yearbook of China*, various issues; Ministry of Agriculture, *Agricultural Yearbook of China*, various issues.

down of the late 1980s and 1990s. Rising off-farm labor opportunities and land use opportunity costs constrained the growth of grain output throughout that period and the growth of cash crops since 1985.

Growing environmental degradation, including erosion, salinization, and loss of cultivated land may also be affecting China's agricultural supply. Both erosion and salinization have increased since the 1970s, to the detriment of the output of grain, rice, and other agricultural products (Huang and Rozelle, 1995).

Agricultural Development Strategy and Policies

Food self-sufficiency has been and will continue to be the central goal of China's agricultural policy. The ninth five-year plan, for 1996–2000, and the National Long Term Economic Plan both called for continued agricultural production growth, annual farmer income growth of 4 percent, maintenance of "near self-sufficiency" in food production, and elimination of absolute poverty. Whether or not all of these development goals can be achieved simultaneously, China's policies, if formulated appropriately, have the capacity to greatly increase agricultural productivity.

Fiscal and Financial Policies

Although government expenditure in agriculture has shown a general increasing trend in the reform period, its share of total investment and the ratio of agricultural investment's share to agricultural GDP's share have shown a declining trend since the 1980s (Huang, 1999b). Officials have stated their intentions to raise the priority of public investment in agriculture. However, due to the weaknesses of the nation's fiscal system, implementation of the new policy to increase public investment in agriculture has been slow (Nyberg and Rozelle, 1999). Many policies and regulations have been promulgated regarding the provision of a minimum level of agricultural and public goods, but there is no budget to back them up. With insufficient budgets, policies almost invariably cannot be carried out effectively.

To gain a better understanding of government policy bias among sectors, we look at both fiscal and financial policies, as well as the state agricultural procurement policy (a policy that we interpret as being an implicit tax on farmers). Table 14.4 shows that government fiscal expenditures on agriculture have been consistently higher than the fiscal revenues generated from the agricultural tax and other official fees collected from agriculture. However, fiscal revenue from the explicit tax on agriculture and fees is only a small portion of the total agricultural capital contribution to industry and to the urban sector.

A significant capital outflow from agriculture to industry occurred in the 1980s and 1990s through the financial system, particularly through rural credit coop-

TABLE 14.4

Capital Flow (billion yuan in 1985 price) from Agriculture/Rural to Industry/Urban Through Fiscal, Financial (banking), and Grain Procurement Systems

	Fiscal System		Financial System		Grain Marketing (implicit tax)	Cash Flow from	
	Agri to Industry	Rural to Urban	Agri to Industry	Rural to Urban		Agri to Industry	Rural to Urban
1978	−15.2	−12.4	—	—	17.9	2.6	5.4
1980	−13.8	−10.8	5.0	1.6	16.6	7.7	7.3
1985	−6.6	4.2	8.3	2.5	5.6	7.3	12.4
1990	−11.2	5.8	19.5	11.9	15.5	23.8	33.2
1995	−7.4	44.4	18.3	10.0	18.1	29.0	72.4
1996	−6.5	42.2	15.7	9.8	11.8	21.0	63.8

NOTES: Capital net flow from agriculture to industry through Agricultural Bank of China, Agricultural Development Bank of China and Rural Credit Cooperative is based on the following formula:

$$[(\text{agricultural enterprises' saving})_t - (\text{agricultural enterprises' saving})_{t-1}] + [(\text{farmer's saving})_t - (\text{farmer's saving})_{t-1}] - [(\text{loan to agriculture})_t - (\text{loan to agriculture})_{t-1}]$$

Capital net flow from rural to urban is based on the following formula:

$$[(\text{TVE's saving})_t - (\text{TVE's saving})_{t-1}] + [(\text{agricultural enterprises' saving})_t - (\text{agricultural enterprises' saving})_{t-1}] + [(\text{farmer's saving})_t - (\text{farmer's saving})_{t-1}] - [(\text{loan to agriculture})_t - (\text{loan to agriculture})_{t-1}]$$

SOURCE: Huang, Ma, and Rozelle (1998).

eratives. A much higher value of capital has flowed from rural to urban areas (as well as the volume that flows from agriculture to industry), clearly showing that capital accumulated from agriculture not only supports industrialization in the urban sector but also provides notable financial resources for the development of rural industry.

After accounting for the implicit tax through the government procurement system, China extracted an accumulated total of 313 billion yuan (in 1985 prices) from the agricultural sector for the nation's industrialization effort in 1978–96 and about 563 billion yuan from the rural sector for the urban economy during the same period. Moreover, the flow of capital from agriculture to industry and from the rural sector to the urban has accelerated since reforms were initiated in the late 1970s. While much more research is needed to analyze the determinants of these trends and inefficiencies (if any) that distortions in the economy are causing, with the projected investment needs of the agricultural economy, it is unclear how officials will be able to mobilize capital to meet the nation's goal of raising agricultural productivity by greater investment in agriculture.

Food Price and Marketing Policies

Price and market reforms are key components of China's development policy shift from a socialist to a market-oriented economy. The price and market reforms initiated in the late 1970s were aimed at raising farm-level prices and gradually liberalizing the market. These reforms included increases in government procurement quota prices; reductions in the quota levels; introduction of above quota bonuses; negotiated procurement of surplus production of grains, oils, and most other commodities; and flexibility in marketing privately the surplus production of all categories of agricultural products. Nonetheless, the limited and differential rates of liberalization of the agricultural markets have had a substantial impact on productivity and commodity composition at the household and national levels (Lin, 1992; Huang, Rosegrant, and Rozelle, 1995). The shift from the collective to the Household Responsibility System also raised the price responsiveness of farm households (Lin, 1991a). As the right to private trading was extended to include surplus output of all categories of agricultural products after contractual obligations to the state were fulfilled, the foundations of the state marketing system began to be undermined (Rozelle et al., 1997).

After record growth in agricultural production in 1984 and 1985, a second stage of price and market reforms was announced in 1985 aimed at radically limiting the scope of government price and market interventions and further enlarging the role of market allocation. Farmers and state commercial departments were to "negotiate" purchase contracts before the planting season at the weighted-average quota and above-quota prices. Other than for grains and cotton, the intention was to gradually eliminate planned procurement of agricultural products; government commercial departments may only continue to buy and sell in the market. The contract system, however, also resulted in a negative impact on agricultural production as the marginal price to the producer declined (Sicular, 1991, 1995).

Because of the sharp drop in the growth of agricultural production and food price inflation in the late 1980s, implementation of the new policy stalled. Mandatory procurement of grains, oil crops, and cotton was continued. To provide more incentive for farmers to raise productivity and sell to the government, contract prices were raised over time. Despite this, the increase in the nominal agricultural procurement price was lower than the inflation rate, which led to a decline in real farm gate prices.

After agricultural production and prices stabilized in 1990–92, another attempt was made in early 1993 to abolish the compulsory quota system and the sale at ration prices to consumers. While the state distribution and procurement systems were both substantially liberalized, the policy was reversed when food price inflation reappeared in 1994. Since then, several new policies have been implemented. Government grain procurement once again became compulsory. The provincial governor's "rice bag" responsibility system was introduced in 1994–95.

With three record levels of grain production in China in 1995, 1996, and 1997, almost zero or negative inflation since 1997, rising grain stocks, declining prices in food markets, and a rising financial burden from state grain marketing, China was in a position to take further steps to liberalize its domestic grain mar-

TABLE 14.5

Nominal and Effective Real Protection Rates of Grain, 1985–98

Year	Quota Procurement Price				Negotiated Procurement Price				Market Price			
	Rice	Wheat	Maize	Soybean	Rice	Wheat	Maize	Soybean	Rice	Wheat	Maize	Soybean
	Nominal protection rate (percent)											
1985–89	−30	4	−13	−13	−5	34	17	15	14	52	37	39
1990–94	−37	−14	−35	−32	−16	14	−7	7	−2	26	12	26
1995–98	−18	−9	−2	−26	−7	0	8	2	4	20	25	13
	Effective real protection rate (percent)											
1985–89	−69	−54	−61	−61	−58	−42	−48	−49	−50	−34	−40	−38
1990–94	−70	−59	−69	−67	−60	−46	−55	−49	−53	−39	−46	−40
1995–98	−41	−35	−29	−48	−34	−29	−23	−28	−26	−14	−10	−20

NOTE: Imputed prices (value of imports or exports divided by quantity of imports or export) are used as the reference prices.
SOURCE: Author's estimates.

ket. Indeed, the "free market" had continued to flourish, notwithstanding the strong control maintained over the grain market before the mid-1990s. However, the central government initiated a controversial policy change in the grain marketing system in 1998.[2] The 1998 policy prohibits individuals and private companies from procuring grain from farmers, but they are allowed to operate in wholesale and retail markets.[3] Commercial arms of grain bureaus and the grain reserve system are the only ones who may procure grain from farmers. The ban on private grain procurement was considered by the government as a precondition for the elimination of its financial burden. Grain quota procurement prices were set 20 to 30 percent higher than market prices. Prices of grain sold by grain bureaus directly to markets or to private traders were to exceed procurement prices sufficiently to cover all operating costs and thereby avoid losses in marketing by grain bureaus. However, few economists believe that the policy achieved any of its goals.

Because of the high costs of monitoring and inspecting the grain market, private traders have continued to purchase grain from farmers since the policy was implemented. The market operating costs of private traders are much lower than those of the grain bureaus, so even though the government grain procurement prices were set at much higher levels than equilibrium market prices in 1998, private traders could offer farmers grain prices higher than government procurement prices and still sell grain in the market at prices lower than those offered by grain bureaus. The results of this policy have been rising transaction costs for private traders, increasing grain stocks held by grain bureaus, adverse effects on resource allocation, and diversification of agricultural production.

Table 14.5 shows our estimates of nominal and real protection rates, based on various producers' prices from 1985 to 1998 for rice, wheat, maize, and soybeans. The nation's policy to require farmers to deliver a mandatory quota at below-market prices has consistently represented a tax on (or disprotection to) farmers. The introduction of negotiated procurement reduced the tax from government procurement operations. Not surprisingly, the most heavily taxed commodities are the exportable ones, especially rice. Wheat, China's main imported commodity, has received more favorable treatment. Aside from the lower quota price for rice, the proportion of grain procurement at the lower quota price is typically higher for rice, compared to maize and soybeans. The nominal protection rates (NPRs) for wheat and maize at free market prices have ranged from 20 to 25 percent since the mid-1990s.

In sum, despite substantial efforts to liberalize the price and market structure of the agricultural sector, most major agricultural commodities continue to be heavily penalized by commodity-specific policies for procurement (except for 1998). When the impact of the overvaluation of the domestic currency due to the trade protection system is factored in, the distortions in agricultural incentives become even worse. Distorted prices depress agricultural production and redistribute income from farmers to urban consumers and the agricultural processing sector. Improving farmer's incentives to produce and raising agricultural productivity and farmers' income require further liberalization of China's agricultural markets, especially the grain market.

Foreign Exchange and Trade Policies

China has become a much more open economy, with foreign trade growing faster than GDP. The trade dependence ratio, the share of exports and imports in GDP, rose from 12 percent in 1980 to 23 percent in 1985 and to 36 percent in 1997 (State Statistical Bureau, 1980–97a). Total value of agricultural trade of China increased from U.S.$11.6 billion in 1980 to $31.2 billion in 1997. However, the share of agricultural trade in the total trade value fell from 30.4 percent in 1980 to 10 percent in 1997 due to the even faster growth of trade in manufactured goods.

China's open door policy contributed to this rapid growth of the external economy and to greater reliance on both domestic and international trade to meet consumer demand. Historically, the overvaluation of domestic currency for trade protection purposes had reduced agricultural incentives. Real exchange rates remained constant and even appreciated during the thirty years prior to the reforms. After the reforms, however, the real exchange rate depreciated rapidly, with the exception of several years of domestic price inflation during the mid-1980s; from 1978 to 1992, it depreciated more than 400 percent. Falling exchange rates increased export competitiveness and have contributed to China's phenomenal export growth record (in nongrain food products) and the spectacular national economic performance of the 1980s.

In recent years, however, the situation has changed. From 1992 to 1997, the real exchange rate has appreciated by about 30 percent. Although the NPRs of agricultural products at free market prices have been positive since 1990s, most agricultural product price protection rates are negative if the real overvaluation of the domestic currency is considered (see the real effective protection rates in Table 14.5). In fact, when viewed from this point of view, China has provided its agricultural sector with little protection in recent years.

Land Use Policy

Nearly every farm household in China is endowed with land or services from land. Land ownership rests with the village (or collective) and is contracted or otherwise allocated to households. Security of legal tenure on contracted land was extended in the 1990s from fifteen to thirty years, but village leaders frequently ignore these policy directives. The dynamics of household and village demographics and other policy pressures often induce local authorities to reallocate land prior to contract expiration. Although there are most likely significant long-term gains to productivity that would be associated with better tenure arrangements, several analyses have demonstrated that China's land tenure system has had only a marginal impact on agricultural production (Brandt et al., 2000). However, the absence of secure tenure rights does prevent farmers from using land as collateral and limits their access to formal credit markets.

Formal land rental markets are infrequently observed in China. Informal arrangements allow households to transfer short-term use rights to others for a fee—including tax and quota liabilities—although the proportion of land rented is very small. As increasing numbers of rural residents migrate or otherwise obtain nonagricultural employment, inefficiencies in land utilization arise when farmers cannot rent out their land. One of the challenges facing the government today is the search for a mechanism that permits the remaining full-time farmers to access additional farmland and so improve their incomes by raising the land-to-labor ratio.

Despite the benefits that farmers would receive if land were privatized or if land rights were more secure, a number of household surveys have determined that most farmers prefer collective ownership and periodic land adjustments based on demographic dynamics (Kung and Liu, 1997). Therefore, an abrupt change in land property rights, such as privatization, might have significant costs. The pressures to privatize agricultural land in China are actually quite low.

The effects on food security and poverty of equitable distribution of land to farmers are obvious. But land fragmentation and small size of farms constrain the growth of labor productivity and farmers' incomes. Probably more than any single feature, the size of farms in China defines its agriculture. More than 70 percent of the population, nearly 900 million people, lives in rural areas. Since only 10 percent of China's land is arable, the enormous number of farm households

TABLE 14.6

Rural Enterprise (RE) Development in China, 1980–97

	REs' Share in Rural Labor (percent)	REs' Share in Total GDP (percent)	REs' Share in Total Export (percent)	Farmland Size (ha/farm)	Non-Farm Income Share (percent)
1980	9	N.A.	N.A.	0.56	17
1985	15	9	N.A.	0.51	25
1990	22	14	15	0.43	26
1995	29	25	43	0.41	37
1996	30	26	48	0.41	38
1997	28	28	46	0.40	39

means that China already has almost the smallest farms in the world, and farm size is falling (see Table 14.6). In 1980, the average size was only 0.56 hectares (about 1.4 acres) per farm, or around 0.15 hectares (a third of an acre) per capita. By 1997, farm size had fallen to 0.40 hectares (1 acre). Despite their minute size, China's farms still produce more than half of the income of rural households. The rise in nonagricultural income, however, accounts for most of the gains in per capita rural incomes in the reform era, and work off the farm is the most likely way for rural residents to escape poverty.

The small scale of farming and increasing importance of the nonagricultural sector have important implications for officials who need farmers to adopt new technology to increase production and raise productivity. In most cases, farmers must incur a fixed cost before they can adopt or efficiently use most new technologies. The cost may be denominated in terms of the time it takes to search for the new technology or in the effort and expenditure it takes to learn how to use it effectively. Since the outcome of adopting a new method of farming is uncertain, part of the cost may be the effort a farmer exerts to protect the household from the risks of the new technology (e.g., partial adoption). If the costs are fixed, the size of the operation on which the new breakthrough will be used is a factor in whether or not a farmer will decide to adopt or not. If the farm size is large, a farmer will be willing to exert a lot of effort and money experimenting with new technologies, since on a per-unit-of-land basis, the cost will be small. In contrast, when the farm is small, unless the prospects of increased profits are large, farmers will be less enthusiastic about investigating new technologies. It is not that farmers resist new technology; it is just that the marginal benefit of the investment required for an appropriate breakthrough is less than its cost. Rising wages off the farm also may slow adoption, since the opportunity cost of adoption will be higher.

In a growing economy characterized by a large number of small farmers, a government that wants to increase the growth rate of agriculture may find that it can play an important role in the creation and delivery of new technology.

The idea is that the government must reduce the cost of discovery and learning. For example, providing extension services to farmers can reduce the cost to the farmer as the information is brought to them. Making technologies available through government-sponsored seed companies that will guarantee the reliability of the product and provide advice through the local seed station or network of township and village leaders can also reduce search and adoption costs and reduce the risk of adoption.

Rural Development and Labor Market Development Policies

China's experience in the development of rural enterprises shows the importance of expanding nonagricultural activities in rural areas both to generate employment for rural labor and to raise agricultural labor productivity (see Table 14.7). Rural industrialization plays a vital role in reducing the agricultural labor surplus. Agricultural labor productivity grew at about 10 percent annually in the entire reform period, and growth has been on a rising trend since the late 1970s. It is regarded as one of the major successes of the country's reforming economy.

The share of rural enterprises (REs) in GDP rose significantly from 2 to 4 percent in the 1970s to 28 percent by 1997 and dominated the export sector by the mid-1990s (see Table 14.6). Now REs employ nearly 30 percent of rural labor and are the major source of rural employment creation. With the rapid growth of REs in China, the diversification of farmer income has been remarkable. The share of nonfarm income in farmers' income rose sharply from 17 percent in 1980 to 39 percent in 1997 (see Table 14.6).

Prior to the rural reforms, underemployment had been a persistent problem in rural China. This became more apparent as efficiency gains in agriculture dur-

TABLE 14.7

Agricultural Labor Productivity in China, 1978–97

	Agriculture		Crop	
	Gross Value	Value Added	Gross Value	Value Added
Labor (yuan/year)				
1978	491	358	557	368
1984	665	475	1,358	915
1992	1,314	831	1,969	1,205
1997	2,990	1,767	2,721	1,749
Annual growth rate (percent)				
1979–84	6.3	4.9	19.8	20.5
1985–92	9.0	7.4	5.0	3.6
1993–97	18.7	16.9	7.1	8.3
1978–97	10.4	8.8	10.2	10.2

NOTE: Values are measured in 1978 constant prices.
SOURCE: Huang (1999b).

ing the reforms reduced the labor input needed for crop production. During the same period, the rural labor force grew by 2 to 2.5 percent annually, with more than 10 million new entrants each year during the 1980s. The increase in rural labor resources, combined with land scarcity, limited the absorptive capacity of agricultural employment and could have caused an enormous labor surplus, slowed farmers' income growth, and limited the extent of poverty reduction if the nonagricultural sector had not grown rapidly.

Many countries typically encouraged rural-to-urban migration to cope with an abundance of rural labor in the early part of the twentieth century. However, massive, unmanaged migration has often resulted in numerous problems for urban society, including rising levels of pollution, increased congestion, housing shortages, inadequate social services, and a rising proportion of the urban population in poverty. China's experience in developing rural enterprise shows how the expansion of nonagricultural activities in the rural areas can generate employment to provide jobs for a growing rural labor force. Indeed, rural enterprises now dominate many industrial sectors in China, including textiles, clothing, farm machinery and equipment, other simple machinery, construction materials, food processing, and a variety of consumer goods.

At the same time, there are still a number of factors hindering adjustments in the labor market. There are natural barriers, such as moving costs, that exist in all economies, regardless of their nature or structure. China's factor markets still contain many structural imperfections, such as employment priority for local workers, housing shortages, and the urban household registration system (Lin, 1991b; Lyons, 1992; Rozelle, 1994; Lohmar, 1999). One of the costs of these imperfections is that they restrict the mobility of factors among alternative economic activities, reducing the efficiency of resource allocation.

Antipoverty Policy

Both central and local governments are committed to poverty alleviation. In the early 1980s, tremendous progress was made in addressing China's poverty problem (Nyberg and Rozelle, 1999). According to government poverty statistics, the number of people under the poverty line in rural areas declined from 260 million in 1978 to 89 million in 1984. The incidence of poverty (the share of the poor in the total population) declined from 32.9 percent to 11.0 percent during this period. Much of the credit for the early reduction in poverty is attributed to the rapid rural economic growth that resulted from better incentives and the government's rural reform program (Lardy, 1983). However, the inadequacy of the financial resources available to develop poor areas is a challenge for officials charged with alleviating poverty in China. Even though total funds for poor areas increased in nominal terms over time, real investment in the poor areas declined in the late 1980s and early 1990s.

With the poor increasingly located in the more remote areas, the change in lending strategy from the household to economic entities, the inadequacy of financial resources, and slower growth of the rural economy, the progress achieved since the early 1980s has slowed. There were about 42 million people still living below the official poverty line in 1998, or approximately 5 percent of the rural population.

The government originally set a goal of eliminating absolute poverty for the remaining 42 million people by the end of the twentieth century. To achieve this, the program called for increased funding for the poor areas, particularly for the 592 counties that are designated as poor by the central government. However, the increase of funds for the poor areas has been limited since 1994. Indeed, real investment in poor areas declined by 33 percent between 1993 and 1996. Although the investment in poor areas rose in 1997, it was still lower than the level of funding allocated in the first year (1994) of the 8–7 program's push to eliminate poverty. (For a more comprehensive review of poverty policy, see Chapter Nine.)

Technology Development Policies

Beginning in the 1960s, China's agricultural research institutions expanded rapidly from virtual nonexistence in the 1950s, producing a steady flow of new varieties and other technologies. China's farmers used semidwarf seed varieties several years before the release of Green Revolution technology elsewhere in the world. China was the first country to develop and extend the use of hybrid rice. Chinese-bred corn, wheat, and sweet potatoes were comparable to the best in the world in the prereform era (Stone, 1988).

Nationwide reforms in research were launched in the mid-1980s. The reforms attempted to increase research productivity by shifting funding from institutional support to competitive grants, supporting research useful for economic development, and encouraging applied research institutes to support themselves by selling the technologies they developed. Although competitive grant programs may have increased the efficacy of China's agricultural research system, reliance on commercial revenue to subsidize research and compensate for public funding shortfalls has weakened it. Empirical evidence demonstrated the declining efficacy of China's agricultural research capabilities in the early 1990s (Jin et al., 1998).

Taking into account the role that science and technology played in raising agricultural productivity and the recent deterioration of the research system, the Chinese government concludes in its long-term plan for 2010 that China will rely on new technology, particularly new crop and livestock varieties, to raise future agricultural production. Technology is at the center of the "advancement of agriculture" (*kejiao xingnong*). The exhortation of Jiang Zemin, then president of China, is widely quoted: "We are counting on breakthroughs of our agricultural research system. We need to begin reinventing China's agricultural sciences

TABLE 14.8

Agricultural Research and Extension Expenditures in China, 1985–96

Year	Agricultural Research Expenditure			Share of State Finance (percent)	Agricultural Research Intensity (percent)	Agricultural Extension Expenditure (billion)	Public Agricultural Research Intensity (percent)
	Total (billion)	State Finance (billion)	Development Income (billion)				
1985	2.20	1.65	0.55	75	0.52	N.A.	N.A.
1986	2.06	1.46	0.59	71	0.48	1.74	0.24
1987	2.00	1.35	0.65	68	0.44	1.81	0.32
1988	2.14	1.43	0.71	67	0.46	1.69	0.24
1989	2.14	1.45	0.71	67	0.47	1.55	0.23
1990	2.05	1.24	0.81	61	0.39	1.74	0.23
1991	2.31	1.25	1.07	54	0.43	1.99	0.25
1992	2.55	1.33	1.22	52	0.44	2.10	0.25
1993	2.67	1.27	1.40	48	0.46	2.08	0.23
1994	2.95	1.39	1.56	47	0.44	2.09	0.24
1995	2.83	1.42	1.41	50	0.39	2.17	0.23
1996	2.88	1.51	1.37	53	0.36	N.A.	N.A.

NOTES: Values are in 1990 constant yuan. Agricultural research (extension) intensity is measured as the percentage of agricultural research (extension) expenditures to agricultural GDP. Agricultural research expenditure includes expenditures from government fiscal accounts (or public agricultural research investment) and commercial revenue generated by agricultural research institutes.
SOURCE: State Sciences and Technology Commission (1985–97).

and technology revolution." The government has begun an ambitious program promoting biotechnology and has pushed a number of high-profile technology projects, such as hybrid rice. It has set ambitious funding growth targets.

At the same time, however, budgetary cutbacks, administrative decentralization, perceptions of inefficiencies, and interministerial infighting has led to falling support for agricultural research, severe reductions in extension staff, and halfhearted attempts to reform the seed industry. Fiscal constraints have limited China's ability to invest more on agricultural research and extension since the mid-1980s (see Table 14.8). Agricultural research investment intensity has been declining over time. By the mid-1990s, the intensity of both agricultural research and extension expenditure was among the lowest in the world (Huang, Hu, and Fan, 1998).

Today, the record on the reform of the agricultural technology system is mixed, and its impact on new technological developments and crop productivity is unclear. Leaders have launched wide-ranging, deeply penetrating reforms in research institutes, commercialized a wide number of extension activities, and begun to liberalize seed markets. Progress in reorganization of the management and financing of research reform varies greatly over time, across space, and among the components of the system. Different indicators of research output and agricultural productivity paint different pictures of the success or failure of the changes (Jin et al., 1998).

Technology Changes and the Growth of Agricultural Productivity

This section reports the results of our own study on the impact of national investment in research and extension in China. Due to the enormous data requirements, we had to limit our attention to four major crops (rice, wheat, soybeans, and maize) in major growing provinces. (For details, see Huang, Rozelle, and Rosegrant, 1999.)

Crop Productivity in China During the Reform

Historically, estimates of China's cropping total factor productivity (TFP) have been controversial. Differences in the estimates between Tang and Stone (1980) and Wiens (1982) triggered a debate on the success of prereform agriculture. The major work documenting TFP growth in the reform era, Wen (1993), showed progress and stagnation, depending on the time period of analysis. On the one hand, Wen's work confirms the efficiency analyses of McMillan et al. (1989) and Lin (1992), showing that rapid TFP growth was at least in part behind the rural economy's miracle growth in the early 1980s. However, Wen's work was based on data through 1990, and it created the impression that the agricultural sector was in trouble, since aggregate TFP growth stagnated after 1985.

Table 14.9 shows a general upward, though variable, trend of TFP in rice, wheat, maize, and soybean productivity. Although the rate of increase varies by

TABLE 14.9

Trends of Output, Input, and Total Productivity for Rice, Wheat, Soybean, and Maize in China, 1979–95

Year	TFP Index (1979 = 100)				Output Index (1979 = 100)				Input Index (1979 = 100)			
	Rice	Wheat	Soybean	Maize	Rice	Wheat	Soybean	Maize	Rice	Wheat	Soybean	Maize
1979	100	100	100	100	100	100	100	100	100	100	100	100
1980	109	103	102	104	97	86	112	104	97	96	103	99
1981	120	123	111	107	100	97	127	101	93	89	115	93
1982	138	148	104	122	112	110	132	104	87	85	124	83
1983	146	178	133	147	118	137	134	118	87	87	100	80
1984	156	192	139	168	122	149	146	129	84	88	102	75
1985	154	191	143	156	115	150	167	111	80	88	118	69
1986	157	202	152	163	117	160	186	125	79	89	118	75
1987	158	206	158	172	117	157	202	141	78	86	126	79
1988	151	199	157	177	115	152	204	141	80	86	129	77
1989	158	200	131	163	123	164	158	138	82	92	125	83
1990	163	197	152	191	127	168	180	177	82	98	117	90
1991	165	195	153	200	123	166	182	181	78	94	117	86
1992	169	205	150	191	121	174	189	166	74	95	129	85
1993	179	223	159	210	117	187	272	179	70	94	177	84
1994	169	215	178	191	116	181	287	179	74	93	160	90
1995	154	221	171	185	121	186	243	195	77	91	147	101

SOURCE: Huang, Rozelle, Hu, and Jin (1999).

time period, in general, the TFP of all crops rose rapidly in the early 1980s, the earliest period of Chinese reform: TFP of wheat increased by more than 90 percent between 1979 and 1985; of rice, by 54 percent; of soybeans, by more than 43 percent; and of maize, by 56 percent.

But such an unparalleled rise in TFP could not be sustained. Average TFP was at about the same level in 1990 as in 1985. Stagnant TFP trends, as described by Wen (1993) for the entire agricultural sector, are also evident in the grain sector. These trends have generated great discussion in China over the causes of yield slowdowns during this period. The debate usually focuses on land rights, commodity pricing policy, the availability and price of inputs, and the structural transformation of the rural economy (i.e., the expansion of rural industries and rural income diversification).

The rise in TFP, however, restarts in the 1990s. Productivity of wheat, the most successful crop, rises by more than 24 percentage points between 1990 and 1995. That of soybeans, a close second, increases by about 20 percentage points, albeit from a lower base. If one discounts 1994 and 1995, the TFP growth rates of rice and maize nearly match those of wheat and soybeans. The productivity of rice, however, moves down sharply in the mid-1990s and ends up below that of soybeans. Maize rises as much as wheat in the early 1990s, but like rice, it falls back in 1994 and 1995.

Although TFP growth patterns for all of the crops aggregated at the national level are similar, trends of the various sample provinces—even within a crop—vary sharply (Jin et al., 2002). For example, in the case of wheat, TFP rises as much as 3 to 4 percent annually in Hebei and Shandong. Productivity gains in Shanxi and Sichuan are less than 1.5 percent annually. The overall gains in rice TFP vary even more, ranging from only 21 percent in Hebei to more than 140 percent in Jilin.

Agricultural Technology in China

China has traditionally had one of the strongest research systems in the world. China's agricultural scientists and the government support system developed and disseminated technology throughout the People's Republic period. By the early 1980s, China's research and development system for agriculture was at its peak. It had just made several major breakthroughs. Its level of national funding had been increasing. Partly as a consequence of past investments, throughout the reform era, breeders turned out a constant stream of new varieties. Since 1982, rice farmers in China have used about four hundred "major" varieties each year. Rice farmers in each province use around twenty-five major varieties per year. In the case of wheat, because there is no single dominant variety (unlike hybrid rice, for which a few varieties account for a large proportion of the nation's sown area), the total number of varieties per year nationally and the number per province might be expected to be larger. In fact, however, wheat farmers in each province use around twenty-three varieties each year, and maize farmers, on average, use thirteen varieties. There are even fewer major soybean varieties in China, both in total and on a per-province basis. One reason may be that the research system has not traditionally centered its attention on the crop. Furthermore, China is the center of origin for soybeans, and there are many more small, traditional varieties that are still being grown.

Chinese farmers adopt new varieties with great regularity. The rate of turnover of varieties of major rice, wheat, maize, and soybeans in China is very impressive.[4] Between the early 1980s and 1995, China's farmers turned over their varieties at a rate that ranges from about 13 to 45 percent. Maize farmers turn over their varieties most, averaging more than 33 percent per year. This means that every three years *on average,* maize farmers replace all of the varieties in their fields. Rice and wheat farmers adopt varieties at a somewhat slower rate, changing their varieties every four to five years. Soybean farmers adopt varieties at the slowest rate, changing their varieties every six years. Again, this might be consistent with the fact that the research system has paid less attention to soybeans. From conversations with those familiar with grain cultivation in the United States, Mexico, and India, as national averages, the turnover rates in China rival those found in the rice bowls and wheat baskets of the developing and developed world.

To examine the nature of technology more closely, we create two measures that can demonstrate the quality of technology being created by the research system and the technological choices being made by farmers. Using the experiment station yield of each major variety during the year that the variety was certified, two measures are developed: a "yield envelope" variable and an "adopted yield potential" variable. The yield envelope, which is created by using the *highest* yield of any *one* major variety in the field in each province during a given year, is a measure of the ultimate yield potential of the current technology of each province's research system. The other variable, adopted yield potential, is the unweighted *average* of the experiment station yields of *all* major varieties that have been adopted by farmers. In our analysis, since farmers are the ones who adopt these varieties, we consider this as a measure of technology adoption. In addition to the rapid adoption of new technology, China's research system has created a steady stream of yield-increasing technologies (see Table 14.10). The yield envelopes for rice and maize, especially, have moved out at nearly 2.5 percent per year largely because of the development of hybrid rice and maize varieties. Albeit more modest, the yield envelopes of wheat and soybeans (both 1.3 percent) have also risen significantly during the reforms.

Farmers, however, have not always chosen (or been able to choose) the highest-yielding varieties. The average yield potential (as measured by the yield at the experiment station of each variety during the year it was certified) of major varieties in the sample area has risen between 0.6 (soybeans) and 1.8 (maize) percent per year during the reforms (see Table 14.10). When compared to the farm-

TABLE 14.10

Experiment Station Yields, Actual Yields, and the Yield Gap in Sample Provinces in China, 1980–95

	1980[c]	1995	Annual Growth Rate (percent)
Rice			
Yield envelope[a] (tons/ha)	6.6	9.1	2.3
Adopted potential yield (*APY*)[b] (tons/ha)	6.1	7.2	1.4
Actual yield (tons/ha)	4.2	6.2	2.6
Gap between "average experiment" and "actual"	31%	14%	
Wheat[c]			
Yield envelope[a] (tons/ha)	6.3	7.5	1.3
Adopted potential yield (*APY*)[b] (tons/ha)	4.6	5.2	0.9
Actual yield (tons/ha)	1.9	3.6	3.2
Gap between "average experiment" and "actual"	58%	31%	
Maize			
Yield envelope[a] (tons/ha)	7.6	11.0	2.5
Adopted potential yield (*APY*)[b] (tons/ha)	6.1	7.9	1.8
Actual yield (tons/ha)	3.0	4.9	3.2
Gap between "average experiment" and "actual"	51%	38%	
Soybeans			
Yield envelope[a] (tons/ha)	2.9	3.5	1.3
Adopted potential yield (*APY*)[b] (tons/ha)	2.7	3.0	0.6
Actual yield (tons/ha)	1.1	1.7	3.1
Gap between "average experiment" and "actual"	59%	43%	

NOTES: [a]Yield envelope is the *highest* experiment station yield of a variety that has been extended to the field. In this table, the figure is the average of sample provinces.
[b]Adopted yield potential is the *average* experiment station yields of *all* varieties being adopted by farmers. In this table, the figure is the average of sample provinces.
[c]Wheat data go back only to 1982, so figures for wheat are for that year, not 1980.
SOURCE: Huang, Rozelle, Hu, and Jin (1999).

ers' actual yields, in 1980 (1982 for wheat), the difference ranged from 31 to 59 percent, gaps that are not high by the standard of developing countries (Pingali, Hossein, and Gerpacio, 1997; Pingali and Rosegrant, 1995). In part reflecting the rapid rise in inputs, the gap fell for all crops.

There are two ways to interpret the yield gaps that currently exist in China. On the one hand, there appears to be a great deal of yield potential left in varieties in the field and even more when considering the differences between actual yields and the yield envelope. On the other hand, the relatively small and narrowing gap (14 to 43 percent) between actual yields and adopted yield potential means that China's yield potential is not that large, and the nation needs more breakthroughs if the pace of yield growth is to be maintained.

In contrast, the gap between the yield envelope and adopted yield frontier has grown bigger, a fact that also has a number of implications for China's future yield growth. It may be that high-yielding varieties are not moving out into the field because of some physical, policy, or infrastructure constraint. On the other hand, it could be that farmers are finding that varieties other than the highest-yielding ones are the most effective at increasing efficient production. Farmers may choose to use varieties that have less than the highest yield because other factors matter more (e.g., the selected variety requires less input or is better-priced).

In addition to producing genetic material itself, China has also drawn heavily on the international research system for genetic material, especially for rice.[5] Material from the International Rice Research Institute (IRRI) comprises a large share of China's rice germplasm. Nationwide, we can trace around 20 percent of the germplasm to IRRI varieties. The proportion varies greatly over time (from 16 to 25 percent) and also varies by province, reaching more than 40 percent in Hunan, one of China's largest rice-growing provinces, in the late 1980s. Although the national use of wheat and maize materials from the CG system (varietals contributed by the Consultative Group for International Agricultural Research centers), mostly from the International Maize and Wheat Improvement Center (CIMMYT), is lower (4 percent is the national average), great variability exists among provinces, in some of which material from the CG system (especially those in CIMMYT's mandate area, for example, Yunnan province for wheat or Guangxi province for maize) makes up around half of the germplasm.

In summary, China's research system has created a lot of new technology and has succeeded in getting farmers to adopt it at a rapid pace. The technology embodies significant levels of yield-increasing material that may prove to be an important determinant of productivity. The national research effort is also aided by the international agricultural research system. The rate of adoption of the highest-yielding material, however, is much slower. China's yields and output certainly have grown due to increased use of inputs.

Technology, Extension, and Productivity

An econometric analysis of the determinants of new technology demonstrates the effectiveness of investments in the research system. The higher level of national stocks both accelerate the pace of varietal turnover and raise the yield potential embodied in major varieties used by farmers. If technology is the engine that will drive China's food supply in the future (Huang, Rozelle, and Rosegrant, 1999), the results in the study emphasize the necessity of maintaining the level and growth of public investment in crop research and development. Regardless of what factors contribute to the creation of China's rice, wheat, maize, and soybean material, technology has a large and positive influence on TFP. The role of extension is less simple. The impact of extension can occur through its effect on spreading new seed technologies and providing other services that enhance farmer productivity.

Examining elasticities of TFP with respect to technology, extension, and the factors that affect technology help us to understand what factors are contribut-

TABLE 14.11

Elasticities of TFP with Respect to Technology, Extension, and Other Factors for Rice, Wheat, Soybean, and Maize for China, 1982–95

	Rice	Wheat	Soybean	Maize
Direct				
Varietal turnover	0.31	0.28	0.27	0.32
Extension expenditure	−0.08	0[a]	0.31	−0.32
Indirect				
Research stock	0.63	0.47	0.6	0.67
CG contribution	0[a]	0.01	0[a]	0[a]
Yield envelope	−0.12	0.14	−0.12	−0.11
Extension expenditure	0.05	0.10	0.08	0[a]

NOTE: [a]The 0 elasticity implies that the coefficient was not significantly different than zero.
SOURCE: Huang, Rozelle, Hu, and Jin (1999).

ing importantly to productivity (see Table 14.11). The elasticities on the technology variable (varietal turnover) and the research investment variable (measured in research stock) are large for all crops. Research investment leads to increases in TFP through its impact on varietal turnover and certainly is one of the reasons recent estimates of the returns to research calculate the internal rate of return to be between 50 percent (Huang et al., 2002) and 70 to 100 percent (Fan, 1997). The fact that research investment increases productivity so much is also good for farmers, who are sometimes hurt by policies that lead to price declines if they are not accompanied by cost reductions.

Although the elasticity on the CG variable is small in examining its effect on TFP through varietal turnover, a direct, more intuitive interpretation can be seen from the marginal effect. In the case of rice, a rise of 1 percentage point in CG material increases TFP by nearly 1 percentage point. However, when its impact through the increase in yield potential is considered (Jin et al., 2002), the marginal impact of CIMMYT material is small.[6] However, it should be noted that this effect is above and beyond the contribution that the CG system's germplasm has had on the varieties in the field. From 4 to 25 percent of China's rice, wheat, and maize germplasm is contributed by CG varieties (Jin et al., 2002); as a result, at least that much credit should be attributed to the CG system for the rise in TFP due to varietal turnover.

Trade Liberalization, Agricultural Technology, and China's Food Deficit

Issues and Debates

China's ability to feed itself in the twenty-first century has been widely discussed and is a subject of much concern among researchers of China's agricultural economy. The preponderance of serious evidence indicates that China will be able to feed itself, although grain imports will probably rise over the next several decades. Yang and Tyers (1989) forecast that China would import roughly 50 metric million tons (mmt) annually in the late 1990s. Rozelle, Huang, and Rosegrant (1996) and Huang, Rozelle, and Rosegrant (1999) predict that China will need to import 30–40 mmt annually to meet domestic demand for the first two decades of the twenty-first century. Most international food trade and production specialists believe that current suppliers can meet China's rising import demands without long-term price increases or threats to world food security.

The impact of trade liberalization and China's accession to the WTO on domestic grain production and grain imports is of increasing concern to China's leaders. While most of the recent studies show that China will gain from joining the WTO, the impact on the economy varies greatly across sectors. Domestic agricultural production, particularly grain, cotton, oil crops and sugar crops, will decline with the trade liberalization (Huang and Chen, 1999).

Some researchers even predict that liberalization will lead to massive imports and a steep fall in China's rate of self-sufficiency. Garnaut and Ma (1992) forecast that China would face a grain shortage of up to 90 mmt in 2000. Brown (1995) argues that China's grain production will have fallen between 216 and 378 mmt short of demand by the end of the first quarter of the twenty-first century, forcing the nation to use foreign exchange earnings from the booming export sector to import enough grain to fill the gap. He predicts that China's imports will drain the world grain supplies, force prices up, and deny poorer nations the grain necessary to feed their populations.

Such a wide range of net import predictions is perplexing. China's emergence as either a major importer or a major exporter could have enormous consequences for world grain markets and prices. China is experiencing rapid development and transformation. Continual reforms and the dynamic nature of China's economy require that researchers update predictions frequently.

Our projections here incorporate recent government policies and trade liberalization based on a projection model developed at the Center for Chinese Agricultural Policy (CCAP), CCAP's Agricultural Policy Simulation and Projection Model (CAPSiM).[7]

Given China's entry into the WTO and the associated process of trade liberalization, we project China's food economy in the early twenty-first century under three alternative scenarios: a baseline run, a free trade regime only, and a free trade regime with an increase in public investment in agricultural research. Although the baseline and complete free trade regime scenarios are extreme, they bound the projections, as the actual situation is likely to fall somewhere in between. The baseline scenario assumes that the current policies will be continued without change even after China's accession to the WTO. The free trade regime assumes that China will liberalize its agricultural sector and be completely unprotected by 2005. We also examine what would happen should China liberalize while increasing public investment. The annual growth rate of agricultural research expenditures in real terms is 4 percent under both the baseline and free trade scenarios; it is 6 percent under the scenario of free trade with an increase in agricultural research expenditure.

Agricultural Production, Demand, and Trade

Baseline Scenario

Our baseline projections show that China's per capita food grain consumption peaked in the late 1990s. The average rural resident will increase consumption until the year 2010 and then reduce demand thereafter. Urban food grain consumption declines over most of the projection period. Rural-to-urban migration leads to overall lower food demand.

Per capita demand for red meat is forecast to rise sharply throughout the projection period. China's consumers will increase their meat consumptions by 65 percent by 2020, from 17 to 28 kilograms per capita for pork, from 2 to 3 kilograms for beef, and 1 to 2 kilograms for mutton.[8] Although rural demand lags the growth of urban demand, urbanization will shift people from rural into high-consumption urban areas. In 1996, an average urban resident consumed about 60 percent more red meat than his or her rural counterpart. Per capita demand for poultry and fish, although initially lower, will rise proportionally faster than red meat demand.

The projected demand increase for red meat, poultry, and other animal products will spur aggregate feed grain demand. The baseline scenario predicts that demand for feed grains will increase to 175 mmt by 2010 and climb to 217 mmt by 2020 (see Table 14.12).[9] Feed grains as a proportion of total grain utilization will grow from 27 percent in the mid-1990s to about 38 percent in 2020.

Aggregate grain demand, taking projected population growth into account, will reach 519 mmt by 2010, an increase of 23 percent over 1996 (see Table 14.12). Although projected food demand levels off over the later projection period, grain demand will continue to increase in response to population growth and increased demand for animal products. Aggregate grain demand is expected to reach 578 mmt by the end of the forecast period. Baseline projections show China's grain production gradually falling behind increasing demand. Our projections forecast rising grain deficits; imports will surge to 20 mmt in 2005 and stay at about 18–20 mmt in 2010–20 (see Table 14.12).

In the livestock and aquatic sector, the increases in domestic production nearly match the increases in demand. The annual production growth rates of various animal products will range from 3 to 7 percent in 2000–20. The growth rates are equivalent to the growth rates of the demand for these products in the same period. The sector will continue to export, but the amounts of exported livestock products and fish will be small compared to total domestic production or consumption.

TABLE 14.12

Projections of Grain Production, Demand, and Net Imports Under Various Scenarios, 2005–2020

	2005	2010	2020
Baseline			
Production (mmt)	464	499	560
Net import (mmt)	20	20	18
Demand (mmt)	484	519	578
Food (mmt)	257	266	279
Feed (mmt)	151	175	217
Others (mmt)	76	78	83
Grain self-sufficiency (percent)	96	96	97
Free trade regime			
Grain net import (mmt)	60	55	48
Maize (mmt)	39	47	64
Grain self-sufficiency (percent)	88	89	92
Free trade regime plus increase in agricultural research expenditure (annual growth rate 4 percent → 6 percent)			
Grain net import (mmt)	60	52	17
Maize (mmt)	39	46	51
Grain self-sufficiency (percent)	88	90	97

SOURCE: Authors' projection.

Impacts of Trade Liberalization

Under the free trade scenario, domestic grain prices (except those for rice) would fall. The fall in the domestic price of grain raises grain consumption and reduces growth in production. Compared to the baseline scenario, the gap between domestic supply and demand of grain would rise. China's net grain imports would increase to 60 mmt in 2005 (a level representing about 12 percent of the total grain consumption in China) and about 48–55 mmt in the period 2010–20 (see Table 14.12).

The most serious impacts of trade liberalization on grain are projected to be on maize, followed by wheat and soybeans. Under the free trade scenario, China's domestic maize production would fall far behind maize consumption. Production would grow annually by only 0.7 percent, while consumption would grow by 5.9 percent as a result of the decline in maize price and surging feed demand for livestock production expansion after trade liberalization (2000–05). Consequently, imports of maize would increase dramatically from less than 2 mmt in 2000 to 39 mmt (nearly one-quarter of maize consumption in China) in 2005. China would likely be the world largest importer of maize in the coming years if the sector were completely liberalized.

Although wheat is a food grain, the consumption response of which to price change is weaker than that of feed grains, the impact of trade liberalization on wheat will also be substantial in the first few years as the wheat price declines. But projected wheat imports will fall after 2005 with the decline in population growth and the drop in demand due to migration (since urban residents consume less grain on a per capita basis than those in rural areas).

In contrast, rice producers are predicted to benefit from the trade liberalization. Under the free trade scenario, rice production will rise from 133 mmt in 2000 to 145 mmt in 2005, with an annual growth rate of 1.8 percent (compared to the baseline of 0.9 percent). The higher rate of production growth results from the rise in the rice price and the decline in the prices of inputs such as fertilizer and pesticide under free trade. In the meantime, the increase in the rice price reduces the annual rice consumption growth rate from 0.8 percent in the baseline to only 0.6 percent in 2000–05. The combined impacts of production and consumption imply that trade liberalization would result in substantial rice exports (7.12 mmt in 2005).

The impacts of trade liberalization on China's animal sector are also significant. But in contrast to the grain sector, trade liberalization will raise domestic prices of pork and poultry substantially and those of eggs and fish moderately. The increase in the prices of these major animal products and a decrease in the feed price resulting from trade liberalization would stimulate the domestic production of these products on the one hand and dampen their consumption on the other hand. The exports of livestock and fish products would expand considerably, assuming that China's exports did not run into other trade barriers (such as phytosanitary regulations). Trade liberalization is also expected to have significantly negative impacts on the productions of sugar crops, oil crops, and cotton and substantial positive impacts on horticulture and food processing industry (Huang and Chen, 1999).

Agricultural Technology and China's Grain Self-Sufficiency

Food security has been and will continue to be one of the central goals of China's policy. While food security has many dimensions, one of the targets set by the Chinese government recently is to achieve a grain self-sufficiency level above 95 percent. Although this level of grain self-sufficiency has been widely debated, any changes (including trade liberalization) that might lower the grain self-sufficiency level below 95 percent in the long-term would get little support from the current leadership.

Table 14.13 presents China's grain self-sufficiency rates under the three scenarios for 1995–2020. The third scenario assumes that the growth rate of agricultural research expenditure in real terms rises from 4 percent (the assumption use in the other scenarios) to 6 percent during the entire projection period.

Under the baseline scenario, while China will be able to achieve one of the major components of its food security target (greater than 95 percent grain self-sufficiency) in the future, the costs associated with this scenario should not be ignored. All grain prices in domestic markets (except for rice) will considerably

TABLE 14.13

Grain Self-Sufficiency Rates Under Various Scenarios,
1994–2020

(percent)

	1994–96	2005	2010	2020
Baseline				
Total grain	98	96	96	97
Rice	100	99	100	101
Wheat	92	92	95	100
Maize	101	94	91	90
Soybean	100	101	102	102
Free trade regime				
Total grain	98	88	90	92
Rice	100	105	107	114
Wheat	92	83	88	97
Maize	101	76	74	72
Soybean	100	92	94	95
Free trade with raise in agricultural research expenditure *				
Total grain	98	88	90	97
Rice	100	105	108	119
Wheat	92	83	89	102
Maize	101	76	75	78
Soybean	100	92	95	101

NOTE: *The third scenario assumes that the growth rate of agricultural research expenditure in real terms rises from 4 percent (the assumption used in the other scenarios) to 6 percent during the entire period of the projection.

exceed prices in the international markets. For example, the domestic prices of maize, wheat, and soybeans will exceed international prices by about 26, 20, and 21 percent, respectively, in 2005, and the gap between the domestic and international prices will widen thereafter, particularly for maize. The domestic price of maize will reach that of wheat by 2020. Whether the government budget and consumers can pay for the grain price protection policy and how livestock production and exports will be affected are issues that need to be considered.

Complete trade liberalization (the free trade scenario) will obviously challenge the government's current food security goal. China's grain self-sufficiency rate will decline rapidly from 98 percent in the mid-1990s to 88.4 percent in 2005 (see Table 14.13), a level unlikely to be accepted by the current government. Although the grain self-sufficiency rate will rise gradually after 2005, some 8 percent of domestic grain demand will still need to be met by imports in 2020.[10]

However, it is important to note that the most effective policy to improve China's food security and raise grain self-sufficiency level in the long run is to invest in agricultural productivity enhancement, such as agricultural R&D, rural infrastructure, and water control (irrigation). Altering assumptions about investment in agricultural research has the greatest impact on production and trade balances in the long run. For example, Table 14.13 shows that China could essentially achieve its long-term grain self-sufficiency target (after 2015) even under the free trade regime, if the annual growth rate in agricultural research investment rises from 4 to 6 percent. The result is hardly surprising, given the large contributions that agricultural research and the technology it has produced have made to agricultural productivity in the past.

Conclusions and Implications for Policy

China, the world's most populous country, is highly acclaimed for its ability to feed over one-fifth of the world's population with only 7 percent of the world's arable land. Despite extremely limited natural resources and a population that has doubled over the past four decades, per capita availability of food, household food security, and nutrition have all improved significantly. Increased domestic production is almost solely responsible for increased per capita food availability. However, China may face great challenges in reaching the goal of feeding its growing population and maintaining high food security in the coming decades if future policies do not further these goals.

Our projections show that while China's importance as a world grain importer will increase over the coming decades, China will neither drain world grain markets nor become a major grain exporter if the future policies are formulated properly. Net grain imports over the next three decades are likely to be between 20 and 35 mmt annually. Accelerating demand for meat and feed grains are the major reasons for rising grain imports. China's grain production will become increasingly oriented toward feed grains. However, in some situations (under complete trade liberalization without substantial increases in agricultural research investment), China could have to import up to 50 million tons or more.

Our estimates of China's net grain imports could also shift, depending on the situation. We expect that relaxing any major policy assumptions or changing factors that we did not consider explicitly, such as competition for agricultural water use and declining returns to investment in agriculture and research, will have a significant impact on China's predicted food supply and demand.

Limited options for increasing food supplies intensify the challenge of meeting China's food security target. Although our policy and literature review has illustrated that institutional reform, water control investments, price policies, and improvements to the environment contribute to higher food production, such matters as scare resources, current agricultural policies, and fiscal constraints may preclude leaders from implementing some of them. Decollectivization and fiscal reform have already been tapped for most of their gains. Likewise, five decades of development have exploited most of the easy gains from land and water investments (World Bank, 1997). Huang and Rozelle (1995) demonstrate the negative impact that increasing environmental stress has on output but conclude that in the current period, gains from launching a major effort to alleviate the problems will add little to supply, at uncertain cost. The nation's budget crises, above all, bind the hands of officials even if investments in agricultural research promise high returns. Chronic budget shortfalls and looming trade agreements also effectively shut off the option of using East Asian–style price policies to maintain production levels.

The constraints imposed on leaders by resource scarcity and politicoeconomic realities increase the need to understand the scope for supply expansion from one of the most important sources of past supply growth, investments in the research system. The huge stock of research created by years of investment and the promising potential of technologies under development (from both domestic researchers and foreign sources) give leaders one solid policy handle.

China's research system has produced a steady flow of new crop varieties and other technologies since the 1950s. The robust growth of China's stock of research capital is in large part responsible for the nation's dramatic agricultural growth rates. Improved technology has been the biggest factor by far, behind grain production growth, and as such is a major source of increased food availability in China.

The analyses and results presented in this chapter establish a basis for China's leaders and policymakers (and those elsewhere in the world) to invest confidently in the nation's agricultural research system. The basis for doing so rests primarily on the important effects that technology and the institutions that create, import, and disseminate it have had on TFP in the past. The picture sketched by several of our recent studies (Huang, Hu, and Fan, 1998; Huang, Rozelle, and Rosegrant, 1999; Huang et al., 2002) demonstrates that investment in new technology is many-faceted. Public investments in breeding and extension pay off in terms of higher TFP. The form of the technology matters, not only in how rich it is in terms of yield-enhancing material but also in whether or not farmers will adopt it.

However, the recent decline in the government's budgetary commitment to research has weakened the system. The extension system is also extremely fragile and needs to be strengthened. Development of an efficient seed industry is not without roadblocks as appropriate supporting institutions (eliminating entry barriers, allowing the market to set prices, phasing out subsidies, and developing intellectual property rights) take time to mature.

After two decades of reform, the grain bureaus still require farmers to deliver specified quantities of grain. Although it is premature to evaluate the impacts of the new grain market reforms in the late 1990s on grain production, prices, and marketing, issues related to the ability and willingness of local governments to hold sufficient buffer stocks for price stabilization need to be addressed. China should allow a greater role for the market to determine trade patterns in order to reap gains from comparative advantage. This would probably mean increased overall agricultural trade domestically among provinces and internationally and a shift toward importing more land-intensive agricultural products and exporting more labor-intensive agricultural products. Policy steps to exploit comparative advantage might include removing implicit taxes on farmers and reforming the domestic grain pricing and marketing system. In the past, China's policy on domestic agricultural product marketing has been biased against producers. Domestic price and marketing policies have consistently taxed farmers in most periods. Moreover, the most heavily taxed commodities are the exportable agricultural commodities.

In short, China's agriculture has achieved enormous gains over the course of twenty years of reform. However, it also faces steep challenges in the future. Good development and transition policies are needed now more than ever.

Notes

1. The crisis did not directly spread to China, in part as a consequence of the more insulated nature of its economy and in part due to the size of its domestic capital market and the strength of its domestic demand.

2. The goals of the grain market reform in 1998 were to improve the efficiency of the grain marketing system and to reduce central government's fiscal burden in financing grain circulation and the reserve system.

3. Under the policy, grain marketed by the private sector in wholesale and retail markets should come from the state grain bureau.

4. Variety turnover is a measure of how fast major varieties that first appear in China's field are able to replace the older varieties; see Jin et al. (2002) for details.

5. It should also be remembered that China also has contributed significantly to the world stock of genetic resources for rice and soybeans, in particular.

6. This may result from the fact that some provinces in southern and western China, where CIMMYT varieties are adopted, are excluded from the analysis due to lack of data. Currently, efforts are under way to collect data for these missing provinces.

7. CAPSiM is a partial equilibrium model. Most of the elasticities are estimated econometrically with imposition of theoretical constraints. CAPSiM explicitly accounts for urbanization and market development (demand side), technology, agricultural investment, environmental trends, and competition for labor and land use (supply side), as well as the price responses of both demand and supply (see Huang and Chen, 1999).

8. A kilogram equals 2.2 pounds.

9. All figures are for trade grain—rice in milled form, not unprocessed grain.

10. However, it is worth noting that this is an extreme case (the free trade regime), representing a maximum impact of the trade liberalization on China's grain economy. The actual impacts of China's joining the WTO will be much lower than the results in this free trade scenario.

References

Anderson, Kym. 1990. *Comparative Advantages in China: Effects on Food, Feed, and Fiber Markets*. Paris: Organization for Economic Cooperation and Development.

Brandt, Loren, Jikun Huang, Guo Li, and Scott Rozelle. 2000. *Land Rights in China: Facts, Fictions, and Issues*. Working Paper, Department of Agricultural and Resource Economics, University of California, Davis.

Brown, Lester. 1995. *Who Will Feed China? Wake-Up Call for a Small Planet*. Washington, D.C.: Worldwatch Institute.

Cheng, Guoqiang. 1998. "The Patterns of China's Agricultural Trade." *Intertrade*, 11, 4–6.

Fan, Shenggen. 1991. "Effects of Technological Change and Institutional Reform in Production Growth of Chinese Agriculture." *American Journal of Agricultural Economy*, 73, 266–75.

———. 1997. "Production and Productivity Growth in Chinese Agriculture: New Measurement and Evidence." *Food Policy*, 22, 213–28.

Fan, Shenggen, and Phil Pardey. 1997. "Research Productivity and Output Growth in Chinese Agriculture." *Journal of Development Economics*, 53, 115–37.

Garnaut, Ross, and Guonan Ma. 1992. *Grain in China: A Report*. Canberra, Australia: East Asian Analytical Unit, Department of Foreign Affairs and Trade.

Huang, Jikun. 1999a. "Allocation Efficiency of Agricultural Resources in the 20-Year Reform." *China's Rural Survey*, 1, 1–9; 2, 29–37.

———. 1999b. *Performance, Prospects, and Challenges for China's Agriculture in the 21st Century*. Report submitted to RAP/FAO, Bangkok.

Huang, Jikun, and Chunlai Chen. 1999. *Agricultural Trade Liberalization in China: Commodity and Local Agriculture Studies*. Project report for the United Nations Economic and Social Commission for Asia and the Pacific.

Huang, Jikun, Ruifa Hu, Linxin Zhang, and Scott Rozelle. 2002. *Agricultural R&D Investment and Policy in China*. Beijing: China Agricultural Press.

Huang, Jikun, Ruifa Hu, and Xiandong Fan. 1998. "Agricultural Research Investment in China." *China Soft Sciences*, 7, 95–101.

Huang, Jikun, Hengyun Ma, and Scott Rozelle. 1998. "Rural Poverty and Investment Policy in the Poor Area in China." *Reform*, 4, 72–83.

Huang, Jikun, Mark Rosegrant, and Scott Rozelle. 1995. *Public Investment, Technological Change, and Agricultural Growth in China*. Working Paper, Food Research Institute, Stanford University.

Huang, Jikun, and Scott Rozelle. 1995. "Environmental Stress and Grain Yields in China." *American Journal of Agricultural Economics*, 77, 853–64.

———. 1996. "Technological Change: Rediscovering the Engine of Productivity Growth in China's Agricultural Economy." *Journal of Development Economics*, 49, 337–69.

Huang, Jikun, Scott Rozelle, and Mark Rosegrant. 1999. "China's Food Economy to the 21st Century: Supply, Demand, and Trade." *Economic Development and Cultural Change*, 47, 737–66.

Huang, Jikun, Scott Rozelle, Ruifa Hu, and Songqing Jin. 1999. *The Creation and Spread of Technology and Total Factor Productivity in China: An Analysis of the Contribution of China's Research System and CG-Supplied Genetic Material*. Paper presented at the annual meeting of the American Agricultural Economics Association, Nashville, Tenn.

Jin, Songqing, Ruifa Hu, Jikun Huang, and Scott Rozelle. 2002. "The Creation and Spread of Technology and Total Factor Productivity in China." *American Journal of Agricultural Economics*, 84, 916–30.

Jin, Songqing, Carl Pray, Jikun Huang, and Scott Rozelle. 1998. *Commercializing Agricultural Research and Fungible Government Investment: Lessons from China.* Working paper, University of California, Davis.

Kung, James, and Shouying Liu. 1997. "Farmers Preferences Regarding Ownership and Land Tenure in Post-Mao China." *China Journal,* 38(July), 33–63.

Lardy, Nicholas R. 1983. *Agriculture in China's Modern Economic Development.* Cambridge: Cambridge University Press.

Lin, Justin Yifu. 1991a. "The Household Responsibility System Reform and the Adoption of Hybrid Rice in China." *Journal of Development Economics,* 36, 353–72.

———. 1991b. "Prohibitions of Factor Market Exchanges and Technological Choice in Chinese Agriculture." *Journal of Development Studies,* 27(4), 1–15.

———. 1992. "Rural Reforms and Agricultural Growth in China." *American Economic Review,* 82, 34–51.

———. 1998. *How Did China Feed Itself in the Past? How Will China Feed Itself in the Future?* Lecture, CIMMYT (International Maize and Wheat Improvement Center) Economics Program, Mexico City.

Lin, Justin Yifu, Mingao Shen, and H. Zhao. 1996. *Agricultural Research Priority in China: A Demand and Supply Analysis of Seed Improvement Research for Major Grain Crops in China.* Beijing: China Agriculture Press.

Lohmar, Bryan. 1999. *Rural Institutions and Labor Movement in China.* Ph.D. dissertation, Department of Agricultural Economics, University of California, Davis.

Lyons, Thomas. 1992. *Market-Oriented Reform in China: Cautionary Tales.* Working Papers on Transitions from State Socialism. Mario Einaudi Center for International Studies, Cornell University.

McMillan, J., J. Whalley, and L. Zhu. 1989. "The Impact of China's Economic Reforms on Agricultural Productivity Growth." *Journal of Political Economy,* 97, 781–807.

Ministry of Agriculture. 1980–98 (published annually). *China Agricultural Yearbook* [in Chinese.] Beijing: China Agricultural Press.

———. 1997. *China's Agricultural Development Report, 1997.* Beijing: Ministry of Agriculture.

———. 1998. *China's Agricultural Development Report, 1998.* Beijing: Ministry of Agriculture.

Nyberg, Albert, and Scott Rozelle. 1999. *Accelerating China's Rural Transformation.* Washington, D.C.: World Bank.

Pingali, P. L., M. Hossein, and R. V. Gerpacio. 1997. *Asian Rice Bowls: The Returning Crisis?* Cambridge, Mass.: CAB International.

Pingali, P. L., and Mark Rosegrant. 1995. "Green Revolution Blues." Paper presented at the annual meeting of the American Agricultural Economics Association, Orlando, Fla.

Rozelle, Scott. 1994. "Decision Making in China's Rural Economy: The Linkages Between Village Leaders and Farm Households." *China Quarterly,* 137(March), 99–124.

Rozelle, Scott, and Jikun Huang. 2000. "Transition, Development and Wheat Supply in China," *Australian Journal of Agricultural Economics,* 44, 543–71.

Rozelle, Scott, Jikun Huang, and Mark Rosegrant. 1996. "Why China Will NOT Starve the World." *Choices,* First Quarter, 18–24.

Rozelle, Scott, Albert Park, Jikun Huang, and Hehui Jin. 1997. "Liberalization and Rural Market Integration in China." *American Journal of Agricultural Economics,* 79, 635–42.

Sicular, Terry. 1991. "China's Agricultural Policy During the Reform Period." In Joint Economic Committee, Congress of the United States, ed., *China's Economic Dilemmas in the 1990s: The Problems of Reforms, Modernization and Interdependence,* vol. 1. Washington, D.C.: Government Printing Office.

———.1995. "Redefining State, Plan and Market: China's Reforms in Agriculture Commerce." *China Quarterly*, 143,1020–46

State Science and Technology Commission. 1985–1997. *Statistical Compendium for Agricultural Research in China*. Beijing: State Science and Technology Commission.

State Statistical Bureau. 1980–99a (published annually). *China Statistical Yearbook*. Beijing: State Statistical Publishing House.

———. 1990–98b (published annually). *China Rural Statistical Yearbook*. Beijing: State Statistical Publishing House.

Stone, Bruce. 1988. "Developments in Agricultural Technology." *China Quarterly*, 116, 705–52.

Tang, Anthony M., and Bruce Stone. 1980. *Food Production in the People's Republic of China*. Washington, D.C.: International Food Policy Research Institute.

Wen, Guangzhong. 1993. "Total Factor Productivity Change in China's Farming Sector, 1952–1989." *Economic Development and Cultural Change*, 42 191–208.

Wiens, T. J. 1982. "Technological Change." In Randolph Barker and Radha Sinha, eds., *The Chinese Agricultural Economy*. Boulder, Colo.: Westview Press.

World Bank. 1997. *At China's Table: Food Security Options*. Washington, D.C.: World Bank.

Yang, Yongzheng, and Rodney Tyers. 1989. "The Economic Costs of Food Self-Sufficiency in China." *World Development*, 17, 237–53.

15

Bending Without Breaking

The Adaptability of Chinese Political Institutions

Jean C. Oi

China eschewed the "big bang" approach to avoid the thorny political and social consequences of economic reform.[1] To a large extent, it succeeded. Compared to the nations of the former Soviet Union and eastern Europe, China's reform process has been relatively smooth. Significant economic progress has been achieved. Yet by the second decade of reform, the regime already faced the problems of consolidation, which is often more difficult than the initiation of reform.[2] The "trickle-down" theory underlying Deng's policy of "let some get rich first" was coming under increasing question, as those who had failed to benefit were becoming more and more anxious as regional and sectoral inequalities increased. After more than two decades of reform, as the leadership is dealing with the most difficult of the economic problems—reforming the state-owned enterprises (SOEs) and the banks—the pressure and discontent generated by reform are getting worse. Workers in SOEs, once the elite of the workforce, are being laid off in large numbers. Perhaps most worrisome to the regime, discontented peasants and workers are taking their grievances to the streets, in cities and the countryside.

Is the political system up to the task of dealing with the mounting economic and political demands? Will the political system be the weak link that prevents China from sustaining the economic gains achieved in the first two decades of reform? That is the big question, but one that cannot be easily answered. One way to begin to get a handle on this big issue is to explore how flexible the regime has been in trying to accommodate, ameliorate, or defuse the sources of political instability that have arisen as the result of the economic reforms.

Limited but Significant Political Change

China's rapid economic growth since 1980 has raised the possibility that economic and political reform do not have to be undertaken together. It is commonly accepted that China achieved economic reforms with minimal political reform. Outwardly, the political system still exhibits many of the same Leninist characteristics that it did when the reforms started. As other observers have noted, it is still a system ruled by the Communist Party, the standing committee of the Politburo still sets policy, and the structure still supports a mobilizational system. The succession problem is unsolved, the Party is separated from neither the government nor the state, and corruption remains a major problem. The continued arrests by the regime of high-profile dissidents and individuals who try to set up opposition parties or who are perceived to present a challenge, such as the Falun Gong, further highlight the continued limits on political reform. These repressive acts reinforce the impression left by the brutal 1989 crackdown on demonstrators in Tiananmen Square and suggest that the regime is brittle and out of touch with its citizens.

Although the infractions of human rights are serious and the regime is vulnerable, both of which suggest a lack of political reform, these problems obscure the limited but significant changes that have taken place in China's political system over the past two decades. A major reason why problems often overshadow advances is that the amount of political change one sees in China varies significantly, depending on where one looks in the system and how one defines political change. The change is least evident at the national level, but even there, as John Burns has argued, there has been forward movement, ranging from the institution of open civil service exams to new roles for mass organizations and people's congresses to a rejuvenated leadership.[3] Efforts are also under way to realize the rule of law.[4] The attempts to streamline the state bureaucracy and raise the qualifications of those who serve in government are yet other examples of the conscious effort to reform the system.

While developments at the national level set the overall tone of the political system, they do not always reflect what is going on within the system, especially at the lower levels. If one looks beyond the national level, beyond the lack of popular national elections and the regime's treatment of dissidents, to the grass roots, to China's villages and cities, one sees modes of articulation and pursuit of interests that suggest significant political change has occurred in China. Citizens cannot elect their national leaders, but a new range of *other* activities and channels have allowed citizens to articulate and pursue their interests in ways that were never before possible in China.[5] Table 15.1 provides a quick summary of some major changes that have taken place.

People familiar with China know that there are still many problems with and limitations on the changes occurring at both the national and local levels. The increased power of the National Peoples' Congress (NPC) is likely due more to personalities than to institutional strengthening. The rule of law is limited by poor implementation and poorly trained legal personnel, including judges. Key posts within the bureaucracy are still subject to the Party-controlled *nomenklatura* approval system. Village elections, in addition to being only selectively and

TABLE 15.1
Toward Political Change in China

Level	Change
National	Increasing autonomy of the National People's Congress (NPC)
	Increasing reliance on rule of law: Passage of administration litigation law
	Increasingly better-educated, more technocratic bureaucracy based on a civil service examination with age-determined mandatory retirement
Local	Passage of the Organic Law on Villagers' Committees that provides for village elections
	Two-ballot system for election of village party secretary
	Overt expressions of discontent in both urban and rural areas
	Rightful resistance, including peasants using laws to combat cadre abuse
	Individual and collective action, including demonstrations, strikes, and attacks on government offices and officials
	More transparency in the management of village affairs, including open accounting and levy cards
	Move from a system of ad hoc fees to standardized taxes on peasants

sometimes poorly implemented, exclude the post of village Party secretary. The two-ballot system, while addressing this problem, is experimental and still limited. Clear boundaries must not be crossed in political action, especially collective action.

Clearly, these changes are far from institutionalized and problem-free, but that does not preclude the possibility that they have opened the door to significant political change. To see how far the door has opened and how far down the new road the system has traveled, let us examine in more detail the nature of the new forms of political activity that are occurring in China and the regime's response.

New Forms of Political Expression

Of the new forms of political expression, the most worrisome and perhaps the most significant is the overt expression of discontent that has occurred in both rural and urban areas. The existence of such expression indicates severe discontent, but what that suggests about the political regime, its power, or its flexibility is less obvious. To know how threatening these incidents of unrest are to the regime, we need to know much more than that they have taken place. What are the sources of discontent? Is the anger directed at the central state or at local officials? Knowing who is being blamed not only sheds light on how threatening these demonstrations are to the central state but also gives important clues into the calculus of the state's response.

Expressions of Peasant Discontent

Peasant grievances against state policies are nothing new. What is new are the ways that peasants manifest this discontent and pursue their interests. Whereas peasants pursued their interests during the Mao period mostly through covert channels, often through the *nonarticulation* of interests and sometimes in collusion with their local cadres to evade exactions by the upper-level state,[6] the post-Mao countryside has witnessed an array of overt, sometimes violent, expressions of peasant discontent.

The more informed and more peacefully inclined peasants use published laws to obtain their rights and to punish their cadres—the "rightful resistance" that Li and O'Brien have described.[7] Others, when provoked, beat their cadres, burn their houses, or march on the upper levels of government. Sometimes whole villages or even groups of villages have marched on township or county governments, such as the Renshou riots in Sichuan, causing serious destruction of property, injuries and even deaths and requiring troops to quell the disturbances.[8]

The number of such incidents and how many individuals participate are difficult to know. Bernstein notes that in "the fall, winter, and early spring of 1996 – 1997, confrontations in the form of demonstrations . . . as well as petitioning. . . erupted in nine provinces in 36 counties; 230 were labeled cases of turmoil or rebellion (*dongluan, saoluan, baodong*)."[9] Between mid-May and mid-June 1997, half a million peasants took part in demonstrations in the provinces of Hunan, Hubei, Anhui, and Jiangxi.[10]

Sources and Character of Rural Discontent

Much of the peasant discontent can be traced to the unintended consequences of the decollectivization of agriculture. It is widely known that decollectivization changed the organization of production and increased the incentives under the Household Responsibility System. What is less often noted is that decollectivization also opened the door to increasing "peasant burdens" when it deprived village officials of the rights to use the income from the harvest for village administrative expenses. If a village has no sources of collective income, such as village enterprises, it is dependent on the "village retained fees" (*tiliu*) for the entirety of the village operating budget.[11] Because villages are not considered an official level of government, they receive no budget allocation from the upper levels, unlike the township level and above. The only right village officials have to household income is the *tiliu* assessment, which the village levies above and beyond the national agricultural tax on each household based on income. The central government legislated rules that forbid these fees to exceed 5 percent of peasant income. The problem is that this limit is routinely exceeded as local cadres raise these levies to meet local needs. The poorer the village, the more likely peasants will be pressed for more fees.

Peasant burdens are further aggravated when local officials falsely report production and income. Such problems are especially prominent in the less developed areas, where officials try to increase their bonuses and prospects for promotions by reporting a good economic performance. Not all cadres who engage in such practices are driven by corruption; some are simply pressured by their superiors at the township or county, who themselves are subject to the same economic pressure, to report higher levels of development than actually achieved.[12]

Cadre corruption can take many forms; false reporting is but one of them. Another that has sparked peasant protest is the issuing of IOUs. Cadres misappropriate funds designated for state procurement of crops, resulting in peasants' being paid IOUs instead of cash when they deliver their grain for sale to the state. Central funds are specially allocated for procurement. The problem is what happens to the funds once they come down to the county and township levels. *Nuoyong*—the misappropriation of funds—has been an ongoing problem between the local and central state since at least the 1980s.[13]

A third area of discontent is the increasing costs of production—costs have reportedly gone up 15 percent a year between 1984 and 1996.[14] The problem cannot be reduced to cadre corruption, but it is aggravated when corrupt local cadres skim off the low-priced state-supplied goods and sell them illegally on the open market at much higher prices.

Expressions of Urban Discontent

Workers, like peasants, have also always had ways to pursue their interests, but as with their rural counterparts, most of their strategies were likely to be covert, often through the use of personal connections.[15] Again, what is new is the degree to which workers are willing to articulate their grievances through overt channels.[16] What is most surprising is that the government has allowed workers to engage in what can be considered collective action to promulgate their demands. Workers have not only visited government offices as individuals or small groups but have also participated in group demonstrations and processions, work slowdowns, strikes, and attacks on government offices and officials.[17]

Another feature of worker unrest that departs from the prereform period is the action of workers independent of their work unit. The cohesion and tight control of workers in the unit system are well known.[18] A common strategy of workers to get ahead was to curry favor with their shop floor and factory leaders. This strategy no doubt still exists, but one also finds that workers now complain and demonstrate openly against their factory manager. Sometimes angry workers take matters directly into their own hands and march their factory director in the streets, sometimes in Cultural Revolution style, forcing them to assume the "airplane" position, roughing them up along the way.[19]

As in rural areas, it is difficult to know how many workers are taking part in collective action. The number of laid-off workers grew from 3 million in 1993 to 11.5 million in 1997.[20] But those numbers tell us little about how many of these are discontented or how many would take political action. We have reports of various incidents of unrest but not a very clear picture of what the situation looks like nationally. Solinger cites a report stating that in 1995, eleven incidents nationwide involved more than ten thousand workers.[21] Later research found that in Shandong province in 1998, the party committee and the government at the county level and above received close to fifteen thousand visits, an increase of more than 40 percent from the previous year; the numbers participating also increased by more than 40 percent. In Liaoning, between January and May 1998, more than eleven hundred collective visits to the government involved more than fifty participants.[22] Most of the time, the actions are contained within a factory, although there are examples where strikes and protests spread beyond a factory's gates. Solinger cites sources that indicate that one strike spread to involve forty enterprises.[23] One factory protest in Sichuan where workers marched their director in the streets reportedly involved twenty thousand people throughout the city by the end of the day.[24]

Sources and Character of Urban Discontent

At this point, the situation in the urban areas is less well understood than for the rural areas. From what we can tell, the sources of discontent in China's cities seem to be a familiar mix of the consequences of economic reform combined with cadre corruption. The disaffected include laid-off workers, workers in factories that have been declared bankrupt and closed, workers in unprofitable but not yet bankrupt factories who are not laid off but who also are not paid because their factory is broke and can't get loans, and retired workers who are not receiving their pensions.[25] The degree of dissatisfaction among these individuals is a much more complex issue. We cannot simply assume that all laid-off workers are discontent. Ongoing research finds that at least a portion of them actually enjoy a higher standard of living than before they were laid off. Some have since found higher-paying jobs in the private sector. Obviously, this is not true in all cases. There are many families whose standard of living has declined dramatically as the result of layoffs, sometimes with the husband and wife both being victims.[26]

We also know that workers are upset with more than the fact that they were laid off or that their factories are not paying owed wages. The financial difficulties of factories are made worse by the corruption that exists or that workers perceive to exist. Workers are upset by the closure of factories and the layoffs, but in some cases, the protests are aimed at specific instances of corruption or the failure of their factories to carry out provisions instituted by the state to protect the welfare of the laid-off workers, such as payment of a portion of a worker's wages during the layoff period. In other instances, the anger is specifically directed at a factory director who is thought to be skimming off funds; wasting scarce funds on frivolous expenses, such as "investigative" trips abroad; or falsely reporting high profits to the higher levels in order to earn personal bonuses while workers go unpaid, sometimes for years. To assess how serious a threat these workers are to the state, we need to know more about what options they have in other sectors to earn a wage and also what proportion of them actually receive the benefits promised by the state, what proportion are getting retooled or retrained, and what proportion are being found jobs and the channels through which their jobs are secured.

Weakening or Adaptation by the Regime?

The demonstrations and other forms of public expressions that I have described, while not examples of legislated political reform, do represent political change. The question is, what kind of political change are we witnessing? Does the emergence of this spontaneous political expression mean that the regime has lost control? Or are we witnessing the adaptation of the Communist system to the new realities that have been created along with the economic reforms?

Urban workers have until now been the privileged members of the working class, so their recent demonstrations may be more understandable. But this is not the case for peasants. What is notable is not peasant discontent; peasants have long suffered injustices in the PRC. Regardless of whether there was discontent before or not, seldom have there been demonstrations by any groups in urban or rural areas. The question that needs to be asked for both workers and peasants is, why are they now willing to pursue overt action, taking to the streets, and going openly to upper levels of government?

One possible explanation is that peasants and workers have reached the end of their patience. The situation has become intolerable. Moreover, and this is key, they feel that the state is less able to impose penalties on them; in other words, they have nothing to lose. The implication is that the state is now weak and can no longer prevent such incidents from occurring.

The ability of the authorities to penalize the peasants and workers has clearly been reduced. Authority relations, particularly in the countryside in the wake of decollectivization and the reopening of markets, have been radically altered. These two institutional reforms gutted the Maoist control system that kept peasants compliant and tied to the farms. Local officials no longer have monopoly control over economic opportunities and resources to gain compliance. In this sense, the state, at both the central and local levels, has become weaker and less effective.

This change in authority relations, however, is masked by the continuity in political form—the same dual power structure of Party secretary and village head,[27] still exists in all villages. The difference is that after the reforms, not all who hold these offices have power. In some villages, the power of these bodies has been eviscerated. The most obvious example is the "paralyzed villages" that are reported in the Chinese press, where peasants are poor and cadres do nothing.[28] In such villages, not only do peasants not fear their cadres, but there is little that cadres can do to those who refuse to cooperate.[29] Such peasants have little to lose but perhaps something to gain by exposing the corruption and incompetence of their local cadres. Control over workers has similarly been loosened as they depend less on their work units, their factory. The bonds are increasingly weakened as these factories fail to live up to their commitments as the "iron rice bowl" cracks more and more.

Although the effectiveness of state controls has been weakened, in itself that is an insufficient explanation for the increase in overt political activity. Peasants and workers still know that the state can effectively use coercion and repression to put down demonstrations. The detention or arrest of known leaders of violent protests is well known. This occurred in the Renshou riots in Sichuan.[30] We cannot know whether the demonstrations are a sign that the state is losing its ability to institute effective controls without knowing how many times the regime has cracked down compared to the total number of demonstrations that have taken place in the rural and urban areas. If, as I suspect, the total number of demonstrations is much higher than arrests, we must look for an alternative explanation for the regime's nonrepressive response.

In spite of the increasing fiscal power of the localities and declining fiscal revenues of the center that some have pointed to with alarm,[31] if one looks more broadly at the overall political and economic system and at the levers the central state does still control, the case for a weakened state on the verge of collapse is dramatically overdrawn and misleading. In contrast to eastern Europe and the nations of the former Soviet Union, local and central governments in China are part of the same functioning unitary state and party. There are no opposition parties ruling the localities to try to overthrow those in power at the center. The central Chinese state remains vertically integrated. The Communist Party still controls the *nomenklatura* system of personnel appointments that secures at least minimal compliance from its agents.[32] The loosening that I have highlighted is in comparison with the Maoist period. This must be kept in mind when talking about the power of the center. This caveat is particularly warranted in the face of theories that predict a "market transition" and the emergence of "civil society" or a "societal takeover." The incidents when the Chinese state has cracked down suggest that it still has the coercive power to quell social unrest.

If the state is strong enough to have the choice of whether to use that force or not, the alternative explanation of the large number of instances of social unrest is that the state has made a conscious decision not to use its full coercive apparatus to stop such demonstrations. We know from its dealing with other groups that it is capable of much more effective silencing. In this alternative explanation, the airing of peasant and worker grievances has become an accepted part of local politics.[33] Overt worker and peasant political action can be understood as stemming from discontent, the fact that they are at the end of their patience and feel that they have little to lose. The difference with this explanation is the changed attitude of the regime. In other words, this alternative explanation posits that an added reason why peasants and workers are more willing to take to the streets is that they feel it is now within bounds, allowed by higher-level authorities. In this interpretation, over the course of the reforms, the state has consciously adopted a complex strategy that includes the use of political changes that on the one hand allow for more political participation and public expression but at the same time serve to strengthen the regime's own position. As the following section will show, this alternative explanation is supported by a number of policies that the state has adopted in recent years to alleviate the discontent that lay at the root of the problems, especially in the countryside.

Defusing Discontent, Redirecting Blame, and Legislating Institutional Protections

As with other aspects of reform, the state shows two faces: it still periodically relies on the stick to ensure stability, but increasingly it has been offering carrots to relieve the pressures and defuse the discontent in order to shore up its legitimacy. It is these carrots that suggest the regime is willing to bend, without breaking, in dealing with societal demands. These actions include simply providing funds to factories so that they can pay demonstrating workers their back pay. In the countryside, instead of paying back wages, the center has provided funds to pay off peasants holding IOUs. In other instances, the state has abolished certain fees in the aftermath of particularly severe peasant unrest, such as occurred in Renshou in 1993, when "the Central Committee and State Council abolished 37 fees and fund-raising programs" and "called for limits on 17 others."[34] More recently, regulations are being put in place that will change the system of ad hoc and variable fees into a system of standardized taxes that will reduce the arbitrariness with which local officials have increased the peasants' burden.

In addition to short-term ameliorative action, the state has also legislated new political institutions that will provide longer-term protection against problems of the type that has been fueling discontent. Perhaps because the SOE reforms are still under way, most of these legislative actions have been with regard to the rural areas.

The best example of the degree to which the regime has been willing to bend in the face of potential unrest is the highly publicized Organic Law on Villagers' Committees, which gives peasants the right to hold free and competitive elections for the village committee and establish legislative assemblies, thus creating a new basis of village power—popular election. Through various methods, some more democratic than others, villagers can nominate candidates for village committee head and the other four to six members of the committee that officially governs the village. Candidates give campaign speeches, often on election day. Voting is by secret ballot, and the votes are counted openly in front of the electorate. Candidates and winners need not be Party members. In some villages, private entrepreneurs have been elected over Party members as peasants look to economically successful individuals to lead them to prosperity. In some areas, the enthusiasm for these elections has gotten to the point where vote buying occurs.

How widely village elections are held and conducted as the law stipulates varies significantly. The most authoritative and likely estimate is somewhere around one-third of China's villages held elections in the mid- to late 1990s. One reason for this relatively low implementation rate is that the law requiring all villages to conduct elections was passed in draft form in 1987 but did not become an official law until 1998, leaving implementation to the local authorities. Whether they have done so and how well they have implemented the law are questions for empirical research.

Despite the continuing problems, the passage of the Organic Law has opened the door to significant and real change. There is evidence that in some villages, particularly as the process proceeds through various rounds of elections and peasants realize that their vote actually carries some weight, these elections have resulted in popularly elected officials who have real power to make decisions. Party candidates have been rejected or voted out of office.[35] The impressive point is that the election legislation emanated from the central state.

The logic behind such a step, albeit perverse, makes good political sense. While this is a clear step toward political change, and some might say a political concession, the reason why the regime has pursued such a policy may have nothing to do with wanting to promote democracy as an end but everything to do with the problems that elections could solve for it. The decision to allow village elections represents a policy choice, a trade-off between the potential for increased peasant instability or amending existing political institutions, giving up the practice under which higher levels select the head of village government, and allowing democratic selection by the villagers themselves. In the end, proponents of the policy won because elections were the most viable *means* for quelling peasant unrest and increasing regime legitimacy.[36] Village elections are a safety value designed to let peasants vent their dissatisfaction, but one meant to point the responsibility for continued poverty and poor village leadership away from the central authorities. Note that it is the poor villages that are targeted in the implementation of this policy.[37] These elections are occurring in those places that the press has dubbed the paralyzed villages mentioned earlier.[38]

The regime is showing signs that it may even be ready to inch forward to complete the democratic process in the selection of village leaders. On a limited and experimental basis, the regime has consented to democratic selection of Party secretaries,[39] who were not subject to democratic election under the Organic Law. There are also signs that the regime may be ready to allow elections to spread to the higher levels, although this is still being controlled and monitored carefully. Experiments have been going on in selected townships, where the population has been allowed to elect township government heads. But there have also been reports that such elections are illegal and such practices have been banned. According to Ministry of Civil Affairs officials, however, the experiments with township elections continue, but they cannot be publicized. Unlike village elections, the regime has yet to decide if the costs of increasing political participation to the township are worth the political risks. The fact that they are even considering this is a positive sign.

The regime has to weigh the costs of legislating new laws and institutions designed to protect peasants from cadre abuse and corruption or risk further peasant discontent and potential uprising. Such measures allow the regime to openly take the peasants' side and support their demands without jeopardizing, and maybe even helping, its own position. For example, requiring that information about village finances, quotas, taxes, fees, and other matters be openly displayed on public village blackboards prevents or at least reduces abuse by village officials.[40] Similarly, peasants are to be issued cards that clearly state how much tax they are supposed to pay and how much they should pay to the township and to the village. In short, such policies are an effective (and clever) way for the regime to discipline its members and promote efficient and honest government. Giving peasants the right to dismiss their leaders protects the reputation of the Party itself and redirects blame to the villagers themselves for choosing poorly. If this can solve some of the problems and lead poor villagers out of poverty, the state will gain in legitimacy. Though risky in the short term, over the longer run, this may force Party members to be better leaders and solidify the Party's control at the local levels. In the absence of political campaigns that characterized the Mao period, the state can use democratic methods—village elections and cadre accountability—not only to ameliorate peasant discontent but also as a relatively low-cost way to combat cadre corruption and improve local government.

In the urban areas, the measures that the regime has taken so far are more ad hoc. As yet, China lacks a fully developed welfare program that would provide guaranteed support for laid-off workers. In the meantime, the state has instituted a three-part program intended as a safety net for workers displaced by the reforms. Laid-off workers are supposed to have access to a reemployment service center, unemployment insurance, and a basic insurance system. But this package is far from fully institutionalized. The provisions are only half-measures in the sense that the center cannot fully fund these programs, putting the burden on the enterprises and the localities. Moreover, the program seems to contain a "catch 22" clause: laid-off workers who decide to participate in the short-term relief and retraining programs will be cut off forever from their state factory. This has become a major stumbling block for many workers who choose not to participate in the state's programs because it would mean that their factory, their *danwei*, would then no longer be responsible for their welfare and would no longer be responsible for reemploying them. After the safety period, workers would have to go it alone.

No doubt because it recognizes that no institutionalized welfare program exists, the state is at this point primarily trying to placate workers by instituting short-term solutions to the problems that have prompted groups of laid-off workers to visit their local government offices or demonstrate in the streets. The solutions are sometimes relatively easy and straightforward. Higher-level officials simply provide a factory with sufficient funds to pay the back wages of its workers. In other cases, in addition to paying off the workers, authorities may fire or fine the factory manager found guilty of corruption or falsely reporting profits. The point is that instead of conducting mass arrests, the state is trying to placate the protesters.

Mediating Risks for the Regime

In assessing the threat of the incidence of political unrest, it is necessary to take into account factors that mediate the seriousness of the situation for the regime. These factors make it easier for the central state to contain the unrest in the urban and rural areas and provide further insights into why the state may be willing to allow demonstrations to occur.

First, most of the incidents of unrest seem to be isolated cases. In sharp contrast to the well-organized Falun Gong, on which the regime has cracked down hard, there seems to be little or nothing in the way of a network in place that is capable of playing a coordinating role among either the workers or the peasants. The protesters seldom expand their activities outside of their local area or factory, although there have been exceptions, as earlier examples suggest. So far, there are no signs that other groups who have grievances against the regime are attempting to coordinate larger-scale collective resistance. Political dissidents and intellectuals do not appear to be involved in these disturbances.[41]

Second, it must be highlighted that because of the variation that exists in the level of economic development, the occurrence of problems is also limited to certain types of localities. For example, rural protests occur mostly in the poor areas of the countryside, not the rich industrialized areas along the coast. China does not face a situation where peasants everywhere or workers everywhere are rising up in protest and taking to the streets. It is seldom noted that among the SOEs, there are segments that are actually doing well. Thus not all factories are doing poorly, and not all workers are suffering. As indicated earlier, not even all laid-off workers are suffering.

Third, to be a laid-off worker in China is not the same as being pushed out into the streets and left homeless, as has sometimes occurred in eastern Europe or the United States. Unlike unemployed in market systems, laid-off workers in China are entitled to keep whatever benefits their factories still provide. For those who were in the large state-owned factories, this is likely to include some sort of housing. The degree to which this mediates discontent cannot be overemphasized. A development to watch is whether this practice continues as more pressure is put on enterprises to cut costs. At what point will all the benefits of the unit system be cut?

Fourth, the threat to the central state is mediated by the fact that in both rural and urban areas, a common target of the protests is local officials. Local cadres, not the central state, are blamed for the problems that the peasants are enduring. The state can take the side of the peasants, as noted earlier, and not only punish corrupt cadres but also pass new regulations to protect peasants in the future. The center can claim to be the shield rather than the sword. In urban areas, such arguments are harder to make: it is clear that layoffs result from the centrally mandated SOE reform. Nonetheless, the state can say that it has tried to provide welfare policies and services for the laid-off workers. It has set up the three-step safety net described earlier. It can point to special offices, such as those in the Ministry of Civil Affairs, to help workers retrain and find new employment, in addition to overseeing welfare payments. Exposing corrupt or inept cadres can help the state's case. This does not absolve the central authorities of responsibility, but again, it redirects blame away from them.

As a side note, blaming local authorities and poor implementation also allow workers and peasants a legitimate excuse to openly call for change without being accused of trying to overthrow the regime or its top leaders. This fact helps explain why the regime is willing to allow more of this expression than we might otherwise expect. This is where the regime can bend and allow its citizens greater participation. The citizens are being solicited to help the regime clean up the corruption that exists at the lower levels.

Fifth, the regime's claims that many of the problems lie with the local officials may be aided by the regional inequalities that emerged with the economic reforms. The tremendous variation in types of economies and corresponding levels of income allows the central authorities to defend the overall thrust of the reforms and to blame problems on local officials who are not carrying out state policies properly. The discontented are unlikely to oppose reform, even if they currently have not fully benefited from the fruits of reform, because it is widely perceived that the reform policies have resulted in successful economic development and wealth in some areas, just not in theirs.

The ambiguous feelings that the poor most likely have toward the regime is reflected in the growth in migration and the large floating population that one finds in cities and in the richer parts of the countryside. The conditions that these migrants endure in the cities certainly can elicit our sympathy.[42] But whether such conditions will lead to potentially violent discontent is questionable. As similar phenomena in other countries have shown, shantytowns do not necessarily lead to increased political activism.[43] The Chinese state may be viewed as rigid and unyielding in not abolishing the *hukou* system that separates these migrants from legal city dwellers and denies migrants social services and education for their children.

But one could argue that the state has in practice acceded to at least some of the migrants' demands by allowing them to remain in the cities most of the time. Except for its sporadic assaults on large communities such as Zhejiangcun in Beijing and the cosmetic migrant sweeps for big international events, authorities have allowed these migrants to slide into niches in the urban areas, to fill unwanted jobs, and to earn more money than they would have otherwise been able to obtain had they stayed in their home localities or had there not been reform. Rather than rigidity, an argument can be made that both the migrants and the political system have worked out ad hoc measures such that the state allows these not quite legal residents into the cities. The migrants are allowed to make the best of admittedly poor conditions to take advantage of the higher incomes in the cities and get what part of the wealth they can. This method of income redistribution may moderate the discontent that might otherwise erupt from the inequalities between the rich and the poor regions and help close the gap. We need to look not just at what is happening in the cities where the migrants work but also at what is happening in their home villages where the money is being remitted.[44]

In assessing the potential for discontent and unrest, one should remember that the plight of these rural migrants, regardless of how poor they are or how bad their living conditions are in the cities, is significantly different from those in other developing countries. All peasant migrants have the security of knowing that they have a safety net. They can always go home to the countryside. They may not like it, but each has land to farm. As I have argued elsewhere, one likely reason why the state has not abolished the *hukou* system and not abolished the land allocation attached to rural *hukou* is the regime's concern about the political consequences of sending migrants home when the urban economy is unable to support them as more workers are laid off from urban enterprises.[45]

A Glass Half-Empty or Half-Full?

Is the political change in China a story of a glass half-empty or half-full? A convincing picture could be presented either way, depending on what aspect of political change one focuses on and the level of the system one examines. The problems, as I indicated at the beginning of the chapter, abound. While reflective of the continued hesitation toward political reform, the problems and periodic crackdowns obscure the much more accommodating stance that the regime is taking toward the many forms of overt and sometimes violent articulation of grievances by hundreds—even thousands—of people in different localities during the last decade or more of the reform process. This is not to say that the regime has been submissive or completely accepting of the disturbances—the state continues to use its considerable coercive powers whenever it feels threatened.

China is a transitional system that is still Leninist and wants to keep one-party control. Change must be compatible, first and foremost, with stability in a rapidly changing economic environment. But as this chapter has shown, that has still left considerable room for China to bend and adopt a range of political reforms. China has rejected the "big bang" approach for political change, as it did in economic reform, in favor of "groping for stones to cross the river." This has resulted in change that is significant but often comes slowly and under the cover of existing institutions that have since lost much of their original character. In some cases, the regime takes more radical steps toward political change, such as the Organic Law, when it is deemed necessary. But even then, the outwardly radical political reform, at the same time that it reduces discontent and may yield better government, especially in the heretofore poor areas, also increases the legitimacy of the Party.

Observers hoping for a more democratic China may bristle that such a policy of popular election is being used, but the end result is that peasants now have the ability to elect at least some of their most important leaders. If the recent experiments continue, free elections may extend also to Party leaders within the villages and may even inch their way up to the townships. One day, elections may reach the national level, but that is not likely anytime soon. Though less exciting than radical political change on a national level, allowing elections at the grass roots first may result in more stable democratic politics if and when elections extend further up the system. The accumulation of gradual reforms may eventually result in a changed political system, much as the many changes to what was still officially a centrally planned economy made China a market-oriented economy, albeit one with Chinese characteristics.

The question is, will the political system be able to withstand the problems and challenges long enough for gradual political reform to run its course? Through a combination of coercion and a large dose of amelioration, the regime has so far been able to weather the incidents of political unrest that have resulted from economic problems and has been willing to bend. The dangers to the regime are mediated greatly by the fact that the problems so far are primarily perceived as local problems. The central state has managed to direct most of the blame away from itself, blaming bad local cadres and improper implementation of policy. The idea that the emperor is good still holds at least some water. The center has managed to portray itself as the actor who will right the system, with better policies that will hold the lower levels more accountable. The regime has also been helped by the negative example of what happened both economically and politically in eastern Europe and Russia. This has no doubt dampened the spirit of those who might otherwise be calling for a quicker pace of political reform. This would include the intellectuals, who until now have not played a role in or tried to connect with any of the rural or urban incidents of political unrest.

But the regime is not home free. I have in this chapter identified a number of problems that the regime must solve if it is to continue to successfully maneuver and sustain its economic gains and complete the reform process. How the state deals with these issues should be the agenda for research if one wants to know whether the regime will be able to continue to muddle through and consolidate the gains that it has made economically. One obvious issue is how long the localities will be willing to play the fall guy and accept blame for the problems that are leading to the current discontent.[46] What will the state do to prolong the legitimacy of such an explanation? For the moment, peasants and workers are venting at least some of their anger at their local officials. But careful analysis of the problems shows that the reasons behind some of the corruption by local officials are the inadequacies and contradictions inherent in central-level policies. The problem of increasing peasant burdens is a case in point. The state needs to provide a solution to village funding. Similarly, state policy calls for laid-off workers to receive a portion of their wages, but the state has failed to provide the enterprises and the localities with sufficient resources to allow them to implement this policy. The state's policy might work in a locality that has only one or two red-ink-ridden SOEs, but what actions will it take in a place like Shengyang, in China's rust belt? When and where will this strategy of passing the blame to the localities backfire? We should be on the lookout for such actions, especially where locals themselves elect their community leaders as they do in some villages.

The biggest problem, and perhaps the ultimate test that will determine whether the regime can consolidate the reforms, is how effectively it can root out the corruption that seems to be growing, or at least is perceived to be growing, in the system. What steps are being taken to curb corruption? How far will the regime be willing to let citizens expose the corruption? Will those at the local levels still have enough power to silence well-meaning citizens?[47] Whose side will the center take? Is former President Jiang's new thought, the "three represents," a vehicle for further cleaning out the bureaucracy?[48] It is not just a matter of moral legitimacy and honesty but also a question of regime capacity. The degree to which the sources of discontent can be traced to cadre corruption and improper policy implementation suggest that the state is extremely vulnerable to the inefficiencies and conflicting interests of its agents at the local levels.[49] The adequacy of a number of state institutions is in question.

One is the state's statistics-gathering system. Many of the problems that I have described as fueling unrest can be traced to the inability of the system to get reliable information from the lower levels. The amount of false reporting strongly points to the need not only to get rid of cadre corruption but also to find new and more accurate sources of information that are less subject to local manipulation. Some efforts are already under way. The State Statistical Bureau has begun to send more of its own people to gather data directly, rather than relying on local officials. It remains to be seen how effective or viable such measures will be. The ability of the center to get accurate information has always been a problem, but the situation may be more difficult now that the reforms have altered the incentives of local officials so that they are more likely to think of local rather than national interests when they fill out statistical reports destined for the upper levels.[50]

Second, and related to the first weakness, how are the holes in the state regulatory system, especially at the lower levels, being closed? The regime still has a considerable degree of control, the *nomenklatura* system remains firmly in place, and the Party still controls the personnel system. The problems are not examples of flagrant abuse of regulations or disregard for central directives. As I have shown elsewhere, local officials still faithfully implement the directives that are sent down. The question is how effectively and completely local officials do their job. The *nomenklatura* system is effective in preventing gross misconduct, but it often only elicits minimum, not maximum, compliance. What measures is the regime taking to close the gap between the two?

Third, the actions that local officials have had to take both to survive and to get ahead, especially in the countryside, at the village level, strongly suggest that the regime needs to rethink how local expenditures should be financed as well as how to compensate local cadres. One question that is ripe for research is whether the recent trend to privatize collectively owned village enterprises will lead to problems stemming from the lack of collective funds and the corresponding lack of public goods, which to this point have been limited to the poor agricultural areas. Will the problems and the discontent spread to the richer areas as sources of collective revenue diminish with the sale of enterprises? The recent decision to turn fees into taxes seems to be a clear response to the need to reform the fiscal system that after decollectivization left villages without a legitimate and fairly stable tax base to fund expenditures.

Whether the glass will become more full or more empty with regard to political reform will depend on China's continued willingness and ability to adapt its political institutions to the new realities that have emerged as the system has evolved from the plan and strict control over its population. China succeeded to a large extent in its economic reforms by adapting existing Maoist institutions to the needs of a market economy. In the process, it radically changed the economic system. Let us hope that the regime will continue to bend and reshape, if slowly, the political system as it comes to those stones that have so far been the barriers to the expansion of legitimate political activity. Without such bending and adaptation, the system is likely to break.

Notes

1. See, for example, Andrew Walder, ed., *China's Transitional Economy* (Oxford: Oxford University Press, 1996).

2. See Joan Nelson, "The Politics of Economic Transformation: Is Third World Experience Relevant in Eastern Europe?" *World Politics*, April 1993, *45*, 433–63.

3. See John P. Burns, "The People's Republic at 50: National Political Reform," *China Quarterly*, September 1999, *159*, 580–94; see also two works by Murray Scott Tanner, "The National People's Congress," in Merle Goldman and Roderick MacFarquhar, eds., *The Paradox of China's Post-Mao Reforms* (Cambridge, Mass.: Harvard University Press,

1999), and "The Erosion of Central Party Control over Lawmaking," *China Quarterly*, June 1994, *38*, 381– 403.

4. See Minxin Pei, "Citizens vs. Mandarins: Administrative Litigation in China," *China Quarterly*, December 1997, *152*, 832– 62; Pitman Potter, "The Chinese Legal System: Continuing Commitment to the Primacy of State Power," *China Quarterly*, September 1999, *159*, 673–83; Stanley Lubman, *Bird in a Cage: Legal Reform in China After Mao* (Stanford, Calif.: Stanford University Press, 1999); and Randall Peerenboom, *China's Long March Toward Rule of Law* (New York: Cambridge University Press, 2002).

5. See Tianjian Shi, *Political Participation in Beijing* (Cambridge, Mass.: Harvard University Press, 1997).

6. For details on the Mao period, see Jean C. Oi, *State and Peasant in Contemporary China: The Political Economy of Village Government* (Berkeley: University of California Press, 1989), esp. ch. 6 and 7.

7. See Kevin O'Brien and Lianjiang Li, "Villagers and Popular Resistance in Contemporary China," *Modern China*, January 1996, *22*(1), 28–61.

8. See Thomas Bernstein, "Instability in Rural China," in *Is China Unstable? Assessing the Factors* (Washington, D.C.: Sigur Center for Asian Studies, 1998), for a detailed study of rural instability; I have also relied on Thomas Bernstein and Xiaobo Lu, *Taxation Without Representation in Contemporary Rural China* (New York: Cambridge University Press, 2003).

9. Bernstein, *Financial Burdens*.

10. Bernstein, "Instability."

11. See Jean C. Oi, *Rural China Takes Off: Institutional Foundations of Economic Reform* (Berkeley: University of California Press, 1999).

12. See Cai Yongshun, "Between State and Peasants: Local Cadres and Statistical Reporting in Rural China," *China Quarterly*, September 2000, *163*, 783–805.

13. See Oi, *State and Peasant*.

14. Peasant dissatisfaction is also likely to have increased when the state suddenly changed its grain marketing policy, once again forcing private grain traders to buy from state grain stores.

15. See Andrew Walder, *Communist Neo-Traditionalism: Work and Authority in Chinese Industry* (Berkeley: University of California Press, 1986).

16. Not all of these are new. Urban residents could always complain to officials in government bureaus, and there were even strikes during the Maoist period.

17. Cai Yongshun, "The Silence of the Dislocated: Chinese Laid-Off Employees in the Reform Period." Ph.D. dissertation, Stanford University, Department of Political Science, 2001. Also see Cai Yongshun, "The Resistance of Chinese Laid-Off Workers in the Reform Period," *China Quarterly*, June 2002, *170*, 327–44; and Dorothy J. Solinger, "The Potential for Urban Unrest, or Will the Fencers Stay on the Piste?" in David Shambaugh, ed., *Is China Unstable? Assessing the Factors* (Armonk, N.Y.: Sharpe, 2000).

18. See, for example, Walder, *Communist Neo-Traditionalism*.

19. Reported in Cai, "Silence of the Dislocated."

20. Ibid.

21. Solinger, "Potential for Urban Unrest."

22. Cai, "Silence of the Dislocated."

23. Solinger, "Potential for Urban Unrest."

24. Cai, "Silence of the Dislocated."

25. A total of 1.5 million retired workers failed to receive their pensions in 1997.

26. See Cai, "Silence of the Dislocated."

27. The village head is officially called the chairman of the village committee.

28. The situation is dramatically different in the rich, industrialized villages, where

cadres still control numerous resources on which peasants depend. See Oi, *Rural China Takes Off.*

29. See O'Brien and Li, "Villagers and Popular Resistance."

30. See Bernstein, "Instability in Rural China."

31. See Wang Shaoguang, "The Rise of the Regions: Fiscal Reform and the Decline of Central-State Capacity in China," in Andrew Walder, ed., *The Waning of the Communist State: Economic Origins of Political Decline in China and Hungary* (Berkeley: University of California Press, 1995).

32. On the *nomenklatura* system as an effective instrument of central state control over the localities, see Yasheng Huang, *Inflation and Investment Controls in China: The Political Economy of Central-Local Relations During the Reform Era* (New York: Cambridge University Press, 1996).

33. In Shenyang, where there are many laid-off workers, demonstrations have become so common that city authorities announce their locations to prevent traffic congestion. "Old-Line Communists at Odds with Party in China," *New York Times*, July 2, 2000, p. 3.

34. Bernstein, *Financial Burdens.*

35. The degree to which elected officials wield effective power varies significantly. See Jean C. Oi and Scott Rozelle, "Elections and Power: The Locus of Decision Making in Chinese Villages," *China Quarterly*, June 2000, *162*, 513–39.

36. I elaborate this argument further in Jean C. Oi, "Economic Development, Stability and Democratic Self-Governance," in Maurice Brace, Suzanne Pepper, and Shu-I Tang, eds., *China Review, 1996* (Hong Kong: Chinese University Press, 1997).

37. The implementation of this policy is still spotty.

38. See Oi and Rozelle, "Elections and Power."

39. This is known as the two-ballot system; see Lianjiang Li, "The Two-Ballot System in Shanxi Province: Subjecting Village Party Secretaries to a Popular Vote," *China Journal*, July 1999, *42*, 103–24.

40. See Kevin O'Brien and Lianjiang Li, "The Politics of Lodging Complaints in Rural China," *China Quarterly*, September 1995, *143*, 756–83.

41. See Merle Goldman, "Politically Engaged Intellectuals in the 1990s," *China Quarterly*, September 1999, *159*, 700–11.

42. See Dorothy J. Solinger, *Contesting Citizenship in Urban China: Peasant Migrants, the State, and the Logic of the Market* (Berkeley: University of California Press, 1999).

43. See, for example, Nelson, "Politics of Economic Transformation."

44. There is already some work suggesting that substantial amounts of money are being sent home; see Elisabeth Croll and Huang Ping, "Migration for and Against Agriculture in Eight Chinese Villages," *China Quarterly*, March 1997, *149*, 128–46.

45. See Jean C. Oi, "Two Decades of Rural Reform." *China Quarterly*, September 1999, *159*, 616–28.

46. On the problem of a discontented mid- and lower-level cadre corps, see Bruce Dickson, "Political Instability at the Middle and Lower Levels: Signs of a Decaying CCP, Corruption, and Political Dissent," in Shambaugh, *Is China Unstable?*

47. For an example of the dangers, see "Old-Line Communists."

48. Jiang Zemin's "three represents" has become part of official Party theory. It calls for the Communist Party "to represent the development trend of China's advanced social productive forces, the orientation of China's advanced culture, and fundamental interests of the overwhelming majority of the people in China."

49. This is particularly dangerous given the increasing resources that are being accumulated in the localities as a result of the fiscal reforms. See Oi, *Rural China Takes Off.*

50. I elaborate the problems of regulation at the local levels in ibid.

Part VI

FURTHER RESEARCH

16

Agenda for Future Research

Nicholas C. Hope, Dennis Tao Yang, and Mu Yang Li

In the past twenty years, policy reform in China characterized by "feeling the stones to cross the river," has profoundly transformed the old economic and institutional structure. Despite the gradual and experimental nature of the process, China's transition from a planned to a market system has penetrated all important aspects of the economy. The contributions in this volume demonstrate amply the complexity of the reform process, and they explore a highly diverse agenda of reform. The authors attribute the remarkable growth of the Chinese economy in the past two decades directly to policy reforms, but they also emphasize that reforms remain incomplete.

China still faces great challenges at the beginning of the twenty-first century. The incomplete nature of reform underlines the potential value of economic research designed to inform policymakers on future choices. And the chapters assembled here orient researchers toward two broad lines of inquiry where analysis would afford insights that shape policy decisions: assessment of experience to date and evaluation of future reform options. In this final chapter, we lay out promising questions for research in these two broad areas. The agenda is not exhaustive; it incorporates research topics identified in this volume and reflects our judgments as well as those of the other authors about areas in which research seems especially worthwhile.

Learning from the Past

Systematic evaluation of experience using quantitative research is an important way to learn how policy programs affect the behavior of economic agents, thereby helping to distinguish policies that raise efficiency from those that do not. Determining what causes successful economic performance would allow policymakers to deepen effective reforms and to reinforce achievements. In situations where reforms have failed to generate the desired outcomes or where their implementation has encountered resistance, investigations into the causes of the failures could help policymakers refine existing policies or otherwise provide remedies. Moreover, evaluating the implementation of reforms could involve estimation of costs and benefits that could guide further reform. In looking ahead, policymakers would benefit from estimates of efficiency losses due to existing distortions and of potential benefits from eliminating distortions. Hence useful policy research would study the causal factors explaining successes and failures, analyze the costs and benefits of specific reform programs, and support these analyses by assembling good economic data.

Better Data as a Priority

The availability of high-quality data is essential for reliable empirical research. Since the inception of Chinese reform in the late 1970s, the release of official data and collection of survey data have spurred empirical research among social scientists. Despite evident improvements, data on crucial aspects of the economy remain scarce. The lack of attention paid to rigorous data analysis has rendered some data, even when they are available, unsuitable for effective use by researchers and policymakers alike.

At the macroeconomic level, as Lardy points out in Chapter Three, there is inadequate information on the volume of nonperforming loans in banks and nonbank financial institutions and on the prospects for recovering some of those loans. The People's Bank of China (PBC) has recently introduced a loan classification system using standard international criteria, but no systematic information on nonperforming loans has been released. In regard to public finance and the overall sustainability of China's fiscal situation, there are no reliable data on the magnitude of the unfunded pension obligations of the state-owned enterprises (SOEs). These estimates are needed for decisions about deepening enterprise reforms because, with the anticipated closure or divestiture of many SOEs, the government needs to raise additional fiscal revenues to take over those firms' obligations.

Good data are needed, too, in analyzing how to provide social insurance. As Hussain emphasizes in Chapter Ten, a major constraint in establishing an effective social safety net is the lack of fiscal recourses, especially in poor areas. One possibly viable way to cope with limited local budgets is resource pooling in the provision of pension and unemployment insurance. But to formulate realistic proposals, researchers need to compile data on the varying fiscal capacities of poor and less poor regions and cities. Timely investigations into these issues are essential in light of the ongoing transition from an enterprise-based system for the provision of social insurance to one based on society and government; the experience of the pilot project introduced in Liaoning province during 2001 should be highly valuable in this regard.

Data required for microeconomic analysis of policy responses includes a series of surveys of households and enterprises that would provide comprehensive information on family activities and firm operations. Due in part to the lack of micro-level data, detailed empirical analysis on family and enterprise behavior is absent in many chapters in this volume.

Rozelle, Zhang, and Huang, for instance, in Chapter Nine point to the desirability of using household-level data to evaluate the cost effectiveness of alternative poverty programs; their analysis is limited by the county-level data employed in their chapter. Better analysis would require detailed demographic information; records on household expenditures, including those on education, health services, and nutrition; and input-output information on production. Then parameters concerning behavioral responses of the families—for example, in choosing what to produce or how much to invest in children—could be estimated. These estimates would in turn facilitate the comparison of the effects of alternative policies—such as subsidizing income directly versus improving local infrastructure—to determine what works best. Similarly, data at comparable levels of detail are required to study the production supply responses of farm families to changes in policies or in the economic environment. An example of the latter change is China's entry into the World Trade Organization, meaning that one must anticipate increases in grain imports due to cost advantages in production in other countries. Research on the responses of China's farm grain supply would help policymakers prepare appropriate adjustment measures.

An examination of how firms respond to policies and incentives requires comprehensive data on such matters as factor utilization, output, and prices. For instance, the availability of good data would enable researchers to investigate how firms would act to reduce pollution when environmental regulations change, a topic discussed by Wheeler, Wang, and Dasgupta in Chapter Twelve. Under certain conditions, a tax on pollution could be equivalent to an increase in the price of an input, meaning that the firm would adjust its factor choices and output level if such a regulation were implemented. Tracing out the possible behavioral responses of firms would help decision makers formulate appropriate regulations and design incentives to encourage policy compliance.

Learning from Success

Better data would also facilitate learning from past achievements. Since policy reform is a complex business with high stakes, much can be learned from quantifying the relative contributions of specific reforms to improved performance. The remarkable agricultural growth in the reform era is an example, which, according to Huang, Lin, and Rozelle in Chapter Fourteen, can be attributed primarily to the adoption of the household responsibility system, appropriate price incentives, and investments in agricultural research. These findings should help policymakers extend effective programs and build on their success.

Research on the causal factors of success can find useful topics in many areas of reform. One remarkable achievement is China's rapid emergence from a state of virtual isolation from the world economy to become a major magnet for foreign direct investment (FDI), currently attracting more than one-third of all FDI annual flows to developing countries. Policymakers could learn from research that identifies the underlying economic and policy factors that have attracted FDI into China and determine its allocation across different provinces and regions. In particular, why do investors from Hong Kong and other countries choose to invest in China despite poor legal protection and various other institutional impediments? Furthermore, there are important issues concerning the structure of FDI and its impact on productivity and growth. To what extent has foreign capital influenced China's industrial composition and boosted its international trade? How has FDI helped enhance industrial productivity and overall growth? Analysis of these questions would complement the research findings reported by Wei in Chapter Seven, which emphasize that reducing red tape and corruption are effective ways to sustain current capital inflows and attract even more investment. In a similar vein, good research might reveal the contributing factors behind the rapid growth of township and village enterprises as well as the growth in interprovincial trade.

Learning from Mistakes

The study of policy failures might also provide useful lessons that help decision makers amend past policies, modify the institutional environment, and avoid future mistakes. Lardy cites inefficiency in fiscal and financial management as an example of institutional failure. By the mid-1990s, China's fiscal and financial apparatus had resulted in both the accumulation of substantial bad loans in the state banks and overcapacity in production. In turn, these have led to low capacity utilization, a massive buildup of inventories, and a deflationary macroeconomic environment. Excessive resources poured into property development, thereby creating a major bubble in the housing and property markets. Although several analysts have depicted the inefficiency of these outcomes, limited research has been conducted to illuminate the structural and institutional causes of the current situation.

A major problem for any command system is that central planners have inadequate information on which to make optimal resource allocation decisions. As a result, serious distortions arise in input allocation and output distribution. The gradual removal of distortions is a painstaking but necessary task that China's policymakers have had to confront throughout the reform process. Two types of information are particularly useful for policymakers: (1) knowing where distortions prevail and the magnitudes of associated efficiency losses and (2) identifying the institutions and policies that create the distortions.

Scholars contributing to this volume agree that China has gone a long way toward introducing competitive forces in the final goods markets. According to Naughton in Chapter Eight, for instance, there is considerable competition among producers of final goods in different regions, intraindustry and inter-provincial trade are both substantial, and goods now reach their consumers through diversified channels. By contrast, serious distortions still remain in the factor markets. Two aspects of input market inefficiency that have drawn particular attention are preferential allocation of credit to favor the state sector, as discussed by Bai, Li, and Wang in Chapter Four, and the fragmented labor market across rural-urban sectors, as reported by Yang and Cai in Chapter Thirteen. Although policymakers and scholars are aware of the distortions, the potential gains from restoring efficiency are still unknown. In particular, by how much does the rate of return to physical capital differ between the state and nonstate sectors? What would be the gain in output if investment funds were allocated optimally across the two sectors? Similarly, how large is the productivity differential for comparable labor across rural-urban regions and provincial borders? If known, that could be used to compute the productivity and welfare gains associated with more efficient allocation of labor. If the potential efficiency gains are large, these estimates could be used, in turn, to persuade policymakers to overcome local resistance and to pursue greater integration in the domestic input markets.

Weighing Costs and Benefits

Systematic assessment of factor market distortions is a special aspect of the cost-benefit analysis called for in assessing specific reform programs. Another example is the investment in agricultural research that (as Huang, Lin, and Rozelle assert in Chapter Fourteen) has been a key factor in China's sustained growth of grain production. But with the government experiencing fiscal weaknesses and with competing uses for government expenditures, how much should be invested in agricultural research? The answer to this question awaits research to determine the potential benefits from and costs of investment in agricultural research.

The value of research on the potential costs and benefits of reform programs is evident in most of the topic areas dealt with in this volume. Housing construction presents a good example. Zax suggests in Chapter Eleven that there has been oversupply in both the quantity and the quality of housing. Therefore, to better inform decision makers who allocate (especially public) funds to property construction, research is needed on construction costs and what households are able and willing to pay for housing services. A wedge between demand and supply prices would reveal the extent of problems in the incentives and institutional underpinnings of the current system.

Cost-benefit analysis is useful too in assessing the effectiveness of alternative approaches to targeting the poor and reducing poverty. Research could indicate whether poverty can be reduced more cost-effectively by allocating funds directly to individual households, rather than by improving the local economic environment. The value of research is also high in assessing the gains and losses to society when local governments choose to protect local economies, enforce laws and regulations, and collect taxes. As Naughton points out, understanding the conditions under which the success of further reforms depends on the behavior of local governments is an important step toward presenting officials with the right incentives.

Informing Future Reforms

The gradual and experimental nature of China's transition implies uneven progress in many areas of reform, which to a certain extent depends as well on when reforms were instituted. Those implemented early, including incentive schemes, household and enterprise autonomy, liberalization of output prices, and opening to foreign trade and investment, have accomplished many of their intended objectives. But in other areas, including the development of factor markets, fiscal and financial systems, privatization of large SOEs, and the provision of social security, reforms, though sometimes well begun, are far from complete. And in a few areas, such as the political system and the introduction and enforcement of new laws, only limited reform has been attempted; arguably, much more remains to be done.

Economic research on policy reforms should involve both the identification of areas where serious inefficiency still remains and also the recognition that slow progress in those areas often indicates major implementation problems or strong resistance to change. Simply knowing which areas need more reform is insufficient. Research must tackle a host of difficult questions involving the causes of implementation failures. Why are certain institutional barriers still in place? What political, social, and economic incentives sustain those barriers? What will be the consequences of breaking them down and further reforming institutions? These questions point to a rich research agenda on the factors that determine the evolution of institutions, the interaction of political and economic reforms, and the coordination of multiple reform programs.

Toward More Effective Institutions

Understanding what motivates the development of Chinese institutions, as well as the conditions that allow them to be reformed effectively, would contribute greatly in developing strategies for future reform. China watchers recognize that certain policy and institutional rigidities have caused inefficient economic outcomes. For instance, exclusive provision to local (urban) residents of such social services as schooling and child care obstructs labor mobility and distorts the labor market. Preferential allocation of investment credits to the state sector lowers the returns to capital for the economy as a whole. Moreover, local governments are often reluctant to enforce environmental regulations in their own jurisdictions because of the potential negative effects on the employment, production, and profits of the enterprises they either own or support. Although these inefficiencies are well documented, more research is needed to formulate policies to change the status quo.

To inform policy makers, one must first identify relevant interest groups. Whose responsibility is it to reform institutions fraught with inefficiency? At what level of administration is the reform relevant, and how do different levels of government interact? Who are the potential winners and losers from specific reforms? Answers to these questions would help policymakers design new rules, induce effort from the parties involved, and compensate losers appropriately to overcome resistance. The benefits from successful policy reforms should create powerful incentives for all parties to implement new rules better and to promote more efficient institutions.

Some of the scholars contributing to this volume have already conducted research designed to create the right incentives for the development of institutions. Qian and Wu, the authors of Chapter Two, for example, suggest that a two-tier judiciary might mitigate the problems of local economic protectionism. Their idea is to make local courts more independent of local governments so that they would exhibit more impartiality in the enforcement of laws and contracts. Another example is Alford's discussion in Chapter Five of the feasibility of establishing "rule by law" in a society where the Party makes the law an instrument of state power. His analysis clarifies the conditions needed for the healthy development of law and legal institutions. In the same vein, a vast array of research topics exists in all areas where reforms have encountered difficulties in implementation. Among those areas are urban-biased policies, the clarification of land use and other property rights, the regulation and practice of interprovincial commerce, and the privatization of enterprises with ambiguous ownership arrangements.

Avoiding "Conflicting Reforms"

Another major area for research is how to coordinate and promote positive interactions of reform programs. Experience suggests that the benefits from reforms in any single area depend crucially on how reforms perform in other areas and in particular on whether related markets function well. All would agree that the payoffs from implementing the household responsibility system for rural families and ceding greater autonomy to enterprises were greatly enhanced by the relaxation of price controls. Equally clearly, price reforms realized much higher payoffs where households and firms had the freedom to respond to market signals. The gradual nature of the Chinese reform process means that there could be large potential gains from deepening reforms in pivotal areas, where the gains come both directly from that area and from enhancing the benefits from reforms in complementary areas. Therefore, when reforms might encounter resistance, knowledge of the potential size of payoffs and where interactions convey the highest mutual benefits would be of great value.

Reform programs where careful coordination may significantly enhance overall benefits can be found in almost every part of the economy. Clearly, the establishment of a social safety net is essential for deepening the reforms of SOEs and promoting the growth of nonstate enterprises. Financial reforms intended to develop a commercial credit culture in the banking sector are prone to fail unless SOEs are required to face effective financial discipline. Moreover, researchers also recognize that poverty amelioration programs will be less effective without a concerted effort to invest more in health services and schooling, which are important determinants of family earnings.

China's accession to the WTO is another area where coordination of reforms will likely have high payoffs. As Martin, Dimaranan, Hertel, and Ianchovichina observe in Chapter Six, reform needs are urgent in the financial sector and telecommunications, where substantial changes in the regulatory frameworks, as well as in trade policies, will be required. This situation is compounded by the fact that for the time being, entry by nonstate enterprises in these industries is restricted—the tilted playing field reduces competition, thus making the industries more vulnerable to future international competition.

Similarly, accession to the WTO will lower Chinese tariffs on a number of agricultural commodities, probably leading China to import more of them. The likely reduction in domestic production that results will add to the challenges in transferring labor out of agriculture. What policy changes would prepare China to respond better to these challenges? Further investigation of the linkages in reform programs will help policymakers establish their reform priorities.

To do so, the timing of research on the coordination of reform programs becomes crucial—research will have the highest value if conducted before isolated initiatives are implemented. As a good example, consider the relationship between housing reforms and the provision of pensions. As Lardy observes, in the mid-1990s, the market value of housing owned by SOEs was roughly equal to the magnitude of their unfunded pension liabilities. Some analysts suggested at the time that the SOEs could sell their housing assets to meet their outstanding pension obligations. But during the frantic period of housing privatization in the late 1990s, much of the public housing was sold to urban households at deeply discounted prices or simply given away. As a result, the value of housing assets now controlled by SOEs is much lower than the value of unfunded pension liabilities. Financing these liabilities remains a challenging task, but the government already seems to have lost an opportunity to resolve the problem partially through housing reforms.

A related example is the possibility that the Chinese government could issue government bonds to write off the nonperforming loans of state-owned banks and to recapitalize them. This option is clearly unattractive while state-owned banks are still required to supply credit to weak SOEs. Timely research is needed, however, to supplement Lardy's work and to investigate for how long this option seems possible in a situation where substantial bond issues are already funding public expenditures to stimulate demand. Ideally, the option should be used before the ratio of domestic debt to gross domestic product reaches the high levels that make it fiscally undesirable or unsustainable.

Reconciling Economic and Political Reforms

In a number of chapters, a common theme is the high payoffs from research that investigates how political and economic reforms interact. In many ways, the Chinese Communist Party continues to interfere with efficient business practices. Examples include the control of senior personnel appointments in large SOEs, Party influence over corporate strategic plans, and control over approval of investment projects and credits. Despite the Party's growing tolerance of overt expressions of grievances from citizens, as Oi records in Chapter Fifteen, it continues to be unwilling to cede or share power, thus raising the question of whether prevailing political institutions are able to complete the remaining reform agenda.

Some authors take the view that reformers within the Party usually opt for economic growth when the objectives of political power and economic development clash. Others observe that the Party still displays inflexibility on any issue that threatens to erode its predominant position. Moreover, in some instances, the interests of the leader or leadership seem to take priority even over the Party. This raises important questions that are yet unanswered: Can the leaders be relied on not to thwart reforms that could have an adverse impact on their leadership? What systemic checks and balances make economically beneficial change irreversible? Will China need a political opening to sustain economic growth? And what are the conditions under which the Party would take further measures to remove itself from business operations?

These questions call for sound research on the Chinese government's incentives and behaviors. One direction for research is empirical analysis of the effects of Party control on enterprise performance. Now that many firms of different ownership types, with varying degrees of Party influence, compete in the same market, firm-level empirical analysis could determine the extent to which Party involvement affects firm performance. Whether Party influence has a significant negative effect on performance is still an open question. However, if the existence of such a negative effect could be established, policymakers would need to reconsider the Party's role in the longer run.

Another purpose for research is to present explicit policy options to the decision makers. For instance, in determining whether to prolong the life of inefficient SOEs, the government needs to consider its options. The state could maintain control over the SOEs and continue to supply credit and subsidies to sustain employment at the expense of rising bad loans, or it could privatize the enterprises and use any funds raised to retrain workers laid off from the SOEs or to provide unemployment benefits (or both). If empirical research establishes on the one hand large efficiency losses from bad loans and on the other hand high economic value from worker retraining and unemployment insurance, Chinese leaders might reap political gains by adopting the latter approach. The results would be improvements in efficiency that stem from actions taken for the political advantage of the Party.

Finally, another important aspect of reforms noted by several authors concerns the provision of public goods and services. Due to the incomplete nature of China's economic reform as it progresses toward a market system, the supply of many public goods and social services has lagged. For instance, the investment in agricultural research has dwindled, with notable drops, in particular, during periods of budgetary difficulty. Conditions in many rural schools have deteriorated due to organizational changes, and social security programs are almost entirely absent in the countryside. The collapse of the system of "barefoot doctors" has severely curtailed even rudimentary health services in poor rural areas. And China needs a reliable system of property registration and more transparent laws and regulations establishing property rights, especially, for example, in developing an efficient housing market.

In a market system with democracy, publicly elected officials would represent the voters of their own constituencies and facilitate the provision of such public goods as investments in health services and education. In the absence of effective democratic representation in China, what policy reforms are needed to induce the socially desirable supply of public goods and services? Research on these questions, as well as quantitative assessments of the value of these and other public goods and services, would provide valuable information on reform priorities and raise the returns from future reforms.

Conclusion

Despite the remarkable success of China's policy reform in the past two decades, many formidable challenges remain. A common observation is that the second stage of reform is frequently more difficult than the first because (1) the first wave of reforms often deals with distortions that are obvious—price liberalization, enterprise incentives and the like—and (2) unlike the first wave, later reforms often cannot be implemented by administrative decree. Second-stage reforms often require more planning and coordination and often encounter more political resistance. In the Chinese case, necessary reforms yet to be implemented are entangled with difficult areas of the legal and political systems, local and central government relationships, and the continued dramatic overhaul of the institutions inherited from central planning. These complications all considerably raise the value of research in designing further reform and emphasize the information that Chinese policymakers need to bring the elusive riverbank ever nearer.

INDEX

Abatement: *See* Pollution abatement
Accession Working Party, 171
Accounting, for urban housing, 342
Accumulation of capital, common vs.
  civil law regimes and, 126
Adaptation, by regime, 456–458
Ad hoc arrangements, vs. rule of law, 57
Administration, under central planning,
  40. *See also* Bureaucracy; Government
Administrative Litigation Law (1989),
  125, 134; actions under, 144n11
Administrative Reconsideration Law, 140
Adverse selection, in municipal health in-
  surance coverage, 303–304
Affordability, of urban housing, 325–327,
  330–331
Afsah, Shakeb, 358
Age structure, of working-age adults,
  278–279, 278 (tab.)
Agrarian economy, 1–2
Agreement on Trade-Related Aspects of
  Intellectual Property Rights (TRIPS),
  166
Agricultural development, in reform
  economy, 418–422; strategy and poli-
  cies for, 422–432; Agricultural economy, growth rate by sector and commodity, 421 (tab.)
Agricultural labor, development of, 429–
  430; productivity of, 429 (tab.)
Agricultural Policy Stimulation and Projection Model (CAPSiM), 439, 446n7

Agricultural pricing policies, 413n1
Agricultural productivity, 419–422, 433–
  438; demand, trade, and, 440–442;
  trends for rice, wheat, soybean, and
  maize, 433 (tab.)
Agricultural technology, 428–429,
  431–432, 434–438, 445; grain self-
  sufficiency and, 442–444, 443 (tab.);
  trade liberalization, food deficit, and,
  438–444
Agriculture, boosting productivity of,
  22–23; capital flow from, 423 (tab.);
  under central planning, 399; collectivized, 99; discrimination against, 389,
  396–397; farm incomes and, 22; final
  tariff bindings on selected products,
  168 (tab.); fixed assets in, 414n9; GDP
  from, 6; government discrimination
  against, 389; growth of, 1, 424; Household Responsibility System and, 3, 400;
  improving productivity of, 417–449;
  land use policy and, 427–429; organized by households, 34; poverty loans
  for, 245, 249 (fig.), 264; price changes
  and SOE wage growth, 402 (fig.);
  prices of, 404; public investment in,
  422; ratio of nonagricultural income
  to agricultural income, 397 (tab.); research in, 431–432, 432 (tab.), 437,
  445; shares of government expenditures and loans to, 407 (fig.); support
  for industry at expense of, 406; taxa-

Agriculture (*continued*)
tion of, for industrialization, 389; urbanization rate and, 280–281; WTO
commitments and, 167–168. *See also*
Agricultural entries; Food; Food
security
Air pollution, 21; ambient concentration
of, 369–370; control of, 354; deaths
from, 355 (fig.), 378 (fig.); externalities
and, 130; intensity of, 359–361, 360
(fig.); levies on, 364–365, 381–382,
383–384; regulation of, 374–375;
value of regulation of, 378–383
Alford, William P., 13, 26n13, 122, 125,
133, 135, 136, 137, 141, 142, 143n1,
143n4, 144n11, 144n15, 145n19,
477
Allocation of capital, through credit to
inefficient SOEs, 412
Almanac of China's Economy, 98
Anderson, Kym, 167, 419
Anhui province, 414n11
Antipoverty policy, in rural areas, 430–
431
Anti-smuggling campaign, 165
Apparel industry, 172–173
Aquatic sector, production and demand
for, 440
Arm's-length government-business rela-
tionship, judiciary protectionism and,
59
ASEAN, 16, 230n5; China exports com-
pared with, 214
Asian Development Bank; Chinese legal
development and, 123; legal develop-
ment assistance from, 138
Asset management companies (AMCs),
5, 26n9, 92n25; nonperforming loans
and, 52, 72
Auction market, 77
Auditing system, 43
Autarkic economic units, Chinese prov-
inces as, 214
Authority relations, 456–458
Automatic import registration (AIR), 163
Automobile fees, 74

Bach, C., 164
Badcock, Blair, 327, 328, 337
Bai, Chong-En, 12, 97, 475
Balanced budget, potential for, 83

Baldwin, R. E., 216
Bangserg, P. T., 201n2
Bank credit, NSE access to, 114–115
Bank guarantees, 144n9
Bank of China, profits of, 70
Bankruptcy, 72–73, 225
Banks and banking, 12; banking system
and, 224; bonds for loans and, 73, 479;
commercial banks and, 44–45; commercial basis for operation, 83; commercial principles in, 5; compliance
with banking ratios and, 86; credit
allocation by, 106–108, 107 (tab.); institutional constraints on, 72–74; portfolios of, 12; profitability of, 70; rates
of return on assets, 70; recapitalization
of state-owned, 85; reform of, 32, 51–
53, 241, 401; regulation and supervision of, 71–72; responsibility for profits
and losses by, 85, 89; selective lending
by, 85; state banks and, 44, 51–53;
working-capital lending to private sector, 86–87
Barefoot doctors, 300, 304, 480
Barefoot lawyers, 142
Barlow, Melinda, 315, 316, 338, 344n2
Barriers to entry of NSEs, 104–110;
credit restrictions as, 106–108; by firm
size, 105 (tab.); legal and bureaucratic
restrictions as, 104–106; NSE development and, 97; poor legal protection
as, 108–109; SOEs and, 109–110;
WTO membership and, 105–106
Barriers to factor mobility, 26n17
Barriers to trade; nontariff, 162–164;
product-specific, 166
Barro, Robert J., 143n6
Basel Agreement, 91n16
Bates, Robert, 389, 413n2
Bates Prize, Shleifer and, 126
Beijing, 206; elite business practitioners
in, 142; pollution abatement bene-
fits and costs in, 379–381. *See also*
Pollution
Berlozi, Antoaneta, 140
Bernstein, Thomas, 453, 467n8, 467n9,
467n10, 468n30, 468n34
"Best practices," 36; international, 137
Bian, Fuqin, 329
Bian, Yianjie, 316, 317, 326, 327, 329,
330, 333, 335, 344n4, 347n33

Bias, among sectors, 422; urban, 389–416
Birdzell, L. E., 48
Bodde, Derk, 137
Bonds, transaction volume in spot market for government bonds, 92n26; treasury, 93n34; treasury debt and, 75; underdeveloped market for, 73–74
Bottelier, Pieter, 26n6
Brace, Maurice, 468n36
Brandt, Loren, 401, 414n10, 427
Breweries, decrease in, 225
Brock, William A., 127
Buckley, Robert M., 333, 335, 339, 346n27, 347n31, 347n38, 348n42
Budgetary review, state vs. nonstate sectors and, 113 (tab.)
Budget constraints, of NSEs, 114
Budget deficit, 75; in increasing government revenues scenario, 80–83
Budgeting, of social security revenue and expenditures, 306
Budget Law (1995), 5, 43
Building, overbuilding and, 68–69. *See also* Property entries
Bulk commodities, 216, 218–220
Bureau of Legislative Affairs of the State Council, 124
Bureaucracy, Party control of, 451–452, 457
Bureaucratic restrictions to entry, of NSEs, 104–106
Bureaucrats, compensating for lost control rights, 117–118
Burns, John P., 466n3
Business, decline in number of firms in, 225; forms of ownership, 34
Business disputes, private firms' handling of, 108–109, 108 (tab.)
Business environment, in selected countries (1990s), 179 (tab.)
Business International Corporation, 129
Business International (BI) index, corruption measured by, 191
Byrd, W., 159

Cadot, O., 154
Cadre abuse, corruption and, 453–454; peasants and, 460
Cadres, as targets of protests, 461–462
Cai Fang, 237, 389, 404, 414n7, 414n8, 415

Cai Yongshun, 467n12, 467n19, 467n22, 467n24, 467n26
Cameron, Judy, 143
Canada, interprovincial sales data in, 213
Cao, Rongquing, 318, 327, 346n23
Capacity, excess, 69; utilization of, 67
Capital, allocation to inefficient SOEs, 412; injection into banking system, 72; NSE needs for, 119
Capital account, convertibility of, 42; provincial, 217
Capital controls, 192
Capital flow, from agriculture to industry, 423 (tab.)
Capital gains tax, on real estate transactions, 343–344
Capitalist societies, legal rationality in, 125
Capital-labor ratio, urban and rural, 414n9
Capital markets, 15
Capital mobility, interprovincial trade and, 208
Carter, C., 162
Carter, M. R., 241
CCP: *See* Chinese Communist Party (CCP)
Center for Chinese Agricultural Policy (CCAP), 439
Central bank, 44. *See also* People's Bank of China (PBC)
Central Bank Law (1995), 5, 44, 75
Central China, developing, 403
Centralization, of social security system, 285
Centrally planned economy
Chinese economy and, 219; after Cultural Revolution, 38–39; focus on heavy industry and, 2; industrial support under, 405–408; Lenin on, 35; replacement with market system, 36; rural-urban disparities under, 398–399
Chaichian, Mohammad A., 315, 326, 327, 330, 331
Chang, Chun, 111
Changchong (asset management company), 72, 73
Channels of distribution, diversification of, 224
Che, Jiahua, 111
Chen, Aimin, 327, 330, 332, 333, 337, 338, 345n9, 345n13, 345n14

Chen, Albert, 143
Chen, Chunlai, 417
Chen, J., 162, 414n7
Chen, Ke, 314, 328, 330
Chen, S., 174
Chen, Xiangming, 326, 346n25
Chen Xitong, 140
Chen Zhiqiang, 95n66
Cheng, Chunlai, 439
Cheng, Guoqiang, 417
Cheung, Tai Ming, 317, 327, 330
China, corruption in, 178; European
  Union trade and, 214; foreign direct
  investment in, 178–203; as host for
  FDI compared to potential, 194 (tab.);
  as host of FDI, 181–188, 189–199,
  190 (tab.); number of poor in rural
  China (1984–98), 251 (tab.); sources
  of FDI in, 187, 188 (tab.)
"China Circle" region, 210
China Development Bank, 76–77, 91n4
China Household Income Project
  (CHIP) surveys, 318, 344–345n6
China Insurance Regulatory Commission,
  92n25
China National People's Congress, Law
  on Individually Owned Enterprises, 54
China National Petroleum Corporation
  (CNPC), 50
China Petrochemical Corporation
  (SINOPEC), 50
China Securities Regulatory Commission,
  50, 92n25
China Telecom, 58
Chinese Communist Party (CCP), 4; cur-
  rent role of, 451; economic reform
  and, 24–25; exemption from legal sys-
  tem, 134–135; judiciary and, 135;
  leadership of, 38; *nomenklatura* system
  and, 457, 466; political will of, 38–39;
  property interests and, 136; rule of law
  and, 13–14
Chiu, Rebecca L. H., 315, 317, 327, 331,
  346n17, 346n20
Chongqing, 62n3. *See also* Pollution
Chooi Tow Kwan, 92n25
Chow, Gregory, 25n2
Chu, David K. Y., 327, 335, 338
Chu, George S.-F., 318, 327, 346n23
Cinda (asset management company), 72,
  73
Cities, policy choices and environmental

consequences in, 371–378. *See also*
  Urban areas; specific cities
Civil law, regimes, 126; sector-specific
  rules and, 123; systems, 128
Civil law model, Soviet-style, 137
Civil servants, professionalization of, 125
Clarke, Donald, 92n21, 135, 141
Clean Water, Blue Skies (World Bank),
  130–131
Closed-end loans, 89
CNPC: *See* China National Petroleum
  Corporation (CNPC)
Coal, 219; mining sector and, 225; pollu-
  tion and, 21
COD: *See* Organic water pollution (COD)
Cohen, Jerome A., 143n3
Collective, 34; NSE registered as, 111
Collective action, workers in, 454–455
Collective enterprises, 12, 99; privatized,
  55; sale of, 96n78
Collective ownership, farmer preference
  for, 427
Collectivized agriculture, 99
Colwell, Peter F., 315
"Comfort letters," 144n9
Command economy, 1; excess capacity
  and, 15–16; transition from, 274, 275
Commerce, state sector and, 34
Commercial banking, 44–45, 224
Commercial Bank Law (1995), 44, 72, 86
Commercially oriented banking prac-
  tices, 82 (tab.), 83, 84 (tab.), 85–90
Commercial owner occupancy, of urban
  housing, 313
Commodities, 230n7; prices of, 159; re-
  stricted to trading firms, 161
Commoditization, housing reform and,
  317; inequities addressed by, 335, 343–
  344
Commodity composition, regional inte-
  gration and, 215–218; types of com-
  modities, 215
Common law, 128, regimes, 126
Commune and brigade enterprises, 99
Communes, collapse of, 408–409; devel-
  opment and, 399; replacement of, 3
Communicable diseases, 298
Communication Bank of China, 52
Communications, upgrades in, 219–220
Communist Parties, in Eastern Europe,
  38; judiciary and, 144n12. *See also*
  Chinese Communist Party (CCP)

Competition, 225, 478; among enterprises, 12–13
Complaints, literacy and, 139
Comprehensive law, of 1999, 123
Consolidation, 225
Constitution, 124, 135; amendment to (1999), 6; Article 5 of, 37; rule of law in, 37, 57
Construction industry, inefficiencies in, 327
Consultative Group for International Agricultural Research centers, 437
Consumption, 87–88; of foods, 440; NSE tax revenues and, 111; from polluting sectors, 363–364, 363 (fig.), 364 (fig.); rural-urban inequity and, 390, 399
Contract employment, 286
"Contracting," between levels of government, 35
Contract law, 136
Contract provisions, in 1980s, 123
Contract system, in agriculture, 424
Contributions, to health care, 301–302, 302 (tab.); outlays and, 308–309; for pensions in cities, 296–297
Contributions to social security system, 288; collecting, 293; defined benefits and, 292; transforming into single social security tax, 305
Cooperative health insurance schemes, 304
Cooperatives, 34; rural credit, 71
Corporate governance, 50–51, 118–119; substantive law of, 128
Corruption, cadre, 453–454, 460; in China, India, and Singapore, 178; curbing, 464; measuring, 191–192; and other measures of public institutions, 195–196, 195 (tab.); private enterprises and, 109; reducing, 200, 201 (tab.); rule of law vs., 57
Cost-benefit analysis, for poverty reduction, 475–476
Costs, of housing, 328–329; of pollution abatement, 371, 379–381; of urban housing, 327–329. *See also* Pollution
Counties, designated as poor, 238
Credit, 12; for housing financing, 347n40; to inefficient SOEs, 412; inventory increases and, 69; subsidized, 241–242
Credit allocation, local government and, 44

Credit analysis, 89
Credit control, 4
Credit culture, commercial, 85–90
Credit guarantee system, 89–90
Creditors, mortgage transactions and, 339
Credit restrictions to entry, of NSEs, 106–108
Crime, increase in, 131
Croll, Elisabeth, 468n44
Crop(s), productivity during reform, 433–434; yields of, 435–437, 436 (tab.). *See also* Agriculture; Grain; specific crops
Cross-province (regional) central bank branches, 32
Cross-regional labor migration, 115, 116
Cruz, Ramoncito de la, 94n52
Cultural Revolution, 38; age structure of working-age adults and, 279; economy after, 408; legal reform after, 123
Currency, value of trade and, 154
Current account convertibility, 6, 42
Customs data, 228
Customs duties, imports subject to, 165. *See also* Tariffs
Cutler, D. M., 276

Dai, Y., 206
Dasgupta, Susmita, 21, 139, 353, 357, 359, 364, 365, 384, 386n5, 473
Data, for microeconomic analysis of policy responses, 473; need for, 472; on poverty programs, 473; on regional integration, 227–229
Davey, W., 167
Deaths, from air pollution, 355, 377–378, 378 (fig.); causes of, 297, 297 (tab.); from SO_2 pollution, 377 (tab.)
Deaton, A., 276
Debt, bond market and, 73–74; for financing government expenditures, 75–76; government, 75–76, 77; nontreasury, 76–78; ratio to gross domestic product, 80; treasury, 73, 75, 76 (tab.), 83, 93n36
Debt-equity swaps, 52, 53
Debt-to-GDP ratio, 83, 95n59
Decentralization; information, 112; intragovernment, 110–111; of social security revenue and expenditure budgeting, 305–306; of trade, 158; urban housing and, 317–318

Deci, Edward, 143
"Decision on Issues Concerning the Establishment of a Socialist Market Economic Structure," 4–6, 9, 10–11, 31, 32, 36; reasons for change and, 35–42
Decollectivization, 99, 420, 444
Defense industry, NSEs in, 105
Deficit, in state pension system, 77–78
Defined benefits and contributions, 292
Deflation, 67; policy response to, 87
De Lisle, Jacques, 144n16
Demand, for foods, 440; for urban housing, 314–315
De Melo, J., 154
Democracy, in China, 464; elections and, 62n4
Demographic transition, 274, 275–279
Demonstrations, by peasants, 453. *See also* Protests
Deng Xiaoping, 31, 181; alternative housing and, 313; housing reform and, 315; inflation and, 4; reforms and, 2, 25; southern tour by, 36
Dependency ratio, 27n20
Dependent population, composition of, 276–278
Depression, 404
Deprivation, social assistance for preventing, 311
Designated trading, 161; products covered by, 162 (tab.)
Developed economies, in East Asia, 129
Developing countries; China and, 273; lack of pressure groups in China and, 406
Developing-country host of FDI; China as, 178–179, 181–188; evolution of India as, 181–188
Development, of modernizing elites, 389
Development policy, heavy-industry-oriented, 405–408
Development Research Center, 206
Dickens, Charles, 31
Dickie, Mure, 92n24
Dicks, Anthony, 135
Dickson, Bruce, 468n46
Dimaranan, Betina, 14, 153, 478
Direct budgetary transfers, to poor areas, 237
Direct foreign investment: *See* Foreign direct investment (FDI)

Direct transfers, to urban dwellers, 411. *See also* Subsidies; Transfers
"Dirty" sectors: *See* Pollution; specific sectors
Discontent, defusing and redirecting blame for, 458–461; local officials as targets of, 461–462; rural, 452–454, 457–458; urban, 454–456, 457–458
Discrimination, against NSEs, 97–98, 104–110, 114–115; against rural areas, 391–397
Disease, health status and, 297–298. *See also* Health care
Disputes, resolution of, 131
Distribution channels, diversification of, 224
Diversification, of banks' ownership structure, 53–54; of distribution channels, 224; of ownership structure, 50
Doctors, in rural areas, 300, 304, 480
Domestic outflows, 230n7; ratio of, 211
Domestic trade estimates, 230n3
Domestic trade ratios, 209 (tab.)
Domestic value added, discrimination against industries relying on, 165
Dongfang (asset management company), 72, 73
Dong Furen, 42, 43, 94n43
Dowall, David E., 316, 317, 327, 328, 329, 331, 337, 344n3
Dual-track approach, 34; to foreign exchange markets, 42
Du Xiaoshan, 241
Dwyer, D. J., 314, 327, 332

East Asian economic miracle, 128
Eastern Europe, failure of pre-1990 reform, 38; privatization of state-owned enterprises in, 54; reforms in, 33
Ecklund, George N., 25n2
Econometric specification, for foreign investment source countries, 192–193
Economic crimes, 131
Economic development, 279–283; agriculture and, 418–419; institutional foundations of, 48; legal institutions and, 126–129; legal reform and, 130–133; pollution control and, 384; as transition, 274, 275; variation by localities, 461

Economic entities, poverty loans redirected to, 241

Economic growth, cumulative percentage growth rates (1995–2005), 170 (tab.); FDI and, 178; rates of, 1; structural change, liberalization and, 169–174

Economic integration, 14

Economic organization, legal protection of, 123

Economic reform "Decision" (1993) and, 10–11; for environmental gains, 383; environmental regulation and, 373–378; political reforms' interactions with, 479–480; pollution and, 355–368; urban bias and, 409–411

Economic rents (surpluses), distribution of, 343

Economic sectors, bans on NSEs in, 104–105

Economic structure, literature on, 206

Economics, Western, 41

Economy, 1–2, agriculture in, 418–419; changes in structure of China's, 420 (tab.); growth of, 418, 419 (tab.); Party-State control of, 48; political system and, 24–25; property rights and, 126; similarity of provincial, 206; small enterprises and, 54; state sector and, 39–40; transformation of sectoral structure of, 7 (fig.). *See also* Regional economies

Efficiency, discrimination against NSEs and, 97–98; eliminating rural-urban gap for, 411; of intermediation, 68–71, 83; 8-7 Program, 16–17, 238, 253

Eisenberger, Robert, 143

Elderly, 276; old-age financial support and, 277–278

Elections, local, 62n4, 458–459

Elite business practitioners, in Beijing, 142

Ellickson, Robert C., 127

Emancipation of mind (1977, 1978), 39

Emissions (industrial), 353–354; intensities and loads of, 369

Employment, contract employment, 286; in health care system, 298–299; labor shift and, 281; in nonstate sector, 116; with NSEs, 111; rural, 429; urban, 414n13

Employment growth, in private sector, 87

Energy and transport, of GDP, 219 (fig.)

Enforcement; of judgments, 144n13; of pollution regulations, 358

Engel, C., 214

Enterprise-level changes, 224–225

Enterprise reform, 36–37, 49; future research on, 226

Enterprise system, government-business relationship and, 33. *See also* Private enterprises

Entrepreneurs, compensating bureaucrats and, 117–118

Entrepreneurship, 54–55; poverty relief and, 264

Entry: *See* Barriers to entry of NSEs

Environment, 353–388; growth and, 20–21; industrial damage to, 353–355; policy choices and consequences in five cities, 371–378; provincial differences in citizen complaints about, 359 (fig.); regulation and, 356–358

Environmental law, 130–131

Environmental regulation, economic reform and, 373–378

Epidemiological transition, 298

Epstein, Richard, 127, 133

European Union (EU), 126; Chinese legal development and, 123; development assistance from, 138; exports compared with China, 214

Everbright Bank, 92n17

Excess capacity, 69; in steel industry, 88

Exchange rates, 159, 426–427; reform of, 32. *See also* Foreign exchange markets

Exemptions, for processing trade and for foreign investment, 165

Expenditures, rise in, 80, 83

Export market, China in, 7, 9

Export ratio, provincial, 210–211

Exports, China's share of world exports, 155 (fig.); composition of, 156, 156 (fig.); of foods, 440; foreign-invested firms and, 178; goods used in production of, 165; of grain, 444; growth of, 154; in 25 provinces, 210 (fig.)

Extension, of agricultural technology, 437–438

Externalities, 130–131

Extrabudgetary fees and funds, 43

Factor endowments, growth of, 169
Factor markets, assessment of distortions in, 475–476; interventions in, 406–407, 411–412
Factor mobility, barriers to, 26n17
Falun Gong, 27n25, 461
Families, Household Responsibility System and, 400; urban housing and, 344n1
Fan, Shenggen, 421, 438
Fan, Xiandong, 432, 445
Fang, Cai, 21–22
Fang Liufang, 141, 142
Farm income, 22
Farming, farm size and, 427–428; household earnings and, 400; Household Responsibility System and, 400; negotiation for market allocation by, 424; new methods of, 428–429; technology for, 428–429, 431–432; welfare of, 402–403. *See also* Agriculture
FDI: *See* Foreign direct investment (FDI)
Fee-for-service health care, 300, 301, 302
Fees, paid by NSEs, 120n2
Fifteenth Party Congress (1997), 6, 37
Financial crisis, in Asia, 42
Financial institutions, loans outstanding from, 68
Financial intermediation, 12
Financial losses, of NSEs, 114
Financial markets, NSE access to, 114–115
Financial policies, for food self-sufficiency, 422–423
Financial reform program, 67–68, 71–90; fiscal sustainability and, 74; government debt and, 75–76; institutional constraints on, 72–74; nontreasury government debt and, 76–78; revenues and, 74–75
Financial sector, performance of, 70–71; SOEs and, 49
Financial sustainability, 1998–2002, 79 (tab.); scenarios for, 80–85
Financial system, intermediation and, 67; recapitalization of, 78–83; reform of, 11–12, 44–45; resource allocation by, 90
Financing, of health care, 301–302, 302 (tab.); mortgage, 338–340; for owner-occupied urban housing, 322 (tab.); of

pensions, 291; of private housing, 317; of rural housing, 315
Finder, Susan, 124
Firm size, entry barriers to NSEs by, 105 (tab.)
Fiscal decentralization, 97–98
Fiscal federalism, 36
Fiscal management, 5
Fiscal policies, for food self-sufficiency, 422–423
Fiscal reform, two-tier tax administration system in, 59
Fiscal revenue, 49
Fiscal sustainability, 81 (tab.); banks and, 74; commercial bank behavior, 82 (tab.); revenue enhancement, 81 (tab.); revenue enhancement and commercial bank behavior, 84 (tab.)
Fiscal system, market-oriented, 41; poverty investment and, 264; reform of, 32, 40, 43–44
Five-Year Plan (eighth), housing reform in, 316
Fixed investment, state vs. nonstate sector shares of, 106 (tab.)
Fleisher, B., 414n7
Fong, Peter K. W., 315, 317, 336, 346n19, 346n25
Food, foreign exchange and, 426–427; price and marketing policies, 423–426. *See also* Food security
Food for Work program, 241, 248, 270n2
Food grain, 440, 441–442
Food production, 23
Food security, 417, 418, food production increases and, 420; policy for, 444–446; self-sufficiency as goal and, 422; trade liberalization, food deficit, and, 438–444; trade policies and, 426–427. *See also* Agriculture
Forced savings, for housing, 316–317
Ford Foundation, Chinese legal development and, 123, 138
Foreclosure, on urban property, 339–340
Foreign contributions, to Chinese legal development, 137–141
Foreign direct investment (FDI), 7–9, 130, 474
Foreign direct investment in China and India, 178–203; China as host of, from major source countries, 189–199;

China as largest developing-country host of, 178–179; contractual amount and realized value (China), 182–183; data on, 189–191, 190 (tab.); economic specification for countries, 192–193; evolution of laws and regulations on FDI, 183–186; flow in, 196; linear regression on, 180; and potential in China, 180–181, 194 (tab.); realized, 181 (tab.); regression results and interpretation, 193–196; sources of, 187

Foreign exchange markets, reforms of, 42

Foreign exchange rate, unification of (1994), 5–6

Foreign exchange system; food products and, 426–427; prereform trade regime and, 157–158; two-tier, 159

Foreign firms, 141; treatment in China, 178

Foreign-invested companies, 99

Foreign investment, 15, 132; exemptions for, 165. *See also* Foreign direct investment (FDI)

Foreign legal models, 137–138

Foreign-owned firms, 34

Foreign trade: *See* Trade

Foreign trade corporations (FTCs), 157; increase in number of, 161; with trading rights for range of commodities, 160, 160 (tab.)

Foreign trade ratios, 209 (tab.)

Foreign trading companies, information on, 228

Formal norms, informal norms and, 142

Foundations, legal development assistance from, 138

Four Dragons of Asia (Four Little Tigers), 39, 408; China contrasted with, 2

Fourteenth Party Congress (1992), 36

Fourth Plenum of Fifteenth Party Central Committee, SOE reform and, 49–50

Frankel, Jeffrey, 201n6

Free enterprise, government-business relationship and, 48

Free ride, in social security system, 306

Free trade, food production and, 441–442; in inputs used in production of exports, 158–159; WTO and, 439–440

Frictional unemployment, 404

FTCs: *See* Foreign trade corporations (FTCs)

Fuel tax, 74, 92–93n31

Fujian, 209, 230n2

Funds, misappropriation of, 454

Gaddy, Cliff, 92n29

Gao, Xiaoyuan, 314, 326, 330, 332, 346n25

Garnaut, Ross, 404

GATT: *See* General Agreement on Tariffs and Trade (GATT)

GDP: *See* Gross domestic product (GDP)

GDP deflator, 87

General Agreement on Tariffs and Trade (GATT), 168

Geopolitics, political will of CCP and, 39

German civil law, 128–129

Germany, investment in China, 191

Getihu, 6

Glass-Steagall Act, 44–45

Global Competitiveness Report, 191 China and India in, 179

Global marketplace, China in, 10, 61. *See also* World economy

Global Trade Analysis Project (GTAP), global general equilibrium model, 153–154

Globalization, world trade and raw materials in, 216

Goldman, Merle, 466n3, 468n41

Gong Xiangrui, 141

Goods, bulk, 218–220; characteristics of goods in interprovincial trade, 217 (tab.); provision of public, 480; share of exports in GDP, 155 (fig.)

Governance, corporate, 50–51; reforms in large SOEs and, 46

Government, control by, 457; foreclosure on urban property and, 339; health care financing from, 301–302; insufficiency of revenue and, 49; social security for employees of, 286; supplementary social insurance funds from, 309

Government bonds, included in measure of government debt outstanding, 93–94n41; for nonperforming loans of state-owned banks, 479; transaction volume in spot market for, 92n26

Government-business relationship, 33; role of, 48–49; transforming SOEs and, 49–53

Government debt, 75–76; nontreasury, 76–78; treasury debt and, 73
Government Health Insurance Service (GIS), 301
Government intervention, political economy of, 405–411
Government revenues, changing variable of, 83
Gradualism, in economic reform, 2
Grain, 440, 441 (tab.); food grain, 440; imports of, 27n24; self-sufficiency in, 442–444, 443 (tab.)
Grain production, 424–425; market monitoring/inspection and, 425; nominal and effective real production rates of grain, 425–426, 425 (tab.)
Grants, to households, 239–240
Great Leap Forward, rural-urban consumption and, 399
Green Revolution technology, 431
Greif, Avner, 127
Griffin, Keith, 344n5
Gross domestic product (GDP), 1; debt ratio to, 80; energy and transport of, 219 (fig.); government revenues and, 74, 78; growth of, 418; "opening" policy and, 34; quadrupling since 1979, 6; real, 218
Gross per capita income, in Sichuan Province, 254 (tab.), 255 (fig.)
Grove, Theodore, 401
Growth, determinants of, 260–264
Growth-oriented activities, local investment in, 241
Growth rate, 95n58; above real rate of interest, 85
Gruen, N., 154
G-7, 126, 136, 137
GTAP Version 4 model of global economy, 169
Gu, Yanxiang Anthony, 314
Guan, Y., 327
Guangdong, 210. *See also* Pollution
Guangdong International Trust and Investment Corporation (GITIC), 45; collapse of, 132
Guangzhou: *See* Pollution
Guanxi, 133

Hainan Development Bank, 45
Hamer, Andrew Marshall, 318, 331, 332, 338, 342, 345n8, 347n30

Harding, James, 92n30
Hartman, Raymond, 357, 359
Hayami, Y., 167
Hays, R. Allen, 315, 316, 317, 324, 330, 333, 335, 336, 344n3, 345n7, 346n21
Health, air pollution and, 369, 370
Health care, financing of, 301–302, 302 (tab.); networks of, 299; provision of, 298–300
Health insurance, 288, 293, 302–304; coverage by, 302–303; social welfare and, 297–304
Health services, rural, 480
Heavy-industry-oriented development policy, 405–408
Hertel, Thomas W., 14, 153, 156, 169, 175n1, 478
Hettige, Mala, 386n10
He Weifang, 141
Higher education, 274
Highway Law, 74; amending, 74–75
Home country effect, in United States, 214
Homeless families, 344n1
Home state effect, 214
Hong Kong, 210; FDI flow and, 199 (tab.); FDI stock and, 198 (tab.); foreign direct investment in China and, 187, 196–201, 197 (tab.); smuggling from, 165
Hope, Nicholas C., 1, 471
Hospitals, 298–299; rural, 300
Household registration system, 27n23; labor and, 407
Household Responsibility System (HRS), 3, 399–400, 409, 420
Households, dwellings purchased by, 345n14; grants to, 239–240; poverty loans to, 245; poverty reduction based on, 267
Household savings, 68
Housing, 19–20; financing of, 317; market bid price for, 346n22; owned by state-owned enterprises, 78; privatization of, 478–479; reforms of, 10; structural conditions of, 318; as work unit wage, 330
Housing market, property rights and, 480
Housing projects, quality of and densities in, 328
Housing reform (urban China), 313–350; conference on, 316; goals of, 317–318

Housing Reform Steering Group, 316
Hu, Ruifa, 432, 445
Hu, Xiaoyi, 284
Hua, Xie Zhao, 337, 338, 341
Huang, Jikun, 17, 23, 235, 417, 421, 422, 424, 432, 433, 437, 438, 439, 445, 473, 475
Huang, Yao Liang, 337, 338, 341
Huang, Yasheng, 132, 468n31
Huang, Yiping, 404
Huang Ping, 468n44
Huang Ying, 94n47, 94n48
Huarong (asset management company), 72, 73
Hui, Eddie Chi Man, 315, 316, 327, 332
Hukou system, 462
Human development, China's record in, 273–274
Human rights, 451
Hungary, economic reforms in, 32
Huq, Mainul, 357, 359, 365, 384, 386n9
Hussain, Athar, 18, 27n20, 273, 285, 472

Ianchovichina, Elena, 14, 153, 169, 478
Ideology, after Decision, 36–38; rhetoric and, 37
Illegal imports, 130
Illegal investments, 130
Import market, China in, 7, 9
Import permits, for NSEs, 105
Imports, free trade in inputs used in production of exports, 158–159; of grain, 27n24, 444; information on, 228; market for, 173–174, 173 (tab.); planned volumes of, 157; share protected by NTBs, 163 (tab.); SOEs and, 161; trade liberalization and, 439
Incentives, for enterprises, 401; for housing purchases, 331; of NSEs, 114; response of firms to, 473
Income, farm, 429; housing and, 346n19; peasant, 453; sharing of rising, 16–17; urban housing market prices and, 324–325
Income gap, rural mobility and, 404; rural-urban, 414n7
Incremental reform, 33–35
Independence, of judiciary, 135
India, corruption in, 178; evolution as host of FDI, 181–188; foreign direct investment and, 178–203, 179
Indirection, 139–140

Individual accounts, for social security, 288, 292
Individual contributions, to health care, 302
Individually owned private enterprises, 99
Industrial air pollution, deaths from, 378 (fig.)
Industrial and Commercial Bank of China, credit from, 86
Industrial enterprises, state-owned (1993), 55 (tab.)
Industrial growth, state and nonstate contributions to, 104 (tab.)
Industrial migration, regulation, pollution abatement, and, 364–367
Industrial output, growth rates of, 100 (tab.); in nonstate sector, 97, 102–103, 103 (tab.); ownership composition in, 53 (tab.); SOE contribution to, 120n1; in state sector, 102–103, 103 (tab.)
Industrial pollution, 353–355
Industrial sector, 1, focus on, 2; GDP from, 6. *See also* Industry
Industrialization, 3; as growth catalyst, 389; rural, 429; specialization of, 216
Industry, bias toward, 422–423; capital flow to, 423 (tab.); excess capacity in, 69; heavy-industry-oriented development policy and, 405–408; imports from pollution-intensive, 363 (fig.); labor shift into, 279; output of, 353; output share of large plants, 361 (fig.); pollution and, 358–367, 369; poverty loans for, 245, 249 (fig.), 264; production and pollution from, 372–373; transfers dominated by, 213
Inefficiency, 67
Infant mortality, 269, 274
Inflation, 4; inflation subsidies and, 401; in 1990s, 40
Inflows, 212–213, 212 (fig.), 213 (fig.); of 25 provinces, 211 (fig.)
Informal housing, 340
Informal norms, formal norms and, 142
Information, gathering, 464
Information decentralization, 112
Information Technology Agreement, 171–172
Infrastructure, creating, 18; of health care system, 298; investment in, 220, 220 (fig.); poverty relief and, 264; upgrades

Infrastructure (*continued*)
    in transportation and communications,
    219–220
Innovation, stable legal order and, 137
Input, trends for rice, wheat, soybean,
    and maize, 433 (tab.)
Input-output tables: *See* Provincial input-
    output (I-O) tables
Input stage of development, 131–132
Institute of Industrial Economics, 221
Institution(s), creating effective, 476–477
Institutional actors, roles and responsibili-
    ties of, 125
Institutional changes, 33–34
Institutional constraints, on bank perfor-
    mance, 72–74
Institutional environment, of private en-
    terprise, 55–56
Institutional features, growth retarded by,
    221–224
Institutional protections, against problems
    causing discontent, 458–461
Insurance, for health care financing, 301;
    health insurance, 302–304; for laid-off
    workers, 460
Insurance companies, assets of, 92n25;
    lack of, for diversification, 73
Integration, economic, 14; regional,
    204–232
Intellectual inputs, leadership mindset
    and, 40–42
Intellectual property rights, 136, 166
Interest groups: *See* Pressure groups
Interest income, 93n33; tax on, 74, 75
Interest rate control, 192
Interest rates, cuts in, 87–88
Interindustry trade, 215–216
Intermediaries, 222
Intermediation, 67; by banking system,
    83; efficiency of, 68–71
Internal market, integrating, 15–16
International consultants, 129
International economy: *See* World
    economy
International Maize and Wheat Improve-
    ment Center (CIMMYT), 437
International trade, agriculture's declining
    role in, 419
Internet, laws concerning, 136
Interprovincial trade, 16, 204–205, 207–
    225; bulk goods and materials in, 218–
    220; characteristics of goods in, 217

(tab.); coal, grain, and iron as, 219;
    commodity composition in, 215–218;
    dominated by intraindustry trade, 217–
    218; enterprise-level changes in, 224–
    225; future work on, 226–227; growth
    rate of, 211–212, 211 (tab.); numbers
    for, 213–214; provincial policies that
    restrain trade in, 220–224; scale of,
    209; significance for all provinces,
    214–215
Interprovincial transfers, literature on, 206
Interregional trade, key problems with,
    221–222; within nations, data on,
    213–214
Interventions: *See* specific interventions;
    specific issues
Intragovernment decentralization, 97–98,
    110–111
Intraindustry trade, 215; dominance of
    interprovincial trade by, 217–218;
    world trade dominated by, 216
Inventories, 67; excess, 69–70
Investment, 87–88; financing of, 4; for-
    eign direct, 130; illegal, 130; misalloca-
    tion of, 12; from overseas Chinese,
    132; poverty relief and, 263–264; in
    property, 68–69; types of, 37
Investment controls, 4
Investment funds, allocation of, 241;
    managerial abuse of, 119
Investment programs, 239, 239 (tab.)
Investment-to-wage spending ratio, in
    Shaanxi, 243 (fig.)
Inward FDI, 178
I-O tables: *See* Provincial input-output
    (I-O) tables
Iron, 219

Japan, 128, 129; economic development
    of, 38–39; investment in China, 191;
    lawyers in, 128
Jefferson, Gary, 401
Ji Weidong, 137
Jianbo, Lou, 337, 338, 339, 340, 347n41
Jiangsu, 40
Jiang Zemin, 36, 125, 468n48; on agri-
    cultural research, 431–432
Jiang Zhongyi, 241, 268, 270n2
Jilin, 209, 230n2
Jin, Songqing, 431, 432, 434, 438, 446
Jin Hehui, 266
Jiujiang, 303

Johnson, D. Gale, 27n22, 418
Joint stock corporations, 37; state firm conversion to, 224
Joint Venture Law (1979), 123
Joint ventures, between domestic and foreign firms, 158; between state-owned enterprises and foreign investors, 99; FDI as, 182–187; with foreign firms, 34
Jolls, Christine, 143
Judicial interpretations, by Supreme People's Court, 124
Judiciary, Communist Party and, 135; lack of independence of, 135; two-tier, 59, 477

Kanbur, R., 414n7
Keller, P., 143n2
Khan, Azizur Rahman, 344n5, 347n32
Kim, Joochul, 327, 330
Kim, S., 207
Kingson, E. R., 285
Kirkby, Richard, 328, 346n25
Korea, 128, 129
Kornai, Janos, 34, 48, 54
Kritzer, Herbert, 127, 132
Krueger, Anne, 408, 413n1, 413n3, 413n4
Kumar, A., 206
Kung, James, 427
Kwok, R. Yin-Wang, 327, 335, 338

La Porta, Rafael, 126, 128, 143n5
Labor, cross-regional migration of, 115, 116; intervention in market for, 406–407, 411; mobility of, 400, 403–404, 411; poverty relief and, 264; in private enterprises, 99; shift into industry and services, 279; in SOEs, 284; urban vs. rural, 412–413. *See also* Migrant labor; Workforce
Labor force, 6; binding members to work units, 284; sectoral distribution of, 281 (tab.), 282
Labor insurance, 289–290; health care insurance as, 289–290; old-age pensions as, 289–292; TVEs and, 296; unemployment insurance as, 289–290, 292–295
Labor market, gains from improving productivity, 411; rural, 394, 429–430; urban, 394

Labor market efficiency, productivity gains from improving, 411
Labor mobility, barriers to rural, 414n12; contributions to GDP growth rate, 415n17; regulations of, 404
Lai, Ok-Kwok, 316, 317, 330, 332, 335, 342
Laid-off workers, 295, 460–461
Lalkaka, Dinyar, 314, 329, 331
Land allocation system, 346n21
Land management, 418
Land rights, private, 3; for urban housing, 336, 341, 347n41
Land tenure system, 427
Land use, policy of, 427–429
Lange, John E., 143n3
Laozi, 122, 133, 143
Laplante, Benoit, 358
Lardy, Nicholas R., 11–12, 67, 91n1, 92n18, 92n22, 92n25, 93n39, 157, 159, 164, 178, 237, 430, 472, 478, 479
Large Enterprise Working Committee, 46
Latest Economic Statistics (China), 226–227
Lau, Laurence, 34
Law(s), economic development and, 126–129; and economic growth, 142–143; evolution of laws and regulations on FDI (China and India), 183–186; FDI (China and India) and, 182; rule of, 13–14; statist orientation of developmental assistance for, 139; uses of, 136–137
Law on Chinese-Foreign Equity Joint Ventures (1979), 181
Law on Individually Owned Enterprises, 54
Law reform, assessing success of, 125–130; directions for further research on, 141–143. *See also* Law(s); Legal development
Lawyers, American lawyers as brokers, 127, 132–133; paraprofessional, 142
Leadership, mind-set of, 40–42; responsiveness after Mao, 408; of village, 459–460
Leading Group for Economic Development in Poor Areas, 237, 238, 239–240, 245, 270n2
Leaf, Michael, 340
Lee, Brian Y., 314, 338, 340, 347n39, 348n43

Lee, M. H., 327
Legal development, foreign contributions to, 137–141; in reform period, 123–125; resources devoted to, 125–126
Legal institutions, and economic development, 126–127; informal norms and, 127
Legal models, customization by China, 137; foreign vs. customized, 137–138
Legal protection, for NSEs, 106–108, 118–119; for property and economic organization, 123
Legal reform, 60, 122–149, dilemmas in, 133–141; economic development and, 130–133; top-down, 133–134. *See also* Law(s)
Legal restrictions to entry, of NSEs, 104–106
Legal systems, classification of, 128; exemption of Communist Party from, 134–135; formal institutions, customs, and, 131
Legislation, law on, 125; to structure and staff legal processes, 125
Lending, 69–70, bad, 12; growth of, 86, 91n4. *See also* Banks and banking; Loans
Lenin, Vladimir Ilyich, 35
Li, David D., 12, 97, 111, 475
Li, Jinyan, 340, 341, 348n47
Li, Lianjiang, 453, 467n7, 468n29, 468n39, 468n40
Li, Ling Hin, 328, 342, 347n34, 347n35, 348n49
Li, Mu Yang, 471
Li, Shuhe, 119
Li, Wei, 406
Li Boxi, 206
Li Guo, 240, 241
Li Jianguang, 240, 241
Li Jinhua, 130
Li Qiang, 209
Li Shi, 344n5, 345n6
Li Zhou, 264, 265
Liang, Echo H., 236, 238
Liang Zhiping, 141
Liaoning province, 213; social security in, 27n19. *See also* Pollution
Liberalization, economic, 3–4; growth, structural change, and, 169–174. *See also* Trade liberalization
Liebman, Benjamin L., 142, 143n4
Life expectancy, 1–2

Lifestyle: *See* Living standards
Lim, G. C., 327
Lin, Justin Yifu, 23, 399, 400, 407, 414n8, 417, 418, 421, 424, 430, 433, 473, 475
Lipton, Michael, 389, 413n2
Literacy, 139
Liu, Shouying, 427
Liu Nanping, 124, 136
Livestock, production and demand for, 440
Living allowance, 295
Living expenses, government allocation of, 94n50
Living space, size of, 317–318, 318 (tab.), 332, 346n17
Living standards, 10; improvement in (1978–1993), 33; protection of urban dwellers, 401
Loan classification system, 472
Loans, allocation to state- and collectively owned companies, 86; closed-end, 89; diversion of poverty monies, 242; non-performing, 71, 72; for poverty, 240; to private and individual firms, 86. *See also* Lending; Poverty
Local elections, by peasants, 458–459
Local governments, debt of, 77; environmental performance of industry and, 367–368; interregional trade and, 220–222; intragovernment decentralization and, 110–111; literature about power of, 206; monetary policy, credit allocation, and, 44; NSEs and, 98, 115, 120n2; poverty relief and, 241, 263–264; urban housing and, 344n3
Logan, John R., 315, 322, 324, 327, 329, 330, 336, 337, 344n3, 345n11, 345n15, 347n35
Lohmar, Bryan, 430
Lou, Jiwei, 40
Low-income economy, China as, 273
Low-wage policy, housing and, 330
Lu, Baifa, 222, 225
Lu, Hanlong, 327
Lu, Xiaobo, 467n8
Lubman, Stanley B., 125, 143n1, 144n11, 467n4
Lucas, Robert, 365
Luo, Bing, 134, 139
Luo Qizhi, 125
Lyons, Thomas, 430

Macaulay, Stewart, 127
MacFarquhar, Roderick, 466n3
Macroeconomic management, 4; market-oriented approach to, 40
Magee, Stephen P., 127
Ma Hong, 222, 225
Maize: *See* Agriculture; Crop(s)
Management: *See* Leadership
Managerial abuse, of investment funds, 119
Mandatory planning targets, 34
Mani, Muthukumara, 386n10
Manion, Melanie, 133, 134
Manufactured goods, reductions in tariff protection for, 167; trade in, 217
Manufacturing sectors, in United States, 207
Mao Zedong, urban per capita consumption and, 27n22
Market(s), nonstate sector and, 34; regional integration and, 204–232
Market economy, as goal, 36; government-business relationship, 33; institutions of, 134; transition to, 2–4, 31–62, 274, 275, 283–286
Market integration, categories of goods and, 216
Market outcomes, local government countermanding of, 223–224
Market prices; defined, 324–325; plan prices and, 159–160; selling urban housing at, 324–331
Market reforms, agriculture and, 400; environment and, 354
Market socialism, socialist market economy differences from, 36
Market value, private housing and, 323, 323 (tab.)
Marketization, future research on, 226
Market-oriented economy, movement to, 423–424
Market-oriented legal development, 137
Market-supporting institutions, building of, 11–12
Martin, Paul, 216, 386n9
Martin, William, 14, 153, 156, 159, 164, 169, 175n1, 478
Mass privatization, of state-owned enterprises, 54
Materials, bulk, 218–220
Maternal mortality rates, 269
McCallum, J., 213–214

McMillan, John, 26n12, 400, 421, 433
Medicine: *See* Health care
Migrant labor, 27n23, 430, 462–463; social security and, 282–283
Ming, Lizhi, 108, 109, 120n2
Ministry of Civil Affairs, 289, 462
Ministry of Finance, bonds and, 73
Ministry of Foreign Trade and Economic Cooperation (MOFTEC), 160
Ministry of Information Industry, 58
Ministry of Justice, 124
Ministry of Labor and Social Security, 285, 287
Miroeconomic analysis, of policy responses, 473
Mobility, of rural labor, 22, 403–404
MOFTEC: *See* Ministry of Foreign Trade and Economic Cooperation (MOFTEC)
Monetary policy, 5
Monetary system, 36; reform of, 44–45
Moral hazard, health care and, 301
Morris, Clarence, 137
Mortality rate, of children under five, 274
Mortgage financing, for urban housing, 338–340, 347n38
Mortgages, 330; multiple, 347n39
Multilateral development banks, 126
Multilevel poverty alleviation network, 240
Multinational regions, trade of, 230n5
Multitier pricing system, for removing distortions in commodity prices and exchange rates, 159
Municipal health insurance, 303–304
Municipalities, industry in, 206
Municipal Labor and Social Security Bureaus, 296, 305
Murie, Alan, 315, 316, 324, 326, 327, 330, 332, 338, 341, 345n10, 345n12, 346n20
Mutual funds, lack of, for diversification, 73

Nadelson, Robert, 317, 327, 330
National defense industry, NSEs in, 105
National integration, 216
National I-O table, 218
National Long Term Economic Plan, food self-sufficiency in, 422

National People's Congress (NPC), 124; committees of, 124; Highway Law amendment and, 75; power of, 451

Natural disaster relief, social assistance and, 310

Natural resources, depletion of, 20–21

Naughton, Barry, 16, 161, 204, 210, 476

Nelson, Joan, 466n2, 468n43

Net per capita income, in Sichuan Province, 256 (tab.), 257 (fig.)

Ng, F., 165

Ni, Siyi, 144n13

Nomenklatura system, 457, 466

Nominal GDP, in 1998, 95n71

Nominal protection rates (NPRs), for wheat and maize, 426

Nonbank financial institutions, financial condition of, 70–71; working-capital lending to private sector, 86–87

Nonfactor services, share in GDP, 155 (fig.)

Nonfarm employment, shift to services, 281

Nongovernment entities, foreclosure on urban property and, 339

Nonperforming loans (NPLs), 5, 74

Nonstate enterprises (NSEs), 34; ambiguous property rights arrangements and, 110–111; compared with state-owned enterprises (SOEs), 97–121; fees paid by, 120n2; government-created difficulties and, 114–115; information available on, 112; intragovernmental decentralization and, 110–111; policy implications for, 119–120; restrictions on entry of, 104–110; rule of law and, 118–119; transitional institutions as obstacles to growth of, 113–119

Nonstate ownership, positive role of, 6

Nonstate sector, 97–121; classified as rural or urban, 99; defined, 98–100; government budgetary review of, 113 (tab.); growth of, 100–104, 100 (tab.), 101 (tab.), 102 (tab.), 103 (tab.), 104 (tab.); share in short-term loans from state banks, 107 (tab.)

Nontariff barriers (NTBs), 162–164

Nontreasury government debt, 76–78

Nonwage benefits, urban and rural, 394

Norms, formal and informal, 142; legal institutions and, 127

North, Douglass C., 48, 125–126

NSEs: *See* Nonstate enterprises (NSEs)

NTBs: *See* Nontariff barriers (NTBs)

Nutrition, recommended, 250

Nyberg, Albert, 422, 430

O'Brien, Kevin, 453, 467n7, 468n29, 468n40

Occupational health care, 299

Occupational health insurance, replacement with municipal schemes, 303

Off-budget fees and funds, 43

Office space, unoccupied, 68–69

Ohnesorge, John K. M., 144n14

Oi, Jean C., 24, 142, 450, 467n6, 467n11, 468n35, 468n36, 468n38, 468n45, 468n49, 479

Olarreaga, M., 154

Old-age pensions, 276, 277, 289–292, 307; extension of, 309; issues in, 292

O'Neill, Mark, 135

One-tier system, of pension financing, 291

Open door policy, of India, 179

"Opening" policy, GDP and, 34

"Opinions Concerning an All-Around Promotion of Housing Reforms in Cities and Towns" (State Council), 316

Organic Law on Villagers' Committees, 458, 459

Organic water pollution (COD), 353. *See also* Pollution

Outflows, 212–213, 213 (fig.); provincial, 212 (fig.); in 25 provinces, 210 (fig.)

Outlays, for social insurance, 308–309

Output, trends for rice, wheat, soybean, and maize, 433 (tab.). *See also* Industrial output; World outputs

Output stage of development, 131–132

Outward FDI, 180

"Over-all open-up strategy," 403

Overinvestment, in steel industry, 88

Overseas Chinese, 182; investment from, 132

Owner-occupied housing (urban), 319, 336–337; housing reform and, 322–324, 322 (tab.), 323 (tab.); inheritance of, 323; purchases on preferential terms, 323; self-built, 323

Ownership, 37; competition among types, 12–13; composition in industrial output, 53 (tab.); diversification of structure for state-controlled, 50; forms of, 34, 99; reforms of, 42, 46; of urban housing, 338

PADOs, *See* Poor Area Development Offices (PADOs)
Pan, Yunkang, 327
"Paralyzed villages," 456
Paraprofessional lawyers, 142
Pargal, Sheoli, 359
Parish, William L., 329
Park, Albert, 237, 238, 240, 241, 242, 270n2
Particulate pollution, 353; abatement costs for, 366–367, 366 (fig.); health damage from, 370
Party-State, 35
Pay-as-you-go system, for pension financing, 291, 309; of social security, 18, 19
Payne, Janice, 138
Peasants, cadres blamed by, 461–462; collective action by, 413n2; discontent expressed by, 452–454; food production quotas for, 399; free local elections by, 458–459; "paralyzed villages" and, 456; penalties for protest, 456; starvation and, 408. *See also* Rural entries
Peerenboom, Randall, 467n4
Pei Minxin, 125, 467n4
Pension(s), 46–47, 276, 277, 289–292
Pension debt, 77
Pension financing, two-tier system of, 291–292, 307
Pension funds, lack of, for diversification, 73
Pension obligations, of workers in liquidated firms, 72–73
Pension problem, growth of, 78
People's Bank of China (PBC), 4, 5, 12, 71; loan classification system of, 472; reorganization of regional branch structure, 71–72
People's Commune system, 99
People's Republic of China, founding of, 1
Pepper, Suzanne, 468n36
Per capita income, results from growth regressions on, 258 (tab.); rural-urban inequity and, 390; total, urban and rural, 394–395, 396 (tab.); urban disposable, 395 (tab.)

Perkins, Dwight, 414n8, 414n9
Personnel, for legal and judicial implementation, 125
Petrochemical companies, 50
PetroChina, 50
Piazza, Alan, 236, 238
Pillar (priority) industries, 222, 223 (tab.)
Pistor, Katharina, 137
Planned economy, 2; transition to market economy and, 31–62
Pleskovic, Boris, 26n7
Poland, 54
Policy, response of firms to, 473
Policy banks, balance outstanding of bonds issued by, 77
Policy failures, study of, 474–475
Policy reform, data on past achievement and, 473–474; economic research on, 476; for food production, 444–446; status of and needs for further, 9–10; sustaining, 20–21
Political change, public expressions as, 456
Political economy, inequality of wealth and, 21–22; of rural-urban divide, 389–416
Political expression, peasant discontent and, 452–454; urban discontent and, 454–456
Political institutions, ability to accommodate change, 60; adaptability of, 450–468
Political power, of urban vs. rural groups, 389
Political reforms, 450–452; economic reforms' interactions with, 479–480; national and local levels, 452 (tab.)
Political system, economic reform and, 24–25; after Mao, 408–409
Political unrest, in 1989, 409–410
Political will, of CCP, 38–39
Pollution, 20–21, consequences of, 354–355; control agencies, 353–354; costs of abatement, 357; deaths from industrial air pollution, 378 (fig.); enforcement of, 384; externalities and, 130–131; future of, 368–371; impact of alternative policies on, 368–369; industrial, 353–355; plant and industry characteristics of, 358–359; policy choices and environmental consequences in five cities, 371–378; pro-

Pollution (*continued*)
jecting damage from, 369–370; provincial levies for, 357–358, 357 (fig.); reduction of, 355–368; trends in pollution intensity factors, 371–372; value of regulation, 378–383. *See also* Environment

Pollution abatement, in Beijing, 379–381; progress in, 368; projecting costs of, 371; regulation, industrial migration, and, 364–367; in Zhengzhou, 381–383

Pollution intensity, comparative significance of factors, 359–361, 360 (fig.)

Poor Area Development Offices (PADOs), 240, 241, 243, 263, 266

Poor area policy, 236–249; area selection and, 237–238; grant and loans to households and, 239–240; investment programs and, 239, 239 (tab.); problems in delivering effective investments, 264–267; reforms to target development projects, 240–241; Shaanxi Province in late 1980s and early 1990s, 242–243; shifts in 1990s, 241–242; Sichuan Province in 1990s, 247–248, 249 (fig.); sources and uses of poverty funds, 242, 243–245; success in delivering effective investments, 267–269; uses of poverty funds, 245–246

Poor area programs, avoiding diversion in, 267–268

Poor areas, impact of China's investments in, 253–264

Population, characteristics in 2020, 19; demographic transition and, 275–276; profile of (1998 and 2020), 275 (tab.)

Posner, Richard, 144–145n17

Potter, Pitman B., 141, 143n1, 467n4

Poverty, 9; China contrasted with Four Dragons of Asia, 2; decline of, 274, 306; extent of, 268–269; measurement in China, 26n18; providing for poor, 17–18; rural antipoverty policy and, 430–431; in Shaanxi, 243 (fig.); urban, 274; urban social relief and, 289; war on, 235–272. *See also* Poor area policy

Poverty alleviation task force, 237

Poverty funds, retargeting, 259; sources and uses of, 242, 243–245, 245–246, 246 (fig.)

Poverty lines, 238, 250, 251; in 1984, 1995, and 1998, 270n4; in urban areas, 289; urbanization rate and, 280–281

Poverty programs, 17; data on, 473; determinants of growth and, 260–264; impact of participation on growth, 260; loans made on noneconomic grounds and, 266–267; project design for, 264–265; quality of participants in, 265–266

Poverty reduction, 10, 16–17, 33, 235–272; economic linkages, policy, and, 252–253; investment per capita and proportion of investment by source, 244 (fig.); new strategy for, 268–269; record on, 250–253; resource allocation for, 264–269; social assistance and, 310

Power, of CCP, 38–39

Predictability, rule of law and, 57

Prereform trade regime, 157–158

Pressure groups, lack of power to affect industrial policy, 406; urban, 409, 410

Price(s), changes in (1994–98), 88 (tab.); devaluations of yuan and, 154; of grains, 443; liberation of, 41; share of goods sold at state-fixed prices, 159 (tab.); for urban housing, 324–325, 328–329

Price controls, 3; urban housing and, 347n35

Price discrimination, against agriculture, 410

Price reforms, agriculture and, 400

Price subsidies: *See* Subsidies

Pricing (housing), arbitrary and comparative, 345n15; three-part housing, 316

Pricing system, multitier and two-tier, 159

Priority industries, 222, 223 (tab.)

Private enterprises, 6, 10, 12, 34, 99; competition among, 12–13; development of, 35; forms in China, 54–55; most important social problems of, 109 (tab.); promoting, 33, 53–57; registered as collective, 111; sources of initial investment, 107–108, 107 (tab.); types of, 99

Private health care, 299–300

Private housing, financing of, 317

Private justice, for wealthy enterprises, 141

Private ownership, in Chinese constitution (1999), 37; of housing, 315, 322–324

Private property rights, 316

Private rental market, in urban housing, 345n9

Private sector, bank and nonbank financial institution loans to, 86–87; employment growth in, 87; sale of collective enterprises and, 96n78

Privately owned private enterprises, 99

Privatization, 225; of collective enterprises, 55; difficulties with, 117–118; of farmland, 427; future research on, 226; of housing, 478–479; housing inequities and, 335; property rights and, 117; SOE contribution to industrial output and, 120n1; of SOEs, 32, 45; use of term, 62n2

Processing trade, 229

Procurement, planned, 424

Production, agricultural, 419–422; structure of, 206–207

Production capacity, financing of excess, 88–89

Productivity, agricultural, 417–449, 433–438; in housing construction, 327

Product-specific barriers, 166

Profits, of banks, 70, 91n15; hidden by NSEs, 112

Profits and losses, bank responsibility for, 89

Progressive taxation, of real estate surpluses, 343–344

Project design, for delivering effective poor relief investments, 264–265

Property, investment in, 68–69; legal protection of, 123; legal protection of NSEs and, 109; national law on, 123; taxation of, 340–342

Property bubble, 67, 68–69, 90

Property registration, 480

Property rights, 13; laws and regulations for, 480; of nonstate enterprises, 117; of NSEs, 108–109, 110–111; protecting private rights, 58; reform of, 42; for urban housing, 336–338; western economies and, 125–126

Protection, reduction of, 167; regional, 16

Protectionism, local, 221–222

Protective barriers, product-specific, 166

Protests, local officials as targets of, 461–462; peasant, 452–454; risks for regime and, 461–463

Protocol of Accession, to WTO, 166

Provinces, citizen environmental complaints in, 359 (fig.); individual, 209–210; pollution intensities in, 356 (fig.); pollution levies in, 357–358, 357 (fig.); pollution regulation in, 357–358; privatization of small SOEs in, 45. *See also* specific provinces

Provincial economies, similarity of, 206

Provincial input-output (I-O) tables, 208–209, 227

Provincial outflows, 212 (fig.)

Provincial policies, trade restrained by, 220–224

Provisional legal measures, 136–137

Public finances, 12

Public goods and services, provision of, 480

Public health, 299; pollution levy reform and, 383–384

Public institutions, justice for, 141; law and, 138

Pudney, Stephen, 345n10, 346n27, 347n33

Pudong, Shanghai, overbuilding in, 69

Pudong Development Bank, 52

Purchase prices, of urban housing, 322–323

Putterman, Louis, 414n8

Qian Yingyi, 3, 10–11, 26n7, 31, 34, 111, 137, 144n15, 477

Qiushi, 125

Quality of life: *See* Living standards

Quantity-driven engineering, for housing, 328

Quotas, in agricultural production, 424; price and marketing reforms and, 424

Railroad infrastructure, upgrades in, 219

Randolph, Patrick A., Jr., 337, 338, 339, 340, 347n41

Rate of return on assets, 91n1; bank assets, 70

Rates of exchange, dual-track approach to, 42

Ratios of loans, 95n64

Ravallion, M., 174
Raw materials, in world trade, 216
Rawski, Thomas G., 91n9, 95n69, 95n74, 401, 414n8
Real estate, managing residential, 317; rights in, 337–338. *See also* Housing
Real estate development, 68–69
Real exchange rate effect, 165–166
Real GDP, Chinese interregional trade and, 218
Real rate of interest, on government bonds, 94n52; growth rate above, 85
Recapitalization, of financial system, 78–83; of state-owned banks, 85
Redevelopments, prices for new housing in, 328–329
Redistribution, in urban areas, 401–403
Red tape, in China and India, 178, 200–201, 201 (tab.)
Reemployment service center, for laid-off workers, 460
Reform(s): agricultural growth and, 421–422; agricultural productivity and, 433–434; assessment of first five years, 48–49; avoiding conflicting, 477–479; banking, 401; central regions in, 414n11; Chinese economic changes and, 102–103; economic, 40, 361–362; enterprise, 224–225; of financial system, 11–12, 71–90; as imperative, 2–4; increase in (1990s), 4–9; legal, 122–149; between 1978 and 1993, 33–35; in 1980s, 41; political, 450–452; political institutions' accommodation of, 60; poverty, 240–242; price, 34; price and marketing, 423–426; process of, 450; research on areas for, 41; rural-urban bias after, 409–411; rural-urban inequities during initial years of, 399–401; second stage of, 42–47; socialist market economy and, 61; of state banks, 51–53; state enterprises and, 285; tariff, 164–166; in taxation, 5; technology development policies and, 431–432, 432 (tab.); of trade regime, 158–160; trends in, 61; of urban housing, 313–350; in urban social security, 286–289; war on poverty and, 235; for WTO accession, 168–169. *See also* Market economy, transition to; specific sectors and reforms

Reform economy, agricultural development in, 418–422
Reform era, production structure during, 207
Regional banks, 44
Regional branch structure, of People's Bank of China, 71–72
Regional development policies, 403, 403 (tab.); urban emphasis of, 401–402
Regional economies, developing central and western, 403; literature on, 205–207
Regional growth models, future research on, 226
Regional integration, 204–232
Regional specialization, implications for, 225
Regulation(s), 4; to attract overseas investment, 182; bank, 71–72; closing holes in, 465–466; discriminatory, 115; environmental, 356–358, 373–378; evolution of laws and regulations on FDI (China and India), 183–186; pollution and, 355–368, 384; reducing, 200–201, 201 (tab.); value of pollution regulation, 378–383. *See also* Law(s); specific laws
Regulatory agencies, legal protection by, 108–109
Regulatory burden, 192
"Releasing the small and the medium" policy, 55
Renaud, Bertrand, 315, 316, 338, 344n2
Rent, as percentage of household income, 317
Rental, of farmland, 427
Rental housing, housing reform and, 320–322, 320 (tab.), 321 (tab.), 345n9
Rents, 344n4
Rent-seeking, rule of law vs., 57
Repayment, on subsidized poverty loans, 240, 241–242
Replacement costs, of urban housing, 347n32
Research: agricultural, 23, 431–432, 432 (tab.), 437, 445; future, 471–481; government oversight of, 145n21; on law reform, 141–143; on policy reform, 476
Residential real estate, managing, 317

Resource allocation, by financial system, 90; for poverty relief, 264–269

Resource flows, urban housing and, 341

Resources, diverting from informal to formal processes, 131; industrialization and, 216

Respiratory disease: *See* Air pollution; Health

Restrictions to entry: *See* Barriers to entry of NSEs

Restructuring, 225

Retirement, pension program and, 46–47; provision for, 18

Retirement age, 311n1

Return on assets, 67; rate of, 91n1

Revenue-producing enterprises, local investment in, 241

Revenues, decline in, 74–75; increase-by-half scenario, 80–83; loan losses absorbed from loan loss reserves, 83; pollution levy and, 383; from real estate, 344

Revenue share, growth by half, 80–83; in Russia, 92n29

Rheinstein, Max, 125

Rhetoric, ideology and, 37

Rice, trade liberalization and, 442. *See also* Agriculture; Crop(s)

"Rice bag" responsibility system, 424

Riskin, Carl, 344n5, 345n6, 414n8

Risk-weighting system, in China, 91n16

Roach, Stephen, 92n27

Road fees, 74

Rogers, J. H., 214

Roland, Gérard, 34

Rong, C., 41, 219

Rosegrant, Mark, 421, 424, 433, 437, 439, 445

Rosen, Daniel, 132, 141

Rosenberg, Nathan, 48

Rozelle, Scott, 17, 23, 158, 162, 235, 237, 238, 241, 260, 263, 266, 417, 421, 422, 424, 430, 433, 437, 439, 445, 468n35, 468n38, 473, 475

Rule of law, 13–14, 126, 140, 477; applying to government, 57–58; in Chinese constitution (1999), 37; consensus on meaning of, 136; economic roles of, 57–58; enforcing, 58–59; establishing, 57–59; for government-business relationship, 33; nonstate enterprises and, 118–119; to protect private property rights, 58. *See also* Law(s); Legal development

Rule-based macroeconomic management, 4

Rural areas, antipoverty policy in, 430–431; bias against, 389; development in, 418, 429–430; discontent expressed in, 452–454; economic growth and poverty in, 252, 252 (tab.); health care in, 300; inequity of, 389–416; labor in, 412–413; labor mobility in, 414n12; out-migration from, 283; per capita consumption expenditures and, 392–394, 393 (tab.); poverty in, 235, 413n2; ratio to urban consumption and income, 396 (fig.); reforms in, 400–401, 408–409; social security in, 18; social security priorities in, 304–305, 306; social security system and, 306–307; technology for, 428–429, 431–432; TVEs in, 101–102; wealth and poverty in, 21–22; worker mobility in, 22. *See also* Labor

Rural credit cooperatives, 71

Rural credit funds, 92n20; closing, 71

Rural discontent, expressions of, 452–453; sources and character of, 453–454

Rural enterprises (REs), 429; development of, 428 (tab.)

Rural Household Survey, 413n5

Rural housing, financing of, 315

Rural industry, 410

Rural nonstate sector, 99

Rural poverty, 17

Rural sector, employment in, 414n9

Rural social security, 296–297

Rural-urban inequities, bridging gap and, 411–413; under central planning, 398–399; closing of gap and, 403–405; determinants of, 398–405; discriminatory policies and, 391–397; from heavy-industry-oriented development strategy, 408; from industrialization policy, 407; during initial years of reform, 399–401; narrowing of, 409; policy formation for, 405–411; political economy of, 389–416

Russia, revenue share in, 92n29

Ryan, Richard, 143

Sanzi yibao system, 414n15
Savings, household, 68; interest income on, 93n33
Saywell, Trish, 95n63
Schiff, Maurice, 413n1
Schulz, J. H., 285
Science, agricultural productivity and, 431–432, 432 (tab.)
"Second economy," nonstate sector as, 34
Sectoral distribution, of labor force, 282
Sectors, bias by, 422; economic, 7 (fig.); output share of industrial pollution by, 363 (fig.). *See also* Rural-urban inequities; specific sectors
Sector-specific rules, 123
Seidman, Ann, 138
Seidman, Robert B., 138
Seignorage gains, in government fiscal revenues, 94n51
Self-employment, 6, 279–280, 282
Self-help housing, 323, 328, 340
Self-sufficiency: *See* Food; Food security; Grain
Sen, A. K., 276
Service sector, GDP from, 6; interprovincial trade and, 208
Services, labor shift into, 279, 281; provision of public, 480
Shaanxi Province, growth in, 263–264; poverty programs in, 17; poverty relief in, 242–243, 246 (fig.), 247 (fig.)
Shanghai, 206; pollution control in, 368. *See also* Pollution
Shareholding enterprises, 99
Shaw, Victor N., 315, 316, 344n4, 346n17
Shen, L., 206
Shen, Mingao, 418
Shenyang: *See* Pollution
Shi, Tianjian, 467n5
Shi Mingshen, 919n15
Shi Tianjian, 139
Shleifer, Andrei, 126, 127, 128, 129, 134, 143n5
Shortages, in Hungarian market reform, 32; of urban housing, 314–315
Sichuan Province, 414n11; gross per capita income in, 254 (tab.), 255 (fig.); growth in, 260–263; income levels and growth in, 261 (tab.); net per capita income in, 256 (tab.), 257 (fig.); pollu-

tion control in, 368; poverty funds for, 247–248, 247 (fig.). 248 (fig.), 249 (fig.), 250 (fig.); poverty programs in, 17. *See also* Pollution
Sichuan Rural Health Experiment, 304
Sicular, Terry, 159, 424
Singapore, corruption in, 178
SINOPEC: *See* China Petrochemical Corporation (SINOPEC)
Site values, of urban housing, 325
Siying qiye, 6
SO_2: *See* Sulfur dioxide emissions
Social assistance, 310–311
Social insurance, 308–310; coverage of, 308; data on, 472; sustainable nature of, 310
Social safety net: *See* Social security system
Social security system, 18–19, 36, 286–295; contributions to, 288, 292; description of suitable system, 307–311; establishment of, 46–47; increase in wage-employment and, 282–283; labor insurance and, 289–290; lack of social safety net and, 49; priorities in reform of, 304–307; reforms in urban social security, 286–289; reforms of, 26–27n19; rural, 296–297. *See also* Social welfare
Social welfare, 10; demographic transition and, 274, 275–279; obligations to workers in liquidated firms, 72–73; population and labor force distribution and, 280; in three transitions context, 273–312
Socialist market economy, 36; differences from market socialism, 36; program for, 61
SOEs: *See* State-owned enterprises (SOEs)
Soileau, William D., 317, 331, 332, 333, 336, 337, 338, 339, 341, 347n38
Sole state ownership form, of banks, 51
Solid wastes, 353
Solinger, Dorothy J., 467n17, 467n21, 467n23, 468n42
Song, Shufeng, 318, 327, 328, 332, 341, 342, 346n23, 348n48
Sovereign bond issues, 95–96n77
Soybeans: *See* Agricultural productivity; Agriculture; Crop(s)

Special economic zones, 158
Special treasury bond, 93n37
Standard of living: *See* Living standards
State and Revolution (Lenin), 35
State Auditing Agency, 43
State banks, reforming, 51–53
State Council, Bureau of Legislative Affairs of, 124; penalties for firms not making pension and other social contributions, 78; poverty network and, 240; on social security program, 47
State Economic and Trade Commission, 222; automatic import registration and, 163; credit guarantee system of, 89–90; deflation and, 88–89
State Economic Commission, 157
State Environmental Protection Agency (SEPA), 353, 357; data from, 369
State firms, conversion to joint stock companies, 224; decrease in, 225
State Land Administration Bureau, 337
State pension debt, 77
State Planning Commission (SPC), 157, 222, 268
State pricing, goods subject to, 175n3
State sector, deterioration of, 285–286; government budgetary review of, 113 (tab.); industrial output of, 34; motivation for reform and, 39–40
State Statistical Bureau (SSB), 392, 413n5, 464; poverty lines from, 250
State trading, 161–162; products covered by, 162 (tab.)
State-led legal reform, 123–125
State-owned banks, 72; commercial behavior of, 72
State-owned enterprises (SOEs), 5, 12; budgetary or credit allocations to inefficient, 410–411; compared with nonstate enterprises, 97–121; corporatization process of, 404; fixed assets in, 414n9; government-business relationship and, 48; industrial enterprises by size (1993), 55; as main source of revenue, 49; mass privatization of, 54; ownership changes in, 99; performance of, 77; pollution from, 359, 372; privatizing, 32; reforming, 33, 36–37, 45–46; reforms in financial relations with, 401; regulation of, 109–110; and restriction to entry of NSEs, 106–108;

share of trade, 161; social role of, 283–284; social security and, 286; transforming, 49–53; workforce in, 222–223
State-owned policy banks, debt of, 76
State-run enterprises, poor performance of, 266–267
State-trading enterprises (STEs), protection and, 167
Statist orientation, of developmental assistance for law, 139
Statistical Yearbook of China, 392
Statistics, on law, 145n20
Steel, 219; excess capacity and overinvestment in, 88
Stein, Ernesto, 201n6
Stevens, J., 164
Stiglitz, Joseph, 26n7
Stone, Bruce, 431, 433
Structural change, economic growth, liberalization, and, 169–174
Structural growth, trade policy, trade growth, and, 153–177
Structural unemployment, 404
Structure, economic, 206
Subprovincial tax, 43
Subsidies, 225; of credit, 241–242; favoring urban sector, 411–412; to insolvent enterprises, 285; local, of poverty loans, 242; monthly housing rents and, 320 (tab.); of poor areas, 237; in urban areas, 409; to urban enterprises, 410; for urban housing, 314, 315–316, 317, 341. *See also* Transfers
Subsidized alternative housing, 329–330
Subsidized loans, as poverty funds, 244
Substantive rules, developing, 145n17
Sulfur dioxide emissions, 353, 354 (fig.), 370, 376 (fig.); abatement in Zhengzhou, 382 (fig.); lives saved by regulation of, 377 (fig.); manufacturing sector share of, 362 (fig.)
Sun Shangwu, 95n70
Sunstein, Cass R., 143
Supernational treatment, of foreign firms (China), 182
Supplementary social insurance funds, from government, 309
Supreme People's Court, 59, 124, 135
Survey research, government oversight of, 145n21

Sustainable housing commoditization,
335–336
"Swap" market exchange rates, 6

Taiwan, 128, 129, 210
Taiwanese investment, 201n4
Tang, Anthony M., 433
Tang, Shu-I, 468n36
Tanner, Murray Scott, 466n3
Targeting, of success and growth effects
in alleviating poverty, 253–259
Tariff barriers, 164–166
Tariff exemptions, on intermediate inputs
used in producing exports, 169
Tariffs, 157, 161; drop in, 174; final bind-
ings on agricultural products, 168
(tab.); rates of, 164 (tab.), 171–172; re-
forms in, 164–166; weighted average,
with and without WTO accession, 172
(tab.); WTO and, 167, 478
Taubman, Wolfgang, 314, 325, 328
Tax bureaus, 5
Tax rates, of host countries, 192
Tax reform, 5, 32, 40, 43–44, 115; NSEs
and, 113
Tax revenue, fuel tax and, 92–93n31
Taxation, from agriculture for industrialization, 423; complaints about, 120n3;
on fuel, 74; information decentralization and, 112; on interest income, 74,
75; market-oriented system, 41; of
NSEs, 111; for pensions, 47; profits
hidden by NSEs and, 112; property,
340–342; for social security, 305; two-
tier tax administration system in, 59;
value-added (VAT), 115–116. *See also*
Tax reform
Technology, agricultural, 428–429, 431–
432, 434–438, 442–444, 445
Temporary legal measures, 136–137
Tenure, in urban housing, 319–320, 319
(tab.)
Ten-Year Scheme of Economic and Social
Development, housing reform in, 316
Textiles, 172–173, 225
Thaler, Richard, 143
Third Plenum of Eleventh Party Congress
(1978), and transformation to market-
oriented economy, 2–4
Third Plenum of the Fourteenth Party
Congress (1993), 4, 31, 36

Thomas, Vinod, 413n4
Three-emphasis *(san jiang)* campaign,
116–117
Three transitions, social welfare in context of, 273–312
Tianjin, 206, 213
Timing, 127–129
Tolley, George S., 318, 325, 328, 329,
333, 336, 337, 346n18, 346n27, 413n4
Tong, Zhong Yi, 315, 316, 317, 324,
330, 333, 335, 336, 344n3, 345n7,
346n21
Tong Zhong, 238, 252, 260
Top-down legal reform, 133–134
Total factor productivity (TFP); crop
productivity and, 433–434, 437–438;
elasticities of, with respect to technology, extension, and other factors, 437–
438, 438 (tab.)
Township and village enterprises (TVEs),
3, 34, 40, 99–100; development of
(1980–95), 101 (tab.); growth rate of
output and employment (1981–95),
102 (tab.); labor insurance and, 296;
loans to, 242; reduction of, 410
Township and village industrial enterprises (TVIEs), pollution and, 386n1,
386n11
Trade: agricultural trade liberalization
and, 417; contributions of firms to,
160, 160 (tab.); domestic and foreign
ratios, 209 (tab.); exemptions for foreign investment, 165; exemptions for
processing, 165; food production and,
426–427; growth of, 426–427; internal, 15–16; interprovincial, 204–205,
207–225; in manufactured goods, 217;
patterns of growth in, 175; processing
of, 158–159; provincial policies re-
straining, 220–224; structural changes
in, 169–174; tariff barriers to, 164–
166
Trade growth, trade policy, structural
growth, and, 153–177
Trade liberalization, 417; agricultural
technology, food deficit, and, 438–
444; domestic grain prices and, 441–
442; industrial pollution and, 362–364
Trade policies, 156–169; nontariff barriers and, 162–164; prereform trade regime and, 157–158; reform of trade re-

gime and, 158–160; structural growth, trade growth, and, 153–177; tariff barriers and, 164–166; trading firms and, 160–162; WTO accession and, 166–169

Trade regime, prereform, 157–158; reform of, 158–160

Trade sector, developments in, 154–156

Trade surplus, on current account, 217

Trading firms, types and numbers of, 160–162

Trading partners, China as market for, 173–174

Transactions, hidden by NSEs, 112

Transaction volume, in spot market for government bonds, 92n26

Transfers, domination by single industry, 213; issues between central and local governments, 43; to poor areas, 237. *See also* Subsidies

Transition, nature of, 476

Transitional economies: China as, 463–464; data needed for, 472; goods and services, raw materials, and, 216–217; manufactured goods in, 217

Transitional institutions, diminishing role of, 115–117, 119; fiscal and intragovernmental decentralization as, 97–98; nonstate sector (NSEs) and, 98, 110–112; as obstacles to nonstate sector's growth, 113–119

Transparency, rule of law and, 57

Transportation, poverty investments in Sichuan, 250 (fig.); upgrades in, 219–220

Transport capacity, 207

Treasury, interest burden of debt, 83

Treasury bonds, 93n34

Treasury debt, 73, 75, 93n36; financing at lower real rate of interest, 85; interest outlays on (1993–98), 76 (tab.); outstanding in 1993, 93n41; stock of, 93n37

TRIPS: *See* Agreement on Trade-Related Aspects of Intellectual Property Rights (TRIPS)

TVEs: *See* Township and village enterprises (TVEs)

Two-ballot system, 452

Two-tier system, judiciary, 59, 477; of pension financing, 291–292, 307

Tyers, Rodney, 439

Tyler, Tom R., 127

Underdeveloped economy, Chinese economy and, 219

Unemployed urban workers, 295

Unemployment, urban, 288, 404, 414n14

Unemployment benefits, expenditure reduction by cutting, 295; laid-off workers category and, 295

Unemployment insurance, 292–295; for laid-off workers, 460

Uniformity, rule of law and, 57

United Nations Development Programme, Chinese legal development and, 123; legal development assistance from, 138

United States, home country effect in, 214; integrated national economy in, 207; interstate travel data in, 213

U.S. Foreign Corrupt Practices Act, 129

Upgrades, in transportation and communications infrastructure, 219–220

Urban areas, bias toward, 389–416; housing reform in, 313–350; inflation subsidies in, 401; labor in, 412–413; per capita consumption expenditures and, 392–394, 393 (tab.); per capita disposable income in, 395 (tab.); poverty in, 18, 21–22, 235; power in, 413n2; ratio to rural consumption and income, 396 (fig.); redistribution in, 401–403; reforms in, 400–401, 409; rural inequity with, 389–416; rural migration to, 430; social security reform priorities in, 305; social security system combined with rural areas, 306–307; unemployment in, 404; wealth in, 21–22. *See also* Cities

Urban bias, pressure-group impact and, 410

Urban discontent, expressions of, 454–455; sources and character of, 455–456

Urban Household Survey, 394, 413n5

Urban housing, accounting deficits and, 334; affordability of, 325–327; allocation system for, 342–343; attraction of alternatives to ownership, 329–330; characteristics of, 318, 319 (tab.); characteristics of stock, 314–315; compari-

Urban housing (*continued*)
sons between housing costs/prices and incomes, 327 (tab.); construction cost estimates, 325 (tab.); densities in, 328; evolution of, 314–318; excess stocks of, 332; forced savings for, 316–317; ideological commitment to quantitative goals, 332; improving affordability of, 330–331; inequality of, 334–335; informal housing and, 340; land use rights and, 336; living space in, 317–318, 318 (tab.); mortgage financing and, 338–340; owner-occupied, 316, 322–324; planning of, 327–328; property rights and, 336–338; property taxation and, 340–342; ratio of costs to household income, 346n18; reasons for costs of, 327–329; reasons for volume of building, 331–332; recent changes in, 318–324; in redevelopments, 328–329; reducing deficit in, 332–335; rental housing and, 320–322; selling at market prices, 324–331; shortage of, 314; structural conditions of, 318; subsidized alternatives to home ownership, 329–330; subsidized and market sale prices, 326 (tab.); tenure and, 319–320
Urban nonstate sector, 99
Urban population, insurance for rural labor force and, 296
Urban poverty, increase in, 274; social assistance and, 310; urban social relief and, 289
Urban sector, employment in, 414n9
Urban social security, government contribution toward, 288; reforms in, 286–289
Urban social welfare system, state enterprises and, 284–285
Urban unemployment, reduction of, 414n14
Urbanization, rate of, 280–281
Uruguay Round, 168

Valdes, Alberto, 413n1
Value, of purchased private housing, 323
Value-added tax (VAT), 115–116
Van Steekelenberg, Ester, 318, 331, 332, 338, 342, 345n8, 347n30
Villages, elections in, 458–459

Vishny, Robert W., 127, 134
Voting: *See* Elections

Wage employment, 279–280, 282
Wages: cash and consumption items, 330; rent subsidies and, 316
Wa Jinglian, 143n7
Walder, Andrew G., 142, 283, 329, 466n1, 467n18
Wan, Z., 163
Wang, Dewen, 415
Wang, Hua, 21, 353, 357, 364, 365, 386n5, 386n8, 473
Wang, Limin, 345n10, 346n27, 347n33
Wang, Sangui, 236, 238, 270n2
Wang, Ya Ping, 315, 316, 324, 326, 327, 330, 332, 338, 341, 345n10, 345n12, 346n20
Wang, Yijiang, 12, 97, 111, 475
Wang, Yukun, 314, 315, 317, 332
Wang Liming, 143n1
Wang Shaoguang, 468n31
Wang Zhuo, 95n76
War on poverty, 235–272
Wastewater pollution, 353
Water pollution, intensity of, 359–361, 360 (fig.); regulation of, 374–375
Waterways, pollution of, 21
Watson, Alan, 137, 205
Wealth, from NSEs, 111
Wealthy enterprises, justice for, 141
Weber, Max, 125
Wedeman, A. H., 205
Weersink, Alfons, 237, 238
Wei, Shang-jin, 15, 132, 178, 201n6
Weitzman, Martin L., 111
Welfare, of farmers, 402–403; poverty reduction based on, 267. *See also* Social welfare
Welfare program, for laid-off workers, 460–461; rural and urban, 394
Welfare system, collapse of enterprise-centered, 18
Wellons, Philip A., 137
Wen, Guangzhong, 433
West, economics in, 41; reasons for rise of, 48
Western China, developing, 403
Western Europe, lawyers in, 128
Whalley, J., 400, 421

Wheat, trade liberalization and, 441–442. *See also* Agriculture; Crop(s)

Wheeler, David, 21, 139, 353, 357, 358, 359, 364, 365, 384, 386n5, 386n6, 386n9, 386n10, 473

Whyte, Martin K., 329

Wiens, T. J., 433

Wilhelm, Kathy, 95n63

Wolf, H. C., 214, 226, 230n4

Wong, Chung Ming, 413n4

Wong, Francis Kwan Wah, 315, 316, 327, 332

Woodruff, Christopher, 26n12

Work units, housing accounts of, 333–334; housing as wages from, 330; separations from, 286; social welfare based on, 287–288, 305; urban housing and, 330, 345n10; workers bound to, 284; worker unrest and, 454

Workers, penalties for protest, 456; urban discontent and, 454–456; welfare for laid-off, 460–461

Workforce, growth of, 171; in state-owned enterprises, 222–223

Working-age adults, age structure of, 278–279, 278 (tab.)

Working-capital lending, 86–87, 87 (tab.), 95n67

World Bank, agricultural pricing research by, 413n1, 413n3; Chinese legal development and, 123; on insulation of high-level bureaucrats, 127–128; legal development assistance from, 138; poverty lines of, 251

World economy, China in, 7, 8 (fig.), 172–173, 173 (tab.)

World export markets, China's share of, 172–173, 173 (tab.)

World Food Programme, 264–265

World outputs, China's share of, 172–173, 173 (tab.)

World trade, China's role in, 14–15. *See also* Trade

World Trade Organization (WTO), 9–10, 14, 23, 61; accession to, 166–169, 172, 173–174; adjustments for entry, 153; China in, 33; coordination of reforms and, 478; NSE restrictions to entry and, 105–106; tariff barriers and, 164; trade liberalization and, 439

Wu, Fulong, 317, 327, 328, 329, 330, 332, 333, 335, 337, 345n10

Wu, Jinglian, 10–11, 31, 34, 41, 477

Wu Guobao, 238, 241, 242, 270n2

Xia Lu, 137

Xia Yong, 141

Xiang Huaicheng, 77

Xiaojun Gao, 267

Xiao Yang, 139

Xie, 44

Xiu Xiaoqi, 414n15

Xu, Chenggang, 111

Xu, Xiping, 369, 370

Yang (prefecture), 245

Yang, Dennis Tao, 1, 21–22, 389, 399, 414n7, 414n12, 471

Yang, Yongzheng, 439

Yang Li, Mu, 1

Yang Shuang, 91n3, 91n4, 94n54

Yang Xu, 93n32

Yao, Shujie, 414n7

Yeats, A., 165

Yeh, Anthony Gar-On, 337

Yields, crop, 435–437, 436 (tab.); on government bonds, 94n52

Yilong microcredit project, 267

Young, A., 206, 207

Young, Leslie, 127

Yulin (prefecture), 245

Yusuf, Shahid, 414n8, 414n9

Zax, Jeffrey S., 19–20, 94n49, 313, 328, 340, 475

Zeng Peiyan, 26n16

Zhang, C. H., 365, 384

Zhang, Houyi, 108, 109, 120n2

Zhang, Linxiu, 17, 235, 236

Zhang, S., 163

Zhang, X., 413n6, 414n7, 473

Zhang, Xinmin, 394n6

Zhang, Y., 163

Zhang, Zongyi, 414n7

Zhang Sai, 209

Zhang Shouyi, 209

Zhao, H., 418

Zhao Renwai, 34, 344n5

Zhejiang Province, 303; private small and medium-sized enterprises in, 56–57

Zheng, Yuxin, 401
Zhengzhou, pollution abatement in,
 381–383
Zhou Binbin, 240
Zhou, Li, 414n8
Zhou, Min, 314, 315, 322, 324, 327,
 330, 336, 337, 344n3, 345n11,
 345n15, 347n35
Zhou, Xiaochuan, 41

Zhou Zhenhua, 208, 229
Zhu, Jieming, 336, 347n35
Zhu, L., 400, 421
Zhu, Xiaodong, 401, 414n10
Zhu Ling, 241, 268, 270n2
Zhu Rongji, 27n22, 125, 223–224
Zhuang, J., 285
Zhuanzhi system, 6